GARDNER'S

ART

THROUGH THE

AGES

BOOK E: MODERN EUROPE AND AMERICA

....

FIFTEENTH EDITION

FRED S. KLEINER

CENGAGE
Learning·

Australia · Brazil · Mexico · Singapore · United Kingdom · United States

Gardner's Art through the Ages, Fifteenth Edition, Book E: Modern Europe and America
Fred S. Kleiner

Product Director: Monica Eckman

Product Manager: Sharon Adams Poore

Content Developer: Rachel Harbour

Associate Content Developer: Erika Hayden

Product Assistant: Rachael Bailey

Media Developer: Chad Kirchner

Marketing Manager: Jillian Borden

Senior Content Project Manager: Lianne Ames

Senior Art Director: Cate Rickard Barr

Manufacturing Planner: Sandee Milewski

IP Analyst: Jessica Elias

IP Project Manager: Farah Fard

Production Service and Layout: Dovetail Publishing Services

Compositor: Cenveo® Publisher Services

Text Designer: Frances Baca

Cover Designer: Mark Fox, Design is Play

Cover Image: Bildarchiv Preussischer Kulturbesitz/Art Resource, NY

Library of Congress Control Number: 2014943688

Book E:
ISBN: 978-1-285-83802-1

Cengage Learning
20 Channel Center Street
Boston, MA 02210
USA

Cengage Learning is a leading provider of customized learning solutions with office locations around the globe, including Singapore, the United Kingdom, Australia, Mexico, Brazil, and Japan. Locate your local office at **www.cengage.com/global.**

Cengage Learning products are represented in Canada by Nelson Education, Ltd.

To learn more about Cengage Learning Solutions, visit **www.cengage.com.**

Purchase any of our products at your local college store or at our preferred online store **www.cengagebrain.com.**

Printed in the United States of America
Print Number: 01   Print Year: 2014

Caspar David Friedrich, *Wanderer above a Sea of Mist*, 1817–1818. Oil on canvas, 3' 1¾" × 2' 5⅜". Hamburger Kunsthalle, Hamburg.

The first painters, who covered the walls and ceilings of the caves of France and Spain beginning around 30,000 years ago, chose animals and occasionally humans as their exclusive subjects. The first landscapes appeared many thousands of years later, but soon became staples of most, but by no means all, artistic cultures worldwide.

Landscape painting was especially popular during the 19th century, when many painters embraced the principles of the artistic movement called Romanticism. Romantic artists, such as the German painter Caspar David Friedrich (1774–1840), sought to capture the transcendental on canvas. In *Wanderer above a Sea of Mist*, Friedrich succeeded in communicating an almost religious awe at the beauty of the natural world. A solitary man stands on a rocky promontory and surveys a vast panorama of clouds, mountains, and thick mist. Because Friedrich chose a point of view on the level of the man's head, the viewer has the sensation of hovering in space behind him—an impossible position that enhances the aura of mystery the artist wanted to convey.

That we know Friedrich's name and details of his career is not surprising, because that has been the norm in Western art since the Renaissance, when the modern notion of individual artistic genius took root. But in many periods of the history of art, artists toiled in anonymity to fulfill the wishes of their patrons, whether Egyptian pharaohs, Roman emperors, or medieval monks. *Art through the Ages* surveys the art of all periods from prehistory to the present, and worldwide, and examines how artworks of all kinds have always reflected the historical contexts in which they were created.

Brief Contents

Contents

30 Modernism and Postmodernism in Europe and America, 1945 to 1980 948

FRAMING THE ERA After Modernism: Postmodernist Architecture 949

TIMELINE 950

The Aftermath of World War II 950

Painting, Sculpture, and Photography 950

Architecture and Site-Specific Art 978

Performance and Conceptual Art and New Media 986

THE BIG PICTURE 993

31 Contemporary Art Worldwide 994

FRAMING THE ERA Art as Sociopolitical Message 995

TIMELINE 996

Art Today 996

Personal and Group Identity 996

Political and Social Commentary 1004

Representation and Abstraction 1009

New Media 1016

Environmental and Site-Specific Art 1019

Architecture 1024

THE BIG PICTURE 1031

Preface

I take great pleasure in introducing the extensively revised and expanded 15th edition of *Gardner's Art through the Ages: A Global History,* which, like the 14th edition, is a hybrid art history textbook—the first, and still the only, introductory survey of the history of art of its kind. This innovative new kind of "Gardner" retains all of the best features of traditional books on paper while harnessing 21st-century technology to significantly increase the number of works examined—without substantially increasing the size of the text or abbreviating the discussion of each work.

When Helen Gardner published the first edition of *Art through the Ages* in 1926, she could not have imagined that nearly a century later, instructors all over the world would still be using her textbook (available even in Mandarin Chinese) in their classrooms. Indeed, if she were alive today, she would not recognize the book that, even in its traditional form, long ago became—and remains—the world's most widely read introduction to the history of art and architecture. I hope that instructors and students alike will agree that this new edition lives up to the venerable Gardner tradition and even exceeds their high expectations.

The 15th edition follows the 14th in incorporating an innovative new online component that includes, in addition to a host of other features (enumerated below), *bonus essays* and *bonus images* (with zoom capability) of more than 300 additional important works of all eras, from prehistory to the present and worldwide. The printed and online components of the hybrid 15th edition are very closely integrated. For example, every one of the more than 300 bonus essays is cited in the text of the traditional book, and a thumbnail image of each work, with abbreviated caption, is inset into the text column where the work is mentioned. The integration extends also to the maps, index, glossary, and chapter summaries, which seamlessly merge the printed and online information.

KEY FEATURES OF THE 15TH EDITION

In this new edition, in addition to revising the text of every chapter to incorporate the latest research and methodological developments, I have added several important features while retaining the basic format and scope of the previous edition. Once again, the hybrid Gardner boasts roughly 1,700 photographs, plans, and drawings, nearly all in color and reproduced according to the highest standards of clarity and color fidelity. Included in this count are updated and revised maps along with hundreds of new images, among them a new series of superb photos taken by Jonathan Poore exclusively for *Art through the Ages* during three photographic campaigns in Germany and Rome in 2012–2014 (following similar forays into France and Tuscany in 2011–2013). The online component also includes custom videos made at architectural sites. This extraordinary new archive of visual material ranges from ancient temples in Rome; to medieval, Renaissance, and Baroque churches in France, Germany, and Italy; to such modernist masterpieces as the Notre-Dame-du-Haut in Ronchamp, France, and the Guggenheim Museum in New York. The 15th edition also features an expanded number of the highly acclaimed architectural drawings of John Burge. Together, these exclusive photographs, videos, and drawings provide readers with a visual feast unavailable anywhere else.

Once again, a scale accompanies the photograph of every painting, statue, or other artwork discussed—another unique feature of the Gardner text. The scales provide students with a quick and effective way to visualize how big or small a given artwork is and its relative size compared with other objects in the same chapter and throughout the book—especially important given that the illustrated works vary in size from tiny to colossal.

Also retained in this edition are the Quick-Review Captions (brief synopses of the most significant aspects of each artwork or building illustrated) that students have found invaluable when preparing for examinations. These extended captions accompany not only every image in the printed book but also all the digital images in the online supplement. Each chapter also again ends with the highly popular full-page feature called *The Big Picture,* which sets forth in bullet-point format the most important characteristics of each period or artistic movement discussed in the chapter. Also retained from the 14th edition are the timeline summarizing the major artistic and architectural developments during the era treated (again in bullet-point format for easy review) and a chapter-opening essay called *Framing the Era,* which discusses a characteristic painting, sculpture, or building and is illustrated by four photographs.

Another pedagogical tool not found in any other introductory art history textbook is the *Before 1300* section that appears at the beginning of the second volume of the paperbound version of the book and at the beginning of Book D of the backpack edition. Because many students taking the second half of a survey course will not have access to Volume I or to Books A, B, and C, I have provided a special (expanded) set of concise primers on architectural terminology and construction methods in the ancient and medieval worlds, and on mythology and religion—information that is essential for understanding the history of art after 1300, both in the West and the East. The subjects of these special boxes are Greco-Roman Temple Design and the Classical Orders; Arches and Vaults; Basilican Churches; Central-Plan Churches; the Gods and Goddesses of Mount Olympus; the Life of Jesus in Art; Early Christian Saints and Their Attributes; Buddhism and Buddhist Iconography; and Hinduism and Hindu Iconography.

Boxed essays once again appear throughout the book as well. These essays fall under six broad categories, two of which are new to the 15th edition:

Architectural Basics boxes provide students with a sound foundation for the understanding of architecture. These discussions are concise explanations, with drawings and diagrams, of the major aspects of design and construction. The information included is essential to an understanding of architectural technology and terminology.

Materials and Techniques essays explain the various media that artists employed from prehistoric to modern times. Because materials and techniques often influence the character of artworks, these discussions contain essential information on why many monuments appear as they do.

Religion and Mythology boxes introduce students to the principal elements of the world's great religions, past and present, and to the representation of religious and mythological themes in painting and sculpture of all periods and places. These discussions of belief systems and iconography give readers a richer understanding of some of the greatest artworks ever created.

Art and Society essays treat the historical, social, political, cultural, and religious context of art and architecture. In some instances, specific monuments are the basis for a discussion of broader themes.

Written Sources present and discuss key historical documents illuminating important monuments of art and architecture throughout the world. The passages quoted permit voices from the past to speak directly to the reader, providing vivid and unique insights into the creation of artworks in all media.

In the *Artists on Art* boxes, artists and architects throughout history discuss both their theories and individual works.

New to the 15th edition are *The Patron's Voice* boxed essays, which underscore the important roles played by the individuals and groups who paid for the artworks and buildings in determining the character of those monuments. Also new are boxes designed to make students think critically about the decisions that went into the making of every painting, sculpture, and building from the Old Stone Age to the present. Called *Problems and Solutions,* these essays address questions of how and why various forms developed; the problems that painters, sculptors, and architects confronted; and the solutions they used to resolve them.

Other noteworthy features retained from the 14th edition are the extensive (updated) bibliography of books in English; a glossary containing definitions of and page references for italicized terms introduced in both the printed and online texts; and a complete museum index, now housed online only, listing all illustrated artworks by their present location. The host of state-of-the-art online resources accompanying the 15th edition are enumerated on page xi).

ACKNOWLEDGMENTS

A work as extensive as a global history of art could not be undertaken or completed without the counsel of experts in all areas of world art. As with previous editions, Cengage Learning has enlisted more than a hundred art historians to review every chapter of *Art through the Ages* in order to ensure that the text lives up to the Gardner reputation for accuracy as well as readability. I take great pleasure in acknowledging here the important contributions to the 15th edition made by the following: Patricia Albers, San Jose State University; Kirk Ambrose, University of Colorado Boulder; Jenny Kirsten Ataoguz, Indiana University–Purdue University Fort Wayne; Paul Bahn, Hull; Denise Amy Baxter, University of North Texas; Nicole Bensoussan, University of Michigan-Dearborn; Amy R. Bloch, University at Albany, State University of New York; Susan H. Caldwell, The University of Oklahoma; David C. Cateforis, The University of Kansas; Thomas B. F. Cummins, Harvard University; Joyce De Vries, Auburn University; Verena Drake, Hotchkiss School; Jerome Feldman, Hawai'i Pacific University; Maria Gindhart, Georgia State University; Annabeth Headrick, University of Denver;

Shannen Hill, University of Maryland; Angela K. Ho, George Mason University; Julie Hochstrasser, The University of Iowa; Hiroko Johnson, San Diego State University; Julie Johnson, The University of Texas at San Antonio; Paul H.D. Kaplan, Purchase College, State University of New York; Rob Leith, Buckingham Browne & Nichols School; Brenda Longfellow, The University of Iowa; Susan McCombs, Michigan State University; Jennifer Ann McLerran, Northern Arizona University; Patrick R. McNaughton, Indiana University Bloomington; Mary Miller, Yale University; Erin Morris, Estrella Mountain Community College; Nicolas Morrissey, The University of Georgia; Basil Moutsatsos, St. Petersburg College–Seminole; Johanna D. Movassat, San Jose State University; Micheline Nilsen, Indiana University South Bend; Catherine Pagani, The University of Alabama; Allison Lee Palmer, The University of Oklahoma; William H. Peck, University of Michigan–Dearborn; Lauren Peterson, University of Delaware; Holly Pittman, University of Pennsylvania; Romita Ray, Syracuse University; Wendy Wassyng Roworth, The University of Rhode Island; Andrea Rusnock, Indiana University South Bend; Bridget Sandhoff, University of Nebraska Omaha; James M. Saslow, Queens College, City University of New York; Anne Rudolph Stanton, University of Missouri; Achim Timmermann, University of Michigan; David Turley, Weber State University; Lee Ann Turner, Boise State University; Marjorie S. Venit, University of Maryland; Shirley Tokash Verrico, Genesee Community College; Louis A. Waldman, The University of Texas at Austin; Ying Wang, University of Wisconsin-Milwaukee; Gregory H. Williams, Boston University; and Benjamin C. Withers, University of Kentucky.

I am especially indebted to the following for creating the instructor and student materials for the 15th edition: Ivy Cooper, Southern Illinois University Edwardsville; Patricia D. Cosper (retired), The University of Alabama at Birmingham; Anne McClanan, Portland State University; Amy M. Morris, The University of Nebraska Omaha; Erika Schneider, Framingham State University; and Camille Serchuk, Southern Connecticut State University. I also thank the more than 150 instructors and students who participated in surveys, focus groups, design sprints, and advisory boards to help us better understand readers' needs in our print and digital products.

I am also happy to have this opportunity to express my gratitude to the extraordinary group of people at Cengage Learning involved with the editing, production, and distribution of *Art through the Ages.* Some of them I have now worked with on various projects for nearly two decades and feel privileged to count among my friends. The success of the Gardner series in all of its various permutations depends in no small part on the expertise and unflagging commitment of these dedicated professionals, especially Sharon Adams Poore, product manager (as well as videographer extraordinaire); Rachel Harbour, content developer; Lianne Ames, senior content project manager; Chad Kirchner, media developer; Erika Hayden, associate content developer; Elizabeth Newell, associate media developer; Rachael Bailey, senior product assistant; Cate Barr, senior art director; Jillian Borden, marketing manager; and the incomparable group of local sales representatives who have passed on to me the welcome advice offered by the hundreds of instructors they speak to daily during their visits to college campuses throughout North America.

I am also deeply grateful to the following out-of-house contributors to the 15th edition: the incomparable quarterback of the entire production process, Joan Keyes, Dovetail Publishing Services; Helen Triller-Yambert, developmental editor; Michele Jones, copy editor; Susan Gall, proofreader; Mark Fox, Design is Play, cover designer; Frances Baca, text designer; PreMediaGlobal, photo researchers; Cenveo Publisher Services; Jay and John Crowley, Jay's Publishing Services;

Mary Ann Lidrbauch, art log preparer; and, of course, Jonathan Poore and John Burge, for their superb photos and architectural drawings.

I also owe thanks to two individuals not currently associated with this book but who loomed large in my life for many years: Clark Baxter, who retired in 2013 at the end of a long and distinguished career, from whom I learned much about textbook publishing and whose continuing friendship I value highly; and former coauthor and long-time friend and colleague, Christin J. Mamiya of the University of Nebraska–Lincoln, with whom I have had innumerable conversations not only about *Art through the Ages* but the history of art in general. Her thinking continues to influence my own, especially with regard to the later chapters on the history of Western art. I conclude this long (but no doubt incomplete) list of acknowledgments with an expression of gratitude to my colleagues at Boston University and to the thousands of students and the scores of teaching fellows in my art history courses since I began teaching in 1975, especially my research assistant, Angelica Bradley. From them I have learned much that has helped determine the form and content of *Art through the Ages* and made it a much better book than it otherwise might have been.

Fred S. Kleiner

CHAPTER-BY-CHAPTER CHANGES IN THE 15TH EDITION

The 15th edition is extensively revised and expanded, as detailed below. Each chapter contains a revised Big Picture feature, and all maps in the text are new to this edition. Instructors will find a very helpful figure number transition guide in the online instructor companion site.

Introduction: What Is Art History? Added 18th-century Benin Altar to the Hand and details of Claude Lorrain's *Embarkation of the Queen of Sheba.*

26: Rococo to Neoclassicism: The 18th Century in Europe and America. New Framing the Era essay "Angelica Kauffman, the Enlightenment, and Neoclassicism." New Art and Society boxes "Poussinistes and Rubénistes," "Joseph Wright of Derby and the Industrial Revolution," and "Vigée-Lebrun, Labille-Guiard, and the French Royal Academy." New Problems and Solutions box "Grand Manner Portraiture." New Written Sources box "Winckelmann and the History of Classical Art." New Patron's Voice box "Thomas Jefferson, Patron and Practitioner." New discussion of the portraits of Pompeo Batoni. New photographs of the exterior and interior of Vierzehnheiligen.

27: Romanticism, Realism, Photography: Europe and America, 1800 to 1870. New Framing the Era essay "The Horror—and Romance—of Death at Sea." New Patron's Voice box "The Coronation of Napoleon." New Written Sources box "Friedrich's *Wanderer above a Sea of Mist.*" New Artists on Art boxes "John Constable on Landscape Painting" and "Thomas Cole on the American Landscape." New Art and Society box "Edmonia Lewis, an African American Sculptor in Rome." New Problems and Solutions boxes "The First Public Art Museum" and "Prefabricated Architecture." New bonus essays on the Arc de Triomphe in Paris and the Brandenburg Gate in Berlin. New photographs of Daumier's *Rue Transnonain*; the Altes Museum in Berlin; the Houses of Parliament in London; and the Brooklyn Bridge.

28: Impressionism, Post-Impressionism, Symbolism: Europe and America, 1870 to 1900. Major rewriting of the sections on Impressionism, Post-Impressionism, and Symbolism. New Framing the Era essay "Modernism at the Folies-Bergère." New Problems and Solutions boxes "Painting Impressions of Light and Color," "Making Impressionism Solid and Enduring," "Painting Psychic Life," and "The First Skyscrapers." New Art and Society boxes "Women Impressionists" and "The Arts and Crafts Movement." New Written Sources box "Albert Aurier on Symbolism." Added Camille Claudel's *The Waltz.* New photograph of the Eiffel Tower in Paris and of Casa Milá in Barcelona.

29: Modernism in Europe and America, 1900 to 1945. New Framing the Era essay "Picasso Disrupts the Western Pictorial Tradition." New Problems and Solutions boxes "Delaunay, Orphism, and the Representation of Modern Life" and "Léger, the Machine Aesthetic, and the Representation of Modern Life." New Art and Society boxes "The Harlem Renaissance" and "Jacob Lawrence's *Migration of the Negro.*" New Written Sources box "André Breton's *First Surrealist Manifesto.*" New Artists on Art boxes "Alfred Stieglitz on 'Straight Photography,'" "Frank Lloyd Wright on Organic Architecture," "Piet Mondrian on Neoplasticism," and "Grant Wood's *Revolt against the City.*" New Patron's Voice box "The Museum of Modern Art as Collector and Patron." Added Adolf Loos's Villa Müller in Prague. New photographs of Rietveld's Schröder House in Utrecht and of the Bauhaus Shop Block in Dessau.

30: Modernism and Postmodernism in Europe and America, 1945 to 1980. New Framing the Era essay "After Modernism: Postmodern Architecture." New Artists on Art box "Jena Dubuffet on Crude Art." New Written Sources box "Greenbergian Formalism." New or expanded Artists on Art boxes "Helen Frankenthaler on Color-Field Painting," "Roy Lichtenstein on Pop Art and Comic Books," "James Rosenquist on *F-111,*" and "Judy Chicago on *The Dinner Party.*" New Problems and Solutions boxes "Robert Venturi and Postmodernist Complexity and Contradiction" and "Rethinking 'Art': Conceptual Art." Added discussions of Gerhard Richter, James Rosenquist, and Pier Luigi Nervi, with new photographs of *Townscape Paris, F-111,* and the Palazzetto dello Sport, Rome, as well as new photographs of the interior of Saarinen's TWA terminal and Graves's Portland Building.

31: Contemporary Art Worldwide. Major reorganization and expansion with the addition of Sandow Birk's *Death of Manuel,* Martha Rosler's *Gladiators,* Fernando Botero's *Abu Ghraib 46,* Zhang Xiaogang's *Big Family No. 2,* Helen Oji's *Mount St. Helens,* Elizabeth Murray's *Can You Hear Me?,* Yayoi Kusama's abstract canvases, El Anatsui's *Bleeding Takari II,* Anish Kapoor's *Cloud Gate,* Do-Ho Suh's *Bridging Home,* Zaha Hadid's Signature Towers project in Dubai, and Norman Foster's Gherkin in London. New Artists on Art boxes "Shirin Neshat on Iran after the Revolution" and "Leon Golub on *Mercenaries.*" New Problems and Solutions boxes "Rethinking the Shape of Painting" and "Norman Foster, the Gherkin, and Green Architectural Design." New photographs of Christo and Jeanne-Claude's *Surrounded Islands,* Stirling's Neue Staatsgalerie and Behnisch's Hysolar Institute in Stuttgart, and Gehry's Guggenheim Museo in Bilbao.

Resources

FOR FACULTY

Instructor Companion Site

Access the Instructor Companion Site to find resources to help you teach your course and engage your students. Here you will find the Instructor's Manual; Cognero computerized testing; and Microsoft PowerPoint slides with lecture outlines and images that can be used as offered or customized by importing personal lecture slides or other material.

Digital Image Library

Display digital images in the classroom with this powerful tool. This one-stop lecture and class presentation resource makes it easy to assemble, edit, and present customized lectures for your course. Available on Flashdrive, the Digital Image Library provides high-resolutions images (maps, diagrams, and the fine art images from the text) for lecture presentations and allows you to easily add your own images to supplement those provided. A zoom feature allows you to magnify selected portions of an image for more detailed display in class, or you can display images side-by-side for comparison.

Google Earth™

Take your students on a virtual tour of art through the ages! Resources for the 15th edition include Google Earth™ coordinates for all works, monuments, and sites discussed in the text, encouraging students to make geographical connections between places and sites. Use these coordinates to start your lectures with a virtual journey to locations all over the globe, or take aerial screenshots of important sites to incorporate in your lecture materials.

FOR STUDENTS

MindTap for *Art through the Ages*

MindTap for *Gardner's Art through the Ages: A Global History*, 15th edition, helps you engage with your course content and achieve greater comprehension. Highly personalized and fully online, the MindTap learning platform presents authoritative Cengage Learning content, assignments, and services offering you a tailored presentation of course curriculum created by your instructor.

MindTap guides you through the course curriculum via an innovative Learning Path Navigator where you will complete reading assignments, annotate your readings, complete homework, and engage with quizzes and assessments. Concepts are brought to life with: zoomable versions of close to 1,500 images; videos to reinforce concepts and expand knowledge of particular works or art trends; numerous study tools, including image flashcards; a glossary complete with an audio pronunciation guide; Google Earth™ coordinate links for all works, monuments, and sites discussed in the text; and much more! Additional features, such as the ability to synchronize your eBook notes with your personal EverNote account, provide added convenience to help you take your learning further, faster.

Slide Guides

The Slide Guide is a lecture companion that allows you to take notes alongside representations of the art images shown in class. This handy resource includes reproductions of the images from the book, with full captions and space for note-taking.

ABOUT THE AUTHOR
Fred S. Kleiner

FRED S. KLEINER (Ph.D., Columbia University) has been the author or coauthor of *Gardner's Art through the Ages* beginning with the 10th edition in 1995. He has also published more than a hundred books, articles, and reviews on Greek and Roman art and architecture, including *A History of Roman Art*, also published by Cengage Learning. Both *Art through the Ages* and the book on Roman art have been awarded Texty prizes as the outstanding college textbook of the year in the humanities and social sciences, in 2001 and 2007, respectively. Professor Kleiner has taught the art history survey course since 1975, first at the University of Virginia and, since 1978, at Boston University, where he is currently professor of the history of art and architecture and classical archaeology and has served as department chair for five terms, most recently from 2005 to 2014. From 1985 to 1998, he was editor-in-chief of the *American Journal of Archaeology*.

Long acclaimed for his inspiring lectures and devotion to students, Professor Kleiner won Boston University's Metcalf Award for Excellence in Teaching as well as the College Prize for Undergraduate Advising in the Humanities in 2002, and he is a two-time winner of the Distinguished Teaching Prize in the College of Arts & Sciences Honors Program. In 2007, he was elected a Fellow of the Society of Antiquaries of London, and, in 2009, in recognition of lifetime achievement in publication and teaching, a Fellow of the Text and Academic Authors Association.

▲ **I-1a** Among the questions art historians ask is why artists chose the subjects they represented. Why would a 17th-century French painter set a biblical story in a contemporary harbor with a Roman ruin?

▲ **I-1b** Why is the small boat in the foreground much larger than the sailing ship in the distance? What devices did Western artists develop to produce the illusion of deep space in a two-dimensional painting?

■ **I-1** **CLAUDE LORRAIN,** *Embarkation of the Queen of Sheba,* 1648. Oil on canvas, 4' 10" × 6' 4". National Gallery, London.

◀ **I-1c** Why does the large port building at the right edge of this painting seem normal to the eye when the top and bottom of the structure are not parallel horizontal lines, as they are in a real building?

What Is Art History?

What is art history? Except when referring to the modern academic discipline, people do not often juxtapose the words *art* and *history*. They tend to think of history as the record and interpretation of past human events, particularly social and political events. In contrast, most think of art, quite correctly, as part of the present—as something people can see and touch. Of course, people cannot see or touch history's vanished human events, but a visible, tangible artwork is a kind of persisting event. One or more artists made it at a certain time and in a specific place, even if no one now knows who, when, where, or why. Although created in the past, an artwork continues to exist in the present, long surviving its times. The first painters and sculptors died 30,000 years ago, but their works remain, some of them exhibited in glass cases in museums built only a few years ago.

Modern museum visitors can admire these objects from the remote past and countless others produced over the millennia—whether a large painting on canvas by a 17th-century French artist (FIG. I-1), a wood portrait from an ancient Egyptian tomb (FIG. I-14), an illustrated book by a medieval German monk (FIG. I-8), or an 18th-century bronze altar glorifying an African king (FIG. I-15)—without any knowledge of the circumstances leading to the creation of those works. The beauty or sheer size of an object can impress people, the artist's virtuosity in the handling of ordinary or costly materials can dazzle them, or the subject depicted can move them emotionally. Viewers can react to what they see, interpret the work in the light of their own experience, and judge it a success or a failure. These are all valid responses to a work of art. But the enjoyment and appreciation of artworks in museum settings are relatively recent phenomena, as is the creation of artworks solely for museum-going audiences to view.

Today, it is common for artists to work in private studios and to create paintings, sculptures, and other objects to be offered for sale by commercial art galleries. This is what American artist CLYFFORD STILL (1904–1980) did when he created his series of paintings (FIG. I-2) of pure color titled simply with the year of their creation. Usually, someone the artist has never met will purchase the artwork and display it in a setting that the artist has never seen. This practice is not a new phenomenon in the history of art—an ancient potter decorating a vase for sale at a village market stall probably did not know who would buy the pot or where it would be housed—but it is not at all typical. In fact, it is exceptional. Throughout history, most artists created paintings, sculptures, and other objects for specific patrons and settings and to fulfill a specific purpose, even if today no one knows the original contexts of those artworks. Museum visitors can appreciate the visual and tactile qualities of these objects, but they cannot understand why they were made or why they appear as they do without knowing the circumstances of their creation. Art *appreciation* does not require knowledge of the historical context of an artwork (or a building). Art *history* does.

ART HISTORY IN THE 21ST CENTURY

Art historians study the visual and tangible objects that humans make and the structures that they build. Scholars traditionally have classified these works as architecture, sculpture, the pictorial arts (painting, drawing, printmaking, and photography), and the craft arts, or arts of design. The craft arts comprise utilitarian objects, such as ceramics, metalwork, textiles, jewelry, and similar accessories of ordinary living—but the fact that these objects were used does not mean that they are not works of art. In fact, in some times and places, these so-called minor arts were the most prestigious artworks of all. Artists of every age have blurred the boundaries among these categories, but this is especially true today, when multimedia works abound.

Beginning with the earliest Greco-Roman art critics, scholars have studied objects that their makers consciously manufactured as "art" and to which the artists assigned formal titles. But today's art historians also study a multitude of objects that their creators and owners almost certainly did not consider to be "works of art." Few ancient Romans, for example, would have regarded a coin bearing their emperor's portrait as anything but money. Today, an art museum may exhibit that coin in a locked case in a climate-controlled room, and scholars may subject it to the same kind of art historical analysis as a portrait by an acclaimed Renaissance or modern sculptor or painter.

The range of objects that art historians study is constantly expanding and now includes, for example, computer-generated images, whereas in the past almost anything produced using a machine would not have been regarded as art. Most people still consider the performing arts—music, drama, and dance—as outside art history's realm because these arts are fleeting, impermanent media. But during the past few decades, even this distinction between "fine art" and "performance art" has become blurred. Art historians, however, generally ask the same kinds of questions about what they study, whether they employ a restrictive or expansive definition of art.

The Questions Art Historians Ask

HOW OLD IS IT? Before art historians can write a history of art, they must be sure they know the date of each work they study. Thus an indispensable subject of art historical inquiry is *chronology,* the dating of art objects and buildings. If researchers cannot determine a monument's age, they cannot place the work in its historical context. Art historians have developed many ways to establish, or at least approximate, the date of an artwork.

Physical evidence often reliably indicates an object's age. The material used for a statue or painting—bronze, plastic, or oil-based pigment, to name only a few—may not have been invented before a certain time, indicating the earliest possible date (the *terminus post quem*: Latin, "point after which") someone could have fashioned the work. Or artists may have ceased using certain materials—such as specific kinds of inks and papers for drawings—at a known time, providing the latest possible date (the *terminus ante quem*: Latin, "point before which") for objects made of those materials. Sometimes the material (or the manufacturing technique) of an object or a building can establish a very precise date of production or construction. The study of tree rings, for instance, usually can determine within a narrow range the date of a wood statue or a timber roof beam.

Documentary evidence can help pinpoint the date of an object or building when a dated written document mentions the work. For

1 ft.

I-2 **CLYFFORD STILL,** *1948-C,* 1948. Oil on canvas, 6' 8$\frac{7}{8}$" × 5' 8$\frac{3}{4}$". **Hirshhorn Museum and Sculpture Garden, Smithsonian Institution, Washington, D.C. (purchased with funds of Joseph H. Hirshhorn, 1992).**

Clyfford Still painted this abstract composition without knowing who would purchase it or where it would be displayed, but throughout history, most artists created works for specific patrons and settings.

Thus a central aim of art history is to determine the original context of artworks. Art historians seek to achieve a full understanding not only of why these "persisting events" of human history look the way they do but also of why the artistic events happened at all. What unique set of circumstances gave rise to the construction of a particular building or led an individual patron to commission a certain artist to fashion a singular artwork for a specific place? The study of history is therefore vital to art history. And art history is often indispensable for a thorough understanding of history. In ways that other historical documents may not, art objects and buildings can shed light on the peoples who made them and on the times of their creation. Furthermore, artists and architects can affect history by reinforcing or challenging cultural values and practices through the objects they create and the structures they build. Although the two disciplines are not the same, the history of art and architecture is inseparable from the study of history.

The following pages introduce some of the distinctive subjects that art historians address and the kinds of questions they ask, and explain some of the basic terminology they use when answering these questions. Readers armed with this arsenal of questions and terms will be ready to explore the multifaceted world of art through the ages.

example, official records may note when church officials commissioned a new altarpiece—and how much they paid to which artist.

Internal evidence can play a significant role in dating an artwork. A painter might have depicted an identifiable person or a kind of hairstyle, clothing, or furniture fashionable only at a certain time. If so, the art historian can assign a more accurate date to that painting.

Stylistic evidence is also very important. The analysis of *style*—an artist's distinctive manner of producing an object—is the art historian's special sphere. Unfortunately, because it is a subjective assessment, an artwork's style is by far the most unreliable chronological criterion. Still, art historians find stylistic evidence a very useful tool for establishing chronology.

WHAT IS ITS STYLE? Defining artistic style is one of the key elements of art historical inquiry, although the analysis of artworks solely in terms of style no longer dominates the field the way it once did. Art historians speak of several different kinds of artistic styles.

Period style refers to the characteristic artistic manner of a specific era or span of years, usually within a distinct culture, such as "Archaic Greek" or "High Renaissance." But many periods do not display any stylistic unity at all. How would someone define the artistic style of the second decade of the new millennium in North America? Far too many crosscurrents exist in contemporary art for anyone to describe a period style of the early 21st century—even in a single city such as New York.

Regional style is the term that art historians use to describe variations in style tied to geography. Like an object's date, its *provenance,* or place of origin, can significantly determine its character. Very often two artworks from the same place made centuries apart are more similar than contemporaneous works from two different regions. To cite one example, usually only an expert can distinguish between an Egyptian statue carved in 2500 BCE and one made in 500 BCE. But no one would mistake an Egyptian statue of 500 BCE for one of the same date made in Greece or Mexico.

Considerable variations in a given area's style are possible, however, even during a single historical period. In late medieval Europe, French architecture differed significantly from Italian architecture. The interiors of Beauvais Cathedral (FIG. I-3) and the church of Santa Croce (Holy Cross, FIG. I-4) in Florence typify the architectural styles of France and Italy, respectively, at the end of the 13th century. The rebuilding of the east end of Beauvais Cathedral began in 1284. Construction commenced on Santa Croce only 10 years later. Both structures employ the *pointed arch* characteristic of this era, yet the two churches differ strikingly. The French church has towering stone ceilings and large expanses of colored-glass windows, whereas the Italian building has a low timber roof and small,

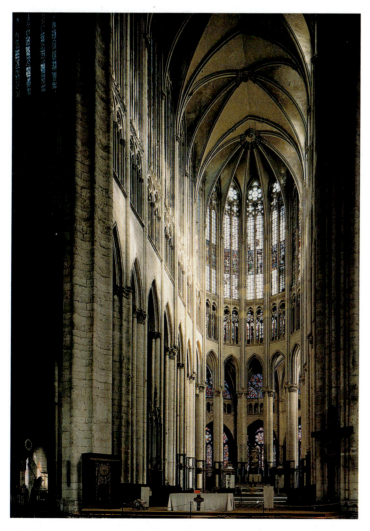

I-3 Choir of Beauvais Cathedral (looking east), Beauvais, France, rebuilt after 1284.

The style of an object or building often varies from region to region. This cathedral has towering stone vaults and large stained-glass windows typical of 13th-century French architecture.

I-4 Interior of Santa Croce (looking east), Florence, Italy, begun 1294.

In contrast to Beauvais Cathedral (FIG. I-3), this contemporaneous Florentine church conforms to the quite different regional style of Italy. The building has a low timber roof and small windows.

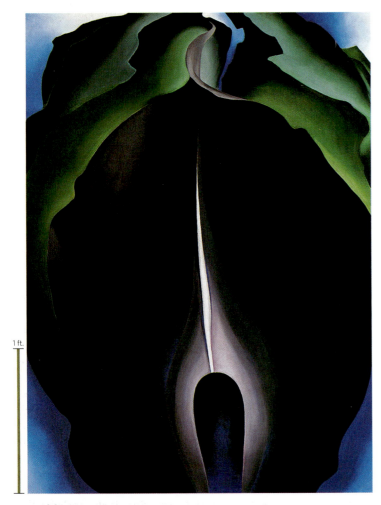

I-5 GEORGIA O'KEEFFE, *Jack-in-the-Pulpit No. 4*, 1930. Oil on canvas, 3' 4" × 2' 6". National Gallery of Art, Washington, D.C. (Alfred Stieglitz Collection, bequest of Georgia O'Keeffe).

O'Keeffe's paintings feature close-up views of petals and leaves in which the organic forms become powerful abstract compositions. This approach to painting typifies the artist's distinctive personal style.

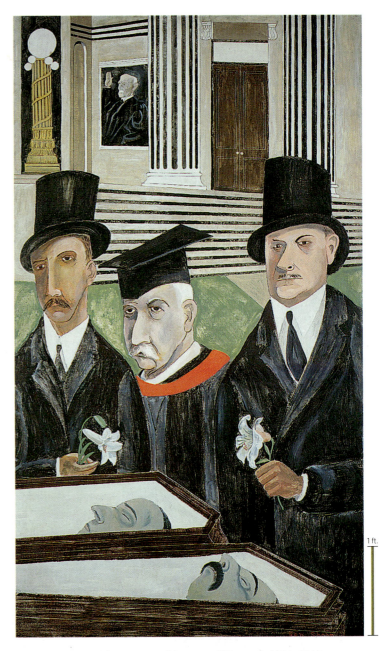

I-6 BEN SHAHN, *The Passion of Sacco and Vanzetti*, 1931–1932. Tempera on canvas, 7' ½" × 4'. Whitney Museum of American Art, New York (gift of Edith and Milton Lowenthal in memory of Juliana Force).

O'Keeffe's contemporary, Shahn developed a style markedly different from hers. His paintings are often social commentaries on recent events and incorporate readily identifiable people.

widely separated clear windows. Because the two contemporaneous churches served similar purposes, regional style mainly explains their differing appearance.

Personal style, the distinctive manner of individual artists or architects, often decisively explains stylistic discrepancies among paintings, sculptures, and buildings of the same time and place. For example, in 1930, the American painter GEORGIA O'KEEFFE (1887–1986) produced a series of paintings of flowering plants. One of them—*Jack-in-the-Pulpit No. 4* (FIG. I-5)—is a sharply focused close-up view of petals and leaves. O'Keeffe captured the growing plant's slow, controlled motion while converting the plant into a powerful abstract composition of lines, forms, and colors (see the discussion of art historical vocabulary in the next section). Only a year later, another American artist, BEN SHAHN (1898–1969), painted *The Passion of Sacco and Vanzetti* (FIG. I-6), a stinging commentary on social injustice inspired by the trial and execution of two Italian anarchists, Nicola Sacco and Bartolomeo Vanzetti. Many people believed that Sacco and Vanzetti had been unjustly convicted of killing two men in a robbery in 1920. Shahn's painting compresses time in a symbolic representation of the trial and its aftermath. The two executed men lie in their coffins. Presiding over them are the three members of the commission (headed by a college president wearing

academic cap and gown) who declared that the original trial was fair and cleared the way for the executions. Behind, on the wall of a stately government building, hangs the framed portrait of the judge who pronounced the initial sentence. Personal style, not period or regional style, sets Shahn's canvas apart from O'Keeffe's. The contrast is extreme here because of the very different subjects that the artists chose. But even when two artists depict the same subject, the results can vary widely. The *way* O'Keeffe painted flowers and the *way* Shahn painted faces are distinctive and unlike the styles of their contemporaries. (See the "Who Made It?" discussion on page 6.)

The different kinds of artistic styles are not mutually exclusive. For example, an artist's personal style may change dramatically during a long career. Art historians then must distinguish among

I-7 GISLEBERTUS, weighing of souls, detail of *Last Judgment* (FIG. 12-15), west tympanum of Saint-Lazare, Autun, France, ca. 1120–1135.

In this high relief portraying the weighing of souls on judgment day, Gislebertus used disproportion and distortion to dehumanize the devilish figure yanking on the scales of justice.

the different period styles of a particular artist, such as the "Rose Period" and the "Cubist Period" of the prolific 20th-century artist Pablo Picasso.

WHAT IS ITS SUBJECT? Another major concern of art historians is, of course, subject matter, encompassing the story, or narrative; the scene presented; the action's time and place; the persons involved; and the environment and its details. Some artworks, such as modern abstract paintings (FIG. I-2), have no subject, not even a setting. The "subject" is the artwork itself—its colors, textures, composition, and size. But when artists represent people, places, or actions, viewers must identify these features to achieve complete understanding of the work. Art historians traditionally separate pictorial subjects into various categories, such as religious, historical, mythological, *genre* (daily life), portraiture, *landscape* (a depiction of a place), *still life* (an arrangement of inanimate objects), and their numerous subdivisions and combinations.

Iconography—literally, the "writing of images"—refers both to the content, or subject, of an artwork, and to the study of content in art. By extension, it also includes the study of *symbols,* images that stand for other images or encapsulate ideas. In Christian art, two intersecting lines of unequal length or a simple geometric cross can serve as an emblem of the religion as a whole, symbolizing the cross of Jesus Christ's crucifixion. A symbol also can be a familiar object that an artist has imbued with greater meaning. A balance or scale, for example, may symbolize justice or the weighing of souls on judgment day (FIG. **I-7**).

Artists may depict figures with unique *attributes* identifying them. In Christian art, for example, each of the authors of the biblical gospel books, the four evangelists (FIG. **I-8**), has a distinctive attribute. People can recognize Saint Matthew by the winged man associated with him, John by his eagle, Mark by his lion, and Luke by his ox.

Throughout the history of art, artists have used *personifications*—abstract ideas codified in human form. Because of the fame of the colossal statue set up in New York City's harbor in 1886, people everywhere visualize Liberty as a robed woman wearing a rayed crown and holding a torch. Four different personifications appear in *The Four Horsemen*

1 in.

I-8 The four evangelists, folio 14 verso of the *Aachen Gospels,* ca. 810. Ink and tempera on vellum, $1' \times 9\frac{1}{2}''$. Domschatzkammer, Aachen.

Artists depict figures with attributes in order to identify them for viewers. The authors of the four gospels have distinctive attributes—winged man (Matthew), eagle (John), lion (Mark), and ox (Luke).

1 in.

I-9 ALBRECHT DÜRER, *The Four Horsemen of the Apocalypse,* ca. 1498. Woodcut, 1' 3¼" × 11". Metropolitan Museum of Art, New York (gift of Junius S. Morgan, 1919).

Personifications are abstract ideas codified in human form. Here, Albrecht Dürer represented Death, Famine, War, and Pestilence as four men on charging horses, each one carrying an identifying attribute.

of the Apocalypse (FIG. I-9) by German artist ALBRECHT DÜRER (1471–1528). The late-15th-century print is a terrifying depiction of the fateful day at the end of time when, according to the Bible's last book, Death, Famine, War, and Pestilence will annihilate the human race. Dürer personified Death as an emaciated old man with a pitch-fork. Famine swings the scales for weighing human souls (compare FIG. I-7). War wields a sword, and Pestilence draws a bow.

Even without considering style and without knowing a work's maker, informed viewers can determine much about the work's period and provenance by iconographical and subject analysis alone. In *The Passion of Sacco and Vanzetti* (FIG. I-6), for example, the two coffins, the trio headed by an academic, and the robed judge in the background are all pictorial clues revealing the painting's sub-ject. The work's date must be after the trial and execution, probably while the event was still newsworthy. And because the two men's deaths caused the greatest outrage in the United States, the painter–social critic was probably an American.

WHO MADE IT? If Ben Shahn had not signed his painting of Sacco and Vanzetti, an art historian could still assign, or *attribute* (make an *attribution* of), the work to him based on knowledge of the artist's personal style. Although signing (and dating) works is quite common (but by no means universal) today, in the history of art, countless works exist whose artists remain unknown. Because per-sonal style can play a major role in determining the character of an artwork, art historians often try to attribute anonymous works to known artists. Sometimes they assemble a group of works all thought to be by the same person, even though none of the objects in the group is the known work of an artist with a recorded name. Art historians thus reconstruct the careers of artists such as "the Achil-les Painter," the anonymous ancient Greek artist whose masterwork is a depiction of the hero Achilles. Scholars base their attributions on internal evidence, such as the distinctive way an artist draws or carves drapery folds, earlobes, or flowers. It requires a keen, highly trained eye and long experience to become a *connoisseur,* an expert in assigning artworks to "the hand" of one artist rather than another. Attribution is subjective, of course, and ever open to doubt. For example, scholars continue to debate attributions to the famous 17th-century Dutch painter Rembrandt van Rijn.

Sometimes a group of artists works in the same style at the same time and place. Art historians designate such a group as a *school.* "School" does not mean an educational institution or art academy. The term connotes only shared chronology, style, and geography. Art historians speak, for example, of the Dutch school of the 17th century and, within it, of subschools such as those of the cities of Haarlem, Utrecht, and Leyden.

WHO PAID FOR IT? The interest that many art historians show in attribution reflects their conviction that the identity of an artwork's maker is the major reason the object looks the way it does. For them, personal style is of paramount importance. But in many times and places, artists had little to say about what form their work would take. They toiled in obscurity, doing the bidding of their *patrons,* those who paid them to make individual works or employed them on a continuing basis. The role of patrons in dictating the content and shaping the form of artworks is also an important subject of art historical inquiry, more so today than at any time in the past.

In the art of portraiture, to name only one category of painting and sculpture, the patron has often played a dominant role in decid-ing how the artist represented the subject, whether that person was the patron or another individual, such as a spouse, son, or mother. Many Egyptian pharaohs and some Roman emperors, for example, insisted that artists depict them with unlined faces and perfect youthful bodies no matter how old they were when portrayed. In these cases, the state employed the sculptors and painters, and the artists had no choice but to portray their patrons in the officially approved manner. This is why Augustus, who lived to age 76, looks so young in his portraits (FIG. I-10). Although Roman emperor for more than 40 years, Augustus demanded that artists always repre-sent him as a young, godlike head of state.

All modes of artistic production reveal the impact of patronage. Learned monks provided the themes for the sculptural decoration of medieval church portals (FIG. I-7). Renaissance princes and popes dictated the subject, size, and materials of artworks destined for display in buildings also constructed according to their specifica-tions. An art historian could make a very long list of commissioned works, and it would indicate that patrons have had diverse tastes and needs throughout history and consequently have demanded different kinds of art. Whenever a patron contracts with an art-ist or architect to paint, sculpt, or build in a prescribed manner, personal style often becomes a very minor factor in the ultimate

1 in.

I-10 Bust of Augustus wearing the corona civica, early first century CE. Marble, 1′ 5″ high. Glyptothek, Munich.

Patrons frequently dictate the form that their portraits will take. Emperor Augustus demanded that he always be portrayed as a young, godlike head of state even though he lived to age 76.

appearance of the painting, statue, or building. In these cases, the identity of the patron reveals more to art historians than does the identity of the artist or school. The portrait of Augustus illustrated here (FIG. I-10)—showing the emperor wearing a *corona civica,* or civic crown—was the work of a virtuoso sculptor, a master wielder of hammer and chisel. But scores of similar portraits of this Roman emperor also exist today. They differ in quality but not in kind from this one. The patron, not the artist, determined the character of these artworks. Augustus's public image never varied.

The Words Art Historians Use

As in all fields of study, art history has its own specialized vocabulary consisting of hundreds of words, but certain basic terms are indispensable for describing artworks and buildings of any time and place. They make up the essential vocabulary of *formal analysis,* the visual analysis of artistic form. Definitions and discussions of the most important art historical terms follow.

FORM AND COMPOSITION *Form* refers to an object's shape and structure, either in two dimensions (for example, a figure painted on a wood panel) or in three dimensions (such as a statue carved from a marble block). Two forms may take the same shape but differ in their color, texture, and other qualities. *Composition* refers to how an artist *composes* (organizes) forms in an artwork, either by placing shapes on a flat surface or by arranging forms in space.

MATERIAL AND TECHNIQUE To create art forms, artists shape materials (pigment, clay, marble, gold, and many more) with tools (pens, brushes, chisels, and so forth). Each of the materials and tools available has its own potentialities and limitations. Part of all artists' creative activity is to select the *medium* and instrument most suitable to the purpose—or to develop new media and tools, such as bronze and concrete in antiquity and cameras and computers in modern times. The processes that artists employ, such as applying paint to canvas with a brush, and the distinctive, personal ways that they handle materials constitute their *technique.* Form, material, and technique interrelate and are central to analyzing any work of art.

LINE Among the most important elements defining an artwork's shape or form is *line.* A line can be understood as the path of a point moving in space, an invisible line of sight. More commonly, however, artists and architects make a line visible by drawing (or chiseling) it on a *plane,* a flat surface. A line may be very thin, wirelike, and delicate. It may be thick and heavy. Or it may alternate quickly from broad to narrow, the strokes jagged or the outline broken. When a continuous line defines an object's outer shape, art historians call it a *contour line.* All of these line qualities are present in Dürer's *Four Horsemen of the Apocalypse* (FIG. I-9). Contour lines define the basic shapes of clouds, human and animal limbs, and weapons. Within the forms, series of short broken lines create shadows and textures. An overall pattern of long parallel strokes suggests the dark sky on the frightening day when the world is about to end.

COLOR Light reveals all colors. Light in the world of the painter and other artists differs from natural light. Natural light, or sunlight, is whole or *additive light.* As the sum of all the wavelengths composing the visible *spectrum,* it may be disassembled or fragmented into the individual colors of the spectral band. The painter's light in art—the light reflected from pigments and objects—is *subtractive light.* Paint pigments produce their individual colors by reflecting a segment of the spectrum while absorbing all the rest. Green pigment, for example, subtracts or absorbs all the light in the spectrum except that seen as green.

Hue is the property giving a color its name. Although the spectrum colors merge into each other, artists usually conceive of their hues as distinct from one another. Color has two basic variables—the apparent amount of light reflected and the apparent purity. A change in one must produce a change in the other. Some terms for these variables are *value* or *tonality* (the degree of lightness or darkness) and *intensity* or *saturation* (the purity of a color, its brightness or dullness).

Artists call the three basic colors—red, yellow, and blue—the *primary colors.* The *secondary colors* result from mixing pairs of primaries: orange (red and yellow), purple (red and blue), and green (yellow and blue). *Complementary colors* represent the pairing of a primary color and the secondary color created from mixing the two other primary colors—red and green, yellow and purple, and blue and orange. They "complement," or complete, each other, one absorbing the colors that the other reflects.

Artists can manipulate the appearance of colors, however. One artist who made a systematic investigation of the formal aspects of art, especially color, was JOSEPH ALBERS (1888–1976), a German-born

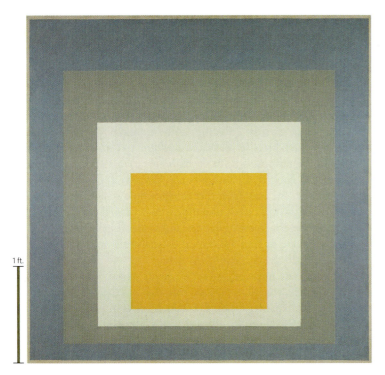

1 ft.

I-11 JOSEF ALBERS, *Homage to the Square: "Ascending,"* 1953. Oil on composition board, 3' 7½" × 3' 7½". Whitney Museum of American Art, New York.

Albers created hundreds of paintings using the same composition but employing variations in hue, saturation, and value in order to reveal the relativity and instability of color perception.

artist who emigrated to the United States in 1933. In connection with his studies, Albers created the series *Homage to the Square*—hundreds of paintings, most of which are color variations on the same composition of concentric squares, as in the illustrated example (FIG. I-11). The series reflected Albers's belief that art originates in "the discrepancy between physical fact and psychic effect."[1] Because the composition in most of these paintings remains constant, the works succeed in revealing the relativity and instability of color perception. Albers varied the hue, saturation, and value of each square in the paintings in this series. As a result, the sizes of the squares from painting to painting appear to vary (although they remain the same), and the sensations emanating from the paintings range from clashing dissonance to delicate serenity. Albers explained his motivation for focusing on color juxtapositions:

> They [the colors] are juxtaposed for various and changing visual effects. . . . Such action, reaction, interaction . . . is sought in order to make obvious how colors influence and change each other; that the same color, for instance—with different grounds or neighbors—looks different. . . . Such color deceptions prove that we see colors almost never unrelated to each other.[2]

TEXTURE The term *texture* refers to the quality of a surface, such as rough or shiny. Art historians distinguish between true texture—that is, the tactile quality of the surface—and represented texture, as when painters depict an object as having a certain texture even though the pigment is the true texture. Sometimes artists combine different materials of different textures on a single surface, juxtaposing paint with pieces of wood, newspaper, fabric, and so forth. Art historians refer to this mixed-media technique as *collage*. Texture

is, of course, a key determinant of any sculpture's character. People's first impulse is usually to handle a work of sculpture—even though museum signs often warn "Do not touch!" Sculptors plan for this natural human response, using surfaces varying in texture from rugged coarseness to polished smoothness. Textures are often intrinsic to a material, influencing the type of stone, wood, plastic, clay, or metal that a sculptor selects.

SPACE, MASS, AND VOLUME *Space* is the bounded or boundless "container" of objects. For art historians, space can be the real three-dimensional space occupied by a statue or a vase or contained within a room or courtyard. Or space can be *illusionistic,* as when painters depict an image (or illusion) of the three-dimensional spatial world on a two-dimensional surface.

Mass and *volume* describe three-dimensional objects and space. In both architecture and sculpture, mass is the bulk, density, and weight of matter in space. Yet the mass need not be solid. It can be the exterior form of enclosed space. Mass can apply to a solid Egyptian pyramid or stone statue; to a church, synagogue, or mosque (architectural shells enclosing sometimes vast spaces); and to a hollow metal statue or baked clay pot. Volume is the space that mass organizes, divides, or encloses. It may be a building's interior spaces, the intervals between a structure's masses, or the amount of space occupied by a three-dimensional object such as a statue, pot, or chair. Volume and mass describe both the exterior and interior forms of a work of art—the forms of the matter of which it is composed and the spaces immediately around the work and interacting with it.

PERSPECTIVE AND FORESHORTENING *Perspective* is one of the most important pictorial devices for organizing forms in space. Throughout history, artists have used various types of perspective to create an illusion of depth or space on a two-dimensional surface. The French painter CLAUDE LORRAIN (1600–1682) employed several perspective devices in *Embarkation of the Queen of Sheba* (FIG. I-1), a painting of a biblical episode set in a 17th-century European harbor with an ancient Roman ruin in the left foreground—an irrationally anachronistic combination that the art historian can explain only in the context of the cultural values of the artist's time and place. In Claude's painting, the figures and boats on the shoreline are much larger than those in the distance, because decreasing the size of an object makes it appear farther away. The top and bottom of the port building at the painting's right side are not parallel horizontal lines, as they are in a real building. Instead, the lines converge beyond the structure, leading the viewer's eye toward the hazy, indistinct sun on the horizon. These three perspective devices—the reduction of figure size, the convergence of diagonal lines, and the blurring of distant forms—have been familiar features of Western art since they were first employed by the ancient Greeks. It is important to state, however, that all kinds of perspective are only pictorial conventions, even when one or more types of perspective may be so common in a given culture that people accept them as "natural" or as "true" means of representing the natural world.

These perspective conventions are by no means universal. In *Waves at Matsushima* (FIG. I-12), a Japanese seascape painting on a six-part folding screen, OGATA KORIN (1658–1716) ignored these Western "tricks" for representing deep space on a flat surface. A Western viewer might interpret the left half of Korin's composition as depicting the distant horizon, as in the French painting, but the sky is an unnatural gold, and the clouds that fill that unnaturally colored sky are almost indistinguishable from the waves below.

I-12 OGATA KORIN, *Waves at Matsushima,* Edo period, ca. 1700–1716. Six-panel folding screen, ink, color, and gold leaf on paper, 4' 11 $\frac{1}{8}$" × 12' $\frac{7}{8}$". Museum of Fine Arts, Boston (Fenollosa-Weld Collection).

Asian artists rarely employed Western perspective (FIG. I-1). Korin was more concerned with creating an intriguing composition of shapes on a surface than with locating boulders, waves, and clouds in space.

The rocky outcroppings decrease in size with distance, but all are in sharp focus, and there are no shadows. The Japanese artist was less concerned with locating the boulders and waves and clouds in space than with composing shapes on a surface, playing the swelling curves of waves and clouds against the jagged contours of the rocks. Neither the French nor the Japanese painting can be said to project "correctly" what viewers "in fact" see. One painting is not a "better" picture of the world than the other. The European and Asian artists simply approached the problem of picture making differently.

Artists also represent single figures in space in varying ways. When Flemish artist PETER PAUL RUBENS (1577–1640) painted *Lion*

Hunt (FIG. I-13), he used *foreshortening* for all the hunters and animals—that is, he represented their bodies at angles to the picture plane. When in life one views a figure at an angle, the body appears to contract as it extends back in space. Foreshortening is a kind of perspective. It produces the illusion that one part of the body is farther away than another, even though all the painted forms are on the same plane. Especially noteworthy in *Lion Hunt* are the gray horse at the left, seen from behind with the bottom of its left rear hoof facing viewers and most of its head hidden by its rider's shield, and the fallen hunter at the painting's lower right corner, whose barely visible legs and feet recede into the distance.

I-13 PETER PAUL RUBENS, *Lion Hunt,* 1617–1618. Oil on canvas, 8' 2" × 12' 5". Alte Pinakothek, Munich.

Foreshortening—the representation of a figure or object at an angle to the picture plane—is a common device in Western art for creating the illusion of depth. Foreshortening is a type of perspective.

seems the right size for the body"). Or proportion can be a mathematical relationship between the size of one part of an artwork or building and the other parts within the work. Proportion in art implies using a *module*, or basic unit of measure. When an artist or architect uses a formal system of proportions, all parts of a building, body, or other entity will be fractions or multiples of the module. A module might be the diameter of a *column*, the height of a human head, or any other component whose dimensions can be multiplied or divided to determine the size of the work's other parts.

In certain times and places, artists have devised *canons*, or systems, of "correct" or "ideal" proportions for representing human figures, constituent parts of buildings, and so forth. In ancient Greece, many sculptors formulated canons of proportions so strict and all-encompassing that they calculated the size of every body part in advance, even the fingers and toes, according to mathematical ratios.

Proportional systems can differ sharply from period to period, culture to culture, and artist to artist. Part of the task that art history students face is to perceive and adjust to these differences. In fact, many artists have used disproportion and distortion deliberately for expressive effect. In the medieval French depiction of the weighing of souls on judgment day (FIG. I-7), the devilish figure yanking down on the scale has distorted facial features and stretched, lined limbs with animal-like paws for feet. Disproportion and distortion make him appear "inhuman," precisely as the sculptor intended.

In other cases, artists have used disproportion to focus attention on one body part (often the head) or to single out a group

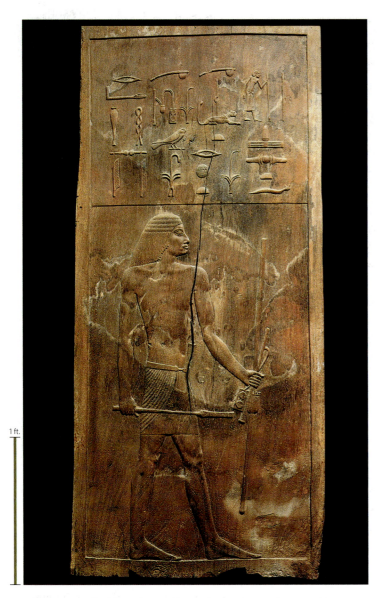

I-14 Hesire, relief from his tomb at Saqqara, Egypt, Dynasty III, ca. 2650 BCE. Wood, 3' 9" high. Egyptian Museum, Cairo.

Egyptian artists combined frontal and profile views to give a precise picture of the parts of the human body, as opposed to depicting how an individual body appears from a specific viewpoint.

The artist who carved the portrait of the ancient Egyptian official Hesire (FIG. I-14) for display in Hesire's tomb did not employ foreshortening. That artist's purpose was to present the various human body parts as clearly as possible, without overlapping. The lower part of Hesire's body is in profile to give the most complete view of the legs, with both the heel and toes of each foot visible. The frontal torso, however, allows viewers to see its full shape, including both shoulders, equal in size, as in nature. (Compare the shoulders of the hunter on the gray horse or those of the fallen hunter in *Lion Hunt*'s left foreground.) The result—an "unnatural" 90-degree twist at the waist—provides a precise picture of human body parts, if not an accurate picture of how a standing human figure really looks. Rubens and the Egyptian sculptor used very different means of depicting forms in space. Once again, neither is the "correct" manner.

PROPORTION AND SCALE *Proportion* concerns the relationships (in terms of size) of the parts of persons, buildings, or objects. People can judge "correct proportions" intuitively ("that statue's head

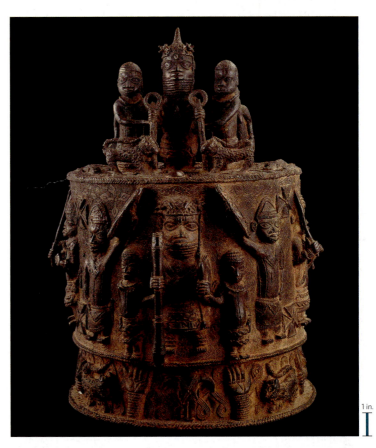

I-15 Altar to the Hand (ikegobo), from Benin, Nigeria, ca. 1735–1750. Bronze, 1' 5½" high. British Museum, London (gift of Sir William Ingram).

One of the Benin king's praise names is Great Head, and on this cast-bronze royal altar, the artist represented him larger than all other figures and with a disproportionately large head.

member (usually the leader). These intentional "unnatural" discrepancies in proportion constitute what art historians call *hierarchy of scale,* the enlarging of elements considered the most important. On the bronze altar from Benin, Nigeria, illustrated here (FIG. I-15), the sculptor varied the size of each figure according to the person's social status. Largest, and therefore most important, is the Benin king, depicted twice, each time flanked by two smaller attendant figures and shown wearing a multistrand coral necklace emblematic of his high office. The king's head is also disproportionately large compared to his body, consistent with one of the Benin ruler's praise names: Great Head.

One problem that students of art history—and professional art historians too—confront when studying illustrations in art history books is that although the relative sizes of figures and objects in a painting or sculpture are easy to discern, it is impossible to determine the absolute size of the work reproduced because they all are printed at approximately the same size on the page. Readers of *Art through the Ages* can learn the exact size of all artworks from the dimensions given in the captions and, more intuitively, from the scales positioned at the lower left or right corner of each illustration.

CARVING AND CASTING Sculptural technique falls into two basic categories, *subtractive* and *additive. Carving* is a subtractive technique. The final form is a reduction of the original mass of a block of stone, a piece of wood, or another material. Wood statues were once

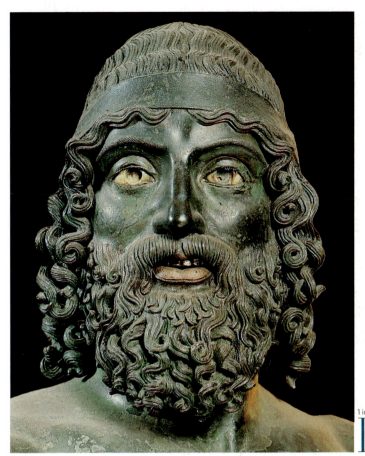

1 in.

I-17 Head of a warrior, detail of a statue (FIG. 5-36) from the sea off Riace, Italy, ca. 460–450 BCE. Bronze, full statue 6' 6" high. Museo Archeologico Nazionale, Reggio Calabria.

The sculptor of this life-size statue of a bearded Greek warrior cast the head, limbs, torso, hands, and feet in separate molds, then welded the pieces together and added the eyes in a different material.

1 ft.

I-16 MICHELANGELO BUONARROTI, unfinished statue, 1527–1528. Marble, 8' 7½" high. Galleria dell'Accademia, Florence.

Carving a freestanding figure from stone or wood is a subtractive process. Michelangelo thought of sculpture as a process of "liberating" the statue contained within the block of marble.

tree trunks, and stone statues began as blocks pried from mountains. The unfinished marble statue illustrated here (FIG. I-16) by renowned Italian artist MICHELANGELO BUONARROTI (1475–1564) clearly reveals the original shape of the stone block. Michelangelo thought of sculpture as a process of "liberating" the statue within the block. All sculptors of stone or wood cut away (subtract) "excess material." When they finish, they "leave behind" the statue—in this example, a twisting nude male form whose head Michelangelo never freed from the stone block.

In additive sculpture, the artist builds up the forms, usually in clay around a framework, or *armature.* Or a sculptor may fashion a *mold,* a hollow form for shaping, or *casting,* a fluid substance such as bronze or plaster. The ancient Greek sculptor who made the bronze statue of a warrior found in the sea near Riace, Italy, cast the head (FIG. I-17) as well as the limbs, torso, hands, and feet (FIG. 5-36) in separate molds and then *welded* them together (joined them by heating). Finally, the artist added features, such as the pupils of the eyes (now missing), in other materials. The warrior's teeth are silver, and his lower lip is copper.

RELIEF SCULPTURE *Statues* and *busts* (head, shoulders, and chest) that exist independent of any architectural frame or setting and that viewers can walk around are *freestanding sculptures,* or *sculptures in the round,* whether the artist produced the piece by carving (FIG. I-10) or casting (FIG. I-17). In *relief sculpture,* the subjects project from the background but remain part of it. In *high-relief* sculpture, the images project boldly. In some cases, such as the medieval weighing-of-souls scene (FIG. I-7), the *relief* is so high that not only do the forms cast shadows on the background, but some parts are even in the round, which explains why some pieces—for example, the arms of the scales—broke off centuries ago. In *low-relief,* or *bas-relief,* sculpture, such as the portrait of Hesire (FIG. I-14), the projection is slight. Artists can produce relief sculptures, as they do sculptures in the round, either by carving or casting. The altar from Benin (FIG. I-15) is an example of bronze-casting in high relief (for the figures on the cylindrical altar) as well as in the round (for the king and his two attendants on the top).

ARCHITECTURAL DRAWINGS Buildings are groupings of enclosed spaces and enclosing masses. People experience architecture both visually and by moving through and around it, so they perceive architectural space and mass together. These spaces and masses can be represented graphically in several ways, including as plans, sections, elevations, and cutaway drawings.

A *plan,* essentially a map of a floor, shows the placement of a structure's masses and, therefore, the spaces they circumscribe and enclose. A *section,* a kind of vertical plan, depicts the placement of the masses as if someone cut through the building along a plane. Drawings showing a theoretical slice across a structure's width are *lateral sections.* Those cutting through a building's length are *longitudinal sections.* Illustrated here are the plan and lateral section of Beauvais Cathedral (FIG. **I-18**), which readers can compare with the photograph of the church's *choir* (FIG. I-3). The plan shows the choir's shape and the location of the *piers* dividing the *aisles* and supporting the *vaults* above, as well as the pattern of the crisscrossing vault *ribs.* The lateral section shows not only the interior of the choir with its vaults and tall *stained-glass* windows but also the structure of the roof and the form of the exterior *flying buttresses* holding the vaults in place.

Other types of architectural drawings appear throughout this book. An *elevation* drawing is a head-on view of an external or internal wall. A *cutaway* combines in a single drawing an exterior view with an interior view of part of a building.

This overview of the art historian's vocabulary is not exhaustive, nor have artists used only painting, drawing, sculpture, and architecture as media over the millennia. Ceramics, jewelry, textiles, photography, and computer graphics are just some of the numerous other arts. All of them involve highly specialized techniques described in distinct vocabularies. As in this introductory chapter, new terms are in *italics* when they first appear. The comprehensive Glossary at the end of the book contains definitions of all italicized terms.

Art History and Other Disciplines

By its very nature, the work of art historians intersects with the work of others in many fields of knowledge, not only in the humanities but also in the social and natural sciences. Today, art historians must go beyond the boundaries of what the public and even professional art historians of previous generations traditionally considered the specialized discipline of art history. In short, art historical research in the 21st century is typically interdisciplinary in nature. To cite one example, in an effort to unlock the secrets of a particular statue, an art historian might conduct archival research hoping to uncover new documents shedding light on who paid for the work and why, who made it and when, where it originally stood, how people of the time viewed it, and a host of other questions. Realizing, however, that the authors of the written documents often were not objective recorders of fact but observers with their own biases and agendas, the art historian may also use methodologies developed in such fields as literary criticism, philosophy, sociology, and gender studies to weigh the evidence that the documents provide.

At other times, rather than attempting to master many disciplines at once, art historians band together with other specialists in multidisciplinary inquiries. Art historians might call in chemists to date an artwork based on the composition of the materials used, or might

I-18 Plan (*left*) and lateral section (*right*) of Beauvais Cathedral, Beauvais, France, rebuilt after 1284.

Architectural drawings are indispensable aids for the analysis of buildings. Plans are maps of floors, recording the structure's masses. Sections are vertical "slices" across a building's width or length.

ask geologists to determine which quarry furnished the stone for a particular statue. X-ray technicians might be enlisted in an attempt to establish whether a painting is a forgery. Of course, art historians often reciprocate by contributing their expertise to the solution of problems in other disciplines. A historian, for example, might ask an art historian to determine—based on style, material, iconography, and other criteria—if any of the portraits of a certain king date after his death. Such information would help establish the ruler's continuing prestige during the reigns of his successors. Some portraits of Augustus (FIG. I-10), the founder of the Roman Empire, postdate his death by decades, even centuries, as do the portraits of several deceased U.S. presidents on coins and paper currency produced today.

DIFFERENT WAYS OF SEEING

The history of art can be a history of artists and their works, of styles and stylistic change, of materials and techniques, of images and themes and their meanings, and of contexts and cultures and patrons. The best art historians analyze artworks from many viewpoints. But no art historian (or scholar in any other field), no matter how broad-minded in approach and no matter how experienced, can be truly objective. Like the artists who made the works illustrated and discussed in this book, art historians are members of a society, participants in its culture. How can scholars (and museum visitors and travelers to foreign locales) comprehend cultures unlike their own? They can try to reconstruct the original cultural contexts of artworks, but they are limited by their distance from the thought patterns of the cultures they study and by the obstructions to understanding—the assumptions, presuppositions, and prejudices peculiar to their own culture—that their own thought patterns raise. Art historians may reconstruct a distorted picture of the past because of culture-bound blindness.

A single instance underscores how differently people of diverse cultures view the world and how various ways of seeing can result in sharp differences in how artists depict the world. Illustrated here are two contemporaneous portraits of a 19th-century Maori chieftain (FIG. I-19)—one by an Englishman, JOHN SYLVESTER (active early 19th century), and the other by the New Zealand chieftain himself, TE PEHI KUPE (d. 1829). Both reproduce the chieftain's facial *tattoo*. The European artist (FIG. I-19, *left*) included the head and shoulders and downplayed the tattooing. The tattoo pattern is one aspect of the likeness among many, no more or less important than the chieftain's European attire. Sylvester also recorded his subject's momentary glance toward the right and the play of light on his hair, fleeting aspects having nothing to do with the figure's identity.

In contrast, Te Pehi Kupe's self-portrait (FIG. I-19, *right*)—made during a trip to Liverpool, England, to obtain European arms to take back to New Zealand—is not a picture of a man situated in space and bathed in light. Rather, it is the chieftain's statement of the supreme importance of the tattoo design announcing his rank among his people. Remarkably, Te Pehi Kupe created the tattoo patterns from memory, without the aid of a mirror. The splendidly composed insignia, presented as a flat design separated from the body and even from the head, is Te Pehi Kupe's image of himself. Only by understanding the cultural context of each portrait can art historians hope to understand why either representation appears as it does.

As noted at the outset, the study of the context of artworks and buildings is one of the central concerns of art historians. *Art through the Ages* seeks to present a history of art and architecture that will help readers understand not only the subjects, styles, and techniques of paintings, sculptures, buildings, and other art forms created in all parts of the world during 30 millennia but also their cultural and historical contexts. That story now begins.

1 in.

I-19 *Left:* JOHN HENRY SYLVESTER, *Portrait of Te Pehi Kupe*, 1826. Watercolor, 8 ¼" × 6 ¼". National Library of Australia, Canberra (Rex Nan Kivell Collection). *Right:* TE PEHI KUPE, *Self-Portrait*, 1826. From Leo Frobenius, *The Childhood of Man: A Popular Account of the Lives, Customs and Thoughts of the Primitive Races* (Philadelphia: J. B. Lippincott, 1909), 35, fig. 28.

These strikingly different portraits of the same Maori chief reveal the different ways of seeing by a European artist and an Oceanic one. Understanding the cultural context of artworks is vital to art history.

◄ 26-1a The Enlightenment fascination with classical antiquity gave rise to the art movement called Neo-classicism. In this painting, Kauffman chose a classical subject and clothed her figures in Roman garb.

► 26-1b Kauffman's heroine is Cornelia, mother of Tiberius and Gaius Gracchus, political reformers during the Roman Republic. The portraits of the mother and her sons are based on ancient statuary.

1 ft.

26-1 ANGELICA KAUFFMAN, *Cornelia Presenting Her Children as Her Treasures*, or *Mother of the Gracchi*, ca. 1785. Oil on canvas, 3' 4" × 4' 2". Virginia Museum of Fine Arts, Richmond (Adolph D. and Wilkins C. Williams Fund).

◄ 26-1c The painting is an Enlightenment exemplum virtutis ("example of virtue"). When a visitor shows Cornelia her jewelry and asks to see Cornelia's, the mother of the Gracchi presents her children as her jewels.

Rococo to Neoclassicism: The 18th Century in Europe and America

THE ENLIGHTENMENT, ANGELICA KAUFFMAN, AND NEOCLASSICISM

The dawn of the *Enlightenment* in the 18th century brought a new way of thinking critically about the world and about men and women, independently of religion, myth, or tradition. Enlightenment thinkers rejected unfounded beliefs in favor of empirical evidence and promoted the questioning of all assertions. This new worldview was a major factor in the revolutionary political, social, and economic changes that swept Europe and America in the mid- to late 1700s. Among these were the wars for independence in America and France, the Industrial Revolution in England, and a renewed admiration in both Europe and America for the art and architecture of classical antiquity. The Enlightenment's emphasis on rationality in part explains this classical focus, because the geometric harmony of classical art and architecture embodied Enlightenment ideals. Moreover, Greece and Rome represented the pinnacle of civilized society— paragons of enlightened political organization. With their traditions of liberty, civic virtue, morality, and sacrifice, these cultures were ideal models during a period of political upheaval.

The Enlightenment interest in classical antiquity in turn gave rise to the artistic movement known as *Neoclassicism,* which incorporated the subjects and styles of Greek and Roman art. One of the pioneers of Neoclassical painting was ANGELICA KAUFFMAN (1741–1807). Born in Switzerland and trained in Italy, Kauffman spent many of her productive years in England. In an era when nearly all successful artists were men, Kauffman enjoyed an enviable reputation and was a founding member of the British Royal Academy of Arts.

Cornelia Presenting Her Children as Her Treasures, or *Mother of the Gracchi* (FIG. 26-1), is perhaps Kauffman's best-known work. The theme of the painting is the virtue of Cornelia, mother of the future political leaders Tiberius and Gaius Gracchus, who, in the second century BCE, attempted to reform the Roman Republic. Cornelia reveals her character in this scene, which takes place after a visitor has shown off her fine jewelry and then haughtily insists that Cornelia show hers. Instead of taking out her own precious adornments, Cornelia brings her sons forward, presenting them as her jewels. *Mother of the Gracchi* is a characteristic example of the Enlightenment embrace of the values of the classical world, an *exemplum virtutis* ("example of virtue") drawn from Greek and Roman history and literature.

To give her retelling of the story an authentic air, Kauffman studied ancient statuary and then clothed her actors in ancient Roman garb and posed them in statuesque attitudes within Roman interiors. The architectural setting is severe, and the composition and drawing have the simplicity and firmness of low-relief carving, qualities that became hallmarks of the Neoclassical style.

A CENTURY OF REVOLUTIONS

In 1700, Louis XIV still ruled France as the Sun King (see page 750), presiding over his realm and French culture from his palatial residence at Versailles (FIG. 25-26). The French king's palace inspired the construction of many other grandiose homes on the Continent and across the English Channel during the early 18th century, including Blenheim Palace (FIG. 26-1A), which SIR JOHN VANBRUGH (1664–1726) and NICHOLAS HAWKSMOOR (1661–

▣ **26-1A** VANBRUGH and HAWKSMOOR, Blenheim Palace, 1705-1725.

1736) designed for the duke of Marlborough. By 1800, however, revolutions had overthrown the monarchy in France and achieved independence for the British colonies in America. The 18th century also gave birth to a revolution of a different kind—the Industrial Revolution, which began in England and soon transformed the economies of continental Europe and North America and eventually the world.

Against this backdrop of revolutionary change, social as well as political, economic, and technological, came major transformations in the arts. Compare, for example, Antoine Watteau's 1717 *Pilgrimage to Cythera* (FIG. 26-7), which unfolds in a lush landscape and celebrates the romantic dalliances of the moneyed elite, with Angelica Kauffman's 1785 *Mother of the Gracchi* (FIG. 26-1), set in an austere home of classical columns and piers and glorifying the maternal virtue of an ancient Roman woman. The two works have little in common other than that both are horizontally oriented oil paintings. In the 18th century, shifts in style and subject matter were both rapid and significant.

ROCOCO

The death of Louis XIV in 1715 brought many changes in French high society. The elite quickly abandoned the court of Versailles for the pleasures of town life. Although French citizens still owed allegiance to a monarch, the early 18th century brought a resurgence of aristocratic social, political, and economic power. Members of the nobility not only exercised their traditional privileges (for example, exemption from certain taxes and from forced labor on public works) but also sought to expand their power. In the cultural realm, aristocrats reestablished their predominance as art patrons. The *hôtels* (elegant private townhouses) of Paris soon became the centers of a new, softer style called *Rococo*. Associated with the regency (1715–1723) following the death of Louis XIV and with the reign of Louis XV (r. 1723–1774), the Rococo style in art and architecture

was the perfect expression of the lighthearted elegance that the wealthy cultivated in their opulent homes (see "Femmes Savantes and Salon Culture," page 765).

Architecture

Rococo appeared in France around 1700, primarily as a style of interior design. The French Rococo exterior was most often simple, or even plain, but Rococo exuberance took over the interior. The term derived from the French word *rocaille* ("pebble"), but it referred especially to the small stones and shells used to decorate grotto interiors. Shells or forms resembling shells were the principal motifs in Rococo ornamentation.

SALON DE LA PRINCESSE A typical French Rococo room is the Salon de la Princesse (FIG. 26-2) in the Hôtel de Soubise in Paris, designed by GERMAIN BOFFRAND (1667–1754) in collaboration with the painter JOSEPH NATOIRE (1700–1777) and the sculptor JEAN-BAPTISTE LEMOYNE (1704–1778). Parisian salons such as this one were the center of Rococo social life. They usurped the role that Louis XIV's Versailles palace (FIG. 25-26) played in the 17th century, when the Sun King set the tone for French culture. In the early 18th century, the centralized and grandiose palace-based culture of Baroque France gave way to a much more intimate and decentralized culture based in private homes.

The new architectural style mirrored this social and cultural shift. A comparison between the Salon de la Princesse and the Galerie des Glaces (FIG. 25-27) at Versailles reveals how Boffrand softened the strong architectural lines and panels of the earlier style into flexible, sinuous curves. The walls melt into the vault. Irregular painted shapes, topped by sculpture and separated by rocaille shells, replace the hall's cornices. Painting, architecture, and sculpture combine to form a single ensemble. The profusion of curving tendrils and sprays of foliage blend with the shell forms to give an effect of freely growing nature, suggesting that the designer permanently bedecked the Rococo room for a festival.

French Rococo interiors were lively total works of art. Exquisitely wrought furniture, enchanting small sculptures (FIG. 26-10), ornamented mirror frames, crystal chandeliers, delightful ceramics and silver plates and goblets, small paintings, and decorative *tapestries* complemented the architecture, relief sculptures, and mural paintings. Unfortunately, the Salon de la Princesse has lost most of the moveable furnishings that once contributed so much to its total ambience. Visitors can nonetheless imagine how this and similar Rococo rooms—with their alternating gilded moldings, vivacious relief sculptures, and daintily colored ornamentation of flowers and garlands, all visually multiplied by their mirror reflections—must have harmonized with the chamber music played in them, with

ROCOCO TO NEOCLASSICISM: THE 18TH CENTURY IN EUROPE AND AMERICA

1700-1725	1725-1750	1750-1775	1775-1800
▪ The Rococo style becomes the rage in the opulent townhouses of Paris ▪ Watteau creates a new painting genre—the fête galante	▪ Neumann adapts the intimate Rococo domestic style to ecclesiastical architecture ▪ Chardin rejects the frivolity of Rococo painting in favor of "natural" art ▪ Canaletto paints views of Venice as souvenirs of the Grand Tour of Italy	▪ The Enlightenment admiration for Greece and Rome prompts a Neoclassical revival in architecture ▪ During the Industrial Revolution, Wright celebrates scientific advances in dramatic paintings ▪ British builders use iron in bridge construction at Coalbrookdale	▪ Reynolds achieves renown for Grand Manner portraits ▪ Vigée-Lebrun and Labille-Guiard gain admission to the French Royal Academy of Painting and Sculpture ▪ David becomes the painter-ideologist of the French Revolution ▪ Jefferson promotes Neoclassicism as the official architectural style of the new American republic

WRITTEN SOURCES
Femmes Savantes and Salon Culture

The feminine look of the Rococo style reflects the taste and social initiative of women, and to a large extent, women dominated the cultural sphere during the Rococo age. In the 18th century, aristocratic women—including Madame de Pompadour (1721–1764), mistress of Louis XV of France; Maria Theresa (1717–1780), archduchess of Austria and queen of Hungary and Bohemia; and Empresses Elizabeth (r. 1741–1762) and Catherine the Great (r. 1762–1796) of Russia—held some of the most influential positions in Europe. Female taste also was a defining factor in numerous smaller courts as well as in the private sphere.

In the early 1700s, Paris was the social capital of Europe, and the Rococo salon (FIG. 26-2) was the center of Parisian society. Wealthy, ambitious, and clever society hostesses competed to attract the most famous and accomplished people to their salons. The medium of social intercourse was conversation spiced with wit and as quick and deft as a fencing match. Artifice reigned supreme, and participants considered enthusiasm or sincerity in bad taste.

The women who hosted these salons, whether in Paris or elsewhere in Europe (FIG. 26-3), referred to themselves as *femmes savants* ("learned women"). Chief among them was Julie de Lespinasse (1732–1776), one of the most articulate, urbane, and intelligent French women of the time. She held daily salons from five o'clock until nine in the evening. The memoirs of Jean François Marmontel (1723–1799), published in 1827, documented the liveliness of these gatherings and the remarkable nature of this hostess.

The circle was formed of persons who were not bound together. She [Julie de Lespinasse] had taken them here and there in society, but so well assorted were they that once [in her salon] they fell into harmony like the strings of an instrument touched by an able hand. Following out that comparison, I may say that she played the instrument with an art that came of genius; she seemed to know what tone each string would yield before she touched it; I mean to say that our minds and our natures were so well known to her that in order to bring them into play she had but to say a word. Nowhere was conversation more lively, more brilliant, or better regulated than at her house. It was a rare phenomenon indeed, the degree of tempered, equable heat which she knew so well how to maintain, sometimes by moderating it, sometimes by quickening it. The continual activity of her soul was communicated to our souls, but measurably; her imagination was the mainspring, her reason the regulator. Remark that the brains she stirred at will were neither feeble nor frivolous. . . . Her talent for casting out a thought and giving it for discussion to men of that class, her own talent in discussing it with precision, sometimes with eloquence, her talent for bringing forward new ideas and varying the topic—always with the facility and ease of a fairy . . . these talents, I say, were not those of an ordinary woman. It was not with the follies of fashion and vanity that daily, during four hours of conversation, without languor and without vacuum, she knew how to make herself interesting to a wide circle of strong minds.*

*Jean François Marmontel, *Memoirs of Marmontel* (1827), translated by Brigit Patmore (London: Routledge, 1930), 270.

26-2 GERMAIN BOFFRAND, Salon de la Princesse, with paintings by CHARLES-JOSEPH NATOIRE and sculpture by JEAN-BAPTISTE LEMOYNE, Hôtel de Soubise, Paris, France, 1737–1740.

Rococo rooms such as this one, featuring sinuous curves, gilded moldings and mirrors, small sculptures and paintings, and floral ornamentation, were the center of Parisian social and intellectual life.

26-3 François de Cuvilliés, **Hall of Mirrors, the Amalienburg, Nymphenburg Palace park, Munich, Germany, early 18th century.**

Designed by a French architect, this circular hall in a German lodge displays the Rococo architectural style at its height, dazzling the eye with the organic interplay of mirrors, crystal, and stucco relief.

the elaborate costumes of satin and brocade, and with the equally elegant etiquette and sparkling wit of the people who graced them.

AMALIENBURG The French Rococo style quickly spread beyond Paris. The Amalienburg, a small lodge that the French architect François de Cuvilliés (1695–1768) built in the park of the Nymphenburg Palace in Munich, is a prime example of Germany's adoption of the Parisian style. The most spectacular room in the lodge is the circular Hall of Mirrors (FIG. **26-3**), a silver-and-blue ensemble of architecture, stucco relief, silvered bronze mirrors, and crystal. The hall dazzles the eye with myriad scintillating motifs, forms, and figurations, and showcases the full ornamental repertoire of the Rococo style at the height of its popularity. Silvery light, reflected and amplified by windows and mirrors, bathes the room and creates shapes and contours that weave rhythmically around the upper walls and the ceiling coves. Everything seems organic, growing, and in motion, an ultimate refinement of illusion with virtuoso flourishes created by the team of architects, artists, and artisans.

VIERZEHNHEILIGEN Rococo style was not exclusively a domestic phenomenon, however. Although some early-18th-century archi-

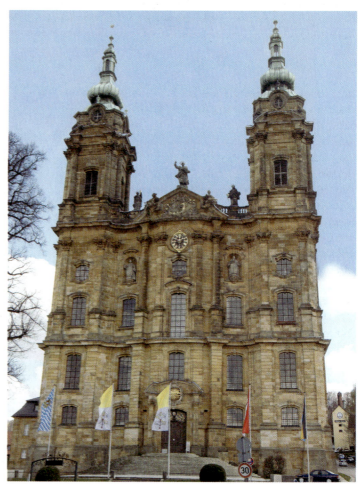

26-4 Balthasar Neumann, **facade of the pilgrimage church of Vierzehnheiligen (looking east), near Bad Staffelstein, Germany, 1743–1772.**

The facade of Neumann's pilgrimage church of Vierzehnheiligen (Fourteen Saints) features the undulating surfaces of Italian Baroque architecture, but its Rococo interior (FIG. 26-6) lacks Baroque drama.

26-5 BALTHASAR NEUMANN, plan of the pilgrimage church of Vierzehnheiligen, near Bad Staffelstein, Germany, 1743–1772.

Vierzehnheiligen's plan features undulating lines and a dynamic composition of tangent ovals and circles. It is even more complex than Borromini's influential church plans (FIGS. 24-11 and 24-13).

26-6 BALTHASAR NEUMANN, interior of the pilgrimage church of Vierzehnheiligen (looking east), near Bad Staffelstein, Germany, 1743–1772.

Neumann adapted the intimate Rococo style to ecclesiastical architecture. Vierzehnheiligen's interior is light and delicate, whereas Italian Baroque church designs are heavy and dynamic.

tects, such as JOHANN BERNHARD FISCHER VON ERLACH (1656–1723), continued to design churches incorporating Baroque and classical elements—for example, Karlskirche (FIG. 26-3A) in Vienna—others eagerly adopted the Rococo style for ecclesiastical architecture. One of the most splendid examples is the pilgrimage church of Vierzehnheiligen (Fourteen Saints; FIGS. 26-4, 26-5, and 26-6) near Bad Staffelstein (MAP 25-1), which the German architect BALTHASAR NEUMANN (1687–1753) began as construction was about to be concluded on the grandiose palace (FIG. 26-6A) he had designed in 1719 for the prince-bishops of Würzburg.

⬈ **26-3A** FISCHER VON ERLACH, Karlskirche, Vienna, 1716–1737.

⬈ **26-6A** NEUMANN, Kaisersaal, Würzburg, 1719–1744.

Vierzehnheiligen's undulating facade (FIG. 26-4) and curve-filled plan (FIG. 26-5) and interior (FIG. 26-6) reveal the influence of the great Italian Baroque architect Francesco Borromini (FIGS. 24-10 to 24-14). Neumann's plan, however, is even more complex than the plans of Borromini's churches in Rome. The German architect deliberately banished all straight lines. The composition, made up of tangent ovals and circles, achieves a quite different interior effect within the essential outlines of a traditional rectilinear basilican church with a nave, transept, and apse. Undulating space is in continuous motion, creating unlimited vistas that are bewildering in their variety and surprise effects, as is also true of the contemporaneous Wieskirche (Church of the Meadow; FIG. 26-6B) by DOMINIKUS ZIMMERMANN (1685–1766). Numerous large windows in Vierzehnheiligen's richly decorated walls flood the interior with an even, bright, and cheerful light. The feeling is one of lightness and delicacy. The church's walls and vaults pulse, flow, and commingle as if they were ceaselessly in the process of being molded. The design's fluidity of line, the floating and hovering surfaces, the interwoven spaces, and the dematerialized masses combine to suggest a "frozen" counterpart to the intricacy of voices in a Baroque fugue by Johann Sebastian Bach (1685–1750). The Bad Staffelstein pilgrimage church is a brilliant ensemble of architecture, painting, sculpture, and music that dissolves the boundaries among the arts.

⬈ **26-6B** ZIMMERMANN, Wieskirche, Füssen, 1745–1754.

Poussinistes and Rubénistes

Pilgrimage to Cythera (FIG. 26-7), the first great fête galante painting, was Antoine Watteau's entry for admission to the French Royal Academy of Painting and Sculpture (see "Academic Salons," page 844). In 1717, the fête galante was not an acceptable category for submission, but rather than reject Watteau's candidacy, the Academy created a new category to accommodate his entry.

At the turn of the 18th century, two competing doctrines sharply divided the membership of the French Royal Academy. Many members followed Nicolas Poussin (FIGS. 25-31, 25-32, and 25-32A) in teaching that form was the most important element in painting, whereas "colors in painting are as allurements for persuading the eyes."* Colors, argued Poussin's admirers, were additions for effect and not really essential. The other group took Rubens (FIGS. 25-2, 25-2A, 25-3, and 25-4) as its model and proclaimed the natural supremacy of color and the coloristic style as the artist's proper guide.

Depending on which doctrine they supported, members of the French Academy were classified as either *Poussinistes* or *Rubénistes*. Watteau was Flemish, and Rubens's coloristic style heavily influenced his work. With Watteau in their ranks, the Rubénistes carried the day, establishing Rococo painting as the preferred style in early-18th-century France.

*Translated by Robert Goldwater and Marco Treves, eds., *Artists on Art*, 3d ed. (New York: Pantheon Books, 1958), 157.

26-7 ANTOINE WATTEAU, *Pilgrimage to Cythera*, 1717. Oil on canvas, 4' 3" × 6' 4$\frac{1}{2}$". Musée du Louvre, Paris.

Watteau's fête galante paintings depict the outdoor amusements of French upper-class society. The haze of color suited the new Rococo taste and was the hallmark of the Royal Academy's Rubénistes.

Painting and Sculpture

The unification of diverse artistic media that characterizes the Rococo style did not preclude the rise to prominence of painters of independent works. Chief among them were Antoine Watteau, François Boucher, and Jean-Honoré Fragonard in France.

ANTOINE WATTEAU The painter whom scholars most closely associate with French Rococo is ANTOINE WATTEAU (1684–1721). Watteau was largely responsible for creating a specific type of Rococo painting genre called a *fête galante* ("amorous festival") (see "Poussinistes and Rubénistes," above). Fête galante paintings depicted the outdoor entertainment or amusements of French high society. The premier example is Watteau's masterpiece (painted in two versions), *Pilgrimage to Cythera* (FIG. 26-7). The canvas presents luxuriously costumed lovers who have made a "pilgrimage" to Cythera, the island of eternal youth and love, sacred to Aphrodite. (Some art historians think the lovers are returning from Cythera rather than having just arrived. Watteau provided few clues to settle the question definitively.) The elegant figures move gracefully from the protective shade of a woodland park filled with playful cupids and voluptuous statuary. The poses of the figures, which blend elegance and sweetness, are hallmarks of Watteau's style, both in ambitious multifigure compositions such as *Pilgrimage to Cythera* and in single-figure studies such as *L'Indifférent* (FIG. 26-7A).

⤴ **26-7A** Watteau, *L'Indifférent*, ca. 1716.

Watteau prepared his paintings using albums of drawings in which he sought to capture slow movement from difficult and unusual angles, searching for the smoothest, most poised, and most refined attitudes. As he experimented with nuances of posture and movement, Watteau also strove for the most exquisite shades of color difference, defining in a single stroke the shimmer of silk at a bent knee or the shine appearing on a glossy surface as it emerges from shadow. The haze of color, the subtly modeled shapes, the gliding motion, and the air of suave gentility tinged with nostalgia appealed greatly to Watteau's wealthy patrons, whom, as he was dying from tuberculosis, he still depicted as carefree and at leisure in his most unusual painting, *Signboard of Gersaint* (FIG. 26-7B).

⤴ **26-7B** Watteau, *Signboard of Gersaint*, 1721.

FRANÇOIS BOUCHER After Watteau's death at age 36 brought his brilliant career to a premature end, FRANÇOIS BOUCHER (1703–1770) rose to the dominant position in French painting, in large part because he was Madame de Pompadour's favorite artist. Although Boucher was an excellent portraitist, his success rested primarily on his graceful canvases depicting shepherds, nymphs, and goddesses cavorting in shady glens engulfed in pink and sky-blue light. *Cupid a Captive* (FIG. 26-8) presents a rosy pyramid of infant and female flesh set off against a cool, leafy background, with fluttering draperies both hiding and revealing the nudity of the figures. Boucher used the full range of Italian and French Baroque devices—the dynamic play of crisscrossing diagonals, curvilinear forms, and slanting recessions—to create his masterful composition. But he dissected powerful Baroque curves into a multiplicity of decorative flourishes, dissipating Baroque drama into sensual playfulness. Lively and lighthearted, Boucher's artful Rococo fantasies became mirrors for his well-to-do French patrons to behold the ornamental reflections of their cherished pastimes.

1 ft.

26-8 FRANÇOIS BOUCHER, *Cupid a Captive*, 1754. Oil on canvas, 5' 6" × 2' 10". Wallace Collection, London.

Boucher was Madame de Pompadour's favorite artist. In this Rococo tableau, he painted a pyramid of rosy infant and female flesh and fluttering draperies set off against a cool, leafy background.

JEAN-HONORÉ FRAGONARD Boucher's greatest student, JEAN-HONORÉ FRAGONARD (1732–1806), was a first-rate colorist whose decorative skill almost surpassed his master's. An example of his

26-9 JEAN-HONORÉ FRAGONARD, *The Swing*, 1766. Oil on canvas, 2' 8⅝" × 2' 2". Wallace Collection, London.

Fragonard's *Swing* exemplifies Rococo style. Pastel colors and soft light complement a scene in which a young lady flirtatiously kicks off her shoe at a statue of Cupid while her lover gazes at her.

Italian Mannerist sculpture. His small group *Nymph and Satyr Carousing* (FIG. **26-10**) depicts two followers of Bacchus, the Roman god of wine. The sensuous nymph who rushes to pour wine from a cup into the open mouth of a semihuman goat-legged satyr is reminiscent of the nude female figures of Benvenuto Cellini (FIGS. 22-52 and 22-52A), who worked at Fontainebleau for Francis I (see page 693), and of Giambologna (FIG. 22-53), a French Mannerist sculptor who moved to Italy. The erotic playfulness of Boucher and Fragonard is also evident in Clodion's 2-foot-tall terracotta group destined for display on a marble tabletop in an elegant Rococo salon.

GIAMBATTISTA TIEPOLO Also small are *The Swing*—less than 3 feet in height—and Watteau's *L'Indifférent* (FIG. 26-7A), which is barely 10 inches tall. Even the figure-packed landscape *Pilgrimage to Cythera* (FIG. 26-7) is only a little more than 4 feet high. But the intimate Rococo style could also be adapted for paintings of huge size, as the work of GIAMBATTISTA TIEPOLO (1696–1770) demonstrates. A Venetian, Tiepolo worked for patrons in Austria, Germany (FIG. 26-4A), and Spain, as well as in Italy. He was a master of illusionistic ceiling decoration in the Baroque tradition, but favored the bright,

manner can stand as characteristic not only of his work but also of the later Rococo in general. In *The Swing* (FIG. 26-9), a young gentleman has convinced an unsuspecting old bishop to swing the young man's pretty sweetheart higher and higher, while her lover (and the work's patron), in the lower left corner, stretches out to admire her from a strategic position on the ground. The young lady flirtatiously kicks off her shoe toward the little statue of Cupid. The infant love god holds his finger to his lips. The landscape emulates Watteau's— a luxuriant perfumed bower in a park that very much resembles a stage scene for comic opera. The glowing pastel colors and soft light convey, almost by themselves, the theme's sensuality.

CLODION Rococo was a style best suited for small-scale works projecting a mood of sensual intimacy. Claude Michel, called CLODION (1738–1814), specialized in small, lively sculptures representing sensuous Rococo fantasies. Clodion lived and worked in Rome for several years after winning a cherished Prix de Rome (Rome Prize) from the French Royal Academy to study art and paint or sculpt in the Eternal City. Clodion's work incorporates echoes of

26-10 CLODION, *Nymph and Satyr Carousing*, ca. 1780–1790. Terracotta, 1' 11¼" high. Metropolitan Museum of Art, New York (bequest of Benjamin Altman, 1913).

The erotic playfulness of Boucher and Fragonard is evident in Clodion's tabletop terracotta sculptures representing sensuous fantasies often involving satyrs and nymphs, the followers of Bacchus.

10 ft.

26-11 GIAMBATTISTA TIEPOLO, *Apotheosis of the Pisani Family,* ceiling painting in the Villa Pisani, Stra, Italy, 1761–1762. Fresco, 77' 1" × 44' 3".

A master of illusionistic ceiling painting in the Baroque tradition, Tiepolo adopted the bright and cheerful colors and weightless figures of Rococo easel paintings for huge frescoes.

THE ENLIGHTENMENT

The aristocratic culture celebrated in Rococo art did not go unchallenged during the 18th century. Indeed, the feudal system that served as the foundation of social and economic life in Europe dissolved, and the rigid social hierarchies that provided the basis for Rococo art and patronage relaxed. By the end of the 18th century, revolutions had erupted in France and America. A major factor in these political, social, and economic changes was the Enlightenment.

Philosophy and Science

Enlightenment thinkers rejected faith in favor of reason and championed an approach to the acquisition of knowledge based on empirical observation and scientific experimentation. Enlightenment-era science had roots in the work of René Descartes (1596–1650), Blaise Pascal (1623–1662), Isaac Newton (1642–1727), and Gottfried Wilhelm von Leibniz (1646–1716) in the 17th century. England and France were the principal centers of the Enlightenment, though its maxims influenced the thinking of intellectuals throughout Europe and in the American colonies. Benjamin Franklin (1706–1790), Thomas Jefferson (1743–1826), and other American notables embraced its principles.

NEWTON AND LOCKE Of particular importance for Enlightenment thought was the work of Isaac Newton and John Locke (1632–1704) in England. In his scientific studies, Newton insisted on empirical proof of his theories and encouraged others to avoid metaphysics and the supernatural—realms that extended beyond the natural physical world. This emphasis on both tangible data and concrete experience became a cornerstone of Enlightenment thought. In addition, Newton's experiments revealed rationality in the physical world, and Enlightenment thinkers transferred that concept to the sociopolitical world by promoting a rationally organized society. Locke, whose works acquired the status of Enlightenment gospel, developed these ideas further. According to Locke's "doctrine of empiricism," knowledge comes through sensory perception of the material world. From these perceptions alone, people form ideas.

Locke asserted that human beings are born good, not cursed by original sin. The laws of nature grant them the natural rights of life, liberty, and property as well as the right to freedom of conscience. Government is by contract, and the purpose of the government is to protect these rights. If and when government abuses these rights, the citizenry has the further natural right of revolution. Locke's ideas empowered people to take control of their own destinies.

PHILOSOPHES The work of Newton and Locke also inspired many French intellectuals, or *philosophes.* These thinkers conceived of individuals and societies as parts of physical nature. They shared the conviction that the ills of humanity could be remedied by

cheerful colors and relaxed compositions of Rococo easel paintings. In *Apotheosis of the Pisani Family* (FIG. **26-11**), a ceiling fresco in the Villa Pisani at Stra in northern Italy (MAP 25-1), Tiepolo depicted seemingly weightless figures fluttering through vast sunlit skies and fleecy clouds, their forms casting dark accents against the brilliant light of high noon. The painter elevated Pisani family members to the rank of gods in a heavenly scene recalling the ceiling paintings of Pozzo (FIG. 24-24). But while retaining 17th-century illusionism in his works, Tiepolo softened the rhetoric and created pictorial schemes of great elegance and grace, unsurpassed for their sheer effectiveness as decor.

ART AND SOCIETY

Joseph Wright of Derby and the Industrial Revolution

The scientific advances of the Enlightenment era affected the lives of everyone, and most people enthusiastically responded to the wonders of the Industrial Revolution such as the steam engine, which gave birth to the modern manufacturing economy and the prospect of a seemingly limitless supply of goods and services.

The fascination that science held for ordinary people as well as for the learned was a favorite subject of the English painter Joseph Wright of Derby (FIGS. **26-11A** and **26-12**). Wright studied painting near Birmingham (MAP 27-2), the center of the Industrial Revolution, and specialized in dramatically lit scenes showcasing modern scientific instruments and experiments.

26-11A WRIGHT OF DERBY, *Experiment on a Bird*, 1768.

A characteristic example of Wright's work is *A Philosopher Giving a Lecture at the Orrery*. In this painting, a scholar demonstrates a mechan-ical model of the solar system called an *orrery*, in which each planet (represented by a metal orb) revolves around the sun (a lamp) at the correct relative velocity. Light from the lamp pours forth from in front of the boy silhouetted in the foreground to create shadows that heighten the drama of the scene. Curious children crowd close to the tiny orbs representing the planets within the curving bands symbolizing their orbits. An earnest listener makes notes, while the lone woman seated at the left and the two gentlemen at the right pay rapt attention. Scientific knowledge mesmerizes everyone in Wright's painting. The artist visually reinforced the fascination with the orrery by composing his image in a circular fashion, echoing the device's orbital design. The postures and gazes of all the participants and observers focus attention on the cosmic model. Wright scrupulously and accurately rendered every detail of the figures, the mechanisms of the orrery, and even the books and curtain in the shadowy background.

Wright's choice of subjects and realism in depicting them appealed to the great industrialists of his day, including Josiah Wedgwood (1730–1795), who pioneered many techniques of mass-produced pottery, and Sir Richard Arkwright (1732–1792), whose spinning frame revolutionized the textile industry. Both men often purchased paintings by Wright featuring scientific advances. To them, the Derby artist's elevation of the theories and inventions of the Industrial Revolution to the plane of history painting was exciting and appropriately in tune with the new era of Enlightenment.

26-12 JOSEPH WRIGHT OF DERBY, *A Philosopher Giving a Lecture at the Orrery*, ca. 1763–1765. Oil on canvas, 4' 10" × 6' 8". Derby Museums and Art Gallery, Derby.

Wright specialized in dramatically lit paintings celebrating the modern scientific instruments of the Industrial Revolution. Here, a scholar demonstrates an orrery, a revolving model of the solar system.

1 ft.

applying reason and common sense to human problems. They criticized the powers of Church and State as irrational limits placed on political and intellectual freedom. They were convinced that by accumulating and propagating knowledge, humanity could advance by degrees to a happier state than it had ever known. This conviction matured into the "doctrine of progress" and its corollary doctrine, the "perfectibility of humankind." Previous societies, for the most part, perceived the future as inevitable—the cycle of life and death. They believed that religious beliefs determined fate. The notion of progress—the systematic and planned improvement of society—first developed during the 18th century and still influences 21st-century thought.

DIDEROT Animated by their belief in human progress and perfectibility, the philosophes took on the task of gathering knowledge and making it accessible to all who could read. Their program was, in effect, the democratization of knowledge. Denis Diderot (1713–1784) greatly advanced the Enlightenment's rationalistic and materialistic thinking. He became editor of the pioneering *Encyclopédie,* a compilation of articles written by more than a hundred contributors, including all the leading philosophes. The *Encyclopédie* was truly comprehensive (its formal title was *Systematic Dictionary of the Sciences, Arts, and Crafts*) and included all available knowledge—historical, scientific, and technical as well as religious and moral—and political theory. (The *Encyclopédie*'s 21st-century descendant is Wikipedia, which has a similar goal of collecting all that is known and making that knowledge universally available.) The first installment of Diderot's 35-volume illustrated encyclopedia appeared in 1751 and the last in 1780. Other Enlightenment authors produced different compilations of knowledge. Diderot's contemporary Georges-Louis Leclerc (1707–1788) undertook a kind of encyclopedia of the natural sciences. His *Natural History,* a monumental work of 44 volumes, was especially valuable for its zoological content. At the same time, Swedish botanist Carolus Linnaeus (1707–1778) established a system of plant classification.

The political, economic, and social consequences of this increase in knowledge and of the doctrine of progress were explosive. It is no coincidence that the French Revolution, the American Revolution, and the Industrial Revolution in England all occurred during this period. These upheavals precipitated yet other major changes, including the growth of cities and of an urban working class, and the expansion of colonialism as the demand for cheap labor and raw materials increased. This enthusiasm for growth gave birth to the doctrine of Manifest Destiny (see page 814)—the ideological justification for continued territorial expansion. Thus the Enlightenment ushered in a new way of thinking and affected historical developments worldwide.

VOLTAIRE François Marie Arouet, better known as Voltaire (1694–1778), was the most representative figure—almost the personification—of the Enlightenment spirit. Voltaire was instrumental in introducing Newton and Locke to the French intelligentsia. He hated, and attacked through his writings, the arbitrary despotic rule of kings, the selfish privileges of the nobility and the Church,

religious intolerance, and, above all, the injustice of the French *ancien régime* (the "old order"). In his numerous books and pamphlets, which the authorities regularly condemned and burned, he protested against government persecution of the freedoms of thought and religion. Voltaire believed that people could never be happy until an enlightened society removed the traditional obstructions to the progress of the human mind. His personal and public involvement in the struggle against established political and religious authority gave authenticity to his ideas. Voltaire persuaded a whole generation that fundamental changes were necessary, paving the way for a revolution in France that he never intended, and probably would not have approved. For example, Voltaire did not believe that "all men are created equal," the credo of Jean-Jacques Rousseau, Thomas Jefferson, and the American Declaration of Independence.

INDUSTRIAL REVOLUTION The Enlightenment emphasis on scientific investigation and technological invention opened up new possibilities for human understanding of the world and for control of its material forces. Research into the phenomena of electricity and combustion, along with the discovery of oxygen and the power of steam, had enormous consequences. Steam power as an adjunct to, or replacement for, human labor initiated a new era in world history. These and other technological advances—admiringly recorded in the paintings of Joseph Wright of Derby (1734–1797; see "Joseph Wright of Derby and the Industrial Revolution," page 772, and figs. 26-11A and 26-12)—exemplified the Enlightenment notion of progress and gave birth to the Industrial Revolution. Most scholars mark the dawn of that technological revolution in the 1740s with the invention in England of steam engines for industrial production. By 1850, England could boast the world's first manufacturing economy. Within a century, the harnessed power of steam, coal, oil, iron, steel, and electricity, working in concert, transformed Europe. These scientific and technological advances also affected the arts, particularly through the invention of photography (see page 832) and the use of new materials for constructing buildings.

COALBROOKDALE BRIDGE The first use of iron in bridge design was in the cast-iron bridge (FIG. 26-13) built over the Severn River, near Coalbrookdale in England (MAP 30-1), where Abraham Darby III (1750–1789), one of the bridge's two designers, ran his family's cast-iron business. The Darby family had spearheaded

26-13 Abraham Darby III and Thomas F. Pritchard, iron bridge (looking northwest), Coalbrookdale, England, 1776–1779.

The first use of iron in bridge design was in this bridge over the Severn River. The Industrial Revolution brought engineering advances and new materials that permanently changed architectural construction.

WRITTEN SOURCES
Diderot on Chardin and Boucher

Denis Diderot was a pioneer in the field of art criticism as well as in the encyclopedic compilation of human knowledge. Between 1759 and 1781, he contributed reviews of the biennial Salon of the French Royal Academy of Painting and Sculpture (see "Academic Salons," page 844) to the Parisian journal *Correspondence littéraire*. In his review of the 1763 Salon, Diderot had the following praise for Chardin's still lifes and for naturalism in painting.

There are many small pictures by Chardin at the Salon, almost all of them depicting fruit with the accoutrements for a meal. This is nature itself. The objects stand out from the canvas and they are so real that my eyes are fooled by them. . . . In order to look at other people's paintings, I feel as though I need different eyes; but to look at Chardin's, I need only keep the ones nature gave me and use them properly. If I had painting in mind as a career for my child, I'd buy this one [and have him copy it]. . . . Yet nature itself may be no more difficult to copy. . . . O Chardin, it's not white, red or black pigment that you grind on your palette but rather the very substance of objects; it's real air and light that you take onto the tip of your brush and transfer onto the canvas. . . . It's magic, one can't understand how it's done: thick layers of color, applied one on top of the other, each one filtering through from underneath to create the effect. . . . Close up, everything blurs, goes flat and disappears. From a distance, everything comes back to life and reappears.*

While Diderot lavished praise on some of the leading artists of his day, he wrote scathing reviews of others. He admired Chardin (FIG. 26-14) because his work was the antithesis of the Rococo manner in painting, which Diderot deplored. Here, for example, is what Diderot had to say about François Boucher (FIG. 26-8), who also exhibited in the Salon of 1763, and his younger protégés emulating his Rococo style:

What a misuse of talent! How much time gone to waste! You could have had twice the effect for half the effort. . . . When one writes, does one have to write everything? And when one paints, does one have to paint everything? . . . This man is the ruination of all young apprentice painters. Barely able to handle a brush and hold a palette, they torture themselves stringing together infantile garlands, painting chubby crimson bottoms, and hurl themselves headlong

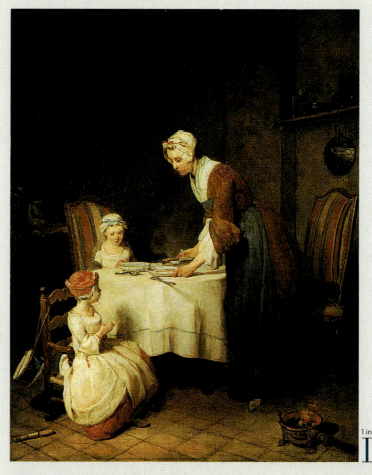

26-14 JEAN-BAPTISTE-SIMÉON CHARDIN, *Grace*, 1740. Oil on canvas, 1' 7" × 1' 3". Musée du Louvre, Paris.

Chardin embraced naturalism and celebrated the simple goodness of ordinary people, especially mothers and children, who lived in a world far from the frivolous Rococo salons of Paris.

into all kinds of follies which cannot be redeemed by originality, fire, tenderness nor by any magic in their models. For they lack all of these.†

*Translated by Kate Tunstall, in Charles Harrison, Paul Wood, and Jason Gaiger, eds., *Art in Theory 1648-1815: An Anthology of Changing Ideas* (Oxford: Blackwell, 2000), 604.
†Ibid., 603-604.

the evolution of the iron industry in England, and they vigorously supported the investigation of new uses for the material. The fabrication of cast-iron rails and bridge elements inspired Darby to work with architect THOMAS F. PRITCHARD (1723–1777) in designing the Coalbrookdale Bridge. The cast-iron armature supporting the roadbed springs from stone pier to stone pier until it leaps the final 100 feet across the Severn River gorge. The style of the graceful center arc echoes the grand arches of Roman *aqueducts* (FIG. 7-33). At the same time, the exposed structure of the bridge's cast-iron parts prefigured the skeletal use of iron and steel in the 19th century, when exposed structural armatures became expressive factors in the design of buildings such as the Crystal Palace (FIG. 27-47) in England and the Eiffel Tower (FIG. 28-40) in France.

"NATURAL" ART

The second key figure of the French Enlightenment, who was also instrumental in preparing the way ideologically for the French Revolution, was Jean-Jacques Rousseau (1712–1778). Voltaire believed that the salvation of humanity lay in the advancement of science and the rational improvement of society. In contrast, Rousseau argued that the arts and sciences, society, and civilization in general had corrupted "natural man"—people in their primitive state. He was convinced that humanity's only salvation lay in a return to something like "the ignorance, innocence and happiness" of its original condition. According to Rousseau, human capacity for feeling, sensibility, and emotions came before reason: "To exist is to feel; our feeling is undoubtedly earlier than our intelligence, and we had feelings before we had ideas." Nature alone must be the guide: "All our natural inclinations are right." Fundamental to Rousseau's thinking was the notion that "Man by nature is good . . . he is depraved and perverted by society." He rejected the idea of progress, insisting that "our minds have been corrupted in proportion as the arts and sciences have improved."[1] Rousseau's elevation of feeling above reason as the most primitive—and hence the most "natural"—human expression led him to exalt as the ideal the peasant's simple life, with its honest and unsullied emotions.

Rousseau's views, popular and widely read, were largely responsible for the turning away from the Rococo sensibility in the arts and the formation of a taste for the "natural," as opposed to the artificial and frivolous.

CHARDIN Reflecting Rousseau's values, JEAN-BAPTISTE-SIMÉON CHARDIN (1699–1779) painted quiet scenes of domestic life in the tradition of 17th-century Dutch genre scenes (see pages 746–747). These subjects offered Chardin the opportunity to praise the simple goodness of ordinary people, especially mothers and young children, who in spirit, occupation, and environment lived far from corrupt society. In *Grace* (FIG. 26-14), Chardin ushers the viewer into a modest room where a mother and her small daughters are about to dine. The mood of quiet attention is at one with the hushed lighting and mellow color and with the closely studied still-life accessories whose worn surfaces tell their own humble domestic history. The viewer witnesses a moment of social instruction, when mother and older sister supervise the younger sister in the simple, pious ritual of giving thanks to God before a meal. The simplicity of the composition reinforces the subdued charm of this scene, with the three figures highlighted against the dark background. Chardin was the poet of the commonplace and the master of its nuances. A gentle sentiment

prevails in all his pictures, an emotion not contrived and artificial but born of the painter's honesty, insight, and sympathy. Chardin's paintings had wide appeal, even in unexpected places. Louis XV, the royal personification of the Rococo in his life and tastes, once owned *Grace*. The painter was also a favorite of Diderot, the leading art critic of the day as well as the editor of the *Encyclopédie* (see "Diderot on Chardin and Boucher," page 774).

JEAN-BAPTISTE GREUZE The sentimental narrative in art became the specialty of French artist JEAN-BAPTISTE GREUZE (1725–1805), whose most popular work, *Village Bride* (FIG. 26-15), sums up the characteristics of the genre. The setting is an unadorned room in a rustic dwelling. In a notary's presence, the elderly father has passed his daughter's dowry to her youthful husband-to-be and blesses the pair, who gently take each other's arms. The old mother tearfully gives her daughter's arm a farewell caress, while the youngest sister melts in tears on the shoulder of the demure bride. An envious older sister broods behind her father's chair. Rosy-faced, healthy children play around the scene. The picture's story is simple—the happy climax of a rural romance. The picture's moral is just as clear—happiness is the reward of "natural" virtue.

Greuze produced this work at a time when the audience for art was expanding. The strict social hierarchy that provided the foundation for Rococo art and patronage gave way to a bourgeois economic and social system. The newly important middle class embraced art, and paintings such as *Village Bride* particularly appealed to ordinary hard-working people. They carefully analyzed each gesture and each nuance of sentiment and reacted with tumultuous enthusiasm. At the 1761 Salon of the Royal Academy, Greuze's picture received enormous attention. Diderot, who reviewed the exhibition for *Correspondence littéraire,* reported that it was difficult to get near the canvas because of the throngs of admirers.

26-15 JEAN-BAPTISTE GREUZE, *Village Bride,* 1761. Oil on canvas, 3' × 3' 10½". Musée du Louvre, Paris.

Greuze was a master of sentimental narrative, which appealed to a new audience that admired "natural" virtue. Here, in an unadorned room, a father blesses his daughter and her husband-to-be.

1 ft.

ART AND SOCIETY

Vigée-Lebrun, Labille-Guiard, and the French Royal Academy

The two most successful woman artists in 18th-century France were Élisabeth-Louise Vigée-Lebrun (FIGS. 26-15A and 26-16) and Adélaïde Labille-Guiard (FIG. 26-17). Although they shared the honor of admission to the French Royal Academy of Painting and Sculpture and enjoyed royal patronage, their careers differed in some significant ways.

Vigée-Lebrun began painting as a young girl under the tutelage of her father, Louis Vigée (1715–1767), a successful portrait painter. By the time she was 15,

🔎 **26-15A** Vigée-Lebrun, *Marie Antoinette*, 1787.

she had already received portrait commissions of her own. After her marriage to Jean-Baptiste Lebrun, a prominent Parisian art dealer, she began to attract wealthy and important clients, whom the couple entertained in salons at their fashionable home. Vigée-Lebrun soon became the favorite painter of Queen Marie Antoinette, whose influence gained the 28-year-old artist admission to the Royal Academy in 1783. She eventually painted some 30 portraits of the queen. Vigée-Lebrun

was famous for the force and grace of her portraits of highborn ladies and royalty throughout Europe. Her induction into the Royal Academy was short-lived, however. After the French Revolution, the Academy rescinded her membership because women were no longer welcome. Nonetheless, Vigée-Lebrun enjoyed continued success owing to her talent, wit, and ability to forge connections with those in power in the postrevolutionary period.

Six years older than Vigée-Lebrun, Labille-Guiard never achieved the renown enjoyed by her younger contemporary. She trained with François-Élie Vincent (1708–1790) and later with his son François-André Vincent (1746–1816), whom she married after her divorce from her first husband, Louis-Nicolas Guiard, a clerk. Like Vigée-Lebrun, Labille-Guiard boasted royal patronage, but not of the same order. She became the official painter of the "mesdames"—the aunts of King Louis XVI—in 1787, four years after she was admitted to the French painting academy on the same day as Vigée-Lebrun. The two painters captured the remaining two of four memberships reserved for women, a quota that Labille-Guiard worked hard to lift after gaining admission. The two artists took opposite sides during the French Revolution, and Labille-Guiard painted portraits of some of the uprising's leaders, including one of the few known portraits of Maximilien Robespierre (1758–1794), the most prominent figure calling for the death of King Louis XVI.

26-16 Élisabeth-Louise Vigée-Lebrun, *Self-Portrait*, 1790. Oil on canvas, 8' 4" × 6' 9". Galleria degli Uffizi, Florence.

Vigée-Lebrun was one of the few women admitted to the Royal Academy of Painting and Sculpture. In this self-portrait, she depicted herself confidently painting the likeness of Queen Marie Antoinette.

26-17 Adélaïde Labille-Guiard, *Self-Portrait with Two Pupils*, 1785. Oil on canvas, 6' 11" × 4' 11$\frac{1}{2}$". Metropolitan Museum of Art, New York (gift of Julia A. Berwind, 1953).

In contrast to Vigée-Lebrun (FIG. 26-16), Labille-Guiard, her older contemporary, depicted herself as a teacher. Her father's bust portrait serves as her muse in a reversal of traditional gender roles.

ÉLISABETH-LOUISE VIGÉE-LEBRUN Another manifestation of the "naturalistic" impulse in 18th-century French art was the emergence of a new more personal and less pretentious mode of portraiture. *Self-Portrait* (FIG. 26-16) by ÉLISABETH-LOUISE VIGÉE-LEBRUN (1755–1842) is a characteristic example of the genre. The painter looks directly at viewers and pauses in her work to return their gaze. Although her mood is lighthearted and her costume's details echo the serpentine curve that Rococo artists and wealthy patrons loved, nothing about Vigée-Lebrun's pose appears contrived. Hers is the self-confident, natural stance of a woman whose art has won her an independent role in society (see "Vigée-Lebrun, Labille-Guiard, and the French Royal Academy," page 776). She portrayed herself in a close-up, intimate view at work on one of the many portraits (for example, FIG. 26-15A) that she painted of her most important patron, Queen Marie Antoinette (1755–1793).

ADÉLAÏDE LABILLE-GUIARD After Vigée-Lebrun, the second most important woman painter in Paris at the end of the 18th century was ADÉLAÏDE LABILLE-GUIARD (1749–1803). A comparison between Labille-Guiard's *Self-Portrait with Two Pupils* (FIG. 26-17) and Vigée-Lebrun's *Self-Portrait* (FIG. 26-16) is instructive. It underscores the two women's different self-images. The younger painter presented herself at work on a portrait of her most important patron, Marie Antoinette. The subject of the canvas that Labille-Guiard is painting is unknown. Her self-portrait focuses instead on her role as a teacher. She had as many as nine women in her studio

at one time. Here, two apprentices—dressed more simply than their elegantly clad instructor—cluster behind her, one intently studying the painting in progress, the other, like Labille-Guiard, gazing at the viewer. The three figures form a classical pyramidal composition, echoed by the easel. In the V formed by the two triangles is a portrait bust of the artist's father. Appropriately for this early feminist, her muse is a man, a reversal of the traditional gender roles.

WILLIAM HOGARTH Across the Channel, a truly English style of painting emerged with WILLIAM HOGARTH (1697–1764), who satirized the lifestyle of the newly prosperous middle class with comic zest. Traditionally, the British imported painters from the Continent—Holbein, Rubens, and Van Dyck among them. Hogarth waged a lively campaign throughout his career against the English feeling of dependence on, and inferiority to, these artists. Although Hogarth would have been the last to admit it, his own painting owed much to the work of his contemporaries in France, the Rococo artists. Yet his subject matter, frequently moral in tone, was distinctively English. This was the great age of English satirical writing, and Hogarth—who admired that literary genre and included Henry Fielding (1701–1754), the author of *Tom Jones* (1749), among his closest friends—clearly saw himself as translating satire into the visual arts.

Hogarth's favorite device was to make a series of narrative paintings and prints, in a sequence similar to chapters in a book or scenes in a play, following a character or group of characters in their encounters with some social evil. *Breakfast Scene* (FIG. 26-18),

26-18 WILLIAM HOGARTH, *Breakfast Scene,* from *Marriage à la Mode,* ca. 1745. Oil on canvas, 2′ 4″ × 3′. National Gallery, London.

Hogarth won fame for his paintings and prints satirizing English life with comic zest. This is one of a series of six paintings in which he chronicled the marital immoralities of the moneyed class.

26-19 Thomas Gainsborough, *Mrs. Richard Brinsley Sheridan,* 1787. Oil on canvas, 7' 2$\frac{5}{8}$" × 5' $\frac{5}{8}$". National Gallery of Art, Washington, D.C. (Andrew W. Mellon Collection).

In this life-size portrait, Gainsborough sought to match Mrs. Sheridan's natural beauty with that of the landscape. The rustic setting, soft-hued light, and feathery brushwork recall Rococo painting.

1 ft.

from *Marriage à la Mode,* is one in a sequence of six paintings satirizing the marital immoralities of the moneyed classes in England. In it, the marriage of a young viscount is just beginning to founder. The husband and wife are tired after a long night spent in separate pursuits. While the wife stayed at home for an evening of cards and music-making, her young husband had been away from the house enjoying the company of another woman. He thrusts his hands deep into the empty money-pockets of his breeches, while his wife's small dog sniffs inquiringly at the other woman's lacy cap protruding from his coat pocket. A steward, his hands full of unpaid bills, raises his eyes in despair at the actions of his noble master and mistress.

The couple's home is palatial, but Hogarth filled it with witty clues to the dubious taste of its occupants. For example, the row of pious religious paintings on the upper wall of the distant room concludes with a curtained canvas undoubtedly depicting an erotic subject. According to the custom of the day, ladies could not view this discretely hidden painting, but at the pull of a cord, the master and his male guests could enjoy a tableau of cavorting figures. In *Breakfast Scene,* as in all his work, Hogarth proceeded as a novelist might, elaborating on his subject with carefully chosen detail, the discovery of which heightens the comedy.

Hogarth designed the marriage series to be published as a set of engravings. The prints of this and his other moral narratives were so popular that unscrupulous entrepreneurs produced unauthorized versions almost as fast as the artist created his originals. The popularity of these prints speaks not only to the appeal of their subjects but also to the democratization of knowledge and culture that the Enlightenment fostered and to the exploitation of new printing technologies that opened the way for a more affordable and widely disseminated visual culture.

THOMAS GAINSBOROUGH A contrasting blend of "naturalistic" representation and Rococo setting is found in *Mrs. Richard Brinsley Sheridan* (FIG. 26-19), a characteristic portrait by British painter THOMAS GAINSBOROUGH (1727–1788). Gainsborough presented Mrs. Sheridan as a lovely, informally dressed woman seated in a rustic landscape faintly reminiscent of Watteau (FIG. 26-7) in its soft-hued light and feathery brushwork. Gainsborough's goal was to match the natural, unspoiled beauty of the landscape with that of his sitter. Mrs. Sheridan's dark brown hair blows freely in the slight wind, and her clear "English complexion" and air of ingenuous sweetness contrast sharply with the pert sophistication of the subjects of Continental Rococo portraits. Gainsborough planned to give the picture a more pastoral air by adding several sheep, but he did not live long enough to complete the canvas. Even with-

out the sheep, the painting clearly expresses Gainsborough's deep interest in the landscape setting. Although he won greater fame in his time for his portraits, as did his slightly older contemporary, SIR JOSHUA REYNOLDS (1723–1792; see "Grand Manner Portraiture," page 779, and FIG. 26-20), Gainsborough had begun as a landscape painter and always preferred painting scenes of nature to depicting individual likenesses.

BENJAMIN WEST Some American artists also became well known in England. BENJAMIN WEST (1738–1820), born in Pennsylvania on what was then the colonial frontier, traveled to Europe early in life to study art and then went to England, where he met with almost immediate success. One of the 36 founding members of the Royal Academy of Arts, West succeeded Sir Joshua Reynolds as its president. He became official painter to George III (r. 1760–1801) and retained that position even during the strained period of the American Revolution.

In *Death of General Wolfe* (FIG. 26-21), West depicted the mortally wounded young English commander just after his defeat of the French in the decisive battle of Quebec in 1759, which gave Canada to Great Britain. Because his subject was a recent event, West

PROBLEMS AND SOLUTIONS
Grand Manner Portraiture

The Enlightenment concept of "nobility," especially in the view of Rousseau (page 774), referred to character, not to aristocratic birth. In an era of revolutions, the virtues of courage and resolution, patriotism, and self-sacrifice assumed greater importance. Having risen from humble origins, the modern military hero joined the well-born aristocrat as a major patron of portrait painting.

Sir Joshua Reynolds was one of those who often received commissions to paint likenesses of key participants in the great events of the latter part of the 18th century. Indeed, he soon specialized in what became known as *Grand Manner portraiture*, echoing the term that Nicolas Poussin used in the previous century to describe his paintings of "grand subjects" (see page 755). Although clearly depicting specific individuals, Grand Manner portraits elevated the sitters by conveying refinement and elegance. Reynolds and other painters communicated a person's grace and class through certain standardized conventions, such as the large scale of the figure relative to the canvas, the controlled pose, the landscape setting, and the low horizon line.

Reynolds painted *Lord Heathfield* (FIG. 26-20) in 1787. The sitter was a perfect subject for a Grand Manner portrait—a burly, ruddy English officer, the commandant of the fortress at Gibraltar. Heathfield had doggedly defended the British stronghold against the Spanish and French, and later received the honorary title Baron Heathfield of Gibraltar. Here, he holds the huge key to the fortress, the symbol of his victory. He stands in front of a curtain of dark smoke rising from the battleground, flanked by one cannon pointing ineffectively downward and another whose tilted barrel indicates that it lies uselessly on its back. Reynolds portrayed the features of the general's heavy, honest face and his uniform with unidealized realism. But Lord Heathfield's posture and the setting dramatically suggest the heroic themes of battle, courage, and patriotism.

26-20 Sir Joshua Reynolds, *Lord Heathfield*, 1787. Oil on canvas, 4' 8" × 3' 9". National Gallery, London.

In this Grand Manner portrait, Reynolds depicted the English commander who defended Gibraltar. As is typical for this genre, Heathfield stands in a dramatic pose, and his figure takes up most of the canvas.

26-21 Benjamin West, *Death of General Wolfe*, 1771. Oil on canvas, 4' 11 $\frac{1}{2}$" × 7'. National Gallery of Canada, Ottawa (gift of the Duke of Westminster, 1918).

West's major innovation was to blend contemporary subject matter and costumes with the grand tradition of history painting. Here, the painter likened General Wolfe's death to that of a martyred saint.

26-22 JOHN SINGLETON COPLEY, *Paul Revere,* ca. 1768–1770. Oil on canvas, 2' 11$\frac{1}{8}$" × 2' 4". Museum of Fine Arts, Boston (gift of Joseph W., William B., and Edward H. R. Revere).

In contrast to Grand Manner portraits, Copley's *Paul Revere* emphasizes the subject's down-to-earth character, differentiating this American work from its European counterparts.

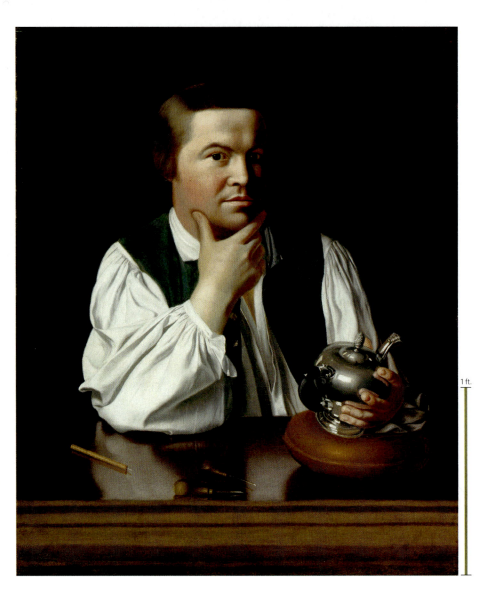

1 ft.

clothed his characters in contemporary costumes (although the military uniforms are not accurate in all details) and included a rare glimpse for his English audience of a Native American warrior, depicted as an exemplary "noble savage." However, West blended this realism of detail with the grand tradition of history painting by arranging his figures in a complex and theatrically ordered composition. His modern hero dies among grieving officers on the field of victorious battle in a way that suggests the death of a saint. (The composition, in fact, derives from paintings of the lamentation over the dead Christ; compare FIG. 20-9.) West wanted to present this hero's death in the service of the state as a martyrdom charged with religious emotions. His innovative and highly effective combination of the conventions of traditional heroic painting with a look of modern realism influenced history painting well into the 19th century.

JOHN SINGLETON COPLEY   American artist JOHN SINGLETON COPLEY (1738–1815) matured as a painter in the Massachusetts Bay Colony. Like West, Copley later emigrated to England, where he absorbed the fashionable English portrait style. But unlike Grand Manner portraits, Copley's *Paul Revere* (FIG. **26-22**), painted before the artist left Boston, conveys a sense of directness and faithfulness to visual fact that marked the taste for honesty and plainness noted by many late-18th- and 19th-century visitors to America. When Copley painted his likeness, Revere was not yet the familiar hero of the American Revolution. In this picture, he is a working professional silversmith. The setting is plain, the lighting clear and revealing. Revere sits in his shirtsleeves, bent over a teapot in progress. He pauses and turns his head to look the observer straight in the eyes. The painter treated the reflections in the polished wood of the tabletop with as much care as he did Revere's figure, his tools, and the teapot resting on its leather graver's pillow. Copley gave special prominence to Revere's eyes by reflecting intense reddish light onto the darkened side of his face and hands. The informality and the sense of the moment link this painting to contemporaneous English and Continental portraits. But the spare style and the emphasis on the sitter's down-to-earth character differentiate this American work from its European counterparts.

THE GRAND TOUR   The 18th-century public also sought "naturalness" in artists' depictions of landscapes. Documentation of specific places became popular, in part due to growing travel opportunities and expanding colonialism. These depictions of geographic settings also served the needs of the many scientific expeditions mounted during the century and satisfied the desires of genteel tourists for

mementos of their journeys. By this time, a "Grand Tour" of the major sites of Europe was an essential part of every well-bred person's education (see "The Grand Tour and Veduta Painting," page 781). Those who embarked on a tour of the Continent wished to return with souvenirs to help them remember their experiences and impress those at home with the wonders they had seen. The English were especially eager collectors of travel pictures. Venetian artists in particular found it profitable to produce paintings of the most characteristic *vedute* ("scenic views") of their city to sell to British visitors. Chief among those artists was ANTONIO CANALETTO (1697–1768), whose works—for example, *Riva degli Schiavoni, Venice (Bank of the Slaves, Venice;* FIG. **26-23**)—English tourists avidly acquired as evidence of their visit to Italy's magical city of water.

POMPEO BATONI   Some of those who embarked on the Grand Tour sought to obtain a more personalized memento of their cultural journey than a portrait of Venice: a portrait of themselves painted by the leading Italian portrait painter of the day, POMPEO BATONI (1708–1787). Born in Lucca and trained in Rome, where he eventually became curator of the papal art collection, Batoni received commissions for "Grand Tour portraits" from prosperous visitors of various nationalities, but especially from Englishmen. More than 150 of Batoni's portraits of English gentlemen with Italian backdrops are in museums and private collections today.

ART AND SOCIETY

The Grand Tour and Veduta Painting

Although travel throughout Europe was commonplace in the 18th century, Italy became an especially popular destination. This "pilgrimage" of aristocrats, the wealthy, politicians, and diplomats from France, England, Germany, Flanders, Sweden, Russia, Poland, Hungary, and even the British colonies in America came to be known as the Grand Tour. Italy's allure fueled the revival of classicism, and the popularity of Neoclassical art drove the fascination with Italy. One British observer noted, "All our religion, all our arts, almost all that sets us above savages, has come from the shores of the Mediterranean."*

The Grand Tour was not simply leisure travel. The education available in Italy to the inquisitive mind made such a tour an indispensable experience for anyone who wished to make a mark in society. The Enlightenment had made knowledge of ancient Greece and Rome imperative, and a steady stream of Europeans and Americans traveled to Italy in the late 18th and early 19th centuries. These tourists aimed to increase their knowledge of literature, the visual arts, architecture, theater, music, history, customs, and folklore. Given this extensive agenda, it is not surprising that a Grand Tour could take a number of years to complete. Most travelers moved from location to location, following an established itinerary, not unlike the pilgrimages to saints' shrines in the late Middle Ages (see "Pilgrimage Roads in France and Spain," page 342).

The British were the most avid travelers, and they conceived the initial "tour code," including required itineraries to important destinations. Although they designated Rome early on as the primary destination in Italy, visitors traveled as far north as Venice and as far south as Naples. Eventually, Paestum, Sicily, Florence, Siena, Pisa, Genoa, Milan, Bologna, and Parma (MAP 25-1) all appeared in guidebooks and in paintings. Joseph Wright of Derby (FIGS. 26-11A and 26-12) and Joseph Mallord William Turner (FIG. 27-22) were among the many British artists to undertake a Grand Tour.

Many visitors to Italy returned home from their Grand Tour with a painting by Antonio Canaletto, the leading painter of scenic views (*vedute*) of Venice. It must have been very cheering on a gray winter afternoon in England to look up and see a sunny, panoramic view such as that in Canaletto's *Riva degli Schiavoni, Venice* (FIG. 26-23), with its cloud-studded sky, picturesque water traffic, and well-known Venetian landmarks painted in scrupulous perspective and minute detail. (The Doge's Palace [FIG. 14-23] is at the left in *Riva degli Schiavoni*.)

Canaletto usually made drawings "on location" to take back to his studio and use as sources for paintings. To help make the on-site drawings true to life, he often used a *camera obscura,* as Vermeer (FIG. 25-18B) did before him. These instruments were darkened chambers (some of them virtually portable closets) with optical lenses fitted into a hole in one wall through which light entered to project an inverted image of the subject onto the chamber's opposite wall. The artist could trace the main details from this image for later reworking and refinement. The camera obscura enabled artists to create convincing representations incorporating the variable focus of objects at different distances. Canaletto's paintings give the impression of capturing every detail, with no "editing." In fact, he presented each site according to Renaissance perspective conventions and exercised great selectivity about which details to include and which to omit to make a coherent and engagingly attractive veduta.

*Cesare de Seta in Andrew Wilton and Ilaria Bignamini, eds., *Grand Tour: The Lure of Italy in the Eighteenth Century* (London: Tate Gallery, 1996), 13.

1 ft.

26-23

ANTONIO CANALETTO, *Riva degli Schiavoni, Venice,* ca. 1735–1740. Oil on canvas, $1'\,6\frac{1}{2}'' \times 2'\,\frac{7}{8}''$. **Toledo Museum of Art, Toledo.**

Canaletto was the leading painter of Venetian vedute, which were treasured souvenirs for 18th-century travelers visiting Italy on a Grand Tour. He used a camera obscura for his on-site drawings.

26-24 Pompeo Batoni, *Charles John Crowle,* ca. 1761–1762. Oil on canvas, 8' 1⅝" × 5' 7¾". Musée du Louvre, Paris.

Prosperous visitors to Rome on the Grand Tour frequently commissioned Batoni to paint their portraits. Here, an English gentleman poses with items attesting to his learning and passion for antiquity.

1 ft.

the excavations of Herculaneum and Pompeii, which the volcanic eruption of Mount Vesuvius had buried (see "The Excavations of Herculaneum and Pompeii," page 783). Soon, murals based on the paintings unearthed in the excavations began to appear in European townhouses, such as the Etruscan Room (FIG. 26-25) by Robert Adam (1728–1792) in Osterley Park House in Middlesex, begun in 1761.

GIBBON AND WINCKELMANN The enthusiasm for classical antiquity also permeated much of the scholarship of the time. In the late 18th century, the ancient world increasingly became the focus of academic research. For example, a visit to Rome inspired Edward Gibbon (1737–1794) to begin his monumental *Decline and Fall of the Roman Empire,* which appeared between 1776 and 1788. The classical world, and specifically classical art, became the lifelong focus of Johann Joachim Winckelmann (1717–1768), whom scholars widely recognize as the first modern art historian (see "Winckelmann and the History of Classical Art," page 784).

Painting

The Enlightenment idea of a participatory and knowledgeable citizenry lay behind the revolt against the French monarchy in 1789, but the immediate causes of the French Revolution were France's economic crisis and the clash between the Third Estate (bourgeoisie, peasantry, and urban and rural workers) and the First and Second Estates (the clergy and nobility, respectively). They fought over the issue of representation in the legislative body, the Estates-General, which had been convened to discuss taxation as a possible solution to the economic problem. However, the ensuing revolution revealed the instability of the monarchy and of French society's traditional structure and resulted in a succession of republics and empires as France struggled to find a way to adjust to these fundamental changes.

JACQUES-LOUIS DAVID The artist who became the painter-ideologist of the French Revolution was Jacques-Louis David (1748–1825). Mengs (FIG. 26-25A) and Kauffman (FIG. 26-1) were pioneers of Neoclassical painting, but David is generally considered the greatest Neoclassical master. A distant relative of François Boucher (FIG. 26-8), David followed the Rococo painter's style until a period of study in Rome won the younger man over to the classical art tradition. David favored academic teachings about using the art of the ancients and of the great Renaissance masters as models. He, like Winckelmann, rebelled against Rococo style as an "artificial taste" and exalted the "perfect form" of Greek art (see "David on Greek Style and Public Art," page 784).

OATH OF THE HORATII David concurred with the Enlightenment belief that the subject of an artwork should have a moral. Paintings representing noble deeds in the past could inspire virtue in the

Batoni's portrait (FIG. 26-24) of Charles John Crowle (1738–1811) is a characteristic example of the type of portrait that his patrons found so appealing. Crowle, a second-generation member of the British Parliament from Yorkshire, stands in a palatial columnar study with a view of the Roman countryside behind him. Attended by his faithful dog, Crowle is surrounded by abundant evidence of his learning and passion for antiquity. Most prominent are copies of reduced size of the *Farnese Hercules* (FIG. 5-66) in Naples and of a statue of the sleeping Ariadne in the Vatican. On the elegant table on which Crowle leans is an astronomical model (compare FIG. 26-12) and an unrolled plan of Saint Peter's (FIG. 24-4). In 1764, after returning from Rome, Crowle was elected a member of the Society of Dilettanti, a prestigious group of British connoisseur-admirers of Greco-Roman art.

NEOCLASSICISM

As Batoni's *Charles John Crowle* (FIG. 26-24) vividly illustrates, the popularity of the Grand Tour among the cultural elite of Europe both reflected and contributed to the heightened interest in classical antiquity during the Enlightenment. Exposure to the art treasures of Italy was also a major factor in the rise of Neoclassicism as the leading art movement of the late 18th century (see "The Enlightenment, Angelica Kauffman, and Neoclassicism," page 763). Further whetting the public appetite for classicism were

ART AND SOCIETY

The Excavations of Herculaneum and Pompeii

Among the developments stimulating the European fascination with classical antiquity was the initiation of systematic excavations at two ancient Roman towns on the Bay of Naples—Herculaneum and Pompeii—in 1738 and 1748, respectively. The violent eruption of Mount Vesuvius in August 79 had buried both sites under volcanic ash and lava (see "An Eyewitness Account of the Eruption of Mount Vesuvius," page 186), protecting the towns for hundreds of years from looters and the ravages of nature. Consequently, the 18th-century excavations yielded an unprecedented number of well-preserved paintings, sculptures, vases, and other household objects, and provided rich evidence for reconstructing Roman art and life. As a result, European ideas about and interest in ancient Rome expanded tremendously, and collectors eagerly acquired as many of the newly discovered antiquities as they could. One of the most avid collectors was Sir William Hamilton (1731–1803), British consul in Naples from 1764 to 1800, who purchased numerous painted vases and other ancient objects soon after taking up his post. Because Hamilton sold his collection to the British Museum in 1772, the finds at Pompeii and Herculaneum quickly became available to a wide public.

"Pompeian" style soon became all the rage in England, as evident, for example, in Robert Adam's Etruscan Room (FIG. 26-25) at Osterley Park House, which was inspired by the frescoes of the Third and early Fourth Styles of Roman mural painting (FIGS. 7-21 and 7-34A). Adam took decorative motifs (medallions, urns, vine scrolls, *sphinxes*, and *tripods*) from Roman art and arranged them sparsely within broad, neutral spaces and slender margins, as in his elegant, linear ancient models. This new Neoclassical style almost entirely displaced the curvilinear Rococo (FIGS. 26-2 and 26-3) in the homes of the wealthy after midcentury. Adam was also an archaeologist, and he had explored and written accounts of the ruins of Diocletian's palace (FIG. 7-72) at Split. Kedleston House in Derbyshire, Adelphi Terrace in London, and a great many other structures that he designed show how the Split palace influenced his work.

The archaeological finds from Herculaneum and Pompeii also affected garden and landscape design, fashion, and tableware. Clothing based on classical garb became popular, and Emma, Lady Hamilton (1761–1815), Sir William's wife, often gave lavish parties dressed in delicate Greek-style drapery (compare the costumes in Angelica Kauffman's *Mother of the Gracchi*; FIG. 26-1).

Neoclassical taste also determined the pottery designs of John Flaxman (1755–1826) and Josiah Wedgwood. Wedgwood established his reputation in the 1760s with his creamware inspired by ancient art. He eventually produced vases based on what were then thought to be Etruscan designs (they were, in fact, imported Greek vases deposited in Etruscan tombs; see page 108) and expanded his business by producing small busts of classical figures as well as cameos and medallions adorned with copies of antique reliefs and statues.

26-25 **Robert Adam**, Etruscan Room, Osterley Park House, Middlesex, England, begun 1761. Reconstructed in the Victoria & Albert Museum, London.

Inspired by archaeological discoveries at Herculaneum and Pompeii in the mid-18th century, Adam incorporated decorative motifs from Roman mural painting into his Etruscan Room at Osterley Park.

Winckelmann and the History of Classical Art

In 1755, Johann Joachim Winckelmann published his groundbreaking *Reflections on the Imitation of Greek Works in Painting and Sculpture*. In this treatise, the German scholar unequivocally designated Greek art as the most perfect to come from human hands. For Winckelmann, classical art was far superior to the "natural" art of his day.

> Good taste, which is becoming more prevalent throughout the world, had its origins under the skies of Greece. . . . The only way for us to become great . . . is to imitate the ancients. . . . In the masterpieces of Greek art, connoisseurs and imitators find not only nature at its most beautiful but also something beyond nature, namely certain ideal forms of its beauty. . . . A person enlightened enough to penetrate the innermost secrets of art will find beauties hitherto seldom revealed when he compares the total structure of Greek figures with most modern ones, especially those modeled more on nature than on Greek taste.*

In his later *History of Ancient Art* (1764), Winckelmann carefully described major works of classical art and positioned each one within a huge inventory organized by subject, style, and period. Before Winckelmann, art historians had focused on biography, as did Giorgio Vasari and Giovanni Pietro Bellori in the 16th and 17th centuries (see "Giorgio Vasari's *Lives*," page 636, and "Giovanni Pietro Bellori on Annibale Carracci and Caravaggio," page 713). Winckelmann thus initiated one modern art historical method thoroughly in accord with Enlightenment ideas of ordering knowledge—a system of description and classification that provided a pioneering model for the understanding of stylistic evolution.

As was the norm at that time, Winckelmann's familiarity with classical art derived predominantly from Roman works and Roman copies of Greek art in Italy. Yet Winckelmann was instrumental in bringing to scholarly attention the differences between Greek and Roman art. Thus he paved the way for more thorough study of the distinct characteristics of the art and architecture of these two cultures.

Winckelmann's influence extended beyond the world of scholarship. He also was instrumental in promoting Neoclassicism as a major stylistic movement in late-18th-century painting. He was, for example, the scholar who advised his countryman ANTON RAPHAEL MENGS (1728–1779) on classical iconography when Mengs painted *Parnassus* (FIG. 26-25A), the fresco that many art historians regard as the first Neoclassical painting. It predates Angelica Kauffman's *Mother of the Gracchi* (FIG. 26-1) by almost a quarter century.

26-25A MENGS, *Parnassus*, 1761.

*Translated by Elfriede Heyer and Roger C. Norton in Charles Harrison, Paul Wood, and Jason Gaiger, eds., *Art in Theory 1648–1815: An Anthology of Changing Ideas* (Oxford: Blackwell, 2000), 451–453.

present. A milestone painting in the Neoclassical master's career, *Oath of the Horatii* (FIG. 26-26), depicts a story from pre-Republican Rome, the heroic phase of Roman history. The topic was not too obscure for David's audience. Pierre Corneille (1606–1684) had retold this story of conflict between love and patriotism, recounted by the ancient Roman historian Livy, in a play performed in Paris several years earlier. According to the story, the leaders of the warring cities of Rome and Alba decided to resolve their conflicts in a series of encounters waged by three representatives from each side.

The Romans chose as their champions the three Horatius brothers, who had to face the three sons of the Curatius family from Alba. A sister of the Horatii, Camilla, was the bride-to-be of one of the Curatius sons, and the wife of the youngest Horatius was the sister of the Curatii. David's painting shows the Horatii as they swear on their swords, held high by their father, to win or die for Rome, oblivious to the anguish and sorrow of the Horatius women.

Oath of the Horatii is a paragon of the Neoclassical style. Not only does the subject matter deal with a narrative of patriotism

David on Greek Style and Public Art

Jacques-Louis David was the leading Neoclassical painter in France at the end of the 18th century. He championed a return to Greek style and the painting of inspiring heroic and patriotic subjects. In 1796, he made the following statement to his pupils:

> I want to work in a pure Greek style. I feed my eyes on antique statues, I even have the intention of imitating some of them. The Greeks had no scruples about copying a composition, a gesture, a type that had already been accepted and used. They put all their attention and all their art on perfecting an idea that had been already conceived. They thought, and they were right, that in the arts the way in which an idea is rendered, and the manner in which it is expressed, is much more important than the idea itself. To give a body and a perfect form to one's thought, this—and only this—is to be an artist.*

David also strongly believed that paintings depicting noble events in ancient history, such as his *Oath of the Horatii* (FIG. 26-26), would serve to instill patriotism and civic virtue in the public at large in postrevolutionary France. In November 1793, he wrote:

> [The arts] should help to spread the progress of the human spirit, and to propagate and transmit to posterity the striking examples of the efforts of a tremendous people who, guided by reason and philosophy, are bringing back to earth the reign of liberty, equality, and law. The arts must therefore contribute forcefully to the education of the public. . . . The arts are the imitation of nature in her most beautiful and perfect form. . . . [T]hose marks of heroism and civic virtue offered the eyes of the people [will] electrify the soul, and plant the seeds of glory and devotion to the fatherland.†

*Translated by Robert Goldwater and Marco Treves , eds., *Artists on Art*, 3d ed. (New York: Pantheon Books, 1958), 206.
†Ibid., 205.

26-26 JACQUES-LOUIS DAVID, *Oath of the Horatii*, 1784. Oil on canvas, 10' 10" × 13' 11". Musée du Louvre, Paris.

David was the Neoclassical painter-ideologist of the French Revolution. This huge canvas celebrating ancient Roman patriotism and sacrifice features statuesque figures and classical architecture.

and sacrifice excerpted from Roman history, but the painter also employed formal devices to present the image with force and clarity. The action unfolds in a shallow space much like a stage setting, defined by a severely simple architectural framework (compare FIG. 26-1). David deployed his statuesque and carefully modeled figures across the space, close to the foreground, in a manner reminiscent of ancient relief sculpture. The rigid, angular, and virile forms of the men on the left effectively contrast with the soft curvilinear shapes of the distraught women on the right. This juxtaposition visually pits the virtues that Enlightenment leaders ascribed to men, such as courage, patriotism, and unwavering loyalty to a cause, against the emotions of love, sorrow, and despair expressed by the women in the painting. The French viewing audience perceived such emotionalism as characteristic of the female nature. The message was clear and of a type readily identifiable to the prerevolutionary French public.

The picture created a sensation at its first exhibition in Paris in 1785. Although David had painted it under royal patronage and did not intend the painting as a revolutionary statement, *Oath of the Horatii* aroused his audience to patriotic zeal. The Neoclassical style soon became the semiofficial voice of the French Revolution.

DEATH OF MARAT When the revolution broke out in 1789, David threw in his lot with the Jacobins, the radical and militant revolutionary faction. He accepted the role of de facto minister of propaganda, organizing political pageants and ceremonies requiring floats, costumes, and sculptural props. David believed that art could play an important role in educating the public and that dramatic paintings emphasizing patriotism and civic virtue would prove effective as rallying calls. However, rather than continuing to create artworks focused on scenes from antiquity, David began to portray scenes from the French Revolution itself.

In 1793, David painted *Death of Marat* (FIG. **26-27**), which he wanted not only to serve as a record of an important event in the struggle to overthrow the monarchy but also to provide inspiration and encouragement to the revolutionary forces. The painting commemorates the assassination that year of Jean-Paul Marat (1743–1793), an influential writer who was David's friend. The artist depicted the martyred revolutionary still holding a quill pen in his right hand after Charlotte Corday (1768–1793), a member of a rival political faction, stabbed him to death while Marat was immersed in a bathtub as he worked. (Marat suffered from a

26-27 JACQUES-LOUIS DAVID, *Death of Marat,* 1793. Oil on canvas, 5' 5" × 4' 2½". Musées Royaux des Beaux-Arts de Belgique, Brussels.

David depicted the revolutionary Marat as a tragic martyr, stabbed to death in his bath. Although the painting displays severe Neoclassical spareness, its convincing realism conveys pain and outrage.

26-28 JACQUES-GERMAIN SOUFFLOT, Panthéon (Sainte-Geneviève; looking northeast), Paris, France, 1755–1792.

Soufflot's Panthéon is a testament to the Enlightenment admiration for Greece and Rome. It combines a portico based on an ancient Roman temple with a colonnaded dome and a Greek-cross plan.

painful skin disease and required frequent medicinal baths.) His "desk" was a board placed across the tub with a wood stand next to it for his writing materials. David presented the scene with directness and clarity. The cold neutral space above Marat's figure slumped in the tub produces a chilling oppressiveness. The painter vividly placed all narrative details in the foreground— the knife, the wound, the blood, the letter with which Corday gained entrance—to sharpen the sense of pain and outrage. David masterfully composed the painting to present Marat as a tragic martyr who died in the service of the revolution. Indeed, the writing stand, which bears the words "To Marat, David," resembles a tombstone, and David based Marat's figure on the dead Christ in Michelangelo's *Pietà* (FIG. 22-12) in Saint Peter's in Rome. The reference to Christ's martyrdom made the painting a kind of "altarpiece" for the new civic "religion," inspiring the French people with the saintly dedication of their slain leader.

Architecture and Sculpture

Architects in the Enlightenment era also formed a deep admiration for the Greco-Roman past. Fairly early in the 18th century, they began to turn away from the theatricality and ostentation of Baroque design, still evident in grandiose structures such as Blenheim Palace (FIG. 26-1A) in England and Karlskirche (FIG. 26-3A) in Austria, as well as from the delicate flourishes of Rococo salons (FIGS. 26-2 and 26-3), palaces (FIG. 26-6A), and churches (FIGS. 26-4 and 26-6B). The style they instead embraced offered a more streamlined antique look.

PANTHÉON The Parisian church of Sainte-Geneviève (FIG. **26-28**), now the Panthéon, designed by JACQUES-GERMAIN SOUFFLOT (1713–1780) stands as testament to the revived interest in classical architecture. The Roman ruins at Baalbek in Syria, especially the gigantic colonnade of the temple of Jupiter, provided much of the inspiration for Soufflot's Neoclassical church. The columns, reproduced with studied archaeological precision, stand out from walls that are severely blank, except for a repeated garland motif near the top. The colonnaded dome, a Neoclassical version of the domes of Saint Peter's (FIG. 22-25) in Rome, the Église du Dôme (FIG. 25-30) in Paris, and Saint Paul's (FIG. 25-38) in London, rises above a Greek-cross plan. Both the dome and the vaults rest on an interior grid of splendid freestanding Corinthian columns, as if the portico's colonnade continued within. Although the whole effect, inside and out, is Roman, the structural principles employed were essentially Gothic. Soufflot was one of the first 18th-century builders to apply the logical engineering of Gothic cathedrals (see "The Gothic Cathedral," page 381) to modern buildings. With few exceptions, however, such as Strawberry Hill (FIG. **26-28A**), owned and largely designed by HORACE WALPOLE (1717–1797), the revival of interest in the Gothic architectural style did not take hold until the following century (see page 828 and FIGS. 27-43 and 27-43A).

26-28A WALPOLE, Strawberry Hill, Twickenham, 1749–1777.

CHISWICK HOUSE The appeal of classical architecture extended well beyond French borders. The popularity of Greek and Roman cultures was due not only to their association with morality, rationality, and integrity but also to their connection to political systems ranging from Athenian democracy to Roman imperial rule. Thus parliamentary England joined revolutionary France in embracing Neoclassicism. In England, Neoclassicism's appeal also was due to its clarity and simplicity. These characteristics provided a stark

26-29 RICHARD BOYLE and WILLIAM KENT, Chiswick House (looking northwest), near London, England, begun 1725.

For this English villa, Boyle and Kent emulated the simple symmetry and unadorned planes of the Palladian architectural style. Chiswick House is a free variation on the Villa Rotonda (FIG. 22-28).

contrast to the complexity and opulence of Baroque art, then associated with the flamboyant rule of absolute monarchy. In English architecture, the preference for a simple and rational style derived indirectly from the authority of the ancient Roman architect Vitruvius (see "Vitruvius's *Ten Books on Architecture*," page 199) through Andrea Palladio (FIGS. 22-28 to 22-31) in the 16th century and Inigo Jones (FIG. 25-37) in the 17th.

RICHARD BOYLE (1695–1753), earl of Burlington, strongly restated Jones's Palladian doctrine in the new Neoclassical idiom in Chiswick House (FIG. **26-29**), which he built on London's outskirts with the help of WILLIAM KENT (ca. 1686–1748). Paving the way for this shift in style was, among other things, the publication of Colin Campbell's *Vitruvius Britannicus* (1715), three volumes of engravings of ancient buildings, prefaced by a denunciation of the Italian Baroque style and high praise for Palladio and Jones. Chiswick House is a free variation on the theme of Palladio's Villa Rotonda (FIG. 22-28). The exterior design provided a clear alternative to the colorful splendor of Versailles (FIG. 25-26). In its simple symmetry, unadorned planes, right angles, and precise proportions, Chiswick House looks very classical and rational. But the Palladian-style villa's setting within informal gardens, where a charming irregularity of layout and freely growing uncropped foliage dominate the scene, balances the classical severity and rationality of the architecture. Just as the owners of English villas cultivated irregularity in the landscaping surrounding their homes, they sometimes preferred interiors ornamented in a style more closely related to Rococo decoration. At Chiswick House, the interior design creates a luxurious Baroque foil to the stern symmetry of the exterior and the plan.

Palladian classicism prevailed in English architecture until about 1760, when it began to evolve into Neoclassicism. Playing a pivotal role in the shift from a dependence on Renaissance examples to ancient models was the publication in 1762 of the first volume of *Antiquities of Athens* by two British painters and architects, JAMES STUART

26-29A STUART, Doric Portico, Hagley Park, 1758.

(1713–1788) and Nicholas Revett (1720–1804). Indeed, the purest expression of Greek-inspired architecture in 18th-century England was Stuart's design for the Doric portico (FIG. **26-29A**) at Hagley Park.

STOURHEAD PARK English architects also made a significant contribution to the history of architecture by developing the *picturesque garden* in the 18th century, a garden designed in accord with the Enlightenment taste for the "natural." This approach to landscape architecture was in strong opposition to the formality and symmetry of Continental gardens such as those of the palace at Versailles (FIG. 25-26), which expressed the French monarch's power to impose rational order on untamed nature. Despite their "unordered" appearance, 18th-century English gardens, like Chinese gardens (see "Planning an Unplanned Garden," page 1055), were carefully planned. But unlike Chinese gardens, English gardens of the Enlightenment era often made allusions to classical antiquity, satisfying the demands of their patrons to surround themselves with mementos of the Grand Tour (see "The Grand Tour," page 781) they undertook in their youth.

26-30 Henry Flitcroft and Henry Hoare, the park at Stourhead, England, 1743–1765.

Flitcroft's design for Hoare's Wiltshire estate included a replica of the Pantheon overlooking an artificial lake, and a grotto alluding to Aeneas's journey to the Underworld from Lake Avernus.

An early masterpiece of this genre is the park at Stourhead (FIG. 26-30), designed by Henry Flitcroft (1697–1769) in collaboration with the property's owner, Henry Hoare (1705–1785), the son of a wealthy banker. Hoare's country estate in Wiltshire overlooked a lush valley in which Flitcroft created an irregularly shaped artificial lake by damming up the Stour River. Around it, he placed a winding path leading to and from a grotto adorned with statues of a river god and a nymph. The twisting road and the grotto conjured for Hoare the voyage of Aeneas and the entrance to the Underworld in Virgil's *Aeneid,* required reading (in the original Latin) for any properly educated British gentleman. Flitcroft also placed around

Hoare's version of Lake Avernus a bridge with five arches modeled on Andrea Palladio's bridge at Vicenza and pavilions that are free variations on famous classical buildings, including the Temple of Venus (FIG. 7-70) at Baalbek and the Pantheon (FIG. 7-49) in Rome. Flitcroft sited all the structures strategically to create vistas resembling those in the paintings of Claude Lorrain (FIG. 25-33), beloved by those who had completed a Grand Tour. In fact, the view reproduced here of Flitcroft's Pantheon beyond the Palladian bridge on the far side of the lake at Stourhead specifically emulates Claude's 1672 *Landscape with Aeneas at Delos* in the National Gallery in London, in turn inspired by the *Aeneid.* Still, consistent with the eclectic

26-31 Thomas Jefferson, Monticello, Charlottesville, Virginia, 1770–1806.

Jefferson led the movement to adopt Neoclassicism as the architectural style of the United States. Although built of local materials, his Palladian Virginia home recalls Chiswick House (FIG. 26-29).

THE PATRON'S VOICE
Thomas Jefferson, Patron and Practitioner

Thomas Jefferson's advocacy of Neoclassicism as the architectural style of the newly independent United States of America was an extension of the Enlightenment belief in the perfectibility of human beings and in the power of art to help achieve that perfection. An accomplished architect in his own right (FIGS. 26-31 and 26-32), as president, Jefferson personally selected Benjamin Latrobe (1764–1820) to complete the commission for the U.S. Capitol in Washington, D.C., specifying that Latrobe use a Roman style. Jefferson's choice reflected in part his admiration for the beauty of the Roman buildings he had seen in Europe and in part his association of those buildings with an idealized Roman republican government and, through that, with the democracy of ancient Greece. As early as 1791, as the first secretary of state under President George Washington, Jefferson expressed his preference for the future design of the Capitol in a letter to Pierre Charles L'Enfant (1754–1825), whom Washington had asked to prepare a plan for the new national capital on the Potomac River.

> Whenever it is proposed to prepare plans for the Capitol, I should prefer the adoption of some one of the models of antiquity, which have had the approbation of thousands of years.*

In his own designs for public buildings, Jefferson also looked to Rome for models. He modeled the State Capitol in Richmond, Virginia, on the Maison Carrée (FIG. 7-32), which he described in 1786 as "the most perfect and precious remain of antiquity in existence."† For the University of Virginia, which he founded, Jefferson turned to the Pantheon (FIG. 7-49). The Rotunda (FIG. 26-32) is the centerpiece of Jefferson's "academical village" in Charlottesville. It sits on an elevated platform at one end of a grassy quadrangle ("the Lawn"), framed by Neoclassical pavilions and colonnades—just as temples in Roman fora (FIGS. 7-12 and 7-44) stood at one short end of a colonnaded square. Each of the ten pavilions (five on each side) resembles a small classical temple. No two are exactly alike. Jefferson experimented with variations of all the different classical orders in his pavilions. He had thoroughly absorbed the principles of classical architecture and clearly delighted in borrowing motifs from major buildings. Jefferson was no mere copyist, however. His designs were highly original—and, in turn, frequently emulated. And, as president and patron, he put his stamp on the character of Washington, D.C., forever.

*Letter of Thomas Jefferson to the commission overseeing the plans for Washington, D.C., January 26, 1786, quoted in Leland M. Roth, ed., *America Builds: Source Documents in American Architecture and Planning* (New York: Harper & Row, 1983), 29.

†Letter of Thomas Jefferson to Madame de Tessé, March 20, 1787, quoted in Harry Francis Mallgrave, ed., *Architectural Theory, Volume I: An Anthology from Vitruvius to 1870* (Malden, Mass.: Blackwell, 2006), 427.

26-32 THOMAS JEFFERSON, Rotunda and Lawn (looking north), University of Virginia, Charlottesville, Virginia, 1819–1826.

Modeled on the Pantheon (FIG. 7-49), Jefferson's Neoclassical Rotunda sits like a temple in a Roman forum on an elevated platform overlooking the colonnaded Lawn of the University of Virginia.

---

tastes of 18th-century patrons, Hoare's park also contains Chinese bridges, a Turkish tent, and a Gothic tower.

THOMAS JEFFERSON Because the appeal of Neoclassicism was due in part to the values with which it was associated—morality, idealism, patriotism, and civic virtue—it is not surprising that in the new American republic, THOMAS JEFFERSON (1743–1826) spearheaded a movement to adopt Neoclassicism as the national architectural style. Jefferson—economist, educational theorist, gifted amateur architect, as well as statesman (see "Thomas Jefferson, Patron and Practitioner," above)—admired Palladio immensely and read carefully the Italian architect's *Four Books of Architecture*. Later, while minister to France, he studied 18th-century French classical architecture and city planning and visited the Maison Carrée (FIG. 7-32), an ancient Roman temple at Nîmes. After his European sojourn, Jefferson decided to completely remodel Monticello (FIG. 26-31), his home near Charlottesville, Virginia, which he originally had designed in a different style. The final version of Monticello is somewhat reminiscent of Palladio's Villa Rotonda (FIG. 22-28) and of Chiswick House (FIG. 26-29), but its materials are the local wood and brick used in Virginia. The single-story home with an octagonal dome set above the central drawing room behind a pediment-capped columnar porch sits on a wooded plot of land with mountain vistas all around. (Monticello means "hillock" or "little mountain" in Italian.) The setting fulfilled another of Jefferson's goals—to build for himself a country villa inspired by the ones described by the first-century Roman author Pliny (see page 186).

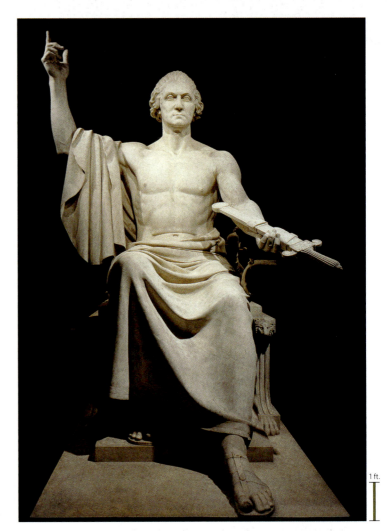

26-33 Jean-Antoine Houdon, *George Washington,* 1788–1792. Marble, 6' 2" high. State Capitol, Richmond.

Houdon portrayed Washington in contemporary garb, but he incorporated the Roman fasces and Cincinnatus's plow in the statue, because Washington similarly had returned to his farm after his war service.

26-34 Horatio Greenough, *George Washington,* 1840. Marble, 11' 4" high. Smithsonian American Art Museum, Washington, D.C.

In this posthumous portrait, Greenough likened Washington to a god by depicting him seminude and enthroned in the manner of Phidias's Olympian statue of Zeus, king of the Greek gods.

JEAN-ANTOINE HOUDON Neoclassicism also became the preferred style for public sculpture in the new American republic. When members of the Virginia legislature wanted to erect a life-size marble statue of Virginia-born George Washington (1732–1799), they awarded the commission to the leading French Neoclassical sculptor of the late 18th century, JEAN-ANTOINE HOUDON (1741–1828). Houdon had already carved a bust portrait of Benjamin Franklin (1706–1790) when Franklin was America's ambassador to France. Houdon's portrait of Washington (FIG. 26-33) is the sculptural equivalent of a painted Grand Manner portrait (FIG. 26-20). But although Washington wears 18th-century garb, the statue makes overt reference to the Roman Republic. The "column" on which Washington leans is a bundle of rods with an ax attached—the ancient Roman *fasces,* an emblem of authority—used much later as the emblem of Mussolini's Fascist government in 20th-century Italy. ("Fascist" derives from "fasces.") The 13 rods symbolize the 13 original states. The plow behind Washington alludes to Cincinnatus, a *patrician* of the early Roman Republic who was elected *dictator* during a time of war and resigned his position as soon as victory had been achieved in order to return to his farm. Washington wears the badge of the Society of the Cincinnati (visible beneath the

bottom of his waistcoat), an association founded in 1783 for officers in the revolutionary army who had resumed their peacetime roles. Tellingly, Washington no longer holds his sword in Houdon's statue.

HORATIO GREENOUGH After his death, Washington gradually took on almost godlike stature as the "father of his country." In 1840, the U.S. Congress commissioned American sculptor HORATIO GREENOUGH (1805–1852) to create a statue (FIG. 26-34) of the country's first president for the Capitol. Greenough used Houdon's portrait as his model for the head, but he portrayed Washington as seminude and enthroned, as Phidias depicted Zeus in the famous lost statue he made for the god's temple at Olympia in ancient Greece. The colossal statue—Washington is more than 11 feet tall, seated—is a supreme example of the Neoclassical style, but it did not win favor with either the Congress that commissioned it or the public. Although no one ever threw Greenough's statue into the Potomac River, as one congressman suggested, the legislators never placed it in its intended position beneath the Capitol dome. In fact, by 1840, the Neoclassical style itself was no longer in vogue. The leading artists of Europe and America had already embraced a new style, *Romanticism,* examined in the next chapter.

ROCOCO TO NEOCLASSICISM: THE 18TH CENTURY IN EUROPE AND AMERICA

Rococo

- In the early 18th century, the centralized and grandiose palace-based culture of Baroque France gave way to the much more intimate Rococo culture based in the townhouses of Paris. There, aristocrats and intellectuals gathered for witty conversation in salons featuring delicate colors, sinuous lines, gilded mirrors, elegant furniture, and small paintings and sculptures.

- The leading Rococo painter was Antoine Watteau, whose usually small canvases feature light colors and elegant figures in ornate costumes moving gracefully through lush landscapes. His fête galante paintings depict the outdoor amusements of French high society.

- Watteau's successors included François Boucher and Jean-Honoré Fragonard, who carried on the Rococo style late into the 18th century. In Italy, Giambattista Tiepolo adapted the Rococo manner to huge ceiling frescoes in the Baroque tradition.

Watteau, *Pilgrimage to Cythera*, 1717

The Enlightenment

- By the end of the 18th century, revolutions had overthrown the monarchy in France and achieved independence for the British colonies in America. A major factor was the Enlightenment, a new way of thinking critically about the world independently of religion and tradition.

- The Enlightenment promoted scientific questioning of all assertions and embraced the doctrine of progress, exemplified by the Industrial Revolution, which began in England in the 1740s. The paintings of Joseph Wright of Derby celebrated the scientific inventions of the Enlightenment era.

- The Enlightenment also made knowledge of ancient Rome imperative for the cultured elite, and Europeans and Americans in large numbers undertook a Grand Tour of Italy. Among the most popular souvenirs of the Grand Tour were Antonio Canaletto's cityscapes of Venice rendered in precise Renaissance perspective with the aid of a camera obscura.

- Rejecting the idea of progress, Rousseau, one of the leading French philosophes, argued for a return to natural values and exalted the simple, honest life of peasants. His ideas had a profound impact on such artists as Jean-Baptiste-Siméon Chardin and Jean-Baptiste Greuze, who painted sentimental narratives about rural families.

- The taste for naturalism also led to the popularity of portrait paintings with landscape backgrounds, a specialty of Thomas Gainsborough, and to a reawakening of interest in realism. Benjamin West represented the protagonists in his history paintings wearing contemporary costumes.

Wright, *A Lecture at the Orrery*, ca. 1763–1765

West, *Death of General Wolfe*, 1771

Neoclassicism

- The Enlightenment revival of interest in Greece and Rome, which spurred systematic excavations at Herculaneum and Pompeii, also gave rise in the late 18th century to the artistic movement known as Neoclassicism, which incorporated the subjects and styles of ancient art.

- One pioneer of the new style was Angelica Kauffman, who often chose subjects drawn from Roman history for her paintings. Jacques-Louis David, who exalted classical art as "the imitation of nature in her most beautiful and perfect form," also favored ancient Roman themes. Painted on the eve of the French Revolution, *Oath of the Horatii,* set in a severe classical hall, served as an example of patriotism and sacrifice.

- Architects also eagerly embraced the Neoclassical style. Ancient Roman and Italian Renaissance structures inspired Jacques-Germain Soufflot's Panthéon in Paris and Richard Boyle's Chiswick House near London. A Greek temple in Athens was the model for James Stuart's Doric portico in Worcestershire.

- In the United States, Thomas Jefferson adopted the Neoclassical style in his designs for Monticello and the University of Virginia. He championed Neoclassicism as the official architectural style of the new American republic because it represented for him idealism, patriotism, and civic virtue.

David, *Oath of the Horatii*, 1784

Jefferson, Monticello, 1770–1806

◄ **27-1a** In this gigantic painting, Géricault rejected Neoclassical compositional principles and, in the Romantic spirit, presented a jumble of writhing bodies in every attitude of suffering, despair, and death.

◄ **27-1b** At the apex of a diagonal axis stretching from the lower left, a heroic seminude black man, one of the few survivors, waves a tattered garment in the hope of attracting the attention of the rescue ship.

27-1 THÉODORE GÉRICAULT, *Raft of the Medusa*, 1818–1819. Oil on canvas, 16' 1" × 23' 6". Musée du Louvre, Paris.

▶ **27-1c** Barely visible in the distance is the ship *Argus*, which would eventually rescue the *Medusa's* 15 survivors, who told Géricault the story of the captain's incompetence and described the horrors of the raft.

FRAMING THE ERA

Romanticism, Realism, Photography: Europe and America, 1800 to 1870

THE HORROR—AND ROMANCE—OF DEATH AT SEA

At the close of the 18th century, Neoclassicism was the dominant artistic style in Europe, but it soon gave way to a movement that historians of art, music, and literature call *Romanticism*. In France, one of the pioneering Romantic painters was THÉODORE GÉRICAULT (1791–1824). Although Géricault retained an interest in the heroic and the epic, and studied drawing in the studio of Neoclassical painter Pierre-Narcisse Guérin (1774–1833), he chafed at the rigidity of the Neoclassical style, instead producing works that captivate viewers with their drama, visual complexity, and emotional force.

Géricault's most ambitious project was *Raft of the Medusa* (FIG. 27-1), an immense (23-foot-wide) canvas with figures larger than life. The painting immortalized the July 2, 1816, shipwreck off the Mauritanian coast of the French frigate *Medusa*, which ran aground on a reef due to the incompetence of its inexperienced captain, a political appointee. The captain and his officers safely abandoned the ship. In an attempt to survive, 147 passengers built a makeshift raft from pieces of the disintegrating frigate. The raft drifted for 13 days, and the starving survivors dwindled to 15, in part because of cannibalism. Finally, the ship *Argus* spotted the raft and rescued those still alive. This horrendous event was political dynamite once it became public knowledge.

In *Raft of the Medusa,* Géricault chose to represent the moment when some of those still alive summon what little strength they have left to flag down the *Argus* far on the horizon, not knowing if the ship's crew could see their raft. Géricault sought to capture accurately the horror, chaos, and emotion of the tragedy yet invoke the grandeur and impact of Neoclassical history painting. He visited hospitals and morgues to study the bodies of the dying and dead, interviewed survivors, and had a model of the raft constructed in his studio. The legacy of Neoclassicism is still evident in the incongruously muscular bodies of the starving. But Géricault rejected Neoclassical composition principles and instead presented a jumble of writhing bodies. He arranged the survivors and several corpses in a powerful X-shaped composition, and piled one body on another in every attitude of suffering, despair, and death. One light-filled diagonal axis stretches from the bodies at the lower left up to the black man raised on his comrades' shoulders and waving a tattered garment toward the horizon. Yet the man, seen from the back and faceless, is an anonymous antihero, in striking contrast to the protagonists of the historical and mythological works then in vogue. The cross axis descends from the dark, billowing sail at the upper left to the shadowed upper torso of the body trailing in the open sea. Géricault's bold decision to place the raft at a diagonal so that a corner juts outward makes it seem as though some of the corpses are sliding off the raft into the viewer's space. *Raft of the Medusa,* like the event itself, caused a sensation. It established Géricault's reputation and reoriented the history of painting.

MAP 27-1

The Napoleonic Empire in 1812.

POLITICAL, INDUSTRIAL, AND ARTISTIC REVOLUTIONS

The revolution of 1789 initiated a new era in France, but the overthrow of the monarchy also opened the door for Napoleon Bonaparte (1769–1821) to exploit the resulting disarray and establish a different kind of monarchy with himself at its head. In 1800, after serving in various French army commands and leading major campaigns in Italy and Egypt, Napoleon assumed a newly created position—First Consul of the French Republic, a title with clear and intentional links to the ancient Roman Republic (see page 179).

During the next 15 years, the ambitious general gained control of almost all of continental Europe in name or through alliances (MAP 27-1). In May 1804, for example, he became king of Italy. Later that year, the pope journeyed to Paris for Napoleon's coronation as Emperor of the French (FIG. 27-3). In 1812, however, Napoleon launched a disastrous invasion of Russia that ended in retreat, and

in 1815 he suffered a devastating defeat at the hands of the British at Waterloo in present-day Belgium. Forced to abdicate the imperial throne, Napoleon went into exile on the island of Saint Helena in the South Atlantic, where he died six years later.

After Napoleon's death, the political geography of Europe changed dramatically (MAP 27-2), but in many ways the more significant changes during the first half of the 19th century were technological and economic. The Industrial Revolution caused a population boom in European cities, and railroads spread to many parts of the Continent, facilitating the transportation of both goods and people.

Transformation also occurred in the art world. The century opened with Neoclassicism still supreme, but by 1870, Romanticism and Realism in turn had captured the imagination of artists and public alike. New construction techniques had a major impact on architectural design, and the invention of photography revolutionized picture making of all kinds.

ROMANTICISM, REALISM, PHOTOGRAPHY: EUROPE AND AMERICA, 1800 TO 1870

1800-1815
- Napoleon appoints David as First Painter of the Empire and brings Italian sculptor Canova to Paris
- Vignon models La Madeleine, Napoleon's Neoclassical "temple of glory," on ancient Roman temples
- David's students Gros, Girodet, and Ingres form a bridge between Neoclassicism and Romanticism

1815-1840
- Romanticism is the leading art movement in Europe. Delacroix and other painters favor exotic and fantastic subjects featuring unleashed emotion, vibrant color, and bold brushstrokes
- Friedrich, Turner, Cole, and other Romantic artists specialize in painting transcendental landscapes
- The Gothic style enjoys a revival in architecture
- Daguerre in France and Talbot in England invent photography

1840-1870
- Courbet exhibits his work in the Pavilion of Realism. He and other Realist painters in Europe and America insist that people and events of their own time are the only valid subjects for art
- Manet's paintings get a hostile reception because of their shocking subjects and nonillusionistic style
- Paxton pioneers prefabricated glass-and-iron construction in the Crystal Palace
- Technological advances enable artists to make on-the-spot photographs of the Civil War

MAP 27-2
Europe around 1850.

ART UNDER NAPOLEON

As soon as Napoleon had consolidated his power, he enlisted France's leading artists and architects to construct a public image of his reign. Not surprisingly, Napoleon, who aspired to rule an empire that might one day rival ancient Rome's, embraced Neoclassicism as the ideal stylistic vehicle for linking his rule with the classical past and for expressing his imperial authority. Napoleon's architectural commissions in Paris included a grandiose triumphal arch (FIG. 27-18A), a commemorative column in the Place Vendôme modeled on the Column of Trajan (FIG. 7-45) in Rome, and a Neoclassical temple.

LA MADELEINE In 1807, Napoleon resumed construction of the church of La Madeleine (Mary Magdalene; FIG. **27-2**) in Paris, which had been interrupted in 1790. However, the new emperor converted the building into a "temple of glory" for France's imperial armies. (The structure reverted again to a church after Napoleon's defeat and long before its completion in 1842.) Designed by PIERRE-ALEXANDRE BARTHÉLÉMY VIGNON (1763–1828), the

grandiose Napoleonic temple includes a high podium and a broad flight of stairs leading to a deep porch in the front. These architectural features, coupled with the Corinthian columns, recall Roman temples in France, such as the Maison Carrée (FIG. 7-32) at Nîmes, making La Madeleine a symbolic link between the Napoleonic and Roman empires. Curiously, the building's classical shell surrounds an interior covered by a sequence of three domes, a feature found in Byzantine and Romanesque churches. Vignon in essence clothed a traditional church in the costume of imperial Rome.

27-2 PIERRE-ALEXANDRE BARTHÉLÉMY VIGNON, La Madeleine, Paris, France, 1807–1842.

Napoleon constructed La Madeleine as a "temple of glory" for his armies. Based on ancient temples (FIG. 7-32) in France, Vignon's Neoclassical design linked the Napoleonic and Roman empires.

27-3 Jacques-Louis David, *Coronation of Napoleon,* 1805–1808. Oil on canvas, 20' 4½" × 32' 1¾". Musée du Louvre, Paris.

At his patron's insistence, David recorded Napoleon at his 1804 coronation crowning his wife with the pope as witness, thus underscoring the emperor's authority and independence from the Church.

NAPOLEON AND DAVID At the fall of the French revolutionary Maximilien Robespierre and his party in 1794, Jacques-Louis David, who had aligned himself personally and through his work (FIGS. 26-26 and 26-27) with the revolutionary forces, barely escaped with his life. He stood trial and went to prison. After his release in 1795, he worked hard to resurrect his career—for example, by painting a series of portraits of Napoleon on horseback crossing the Alps (FIG. 27-2A). When the new emperor

⤴ **27-2A** David, *Napoleon Crossing Saint-Bernard,* 1800–1801.

approached David immediately after his 1804 coronation and offered him the position of First Painter of the Empire, David seized the opportunity. The most grandiose work David produced for his new imperial patron was an immense (20-by-32-foot) canvas (FIG. 27-3) documenting the pomp and pageantry of that coronation (see "The Coronation of Napoleon," page 797). The work took the artist three years to complete.

ANTONIO CANOVA Neoclassical sculpture also was in vogue under Napoleon. His favorite sculptor was Antonio Canova (1757–1822), who somewhat reluctantly left his native Italy to settle in Paris and serve the emperor. Canova had gained renown for his sculptures

of classical gods and heroes (for example, *Cupid and Psyche,* FIG. 27-3A). In Paris, he made numerous portraits of the emperor and his family in the Neoclassical style, including a nude statue of the emperor in the guise of the Roman war god Mars. The most famous portrait that Canova carved is, however, the marble statue (FIG. 27-4) of Napoleon's sister Pauline Borghese (1780–1825) in the guise of Venus Victorious. Initially,

⤴ **27-3A** Canova, *Cupid and Psyche,* 1787–1793.

Canova had suggested depicting Pauline clothed as Diana, goddess of the hunt. She demanded, however, that she be portrayed nude as Venus, the goddess of love. Thus Pauline appears, reclining on a divan and gracefully holding the golden apple, the symbol of the goddess's triumph in the judgment of Paris. Canova clearly based his work on Greek statuary—the sensuous pose and seminude body recall Hellenistic works such as *Venus de Milo* (FIG. 5-84)—and the reclining figure has parallels on Roman sarcophagus lids (FIG. 7-59; compare FIG. 6-6).

The French public never had the opportunity to admire Canova's portrait, however. Napoleon had arranged the marriage of his sister to an heir of the noble Roman Borghese family. Once Pauline was in Rome, she took several lovers, and the public gossiped extensively about her affairs. Pauline's insistence on being represented

THE PATRON'S VOICE
The Coronation of Napoleon

Napoleon's coronation on December 2, 1804, was a carefully staged pageant filled with symbolism. By securing the participation of Pope Pius VII (r. 1800–1823), Napoleon legitimized his assumption of absolute power by linking his crowning to Charlemagne's coronation as Roman emperor by Pope Leo III (r. 795–816) almost exactly 1,000 years before. Moreover, to dissociate himself from the monarchy, Napoleon held his ceremony in Notre-Dame Cathedral (FIG. 13-10) in Paris instead of in Reims Cathedral (FIGS. 13-1 and 13-23A), the traditional setting for the coronation of French kings (see page 373). Napoleon's crown, made for the occasion, also broke with royal tradition. He chose a gold laurel wreath of the kind worn by Roman emperors.

To a large extent, in *Coronation of Napoleon* (FIG. 27-3) First Painter David adhered to historical fact in depicting the event, duly recording, for example, the appearance of the interior of Paris's Notre-Dame Cathedral as the emperor's architects Charles Percier (1764–1838) and Pierre-François-Léonard Fontaine (1762–1853) had decorated it for the occasion. David also faithfully portrayed those in attendance: scores of people, all at approximately life size, including Napoleon; his wife Josephine (1763–1814), who kneels to receive her crown; the pope, seated behind Napoleon; Joseph (1768–1814) and Louis (1778–1846) Bonaparte; Napoleon's ministers; the retinues of the emperor and empress; a representative group of the clergy; and David himself, seated among the rows of spectators in the balconies.

Preliminary studies and drawings reveal, however, that, at Napoleon's direction, David made changes to his initially accurate record of the event. For example, the emperor insisted that the painter depict the pope with his hand raised in blessing, instead of as the inactive witness he was. Further, Napoleon's mother, who had refused to attend the coronation, appears prominently in the center background. The *Gazette nationale* of January 16, 1808, diplomatically described Napoleon's "suggestions" as follows:

> His Majesty, employing expressions full of kindness and taking the most delicate care, communicated to Monsieur David several observations. The painter, recognizing the fine tact, the exquisite taste, and the profound thinking that His Majesty the Emperor manifests in all his engagements with the sciences and the arts, took it upon himself to conform it to these opinions that enlightened him and thus to perfect his painting.*

Given the number of figures and details David had to incorporate in his painting, it is remarkable that he was able to impose upon the lavish pageant the structured composition that was central to the Neoclassical style. As in his *Oath of the Horatii* (FIG. 26-26), David presented the action as if on a theater stage—which in this instance was literally the case, even if the stage Percier and Fontaine constructed was inside a church. In addition, as he did in his arrangement of the men and women in *Oath of the Horatii,* David conceptually divided the painting to highlight polarities. The pope, prelates, and priests representing the Catholic Church appear on the right. The members of Napoleon's imperial court are on the left. The relationship between Church and State was one of this period's most contentious issues. Napoleon's decision to crown himself, rather than to allow the pope to perform the coronation, as was traditional, reflected Napoleon's concern about the Church-State power relationship. For the painting commemorating the occasion, David had initially planned to show Napoleon crowning himself. But the emperor insisted that the artist instead depict the

Detail of *Coronation of Napoleon* (FIG. 27-3).

27-3B INGRES, *Napoleon on His Imperial Throne*, 1806.

moment after, when Napoleon placed a crown on his wife's head, further underscoring his authority and independence from the Church. Moreover, Napoleon instructed David to portray Josephine as looking younger than her real age. David also reduced the scale of Notre-Dame so that the protagonists would not seem dwarfed by the towering interior of the cathedral.

Thus, although this painting appears at first to be a detailed, objective record of a historical event, it is, in fact, a carefully crafted tableau designed to present Napoleon in the way he wished to be seen. In that respect, as well as stylistically, David was emulating the artists in the employ of the ancient Roman emperors (see Chapter 7), as was his pupil, Ingres, in a contemporaneous portrait (FIG. 27-3B) of Napoleon enthroned.

*Todd Porterfield and Susan L. Siegfried, *Staging Empire: Napoleon, Ingres, and David* (University Park: Pennsylvania State University Press, 2006), 196.

27-4 ANTONIO CANOVA, *Pauline Borghese as Venus Victorious,* from the Villa Borghese, Rome, Italy. 1808. Marble, 6' 7" long. Galleria Borghese, Rome.

Canova was Napoleon's favorite sculptor. Here, the artist depicted the emperor's sister—at her insistence—as the nude Roman goddess of love in a marble statue inspired by classical models.

1 ft.

as the goddess of love erotically posed on a 19th-century couch, meticulously reproduced by Canova, reflected her self-perception. Because of his wife's notoriety, Prince Camillo Borghese (1775–1832), the work's official patron, kept the sculpture in his palatial villa in Rome, now the Galleria Borghese, a public museum. The prince allowed relatively few people to see the portrait, and only at night by torchlight.

DAVID'S STUDENTS Given David's stature as an artist in Napoleonic France, along with the popularity of Neoclassicism, it is not surprising that the First Painter attracted numerous students and developed an active and flourishing teaching studio (see "David on Greek Style," page 784). He gave practical instruction to and deeply influenced many important artists of the period. So strong was David's commitment to classicism that he encouraged all his students to learn Latin, the better to immerse themselves in and understand classical culture. David even initially demanded that his pupils select their subjects from Plutarch, the ancient author of *Lives of the Noble Greeks and Romans* and a principal source of Neoclassical subject matter. Due to this thorough classical foundation, David's students all produced work that at its core retains Neoclassical elements. Yet the work of his three most famous students—Ingres (FIGS. 27-3B, 27-7, and 27-8), Gros (FIG. 27-5), and Girodet-Trioson (FIGS. 27-6 and 27-6A)—represents a departure from the structured confines of Neoclassicism. David's pupils laid the foundation for the Romantic movement (see page 801) by exploring the realm of the exotic and the erotic, and often by turning to fictional narratives for the subjects of their paintings, as the Romantic artists would also do.

ANTOINE-JEAN GROS As did his teacher, ANTOINE-JEAN GROS (1771–1835) produced several paintings that contributed to Napoleon's growing mythic status. In *Napoleon Visiting the Plague-Stricken in Jaffa* (FIG. 27-5), the artist, on commission from Napoleon, recorded an incident during an outbreak of the bubonic plague in the course of the general's Syrian campaign of 1799. This fearsome disease struck Muslim and French forces alike, and to quell the growing panic and hysteria, on March 11, 1799, Napoleon himself visited the mosque at Jaffa that had been converted into a hospital for those who had contracted the dreaded disease. Gros depicted Napoleon's staff officers covering their noses against the stench of the place, whereas Napoleon, amid the dead and dying, is fearless and in control. He comforts those still alive, who are clearly awed by his presence and authority. Indeed, by depicting the French leader as having removed his glove to touch the sores of a French plague victim, Gros implied that Napoleon possessed the miraculous power

to heal. The composition recalls scenes of the doubting Thomas touching Christ's wound. Here, however, Napoleon is not Saint Thomas but a Christlike figure tending to the sick, as in Rembrandt's *Hundred-Guilder Print* (FIG. 25-16), which Gros certainly knew. The French painter also based the despairing seated Arab figure at the lower left on the comparable figure (one of the damned) in Michelangelo's *Last Judgment* (FIG. 22-19). The kneeling nude Frenchman with extended arm at the right recalls the dead Christ in Michelangelo's late *Pietà* (FIG. 22-20).

The action in *Napoleon in Jaffa* unfolds against the exotic backdrop of the horseshoe arches and Moorish arcades of the mosque-hospital's courtyard (compare FIG. 10-11). On the left are Muslim doctors distributing bread and ministering to plague-stricken Arabs in the shadows. On the right, in radiant light, are Napoleon and his soldiers in their splendid tailored uniforms. David had used this polarized compositional scheme and an arcaded backdrop to great effect in his *Oath of the Horatii* (FIG. 26-26), and Gros emulated those features in this painting, but employed brighter colors and looser brushstrokes. The younger artist's fascination with the exoticism of the Muslim world, as is evident in his attention to the details of architecture and costume, also represented a departure from his teacher's Neoclassicism and reflects a growing interest among the French in the Near East and North Africa, spurred in large measure by Napoleon's eastern campaigns. Historians and art historians alike refer to this European curiosity about the decidedly non-Western culture of the East as *Orientalism.* The setting of *Napoleon in Jaffa,* along with Gros's emphasis on death, suffering, and an emotional rendering of the scene, also foreshadowed core elements of the artistic movement that would soon displace Neoclassicism—Romanticism.

GIRODET-TRIOSON *Burial of Atala* (FIG. 27-6) by ANNE-LOUIS GIRODET-TRIOSON (1767–1824) is an important bridge between Neoclassicism and Romanticism. Girodet based the painting on *The Genius of Christianity,* a novel by François René de Chateaubriand (1768–1848). The section of the novel dealing with Atala appeared as an excerpt a year before the publication of the entire book in 1802.

27-5 ANTOINE-JEAN GROS, *Napoleon Visiting the Plague-Stricken in Jaffa,* 1804. Oil on canvas, 17' 5" × 23' 7". Musée du Louvre, Paris.

In his depiction of Napoleon as a Christlike healer, Gros foreshadowed Romanticism by recording the exotic people, costumes, and architecture of Jaffa, including the striped horseshoe arches of the mosque-hospital.

Both the excerpt and the novel were enormously successful, and as a result, Atala became almost a cult figure. The exoticism and eroticism integral to the narrative accounted in large part for the public's interest in *The Genius of Christianity.* Set in Louisiana, Chateaubriand's story focuses on the young Native American Chactas and Atala, a Christian girl of mixed European and Native American descent, who had promised her mother on her deathbed that, like the Virgin Mary, she would remain chaste her entire life. However, she falls in love with Chactas, and they run away together through the wilderness. Erotic passion permeates the story, and Atala

27-6 ANNE-LOUIS GIRODET-TRIOSON, *Burial of Atala,* 1808. Oil on canvas, 6' 11" × 8' 9". Musée du Louvre, Paris.

Girodet's depiction of Native American lovers in the Louisiana wilderness appealed to the French public's fascination with what it perceived as the passion and primitivism of the New World.

finally commits suicide rather than break her oath. Girodet's painting depicts this tragedy. Atala's grief-stricken lover, Chactas, buries the heroine in the shadow of a cross. Assisting in the burial is a cloaked priest, whose presence is appropriate given Chateaubriand's emphasis on the revival of Christianity (and the Christianization of the New World) in his novel. Like Gros's depiction of the exotic Muslim world of Jaffa (FIG. 27-5), Girodet's representation of Native American lovers in the Louisiana wilderness appealed to the public's fascination (whetted by the Louisiana Purchase in 1803) with what it perceived as the passion and primitivism of native life in the New World. *Burial of Atala* speaks here to emotions, rather than inviting philosophical meditation or revealing some grand order of nature and form. Unlike David's appeal in *Oath of the Horatii* (FIG. 26-26) to feelings that inspire public action, the appeal here is to the viewer's private world of fantasy and emotion. But Girodet-Trioson also occasionally addressed contemporary themes in his work, as he did in his portrait (FIG. 27-6A) of Jean-Baptiste Belley, a French legislator and former slave.

⊡ **27-6A** GIRODET-TRIOSON, *Jean-Baptiste Belley,* 1797.

J.-A.-D. INGRES David's greatest pupil, JEAN-AUGUSTE-DOMINIQUE INGRES (1780–1867), arrived at David's studio in the late 1790s after Girodet-Trioson had left to establish an independent career. Ingres's study there was to be short-lived, however, as he soon broke with David on matters of style. Ingres adopted what he believed to be a truer and purer Greek style than David's Neoclassical manner. The younger artist employed linear forms approximating those found in Greek vase painting (for example, FIGS. 5-23, 5-23A, 5-24, and 5-24A), and often placed the main figures in the foreground of his composition, emulating classical low-relief sculpture.

APOTHEOSIS OF HOMER Ingres exhibited *Apotheosis of Homer* (FIG. 27-7) at the Salon of 1827 (see "Academic Salons," page 844). The huge painting, intended for a ceiling in the Louvre, incorporates none of the perspective devices of Baroque ceiling painting. Rather, the canvas presents in a single statement the Neoclassical doctrines of ideal form and composition. It is the artist's attempt to wed the styles of Raphael and classical antiquity. Winged Victory (or Fame) crowns the epic poet Homer, who sits like a god on a throne before an Ionic temple. At Homer's feet are two statuesque women, personifications of the *Iliad* (holding a sword) and the *Odyssey* (holding an oar), the offspring of his imagination. Symmetrically grouped about him is a company of the "sovereign geniuses"—as Ingres called them—who expressed humanity's highest ideals in philosophy, poetry, music, and art. To Homer's left are the Greek poet Pindar with his lyre, Phidias with his sculptor's hammer, the philosophers Plato and Socrates, and other ancient worthies of different eras. They gather together in the painter's world of suspended time as Raphael united them in *School of Athens* (FIG. 22-9), which was the inspiration for *Apotheosis of Homer*. To the far right in Ingres's assembly of literary and artistic giants are the Roman poets Horace and Vergil, and two Italians: Dante, and, conspicuously, Raphael. Among the forward group on the painting's left side are Poussin (pointing) and Shakespeare (half concealed). At the right are French writers Jean Baptiste Racine, Molière, Voltaire, and François de Salignac de la Mothe Fénelon. Ingres had planned a much larger and more inclusive group, but limited the cast of characters for the Salon exhibition.

GRANDE ODALISQUE Despite his commitment to ideal form and careful compositional structure, Ingres also produced works that, like those of Gros and Girodet, his contemporaries saw as departures from Neoclassicism. The most famous is *Grande Odalisque* (FIG. 27-8), painted for Napoleon's sister Caroline Murat

27-7 JEAN-AUGUSTE-DOMINIQUE INGRES, *Apotheosis of Homer,* 1827. Oil on canvas, 12' 8" × 16' 10¾". Musée du Louvre, Paris.

Inspired by *School of Athens* (FIG. 22-9) by Raphael, Ingres's favorite painter, this huge canvas is a Neoclassical celebration of Homer and other ancient worthies, Dante, and select French authors.

27-8 Jean-Auguste-Dominique Ingres, *Grande Odalisque*, 1814. Oil on canvas, 2' 11$\frac{7}{8}$" × 5' 4". Musée du Louvre, Paris.

The reclining female nude was a Greco-Roman subject, but Ingres converted his Neoclassical figure into an odalisque in a Turkish harem, consistent with the new Romantic taste for the exotic.

(1782–1839), queen of Naples. The subject—the reclining nude female figure—followed the grand tradition of antiquity and the Renaissance (FIGS. 22-16 and 22-39) in sculpture as well as painting, as did Canova's *Pauline Borghese as Venus* (FIG. 27-4). *Grande Odalisque* again shows Ingres's admiration for Raphael in his borrowing of that master's type of female head (FIGS. 22-7 and 22-8). The figure's languid pose, small head, and elongated limbs and torso, and the generally cool color scheme reveal the painter's debt to Parmigianino (FIG. 22-44) and the Italian Mannerists, sculptors (FIGS. 22-52 and 22-52A) as well as painters. However, by converting the figure to an *odalisque* (woman in a Turkish harem), Ingres, unlike Canova, made a strong concession to the burgeoning Romantic taste for Orientalist subjects.

This rather strange mixture of artistic allegiances—the combination of precise classical draftsmanship, Mannerist proportions, and Romantic themes—prompted confusion, and when Ingres first exhibited *Grande Odalisque* in 1814, the painting drew acid criticism. Critics initially saw Ingres as a rebel in terms of both the form and content of his works. They did not cease their attacks until the mid-1820s, when a greater enemy of David's Neoclassical style, Eugène Delacroix, appeared on the scene (see page 805). Critics suddenly perceived that Ingres's art, despite its innovations and deviations, still contained crucial elements adhering to the Neoclassical taste for the ideal. In fact, on the basis of works such as *Apotheosis of Homer* (FIG. 27-7), Ingres soon became the leader of the academic forces in their battle against the "barbarism" of Delacroix, Théodore Géricault, and the Romantic movement.

ROMANTICISM

Whereas Neoclassicism's rationality reinforced Enlightenment thought (see page 763), particularly Voltaire's views, Romanticism owed much to the ideas of Jean-Jacques Rousseau (see page 774). Rousseau's exclamation "Man is born free, but is everywhere in chains!"—the opening line of his *Social Contract* (1762)—summarizes a fundamental Romantic premise. Romanticism emerged from a desire for freedom—not only political freedom but also freedom of thought, feeling, action, worship, speech, and taste. Romantics

asserted that freedom was the right and property of all. They believed that the path to freedom was through imagination and feeling rather than reason.

The allure of the Romantic spirit grew dramatically during the late 18th century, when the term originated among German literary critics. Their aim was to distinguish peculiarly "modern" traits from the Neoclassical traits that already had displaced Baroque and Rococo design elements. Consequently, some scholars refer to Romanticism as a phenomenon that began around 1750 and ended about 1850, but most use the term more narrowly to denote an art movement that flourished from about 1800 to 1840, between Neoclassicism and Realism.

Roots of Romanticism

The transition from Neoclassicism to Romanticism represented a shift in emphasis from reason to feeling, from calculation to intuition, and from objective nature to subjective emotion. Among the leading manifestations of Romanticism was heightened interest in the medieval period and in the sublime. For people living in the 18th century, the Middle Ages were the "dark ages," a time of barbarism, superstition, mystery, and miracle. The Romantic imagination stretched its perception of the Middle Ages into all the worlds of fantasy open to it, including the ghoulish, infernal, terrible, nightmarish, grotesque, and sadistic—the imagery that comes from the chamber of horrors when reason sleeps. Related to the imaginative sensibility was the period's notion of the sublime. Among the individuals most involved in studying the sublime was the British politician and philosopher Edmund Burke (1729–1797). In *A Philosophical Enquiry into the Origins of Our Ideas of the Sublime and Beautiful* (1757), Burke articulated his definition of the sublime—feelings of awe mixed with terror. Burke observed that pain or fear evoked the most intense human emotions and that these emotions could also be thrilling. Thus raging rivers and great storms at sea could be sublime to their viewers. Accompanying this taste for the sublime was the taste for the fantastic, the occult, and the macabre—for the adventures of the soul voyaging into the dangerous reaches of the imagination.

27-9 JOHN HENRY FUSELI, *The Nightmare*, 1781. Oil on canvas, 3' 3¾" × 4' 1½". Detroit Institute of the Arts (Founders Society purchase with funds from Mr. and Mrs. Bert L. Smokler and Mr. and Mrs. Lawrence A. Fleishman).

The transition from Neoclassicism to Romanticism marked a shift in emphasis from reason to feeling. Fuseli was among the first painters to depict the dark terrain of the human subconscious.

JOHN HENRY FUSELI The concept of the nightmare is the subject of a 1781 painting (FIG. **27-9**) by the Swiss painter Johann Heinrich Fuseli, better known by his English name JOHN HENRY FUSELI (1741–1825). Fuseli lived in Rome from 1770 to 1778 and settled in England in 1799 and eventually became a member of the Royal Academy and one of its instructors. Largely self-taught, he contrived a distinctive manner to express the fantasies of his vivid imagination. Fuseli specialized in night moods of horror and in dark fantasies—in the demonic, the macabre, and often the sadistic. In *The Nightmare*, a beautiful young woman lies asleep, draped across the bed with her limp arm dangling over the side. An *incubus,* a demon believed in medieval times to prey, often sexually, on sleeping women, squats ominously on her body. In the background, a ghostly horse with flaming eyes bursts into the scene from beyond the curtain. Despite the temptation to see the painting's title as a pun because of this horse, the word *nightmare* in fact derives from "night" and "Mara." Mara was a spirit in Scandinavian mythology who tormented and suffocated sleepers. Fuseli was among the first to attempt to depict the dark terrain of the human subconscious that became fertile ground for later artists.

WILLIAM BLAKE In their images of the sublime and the terrible, Romantic artists often combined something of Baroque dynamism with naturalistic details in their quest for grippingly moving visions. These elements became the mainstay of Romantic art and contrasted with the more intellectual, rational Neoclassical themes and compositions. The two were not mutually exclusive, however. Gros, Girodet-Trioson, and Ingres effectively integrated elements of Neoclassicism with Romanticism. So, too, did the visionary English poet, painter, and engraver WILLIAM BLAKE (1757–1827). Blake greatly admired ancient Greek art because it exemplified for him the mathematical and thus the eternal, and his work often incorporated

27-10 WILLIAM BLAKE, *Ancient of Days*, frontispiece of *Europe: A Prophecy*, 1794. Metal relief etching, hand colored, 9½" × 6¾". Pierpont Morgan Library, New York.

Although art historians classify Blake as a Romantic artist, he incorporated classical references in his works. Here, ideal classical anatomy merges with the inner dark dreams of Romanticism.

classical references. Yet Blake did not align himself with prominent Enlightenment figures. As did many other Romantic artists, he also found the art of the Middle Ages appealing. Blake derived the inspiration for many of his paintings and poems from his dreams. The importance he attached to these nocturnal experiences led him to believe that the rationalist search for material explanations of the world stifled the spiritual side of human nature. He also believed that the stringent rules of behavior that orthodox religions imposed had killed the individual creative impulse.

Blake's vision of the Almighty in *Ancient of Days* (FIG. **27-10**) combines his ideas and interests in a highly individual way. For Blake, this figure united the concept of the Creator with that of wisdom as a part of God. He chose *Ancient of Days* as the frontispiece for his book *Europe: A Prophecy,* and juxtaposed it with a quotation ("When he set a compass upon the face of the deep") from Proverbs 8:27. The speaker is Wisdom, who tells the reader how she was with the Lord through all the time of the creation (Prov. 8:22–23, 27–30). Energy fills Blake's composition. The Almighty leans forward from a fiery orb, peering toward earth and unleashing power through his outstretched left arm into twin rays of light. These emerge between his spread fingers like an architect's measuring instrument—a conception of creation with precedents in Gothic manuscript painting (FIG. 13-32). Here, however, a mighty wind surges through the

Creator's thick hair and beard. Only the strength of his Michelangelesque physique keeps him firmly planted on his heavenly perch. In this image Blake merged ideal classical anatomy with the inner dark dreams of Romanticism.

Spain and France

From its roots in the work of Fuseli, Blake, and other late-18th-century artists, Romanticism gradually displaced Neoclassicism as the dominant painting style of the first half of the 19th century. Romantic artists, including Francisco Goya in Spain and Théodore Géricault (FIG. 27-1) and Eugène Delacroix in France, reveled in exploring the exotic, erotic, and fantastic.

FRANCISCO GOYA Although FRANCISCO JOSÉ DE GOYA Y LUCIENTES (1746–1828) was David's contemporary, their work has little in common. Goya spent more than a year in Italy in 1770–1771 and worked with the influential Neoclassical painter Anton Raphael Mengs (FIG. 26-25A) in Madrid. He did not arrive at his general dismissal of Neoclassicism without considerable thought about the Enlightenment and the Neoclassical penchant for rationality and order. In *The Sleep of Reason Produces Monsters* (FIG. **27-11**), an etching from a series titled *Los Caprichos* (*The Caprices*), Goya depicted an artist, probably himself, asleep, slumped onto a desk, while threatening creatures converge on him, at least in his dream. The subject is a variation on the theme of Fuseli's *Nightmare* (FIG. 27-9), but without that painting's sexuality. Seemingly poised to attack the artist are owls (symbols of folly) and bats (symbols of ignorance). The viewer might read this as a portrayal of what emerges when reason is suppressed and, therefore, as advocating Enlightenment ideals. However, the print is ambiguous, probably intentionally so. *The Sleep of Reason* can also be interpreted as Goya's commentary on the creative process and a testament to his embrace of the Romantic spirit—the unleashing of imagination, emotions, and even nightmares. Goya's explanatory caption for the print reads: "Imagination abandoned by reason produces impossible monsters; united with her, she is the mother of the arts and the source of their wonders."

⊞ **27-11A** GOYA, *Family of Charles IV*, 1800.

THIRD OF MAY, 1808 Much of Goya's multifaceted work deals not with Romantic fantasies but with contemporary events. In 1786, he became an official artist in the court of Charles IV (r. 1788–1808) and produced portraits of the king and his family (FIG. **27-11A**). Dissatisfaction with the king's rule increased dramatically during Goya's tenure at the court, and the Spanish people eventually threw their support behind the king's son, Ferdinand VII, in the hope that he would initiate reform. To overthrow

27-11 FRANCISCO GOYA, *The Sleep of Reason Produces Monsters*, no. 43 from *Los Caprichos*, ca. 1798. Etching and aquatint, $8\frac{1}{2}'' \times 5\frac{7}{8}''$. **Metropolitan Museum of Art, New York (gift of M. Knoedler & Co., 1918).**

In this print, Goya depicted himself asleep while threatening creatures converge on him, revealing his embrace of the Romantic spirit—the unleashing of imagination, emotions, and nightmares.

27-12 Francisco Goya, *Third of May, 1808*, 1814–1815. Oil on canvas, 8' 9" × 13' 4". Museo Nacional del Prado, Madrid.

Goya encouraged empathy for the Spanish peasants massacred on May 3, 1808, by portraying horrified expressions on their faces, endowing them with a humanity lacking in the French firing squad.

1 ft.

his father and mother, Queen Maria Luisa (1751–1819), Ferdinand enlisted the aid of Napoleon Bonaparte. Because he had designs on the Spanish throne, Napoleon readily agreed to send French troops to Spain. Not surprisingly, as soon as he ousted Charles IV, Napoleon installed his brother Joseph Bonaparte (r. 1808–1813) on the Spanish throne as his surrogate.

The Spanish people, finally recognizing the French as invaders, sought a way to expel the foreign troops. On May 2, 1808, Spaniards attacked Napoleon's soldiers in a chaotic and violent clash. In retaliation and as a show of force, the French responded the next day by rounding up and executing Spanish citizens. This tragic event is the subject of Goya's most famous painting, *Third of May, 1808* (FIG. 27-12), commissioned in 1814 by Ferdinand VII (r. 1813–1833), who had reclaimed the throne after the ouster of the French. In emotional fashion, following the lead of Callot (FIG. 25-35) in the 18th century, Goya depicted the anonymous murderous wall of Napoleonic soldiers ruthlessly executing the unarmed and terrified Spanish peasants. The artist encouraged empathy for the Spaniards by portraying horrified expressions and anguish on their faces, endowing them with a humanity lacking in the faceless French firing squad in the shadows. Moreover, the peasant about to be shot throws his arms out in a cruciform gesture reminiscent of Christ's position on the cross. (The anonymous martyr's right hand also bears Christ's stigmata.) Goya enhanced the emotional drama of the massacre by sharply contrasting the darkness of the night with the focused illumination of the French squad's lantern and by extending the time frame depicted. Although Goya captured the specific moment when one man is about to be executed, he also recorded the bloody bodies of others lying dead on the ground. Still others have been herded together to be shot in a few moments. The horrible massacre will continue indefinitely.

SATURN Goya painted *Third of May* when he was already totally deaf as a result of a mysterious illness he suffered in 1792 that also rendered him temporarily blind and paralyzed as well. Although he recovered all but his hearing, over time Goya became increasingly disillusioned and pessimistic. This state of mind emerges forcefully especially in his late works known as the "Black Paintings," frescoes he painted on the walls of his farmhouse called Quinta del Sordo (House of the Deaf Man), outside Madrid. Because Goya created the Black Paintings solely on his terms and for his private viewing, they provide great insight into the artist's outlook, which is terrifying and disturbing.

Saturn Devouring One of His Children (FIG. 27-13) depicts the raw carnage and violence of Saturn (the Greek god Kronos; see "The Gods and Goddesses of Mount Olympus," page 105), wild-eyed and monstrous, as he consumes one of his sons in reaction to a prophecy that one of his children would dethrone him. Because of the similarity of Kronos and *khronos* (the Greek word for "time"), Saturn has come to be associated with time. This has led some to interpret Goya's painting as an expression of the artist's despair over the passage of time. Despite the simplicity of the image, it conveys a wildness, boldness, and brutality that evoke an elemental response from all viewers. Goya's work, rooted both in personal and national history, presents darkly emotional images well in keeping with Romanticism.

THÉODORE GÉRICAULT In a tragically brief career lasting only a dozen years, Théodore Géricault (see page 793) had a major influence on the course of French painting in the 19th century. Independently wealthy, he spent only a short time as an apprentice in painting studios, preferring to learn his craft by studying in the Louvre. The former royal palace then housed the recently installed Musée Napoléon and its treasure trove of works by Jan van Eyck, Titian, Caravaggio, Rembrandt, and Peter Paul Rubens, which the emperor had triumphantly brought to Paris as the spoils of his successful military campaigns. Géricault was drawn especially to Rubens, in whose canvases the young painter saw an alternative to the classical compositions, smooth finish, and invisible brushstrokes of David. Géricault also studied Renaissance and Baroque art in Florence, Rome, and

27-14 THÉODORE GÉRICAULT, *Charging Chasseur*, 1812. Oil on canvas, 11' 5" × 8' 8¾". Musée du Louvre, Paris.

Painted when he was 21, Géricault's huge canvas, with its foreshortened rider and loose brushwork influenced by Rubens, differs sharply from David's equestrian portrait of Napoleon (FIG. 27-2A).

27-13 FRANCISCO GOYA, *Saturn Devouring One of His Children,* from Goya's Quinto del Sordo farmhouse, near Madrid, Spain, 1819–1823. Fresco, later detached and mounted on canvas, 4' 9⅛" × 2' 8⅝". Museo Nacional del Prado, Madrid.

This disturbing fresco from Goya's farmhouse uses a mythological tale to express the aging artist's despair over the passage of time. Saturn's Greek name, Kronos, is similar to the Greek word for "time."

Naples in 1816 on a self-funded trip to Italy after failing to win a Rome Prize, but he also explored themes with few if any precedents—for example, portraits of the insane (FIG. **27-13A**).

At the time of his death at age 32, Géricault had exhibited only three works in the Parisian Salons. The last, in 1819, was his greatest work, *Raft of the Medusa* (FIG. 27-1). The first, submitted to the Salon of 1812, was *Charging Chasseur* (FIG. **27-14**). Painted

27-13A GÉRICAULT, *Insane Woman*, 1822–1823.

when he was 21, the gigantic (more than 11-foot-tall) canvas depicts a French cavalry officer (*chasseur*). Because Géricault had to enter the work in the portrait category, he identified the chasseur as Lieutenant Alexandre Dieudonné, but the painting could represent any heroic French soldier during Napoleon's Russian campaign. The chasseur and his rearing horse seen in a three-quarter view from behind fill almost the entire canvas. Inspired by Rubens's boldly foreshortened figures (FIG. I-13) as well as the Flemish master's palette and brushwork, Géricault's painting recalls but differs markedly from David's portrait of Napoleon on horseback (FIG. 27-2A), in which the emperor and his steed occupy a narrow space parallel to the picture plane, as in classical relief sculpture (FIG. 5-50, *top*). Amid the tumult and horror of the raging battle, the officer twists on his mount to fend off an attack from behind. The high drama and violent action disguise how carefully Géricault posed the chasseur and his horse, creating, for example, a continuous arc from the officer's sword to the horse's head and forming three parallel lines from the chasseur's right leg and the horse's two right legs. *Charging Chasseur* impressed the judges at the 1812 Salon and earned the then-unknown Géricault a gold medal.

EUGÈNE DELACROIX Art historians often present the history of painting during the first half of the 19th century as a contest between two major artists—Ingres, the Neoclassical draftsman, and EUGÈNE DELACROIX (1798–1863), the Romantic colorist. Their

ART AND SOCIETY

The Romantic Spirit in Art, Music, and Literature

The appeal of Romanticism, with its emphasis on freedom and feeling, extended well beyond the realm of the visual arts. The imagination and vision that characterized Romantic paintings and sculptures were equally moving and riveting in musical or written form. In European music, literature, and poetry, the Romantic spirit was a dominant presence during the late 18th and early 19th centuries. Composers and authors alike rejected classicism's structured order in favor of the emotive and expressive. In music, the compositions of Franz Schubert (1797–1828), Franz Liszt (1811–1886), Frédéric Chopin (1810–1849), and Johannes Brahms (1833–1897) emphasized the melodic or lyrical. For these composers, music had the power to express what cannot be expressed with words and to communicate the subtlest and most powerful human emotions.

In literature, Romantic poets such as John Keats (1795–1821), William Wordsworth (1770–1850), and Samuel Taylor Coleridge (1772–1834) published volumes of poetry manifesting the Romantic interest in lyrical drama. *Ozymandias,* by Percy Bysshe Shelley (1792–1822), transported readers to faraway, exotic locales. The setting of Lord Byron's *Sardanapalus* is the ancient Assyrian Empire (see page 48). Byron's poem conjures images of eroticism and fury unleashed—images Eugène Delacroix made concrete in his painting *Death of Sardanapalus* (FIG. 27-15). One of the best examples of the Romantic spirit is the engrossing novel *Frankenstein,* written in 1818 by Shelley's wife, Mary Wollstonecraft Shelley (1797–1851). This fantastic tale of a monstrous creature run amok remains popular to the present day. As was true of many Romantic artworks, the novel not only embraced emotionalism but also rejected the rationalism underlying Enlightenment thought. Dr. Frankenstein's monster was a product of science, and the novel is an indictment of the deep faith in science that Voltaire and other Enlightenment thinkers promoted. *Frankenstein* served as a cautionary tale of the havoc that could result from unrestrained scientific experimentation and from the arrogance of scientists.

27-15 Eugène Delacroix, *Death of Sardanapalus,* 1827. Oil on canvas, 12' 1$\frac{1}{2}$" × 16' 2$\frac{7}{8}$". Musée du Louvre, Paris.

Inspired by Lord Byron's 1821 poem, Delacroix painted the Romantic spectacle of an Assyrian king on his funeral pyre. The richly colored and emotionally charged canvas is filled with exotic figures.

1 ft.

dialogue recalls the quarrel between the Poussinistes and the Rubénistes at the end of the 17th century and the beginning of the 18th (see "Poussinistes and Rubénistes," page 768). The Poussinistes were conservative defenders of academism who insisted that drawing was superior to color, whereas the Rubénistes proclaimed the importance of color over line (line quality being more intellectual and thus more restrictive than color). Delacroix's works were products of his view that the artist's powers of imagination would in turn capture and inflame the viewer's imagination. Literature of imagi-

native power served Delacroix (and many of his contemporaries) as a useful source of subject matter (see "The Romantic Spirit in Art, Music, and Literature," above). Théophile Gautier (1811–1872), the prominent Romantic critic and novelist, recalled:

In those days painting and poetry fraternized. The artists read the poets, and the poets visited the artists. We found Shakespeare, Dante, Goethe, Lord Byron and Walter Scott in the studio as well as in the study. There were as many splashes of color as there were blots of ink in the margins of those beautiful books which we endlessly perused. Imagination, already excited, was further fired by reading those foreign works, so rich in color, so free and powerful in fantasy.[1]

DEATH OF SARDANAPALUS Delacroix's 1827 *Death of Sardanapalus* (FIG. **27-15**) is perhaps the grandest Romantic pictorial drama ever painted. Although inspired by the 1821 narrative poem *Sardanapalus* by Lord Byron (George Gordon Byron, 1788–1824), the painting does not illustrate that text faithfully. Delacroix depicted the last hour of the Assyrian king Ashurbanipal (r. 668–627 BCE; FIG. 2-23), whom the Greeks called Sardanapalus. The king has just received news of his army's defeat and the enemy's entry into his city. The setting that Delacroix painted is much more tempestuous and crowded than Byron described, and orgiastic destruction has replaced the sacrificial suicide of the poem. Sardanapalus reclines on his funeral pyre, soon to be set alight, and gloomily watches the carrying out of his order to destroy all of his most precious possessions—his women, slaves, horses, and treasure. The king's favorite concubine throws herself on the bed, determined to go up in flames with her master. The Assyrian ruler presides like a genius of evil over the tragic scene. Most conspicuous are the tortured and dying bodies of the harem women. In the foreground, a muscular slave plunges his knife into the neck of one woman. Delacroix filled this awful spectacle of suffering and death with the most daringly difficult and tortuous poses, and chose the richest intensities of hue. With its exotic and erotic overtones and violent Orientalist subject, *Death of Sardanapalus* tapped into the Romantic fantasies of 19th-century viewers.

Although *Death of Sardanapalus* is a seventh-century BCE drama, Delacroix, like Géricault, also turned to current events, particularly tragic or sensational ones, for his subject matter. For example, he produced several images based on the Greek War for Independence (1821–1829), including a huge canvas that he painted while the war was still in progress recording the Turkish massacre of the Greeks of Chios (FIG. **27-15A**). The French perception of the Greeks as locked in a brutal struggle for freedom from the cruel and exotic Ottoman Turks generated great interest in Romantic circles.

⬈ **27-15A** DELACROIX, *Massacre at Chios*, 1822–1824.

LIBERTY LEADING THE PEOPLE Closer to home, Delacroix captured the passion and energy of the 1830 revolution in *Liberty Leading the People* (FIG. **27-16**). Based on the July 27–29, 1830, Parisian uprising against Charles X (r. 1824–1830), it is at once a record of a contemporaneous event and a Romantic allegory. Dominating the composition is the bare-breasted personification of Liberty defiantly thrusting forth the republic's tricolor banner as she urges the masses to fight on. She wears a scarlet Phrygian cap (the symbol of a freed slave in antiquity), reinforcing the urgency of this struggle. Arrayed around Liberty are bold Parisian types—the street boy brandishing his pistols, the menacing worker with a cutlass, and the intellectual dandy in top hat brandishing a musket. As in Géricault's *Raft of the Medusa* (FIG. 27-1), dead bodies are all around. In the background, the towers of Notre-Dame (FIG. 13-10) rise through the smoke and haze. The painter's inclusion of this recognizable Parisian landmark announces the specificity of locale and event, balancing historical fact with poetic allegory.

WOMEN OF ALGIERS An enormously influential event in Delacroix's life that affected his art in both subject and form was his visit to North Africa in 1832. Delacroix was the official artist in the entourage of the count of Mornay, who led a diplomatic mission to Morocco to seek the support of Sultan Abd al-Rahman (r. 1822–1859) for the French annexation of Algeria. What Delacroix saw in North Africa excited his imagination with fresh impressions that lasted throughout his life and resulted in paintings such as *Tiger Hunt* (FIG. **27-16A**), which he completed more than two decades after his trip.

1 ft.

⬈ **27-16A** DELACROIX, *Tiger Hunt*, 1854.

27-16 EUGÈNE DELACROIX, *Liberty Leading the People*, 1830. Oil on canvas, 8' 6" × 10' 8". Musée du Louvre, Paris.

In a balanced mix of history and poetic allegory, Delacroix captured the passion and energy of the 1830 revolution in this painting of Liberty leading the Parisian uprising against Charles X.

In both subject and style, Delacroix's painting of three odalisques and a black servant in a sumptuous Algiers harem exemplifies Romantic painting, in contrast to Ingres's Neoclassicism (FIG. 27-8).

Among the canvases Delacroix painted immediately upon his return to France is *Women of Algiers* (FIG. **27-17**), which captivated the public when exhibited in the 1834 Salon. For viewers of the exhibition, the painting was their first "eyewitness account" of a harem—an exotic locale that had special appeal because Western men were normally not permitted to enter harems. (Delacroix was able to gain entry because of the official nature of his visit to Morocco. The seated woman at the left seems to acknowledge the artist's presence.) The painting depicts three odalisques—modestly dressed, unlike the harem girl in Ingres's earlier imaginary and coolly classical rendition of the same theme (FIG. 27-8)—and a black servant in an incense-filled room with tiled walls and sumptuous carpets. The woman at the left reclines languorously. Her two seated companions share the intoxicating smoke of a *hookah* (water pipe). Delacroix's "documentation" of the opulent interior of a harem reinforced all the stereotypes that his countrymen held dear, especially their fantasies about Oriental harems as places where men could freely indulge their sexual appetites in the company of exotic women.

Delacroix's style perfectly suits this sensuous subject. Relying on large patches of rich color to define his figures, in striking contrast to Ingres's emphasis on line and contour, his technique is as lush as the harem. What Delacroix knew about color he passed on to later painters of the 19th century, particularly the Impressionists (see page 843). He observed that pure colors are as rare in nature as lines and that color appears only in an infinitely varied scale of different tones, shadings, and reflections, which he tried to re-create in his paintings. He recorded his observations in his journal, which became for later painters and scholars a veritable handbook of pre-Impressionist color theory. Although Delacroix anticipated the later development of Impressionist color science, that art-science had to await the discoveries by Michel Eugène Chevreul (1786–1889) and Hermann von Helmholtz (1821–1894) of the laws of light decomposition and the properties of complementary colors. Only then could the problems of color perception and juxtaposition in painting be properly formulated (see "19th-Century Color Theory," page 855). Nevertheless, Delacroix's observations were significant, and he advised other artists not to fuse their brushstrokes, as those strokes would appear to fuse naturally from a distance.

No other painter of the time explored the domain of Romantic subject and mood as thoroughly and definitively as Delacroix. His technique was impetuous, improvisational, and instinctive, rather than deliberate, studious, and cold. It exemplified Romantic colorist painting, catching the impression quickly and developing it in the execution process. His contemporaries commented on how furiously Delacroix worked once he had an idea, keeping the whole painting progressing at once. One critic described Delacroix's brushwork as painting "with a drunken broom." The fury of the artist's attack matched the fury of his imagination and his subjects.

27-18 François Rude, *Departure of the Volunteers of 1792* (*La Marseillaise*), northeast pier relief of the Arc de Triomphe, Paris, France, 1833–1836. Limestone, 41' 8" high.

This historical-allegorical sculpture features the Roman war goddess Bellona, but the violent motion, jagged contours, and densely packed masses typify Romantic painting compositions.

FRANÇOIS RUDE The Romantic spirit pervaded all media during the early 19th century. As did the painters of the period, many sculptors produced work incorporating both Neoclassical and Romantic elements. The colossal limestone group *Departure of the Volunteers of 1792* (FIG. 27-18), also called *La Marseillaise,* is one example. The relief, the work of FRANÇOIS RUDE (1784–1855), decorates one of the gigantic piers of the Arc de Triomphe (FIG. 27-18A) in Paris, designed for Napoleon by JEAN-FRANÇOIS-THÉRÈSE CHALGRIN (1739–1811). The sculpture depicts the volunteers of 1792 departing from Marseilles to defend France's borders against the foreign enemies of the revolution. A composite personification of Bellona, the Roman goddess of war;

27-18A CHALGRIN, Arc de Triomphe, Paris, 1806–1836.

Liberty; and the Marseillaise, the revolutionary hymn that since 1879 has been France's national anthem, soars above patriots of all ages, exhorting them forward with a thundering battle cry emerging from her wide-open mouth. The figures recall David's classically armored (FIG. 26-26) or nude heroes, as do the rhetorical gestures of the wide-flung arms and the striding poses. Yet the violence of motion, the jagged contours, and the densely packed, overlapping masses relate more closely to the compositional method of dramatic Romanticism, as found in the canvases of Géricault (FIG. 27-1) and Delacroix (FIG. 27-16). Indeed, the allegorical figure in *La Marseillaise* is the spiritual sister of Delacroix's Liberty. Rude's stone figure shares the same Phrygian cap, the badge of liberty, with Delacroix's earlier painted figure, but Rude's soldiers wear classical costumes or are heroically nude, whereas those in Delacroix's painting appear in modern Parisian dress. Both works are allegorical, but one looks to the past and the other to the present.

Landscape Painting

Landscape painting came into its own in the 19th century as a fully independent and respected genre. Briefly eclipsed at the century's beginning by the taste for ideal form, which favored figural composition and history, landscape painting flourished as leading painters adopted the genre as their specialty. Increasing tourism, which came courtesy of improved and expanded railway systems both in Europe (MAP 27-2) and America, contributed to the popularity of landscape painting. So too did the growth of cities. As urban populations expanded, city dwellers increasingly took pleasure in "picturesque" views of the unspoiled countryside. To be sure, earlier artists, especially in the 18th century, regarded the comforting, aesthetic mood that nature inspired as making the landscape itself picturesque—that is, worthy of being painted. But Romantic painters often used nature as allegory and embraced landscape as a vehicle to comment on spiritual, moral, historical, or philosophical issues.

In the early 19th century, most northern European landscape painting to some degree expressed the Romantic view (first extolled by Rousseau) of nature as a "being" that included the totality of existence in organic unity and harmony. German painters, who were primarily Lutherans, were especially attracted to nature, where they could communicate directly with God without the need of a Catholic priest as intermediary. In nature—"the living garment of God," as German poet and dramatist Johann Wolfgang von Goethe (1749–1832) called it—artists found an ideal subject to express the Romantic theme of the soul unified with the natural world. As all nature was mysteriously permeated by "being," landscape artists had the task of interpreting the signs, symbols, and emblems of universal spirit disguised within visible material things. Artists no longer merely beheld a landscape but participated in its spirit, becoming translators of nature's transcendent meanings.

CASPAR DAVID FRIEDRICH Among the first northern European artists to depict the Romantic transcendental landscape was CASPAR DAVID FRIEDRICH (1774–1840), who was born in Greifswald, Germany, near the Baltic Sea; studied art in Copenhagen; and settled in Dresden. For Friedrich, the personal experience of nature led to a deeper understanding of God, nature's creator. The reverential mood of his works demands from the viewer the silence appropriate to sacred places filled with a divine presence.

Abbey in the Oak Forest (FIG. 27-19) is a characteristic example. It is the pictorial equivalent of a solemn requiem. Under a winter sky, through the leafless oaks of a snow-covered cemetery, a procession

27-19 CASPAR DAVID FRIEDRICH, *Abbey in the Oak Forest,* 1810. Oil on canvas, 4' × 5' 8½". Alte Nationalgalerie, Staatliche Museen zu Berlin, Berlin.

Friedrich was a master of the Romantic transcendental landscape. The reverential mood of this winter scene with a ruined Gothic church and cemetery demands the silence appropriate to sacred places.

1 ft.

WRITTEN SOURCES

Friedrich's *Wanderer above a Sea of Mist*

In *Abbey in the Oak Forest* (FIG. 27-19) and most of Caspar David Friedrich's landscapes, the human figure plays an insignificant role. Indeed, in many instances the human actors are difficult even to discern. But in other paintings, one or more figures seen from behind gazing at the natural vista dominate the canvas. In *Wanderer above a Sea of Mist* (FIG. 27-20), probably Friedrich's most famous painting, a solitary man dressed in German attire suggestive of a bygone era stands on a rocky promontory and leans on his cane. He surveys a vast panorama of clouds, mountains, and thick mist. Because Friedrich chose a point of view on the level of the man's head, the viewer has the sensation of hovering in space behind him—an impossible position that enhances the aura of mystery that the scene conveys. Art historians dispute whether Friedrich intended the viewer to identify with the man seen from behind or if he wanted the viewer to contemplate the man gazing at the misty landscape. Some think that the man is not an anonymous hiker but a specific Prussian war hero contemplating the scenery of his native land. In any interpretation, the painter communicated an almost religious awe at the beauty and vastness of the natural world.

Carl Gustav Carus (1789–1869), a German physician and sometime painter who was a friend of Friedrich's, published in Dresden in 1831 *Nine Letters on Landscape Painting, Written in the Years 1815 to 1824*. In one of the letters, he described the essence of Friedrich's approach to landscape painting in a passage that could serve as a description of *Wanderer above a Sea of Mist*:

[T]he solid earth, with all of its varied shapes and features like rocks and mountains, valleys and plains, its placid and its rushing waters, the clouds and airy breezes, these are more or less the forms through which the life of the earth reveals itself to us; a life of such immeasurable dimensions in comparison with our own smallness . . . Go up then to the summit of the mountain, look out across all the distant hilly peaks, contemplate the steady progress of the rivers and every splendor that reveals itself to your gaze, and what feeling is it that then seizes hold of you? There is a quiet sense of devotion within you, you lose yourself in boundless space, your whole being experiences a gentle elevation and purification, your very self vanishes away, you are nothing and God is everything.*

27-20 CASPAR DAVID FRIEDRICH, *Wanderer above a Sea of Mist*, 1817–1818. Oil on canvas, 3' 1¾" × 2' 5⅜". Hamburger Kunsthalle, Hamburg.

Friedrich's painting of a solitary man on a rocky promontory gazing at a vast panorama of clouds, mountains, and thick mist perfectly expresses the Romantic notion of the sublime in nature.

Wanderer above a Sea of Mist perfectly expresses the Romantic notion of the sublime in nature.

*Translated by Nicholas Walker, in Charles Harrison, Paul Wood, and Jason Gaiger, *Art in Theory 1815–1900: An Anthology of Changing Ideas* (Oxford: Blackwell, 1998), 104.

---

of monks bears a coffin into the ruins of a Gothic church that Friedrich based on the remains of Eldana Abbey near Greifswald. The emblems of death are everywhere—the season's desolation, the leaning crosses and tombstones, the black of mourning that the grieving wear, the skeletal trees, and the destruction that time has wrought on the church. The painting is a kind of meditation on human mortality. As Friedrich himself remarked: "Why, it has often occurred to me to ask myself, do I so frequently choose death, transience, and the grave as subjects for my paintings? One must submit oneself many times to death in order some day to attain life everlasting."[2] The artist's sharp-focused rendering of details demonstrates his keen perception of everything in the physical environment relevant to his message. Friedrich's work balances inner and outer experience. "The artist," he wrote, "should paint not only what he sees before him, but also what he sees within him. If, however, he sees nothing within him, then he should also refrain from painting that which he sees before him."[3] Although *Abbey in the Oak Forest* and Friedrich's other works—for

example, *Wanderer above a Sea of Mist* (FIG. 27-20)—may not have the theatrical energy of the paintings of Géricault or Delacroix, a resonant and deep emotion pervades them (see "Friedrich's *Wanderer above a Sea of Mist*," above).

JOHN CONSTABLE In England, one of the most momentous developments in Western history—the Industrial Revolution—had a profound impact on the evolution of Romantic landscape painting. Although discussion of the Industrial Revolution invariably focuses on technological advances, factory development, and growth of urban centers (see page 773), industrialization had no less pronounced an effect on the countryside and the land itself. The detrimental economic effect that the Industrial Revolution had on prices for agrarian products created significant unrest in the English countryside. In particular, increasing numbers of farmers could no longer afford to farm their small plots and had to abandon their land.

John Constable on Landscape Painting

In the early 1820s, John Constable corresponded with his friend John Fisher, the archdeacon of Salisbury Cathedral (FIGS. 13-39 to 13-41), on various topics, including his views on landscape painting. The following excerpts from a letter he wrote to Fisher on October 23, 1821, provide invaluable insight into the artist's goals and values.

> I am most anxious to get into my London painting-room. . . . I have done a good deal of skying, for I am determined to conquer all difficulties. . . . The landscape painter who does not make his skies a very material part of his composition, neglects to avail himself of one of his greatest aids. . . . Certainly, if the sky is obtrusive, as mine are, it is bad; but if it is evaded, as mine are not, it is worse; it must and always shall with me make an effectual part of the composition. . . . The sky is the force of light in nature, and governs every thing; even our common observations on the weather of every day are altogether suggested by it. . . . Shakespeare could make every thing poetical; he tells us of poor Tom's haunts among "sheep cotes and mills." As long as I do paint, I shall never cease to paint such places. . . . Still I should paint my own places best; painting is with me but another word for feeling, and I associate "my careless boyhood" with all that lies on the banks of the Stour; those scenes made me a painter, and I am grateful.*

*Charles Harrison, Paul Wood, and Jason Gaiger, *Art in Theory 1815–1900: An Anthology of Changing Ideas* (Oxford: Blackwell, 1998), 118–119.

27-21 JOHN CONSTABLE, *The Hay Wain*, 1821. Oil on canvas, 4' 3$\frac{1}{4}$" × 6' 1". National Gallery, London.

The Hay Wain is a nostalgic view of the disappearing English countryside during the Industrial Revolution. Constable had a special gift for capturing the texture that climate and weather give to landscapes.

1 ft.

JOHN CONSTABLE (1776–1837) devoted his career to painting the English countryside during this agrarian crisis. He made countless studies from nature for each of his canvases, which helped him produce in his paintings a convincing sense of reality. In his quest for the authentic landscape, Constable studied nature as a meteorologist (he was an accomplished amateur "weatherman"). Although he produced his paintings in his London studio, the norm at the time, he was one of the first to make his sketches outdoors using oil paints instead of watercolors or pencil drawings. His special gift was for capturing the texture that climate and weather, which delicately veil what is seen, give to landscapes. Constable's oil studies of clouds under different weather conditions are especially remarkable. His use of tiny dabs of local color, stippled with white, created a sparkling shimmer of light and hue across the canvas surface—the vibration itself suggestive of movement and process.

The Hay Wain (FIG. **27-21**) is representative of Constable's art and reveals much about his outlook. His subjects are Romantic but not sublime. Here, a small cottage sits on the left of a serenely pastoral scene of the countryside. In the center foreground, a man slowly leads a horse and hay-filled wagon (a *hay wain*) across a shallow stretch of the Stour River. Billowy clouds float lazily across the sky. The muted greens and golds and the delicacy of Constable's brushstrokes complement the scene's tranquility. The artist portrayed the oneness with nature that the Romantic poets sought. The relaxed figures are not observers but participants in the landscape's "being."

In terms of content, *The Hay Wain* is significant for precisely what it does not show—the civil unrest of the agrarian working class and the resulting outbreaks of violence and arson. The people populating Constable's landscapes blend into the scenes and become one with nature. Rarely does the viewer see workers engaged in tedious labor (compare, in France, Jean-François Millet's portrayal of the menial and backbreaking work of women gathering scraps after a harvest; FIG. 27-28). Indeed, this painting has a nostalgic, wistful air to it, and reflects Constable's memories of a disappearing rural pastoralism.

PROBLEMS AND SOLUTIONS
Unleashing the Emotive Power of Color

The passion and energy of Turner's landscapes and seascapes reveal the sensibility that was the foundation for much of the art of the Romantic era, but Turner discovered a new means of capturing in painting Edmund Burke's concept of the sublime—awe mixed with terror.

Turner's *The Slave Ship* (FIG. 27-22), although strikingly different in form from Géricault's *Raft of the Medusa* (FIG. 27-1), also has as its subject a politically explosive disaster at sea. *The Slave Ship* depicts a 1781 incident reported in the widely read *History of the Abolition of the Slave Trade*, by Thomas Clarkson (1760–1846). Clarkson's account, reprinted in 1839, undoubtedly was the reason Turner chose this subject for this 1840 painting. The incident involved the slave ship *Zong*, en route from Africa to Liverpool. The ship's captain, on realizing that his insurance would reimburse him only for slaves lost at sea but not for those who died en route, ordered more than 50 sick and dying slaves to be thrown overboard. Appropriately, the painting's subtitle is *Slavers Throwing Overboard the Dead and Dying, Typhoon Coming On*. Slavery had been a powerful political issue in England for some time. For example, in the 1780s, fashionable women wore brooches depicting a kneeling, shackled African slave and carrying the words "Am I Not a Man and a Brother?"—the seal of the Society for the Abolition of Slavery in England. (Brooches and medallions bearing the motif were produced in great numbers in the ceramic factory of Josiah Wedgwood, much better known for his Neoclassical designs featuring Greco-Roman gods and heroes; see page 783.)

Turner's frenzied emotional depiction of the dumping of the sick slaves into the sea matches its barbaric nature. The artist transformed the sun into an incandescent comet amid flying scarlet clouds. The slave ship moves into the distance, leaving in its wake a turbulent sea choked with the bodies of slaves sinking to their deaths. The relative scale of the minuscule human forms compared with the vast sea and overarching sky reinforces the sense of the sublime, especially the immense power of nature over humans. *The Slave Ship* is the polar opposite of *Raft of the Medusa*, in which heroic, over-life-size bodies fill the canvas and block out most of the ocean. Almost lost in the boiling colors of Turner's painting are the event's particulars, but on close inspection, the viewer can discern the iron shackles and manacles around the wrists and ankles of the drowning slaves, cruelly denying them any chance of saving themselves from the predatory fish circling about them.

A key ingredient of Turner's highly personal style is the emotive power of pure color. The haziness of the painter's forms and the indistinctness of his compositions intensify the colors and energetic brushstrokes. Turner's innovation in works such as *The Slave Ship* was to release color from any defining outlines so as to express both the forces of nature and the painter's emotional response to them. In his paintings, the reality of color is at one with the reality of feeling.

Turner's methods had an incalculable effect on the later development of painting. His discovery of the aesthetic and emotive power of pure color and his pushing of the medium's fluidity to a point where the paint itself is almost the subject were important steps toward 20th-century Abstract Expressionist art, which dispensed with identifiable forms altogether (see page 953).

27-22 JOSEPH MALLORD WILLIAM TURNER, *The Slave Ship (Slavers Throwing Overboard the Dead and Dying, Typhoon Coming On)*, 1840. Oil on canvas, 2' 11$\frac{1}{4}$" × 4'. Museum of Fine Arts, Boston (Henry Lillie Pierce Fund).

The essence of Turner's innovative style is the emotive power of color. He released color from any defining outlines to express both the forces of nature and the painter's emotional response to them.

1 ft.

Thomas Cole on the American Landscape

Although—or perhaps because—he was born in England, Thomas Cole (FIG. 27-23), the most prominent member of the Hudson River School of landscape painting, best defined those qualities that distinguished American landscapes from European ones. In his "Essay on American Scenery" published in the January 1836 issue of *American Monthly Magazine*, Cole described the unique nature of the American countryside.

> There are those who through ignorance or prejudice strive to maintain that American scenery possesses little that is interesting or truly beautiful, . . . that being destitute of those vestiges of antiquity, whose associations so strongly affect the mind, it may not be compared with European scenery. . . . I am by no means desirous of less-

> ening in your estimation the glorious scenes of the old world . . . over which time and genius have suspended an imperishable halo. No! But I would have it remembered that nature has shed over *this* land beauty and magnificence, and although the character of its scenery may differ from the old world's, yet inferiority must not therefore be inferred; for though American scenery is destitute of many of those circumstances that give value to the European, still it has features, and glorious ones, unknown to Europe. . . . The most distinctive, and perhaps the most impressive, characteristic of American scenery is its wildness. It is the most distinctive, because in civilized Europe the primitive features of scenery have long since been destroyed or modified . . . [In America] nature is still predominant . . . [T]hose scenes of solitude from which the hand of nature has never been lifted affect the mind with a more deep toned emotion than aught which the hand of man has touched. Amid them the consequent associations are of God the creator— they are his undefiled works, and the mind is cast into the contemplation of eternal things.[*]

[*]Charles Harrison, Paul Wood, and Jason Gaiger, *Art in Theory 1815–1900: An Anthology of Changing Ideas* (Oxford: Blackwell, 1998), 136–137.

27-23 THOMAS COLE, *The Oxbow* (*View from Mount Holyoke, Northampton, Massachusetts, after a Thunderstorm*), 1836. Oil on canvas, 4' 3$\frac{1}{2}$" × 6' 4". Metropolitan Museum of Art, New York (gift of Mrs. Russell Sage, 1908).

Cole championed the idea of America having a landscape distinct from Europe's. Here, he contrasted dark wilderness on the left and sunlit civilization on the right, with a minuscule painter at the bottom center.

The artist's father was a successful miller and flour merchant and a rural landowner of considerable wealth. Many of the scenes that Constable painted (*The Hay Wain* included) depict his family's property near East Bergholt in Suffolk, East Anglia. This nostalgia, presented in such naturalistic terms, renders Constable's works Romantic in tone. That the painter felt a kindred spirit with the Romantic artists is revealed by his comment, "painting is with me but another word for feeling" (see "John Constable on Landscape Painting," page 811).

J.M.W. TURNER Constable's great contemporary in the English school of landscape painting was JOSEPH MALLORD WILLIAM TURNER (1775–1851). Both artists tirelessly sought to raise the prestige of landscape painting in the Royal Academy. However, whereas Constable's canvases are serene and precisely painted, and have as their exclusive subject the rural countryside of his birthplace, Turner's paintings have a much wider range of themes and, as in *The Slave Ship* (FIG. 27-22), feature turbulent swirls of frothy pigment (see "Unleashing the Emotive Power of Color," page 812).

THOMAS COLE In America, landscape painting was the specialty of a group of artists known as the Hudson River School, so named because its members drew their subjects primarily from the uncultivated regions of New York's Hudson River Valley, although many of these painters depicted scenes from across the country. As did the early-19th-century landscape painters in Germany and England, the artists of the Hudson River School not only presented Romantic panoramic landscape views but also participated in the ongoing exploration of the individual's and the country's relationship to the land. American landscape painters frequently focused on identifying qualities that made America unique. THOMAS COLE (1801–1848), often referred to as the leader of the Hudson River School, best articulated this idea (see "Thomas Cole on the American Landscape," above).

Another issue that surfaced frequently in Hudson River School paintings was the moral question of America's direction as a civilization. Cole addressed this question in *The Oxbow* (*View from Mount Holyoke, Northampton, Massachusetts, after a Thunderstorm*; FIG. 27-23). A splendid scene opens before the viewer, dominated

1 ft.

27-24 ALBERT BIERSTADT, *Among the Sierra Nevada Mountains, California,* 1868. Oil on canvas, 6' × 10'. National Museum of American Art, Smithsonian Institution, Washington, D.C.

Bierstadt's panoramic landscape presents the breathtaking natural beauty of the American West, reinforcing the 19th-century doctrine of Manifest Destiny, which justified America's western expansion.

by the lazy oxbow-shaped turning of the Connecticut River. Cole divided the composition in two, with the dark, stormy wilderness on the left and the more developed civilization on the right. The minuscule artist wearing a top hat in the bottom center of the painting, dwarfed by the landscape's scale, turns to the viewer as if to ask for input in deciding the country's future course. Cole's depictions of expansive wilderness incorporated reflections and moods romantically appealing to the public.

ALBERT BIERSTADT Other Hudson River artists used the landscape genre as an allegorical vehicle to address moral and spiritual concerns. ALBERT BIERSTADT (1830–1902) traveled west in 1858 and produced many paintings depicting the Rocky Mountains, Yosemite Valley, and other dramatic locales. These works, such as *Among the Sierra Nevada Mountains, California* (FIG. **27-24**), present breathtaking scenery and natural beauty. This panoramic view (the painting is 10 feet wide) is awe inspiring. Deer and waterfowl appear at the edge of a placid lake, and steep and rugged mountains soar skyward on the left and in the distance. A stand of trees, uncultivated and wild, frames the lake on the right. To underscore the transcendental nature of this scene, Bierstadt depicted the sun's rays breaking through the clouds overhead, suggesting a heavenly consecration of the land. That Bierstadt's focus was the American West is not insignificant. By calling national attention to the splendor and uniqueness of the regions beyond the Rocky Mountains,

Bierstadt's paintings reinforced the idea of Manifest Destiny. This popular 19th-century doctrine held that westward expansion across the continent was the logical destiny of the United States. As John L. O'Sullivan (1813–1895) expounded in the earliest known use of the term in 1845, "Our manifest destiny [is] to spread over and to possess the whole of the continent which Providence has given us for the development of the great experiment of liberty and federal development of self-government entrusted to us."[4] Paintings of the scenic splendor of the West helped to mute growing concerns over the realities of conquest, the displacement of Native Americans, and the exploitation of the environment. It should come as no surprise that among those most eager to purchase Bierstadt's work were mail-service magnates and railroad builders—entrepreneurs and financiers involved in westward expansion.

FREDERIC CHURCH Another painter usually associated with the Hudson River School was FREDERIC EDWIN CHURCH (1826–1900), but his interest in landscape scenes extended beyond America. He traveled widely—to South America, Mexico, Europe, the Middle East, Newfoundland, and Labrador. Church's paintings are firmly in the idiom of the Romantic sublime, yet they also reveal contradictions and conflicts in the constructed mythology of American providence and character. *Twilight in the Wilderness* (FIG. **27-25**) presents a panoramic view of the sun setting over the majestic landscape. Beyond Church's precise depiction of the magnificent

27-25 Frederic Edwin Church, *Twilight in the Wilderness*, 1860s. Oil on canvas, 3' 4" × 5' 4". Cleveland Museum of Art, Cleveland (Mr. and Mrs. William H. Marlatt Fund).

Church's paintings eloquently express the Romantic notion of the sublime. This wilderness landscape presents a glorious sunset in America, but the dead trees may be a reference to the Civil War.

spectacle of nature, the painting, like Constable's *Hay Wain* (FIG. 27-21), is remarkable for what it does not depict. Like Constable, Church and the other Hudson River School painters worked in a time of great upheaval. *Twilight in the Wilderness* dates to the 1860s, when the Civil War was tearing apart the no-longer-united states. Church's painting does not overtly display evidence of turbulence or discord. Indeed, it does not include even a single figure. But the view of nature that Church provides is not entirely comforting. Beside the rich vegetation and glorious sunset, there are also dead trees, perhaps symbolizing the casualties of the Civil War.

REALISM

Advances in industrial technology during the early 19th century reinforced Enlightenment faith in the connection between science and progress. Both intellectuals and the general public increasingly embraced *empiricism* and *positivism*. To empiricists, the basis of knowledge is observation and direct experience. Positivists ascribed to the philosophical model developed by Auguste Comte (1798–1857), who believed that scientific laws governed the environment and human activity and could be revealed through careful recording and analysis of observable data. Comte's followers promoted science as the mind's highest achievement and advocated a purely empirical approach to nature and society.

France

Realism was a movement that developed in France around midcentury against this backdrop of an increasing emphasis on science. Consistent with the philosophical tenets of the empiricists and positivists, Realist artists argued that only the contemporary world—what people can see—was "real." Accordingly, Realists focused their attention on the people and events of their own time and disapproved of historical and fictional subjects on the grounds that they were neither visible nor present and therefore were not real.

GUSTAVE COURBET The leading figure of the Realist movement in 19th-century art was GUSTAVE COURBET (1819–1877). In fact, even though he shunned labels, Courbet used the term *Realism* when exhibiting his own works (see "Gustave Courbet on Realism," page 816). The Realists' sincerity about scrutinizing their environment led them to paint mundane and trivial subjects that artists had traditionally deemed unworthy of depiction—for example, working-class laborers and peasants, and similar "low" themes. Moreover, by depicting these subjects on a scale and with a seriousness previously reserved for historical, mythological, and religious painting, Realist artists sought to establish parity between contemporary subject matter and the traditional themes of "high art."

Gustave Courbet on Realism

The academic jury selecting work for the 1855 Salon (part of the Exposition Universelle in Paris that year) rejected 3 of the 14 paintings that Gustave Courbet submitted, declaring that his subjects and figures were too coarse (so much so as to be plainly "socialistic") and too large. Typical of Courbet's work are *The Stone Breakers* (FIG. 27-26), which depicts menial laborers, and *Burial at Ornans* (FIG. 27-27), which represents the funeral of an ordinary man and is nearly 22 feet long. In response to the jury's decision, Courbet withdrew all of his works, including those that had been accepted, and set up his own exhibition outside the grounds, calling it the Pavilion of Realism, featuring not 14 but 40 of his own works. This was in itself a bold action. Courbet was the first artist ever known to have staged a private exhibition of his own work. His pavilion and the statement he issued to explain the paintings shown there amounted to the Realist movement's manifesto. Although Courbet maintained that he founded no school and was of no school, he did, as the name of his pavilion suggests, accept the term *Realism* as descriptive of his art.

The statement that Courbet distributed at his pavilion reads in part:

> The title of "realist" has been imposed upon me. . . . Titles have never given a just idea of things; were it otherwise, the work would be superfluous. . . . I have studied the art of the ancients and the moderns, avoiding any preconceived system and without prejudice. I have no more wanted to imitate the former than to copy the latter; nor have I thought of achieving the idle aim of "art for art's sake." No! I have simply wanted to draw from a thorough

knowledge of tradition the reasoned and free sense of my own individuality. . . . To be able to translate the customs, ideas, and appearances of my time as I see them—in a word, to create a living art—this has been my aim.*

Six years later, on Christmas Day, 1861, Courbet wrote an open letter, published a few days later in the *Courier du dimanche*, addressed to prospective students. In the letter, the painter reflected on the nature of his art:

> [An artist must apply] his personal faculties to the ideas and the events of the times in which he lives. . . . [A]rt in painting should consist only of the representation of things that are visible and tangible to the artist. Every age should be represented only by its own artists, that is to say, by the artists who have lived in it. I also maintain that painting is an essentially concrete art form and can consist only of the representation of both real and existing things. . . . An abstract object, not visible, nonexistent, is not within the domain of painting.†

Courbet's most famous statement, however, is his blunt dismissal of academic painting, in which he concisely summed up the core principle of Realist painting:

> I have never seen an angel. Show me an angel, and I'll paint one.‡

*Translated by Robert Goldwater and Marco Treves, eds., *Artists on Art from the XIV to the XX Century* (New York: Pantheon, 1958), 295.
†Translated by Petra ten-Doesschate Chu, *Letters of Gustave Courbet* (Chicago: University of Chicago Press, 1992), 203–204.
‡Quoted by Vincent van Gogh in a July 1885 letter to his brother, Theo, in Ronald de Leeuw, *The Letters of Vincent van Gogh* (New York: Penguin, 1996), 302.

27-26 GUSTAVE COURBET, *The Stone Breakers*, 1849. Oil on canvas, 5' 3" × 8' 6". Formerly Gemäldegalerie, Dresden (destroyed in 1945).

Courbet was the leading figure in the Realist movement. Using a palette of dirty browns and grays, he conveyed the dreary and dismal nature of menial labor in mid-19th-century France.

STONE BREAKERS An early work that exemplifies Courbet's championing of everyday life as the only valid subject for the modern artist is *The Stone Breakers* (FIG. 27-26), in which the Realist painter presented a glimpse into the life of rural menial laborers. Courbet represented in a straightforward manner, and nearly at life size, two men—one about 70, the other quite young—in the decidedly nonheroic act of breaking stones to provide paving for provincial roads. Traditionally, this backbreaking, poorly paid work fell to the lowest members of French society, as the stone breakers' tattered garments and utensils for a modest meal of soup confirm. By juxtaposing youth and age, Courbet suggested that those born to poverty will remain poor their entire lives. The artist neither romanticized

27-27 GUSTAVE COURBET, *Burial at Ornans*, 1849. Oil on canvas, 10' 3$\frac{1}{2}$" × 21' 9$\frac{1}{2}$". Musée d'Orsay, Paris.

Although as imposing in scale as a traditional history painting, *Burial at Ornans* horrified critics because of the ordinary nature of the subject and Courbet's starkly antiheroic composition.

nor idealized the men's work but depicted their thankless toil with directness and accuracy. Courbet's palette of dirty browns and grays further conveys the dreary and dismal nature of the task, and the angular positioning of the older stone breaker's limbs suggests a mechanical monotony.

Courbet's interest in the working poor as subject matter had a special resonance for his mid-19th-century French audience. In 1848, laborers rebelled against the bourgeois leaders of the newly formed Second Republic and against the rest of the nation, demanding better working conditions and a redistribution of property. The army quelled the uprising in three days, but not without long-lasting trauma and significant loss of life. The 1848 revolution raised the issue of labor as a national concern. Courbet's depiction of stone breakers in 1849 was thus timely, populist, and, in the view of the conservative Salon jurors, "socialistic."

BURIAL AT ORNANS Many art historians regard Courbet's *Burial at Ornans* (FIG. **27-27**) as his masterpiece. The huge (10-by-22-foot) canvas depicts a funeral set in a bleak provincial landscape outside the artist's hometown near Besançon in eastern France. Attending the funeral are the types of ordinary people that Honoré de Balzac (1799–1850) and Gustave Flaubert (1821–1880) presented in their novels. While a robed clergyman recites the Office of the Dead, those attending cluster around the excavated gravesite. Although the painting has the imposing scale of a traditional history painting, the subject's ordinariness and the starkly antiheroic composition horrified critics. *Burial at Ornans* is not a record of the burial of a Christian martyr or a heroic soldier. It commemorates a recurring event involving common folk, and it does not ennoble or romanticize death. No one had ever painted a genre subject on this scale. Furthermore, Courbet had the audacity to submit *Burial at Ornans* to the 1851 Salon in the category of history painting, but declined to identify the deceased.

Arranged in a wavering line extending across the enormous breadth of the canvas are three groups—the somberly clad women at the back right; a semicircle of similarly clad men, including town officials and a hunting dog, by the open grave; and assorted churchmen at the left. The seemingly equal stature of all at the funeral also offended the hierarchical social sensibility of the Salon audience. This wall of figures blocks any view into deep space. The faces are portraits. Some of the models were Courbet's father, sisters, and friends. Behind and above the figures are bands of overcast sky and barren cliffs. The dark pit of the grave opens into the viewer's space in the center foreground.

Despite the unposed look of the figures, Courbet controlled the composition in a masterful way by his sparing use of bright color. In place of the heroic, the sublime, and the dramatic (the mourners are all emotionally detached), Courbet aggressively presented Salon viewers with the mundane realities of daily life and death. In 1857, Jules-François-Félix Husson Champfleury (1821–1889), one of the first critics to recognize and appreciate Courbet's work, wrote of *Burial at Ornans,* "[I]t represents a small-town funeral and yet reproduces the funerals of *all* small towns."[5] Unlike the theatricality of Romanticism, Realism captured the ordinary rhythms of daily life.

Of great importance for the later history of art, Realism also involved a reconsideration of the painter's primary goals and departed from the established emphasis on illusionism. Accordingly, Realists called attention to painting as a pictorial construction by the ways they applied pigment or manipulated composition. Courbet's intentionally simple and direct methods of expression in composition and technique seemed unbearably crude to many of his more traditional contemporaries, who called him a primitive. Although his bold, somber palette was essentially traditional, Courbet often used the *palette knife* to quickly place and unify large daubs of paint, producing a roughly wrought surface. His example inspired the young artists who worked for him (and later Impressionists such as Claude Monet and Auguste Renoir; see Chapter 28), but the public accused him of carelessness, and critics wrote of his "brutalities."

27-28 Jean-François Millet, *The Gleaners*, 1857. Oil on canvas, 2′ 9″ × 3′ 8″. Musée d'Orsay, Paris.

Millet and the Barbizon School painters specialized in depictions of French country life. Here, Millet portrayed three impoverished women gathering the scraps left in the field after a harvest.

JEAN-FRANÇOIS MILLET Like Courbet, Jean-François Millet (1814–1878) found his subjects in the people and occupations of the everyday world. Millet was one of a group of French painters of country life who, to be close to their rural subjects, settled near the village of Barbizon in the forest of Fontainebleau. This Barbizon School specialized in detailed pictures of forest and countryside. Millet, their most prominent member, was born into a prosperous farming family in Normandy, but was keenly aware of the hard lot of the country poor. In *The Gleaners* (FIG. 27-28), he depicted three impoverished women—members of the lowest level of peasant society—performing the backbreaking task of *gleaning*. Landowning nobles traditionally permitted peasants to glean, or collect, the wheat scraps left in the field after the harvest. Millet characteristically placed his large figures in the foreground, against a broad sky. Although the field stretches back to a rim of haystacks, cottages, trees, and distant workers and a flat horizon, the gleaners quietly doing their tedious and time-consuming work dominate the canvas. It is hard to imagine a sharper contrast with the almost invisible agricultural workers in Constable's *Hay Wain* (FIG. 27-21).

Although Millet's paintings evoke a sentimentality absent from Courbet's, the French public still reacted to his work with disdain and suspicion. In the aftermath of the 1848 revolution, Millet's investiture of the poor with solemn grandeur did not meet with approval from the prosperous classes. In particular, middle-class landowners resisted granting gleaning rights, and thus Millet's relatively dignified depiction of gleaning antagonized them. The middle class also linked the poor with the dangerous, newly defined working class, which was finding outspoken champions in men such as Karl Marx (1818–1883), Friedrich Engels (1820–1895), and the novelists Émile Zola (1840–1902) and Charles Dickens (1812–1870). Socialism was a growing movement, and both its views on property and its call for social justice, even economic equality, threatened and frightened the bourgeoisie. Millet's sympathetic portrayal of the poor seemed to much of the public to be a political manifesto.

HONORÉ DAUMIER Because people widely recognized the power of art to serve political ends, the political and social agitation accompanying the violent revolutions in France and the rest of Europe in the later 18th and early 19th centuries prompted the French people to suspect artists of subversive intentions. A person could be jailed for too bold a statement in the press, in literature, in art—even in music and drama. Realist artist Honoré Daumier (1808–1879) was a defender of the urban working class, and in his art he boldly confronted authority with social criticism and political protest. In response, the authorities imprisoned him. A painter, sculptor, and, like Dürer, Rembrandt, and Goya, one of history's great printmakers, Daumier produced *lithographs* (see "Lithography," page 819) that enabled him to create an unprecedented number of prints, thereby reaching an exceptionally large and broad audience. In addition to producing individual prints for sale, Daumier also contributed satirical lithographs to the widely read, liberal French Republican journal *Caricature*, further increasing the number of people exposed to his work. In *Caricature*, Daumier mercilessly lampooned the foibles and misbehavior of politicians, lawyers, doctors, and the rich bourgeoisie in general.

RUE TRANSNONAIN Daumier's lithograph *Rue Transnonain, April 15, 1834* (FIG. 27-29), published in the August 1834 issue of *L'association mensuelle*, a monthly French newspaper, had the same shocking impact as Goya's *Third of May, 1808* (FIG. 27-12). The title refers to the day when, on that street in Paris, an unknown sniper killed a civil guard, part of a government force trying to repress a worker demonstration. Because the fatal shot had come from a workers' housing block, the remaining guards immediately stormed the building and massacred all of its inhabitants. With Goya's power, Daumier created a view of the atrocious slaughter from a sharp angle of vision. But unlike Goya, he depicted not the dramatic moment of execution but the terrible, quiet aftermath. The limp bodies of the workers—and of a child crushed beneath his father's corpse—lie amid violent disorder. The print's power derives from its factualness. Daumier's pictorial manner is rough and spontaneous, and that approach to representation, which is a central characteristic of Realist art, accounts in large measure for the print's remarkable force.

MATERIALS AND TECHNIQUES
Lithography

In 1798, the German printmaker Alois Senefelder (1771–1834) created the first prints using stone instead of metal plates or wood blocks. In contrast to earlier printing techniques (see pages 577 and 578), in which the artist applied ink either to a raised or incised surface, in *lithography* (Greek, "stone writing or drawing") the printing and non-printing areas of the plate are on the same plane.

The chemical phenomenon fundamental to lithography is the repellence of oil and water. The lithographer uses a greasy, oil-based crayon to draw directly on a stone plate and then wipes water onto the stone, which clings only to the areas the drawing does not cover. Next, the artist rolls oil-based ink onto the stone, which adheres to the drawing but is repelled by the water. When the artist presses the stone against paper, only the inked area—the drawing—transfers to the paper. Color lithography requires multiple plates, one for each color, and the printmaker must take special care to make sure each impression lines up perfectly with the previous one so that each color prints in its proper place.

One of the earliest masters of this new printmaking process was Honoré Daumier, whose lithographs (FIGS. 27-29 and 27-49A), often published in leading French journals such as *Caricature* and *L'association mensuelle*, reached an audience of unprecedented size.

27-29 HONORÉ DAUMIER, *Rue Transnonain, April 15, 1834*, 1834. Lithograph, 1' 1$\frac{3}{8}$" × 1' 6$\frac{1}{4}$". Yale University Art Gallery, New Haven (Everett V. Meeks, B.A. 1901, Fund).

Daumier used the recent invention of lithography to reach a wide audience for his social criticism and political protest. This print records the horrific 1834 massacre in a workers' housing block.

27-30 HONORÉ DAUMIER, *Third-Class Carriage*, ca. 1862. Oil on canvas, 2' 1$\frac{3}{4}$" × 2' 11$\frac{1}{2}$". Metropolitan Museum of Art, New York (H. O. Havemeyer Collection, bequest of Mrs. H. O. Havemeyer, 1929).

Daumier frequently depicted the plight of the disinherited masses, the victims of 19th-century industrialization. Here, he portrayed the anonymous poor cramped together in a grimy third-class railway carriage.

THIRD-CLASS CARRIAGE For his paintings, Daumier chose the same kind of subjects and representational manner as in his graphic work, especially after the 1848 revolution. His unfinished *Third-Class Carriage* (FIG. 27-30) provides a glimpse into the cramped and grimy railway cars of the 1860s. The riders are poor and can afford only third-class tickets. First- and second-class carriages had closed compartments, but third-class passengers had to cram

27-31 Rosa Bonheur, *The Horse Fair*, 1853–1855. Oil on canvas, 8' $\frac{1}{4}$" × 16' 7 $\frac{1}{2}$". Metropolitan Museum of Art, New York (gift of Cornelius Vanderbilt, 1887).

Bonheur was the most celebrated woman artist of the 19th century. A Realist, she went to great lengths to record accurately the anatomy of living horses, even studying carcasses in slaughterhouses.

together on hard benches stretching from one end of their carriage to the other. The disinherited masses, the victims of 19th-century industrialization, were Daumier's indignant concern. He depicted them in the unposed attitudes and unplanned arrangements of the millions thronging the modern cities—anonymous, insignificant, dumbly patient with a lot they cannot change. Daumier saw people as they ordinarily appeared, their faces vague, impersonal, and blank—unprepared for any observers. He tried to achieve the real by isolating a random collection of the unrehearsed details of human existence from the continuum of ordinary life. Daumier's vision anticipated the spontaneity and candor of scenes captured with the camera at the end of the century.

ROSA BONHEUR The most celebrated woman artist of the 19th century was MARIE-ROSALIE (ROSA) BONHEUR (1822–1899). Born in Bordeaux, she won the gold medal at the Salon of 1848 and became the director of France's state-sponsored drawing school for women the same year, a post she held until 1859. (Admission to the École des Beaux-Arts was nearly impossible for women, as it was in Britain's Royal Academy.) In 1865, Bonheur became the first woman to be awarded the Grand Cross of the French Legion of Honor. As was typical for women since the Renaissance (see "The Artist's Profession," page 566), Bonheur received her artistic training from her father, Oscar-Raymond Bonheur (1796–1849), who was a proponent of *Saint-Simonianism,* an early-19th-century utopian socialist movement that championed the education and enfranchisement of women. As a result of her father's influence, Bonheur launched her career believing that as a woman, an artist, and a lesbian who frequently wore male attire, she had a special role to play in creating a new and perfect society. A Realist passion for accuracy in painting drove Bonheur, but she resisted depicting the problematic social and political themes seen in the work of Courbet, Millet, Daumier,

and other Realists. Rather, she turned to the animal world—not, however, to the exotic wild animals that so fascinated Delacroix (FIG. 27-16A), but to animals common in the French countryside, especially horses, but also rabbits, cows, and sheep. She went to great lengths to observe the anatomy of living horses at the twice-weekly Parisian horse market and spent long hours studying the anatomy of carcasses in the Paris slaughterhouses. (Women were not permitted in the French stockyards and slaughterhouses, but Bonheur's male garb gained her access.)

For *The Horse Fair* (FIG. **27-31**), Bonheur's best-known work, the artist chose a panoramic composition similar to that in Courbet's *Burial at Ornans* (FIG. 27-27). She filled her broad canvas with the sturdy farm Percherons of Normandy and their grooms on parade. Some horses, not quite broken, rear up. Others plod or trot, guided on foot or ridden by their keepers. Bonheur recorded the Percherons' uneven line of march, their thunderous pounding, and their seemingly overwhelming power based on her close observation of living animals, even though she acknowledged some inspiration from the Parthenon frieze (FIG. 5-50, *top*). The dramatic lighting, loose brushwork, and rolling sky also reveal her admiration of Géricault's style (FIG. 27-1 and 27-14). Bonheur's masterful depiction of horses at life size and seen from multiple angles captivated viewers, who eagerly bought engraved reproductions of *The Horse Fair,* making it one of the most popular artworks of the century.

ÉDOUARD MANET As pivotal a figure in 19th-century European art as Gustave Courbet was the painter ÉDOUARD MANET (1832–1883). Like Courbet, Manet was influential in articulating Realist principles, but the younger artist also played an important role in the development of Impressionism in the 1870s (see page 841). Manet's *Le Déjeuner sur l'Herbe* (*Luncheon on the Grass;* FIG. **27-32**), widely recognized only later as a seminal work in the history of art,

27-32 ÉDOUARD MANET, *Le Déjeuner sur l'Herbe* (*Luncheon on the Grass*), 1863. Oil on canvas, 7' × 8' 8".
Musée d'Orsay, Paris.

Manet shocked his contemporaries with both his subject matter and manner of painting. Moving away from illusionism, he used colors to flatten form and to draw attention to the painting surface.

was rejected by the jury for the 1863 Salon. It depicts two clothed men and one nude and one clothed woman at a picnic. Consistent with Realist principles, Manet depicted a contemporary genre scene and based all four figures on real people, including Victorine Meurent (1844–1927), Manet's favorite model at the time, and his brother. The two men wear fashionable Parisian attire of the 1860s. The nude woman—she has undressed in the park and tossed her clothes on the grass—is a distressingly unidealized figure who also seems completely unfazed by her nakedness. She gazes directly at the viewer without shame or flirtatiousness. Her companion looks in the same direction. Neither pays any attention to what the second man is saying to them. Nor is it clear what relationship, if any, the second woman has to the trio "at lunch." She appears to be looking for something in a pool of water, while attempting unsuccessfully to keep her garment dry. No one has any interest in the picnic food. This is no luncheon on the grass, although it may be the aftermath of a meal. Nor is this truly Realism, because the subject is incomprehensible—as Manet wished it to be. In this work, he sought to reassess the nature of painting. The composition contains

sophisticated references and allusions to many artistic genres—history painting, portraiture, pastoral scenes, nudes, and even religious scenes. *Le Déjeuner sur l'Herbe* is Manet's impressive synthesis and critique of the entire history of painting.

This audacious painting outraged the French public. Rather than a traditional pastoral scene—for example, Titian's *Pastoral Symphony* (FIG. 22-35), with which Manet no doubt wished his canvas to be compared—*Le Déjeuner* is not populated by anonymous idealized figures in an idyllic setting. Instead, it features ordinary men and promiscuous women in a Parisian park. One hostile critic, no doubt voicing public opinion, said: "A commonplace woman of the demimonde, as naked as can be, shamelessly lolls between two dandies dressed to the teeth. These latter look like schoolboys on a holiday, perpetrating an outrage to play the man. . . . This is a young man's practical joke—a shameful, open sore."[6]

The negative response to Manet's painting on the part of public and critics alike extended beyond subject matter. The painter's manner of presenting his figures also elicited severe criticism. He rendered the men and women in soft focus and broadly painted the

27-33 ÉDOUARD MANET, *Olympia,* 1863. Oil on canvas, 4' 3" × 6' 2¼". Musée d'Orsay, Paris.

Manet's painting of a nude prostitute and her black maid carrying a bouquet from a client scandalized the public. Critics also faulted his rough brushstrokes and abruptly shifting tonalities.

landscape. The loose manner of painting contrasts with the clear forms of the harshly lit foreground trio and of the pile of discarded female clothes and picnic foods at the lower left. The lighting creates strong contrasts between dark and highlighted areas. In the main figures, many values are summed up in one or two lights or darks. The effect is both to flatten the forms and set them off sharply from the setting. Manet aimed to move away from illusionism toward an open acknowledgment of painting's properties, such as the flatness of the painting surface, which would become a core principle of many later 19th-century painters as well as their successors to the present day. The mid-19th-century French public, however, saw only a crude sketch lacking the customary finish of paintings exhibited in the Paris Salon. The style of the painting, coupled with the unorthodox subject matter, made *Le Déjeuner sur l'Herbe* one of the most controversial artworks ever created.

OLYMPIA Even more scandalous to the French viewing public, however, was Manet's *Olympia* (FIG. **27-33**), painted the same year and also loosely based on a painting by Titian—*Venus of Urbino* (FIG. 22-39). Manet's subject was a young white prostitute. (Olympia was a common "professional" name for prostitutes in 19th-century France.) She reclines on a bed that extends across the full width of the painting (and beyond) and is nude except for a thin black ribbon tied around her neck, a bracelet on her arm, an orchid in her hair, and fashionable slippers on her feet. Like the seated nude in *Le Déjeuner* (Victorine Meurent served again as Manet's model), Olympia meets the viewer's eye with a look of cool indifference. The only other figure in the painting is a black maid, who presents Olympia a bouquet of flowers from a client.

Olympia horrified the public and critics alike. One reviewer of the Salon of 1865 (remarkably, the jury accepted Manet's painting

for inclusion) described the painter as "the apostle of the ugly and repulsive."[7] Although images of prostitutes were not unheard of during this period, the shamelessness of Olympia and her look verging on defiance shocked viewers. The depiction of a black woman was also not new to painting, but the French public perceived Manet's inclusion of both a black maid and a nude prostitute as evoking moral depravity, inferiority, and animalistic sexuality. The contrast of the black servant with the fair-skinned courtesan also conjured racial divisions.

An anonymous critic in *Le Monde Illustré* described Olympia as "a courtesan, with dirty hands and wrinkled feet . . . her body has the livid tint of a cadaver displayed in the morgue; her outlines are drawn in charcoal and her greenish, bloodshot eyes appear to be provoking the public, protected all the while by a hideous Negress."[8] From this and similar reviews, it is clear that critics and the public were responding not solely to the subject matter but to Manet's artistic style as well. The painter's brushstrokes are much rougher and the shifts in tonality are far more abrupt than those found in traditional academic painting.

This departure from accepted practice exacerbated the audacity of the subject matter. *Olympia*—indeed, all of Manet's work—represented a radical departure from the academic style then in favor, as exemplified by the work of ADOLPHE-WILLIAM BOUGUEREAU (1825–1905; FIG. **27-33A**), an artist largely forgotten today, although he was a towering figure in the French art world during the second half of the 19th century.

27-33A BOUGUEREAU, *Nymphs and a Satyr,* 1873.

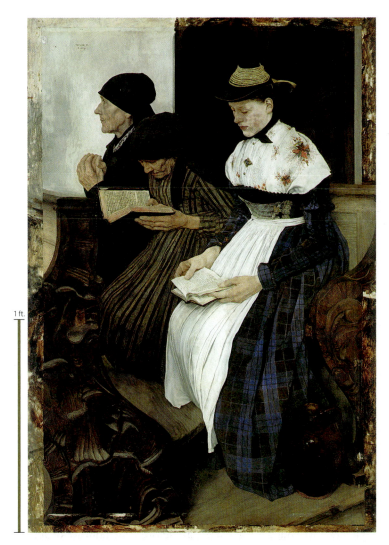

1 ft.

27-34 WILHELM LEIBL, *Three Women in a Village Church*, 1878–1882. Oil on canvas, 2' 5" × 2' 1". Kunsthalle, Hamburg.

French Realism spread quickly to Germany, where Leibl painted this moving depiction of simple peasant women of different generations holding their prayer books in hands roughened by work.

Germany and the United States

Although French artists took the lead in promoting the depiction of the realities of modern life as the only valid goal for artists, the Realist movement was neither exclusively French nor confined to Europe.

WILHELM LEIBL In Germany, WILHELM LEIBL (1844–1900) shared the French Realists' commitment to representing the contemporary world and real people in his paintings. *Three Women in a Village Church* (FIG. **27-34**) is Leibl's most famous work and characteristically depicts the life of rural peasants in Bavaria. The painting, which took three years to complete, records a sacred moment—the moment of prayer—in the life of three women of different generations. Dressed in rustic costume, their Sunday-church best, they quietly pursue their devotions in the village church, their prayer books held in large hands roughened by work. Their manners and their dress reflect their unaffected nature, untouched by the refinements of urban life. Leibl highlighted their natural virtues: simplicity, honesty, steadfastness, and patience. The picture is a moving expression of the artist's compassionate view of his subjects, a reading of character without sentimentality.

WINSLOW HOMER Realism received an especially warm welcome in the United States. One of the leading American Realist painters was WINSLOW HOMER (1836–1910) of Boston. Homer experienced at first hand the most momentous event of his era—the Civil War. In October 1862, he joined the Union campaign as an artist-reporter for *Harper's Weekly*. At the end of the war, he painted *Veteran in a New Field* (FIG. **27-35**). Although it is simple and direct, Homer's painting is a significant commentary on the effects and aftermath of America's catastrophic national conflict. At the center of the canvas is a man with his back to the viewer, harvesting wheat. Homer identified him as a veteran by including his uniform and canteen carelessly thrown on the ground in the lower right corner. The man's current occupation, however, is as a farmer, and he has cast aside his former role as a soldier, as did the veterans of America's Revolutionary War in the previous century. The Civil War veteran's involvement in meaningful and productive work implies a smooth

1 ft.

27-35 WINSLOW HOMER, *Veteran in a New Field*, 1865. Oil on canvas, $2' \frac{1}{8}" \times 3' 2 \frac{1}{8}"$. Metropolitan Museum of Art, New York (bequest of Miss Adelaide Milton de Groot, 1967).

This veteran's productive work implies a smooth transition to peace after the Civil War, but Homer placed a single-bladed scythe—the Grim Reaper's tool—in his hands, symbolizing the deaths of soldiers.

transition from war to peace. This postwar transition to work and the fate of disbanded soldiers were national concerns. Echoing the sentiments behind Houdon's portrayal of George Washington as the new Cincinnatus (FIG. 26-33), the *New York Weekly Tribune* commented: "Rome took her great man from the plow, and made him a dictator—we must now take our soldiers from the camp and make them farmers."[9] America's ability to effect a smooth transition was seen as evidence of its national strength. "The peaceful and harmonious disbanding of the armies in the summer of 1865," wrote poet Walt Whitman (1819–1892), was one of the "immortal proofs of democracy, unequall'd in all the history of the past."[10] Homer's painting thus reinforced the perception of the country's greatness.

Veteran in a New Field also comments symbolically about death. By the 1860s, farmers used cradled scythes to harvest wheat. For this detail, however, Homer rejected realism in favor of symbolism. The former soldier's tool is a single-bladed scythe. The artist thus transformed the man who lived through the Civil War into a symbol of Death—the Grim Reaper himself. In addition to being a tribute to the successful transition to peace, *Veteran in a New Field* is an elegy to the thousands of soldiers who did not return from the war (compare FIG. 27-52). It may also be a lamentation on the recent assassination of President Abraham Lincoln.

THOMAS EAKINS Even more determined a Realist than Homer was Philadelphia-born THOMAS EAKINS (1844–1916), whose paintings reflect his keen appetite for recording the realities of the human experience. Eakins studied both painting and medical anatomy in Philadelphia before undertaking further study under French artist Jean-Léon Gérôme (1824–1904). Eakins aimed to paint things as he saw them rather than as the public might wish them portrayed. This attitude was very much in tune with 19th-century American taste, combining an admiration for accurate depiction with a hunger for truth.

The too-brutal Realism of Eakins's early masterpiece, *The Gross Clinic* (FIG. 27-36), perhaps inspired by Rembrandt's *Anatomy Lesson of Dr. Nicolaes Tulp* (FIG. 25-12), prompted the art jury to reject it for the Philadelphia exhibition celebrating the American independence centennial in 1876. The painting portrays the renowned surgeon Dr. Samuel Gross in the operating amphitheater of the Jefferson Medical College in Philadelphia, where the painting

hung for 130 years until its sale in 2006 to raise funds for the college. Eakins's decision to depict an operation in progress reflects the public's increasing faith that scientific and medical advances could enhance—and preserve—lives. Dr. Gross, with bloody fingers and scalpel, lectures about his surgery on a young man's leg. The patient suffered from osteomyelitis, a bone infection. Watching the surgeon, acclaimed for his skill in this specific operation, are several colleagues—all of whom historians have identified—and the patient's mother, who covers her face. Eakins, who considered becoming a physician and studied at the college, included his self-portrait (in the doorway at the right) to underscore the accuracy of what he recorded as an eyewitness. Also present is an anesthetist, who holds a cloth over the patient's face. Anesthetics had been introduced in 1846, and their development eliminated a major obstacle to extensive surgery. The painting, made more dramatic by the lighting, is an unsparing description of an unfolding event, with a good deal more reality than many viewers could endure. "It is a picture," one critic said, "that even strong men find difficult to look at long, if they can look at it at all."[11]

Consistent with the dominance of empiricism in the latter half of the 19th century, Eakins believed that careful observation and, where relevant, scientific knowledge were prerequisites for his art,

27-36 THOMAS EAKINS, *The Gross Clinic,* from Jefferson Medical College, Philadelphia, Pennsylvania, 1875. Oil on canvas, 8' × 6' 6". Philadelphia Museum of Art, Philadelphia.

The too-brutal realism of Eakins's depiction of a medical college operating amphitheater caused this painting's rejection from the Philadelphia exhibition celebrating America's centennial.

1 ft.

and he created his paintings in a deliberate, methodical way based on firsthand study of his subject. For example, Eakins's focus on anatomical correctness led him to investigate the human form and humans in motion, both with regular photographic apparatuses and with a special camera devised by the French kinesiologist (a person who studies the physiology of body movement) Étienne-Jules Marey (1830–1904). Eakins later collaborated with Eadweard Muybridge (FIG. 27-53) in the photographic study of animal and human action of all types, anticipating the 20th-century invention of the motion picture.

JOHN SINGER SARGENT The expatriate American artist JOHN SINGER SARGENT (1856–1925), born in Florence, Italy, was a younger contemporary of Eakins. Sargent developed a looser, more dashing Realist painting style, in contrast to Eakins's carefully rendered details. Sargent studied art in Paris before settling in London, where he won renown both as a cultivated and cosmopolitan gentleman and as an accomplished portrait painter. He learned his adept application of paint in thin layers and his effortless achievement of quick and lively illusion from his study of Velázquez, whose masterpiece, *Las Meninas* (FIG. 24-31), may have influenced Sargent's family portrait *The Daughters of Edward Darley Boit* (FIG. 27-37). The four girls (the children of one of Sargent's close friends) appear in a hall and small drawing room in their Paris home. The informal, eccentric arrangement of their slight figures suggests how much at ease they are within this familiar space and with objects such as the enormous Japanese vases, the red screen, and the fringed rug, whose scale subtly emphasizes the children's diminutive stature. Sargent must have known the Boit daughters well. Relaxed and trustful, they gave the artist an opportunity to record a gradation of young innocence. He sensitively captured the naive, wondering openness of the little girl in the foreground, the grave artlessness of the 10-year-old child, and the slightly self-conscious poise of the adolescents.

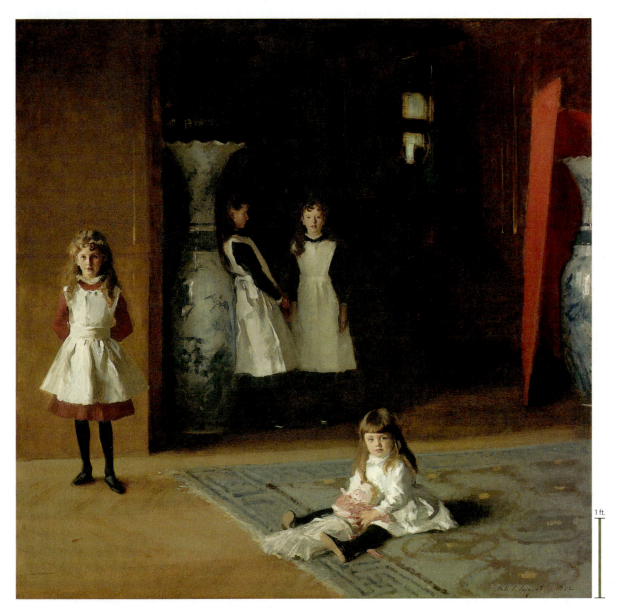

27-37 JOHN SINGER SARGENT, *The Daughters of Edward Darley Boit,* 1882. Oil on canvas, 7' 3$\frac{3}{8}$" × 7' 3$\frac{5}{8}$". Museum of Fine Arts, Boston (gift of Mary Louisa Boit, Florence D. Boit, Jane Hubbard Boit, and Julia Overing Boit, in memory of their father, Edward Darley Boit).

Sargent's casual positioning of the Boit sisters creates a sense of the momentary and spontaneous, consistent with Realist painters' interest in recording modern people in modern contexts.

27-38 Henry Ossawa Tanner, *The Thankful Poor*, 1894. Oil on canvas, 2' 11½" × 3' 8¼". Collection of William H. and Camille Cosby.

Tanner combined the Realists' belief in careful study from nature with a desire to portray with dignity the life of African American families. The lighting reinforces the painting's reverent spirit.

Sargent's casual positioning of the figures and seemingly random choice of the setting communicate a sense of spontaneity. The children seem to be attending momentarily to an adult who has asked them to interrupt their activity. The painting embodies the Realist belief that the artist's business is to record modern people in modern contexts.

HENRY OSSAWA TANNER Typical of the Realist painter's desire to depict the lives of ordinary people engaged in everyday activities is *The Thankful Poor* (FIG. **27-38**), an early work by African American artist HENRY OSSAWA TANNER (1859–1937). Tanner

ART AND SOCIETY
Edmonia Lewis, an African American Sculptor in Rome

About 15 years older than Henry Ossawa Tanner (FIG. 27-38), the sculptor Edmonia Lewis was the daughter of a Chippewa mother and African American father. Born in upstate New York and given the name Wildfire, Lewis became an orphan when she was four years old, and was raised by the Chippewa.

Lewis produced sculptures stylistically indebted to Neoclassicism but depicting contemporary Realist themes. *Forever Free* (FIG. 27-39) is a marble statue that she carved while living in Rome, surrounded by examples of both classical and Renaissance art. It represents two freed African American slaves immediately after President Lincoln's issuance of the Emancipation Proclamation. The man stands triumphantly in a contrapposto stance reminiscent of classical statues. His right hand rests on the shoulder of the kneeling woman with her hands clasped in thankful prayer. The man holds aloft in his left hand a broken manacle and chain as literal and symbolic references to his former servitude. Produced four years after Lincoln's proclamation, *Forever Free* (originally titled *The Morning of Liberty*) was widely perceived as an abolitionist statement. ("Forever free" is a phrase that Lincoln used in both his preliminary September 1862 and final January 1863 emancipation proclamations.) Although emancipated, the former slaves still have shackles attached, in contrast to those born free. However, other factors caution against an overly simplistic reading. For example, scholars have debated the degree to which the sculptor attempted to inject a statement about gender relationships into this statue and whether the kneeling position of the woman is a reference to female subordination in the African American community.

Lewis's accomplishments as a sculptor speak to the increasing access to training available to women in the 19th century. She adopted the name Edmonia Lewis in 1859 when she was admitted to Oberlin College (the first American college to grant degrees to women and among the first to admit African Americans). After Oberlin, Lewis became an

27-39 EDMONIA LEWIS, *Forever Free*, 1867. Marble, 3' 5¼" high. James A. Porter Gallery of Afro-American Art, Howard University, Washington, D.C.

African American–Chippewa Lewis's sculptures owe a stylistic debt to Neoclassicism but depict contemporary Realist themes. She carved *Forever Free* four years after Lincoln's Emancipation Proclamation.

apprentice in a sculpture studio in Boston. She financed her 1865 trip to Rome, which became her permanent home, with the sale of portrait medallions and marble busts, mostly representing abolitionist leaders. Lewis's success in a field dominated by white European and American men is a testament to both her artistic skill and her determination.

27-40 John Everett Millais, *Ophelia*, 1852. Oil on canvas, 2' 6" × 3' 8". Tate Gallery, London.

Millet was a founder of the Pre-Raphaelite Brotherhood, whose members refused to be limited to the contemporary scenes that strict Realists portrayed. The drowning of Ophelia is a Shakespearean subject.

studied art with Eakins at the Pennsylvania Academy of Fine Arts before moving to Paris in 1891. There he combined Eakins's belief in careful study from nature with a desire to portray with dignity the life of the working people he had been raised among as a minister's son in Pennsylvania. The mood in *The Thankful Poor* is one of quiet devotion not far removed from the Realism of Millet (FIG. 27-28) and Leibl (FIG. 27-34), but quite different from the mood of the sculptures of Edmonia Lewis (ca. 1844–ca. 1911), Tanner's older contemporary (see "Edmonia Lewis, an African American Sculptor in Rome," page 826, and FIG. 27-39). Tanner painted the grandfather, grandchild, and main objects in the room in great detail, whereas everything else dissolves into loose strokes of color and light. The lighting reinforces the painting's reverent spirit, with deep shadows intensifying the man's devout concentration. The golden rays pouring in the window illuminate the quiet expression of thanksgiving on the younger face. The deep sense of sanctity evoked here in terms of everyday experience became increasingly important for Tanner. Within a few years of completing *The Thankful Poor,* he began painting biblical subjects grounded in direct studies from nature and in the love of Rembrandt that had inspired him from his days as a Philadelphia art student.

Pre-Raphaelite Brotherhood

Realism did not appeal to all artists, of course. In England, a group of painters who called themselves the *Pre-Raphaelite Brotherhood* refused to be limited to the contemporary scenes that strict Realists portrayed. These artists chose instead to represent fictional, historical,

and fanciful subjects, but with a significant degree of convincing illusion. Organized in 1848, the Pre-Raphaelite artists wished to create fresh and sincere art, free from what its members considered the tired and artificial manner propagated in the academies by the successors of Raphael. Influenced by the critic, artist, and writer John Ruskin (1819–1900), the Pre-Raphaelites shared his distaste for the materialism and ugliness of the contemporary industrializing world. They also expressed appreciation for the spirituality and idealism (as well as the art and artisanship) of past times, especially the Early Renaissance.

JOHN EVERETT MILLAIS One of the founders of the Pre-Raphaelite Brotherhood was John Everett Millais (1829–1896). Millais's *Ophelia* (FIG. 27-40) garnered enthusiastic praise when the painter exhibited it in the Exposition Universelle in Paris in 1855—the exhibition at which Courbet set up his Pavilion of Realism. The subject, from Shakespeare's *Hamlet* (4.7.174–183), is the drowning of Ophelia, who, in her madness, is unaware of her plight:

> *When down her weedy trophies and herself*
> *Fell in the weeping brook. Her clothes spread wide;*
> *And, mermaid-like, awhile they bore her up . . .*
> *Till that her garments, heavy with their drink,*
> *Pull'd the poor wretch from her melodious lay*
> *To muddy death.*

To make the pathos of the scene visible, Millais became a faithful and feeling witness of its every detail, reconstructing it

1 ft.

27-41 Dante Gabriel Rossetti, *Beata Beatrix*, ca. 1863. Oil on canvas, 2' 10" × 2' 2". Tate Gallery, London.

This painting of a beautiful and sensuous woman is ostensibly a literary portrait of Dante's Beatrice, but the work also served as a memorial to Rossetti's wife, who died of an opium overdose.

literary figure—Beatrice, from Dante's *Vita Nuova*. In Rossetti's painting, Dante's heroine overlooks Florence in a trance after being mystically transported to Heaven. Yet the portrait also had personal resonance for Rossetti. It served as a memorial to his wife, Elizabeth Siddal (1829–1862), the model for Millais's *Ophelia*. Siddal had died shortly before Rossetti began this painting in 1862. In the image, a red dove (a messenger of both love and death) deposits a poppy (symbolic of sleep and death) in the hands of the seated woman (Siddal-Beatrice), who has a faraway look on her face. Because Siddal died of an opium overdose, the presence of the poppy assumes greater significance.

ARCHITECTURE

At the opening of the 19th century, Napoleon had co-opted the classical style as the official architectural expression of his empire. Neoclassicism was in vogue elsewhere in Europe, especially in the Prussian capital of Berlin (see "The First Public Art Museum," page 829, and FIGS. **27-41A** and **27-42**) and in the new American republic too, but other historical styles, Gothic chief among them, also enjoyed revivals at the same time that architects were exploring the expressive possibilities that new construction technologies had made possible. The buildings constructed during the 19th century are consequently among the most stylistically diverse in history.

GOTHIC REVIVAL As 19th-century scholars gathered the documentary materials of European history in encyclopedic enterprises, each nation came to value its past as evidence of the validity of its ambitions and claims to greatness. Intellectuals appreciated the art of the remote past as a product of cultural and national genius. Italy, of course, had its Roman ruins, which had long inspired later architects. A reawakening of interest in Gothic architecture also surfaced at this time, even in France under Napoleon. In 1802, Chateaubriand published his influential *Genius of Christianity*—the source for

with a lyricism worthy of the original poetry. (Charles Baudelaire [1821–1867] called him "the poet of meticulous detail.") Although the scene is fictitious and therefore one that Realist painters would have rejected, Millais worked diligently to present it with unswerving fidelity to visual fact. He painted the background on site at a spot along the Hogsmill River in Surrey. For the figure of Ophelia, Millais had a friend lie in a heated bathtub full of water for hours at a time.

DANTE GABRIEL ROSSETTI Another founder of the Pre-Raphaelite Brotherhood was DANTE GABRIEL ROSSETTI (1828–1882), who established an enviable reputation as both a painter and poet. Like other members of the group, Rossetti focused on literary and biblical themes in his art. He also produced numerous portraits of women that projected an image of ethereal beauty and melded apparent opposites—for example, a Victorian prettiness with sensual allure. His *Beata Beatrix* (FIG. **27-41**) is ostensibly a portrait of a

PROBLEMS AND SOLUTIONS
The First Public Art Museum

After the fall of Napoleon, who had occupied the Prussian capital of Berlin from 1806 to 1808, a fervent nationalistic spirit emerged in Germany. One manifestation of Prussian nationalism was the decision to build Europe's first public art museum to house the extensive and growing royal collection. The commission went to KARL FRIEDRICH SCHINKEL (1781–1841), who worked in many revival styles during his career. But which one would be the best choice for an art museum? Although he had designed buildings in the Romanesque, Gothic, and Italian Renaissance styles, Schinkel chose the Neoclassical style for what he and Crown Prince Friedrich Wilhelm III (1755–1861) conceived as a "temple of culture." (The prince's father, King Friedrich Wilhelm II [r. 1786–1797], had earlier commissioned one of the world's most famous Neoclassical monuments, Berlin's Brandenburg Gate [FIG. 27-41A], designed by CARL GOTTHARD LANGHANS [1732–1808].)

27-41A LANGHANS, Brandenburg Gate, Berlin, 1788–1791.

The Altes (Old) Museum (FIG. 27-42), constructed on an island in the Spree River across from the royal palace in Berlin, is not truly temple-like, however. Rather, with its broad facade of 18 Ionic columns on a high podium, it more closely resembles a Greek stoa (FIG. 5-78) than a pediment-capped classical temple. Noteworthy for its perfect proportions, Schinkel's austere design expresses nobility, tradition, and elite culture, now made accessible to the public in a building whose style Europeans associated with the democratic values of ancient Greece and Rome.

The Neoclassical facade masks a very practical plan that has no model in classical temples or stoas, however. A broad central staircase leads into a foyer and then a cubical central block, which projects above the facade's colonnade. The central block houses a sculpture-filled domed rotunda loosely based on the Pantheon (FIG. 7-51) in Rome (a mixing of historical sources characteristic of 19th-century European architecture in general). To either side is a courtyard whose windows provide light to the painting galleries all around. Large windows on the side and rear walls of the Altes Museum also illuminate the galleries.

The Altes Museum is also significant in terms of exhibition theory and practice. This first public art museum was also the first museum of any kind in which the artworks it contained were organized and displayed in chronological order, emphasizing the history of art, as opposed to simply exhibiting aesthetic treasures (compare FIG. 25-1A).

27-42 KARL FRIEDRICH SCHINKEL, Altes Museum (looking northwest), Berlin, Germany, 1822–1830.

Schinkel conceived the first public art museum in Europe as a Neoclassical "temple of culture." The Altes Museum's facade of 18 Ionic columns resembles an ancient Greek stoa (FIG. 5-78).

Girodet's *Burial of Atala* (FIG. 27-6)—which defended religion on the grounds of its beauty and mystery rather than on the grounds of truth. Gothic cathedrals, according to Chateaubriand, were translations of the sacred groves of the ancient Gauls into stone and should be cherished as manifestations of France's holy history. One result of this new nationalistic respect for the Gothic style was that Eugène Emmanuel Viollet-le-Duc (1814–1879) received a commission in 1845 to restore the interior of Paris's Notre-Dame

to its Gothic splendor after later alterations, including those made for Napoleon's coronation (see "The Coronation of Napoleon," page 797).

HOUSES OF PARLIAMENT England also celebrated its medieval heritage with *Neo-Gothic* buildings. In London, when the old Houses of Parliament burned in 1834, the Parliamentary Commission decreed that proposed designs for the

27-43 CHARLES BARRY and AUGUSTUS WELBY NORTHMORE PUGIN, Houses of Parliament (looking southwest), London, England, designed 1835.

During the 19th century, architects revived many historical styles, often reflecting nationalistic pride. The Houses of Parliament have an exterior veneer and towers that recall English Late Gothic style.

new building had to be either Gothic or Elizabethan. CHARLES BARRY (1795–1860), with the assistance of AUGUSTUS WELBY NORTHMORE PUGIN (1812–1852), won the commission for the new Houses of Parliament (FIG. 27-43) in 1835. By this time, architectural style had become a matter of selection from the historical past. Barry had traveled widely in Europe, Greece, Turkey, Egypt, and Palestine, studying the architecture of each place. He preferred the classical Renaissance styles, but he had designed some earlier Neo-Gothic buildings, and Pugin successfully influenced him in the direction of English Late Gothic. Pugin was one of a group of English artists and critics who saw moral purity and spiritual authenticity in the religious architecture of the Middle Ages and revered the careful medieval artisans who built the great cathedrals. The Industrial Revolution was flooding the market with cheaply made and ill-designed commodities. Machine work was replacing handicraft. Many, Pugin included, believed in the necessity of restoring the old artisanship, which they felt embodied honesty as well as quality. Pugin was also the author of the influential *True Principles of Pointed or Christian Architecture* (1841), which RICHARD UPJOHN (1802–1878) consulted for his Neo-Gothic Trinity Church (FIG. 27-43A) in New York City. The design of the Houses of Parliament, however, is not genuinely Gothic, despite its picturesque tower groupings (the Clock Tower, housing Big Ben, at one end, and the Victoria Tower at the other). The building has a formal axial plan and a kind of Palladian regularity beneath its Neo-Gothic detail. Pugin himself said of it, "All Grecian, Sir. Tudor [late English Gothic] details on a classical body."[12]

⤢ **27-43A** UPJOHN, Trinity Church, New York, 1841–1852.

ROYAL PAVILION Although the Neoclassical and Neo-Gothic styles dominated early-19th-century architecture, exotic new approaches of all manner soon began to appear, due in part to European imperialism and in part to the Romantic spirit permeating all the arts.

Great Britain's forays throughout the world, particularly in India, had exposed English culture to a broad range of non-Western artistic styles. The Royal Pavilion (FIG. 27-44), designed by JOHN NASH (1752–1835), exhibits a wide variety of these styles. Nash was an established architect, known for Neoclassical buildings in London, when the prince regent (later King George IV) asked him to design a royal pleasure palace in the seaside resort of Brighton. The architecture of Greece, Egypt, and China influenced the interior decor of the Royal Pavilion, but the fantastic exterior is a conglomeration of Islamic domes, minarets, and screens that some architectural historians describe as "Indian Gothic." Underlying the exotic facade is a cast-iron skeleton, an early (if hidden) use of this material in noncommercial construction. Nash also put this metal to fanciful use, creating life-size palm-tree columns in cast iron to support the Royal Pavilion's kitchen ceiling. The building, an appropriate enough backdrop for gala throngs pursuing pleasure by the seaside, has served as a prototype for countless playful architectural exaggerations still found in European and American resorts.

PARIS OPÉRA Another style that found favor in 19th-century architecture was the Baroque, because it was well suited to conveying a grandeur worthy of the riches that the European elite acquired during this age of expansion. The Paris Opéra (FIG. 27-45), designed by CHARLES GARNIER (1825–1898), is the leading example of *Neo-Baroque* architecture. Garnier, who had traveled extensively in Italy as a Rome Prize recipient, had submitted the winning design (out of 171 entrants) in a competition sponsored by Napoleon III. Garnier's opera house has a festive and spectacularly theatrical Neo-Baroque front and two wings resembling Baroque domed central-plan churches (not visible in FIG. 27-45). Inside, intricate arrangements of corridors, vestibules, stairways, balconies, alcoves, entrances, and exits facilitate easy passage throughout the building and provide space for entertainment and socializing at intermissions.

The Baroque grandeur of the layout and of the building's ornamental appointments is characteristic of an architectural style called

27-44 JOHN NASH, Royal Pavilion (looking northwest), Brighton, England, 1815–1818.

British territorial expansion brought a familiarity with many exotic styles. This palatial "Indian Gothic" seaside pavilion is a conglomeration of Islamic domes, minarets, and screens.

Beaux-Arts, which was most popular in the late 19th and early 20th centuries in France. Based on ideas taught at the dominant École des Beaux-Arts (School of Fine Arts) in Paris, the Beaux-Arts style incorporated classical principles (such as symmetry in design, including interior spaces extending radially from a central core or axis) and featured extensive exterior ornamentation. As an example of a Beaux-Arts building, Garnier's Opéra proclaims, through its majesty and lavishness, its function as a gathering place for fashionable audiences in an era of conspicuous wealth. The style was so attractive to the moneyed classes who supported the arts that theaters and opera houses continued to reflect the Paris Opéra's design until World War I transformed society.

27-45 CHARLES GARNIER, Opéra (looking north), Paris, France, 1861–1874.

For Paris's opera house, Garnier chose a festive and spectacularly theatrical Neo-Baroque facade well suited to a gathering place for fashionable audiences in an age of conspicuous wealth.

27-46 Henri Labrouste, reading room of the Bibliothèque Sainte-Geneviève, Paris, France, 1843–1850.

The exterior of this Parisian library looks like a Renaissance palazzo, but the interior has an exposed cast-iron skeleton, which still incorporates classical Corinthian capitals and Renaissance scrolls.

SAINTE-GENEVIÈVE LIBRARY Work on Garnier's opera house began in 1861, but by the middle of the 19th century, many architects had already abandoned sentimental and Romantic designs from the past. Since the 18th century, bridges had been constructed of cast iron (FIG. 26-13) because of its tensile strength and resistance to fire. Another new building material—steel—became available after 1860. Steel enabled architects to create new designs involving vast enclosed spaces, as in the great train sheds of railroad stations (FIG. 28-4) and in exposition halls. Most other utilitarian architecture— factories, warehouses, dockyard structures, mills, and the like—long had been built simply and without historical ornamentation.

The Bibliothèque Sainte-Geneviève, designed by HENRI LABROUSTE (1801–1875), is an interesting mix of Renaissance revival style and modern cast-iron construction. The library's two-story facade with arched windows recalls Renaissance *palazzo* designs, but Labrouste exposed the structure's metal skeleton on the interior. The lower story of the building housed the book stacks. The upper floor featured a spacious reading room (FIG. 27-46) consisting essentially of two barrel-vaulted halls, roofed in terracotta and separated by a row of slender cast-iron Corinthian columns on concrete pedestals. The columns support the iron roof arches pierced with intricate vine-scroll ornamentation derived from the Renaissance architectural repertoire. Labrouste's design highlights how the peculiar properties of the new structural material aesthetically transformed the shapes of traditional masonry architecture. But it is also clear how reluctant some 19th-century architects were to surrender traditional forms, even when fully aware of new possibilities for design and construction. Architects scoffed at "engineers'

27-46A ROEBLING, Brooklyn Bridge, 1867–1883.

architecture" for many years and continued to clothe their steel-and-concrete structures in the Romantic "drapery" of a historical style. For example, the Brooklyn Bridge (FIG. **27-46A**), designed and constructed by JOHN AUGUSTUS ROEBLING (1806–1869) and WASHINGTON ROEBLING (1837–1926), combined the latest steel technology with motifs from Gothic and Egyptian architecture. JOSEPH PAXTON (1801–1865) was an exception as a proponent of "undraped" architecture (see "Prefabricated Architecture," page 833, and FIG. **27-47**).

PHOTOGRAPHY

A technological device of immense consequence for the modern experience was invented shortly before the mid-19th century: the camera, with its attendant art of photography. From the time Frenchman LOUIS-JACQUES-MANDÉ DAGUERRE (1789–1851) and Englishman WILLIAM HENRY FOX TALBOT (1800–1877) announced the first practical photographic processes in 1839, people have celebrated photography's ability to make convincing pictures of people, places, and things. The relative ease of the process, even in its earliest and most primitive form, seemed a dream come true for 19th-century scientists and artists, who for centuries had grappled with less satisfying methods of capturing accurate images of their subjects. Photography also perfectly suited an age that saw the emergence of Realism as an art movement and a pronounced shift of artistic patronage away from the elite few toward a broader base of support. The growing and increasingly powerful middle class embraced both the comprehensible images of the new medium and their lower cost.

For the traditional artist, photography suggested new answers to the great debate about what is real and how to represent the real in art. Because photography easily and accurately enabled the reproduction of three-dimensional objects on a two-dimensional

PROBLEMS AND SOLUTIONS
Prefabricated Architecture

Completely "undraped" construction—that is, the erection of buildings that did not conceal their cast-iron structural skeletons—first became popular in the conservatories (greenhouses) of English country estates. Joseph Paxton built several of these structures for his patron, the duke of Devonshire. In the largest—300 feet long—he used an experimental system of glass-and-metal roof construction. Encouraged by the success of this system, Paxton submitted a winning glass-and-iron building design in the competition for the hall to house the 1851 Great Exhibition of the Works of Industry of All Nations in London.

As innovative as Paxton's use of modern materials in place of stone was his adoption of a new cost-effective way to erect his exhibition building, the Crystal Palace (FIG. 27-47). Paxton was the champion of *prefabricated architecture*—the use of structural elements manufactured in advance and transported to the construction site ready for assembly. In traditional stone architecture, masons carved the column capitals, moldings, and the like on site to ensure that these delicate features would not be damaged during transport. This slowed down construction considerably. Paxton's use of prefabricated parts—primarily glass panes in wood frames and cast-iron pillars and beams—for the Crystal Palace enabled workers to build the vast (18-acre) structure in the then unheard-of time of six months and to dismantle it quickly at the exhibition's closing to avoid permanent obstruction of the park. The building was the perfect expression of the new industrial age that the Great Exhibition celebrated.

Paxton's design, nonetheless, borrowed much from traditional architecture, especially Roman and Christian basilicas. The Crystal Palace had a central flat-roofed "nave" and a barrel-vaulted crossing "transept," providing ample interior space to contain displays of huge machines as well as to accommodate decorative touches in the form of large working fountains and giant trees. The public admired the Crystal Palace so much that the workers who dismantled it put up an enlarged version of the glass-and-iron exhibition hall at a new location on the outskirts of London at Sydenham, where it remained until fire destroyed it in 1936. Fortunately, a few old black-and-white photographs and several color lithographs (FIG. 27-47) preserve a record of the Crystal Palace's appearance.

27-47 JOSEPH PAXTON, Crystal Palace, London, England, 1850–1851; enlarged and relocated at Sydenham, England, 1852–1854. Color lithograph, 8" × 11¾", by ACHILLE-LOUIS MARTINET, ca. 1862. Private collection.

The tensile strength of iron enabled Paxton to experiment with a new system of glass-and-metal roof construction. Constructed of prefabricated parts, the vast Crystal Palace required only six months to build.

MATERIALS AND TECHNIQUES

Daguerreotypes, Calotypes, and Wet-Plate Photography

The earliest photographic processes were the *daguerreotype* (FIGS. 27-48 and 27-49), named after L.J.M. Daguerre, and the *calotype* (FIG. 27-53).

Daguerre was an architect and theatrical set painter and designer. This background led Daguerre and a partner to open a popular entertainment called the Diorama. Audiences witnessed performances of "living paintings" created by changing the lighting effects on a "sandwich" composed of a painted backdrop and several layers of painted translucent front curtains. Daguerre used a camera obscura for the Diorama, but he wanted to find a more efficient and effective procedure. Through a mutual acquaintance, he met Joseph Nicéphore Niépce (1765–1833), who in 1826 had successfully made a permanent picture of the cityscape outside his upper-story window by exposing, in a camera obscura, a metal plate covered with a light-sensitive coating. Niépce's process, however, had the significant drawback that it required an eight-hour exposure time. After Niépce died in 1833, Daguerre continued his work, making two important discoveries. Latent development—that is, bringing out the image through treatment in chemical solutions—considerably shortened the length of time needed for exposure. Daguerre also discovered a better way to "fix" the image by chemically stopping the action of light on the photographic plate, which otherwise would continue to darken until the image turned solid black.

The daguerreotype reigned supreme in photography until the 1850s, but the second major photographic invention, the ancestor of the modern negative-print system, eventually replaced it. On January 31, 1839, less than three weeks after Daguerre unveiled his method in Paris, William Henry Fox Talbot presented a paper on his "photogenic drawings" to the Royal Institution in London. As early as 1835, Talbot made "negative" images by placing objects on sensitized paper and exposing the arrangement to light. This created a design of light-colored silhouettes recording the places where opaque or

translucent objects had blocked light from darkening the paper's emulsion. In his experiments, Talbot next exposed sensitized papers inside simple cameras and, with a second sheet, created "positive" images. He further improved the process with more light-sensitive chemicals and a chemical development of the negative image. This technique enabled multiple prints. However, in Talbot's process, which he named the *calotype* (from the Greek word *kalos*, "beautiful"), the photographic images incorporated the texture of the paper. This produced a slightly blurred, grainy effect very different from the crisp detail and wide tonal range available with the daguerreotype. Also discouraging widespread adoption of the calotype were the stiff licensing and equipment fees charged for many years after Talbot patented his new process in 1841.

One of the earliest masters of an improved kind of calotype photography was the multitalented Frenchman known as Nadar (FIGS. 27-49A and 27-50). He used glass negatives and albumen (egg-white-based) printing paper (FIGS. 27-51 and 27-52), which could record finer detail and a wider range of light and shadow than Talbot's calotype process. The new *wet-plate* technology (so named because the photographic plate was exposed, developed, and fixed while wet) almost at once became the universal way of making negatives until 1880. However, wet-plate photography had drawbacks. The plates had to be prepared and processed on the spot. Working outdoors meant taking along a portable darkroom—a wagon, tent, or box with light-tight sleeves for the photographer's arms.

Refinements of these early processes served photographers well for a century and a half, but have been almost completely supplanted today by digital photography (see page 1016).

27-48 LOUIS-JACQUES-MANDÉ DAGUERRE, *Still Life in Studio*, 1837. Daguerreotype, $6\frac{1}{4}$" × $8\frac{1}{4}$". Société Française de Photographie, Paris.

One of the first plates Daguerre produced after perfecting his new photographic process was this still life, in which he was able to capture amazing detail and finely graduated tones of light and shadow.

1 in.

surface, the new medium also challenged the place of traditional modes of pictorial representation originating in the Renaissance. Artists as diverse as Delacroix, Ingres, Courbet, and the Impressionist Edgar Degas (see page 849) welcomed photography as a helpful auxiliary to painting. Other artists, however, feared that the camera was a mechanism that would displace the painstaking

work of skilled painters. From the moment of its invention, photography threatened to expropriate the realistic image, until then the exclusive property of painting. But just as some painters looked to the new medium of photography for answers on how best to render an image in paint, so some photographers looked to painting for suggestions about ways to imbue the photographic image with qualities beyond simple reproduction. Indeed, the first subjects that photographers chose to record were traditional painting themes—for example, still lifes and portraits—in part to establish photography as a legitimate artistic medium on a par with painting. A debate immediately began over whether the photograph was an art form or whether the camera was merely a scientific instrument. An 1862 court case provided the answer: photography was an art, and photographs were entitled to copyright protection (see FIG. 27-49A).

Artists themselves were instrumental in the development of the new photographic technology. The camera obscura was familiar to 18th-century artists. In 1807, the invention of the *camera lucida* (lighted room) replaced the enclosed chamber of the camera obscura. Now the photographer aimed a small prism lens, hung on a stand, downward at an object. The lens projected the image of the object onto a sheet of paper. Artists using either of these devices found the process long and arduous, no matter how accurate the resulting work. All yearned for a more direct way to capture a subject's image. Two very different scientific inventions that accomplished this—the *daguerreotype* and the *calotype* (see "Daguerreotypes, Calotypes, and Wet-Plate Photography," page 834)—appeared almost simultaneously in France and England in 1839.

DAGUERREOTYPES The French government presented the new daguerreotype process at the Academy of Science in Paris on January 7, 1839, with the understanding that its details would be made available to all interested parties without charge (although the inventor received a large annuity in appreciation). Soon, people worldwide began making pictures with the daguerreotype "camera" (a name shortened from camera obscura) in a process almost immediately christened "photography," from the Greek *photos* ("light") and *graphos* ("writing or drawing"). From the start, the possibilities of the process as a new art medium intrigued painters. Paul Delaroche (1797–1856), a leading academic painter of the day, wrote in an official report to the French government that anticipated the 1862 legal ruling:

Daguerre's process completely satisfies all the demands of art, carrying certain essential principles of art to such perfection that it must become a subject of observation and study even to the most accomplished painters. The pictures obtained by this method are as remarkable for the perfection of the details as for the richness and harmony of the general effect. Nature is reproduced in them not only with truth, but also with art.[13]

Unlike photographs that people make today, whether printed from traditional film negatives or from digital images, each daguerreotype is a unique work. *Still Life in Studio* (FIG. **27-48**) is one of the first successful plates Daguerre produced after perfecting his method. The process captured every detail—the subtle forms, the varied textures, the finely graduated tones of light and shadow—in Daguerre's carefully constructed tableau. The three-dimensional forms of the sculptures, the basket, and the bits of cloth spring into high relief. The inspiration for the composition came from 17th-century Dutch *vanitas* still lifes, such as those of Pieter Claesz (FIG. 25-21). Like Claesz, Daguerre arranged his objects to reveal their textures and shapes clearly. Unlike a painter, Daguerre could not alter anything within his arrangement to create a stronger image. However, he could suggest a symbolic meaning through his choice of objects. Like the skull and timepiece in Claesz's painting, Daguerre's sculptural and architectural fragments and the framed print of a couple embracing suggest that even art is vanitas and will not endure forever.

HAWES AND SOUTHWORTH In the United States, photographers began to make daguerreotypes within two months of Daguerre's presentation in Paris. Two particularly avid and resourceful advocates of the new medium were JOSIAH JOHNSON HAWES (1808–1901), a painter, and ALBERT SANDS SOUTHWORTH (1811–1894), a pharmacist and teacher. Together, they ran a daguerreotype studio in Boston specializing in portraiture, then popular due to the shortened exposure time required for the process (although it was still long enough to require head braces to help subjects remain motionless while photographers recorded their images).

The partners also took their equipment outside the studio to record places and events of particular interest to them. One resultant image is *Early Operation under Ether, Massachusetts General Hospital* (FIG. **27-49**).

27-49 JOSIAH JOHNSON HAWES and ALBERT SANDS SOUTHWORTH, *Early Operation under Ether, Massachusetts General Hospital*, ca. 1847. Daguerreotype, $6\frac{1}{2}" \times 8\frac{1}{2}"$. Massachusetts General Hospital Archives and Special Collections, Boston.

In this early daguerreotype, which predates Eakins's *Gross Clinic* (FIG. 27-36) by almost 30 years, Hawes and Southworth demonstrated the documentary power of the new medium of photography.

1 in.

This daguerreotype, taken from the vantage point of the gallery of a hospital operating room, puts the viewer in the position of medical students looking down on the type of lecture-demonstration that was typical throughout the 19th century. An image of historical record, this early daguerreotype predates Eakins's *Gross Clinic* (FIG. 27-36) by almost three decades, but the theme had been explored in painting much earlier by Rembrandt (FIG. 25-12). The focus of attention in *Early Operation* is the white-draped patient surrounded by a circle of darkly clad doctors. The details of the figures and the room's furnishings are in sharp focus, but the slight blurring of several of the figures betrays motion during the exposure. The elevated viewpoint flattens the spatial perspective and emphasizes the relationships of the figures in ways that the Impressionists, especially Degas (FIG. 28-8), found intriguing.

NADAR Portraiture was one of the first photography genres to use the new wet-plate technology that improved on the calotype. Making portraits was an important economic opportunity for most photographers, as Southworth and Hawes proved, but the greatest early portrait photographer was undoubtedly Gaspar-Félix Tournachon. Known simply as NADAR (1820–1910), Tournachon was a French novelist, journalist, enthusiastic balloonist (FIG. 27-49A), and caricaturist, who became an early champion of photography. Photographic studies for his caricatures led Nadar to open a portrait

studio. So talented was he at capturing the essence of his subjects that the most important people in France, including Delacroix, Daumier, Courbet, and Manet, flocked to his studio to have their portraits made. Nadar said that he sought in his work "that instant of understanding that puts you in touch with the model—helps you sum him up, guides you to his habits, his ideas, and character and enables you to produce . . . a really convincing and sympathetic likeness, an intimate portrait."[14]

27-49A DAUMIER, *Nadar Raising Photography*, 1862.

Nadar's *Eugène Delacroix* (FIG. 27-50) shows the painter at the height of his career. In this photograph, the artist appears with remarkable presence. Even in half-length, his gesture and expression create a mood that seems to reveal much about him. Perhaps Delacroix responded to Nadar's famous gift for putting his clients at ease by assuming the pose that best expressed his personality. The new photographic materials made possible the rich range of tones in Nadar's images.

JULIA MARGARET CAMERON Among the most famous portrait photographers in 19th-century England was JULIA MARGARET CAMERON (1815–1879), who did not take up photography seriously

1 in.

27-50 NADAR, *Eugène Delacroix*, ca. 1855. Modern print, 8½" × 6⅔", from the original negative. Bibliothèque Nationale, Paris.

Nadar was one of the earliest portrait photographers. His prints of the leading artists of the day, such as this one of Delacroix, reveal the sitters' personalities as well as record their features.

1 in.

27-51 JULIA MARGARET CAMERON, *Ophelia, Study No. 2*, 1867. Albumen print, 1' 1" × 10⅔". George Eastman House, Rochester (gift of Eastman Kodak Company; formerly Gabriel Cromer Collection).

Cameron was a prominent 19th-century photographer who often depicted her female subjects as characters in literary or biblical narratives. The slightly blurred focus is a distinctive feature of her work.

until the age of 48. Although she produced images of many well-known men of the period, including Charles Darwin, Alfred Tennyson, and Thomas Carlyle, she photographed more women than men, as was true of many women photographers. *Ophelia, Study No. 2* (FIG. 27-51) typifies her portrait style. Cameron often depicted her female subjects as characters in literary or biblical narratives. The slightly blurred focus also became a distinctive feature of her work—the by-product of photographing with a lens with a short focal length, which allowed only a small area of sharp focus. The blurriness adds an ethereal, dreamlike tone to the photographs, appropriate for Cameron's fictional "characters." Her photograph of Ophelia has a mysterious, fragile quality reminiscent of Pre-Raphaelite paintings (FIG. 27-41) of literary heroines.

TIMOTHY O'SULLIVAN Photographers were quick to realize the documentary power of their new medium. Thus began the story of photography's influence on modern life and of the immense changes it brought to communication and information management. With photography, historical events could for the first time be recorded in

permanent form on the spot. The photographs taken of the Crimean War (1856) by Roger Fenton (1819–1869) and of the American Civil War by Mathew B. Brady (1823–1896), ALEXANDER GARDNER (1821–1882), and TIMOTHY O'SULLIVAN (1840–1882) remain unsurpassed as incisive accounts of military life, unsparing in their truthful detail and poignant as expressions of human experience.

Of the Civil War photographs, the most moving are the inhumanly objective records of combat deaths. Perhaps the most reproduced of these Civil War photographs is Gardner's print of O'Sullivan's *A Harvest of Death, Gettysburg, Pennsylvania* (FIG. 27-52). Although viewers could regard this image as simple reportage, it also functions to impress on people the high price of war. Corpses litter the battlefield as far and wide as the eye can see. As O'Sullivan's photograph modulates from the precise clarity of the bodies of Union soldiers in the foreground, boots stolen and pockets picked, to the indistinct corpses in the distance, the suggestion of innumerable other dead soldiers is unavoidable. This "harvest" is far more sobering and depressing than that in Winslow Homer's Civil War painting, *Veteran in a New Field* (FIG. 27-35). Though it was

Negative by T. H. O'SULLIVAN.   Entered according to act of Congress, in the year 1865, by A. Gardner, in the Clerk's Office of the District Court of the District of Columbia.   Positive by A. GARDNER, 511 7th St., Washington.

1 in.

A HARVEST OF DEATH, GETTYSBURG, PENNSYLVANIA.

27-52 TIMOTHY O'SULLIVAN, *A Harvest of Death, Gettysburg, Pennsylvania*, 1863. Negative by Timothy O'Sullivan. Albumen print by ALEXANDER GARDNER, $6\frac{3}{4}'' \times 8\frac{3}{4}''$. New York Public Library (Astor, Lenox and Tilden Foundations, Rare Books and Manuscript Division), New York.

Wet-plate technology enabled photographers to record historical events on the spot—and to comment on the high price of war, as in this photograph of dead Union soldiers at Gettysburg in 1863.

1 in.

27-53 EADWEARD MUYBRIDGE, *Horse Galloping*, 1878. Calotype print, 9" × 12". George Eastman House International Museum of Photography and Film, Rochester.

Muybridge specialized in photographic studies of the successive stages in human and animal motion—details too quick for the human eye to capture. Modern cinema owes a great deal to his work.

years before photolithography could reproduce photographs such as this one in newspapers, photographers exhibited them publicly. They made an impression that newsprint engravings never could.

EADWEARD MUYBRIDGE The Realist photographer and scientist EADWEARD MUYBRIDGE (1830–1904) came to the United States from England in the 1850s and settled in San Francisco, where he established a prominent international reputation for his photographs of the western United States. In 1872, the governor of California, Leland Stanford (1824–1893), sought Muybridge's assistance in settling a bet about whether, at any point in a stride, all four feet of a horse galloping at top speed are off the ground. Through his sequential photography, as seen in *Horse Galloping* (FIG. **27-53**), Muybridge proved that racing horses did in fact at times have all four feet in midair. This experience was the beginning of Muybridge's photographic studies of the successive stages in human and animal motion—details too quick for the human eye to capture. These investigations culminated in 1885 at the University of Pennsylvania with a series of multiple-camera motion studies that produced separate photographs of progressive moments in a single action. Muybridge's discoveries received extensive publicity

through the book *Animal Locomotion* (1887), and his motion photographs earned him a place in the history of science, as well as art. These sequential motion studies, along with those of Eakins and Marey (see page 825), influenced many other artists, including their contemporary, the painter and sculptor Edgar Degas (FIG. 28-8), and 20th-century artists such as Marcel Duchamp (FIG. 29-35).

Muybridge presented his work to scientists and general audiences with a device called the *zoopraxiscope*, which he invented to project his sequences of images (mounted on special glass plates) onto a screen. The result was so lifelike that one viewer said it "threw upon the screen apparently the living, moving animals. Nothing was wanting but the clatter of hoofs upon the turf."[15] The illusion of motion in Muybridge's photographic exhibits was the result of a physical fact of human eyesight called "persistence of vision." Stated simply, it means that the brain retains whatever the eye sees for a fraction of a second after the eye stops seeing it. Thus viewers saw a rapid succession of different images merging one into the next, producing the illusion of continuous change. This illusion lies at the heart of the motion-picture industry that debuted in the 20th century. Thus, with Muybridge's innovations in photography, yet another new art form was born—cinema.

ROMANTICISM, REALISM, PHOTOGRAPHY: EUROPE AND AMERICA, 1800 TO 1870

Art under Napoleon

- As Emperor of the French from 1804 to 1815, Napoleon embraced the Neoclassical style in order to associate his regime with the empire of ancient Rome. Roman temples were the models for La Madeleine in Paris, which Pierre Vignon built as a temple of glory for France's imperial armies.

- Napoleon chose Jacques-Louis David as First Painter of the Empire. His favorite sculptor was Antonio Canova, who carved marble Neoclassical portraits of the imperial family, including a reclining image of Napoleon's sister Pauline Borghese in the guise of Venus.

- The beginning of a break from Neoclassicism can already be seen in the work of several of David's students, including Gros, Girodet-Trioson, and Ingres, all of whom painted some exotic subjects reflecting Romantic taste.

Canova, *Pauline Borghese as Venus*, 1808

Romanticism

- The roots of Romanticism are in the 18th century, but usually the term more narrowly denotes the artistic movement that flourished from 1800 to 1840, between Neoclassicism and Realism. Romantic artists gave precedence to feeling and imagination over Enlightenment reason. Romantic painters explored the exotic, erotic, and fantastic in their art.

- In Spain, Francisco Goya's *Caprichos* series celebrated the unleashing of imagination, emotions, and even nightmares. In France, Eugène Delacroix led the way in depicting Romantic narratives set in faraway places and distant times. Ancient Assyria, for example, is the subject of his *Death of Sardanapalus*.

- Romantic painters often chose landscapes as an ideal subject to express the theme of the soul unified with the natural world. Masters of the transcendental landscape include Friedrich in Germany, Constable and Turner in England, and Cole, Bierstadt, and Church in the United States.

Friedrich, *Wanderer above a Sea of Mist*, 1817–1818

Realism

- Realism developed as an artistic movement in mid-19th-century France. Its leading proponent was Gustave Courbet, whose paintings of menial laborers and ordinary people exemplify his belief that painters should depict only their own time and place. Honoré Daumier boldly confronted authority with his satirical lithographs commenting on the plight of the urban working class. Édouard Manet shocked the public with his paintings' subjects—for example, promiscuous women—and with his technique, especially his rough brushstrokes, which emphasized the flatness of the painting surface, paving the way for modern abstract art.

- Among the leading American Realists were Winslow Homer, Thomas Eakins, and John Singer Sargent. Eakins's painting of surgery in progress was too brutally realistic for the Philadelphia art jury that rejected it.

Manet, *Olympia*, 1863

Architecture

- Territorial expansion, the Romantic interest in exotic locales and earlier eras, and nationalistic pride led to the revival in the 19th century of older architectural styles, especially the Gothic, exemplified by London's Houses of Parliament.

- By the middle of the century, many architects had already abandoned sentimental and Romantic designs from the past in favor of exploring the possibilities of cast-iron construction, as in Henri Labrouste's Sainte-Geneviève Library in Paris and Joseph Paxton's prefabricated Crystal Palace in London.

Paxton, Crystal Palace, London, 1850–1851

Photography

- In 1839, Daguerre in Paris and Talbot in London invented the first practical photographic processes. In 1862, a French court formally recognized photography as an art form subject to copyright protection. Many of the earliest photographers, including Nadar and Cameron, specialized in portrait photography, but others, including Hawes, Southworth, and O'Sullivan in the United States, quickly realized the documentary power of the new medium. Muybridge's sequential photos of human and animal motion were the forerunners of modern cinema.

Cameron, *Ophelia*, 1867

28-1a The Folies-Bergère was a popular café and music hall where Parisians enjoyed their leisure—a characteristic Impressionist subject that broke sharply with tradition, as did Manet's sketchy application of paint.

28-1b The central figure in *A Bar at the Folies-Bergère* is a young barmaid who looks out from the canvas but seems detached both from the viewer and the gentleman in a top hat who may be propositioning her.

28-1 ÉDOUARD MANET, *A Bar at the Folies-Bergère*, 1882. Oil on canvas, 3' 1" × 4' 3". Courtauld Gallery, London.

28-1c In accord with modernist principles, Manet called attention to the canvas surface by creating spatial inconsistencies, such as the relationship between the barmaid and her apparent reflection in the mirror.

Impressionism, Post-Impressionism, Symbolism: Europe and America, 1870 to 1900

MODERNISM AT THE FOLIES-BERGÈRE

Between 1800 and 1900, the population of Europe's major cities exploded. In Paris, for example, the number of residents expanded from 500,000 to 2,700,000. It was there that the art movement called *Impressionism* was born, an aesthetic by-product of the sometimes brutal and chaotic transformation of French life, which made the world seem unstable and insubstantial. As the poet and critic Charles Baudelaire (1821–1867) observed in his 1860 essay *The Painter of Modern Life*: "[Modernity is] the ephemeral, the fugitive, the contingent, the half of art whose other half is the eternal and the immutable."[1] Accordingly, Impressionist painters built on the innovations of the Realists in turning away from traditional mythological and religious themes in favor of the daily life of the newly industrialized French capital and its suburbs along the Seine. But, in contrast to the Realists, the Impressionists sought to convey the elusiveness and impermanence of the subjects they portrayed.

One of the most popular Impressionist subjects was Paris's vibrant nightlife. The immensely versatile Édouard Manet (FIGS. 27-32 and 27-33), whose career bridged Realism and Impressionism, painted his last great work—*A Bar at the Folies-Bergère* (FIG. 28-1)—under the influence of the younger Impressionists. The Folies-Bergère was a popular café with music-hall performances, one of Paris's most fashionable gathering places. At the center of Manet's *Folies-Bergère* is a barmaid, who looks out from the canvas but seems disinterested or lost in thought, divorced from her patrons as well as from the viewer. In front of her, Manet painted a marvelous still life of bottles, flowers, and fruit—all for sale to the bar's customers. In the mirror is the reflection of a gentleman wearing a dapper top hat and carrying an elegant walking stick. He has approached the barmaid, perhaps to order a drink, but more likely to ask the price of her company after the bar closes. Also visible in the mirror, at the upper left corner of the canvas, are the lower legs of a trapeze artist and a woman in the nightclub's balcony watching some other performance through opera glasses.

What seems at first to be a straightforward representation of the bar, barmaid, and customers quickly fades as visual discrepancies immediately emerge. For example, is the reflection of the woman on the right the barmaid's? If both figures are the same person, it is impossible to reconcile the spatial relationship among the gentleman, the bar, the barmaid, and her seemingly displaced reflection. These visual contradictions complement Manet's blurred brushstrokes and rough application of paint. Together, they draw attention to the tactile surface of the canvas, consistent with late-19th-century artists' emerging insistence on underscoring the artifice of the act of painting, one of the central principles of *modernist* art.

MARXISM, DARWINISM, MODERNISM

The momentous developments of the early 19th century in Europe—urbanization, industrialization, and increased economic and political interaction worldwide—matured during the latter half of the century. The Industrial Revolution that began in England spread so rapidly to the Continent and the United States that historians often refer to the third quarter of the 19th century as the second Industrial Revolution. Whereas the first Industrial Revolution centered on textiles, steam, and iron, the second focused on steel, electricity, chemicals, and oil. The discoveries in these fields provided the foundation for developments in plastics, machinery, building construction, and automobile manufacturing and paved the way for the invention of the radio, telephone, electric lightbulb, and electric streetcar.

Expanding industrialization was closely tied to rapid urbanization. The number and size of European cities grew dramatically during the latter part of the 19th century, largely due to migration from the countryside. Farmers in large numbers relocated to urban centers because expanded agricultural enterprises squeezed smaller property owners from their land. The widely available work opportunities in the cities, especially in the factories, were also a major factor in this population shift. Improving health and living conditions in the cities further contributed to their explosive growth.

MARXISM AND DARWINISM The rise of the urban working class was fundamental to the ideas of Karl Marx (1818–1883), one of the era's dominant figures. Born in Trier, Germany, Marx received a doctorate in philosophy from the University of Berlin. After moving to Paris, he met fellow German Friedrich Engels (1820–1895), who became his lifelong collaborator. Together they wrote *The Communist Manifesto* (1848), which called for the working class to overthrow the capitalist system. Marx believed that in all societies, those who controlled the means of production conflicted with those whose labor they exploited for their own enrichment—a dynamic he called "dialectical materialism." Marx advocated the creation of a socialist state in which the working class seized power and destroyed capitalism. This new political, social, and economic system—Marxism—held great appeal for the working poor as well as for many intellectuals.

Equally influential was the English naturalist Charles Darwin (1809–1882), who postulated the theory of natural selection. Darwin and his compatriot Alfred Russel Wallace (1823–1913), working independently, proposed a rational model for the process of evolution, rather than attributing evolution to random chance or God's plan. They argued that evolution was the natural result of a competitive system in which only the fittest survived. Darwin's controversial ideas, as presented in *On the Origin of Species by Means of Natural Selection* (1859), contradicted the biblical narrative of creation and were greeted with hostility by many people.

MODERNISM Marx's emphasis on social conflict and Darwin's ideas about evolution were consistent with the growing sense of the world's impermanence and of a constantly shifting reality, which Baudelaire insisted was the essential characteristic of the modern world and the proper subject of a modernist painter (see page 841). *Modernism* in art, however, transcends the simple depiction of the contemporary world—the goal of Realism. Modernists also critically examine the premises of art itself, as Manet did in his groundbreaking 1863 painting *Le Déjeuner sur l'Herbe* (FIG. 27-32) and carried further in his 1882 *A Bar at the Folies-Bergère* (FIG. 28-1). Modernism thus implies certain concerns about art and aesthetics internal to art production, regardless of whether the artist is portraying modern life.

In an important 1965 article, Clement Greenberg (1909–1994), an influential American art critic who wrote about the revolutionary art movements of the decades following World War II (see "Greenbergian Formalism," page 954), explained modernism as follows:

> The essence of Modernism lies . . . in the use of the characteristic methods of a discipline to criticize the discipline itself—not in order to subvert it, but to entrench it more firmly in its area of competence. . . . [T]he unique and proper area of competence of each art coincide[s] with all that [is] unique to the nature of its medium. . . . Realistic, illusionist art had dissembled the medium, using art to conceal art. Modernism used art to call attention to art. The limitations that constitute the medium of painting—the flat surface, the shape of the support, the properties of pigment—were treated by the Old Masters as negative factors that could be acknowledged only implicitly or indirectly. Modernist painting has come to regard these same limitations as positive factors that are to be acknowledged openly. Manet's paintings became the first Modernist ones by virtue of the frankness with which they declared the surfaces on which they were painted. The Impressionists, in Manet's wake, abjured underpainting and glazing, to leave the eye under no doubt as to the fact that the colors used were made of real paint that came from pots or tubes.[2]

IMPRESSIONISM

A hostile critic applied the term *Impressionism* in response to *Impression: Sunrise* (FIG. 28-2), one of the paintings exhibited in the first Impressionist show in 1874 (see "Academic Salons and Independent Art Exhibitions," page 844). Although the critic intended

IMPRESSIONISM, POST-IMPRESSIONISM, SYMBOLISM: EUROPE AND AMERICA, 1870 TO 1900

1870–1880
- Claude Monet and the Impressionists mount their first independent exhibition in Paris
- The Impressionists paint subjects that capture the transitory nature of modern life in urbanized Paris and its suburbs
- European artists begin to collect Japanese prints and emulate Japanese compositions
- Gustave Moreau explores eroticism and fantasy in Symbolist paintings

1880–1890
- Édouard Manet completes his career with paintings in the Impressionist mode
- Georges Seurat investigates color theory and develops pointillism
- Vincent van Gogh moves to France and explores the expressive power of color
- Auguste Rodin receives the commission for *Gates of Hell*
- Alexandre-Gustave Eiffel builds the Eiffel Tower in Paris

1890–1900
- Henri de Toulouse-Lautrec pioneers the art of the poster
- Paul Cézanne seeks "to do Poussin over entirely from nature"
- The Art Nouveau movement emerges in architecture and the decorative arts
- Gustav Klimt's paintings epitomize fin-de-siècle culture in Austria
- Louis Sullivan builds steel, glass, and stone skyscrapers in America

PROBLEMS AND SOLUTIONS
Painting Impressions of Light and Color

In striking contrast to traditional studio artists, Monet began and completed *Impression: Sunrise* (FIG. **28-2**)—a view of the harbor of his boyhood home in Le Havre—outdoors. Closer to Paris, he often set up his easel on the banks of the Seine (FIG. **28-2A**) or in a boat on the river (FIG. **28-2B**). Painting *en plein air* was how Monet was able to meet his goal of capturing an instantaneous representation of atmosphere and climate, which he concluded was impossible to do in a studio. Of course, landscape painters had always drawn and made preliminary color studies outdoors and then used those sketches to produce formal paintings in their studios. Finishing as well as beginning his landscapes outdoors sharpened Monet's focus on the roles that light and color play in the way nature appears to the eye. The systematic investigation of light and color and the elimination of the traditional distinction between a sketch and a formal painting enabled Monet to paint images that truly conveyed a sense of the momentary and transitory. Lilla Cabot Perry (1848–1933), a student of Monet's late in his career, gave this description of Monet's approach:

⊿ **28-2A** MONET, *Bank of the Seine, Bennecourt,* 1868.

⊿ **28-2B** MANET, *Monet in His Studio Boat,* 1874.

> I remember his once saying to me: "When you go out to paint, try to forget what objects you have before you—a tree, a house, a field, or whatever. Merely think, here is a little square of blue, here an oblong of pink, here a streak of yellow, and paint it just as it looks

to you, the exact color and shape, until it gives your own naïve impression of the scene before you."*

Another factor encouraging Monet and some of his contemporaries to paint outdoors was the introduction of premixed pigments conveniently sold in easily portable tubes. The newly available oil paints gave artists new colors for their work and heightened their sensitivity to the multiplicity of colors in nature. After scrutinizing the effects of light and color on forms, Monet and other late-19th-century painters concluded that *local color*—an object's color in white light—becomes modified by the quality of the light shining on it, by reflections from other objects, and by the effects that juxtaposed colors produce. Shadows do not appear gray or black, as many earlier painters thought, but seem to be composed of colors modified by reflections or other conditions. If artists use complementary colors (see "19th-Century Color Theory," page 855) side by side over large enough areas, the colors intensify each other, unlike the effect of small quantities of adjoining mixed pigments, which blend into neutral tones. Furthermore, the "mixing" of colors by juxtaposing them directly on a white canvas without any preliminary sketch—also a sharp break from traditional painting practice—produces a more intense hue than the same colors mixed on the palette. Although it is not true, as some have maintained, that Monet exclusively used primary hues, placing them side by side to create secondary colors (blue and yellow, for example, to create green), he did achieve remarkably brilliant effects with his characteristically short, choppy brushstrokes, which so accurately catch the vibrating quality of light. The reason for much of the early adverse criticism leveled at Monet's paintings was that they lacked the polished surfaces and sharp contours of academic painting. In Monet's canvases, in sharp contrast to traditional oil paintings, the forms take on clarity only when the eye fuses the brushstrokes at a certain distance.

*Quoted in Linda Nochlin, *Impressionism and Post-Impressionism 1874–1904: Sources and Documents* (Englewood Cliffs, N.J.: Prentice Hall, 1966), 35.

28-2 CLAUDE MONET, *Impression: Sunrise,* 1872. Oil on canvas, 1′ 7½″ × 2′ 1½″. Musée Marmottan, Paris.

Fascinated by reflected sunlight on water, Monet broke with traditional studio practice and painted his "impression" en plein air, using short brushstrokes of pure color on canvas without any preliminary sketch.

1 in.

ART AND SOCIETY

Academic Salons and Independent Art Exhibitions

For both artists and art historians, modernist art stands in marked contrast to, indeed in forceful opposition to, academic art—that is, to the art promoted by the established art schools such as the Royal Academy of Painting and Sculpture in France (founded in 1648) and the Royal Academy of Arts in Britain (founded in 1768). These academies provided instruction for art students and sponsored exhibitions, exerting tight control over the art scene. The annual exhibitions, called "Salons" in France, were highly competitive, as was membership in these academies. Subsidized by the government, the French Royal Academy supported a limited range of artistic expression, focusing on traditional subjects and highly polished technique. Because of the challenges that modernist art presented to established artistic conventions, the juries for the Salons and other exhibitions routinely rejected the works that more adventurous artists wished to display, thereby preventing the public from viewing any art other than the officially sanctioned forms of expression. When, however, the 1855 jury rejected some of Gustave Courbet's paintings, the artist reacted by setting up his own Pavilion of Realism (see "Courbet on Realism," page 816). Years later, he wrote:

> [I]t is high time that someone have the courage to be an honest man and that he say that the Academy is a harmful, all-consuming institution, incapable of fulfilling the goal of its so-called mission.*

Growing dissatisfaction with the decisions of the French Academy's jurors prompted Napoleon III (r. 1852–1870) in 1863 to establish the Salon des Refusés (Salon of the Rejected) to show all of the works not accepted for exhibition in the regular Salon. Édouard Manet's *Le Déjeuner sur l'Herbe* (FIG. 27-32) was among them. The public greeted it and the entire exhibition with contempt. One reviewer of the rejected works summed up the prevailing attitude:

> This exhibition, at once sad and grotesque, . . . offers abundant proof . . . that the jury always displays an unbelievable leniency. Save for one or two questionable exceptions there is not a painting which deserves the honor of the official galleries . . . There is even something cruel about this exhibition; people laugh as they do at a farce.†

In 1867, after further rejections, Manet, following Courbet, mounted a private exhibition of 50 of his paintings outside the Paris World's Fair. Six years later, Claude Monet (FIGS. 28-2 to 28-4) and the other Impressionists formed their own society—essentially a painters' union modeled on other workers' unions of the era—and began mounting shows of their works in Paris. This action provided the Impressionists with great freedom because they did not have to contend with the Royal Academy's authoritative and confining viewpoint, which condemned not only the Impressionists' techniques but their modernist subject matter as well. Salon jurors regarded landscapes and cityscapes and the leisure pursuits of the middle class as unworthy themes for important artworks. The Impressionist exhibitions took place at one- or two-year intervals from 1874 until 1886. The Impressionists also displayed their work in private venues, such as the Parisian gallery owned by Paul Durand-Ruel (1831–1922), who was one of the first to recognize the important innovations of the Impressionists and who regularly exhibited their paintings.

Another group of artists unhappy with the official Salon's conservative nature adopted the same renegade idea. In 1884, these artists formed the Société des Artistes Indépendants (Society of Independent Artists) and held annual Salons des Indépendants. Georges Seurat's

1 ft.

28-3 CLAUDE MONET, *Rouen Cathedral: The Portal (in Sun)*, 1894. Oil on canvas, 3' 3 $\frac{1}{4}$" × 2' 1 $\frac{7}{8}$". Metropolitan Museum of Art, New York (Theodore M. Davis Collection, bequest of Theodore M. Davis, 1915).

Monet exhibited 20 paintings of Rouen Cathedral in Paul Durand-Ruel's commercial art gallery in Paris. The canvases show the facade at different times of day and under various climatic conditions.

A Sunday on La Grande Jatte (FIG. 28-17) was one of the paintings in the Independents' 1886 Salon.

As the art market expanded, venues for the exhibition of art increased. Art circles and societies sponsored private shows in which both amateurs and professionals participated. Dealers became more aggressive in promoting the artists they represented by mounting exhibitions in a variety of spaces, some fairly intimate and small, others large and grandiose. Even nightclub owners displayed paintings for sale to their customers, following the example of Dutch innkeepers of the Baroque era (see "Middle-Class Patronage and the Art Market in the Dutch Republic," page 738). All of these proliferating opportunities for exhibition gave French artists alternatives to the traditional constraints of the Salon and provided fertile breeding ground for the development of radically new art forms and styles.

*Letter to Jules-Antoine Castagnary, October 17, 1868. Translated by Petra ten-Doesschate Chu, *Letters of Gustave Courbet* (Chicago: University of Chicago Press, 1992), 346.

†Maxime du Camp, in *Revue des deux mondes*, 1863, quoted in George Heard Hamilton, *Manet and His Critics* (New Haven: Yale University Press, New Haven, Conn., 1986), 42–43.

1 ft.

the label to be derogatory, by the third Impressionist show in 1878, the artists had embraced it and were calling themselves Impressionists. Both artists and critics had used the term before, but only in relation to sketches. Impressionist paintings do incorporate the qualities of sketches—abbreviation, speed, and spontaneity—but the artists considered their sketchlike works to be finished paintings, a radically modernist idea at the time.

CLAUDE MONET The painter of *Impression: Sunrise* was Claude Monet (1840–1926), who grew up on the Normandy coast of France at Le Havre, the great seaport at the mouth of the Seine (map 28-1, page 846), where his father sold groceries in bulk to shipping companies. Monet began to paint at an early age, and moved to Paris in late 1862 to pursue a career as an artist, returning to Le Havre on several occasions. *Impression: Sunrise,* which is a view of that harbor, represented a sharp break from traditional landscape painting. In recording the boats, water, and sky, Monet made no attempt to disguise the brushstrokes or blend the pigment to create smooth tonal gradations and an optically accurate scene. This concern with acknowledging the paint and the canvas surface continued the modernist exploration that the Realists had begun.

The "impressionistic" application of paint is, however, only one aspect of Impressionism. Beyond its affinity with sketches, Impressionism operated at the intersection of what the artists saw and what they felt. In other words, the "impressions" these artists recorded in their paintings were neither purely objective descriptions of the exterior world nor solely subjective responses, but the interaction between the two. They were sensations, the Impressionists' subjective and personal responses to nature, formed and recorded *en plein air*—that is, outdoors (see "Painting Impressions of Light and Color," page 843).

ROUEN CATHEDRAL Monet's intensive study of the phenomena of light and color is especially evident in several series of paintings he made of the same subject. In one series, he painted more than 30 views of Rouen Cathedral, northwest of Paris, 20 of which he exhibited for sale in 1895 in a private commercial art gallery (see "Academic Salons and Independent Art Exhibitions," page 844). The subject evoked powerful associations in the popular imagination: the grandeur of France's Gothic past and of its great martyr saint, Joan of Arc, who was executed at Rouen in 1431. For each canvas in the series, Monet observed the cathedral from nearly the same viewpoint, but at different times of the day and under various climatic conditions. Often, he would work on as many as eight canvases at once, switching from one to another as the atmospheric conditions changed during the course of the day. In the painting illustrated here (fig. 28-3), Monet depicted the church bathed in bright light. In the series as a whole, he carefully recorded the passing of time as seen in the movement of light over identical forms. To a certain degree, the real subject of Monet's painting—as the title *Rouen Cathedral: The Portal (in Sun)* implies—is not the cathedral, which he showed only in part, but the sunlight on the building's main portal. Consequently, many critics accused Monet of destroying form for fleeting atmospheric effects—an assertion that the painter probably would not have disputed, although he would have vigorously defended his approach to representation as well as his rejection of academic standards of judgment.

SAINT-LAZARE Most of the Impressionists painted scenes in and around Paris, the heart of modern life in France. Monet's *Saint-Lazare Train Station* (fig. 28-4) depicts a characteristic aspect of the contemporary urban scene. The expanding railway network had made travel more convenient, bringing large numbers of people into Paris and enabling city dwellers to reach suburban areas, such as Bennecourt (FIG. 28-2A) and Argenteuil (FIG. 28-2B), quickly (MAP 28-1). In his "impression" of the Saint-Lazare railway terminal, Monet captured the energy and vitality of Paris's modern transportation hub. The train, emerging from the steam and smoke it emits, rumbles into the station. In the background haze are the tall buildings that were becoming a major component of the Parisian landscape. Monet's agitated paint application contributes to the sense of energy and conveys the atmosphere of urban life.

Georges Rivière (1855–1943), an art critic and friend of some of the Impressionists, saw this painting in the third Impressionist exhibition and recorded the essence of what Monet had tried to achieve:

> Like a fiery steed, stimulated rather than exhausted by the long trek that it has only just finished, [the locomotive] tosses its mane of smoke, which lashes the glass roof of the main hall. . . . We see the vast and manic movements at the station where the ground shakes with every turn of the wheel. The platforms are sticky with soot, and the air is full of that bitter scent exuded by burning coal. As we look at this magnificent picture, we are overcome by the same feelings as if we were really there, and these feelings are perhaps even more powerful, because in the picture the artist has conveyed his own feelings as well.[3]

GUSTAVE CAILLEBOTTE Monet was not the only Impressionist who considered the buildings and streets of contemporary Paris worthy subjects for their paintings. Manet, in fact, even proposed to the municipal authorities that he decorate Paris's remodeled city hall with murals depicting the metropolis's railroad stations and other emblems of modernity. (His proposal was rejected, however.) Indeed, a common interest in subjects drawn from contemporary city life bound the Impressionists together as a group more than did shared style and technique. The work of GUSTAVE CAILLEBOTTE (1849–1893), the heir to a fortune and an early collector of Impressionist paintings, is a case in point. The brushwork in his 1877 *Paris: A Rainy Day* (FIG. 28-5) bears little resemblance to Monet's or Manet's, but the subject is unmistakably Impressionist.

MAP 28-1 France around 1870 with towns along the Seine.

The setting of Caillebotte's painting is a junction of new boulevards resulting from the redesigning of Paris begun in 1852. The city's population had reached close to 1.5 million by midcentury and nearly doubled by 1900. To accommodate this congregation of humanity and relieve the overcrowding that many believed was a major cause of the cholera epidemic of 1849—and to facilitate the movement of troops in the event of another revolution—Napoleon III ordered Paris rebuilt. The emperor named Baron Georges Haussmann (1809–1891), superintendent of the Seine district, to oversee

28-5 GUSTAVE CAILLEBOTTE, *Paris: A Rainy Day,* 1877. Oil on canvas, 6′ 9″ × 9′ 9″. Art Institute of Chicago, Chicago (Worcester Fund).

Although Caillebotte did not use Impressionistic broken brushstrokes, in his view of the new "Haussmannized" Paris, the composition featuring cutoff buildings and figures suggests the transitory nature of modern life.

1 ft.

28-6 CAMILLE PISSARRO, *La Place du Théâtre Français,* 1898. Oil on canvas, 2′ 4 ½″ × 3′ ½″. Los Angeles County Museum of Art, Los Angeles (Mr. and Mrs. George Gard De Sylva Collection).

This Impressionist view of a busy Paris square seen from several stories above street level has much in common with photographs, especially the flattening spatial effect of the high viewpoint.

the entire project, which the emperor hoped would establish Paris as a world capital surpassing London. In addition to new water and sewer systems, new parks and paved plazas, street lighting, and new residential and commercial buildings, a major component of the new Paris was the creation of the wide, open boulevards seen in Caillebotte's painting. These great avenues, whose construction caused the demolition of thousands of old buildings and streets, transformed medieval Paris into the present-day city, with its superb vistas and wide, uninterrupted arteries for the flow of vehicular and pedestrian traffic. Caillebotte chose to focus on these markers of the new Paris and to commemorate them in a canvas of a size that rivaled traditional history painting.

Although Caillebotte did not dissolve his image into the broken color and brushwork characteristic of Monet's version of Impressionism, his composition is, save for the central lamppost, strongly asymmetrical and in violation of academic norms of design. The major building in the painting is at the upper left, a large empty space is at the lower left, and the largest figures are at the lower right. The frame also cuts off parts of Caillebotte's figures, underscoring that the men and women in this painting are moving and that this is a transitory moment in the life of the city and its residents. Significantly, those residents are all well-dressed Parisians of the leisure class—the only ones who could afford to live in the elegant new neighborhoods that Haussmann created. Thus, despite the sharp focus of *Paris: A Rainy Day,* the picture is the artist's "impression" of modern urban life. In fact, many city dwellers of the time complained that the new Paris was too impersonal and anonymous. Caillebotte incorporated that less celebratory view of the city by showing the pedestrians moving through Haussmann's Paris on a dreary, rainy day and by depicting all of them in similar dress and carrying identical umbrellas.

CAMILLE PISSARRO Other Impressionists also found the spacious boulevards and avenues that were the result of the "Haussmannization" of Paris attractive subjects for paintings. *La Place du Théâtre Français* (FIG. 28-6) is one of many panoramic scenes of the city painted by CAMILLE PISSARRO (1830–1903), the only Jewish member of the Impressionist movement and the only painter to submit his work to all eight Impressionist exhibitions. Born in the Danish West Indies, he settled in Paris in 1855 and was largely self-taught. Pissarro's approach to recording the new look of Paris was quite different from Caillebotte's. Using larger, rougher brushstrokes and a brighter palette, Pisarro captured his visual sensations of a crowded Parisian square viewed from several stories above street level. Unlike Monet, Pissarro did not seek to record fugitive light effects as much as the fleeting motion of street life, which he achieved through a seemingly casual arrangement of figures and horse-drawn carriages. Ironically, to accomplish this sense of spontaneity, Pissarro sometimes used photography to record the places he wished to paint, as did many of his fellow Impressionists. Indeed, the visual parallels between Impressionist paintings and photographs are striking, including, in *La Place du Théâtre Français,* the flattening spatial effect produced by the high viewpoint.

PIERRE-AUGUSTE RENOIR Ample time for leisure activities was another facet of the new, industrialized Paris, and, as noted in the opening discussion of Manet's *A Bar at the Folies-Bergère* (see page 841 and FIG. 28-1), scenes of dining and dancing, café-concerts, opera, ballet, and other forms of urban recreation became mainstays of Impressionism. Although seemingly unrelated, industrialization facilitated these pursuits. With the widespread adoption of set working hours, people's schedules became more regimented, enabling them to plan their favorite pastimes. One Impressionist

ARTISTS ON ART
Renoir on the Art of Painting

Many 19th-century artists were concerned with the theoretical basis of picture making. One of the most cogent statements on this subject is Pierre-Auguste Renoir's concise summary of how he, as an Impressionist, painted pictures and what he hoped to achieve as an artist.

> I arrange my subject as I want it, then I go ahead and paint it, like a child. I want a red to be sonorous, to sound like a bell; if it doesn't turn out that way, I add more reds and other colors until I get it. I am no cleverer than that. I have no rules and no methods; . . . I have no secrets. I look at a nude; there are myriads of tiny tints. I must find the ones that will make the flesh on my canvas live and quiver. [I]f they could explain a picture, it wouldn't be art. Shall I tell you what I think are the two qualities of art? It must be indescribable and it must be inimitable. . . . The work of art must seize upon you, wrap you up in itself, carry you away. It is the means by which the artist conveys his passions. . . . I want people to feel that neither the setting nor the figures are dull and lifeless.*

*Quoted in Eric Protter, ed., *Painters on Painting* (New York: Grosset & Dunlap, 1971), 145.

There is certainly nothing dull or lifeless about *Dance at Le Moulin de la Galette* (FIG. **28-7**), in which Renoir depicted throngs of ordinary working-class people gathered in the popular Parisian dance hall of that name. Some crowd the tables and chatter, while others dance energetically. So lively is the atmosphere that the viewer can virtually hear the sounds of music, laughter, and tinkling glasses. Unlike Manet's Folies-Bergère, a nightclub where people went to seek a new mate or the company of a prostitute, the Moulin de la Galette (Cake Mill) was a gathering place for friends, here seen on a sunny Sunday afternoon, their only day off from work. Renoir dappled the whole scene with sunlight and shade, artfully blurred into the figures to produce precisely the effect of floating and fleeting light that the Impressionists cultivated. The casual poses and asymmetrical placement of the figures and the suggested continuity of space, spreading in all directions and only accidentally limited by the frame, position the viewer as a participant rather than as an outsider. Whereas the artists favored by the French Academy frequently sought to express universal and timeless qualities (Baudelaire's "other half of art;" see page 841), the Impressionists attempted to depict just the opposite— the incidental, momentary, and passing aspects of reality. For Renoir's friends, that "reality" rang true. Several of them posed for individual figures in the painting.

28-7 PIERRE-AUGUSTE RENOIR, *Dance at Le Moulin de la Galette,* 1876. Oil on canvas, 4' 3" × 5' 8". Musée d'Orsay, Paris.

Renoir's painting of this popular Parisian dance hall is dappled by sunlight and shade, artfully blurred into the figures to produce the effect of floating and fleeting light that many Impressionists cultivated.

1 in. I

28-8 EDGAR DEGAS, *The Rehearsal,* 1874. Oil on canvas, 1' 11" × 2' 9". Glasgow Art Galleries and Museum, Glasgow (Burrell Collection).

Degas favored subjects, such as the Paris ballet, that gave him the opportunity to study the human body in motion. The high viewpoint and off-center placement of figures are characteristic aspects of his work.

who turned repeatedly to Parisian cafés and clubs for the subjects of his canvases was PIERRE-AUGUSTE RENOIR (1841–1919), whose father and mother, a tailor and dressmaker in Limoges, moved their large family to Paris in 1844 in search of a better future—the kind of individual decision that, multiplied hundreds of thousands of times, caused the population boom in Paris. Renoir trained as a porcelain painter and then entered the École des Beaux-Arts in 1862. In Paris, he met several of the Impressionists and, in 1874, painted en plein air alongside Monet and Manet at Argenteuil (FIG. 28-2B). In addition to achieving a reputation as one of the leading Impressionist painters, Renoir also became one of the most eloquent writers on the aims of Impressionism (see "Renoir on the Art of Painting," page 848). His *Dance at Le Moulin de la Galette* (FIG. 28-7) of 1876, shown in the third Impressionist exhibition, is a prime example of an Impressionist canvas portraying ordinary Parisians at leisure on Sunday afternoon at an open-air dance club. It was one of the paintings that Caillebotte purchased for himself and bequeathed to France in his will.

EDGAR DEGAS Dancing of a very different kind—ballet—was one of the favorite subjects of EDGAR DEGAS (1834–1917), the eldest son of a wealthy banker, who studied painting with a pupil of Ingres, attended the École des Beaux-Arts, and traveled extensively in Italy, but eventually rejected classicism in favor of Impressionism—or, at least, in favor of Impressionist subject matter. Unlike Monet, who personifies Impressionism for most museum-goers, Degas was not concerned with light and atmosphere. Indeed, he specialized in indoor subjects and made many preliminary studies for his finished paintings. Degas's interests were primarily recording body movement and exploring unusual angles of viewing. He was fascinated by

the formalized patterns of motion of the classical ballet performed at the Paris Opéra (FIG. 27-45) and with the training of ballerinas at its ballet school.

The Rehearsal (FIG. 28-8) is perhaps Degas's finest painting of this genre. In it and similar works, he recorded with care the unstable postures of the ballerinas, who stretch, bend, and swivel. But most of the dancers are hidden from the viewer by other figures or by the spiral stairway at the left. *The Rehearsal* is the antithesis of a classically balanced composition. The center is empty, and the floor takes up most of the canvas surface. At the margins, Degas arranged the ballerinas and their teachers in a seemingly random manner. As in other Impressionist paintings, the cutting off of figures at the left and right enhances the sense that the viewer is witnessing a fleeting moment. The implied position of that viewer is in a balcony looking down at the figures, as opposed to the head-on views of statuesque figures that were the norm in traditional paintings.

Because of his interest in patterns of movement, Degas became fascinated by photography and regularly used a camera to make preliminary studies for his works. Japanese *woodblock* prints, such as those by Suzuki Harunobu (FIG. 34-1), were another inspirational source for paintings such as *The Rehearsal.* Japanese artists used diverging lines not only to organize the flat shapes of figures but also to direct the viewer's attention into the picture space. The Impressionists, and later the Post-Impressionists, who became acquainted with these prints as early as the 1860s, greatly admired the spatial organization, familiar and intimate themes, and flat unmodeled color areas of the Japanese prints, and Degas and others avidly incorporated these features into their own paintings (see "Japonisme," page 850).

ART AND SOCIETY

Japonisme

Despite Europe's and America's extensive colonization in Asia, as elsewhere, during the 19th century, Japan's interactions with the West were very limited until 1853–1854, when Commodore Matthew Perry (1794–1858) and American naval forces exacted trading and diplomatic privileges from the Japanese court. Only then did Europeans become familiar with Japanese culture and Japanese art. The French in particular became so intrigued with everything Japanese that they coined a specific term—*Japonisme*—to describe the Japanese aesthetic, which, because of both its beauty and its exoticism, greatly appealed to the fashionable segment of Parisian society. In 1867 at the Exposition Universelle in Paris, the Japanese pavilion garnered enormous interest. Soon, Japanese kimonos, fans, lacquer cabinets, tea caddies, folding screens, tea services, and jewelry flooded Paris. Japanese-themed novels and travel books were immensely popular as well. As demand for Japanese merchandise grew in the West, the Japanese began to develop import-export businesses, and the foreign currency flowing into Japan helped finance much of its industrialization.

Artists in particular were great admirers of Japanese art. Among those influenced by the Japanese aesthetic were the Impressionists and Post-Impressionists, especially Manet, Degas, Mary Cassatt, James Abbott McNeill Whistler, Henri de Toulouse-Lautrec, Paul Gauguin,

and Vincent van Gogh. Indeed, van Gogh collected and copied Japanese prints (FIG. 28-17B; compare FIG. 34-14), which were more readily available in the West than any other Asian art form. The Japanese presentation of space in woodblock prints (see "Japanese Woodblock Prints," page 1007) intrigued these artists. Because of the simplicity of the woodblock printing process, the Japanese prints feature broad areas of flat color with a limited amount of modulation or gradation. This flatness captured the imagination of modernist painters, who were seeking ways to call attention to the picture surface. The right side of Degas's *The Tub* (FIG. 28-9), for example, has this two-dimensional quality. Degas, in fact, owned a print by Japanese artist Torii Kiyonaga depicting eight women at a bath in various poses and states of undress. That print inspired Degas's painting. A comparison between Degas's bather and a detail (FIG. 28-10) of a bather from another of Kiyonaga's prints is striking, although Degas did not closely copy any of the Japanese artist's figures. But he did emulate Japanese compositional style and the distinctive angles that Japanese printmakers employed in representing human figures.

The decorative quality of Japanese images also appealed to the artists associated with the Arts and Crafts movement in England. Artists such as William Morris (FIG. 28-36) and Charles Rennie Mackintosh (FIG. 28-37) found Japanese prints attractive because those artworks intersected nicely with two fundamental Arts and Crafts principles: art should be available to the masses, and functional objects should be artistically designed.

28-9 Edgar Degas, *The Tub*, 1886. Pastel, 1' 11½" × 2' 8⅜". Musée d'Orsay, Paris.

The Tub reveals the influence of Japanese prints, especially the sharp angles that artists such as Kiyonaga used in representing figures. Degas translated his Japanese model into the Impressionist mode.

28-10 Torii Kiyonaga, detail of *Two Women at the Bath*, ca. 1780. Color woodblock print; full print 10½" × 7½", detail 3¾" × 3½". Musée Guimet, Paris.

THE TUB The impact of Japanese prints on Degas is evident in *The Tub* (FIG. 28-9), inspired by a Japanese woodblock print similar to the one illustrated here (FIG. 28-10) by Torii Kiyonaga (1752–1815). In Degas's picture, a young woman crouches in a tub as she washes her neck with a sponge, unaware of the viewer's presence (also the case with the dancers in *The Rehearsal*). The angle of vision is so sharp that the floor and the tabletop or shelf at the right almost seem to be vertical surfaces parallel to the picture plane. Degas's combination of

Whistler on "Artistic Arrangements"

Underscoring the emerging modernist idea, both in Europe and America, that paintings are independent two-dimensional artworks and not windows opening onto the three-dimensional world, American-born James Abbott McNeil Whistler, who produced his most famous works in London, named many of his paintings not according to the subjects they depicted but in abstract terms—for example, "arrangements" or "nocturnes." *Nocturne in Black and Gold* (FIG. 28-11) is a daring painting with gold flecks and splatters representing an exploded firework punctuating the darkness of the night sky. More interested in conveying the atmospheric effects than in providing details of the scene, Whistler emphasized creating a harmonious arrangement of shapes and colors on the rectangle of his canvas, an approach that many 20th-century artists adopted. Whistler's works angered conservative 19th-century critics, however. In England, John Ruskin (1819–1900) responded to *Nocturne in Black and Gold* by writing a scathing review accusing Whistler of "flinging a pot of paint in the public's face." In reply, Whistler sued Ruskin for libel. During the trial, Ruskin's attorney asked Whistler about the subject of *Nocturne*:

"What is your definition of a Nocturne?"

"It is an arrangement of line, form, and color first; . . . Among my works are some night pieces; and I have chosen the word Nocturne because it generalizes and amplifies the whole set of them. . . . The nocturne in black and gold is a night piece and represents the fireworks at Cremorne [Gardens in London]."

"Not a view of Cremorne?"

"If it were a view of Cremorne, it would certainly bring about nothing but disappointment on the part of the beholders. It is an artistic arrangement."*

The court transcript notes that the spectators in the courtroom laughed at that response, but Whistler won the case. However, his victory had sadly ironic consequences for him. The judge in the case, showing where his—and the public's—sympathies lay, awarded the artist only one farthing (less than a penny) in damages and required him to pay all of the court costs, which ruined him financially.

28-11 JAMES ABBOTT MCNEILL WHISTLER, *Nocturne in Black and Gold* (*The Falling Rocket*), ca. 1875. Oil on panel, 1' 11$\frac{5}{8}$" × 1' 6$\frac{1}{2}$". Detroit Institute of Arts, Detroit (gift of Dexter M. Ferry Jr.).

In this painting, Whistler displayed an Impressionist's interest in conveying the atmospheric effects of fireworks at night, but he also emphasized the abstract arrangement of shapes and colors.

*Quoted in Charles Harrison, Paul Wood, and Jason Gaiger, *Art in Theory, 1815–1900* (Oxford: Blackwell, 1998), 835–836.

the fully modeled figure of the bather and the flatness of the tub and shelf creates a visual perplexity fully consistent with the modernist exploration of the tension between illusionism and the acknowledgment that painting is a two-dimensional art form.

JAMES WHISTLER One of the important American expatriate artists in Europe during the closing decades of the 19th century was JAMES ABBOTT MCNEILL WHISTLER (1834–1903), who spent time in Paris before settling finally in London. He met several of the French Impressionists, and his art—for example, *Nocturne in Black and Gold,* or *The Falling Rocket* (FIG. 28-11)—incorporates some of their concerns and his own. Whistler shared the Impressionists' fondness for recording contemporary life and the sensations that color produces on the eye. To these interests he added his own

desire to create harmonies paralleling those achieved in music (see "Whistler on 'Artistic Arrangements,'" above). He believed that

Nature contains the elements, in color and form, of all pictures, as the keyboard contains the notes of all music. But the artist is born to pick, and choose, and group with science, these elements, that the result may be beautiful—as the musician gathers his notes, and forms his chords, until he brings forth from chaos glorious harmony.[4]

CASSATT AND MORISOT The Impressionists were a diverse group of artists, women as well as men, from disparate economic, social, national, and religious backgrounds, united by a shared interest in the modern world that they experienced daily and a distaste for the stylistic constraints and restricted themes of academic art. The

Women Impressionists

Two of the best-known Impressionists were women. Although they came from very different backgrounds and their paintings could never be confused, both Mary Cassatt and Berthe Morisot brought a distinctively feminine viewpoint to their work, especially with regard to the subjects they chose and the way they portrayed women.

Cassatt, the daughter of a wealthy Philadelphia banker, was fortunate to live at a time when formerly all-male American colleges and art academies were opening their doors to women. She trained at the Pennsylvania Academy of the Fine Arts and then moved to Europe to study masterworks in France and Italy. Cassatt came to the attention of Degas when he saw a painting of hers in the Salon of 1874. Thereafter, she exhibited regularly with the Impressionists, but as a woman, she could not easily frequent the cafés with her male artist friends, and she had the responsibility of caring for her aging parents, who had moved to Paris to join her. Because of these restrictions, Cassatt's subjects were principally women and children, whom she presented with a combination of objectivity and genuine sentiment.

Cassatt's *The Child's Bath* (FIG. **28-12**) invites comparison with Degas's *The Tub* (FIG. 28-9). The two paintings have much in common stylistically. As in Degas's painting, the unseen artist looks down at the bathing scene from above and, similar to the contrast between the bather and the shelf in *The Tub*, the visual solidity of Cassatt's mother and child contrasts with the flattened patterning of the wallpaper and rug. Indeed, *The Child's Bath* owes much to the compositional devices of

1 ft.

28-12 MARY CASSATT, *The Child's Bath*, 1893. Oil on canvas, 3' 3½" × 2' 2". Art Institute of Chicago, Chicago (Robert A. Walker Fund).

Cassatt's compositions owe much to Degas and Japanese prints, but her subjects differ from those of most Impressionists, in part because, as a woman, she could not frequent cafés with her male friends.

two most accomplished Impressionist women were MARY CASSATT (1844–1926), an American, who painted *The Child's Bath* (FIG. 28-12), and Frenchwoman BERTHE MORISOT (1841–1895), two of whose best paintings are *Summer's Day* (FIG. 28-13) and *In a Villa at the Seaside* (FIG. 28-13A). Their works, while having much in common with those of their male colleagues, differed from the paintings of Monet, Renoir, Degas, and the other Impressionists in important ways (see "Women Impressionists," pages 852–853).

POST-IMPRESSIONISM

By the mid-1880s, just as the Impressionists' sketchlike paintings of contemporary life in and around Paris were gaining wider acceptance, a group of younger painters—and even some of the Impressionists themselves—came to feel that in attempting to capture momentary sensations of light and color on canvas, too many important elements of traditional painting were being sacrificed. For example, in a conversation with the influential art dealer Ambroise Vollard (1866–1939) in about 1883, Renoir commented: "I had wrung Impressionism dry, and I finally came to the conclusion that I knew neither how to paint nor how to draw. In a word, Impressionism was a blind alley, as far as I was concerned."[5] Renoir's work took a different turn at that point, and other artists began to

examine more systematically the properties and expressive qualities of line, pattern, form, and color. Among them were Dutch-born Vincent van Gogh and the French painter Paul Gauguin, who focused their artistic efforts on exploring the expressive capabilities of formal elements, and Georges Seurat and Paul Cézanne, also from France, who were more analytical in orientation. Because their art had its roots in Impressionist precepts and methods, but was not stylistically homogeneous, these artists and others, including Henri de Toulouse-Lautrec, became known as the *Post-Impressionists*.

HENRI DE TOULOUSE-LAUTREC One Post-Impressionist who shared the keen interest of some of the Impressionists in Parisian nightlife was HENRI DE TOULOUSE-LAUTREC (1864–1901). His work, however, has an added satirical edge to it and often borders on caricature. Descended from the medieval counts of Toulouse, Toulouse-Lautrec began to paint as a child (his father and uncles were all amateur artists). He moved to Paris in 1882 and studied with two little-known painters, and in 1884, he set up his own studio in the Montmartre district. Genetic defects had stunted his growth and partially crippled him, leading to his self-exile from the high society that his ancient aristocratic name and wealth entitled him to enter. In Paris, he instead embraced the bohemian lifestyle and frequented Montmartre's cafés, dance halls, theaters, and brothels.

28-13 BERTHE MORISOT, *Summer's Day*, 1879. Oil on canvas, 1' 5$\frac{3}{4}$" × 2' 5$\frac{3}{8}$". National Gallery, London (Lane Bequest, 1917).

Morisot's subject (Parisians at leisure), bright palette, and sketchy brushstrokes typify Impressionism, but the people who inhabit her paintings are almost exclusively well-dressed, thoughtful women.

1 in.

Degas as well as to Degas's sources—Japanese prints. But rather than providing a view of a nude woman unaware of the male artist-voyeur who has intruded into her private sphere, Cassatt's canvas celebrates the tender relationship between a mother and her child, both of whom gaze at their joint reflection in the tub of water.

In contrast to the expatriate American Cassatt, Morisot was raised in an upper-middle-class home in Paris, and she could not study painting at the École des Beaux-Arts because the European academies were still closed to women. Instead, she and her sister Edma took lessons from a private tutor. Berthe enjoyed some early success exhibiting in the official salons, but after meeting Édouard Manet in late 1867 or 1868 (she married his brother Eugène in 1874), she came in contact with the Impressionists and submitted nine paintings to their first exhibition in 1874 and many more to all but one of the next seven Impressionist shows.

Morisot's subject matter—the leisure activities of Parisians at resorts along the Seine or in Paris's great park called the Bois de

Boulogne—typifies the interests of many of the Impressionists. But the people who inhabit her canvases are almost exclusively women and their children, always well dressed and thoughtful, never frivolous or objects of male desire. *Summer's Day* (FIG. 28-13), originally titled *The Lake of the Bois de Boulogne* and shown in the fifth Impressionist exhibition of 1880, depicts two women in a boat on that lake. It is similar in spirit to Claude Monet's *On the Bank of the Seine, Bennecourt* (FIG. 28-2A), but Morisot's focus is the women, not the setting. Morisot herself is in the same boat, unseen, and she represented the women at a sharp angle, with parts of their bodies and most of the boat cut off by the frame, using the compositional format pioneered by Edgar Degas (FIG. 28-8) and adopted also by Cassatt. As in her other works (FIG. 28-13A), Morisot rejected contour lines in favor of patches of color that define the shapes of her figures. The sketchy brushstrokes used to paint the women merge with those of the water, unifying figure and ground in a striking two-dimensional composition that also captures all the freshness of a brightly lit summer day en plein air.

28-13A MORISOT, *Villa at the Seaside*, 1874.

He became a denizen of the night world, consorting with the underclass of entertainers, prostitutes, and other social outcasts, bringing his sketchbook everywhere, and drinking heavily. Before dying of alcoholism at age 37, Toulouse-Lautrec devoted his brief career to depicting the city's after-hours entertainment centers, such as the Moulin Rouge (Red Mill), the subject of one of his best paintings.

At the Moulin Rouge (FIG. 28-14) reveals the influences of Degas, of Japanese prints, and of photography in the oblique and asymmetrical composition, the spatial diagonals, and the strong line patterns with added dissonant colors. But although Toulouse-Lautrec based everything he painted on firsthand

1 ft.

28-14 HENRI DE TOULOUSE-LAUTREC, *At the Moulin Rouge*, 1892–1895. Oil on canvas, 4' × 4' 7". Art Institute of Chicago, Chicago (Helen Birch Bartlett Memorial Collection).

Toulouse-Lautrec devoted his brief career to depicting the bohemian lifestyle of Paris at night. The oblique composition, glaring lighting, masklike faces, and dissonant colors of *Moulin Rouge* typify his work.

observation, and the scenes he captured were already familiar to viewers in the work of the Impressionists, he so emphasized or exaggerated each element that the tone is new. Compare, for instance, the mood of *At the Moulin Rouge* with the relaxed and casual atmosphere of Renoir's *Dance at Le Moulin de la Galette* (FIG. 28-7). Toulouse-Lautrec's scene is decadent nightlife, with its glaring artificial light, brassy music, and assortment of corrupt, cruel, and masklike faces. (He included himself in the background—the diminutive man wearing a derby hat accompanying the very tall man, his cousin.) Such distortions by simplification of the figures and faces anticipated Expressionism (see page 885), when artists' use of formal elements—for example, brighter colors and bolder lines than ever before—increased the effect of the images on observers.

POSTER ART Toulouse-Lautrec produced many of his major works using oil-based paints on canvas, the preferred medium of Western art since the Renaissance (see "Tempera and Oil Painting," page 559), but he experimented with other media. Most notably, he explored the new art form of the poster, made possible by the perfection of multicolor lithography (see "Lithography," page 819) in the late 1870s and the development of printing presses capable of handling extra-large sheets of paper. Toulouse-Lautrec became the first great master of poster art, receiving numerous commissions from the concert-hall proprietors he befriended.

Jane Avril (FIG. 28-15), a five-color lithographic poster that appeared on hundreds of walls and windows in Paris in 1893, advertises the celebrated dancer who performed at the Jardin de Paris (Garden of Paris) cabaret. The composition reveals Toulouse-Lautrec's debt to Degas (FIGS. 28-8 and 28-9) in its oblique view from above, exaggerated foreshortening, and figures cut off by the frame. Most severely truncated is the bass viol player at the lower right, whom the artist reduced to a forearm and head and the upper part of his instrument. In fact, the musician and viol became in Toulouse-Lautrec's hands almost abstract shapes, and the lines extending from the instrument became the frame for the figure of Avril, whose left leg, kicking in the air, redirects the viewer's attention to the viol player. The composition, and especially the flat colors within prominent outlines, also owes a great deal to Japanese woodblock prints (FIGS. 34-1 and 34-12A), which late-19th-century French artists collected and admired (see "Japonisme," page 850) and even copied (FIG. 28-17B).

GEORGES SEURAT Of much more modest ancestry was the regrettably short-lived GEORGES SEURAT (1859–1891), the son of a customs official. He studied at the École des Beaux-Arts under one of Ingres's pupils, but was more intrigued by Delacroix's use of color. The subjects of Seurat's paintings of the 1880s were essentially Impressionist themes, but unlike the Impressionists and Toulouse-Lautrec, Seurat depicted modern life in a resolutely intellectual way. He devised a disciplined and painstaking system of painting focused on color analysis. Seurat was less concerned with the recording of immediate color sensations than he was with their careful and systematic organization into a new kind of pictorial order. He disciplined the free and fluent play of color characterizing Impressionism into a calculated arrangement based on scientific color theory. Seurat's system, which he called *divisionism,* but which is better known as *pointillism,* involves carefully observing color and separating it into its component parts (see "Pointillism and 19th-Century Color Theory," page 855). The artist then applies these pure component colors to the canvas in tiny dots (points) or daubs. Thus the shapes, figures, and spaces in the image become comprehensible only from a distance, when the viewer's eyes blend the many pigment dots.

1 ft.

28-15 HENRI DE TOULOUSE-LAUTREC, *Jane Avril,* 1893. Color lithograph, 4' 2½" × 3' 1". San Diego Museum of Art, San Diego (gift of the Baldwin M. Baldwin Foundation).

Multicolor lithography made possible posters such as those Toulouse-Lautrec created to advertise Parisian nightclubs. The composition of *Jane Avril* owes a debt to Degas and Japanese prints.

Seurat introduced pointillism to the French public at the eighth and last Impressionist exhibition in 1886, where he displayed *A Sunday on La Grande Jatte* (FIGS. 28-16 and 28-17). According to one report, the painting attracted huge crowds, and it was impossible to get close enough to study it. La Grande Jatte (The Big Bowl) is an island in the Seine River near Asnières, one of late-19th-century Paris's rapidly growing industrial suburbs. It is the setting for a typically Impressionist recreational theme, populated by "modern people" from various classes and wearing different kinds of clothes. A sleeveless worker lounges in the left foreground next to a middle-class couple. In the center is a little girl in a spotless white dress accompanied by her fashionably attired nanny. Also present is a woman with a monkey on a leash who is almost certainly a prostitute. In short, the Sunday visitors to La Grande Jatte are a cross-section of Parisian society in the 1880s.

Seurat also shared the Impressionists' interest in analyzing light and color. But his rendition of Parisians at leisure is rigid and impersonal, unlike the spontaneous representations of Impressionism. Seurat's pointillism (FIG. 28-16) produced a carefully composed and painted image, in sharp contrast to Impressionist "sketches," incorporating repeated motifs—for example, similarly dressed women, identical parasols—to establish a rhythmic movement across the

MATERIALS AND TECHNIQUES
Pointillism and 19th-Century Color Theory

In the 19th century, advances in the sciences contributed to changing theories about color and how people perceive it. Many physicists and chemists immersed themselves in studying optical reception and the behavior of the human eye in response to light of differing wavelengths. They also investigated the psychological dimension of color. These new ideas about color and its perception provided a framework within which artists such as Georges Seurat (FIGS. 28-16 and 28-17) worked. Although historians do not know which publications on color Seurat himself read, he no doubt relied on aspects of these evolving theories to develop *pointillism*.

Discussions of color often focus on *hue* (for example, red, yellow, and blue), but it is important to consider the other facets of color— *saturation* (the hue's brightness or dullness) and *value* (the hue's lightness or darkness). Most artists during the 19th century understood the concepts of *primary colors* (red, yellow, and blue), *secondary colors* (orange, purple, and green), and *complementary colors* (red and green, yellow and purple, blue and orange; see page 7).

Chemist Michel-Eugène Chevreul (1786–1889) extended artists' understanding of color dynamics by formulating the law of *simultaneous contrasts* of colors. Chevreul asserted that juxtaposed colors affect the eye's reception of each, making the two colors as dissimilar as possible, both in hue and value. For example, placing light green next to dark green has the effect of making the light green look even lighter and the dark green darker. Chevreul further provided an explanation of *successive contrasts*—the phenomenon of colored afterimages. When a person looks intently at a color (green, for example) and then shifts to a white area, the fatigued eye momentarily perceives the complementary color (red).

Charles Blanc (1813–1882), who coined the term *optical mixture* to describe the visual effect of juxtaposed complementary colors, asserted that the smaller the areas of adjoining complementary colors, the greater the tendency for the eye to "mix" the colors, so that

28-16 Detail of *A Sunday on La Grande Jatte* (FIG. 28-17).

Seurat's color system— pointillism—involved dividing colors into their component parts and applying those colors to the canvas in tiny dots. The forms become comprehensible only from a distance.

the viewer perceives a grayish or neutral tint. Seurat used this principle frequently in his paintings.

Also influential for Seurat was the work of physicist Ogden Rood (1831–1902), who published his ideas in *Modern Chromatics, with Applications to Art and Industry* in 1879. Expanding on the ideas of Chevreul and Blanc, Rood constructed an accurate and understandable diagram of contrasting colors. Further (and particularly significant to Seurat), Rood explored representing color gradation. He suggested that artists could achieve gradation by placing small dots or lines of color side by side, which he observed blended in the eye of the beholder when viewed from a distance.

The color experiments of Seurat and other late-19th-century artists were also part of a larger discourse about human vision and how people see and understand the world. The theories of physicist Ernst Mach (1838–1916) focused on the psychological experience of sensation. He believed that humans perceive their environments in isolated units of sensation that the brain then recomposes into a comprehensible world. Another scientist, Charles Henry (1859–1926), also pursued research into the psychological dimension of color—how colors affect people, and under what conditions. He went even further to explore the physiological effects of perception. Seurat's work, though characterized by a systematic and scientifically minded approach, also incorporated his concerns about the emotional tone of the images.

1 ft.

28-17 GEORGES SEURAT, *A Sunday on La Grande Jatte*, 1884–1886. Oil on canvas, 6' 9" × 10'. Art Institute of Chicago, Chicago (Helen Birch Bartlett Memorial Collection, 1926).

huge (almost 7-by-10-foot) canvas. Indeed, the scale of *A Sunday on La Grande Jatte* is firmly in the tradition of the Salon, unlike the intimate easel paintings of the Impressionists. Sunshine fills the picture, but Seurat did not break the light into transient patches of color. Light, air, people, and landscape are formal elements in an abstract design in which line, color, value, and shape cohere in a precise and tightly controlled organization.

VINCENT VAN GOGH In marked contrast to Seurat, VINCENT VAN GOGH (1853–1890) explored the capabilities of colors and distorted forms to express his emotions as he confronted nature. The son of a Dutch Protestant pastor, van Gogh believed he had a reli-gious calling and did missionary work in the coal-mining area of Belgium. Repeated professional and personal failures brought him close to despair. Only after he turned to painting did he find a way to communicate his experiences. He completed his first major work, *The Potato Eaters* (FIG. **28-17A**), when he was 32 years old. Five years later, considering himself a failure as an artist and an outcast not only from artistic circles but also from society

🔎 **28-17A** VAN GOGH, *The Potato Eaters*, 1885.

ARTISTS ON ART
The Letters of Vincent van Gogh

Throughout his life, Vincent van Gogh wrote letters to his brother Theo van Gogh (1857–1891), a Parisian art dealer, on matters both mundane and philosophical. The letters are precious documents of the vicissi-tudes of the painter's life and reveal his emotional anguish. In many of the letters, van Gogh also forcefully stated his views about art, includ-ing his admiration for Japanese prints (FIG. 28-17B). In one letter, he told Theo: "In both my life and in my painting, I can very well do without God but I cannot, ill as I am, do without something which is greater than I, . . . the power to create."*

For van Gogh, the power to create involved the expressive use of color. "Instead of trying to reproduce exactly what I have before my eyes, I use color more arbitrarily so as to express myself forcibly."† Color in painting, he argued, is "not locally true from the point of view of the delusive realist, but color suggesting some emotion of an ardent temperament."‡ "[It is better for a painter to] start from the colors on his palette than from the colors in nature. . . . I study nature, so as not to do foolish things . . . however, I don't care so much whether my color is exactly the same, as long as it looks beautiful on my canvas . . . I repeat, starting from one's palette, from one's knowledge of the harmony of colors is quite different from following nature mechanically and servilely."§

Some of van Gogh's letters con-tain vivid descriptions of his paintings, which are invaluable to art historians in gauging his intentions and judging his success. For example, about *Night Café* (FIG. **28-18**), he wrote:

> I have tried to express the terrible passions of humanity by means of red and green. The room is blood-red and dark yellow with a green billiard table in the middle; there are four citron-yellow lamps with a glow of orange and green. Everywhere there is a clash and contrast of the most disparate reds and greens in the figures of little sleeping hooligans, in the empty, dreary room, in violet and blue. The blood-red and the yellow-green of the billiard table, for instance, contrast with the soft, tender Louis XV green of the counter, on which there is a pink nosegay. The white coat of the landlord, awake in a corner of that furnace, turns citron-yellow, or pale luminous green.**

*Vincent van Gogh to Theo van Gogh, September 3, 1888, in W. H. Auden, ed., *Van Gogh: A Self-Portrait. Letters Revealing His Life as a Painter* (New York: Dutton, 1963), 319.
†August 11, 1888. Ibid., 313.
‡September 8, 1888. Ibid., 321.
§October 2, 1885. Ibid., 253–254.
**September 8, 1888. Ibid., 320.

28-18 VINCENT VAN GOGH, *Night Café*, 1888. Oil on canvas, 2' 4$\frac{1}{2}$" × 3'. Yale University Art Gallery, New Haven (bequest of Stephen Carlton Clark).

In *Night Café*, van Gogh explored ways that colors and distorted forms can express emotions. The thickness, shape, and direc-tion of the brushstrokes create a tactile counterpart to the intense colors.

1 ft.

at large, van Gogh fatally shot himself. He sold only one painting during his lifetime. Since his death, however, van Gogh's reputation and the appreciation of his art have grown dramatically. Subsequent painters, especially the Fauves and German Expressionists (see pages 883 and 885), built on van Gogh's expressive use of color. This kind of influence is an important factor in determining artistic significance, and it is no exaggeration to state that today van Gogh is one of the most revered artists in history.

NIGHT CAFÉ Van Gogh moved to Paris in 1886, where he began to collect—and copy (FIG. **28-17B**)—Japanese prints. In 1881, he relocated to Arles in southern France, where he painted *Night Café* (FIG. **28-18**), one of his most important and innovative canvases. Although the subject is apparently benign, van Gogh invested it with a charged energy. As he stated in a letter to his brother Theo (see "The Letters of Vincent van Gogh," page 856), he wanted the painting to convey an oppressive atmosphere—"a place where one can ruin one's self, go mad, or commit a crime. . . . [I want] to express the power of darkness in a low drinking spot . . . in an atmosphere like a devil's furnace."[6] The room is seen from above, and the floor takes up a large portion of the canvas, as in the paintings of Degas (FIG. 28-9). The ghostlike proprietor stands at the edge of the café's billiard table, disengaged from his customers, as they are from each other. Van Gogh depicted the billiard table in such a steeply tilted perspective that it threatens to

⬆ **28-17B** VAN GOGH, *Flowering Plum Tree*, 1887.

slide out of the painting into the viewer's space. He communicated the "madness" of the place by selecting vivid hues whose juxtaposition augmented their intensity.

Van Gogh's insistence on the expressive values of color led him to develop a corresponding expressiveness in his paint application. The thickness, shape, and direction of his brushstrokes created a tactile counterpart to his intense color schemes. He moved the brush vehemently back and forth or at right angles, giving a textilelike effect, or squeezed dots or streaks onto the canvas directly from his paint tube. This bold, almost slapdash attack enhanced the intensity of his colors.

STARRY NIGHT Similarly illustrative of van Gogh's "expressionist" method is *Starry Night* (FIG. **28-19**), which the artist painted in 1889, the year before his death. At this time, van Gogh was living at the asylum of Saint-Paul-de-Mausole in Saint-Rémy, near Arles, where he had committed himself. In *Starry Night,* the artist did not represent the sky's appearance. Rather, he communicated his feelings about the electrifying vastness of the universe, filled with whirling and exploding stars, with the earth and humanity huddling beneath it. The church nestled in the center of the village is, perhaps, van Gogh's attempt to express or reconcile his conflicted views about religion. Although the style of *Starry Night* suggests a very personal vision, this work does correspond in many ways to the view available to the painter from the window of his room in Saint-Paul-de-Mausole. The existence of cypress trees and the placement of the constellations have been confirmed as matching the view visible to van Gogh during his stay in the asylum. Still, the artist translated everything he saw into his singular vision. Given van Gogh's determination to "use color . . . to express [him]self forcibly," the dark, deep blue suffusing the entire painting cannot be overlooked.

28-19 VINCENT VAN GOGH, *Starry Night,* 1889. Oil on canvas, 2' 5" × 3' $\frac{1}{4}$". Museum of Modern Art, New York (acquired through the Lillie P. Bliss Bequest).

In this late work, van Gogh painted the vast night sky filled with whirling and exploding stars, the earth huddled beneath it. The painting is an almost abstract pattern of expressive line, shape, and color.

1 ft.

Together with the turbulent brushstrokes, the color suggests a quiet but pervasive depression. A letter van Gogh wrote to his brother on July 16, 1888, reveals his contemplative state of mind:

> Perhaps death is not the hardest thing in a painter's life. . . . [L]ooking at the stars always makes me dream, as simply as I dream over the black dots representing towns and villages on a map. Why, I ask myself, shouldn't the shining dots of the sky be as accessible as the black dots on the map of France? Just as we take the train to get to Tarascon or Rouen, we take death to reach a star.[7]

PAUL GAUGUIN Until he lost his job in the stock market crash of 1882, PAUL GAUGUIN (1848–1903) was a stockbroker in Paris. In 1883, penniless, he decided to try to make his living as an artist, having painted as an amateur for many years. Three years later, attracted by Brittany's unspoiled culture, its ancient Celtic folkways, the still-medieval Catholic piety of its people, and its much lower cost of living, Gauguin moved to Pont-Aven, which had become a popular artists' colony. Although in the 1870s and 1880s, Brittany had been transformed into a profitable market economy focused on tourism, Gauguin still viewed the Bretons as "natural" men and women, perfectly at ease in what he regarded as their unspoiled peasant environment.

At Pont-Aven, Gauguin painted *Vision after the Sermon* (FIG. 28-20), also known as *Jacob Wrestling with the Angel,* his most important early work. The painting shows Breton women, wearing their starched white Sunday caps and black dresses, visualizing the sermon they have just heard in church on Jacob's encounter with the Holy Spirit (Gen. 32:24–30). Joining the women, at the far right, is a tonsured monk who has Gauguin's features. The women and the monk pray devoutly before the apparition, as they would have before the roadside crucifix shrines that were characteristic features of the Breton countryside. Gauguin departed from optical realism and composed the picture elements to focus the viewer's attention on the idea and intensify its message. The images are not what the Impressionist eye would have seen and replicated but what Gauguin's memory recalled and his imagination modified. Thus the artist twisted the perspective and allotted most of the space to emphasize the innocent faith of the unquestioning women, and he shrank Jacob and the angel, wrestling in a ring enclosed by a Breton stone fence. Wrestling matches were regular features at the entertainment held after high mass, so Gauguin's women are spectators at a contest that was, for them, a familiar part of their culture.

28-20 PAUL GAUGUIN, *Vision after the Sermon* (*Jacob Wrestling with the Angel*), 1888. Oil on canvas, 2' 4 $\frac{3}{4}$" × 3' $\frac{1}{2}$". National Gallery of Scotland, Edinburgh.

Gauguin admired Japanese prints, stained glass, and cloisonné enamels. Their influences are evident in this painting of Breton women, in which firm outlines enclose large areas of unmodulated color.

Gauguin did not unify the picture with a horizon perspective, light and shade, or naturalistic use of color. Instead, he abstracted the scene into a pattern, with the diagonal tree limb symbolically dividing the spiritual from the earthly realm. Pure unmodulated color fills flat planes and shapes bounded by firm line: white caps, black dresses, and the red field of combat. Gauguin admired Japanese prints and medieval *cloisonné* metalwork (see "Cloisonné," page 313) and *stained glass* (see "Stained-Glass Windows," page 384). These art forms contributed significantly to his daring experiment to transform traditional painting and Impressionism into abstract, expressive patterns of line, shape, and pure color. Like van Gogh, with whom he painted for a brief period in Arles in 1888, Gauguin rejected objective representation in favor of subjective expression. For Gauguin, the artist's power to determine the colors in a painting was a central element of creativity. However, whereas van Gogh's heavy, thick brushstrokes were an important component of his expressive style, Gauguin's color areas appear flatter, often visually dissolving into abstract patches or patterns.

WHERE DO WE COME FROM? In 1888, Gauguin, continuing his restless search for an inexpensive and unspoiled place to live, settled in Tahiti (MAP 36-1). The Polynesian island attracted Gauguin because he believed that it offered him a life far removed from materialistic Europe as well as an opportunity to reconnect with nature. On his arrival, he discovered that Tahiti, under French control since 1842, had been extensively colonized and that its capital, Papeete, was filthy and dangerous. Deeply disappointed, Gauguin tried to maintain his vision of an untamed paradise by moving to the Tahitian countryside, where he expressed his fascination with primitive life in a series of canvases in which he often based the design, though indirectly, on native motifs. The tropical flora of the island inspired the colors he chose for these paintings—unusual harmonies of lilac, pink, and lemon.

1 ft.

ARTISTS ON ART

Gauguin on *Where Do We Come From?*

Paul Gauguin's *Where Do We Come From? What Are We? Where Are We Going?* (FIG. 28-21), painted in Tahiti in 1897, was, in the artist's judgment, his most important work. The scene is a tropical landscape, populated with native women and children. Despite the setting, most of the canvas surface, other than the figures, consists of broad areas of flat color, which convey a lushness and intensity.

Two of Gauguin's letters to friends contain lengthy discussions of this work and shed important light on the artist's intentions and on the painting's meaning.

> Where are we going? Near to death an old woman. . . . What are we? Day to day existence. . . . Where do we come from? Source. Child. Life begins. . . . Behind a tree two sinister figures, cloaked in garments of somber color, introduce, near the tree of knowledge, their note of anguish caused by that very knowledge in contrast to some simple beings in a virgin nature, which might be paradise as conceived by humanity, who give themselves up to the happiness of living.*

> I wanted to kill myself. I went to hide in the mountains, where my corpse would have been eaten up by ants. I didn't have a revolver but I did have arsenic . . . Was the dose too large, or was it the fact of vomiting, which overcame the effects of the poison by getting rid of it? I know not. . . . . Before I died I wanted to paint a large canvas that I had worked out in my head, and all month long I worked day

and night at fever pitch. I can assure you it's nothing like a canvas by Puvis de Chavannes [FIG. 28-24], with studies from nature, then a preparatory cartoon, etc. No, it's all done without a model, feeling my way with the tip of the brush on a piece of sackcloth that is full of knots and rough patches; so it looks terribly unpolished. People will say it is slipshod, unfinished . . . [but] I do believe that not only is this painting worth more than all the previous ones but also that I will never do a better one or another like it. I put all my energy into it before dying, such painful passion amid terrible circumstances . . . and life burst from it.†

Some details of the painting have resisted interpretation because Gauguin's symbolism is so personal, but the general meaning of *Where Do We Come From?* is clear. It is a sobering, pessimistic image of the inevitability of the life cycle, beginning, at the right, with infancy. At the center is a Polynesian Eve in the prime of youth picking fruit from a tree. At the left, with a Tahitian idol in the background, is a crouching old woman contemplating death.

It is noteworthy that, contrary to Gauguin's assertion in the quoted letter, he did make a detailed preliminary drawing, now in the Louvre, for *Where Do We Come From?* He is here altering the facts in order to establish a persona for himself as an inspired genius who created great works without recourse to traditional studio methods. Some scholars have even suggested that he intended his suicide attempt to fail.

*Letter to Charles Morice, March 1898. Translated by Belinda Thompson, *Gauguin by Himself* (Boston: Little, Brown, 1993), 270–271.

†Letter to Daniel de Monfried, February 1898. Translated by Thompson, ibid., 257–258.

1 ft.

28-21 PAUL GAUGUIN, *Where Do We Come From? What Are We? Where Are We Going?* 1897. Oil on canvas, 4' 6¾" × 12' 3". Museum of Fine Arts, Boston (Tompkins Collection).

In search of a place far removed from European materialism, Gauguin moved to Tahiti, where he used native women and tropical colors to present a pessimistic view of the inevitability of the life cycle.

Despite the allure of the South Pacific, Gauguin continued to struggle with life. His health suffered, and his art had a hostile reception. In 1897, worn down by these obstacles, Gauguin decided to poison himself, but not before painting a mural-sized canvas titled *Where Do We Come From? What Are We? Where Are We Going?* (FIG. 28-21), which he wrote about in letters to his friends (see "Gauguin on *Where Do We Come From?*" above). His attempt to commit suicide in Tahiti was unsuccessful, but Gauguin died a few years later, in 1903, in the Marquesas Islands, his artistic genius still unrecognized.

PROBLEMS AND SOLUTIONS
Making Impressionism Solid and Enduring

Paul Cézanne's desire to "make of Impressionism something solid and enduring" led him to formulate a new approach to the art of painting, whether his subject was landscape (FIG. 28-22), still life (FIG. 28-23), or the human figure (FIG. 28-23A). Cézanne's distinctive way of studying nature is evident in *Mont Sainte-Victoire* (FIG. 28-22), one of many views that he painted of this mountain near his home in Aix-en-Provence. His aim was not truth in appearance, especially not photographic truth, nor was it the "truth" of Impressionism. Rather, he sought a lasting structure behind the formless and fleeting visual information that the eyes absorb. Instead of employing the Impressionists' random approach when he was face-to-face with nature, Cézanne, like Seurat, developed a more analytical style. His goal was to order the lines, planes, and colors of nature. He constantly and painstakingly checked his painting against the part of the scene—he called it the "motif"—that he was studying at the moment.

In a March 1904 letter, Cézanne stated his goal as a painter: "[to do] Poussin over entirely from nature . . . in the open air, with color and light, instead of one of those works imagined in a studio, where everything has the brown coloring of feeble daylight without reflections from the sky and sun."* He sought to achieve Poussin's effects of distance, depth, structure, and solidity, not by using traditional perspective and chiaroscuro, but rather by recording the color patterns that he deduced from an optical analysis of nature.

Cézanne set out to explore the properties of line, plane, and color, and their interrelationships. He studied the capacity of lines and planes to create the sensation of depth, the intrinsic qualities of color, and the power of colors to modify the direction and depth of lines and planes. To create the illusion of three-dimensional form and space, Cézanne focused on carefully selecting colors. He understood that the visual properties—hue, saturation, and value—of different colors vary (see "Color Theory," page 855). Cool colors tend to recede, whereas warm ones advance. By applying to the canvas small patches of juxtaposed colors, some advancing and some receding, Cézanne created volume and depth in his works. On occasion, the artist depicted objects chiefly in one hue and achieved convincing solidity by modulating the intensity (or saturation). At other times, he juxtaposed contrasting colors—for example, green, yellow, and red—of similar saturation to compose specific objects, such as fruit or bowls.

For example, in *Mont Sainte-Victoire,* Cézanne replaced the transitory visual effects of changing atmospheric conditions, effects that preoccupied Monet, with a more concentrated, lengthier analysis of the colors in large lighted spaces. The main space stretches out behind and beyond the canvas plane and includes numerous small elements, such as roads, fields, houses, and the viaduct at the far right, each seen from a slightly different viewpoint. Above this shifting, receding perspective—so different from traditional Renaissance perspective with the viewer standing in a fixed position and with a single vanishing point (see "Linear Perspective," page 587)—the largest mass of all, the mountain, seems simultaneously to be both near and far away, an effect achieved by equally stressing background and foreground contours. Cézanne's rendition of nature approximates the experience that a person has when viewing the forms of nature piecemeal. The relative proportions of objects vary, rather than being fixed by strict linear perspective. Cézanne immobilized the shifting colors of Impressionism into an array of clearly defined planes composing the objects and spaces in his scene. Describing his method in a letter to a fellow painter, he wrote:

> [T]reat nature by the cylinder, the sphere, the cone, everything in proper perspective so that each side of an object or a plane is directed towards a central point. Lines parallel to the horizon give breadth . . . Lines perpendicular to this horizon give depth. But nature for us men is more depth than surface, whence the need of introducing into our light vibrations, represented by reds and yellows, a sufficient amount of blue to give the impression of air.[†]

---

*Cézanne to Émile Bernard, March 1904. Quoted in Robert Goldwater and Marco Treves, eds., *Artists on Art, from the XIV to the XX Century* (New York: Pantheon, 1945), 363.

[†]Cézanne to Émile Bernard, April 15, 1904. Ibid., 363.

1 ft.

28-22 PAUL CÉZANNE, *Mont Sainte-Victoire*, 1902–1904. Oil on canvas, 2' 3½" × 2' 11¼". Philadelphia Museum of Art, Philadelphia (George W. Elkins Collection).

In his landscapes, Cézanne replaced the transitory visual effects of changing atmospheric conditions—the Impressionists' focus—with careful analysis of the lines, planes, and colors of nature.

28-23 Paul Cézanne, *Basket of Apples,* ca. 1895. Oil on canvas, 2' $\frac{3}{8}$" × 2' 7". Art Institute of Chicago, Chicago (Helen Birch Bartlett Memorial Collection, 1926).

Cézanne's still lifes reveal his analytical approach to painting. He captured the solidity of bottles and fruit by juxtaposing color patches, but the resulting abstract shapes are not optically realistic.

PAUL CÉZANNE Trained as a painter in his native Aix-en-Provence in southern France, Paul Cézanne (1839–1906) allied himself early in his career with the Impressionists, especially Pissarro (FIG. 28-6), and participated in the first (1874) and third (1877) Impressionist exhibitions in Paris. Initially, Cézanne accepted the Impressionists' color theories and their faith in subjects chosen from everyday life, but his own studies of traditional works of Western art in the Louvre persuaded him that Impressionism lacked form and structure. Cézanne declared that he wanted to "make of Impressionism something solid and enduring like the art in the museums."[8] In works such as *Mont Sainte-Victoire* (FIG. 28-22), he achieved that goal (see "Making Impressionism Solid and Enduring," page 860).

BASKET OF APPLES Still life, even more than landscape, proved to be a very effective vehicle for Cézanne's experiments in remaking Impressionism to emphasize the permanent instead of the transitory. In still-life painting, Cézanne could arrange a limited number of selected objects to provide a well-ordered point of departure. So analytical was Cézanne in preparing, observing, and painting still lifes (in contrast to the Impressionist emphasis on spontaneity) that he had to abandon using real fruit and flowers because they tended to rot. In *Basket of Apples* (FIG. 28-23), the objects have lost something of their individual character as bottles and fruit and have almost become cylinders and spheres. Cézanne captured the solidity of each object by juxtaposing color patches. His interest in the study of volume and solidity is evident from the disjunctures in the painting—the table edges are discontinuous, and various objects seem to be depicted from different vantage points. In his zeal to understand three-dimensionality and to convey the placement of forms relative to the space around them, Cézanne explored his still-life

arrangements from different viewpoints. This resulted in paintings that, though conceptually coherent, do not appear optically realistic.

Cézanne's approach to painting was consistent with the concern of 19th-century modernist painters with the integrity of the painting surface. Viewers of Cézanne's paintings are always aware that the three-dimensional forms they see are in reality two-dimensional patterns of line and color on a flat picture plane. Cézanne's legacy was significant. Especially his late works, such as the unfinished *The Large Bathers* (FIG. 28-23A), profoundly influenced the development of Cubism in the early 20th century (see page 892).

⬈**28-23A** Cézanne, *Large Bathers,* 1906.

SYMBOLISM

The Impressionists and Post-Impressionists believed that their emotions and sensations were important elements for interpreting the world around them, but the depiction of what they could see—people, buildings and boulevards, landscapes, still lifes—remained their primary focus, as it had for the Realists before them. By the end of the 19th century, however, many artists turned their attention away from the real world to the imaginary. These artists, seeking to express their individual spirit, rejected the optical world of daily life in favor of a fantasy world, of forms they conjured in their free imagination. Color, line, and shape, divorced from conformity to the optical image, became symbols of personal emotions in response to

WRITTEN SOURCES
Albert Aurier on Symbolism

An early champion of Paul Gauguin, Albert Aurier published an influential essay in March 1891 in the journal *Mercure de France* in which he described the singular contribution of Gauguin to modern painting and used Gauguin's work to define Symbolism in painting. Aurier argued that

> The goal of painting . . . cannot be the direct representation of objects. Its end purpose is to express ideas as it translates them into a special language. Indeed, in the eyes of the artist . . . objects . . . have a significance only insofar as they are objects. The artist sees them only as *signs,* letters of an immense alphabet that only the genius knows how to read. To write one's thought, one's poem, with those signs, all the while remembering that the sign, however indispensable, is nothing in itself and the idea alone is everything—such appears to be the task of the artist whose eye can determine the evocative potential of tangible objects. . . . As a result, certain laws must govern pictorial imitation. The artist, in every form of art, must carefully avoid . . . concrete truth, illusionism, trompe-l'oeil. Indeed, he must not convey in his picture a false impression of nature that would act on the spectator like nature itself. . . . In consequence, the strict duty of the ideist painter is to make a reasoned selection from the multiple elements of objective reality, to use in his work only the lines, forms, general and distinctive colors that enable him to describe precisely the ideic significance of the object . . . To sum up and conclude, the work

of art as I have evoked it logically, is *Ideist* . . . *Symbolist* . . . *Synthetic* . . . and *Decorative.**

Although he never formally identified himself with the Symbolists, the French painter Pierre Puvis de Chavannes (1824–1898) became a major inspiration for those artists. In striking contrast to the Impressionists and Post-Impressionists, whose work was routinely rejected by the official Salons, Puvis served as a Salon juror until he resigned in 1872 to protest the narrowness of the other jurors. Puvis, nevertheless, was no admirer of Realism or Impressionism, producing instead an ornamental and reflective art incorporating classical imagery—a categorical rejection of the Realist and Impressionist focus on the everyday world.

In *Sacred Grove* (FIG. **28-24**), which may have influenced Seurat's *Grande Jatte* (FIG. 28-17), Puvis deployed statuesque figures in a tranquil landscape with a Greco-Roman shrine. Suspended in timeless poses, the figures have simple and sharp contours, and their modeling is as shallow as *bas-relief* sculpture. The calm and still atmosphere suggests some consecrated place where all movements and gestures have a permanent ritual significance. The stillness and simplicity of the forms, the linear patterns that their rhythmic contours create, and the suggestion of their symbolic weight constitute a type of anti-Realism. Puvis garnered support from a wide range of artists, from, at one extreme, the conservative members of the French Academy and the government, who applauded his classicism, to the Symbolists, who revered Puvis for his vindication of imagination and his independence from the capitalist world of materialism and the machine.

*Translated by Henri Dorra, ed., *Symbolist Art Theories: A Critical Anthology* (Berkeley and Los Angeles: University of California Press, 1995), 199–200.

28-24 Pierre Puvis de Chavannes, *Sacred Grove,* 1884. Oil on canvas, 2' 11½" × 6' 10". Art Institute of Chicago, Chicago (Potter Palmer Collection).

The Symbolists revered Puvis de Chavannes for his rejection of Realism. His statuesque figures in timeless poses inhabit a tranquil landscape, their gestures suggesting a symbolic ritual significance.

the world. Deliberately choosing to stand outside of convention and tradition, these artists spoke in signs and symbols.

Many of the artists following this path adopted an approach to subject and form that associated them with a general European movement called *Symbolism*. Symbolists, whether painters or writers, disdained Realism as trivial. The task of Symbolist artists, both visual and verbal, was not to see things but to see through them to a significance and reality far deeper than what superficial appearance revealed. In so doing, as the poet Arthur Rimbaud (1854–1891) insisted, artists became beings of extraordinary insight. (One group of Symbolist painters called itself the *Nabis*, the Hebrew word for "prophet.") Rimbaud, whose poems had great influence on the artistic community, went so far as to say, in his *Letter from a Seer* (1871), that to achieve the seer's insight, artists must become deranged. In effect, they must systematically unhinge and confuse the everyday faculties of sense and reason, which serve only to blur artistic vision. The artists' mystical vision must convert the objects of the commonsense world into symbols of a reality beyond that world and, ultimately, a reality from within the individual. Elements of Symbolism were already present in the works of van Gogh and especially Gauguin—for example, *Vision after the Sermon* (FIG. 28-20) and *Where Do We Come From?* (FIG. 28-21). In fact, one of the most coherent and influential definitions of Symbolist art appeared in an 1891 essay, "Symbolism in Painting: Paul Gauguin," by Albert Aurier (1865–1892), a leading Symbolist poet and art critic (see "Albert Aurier on Symbolism," page 862).

The extreme subjectivism of the Symbolists led them to cultivate all the resources of fantasy and imagination, no matter how deeply buried or obscure. Moreover, they urged artists to stand against the vulgar materialism and conventional values of industrial and middle-class society. Above all, the Symbolists wished to purge literature and art of anything utilitarian, to cultivate an exquisite aesthetic sensitivity. The subjects of the Symbolists, conditioned by this reverent attitude toward art and exaggerated aesthetic sensation, became increasingly esoteric and exotic, mysterious, visionary, dreamlike, and fantastic—the opposite of "concrete truth, illusionism, trompe-l'oeil." Perhaps not coincidentally, contemporary with the Symbolists, Sigmund Freud (1856–1939), the founder of psychoanalysis, began the age of psychiatry with his *Interpretation of Dreams* (1900), an introduction to the concept and the world of unconscious experience.

GUSTAVE MOREAU One of the foremost Symbolist painters was GUSTAVE MOREAU (1826–1898), who entered the École des Beaux-Arts at age 20. Toward the end of his career, in 1892, Moreau became a professor there, but he lived most of his life as a recluse in his townhouse at 14 rue de la Rochefoucauld in Paris, today the Musée Gustave Moreau. An admirer of Eugène Delacroix, Moreau loved exotic settings and rich colors, but his subjects, often drawn from classical mythology and the Bible, transcend those of Romanticism to embrace the world of imagination and spirituality celebrated by Symbolist writers.

The Apparition (FIG. **28-25**), one of two versions of the same subject that Moreau submitted to the Salon of 1876, treats a theme that fascinated him and many of his contemporaries—the *femme fatale* ("fatal woman"), the destructive temptress of men. The seductive heroine here is the biblical Salome (Mark 6:21–28), who pleased her stepfather, King Herod, by dancing enticingly before him and demanded in return the head of Saint John the Baptist (compare FIG. 21-8). In Moreau's representation of the story, Herod sits in

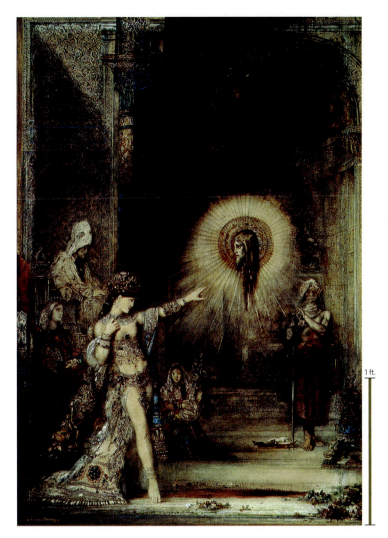

28-25 GUSTAVE MOREAU, *The Apparition*, 1874–1876. Watercolor on paper, 3' 5¾" × 2' 4⅜". Musée du Louvre, Paris.

Moreau's painting of Salome, a biblical femme fatale, combines hallucinatory imagery, eroticism, precise drawing, rich color, and an opulent setting—hallmarks of Moreau's Symbolist style.

the background, enthroned not in a Middle Eastern palace but in a classical columnar hall resembling a Roman triumphal arch. Salome is in the foreground, scantily clad in a gold- and gem-encrusted costume. She points to an apparition hovering in the air at the level of Herod's head. In a radiant circle of light is what Salome desired—the halo-framed head of John the Baptist, dripping with blood but with eyes wide open. The combination of hallucinatory imagery, eroticism, precise drawing, rich color, and opulent setting is the hallmark of Moreau's highly original style. *The Apparition* and Moreau's other major paintings—for example, *Jupiter and Semele* (FIG. **28-25A**)—foreshadow the work of the Surrealists in the next century (see page 921).

28-25A MOREAU, *Jupiter and Semele*, ca. 1875.

28-26 ODILON REDON, *The Cyclops*, 1898. Oil on canvas, 2' 1" × 1' 8". Kröller-Müller Foundation, Otterlo.

In *The Cyclops,* the Symbolist painter Odilon Redon represented the mythical one-eyed giant Polyphemus shyly observing the beautiful sleeping Galatea. The rich profusion of hues is the legacy of Impressionism.

ODILON REDON Like Moreau, fellow French Symbolist ODILON REDON (1840–1916) was a visionary. He had been aware of an intense inner world since childhood, and later wrote of "imaginary things" haunting him. Redon adapted the Impressionist palette and stippling brushstroke for a very different purpose—the representation of dreamlike narratives. In *The Cyclops* (FIG. 28-26), Redon represented the mythological one-eyed giant Polyphemus emerging from behind a rocky outcropping in a landscape with a rich profusion of fresh saturated hues that harmonized with the mood that Redon felt fitted the subject. In Homer's *Odyssey,* Polyphemus is a monstrous giant whom the Greek hero Odysseus must vanquish on his journey home from Troy. Redon chose, however, the less familiar tale of Polyphemus's love for the nymph Galatea. Redon's Cyclops is a shy, simpering creature with its single huge loving eye set into a misshapen head. He rises baloonlike above the beautiful sleeping Galatea. The contrast with Raphael's representation of the same subject (FIG. 22-11) could hardly be more striking. As Redon himself observed: "All my originality consists . . . in making unreal creatures live humanly by putting, as much as possible, the logic of the visible at the service of the invisible."[9]

HENRI ROUSSEAU The imagination of HENRI ROUSSEAU (1844–1910) engaged a different but equally powerful world of personal fantasy. Gauguin had journeyed to the South Seas in search of primitive innocence. Rousseau was a "primitive" without leaving Paris—a self-taught amateur who turned to painting full-time only after his retirement from service in the French government. Nicknamed "Le Douanier" (The Customs Inspector), he first exhibited in the Salon of 1885 when he was 41. Derided by the critics, Rousseau turned to the Salon des Indépendants in 1886 and thereafter exhibited his works there almost every year until his death. Even in that more liberal showcase, Rousseau still received almost universally unfavorable reviews because of his lack of formal training, imperfect perspective, doll-like figures, and settings resembling constructed

28-27 HENRI ROUSSEAU, *Sleeping Gypsy,* 1897. Oil on canvas, 4' 3" × 6' 7". Museum of Modern Art, New York (gift of Mrs. Simon Guggenheim).

In *Sleeping Gypsy,* Rousseau depicted a doll-like but menacing lion sniffing at a recumbent dreaming figure in a mysterious landscape. The painting suggests the vulnerable subconscious during sleep.

theater sets more than natural landscapes. Rousseau compensated for his apparent visual, conceptual, and technical naiveté with a natural talent for design and an imagination teeming with exotic, mysterious images.

Tropical landscapes are the setting for two of Rousseau's most famous works, *Sleeping Gypsy* (FIG. 28-27) of 1897 and *The Dream* (FIG. 28-27A), painted 13 years later. In the earlier painting, the recumbent figure occupies a desert world, silent and secret, and dreams beneath a pale, perfectly round moon. In the foreground, a lion resembling a stuffed, but somehow menacing, animal doll sniffs at the gypsy. A critical encounter impends—an encounter of the type that recalls the uneasiness of a person's vulnerable subconscious self during sleep—a subject of central importance to Rousseau's contemporary, Sigmund Freud. Rousseau's art of drama and fantasy has its own sophistication and, after the artist's death, influenced the development of Surrealism (see page 921).

28-27A ROUSSEAU, *The Dream*, 1910.

JAMES ENSOR Although the Symbolist movement in art and literature began in France, it quickly expanded throughout Europe. The leading Belgian Symbolist was JAMES ENSOR (1860–1949), the son of an expatriate Englishman and a Flemish mother, who spent most of his life in the seaside resort village of Ostend, far from the artistic centers of Europe. In 1883 he cofounded Les Vingts (The Twenty), a group of Belgian artists who staged unjuried exhibitions in Brussels modeled on the independent salons of Paris. A fervent nationalist, he left the group when it began to exhibit the work of foreign artists. In fact, Ensor's most monumental work, *Christ's Entry into Brussels in 1889* (FIG. 28-28), is very likely a critical response to Georges Seurat's *Grande Jatte* (FIG. 28-17), exhibited by Les Vingt in 1887.

Whereas Seurat's canvas celebrates the leisure activities of contented bourgeois Parisians, a typical Impressionist theme, Ensor's even larger (14-foot-long) painting portrays an event that occurred only in the painter's imagination. In fact, it was a future event that Ensor imagined. *Christ's Entry into Brussels in 1889*, painted in 1888, is a socialist commentary on the decadence and alienation of urban life at the end of the 19th century. The mural-sized canvas is the artist's pessimistic vision of how Christ would be greeted if he entered the modern Belgian capital. Christ is a small and insignificant figure on a donkey in the background of the painting, ignored by the dense crowd of soldiers and citizens wearing grotesque masks inspired by the papier-mâché carnival masks that Ensor's family sold in their curio shop in Ostend. Some of the people carry banners and signs. One reads "Long Live Jesus, King of Brussels," another "Long Live the Socialist State." Complementing the ugly, grimacing masked faces of the anonymous crowd, which eloquently express Ensor's condemnation of the corrupt values of modern society, are the discordant combination of reds, blues, and greens and the coarse texture of the thickly applied oil pigment. As an indictment of the immorality of modern life, Ensor's *Christ's Entry* has few equals.

28-28 JAMES ENSOR, *Christ's Entry into Brussels in 1889,* 1888. Oil on canvas, 8' 3½" × 14' 1½". J. Paul Getty Museum, Los Angeles.

Ensor's mural-sized canvas is an indictment of corrupt modern values. Christ enters Brussels on a donkey in 1889, ignored by the dense crowd of soldiers and citizens wearing grotesque, grimacing masks.

EDVARD MUNCH Also linked in spirit to the Symbolists were the English artist AUBREY BEARDSLEY (1872–1898; FIG. 28-28A) and the Norwegian painter EDVARD MUNCH (1863–1944). Munch felt deeply the pain of human life and believed that people were powerless before the great natural forces of death and love. The emotions associated with those forces—jealousy, loneliness, fear, desire, despair—became the theme of most of his art (see "Painting Psychic Life," below).

🔁 **28-28A** BEARDSLEY, *The Peacock Skirt*, 1894.

FIN-DE-SIÈCLE Historians have adopted the term *fin-de-siècle*, which literally means "end of the century," to describe European culture of the late 1800s. This designation is not merely chronological but also refers to a certain sensibility. At that time, the increasingly large and prosperous middle classes were aspiring to gain the advantages that the aristocracy traditionally enjoyed. The masses, striving to live "the good life," embraced a culture of decadence and indulgence. Characteristic of the fin-de-siècle period was an intense preoccupation with sexual drives, powers, and perversions. People at the end of the century also immersed themselves in the exploration of the unconscious. This culture was unrestrained and freewheeling, but the determination to enjoy life masked an anxiety prompted by significant political upheaval and an uncertain future. The country most closely associated with fin-de-siècle culture was Austria.

PROBLEMS AND SOLUTIONS
Painting Psychic Life

Few painters in history have been as successful as Edvard Munch in portraying primal emotions in works of art. In 1877, as a teenager, Munch endured the painful, slow death of his sister from tuberculosis, a wrenching experience that inspired his *Sick Child* of 1886. Munch's mother had died of the same disease a decade earlier, and those tragic events profoundly shaped the painter's outlook on life and his artistic vision.

Munch's goal as an artist was, in his own words, to describe the conditions of "modern psychic life." To achieve that goal, Realist and Impressionist techniques were inappropriate, focusing as they did on the tangible world. Instead, in the spirit of Symbolism, Munch used color, line, and figural distortion for expressive ends. Influenced by Gauguin, whose paintings he saw in an 1884 exhibition in Oslo, Munch produced both paintings and prints whose high emotional charge was a major source of inspiration for the German Expressionists in the early 20th century (see page 885).

Munch's *The Scream* (FIG. 28-29), painted in 1893 when he was 30 years old, exemplifies his style and remains to this day one of the most potent symbols of the unbearable pressures of modern life on individual people. The image—a man standing on a bridge—belongs to the real world. In fact, the inspiration for the painting came after Munch had experienced a fit of anxiety after walking, intoxicated, across an Oslo bridge on a summer evening. However, his depiction of the scene departs significantly from visual reality. *The Scream* evokes a powerful emotional response from the viewer because of the painter's dramatic presentation. The man in the foreground, simplified to almost skeletal form, emits a primal scream. The landscape's sweeping curvilinear lines reiterate the shapes of the man's mouth and head, almost like an echo, as the cry seems to reverberate through the setting. The fiery red and yellow stripes that give the sky an eerie glow also contribute to this work's resonance.

Munch wrote a revealing epigraph to accompany the painting:

> I was walking along the road with two friends. The sun was setting.
> I felt a breath of melancholy—Suddenly the sky turned blood-red.
> I stopped, and leaned against the railing, deathly tired—looking out across the flaming clouds that hung like blood and a sword over the blue-black fjord and town. My friends walked on—I stood there, trembling with fear. And I sensed a great, infinite scream pass through nature.*

Appropriately, the original title of this work was *Despair*.

*Quoted in Petra ten-Doesschate Chu, *Nineteenth-Century European Art*, 3d ed. (Upper Saddle River, N.J.: Pearson, 2011), 515.

1 ft.

28-29 EDVARD MUNCH, *The Scream*, 1893. Tempera and pastels on cardboard, 2' 11¾" × 2' 5". National Gallery, Oslo.

Although grounded in the real world, *The Scream* departs significantly from visual reality. Munch used color, line, and figural distortion to evoke a strong emotional response from the viewer.

28-30 Gustav Klimt, *The Kiss,* 1907–1908. Oil on canvas, 5' 10¾" × 5' 10¾". Österreichische Galerie Belvedere, Vienna.

Klimt's paintings exemplify the Viennese fin-de-siècle spirit. In *The Kiss,* he revealed only a small segment of each lover's body. The rest of the painting dissolves into shimmering, extravagant flat patterning.

GUSTAV KLIMT The Viennese artist Gustav Klimt (1863–1918) captured this period's flamboyance in his work, but tempered it with unsettling undertones. In *The Kiss* (FIG. **28-30**), his best-known work, Klimt depicted a kneeling couple locked in an embrace. The setting is ambiguous, an indeterminate place apart from time and space, perhaps a garden of flowers. Moreover, all the viewer sees of the embracing couple is a small segment of each body—and virtually nothing of the man's face. The rest of the canvas dissolves into shimmering, extravagant flat patterning. This patterning has clear ties to Art Nouveau and to the Arts and Crafts movement (discussed later) and also evokes the conflict between two- and three-dimensionality intrinsic to the work of Degas and other modernists. In *The Kiss,* however, those patterns also signify gender contrasts—rectangles for the man's garment, circles for the woman's. Yet the patterning

also unites the two lovers into a single formal entity, underscoring their erotic union.

GERTRUDE KÄSEBIER Photography, which during the 19th century most people regarded as the ultimate form of Realism, could also be manipulated by artists to produce effects more akin to painting than to factual records of contemporary life. After the first great breakthroughs (see page 834), which bluntly showed what was before the eye, some photographers began to pursue new ways of using the medium as a vehicle of artistic expression. A leading practitioner of what might be called the pictorial style in photography was the American Gertrude Käsebier (1852–1934), who took up the camera in 1897 after raising a family and working as a portrait painter. She soon became famous for photographs with Symbolist themes, such

28-31 GERTRUDE KÄSEBIER, *Blessed Art Thou among Women*, 1899. Platinum print on Japanese tissue, $9\frac{3}{8}$" × $5\frac{1}{2}$". Museum of Modern Art, New York (gift of Mrs. Hermine M. Turner).

Symbolist Käsebier injected a sense of the spiritual and the divine into scenes from everyday life. The deliberately soft focus of this photograph invests the scene with an aura of otherworldly peace.

as *Blessed Art Thou among Women* (FIG. 28-31). The title repeats the phrase that the angel Gabriel used to announce to the Virgin Mary that she would be the mother of the Messiah. In the context of Käsebier's photography, the words suggest a parallel between the biblical Mother of God and the modern mother in the image, who both protects and sends forth her daughter from her secure home into the unfamiliar world at large. The white setting and the mother's pale gown shimmer in soft focus behind the girl, who wears darker tones and whom the photographer captured with sharper focus. Käsebier deliberately combined an out-of-focus background with a sharp or almost-sharp foreground, thereby blurring the entire image slightly. In *Blessed Art Thou,* the soft focus invests the scene with an aura of otherworldly peace. The photograph showcases Käsebier's ability to inject a sense of the spiritual and the divine into scenes from everyday life.

SCULPTURE

The names of the sculptors of the late 19th century are not as familiar as those of the painters of the same era, in part because their work was less revolutionary in nature, in part because their biographies are not as colorful as the tormented and nomadic lives of van Gogh and Gauguin. But the quality of the statues and reliefs created by the leading sculptors of this period is uncontested.

JEAN-BAPTISTE CARPEAUX In France, JEAN-BAPTISTE CARPEAUX (1827–1875) received his training as a sculptor at the École des Beaux-Arts under the direction of François Rude, best known for *La Marseillaise* (FIG. 27-18), his colossal relief on the Arc de Triomphe (FIG. 27-18A) in Paris. Although it took him a decade to achieve, Carpeaux won the Rome Prize in 1854 and spent the next eight years in Italy honing his technical skills. In his mature work, Carpeaux combined his love for the ancient, Renaissance, and Baroque sculpture he saw in Italy with a strong interest in Realism.

All of those sources are evident in his group *Ugolino and His Children* (FIG. 28-32), which he based on a passage in Dante's *Inferno* (33.58–75) in which Count Ugolino and his four sons starve to death while shut up in a tower. In Hell, Ugolino relates to Dante

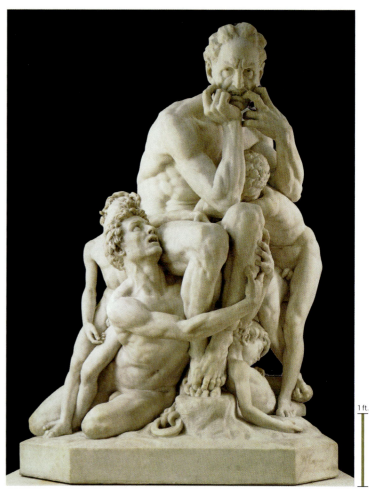

28-32 JEAN-BAPTISTE CARPEAUX, *Ugolino and His Children,* 1865–1867. Marble, 6' 5" high. Metropolitan Museum of Art, New York (Josephine Bay Paul and C. Michael Paul Foundation, Inc., and the Charles Ulrich and Josephine Bay Foundation, Inc., gifts, 1967).

As in Dante's *Inferno,* Carpeaux's Ugolino bites his hands in despair as he and his four sons await death by starvation. The twisted forms suggest the self-devouring torment of frustration.

how, in a moment of extreme despair, he bit both his hands in grief. His children, thinking he did it because of his hunger, offered him their own flesh as food. In Carpeaux's statuary group, the powerful forms—twisted, intertwined, and densely concentrated—suggest the self-devouring torment of frustration and despair wracking the unfortunate Ugolino. A careful student of Michelangelo's male figures, Carpeaux also said he had the ancient *Laocoön* (FIG. 5-89) in mind when he conceived *Ugolino and His Children,* which he hoped would be "a masterpiece of the human spirit." Certainly, the storm and stress captured in his *Ugolino* recall similar characteristics of the group of Laocoön and his two sons. Nevertheless, the sense of vivid reality in the anatomy of Carpeaux's figures shows that the artist had studied the human figure from life, not solely from other statues. However, the French public did not share Carpeaux's interest in Realism. They preferred the idealized bodies of classical sculptures—one of the reasons that Carpeaux was forced to remove another of his best works, *The Dance* (FIG. 28-32A), from the facade of the Paris opera house (FIG. 27-45).

⬀ **28-32A** CARPEAUX, *The Dance,* 1867–1869.

AUGUSTE RODIN As talented as he was, Carpeaux was not the leading French sculptor of the later 19th century. That honor belongs to AUGUSTE RODIN (1840–1917), who conceived and executed his sculptures with a Realist sensibility. The human body in motion fascinated Rodin, as it did Eakins and Muybridge (FIG. 27-53) before him (see "Rodin on Movement in Art and Photography," below). Rodin was also well aware of the Impressionists' innovations. Although color was not a significant factor in Rodin's work, the influence of Impressionism is evident in the artist's interest in the effect of light on sculpted surfaces. When focusing on the human form, he joined his profound knowledge of anatomy and movement with special attention to the body's exterior, saying, "The sculptor must learn to reproduce the surface, which means all that vibrates on the surface, soul, love, passion, life. . . . Sculpture is thus the art of hollows and mounds, not of smoothness, or even polished planes."[10] Primarily a modeler of pliable material rather than a carver of hard wood or stone, Rodin worked his surfaces with fingers sensitive to the subtlest variations of texture, catching the fugitive play of constantly shifting light on metal. In his studio, he often would have a model move around in front of him while he created preliminary versions of his sculptures with coils of clay.

In *Walking Man* (FIG. 28-33), a preliminary study for the sculptor's *Saint John the Baptist Preaching,* Rodin succeeded in representing a fleeting moment in cast bronze. He portrayed a headless and armless figure in midstride at the moment when weight is transferred across the pelvis from the back leg to the front. In addition to capturing the sense of the transitory, Rodin demonstrated his mastery of realistic detail in his meticulous rendition of muscle, bone, and tendon.

ARTISTS ON ART
Rodin on Movement in Art and Photography

Photography had a profound effect on 19th-century art, and many artists used photographs as an aid in capturing "reality" on canvas or in stone. Eadweard Muybridge's photographs of a galloping horse (FIG. 27-53), for example, definitively established that at certain times, all four hooves of the animal are in the air. But not all artists believed that photography was "true to life." The sculptor Auguste Rodin (FIGS. 28-33, 28-33A, and 28-34) was one of the doubters.

> I have always sought to give some indication of movement [in my statues]. I have very rarely represented complete repose. I have always endeavored to express the inner feelings by the mobility of the muscles. . . . The illusion of life is obtained in our art by good modeling and by movement. . . . [M]ovement is the transition from one attitude to another. . . . Have you ever attentively examined instantaneous photographs of walking figures? . . . [Photographs] present the odd appearance of a man suddenly stricken with paralysis and petrified in his pose. . . . If, in fact, in instantaneous photographs, the figures, though taken while moving, seem suddenly fixed in mid-air, it is because, all parts of the body being reproduced exactly at the same twentieth or fortieth of a second, there is no progressive development of movement as there is in art. . . . [I]t is the artist who is truthful and it is photography which lies, for in reality time does not stop.*

*Translated by Robin Fedden, in Elizabeth Gilmore Holt, ed., *From the Classicists to the Impressionists: Art and Architecture in the 19th Century* (New Haven, Conn.: Yale University Press, 1966; reprint 1986), 406–409.

1 ft.

28-33 AUGUSTE RODIN, *Walking Man,* 1905. Bronze, 6' 11¾" high. Musée d'Orsay, Paris.

In this study for a statue of Saint John the Baptist, Rodin depicted a headless and armless figure in midstride. *Walking Man* demonstrates Rodin's mastery of anatomy and ability to capture transitory motion.

GATES OF HELL Rodin also made many
nude and draped studies for each of the
figures in two of his most ambitious
works—the life-size group *Burghers
of Calais* (FIG. **28-33A**) and the *Gates
of Hell* (FIG. **28-34**), which occupied
the sculptor for two decades. After he
failed to gain admission to the École des
Beaux-Arts, Rodin enrolled in the École
Impériale Spéciale de Dessin et Mathé-
matiques (Special Imperial School of
Drawing and Mathematics), the French
school of decorative arts, known as the
"Petit École" (Little School) because it
was a lesser version of the more prestigious Beaux-Arts academy. However,
Rodin's talent could not be suppressed
by rejection. He soon gained attention
for the outstanding realism of some of
his early sculptures, and on August 16,
1880, received a major governmental
commission to design a pair of doors for
a planned Museum of Decorative Arts
in Paris. Rodin worked on the project
for 20 years, but the museum was never
built (the Musée d'Orsay now occupies
the intended site). It was not until after
the sculptor's death that others cast his
still-unfinished doors in bronze.

The commission granted Rodin
permission to choose his own subject.
He selected *The Gates of Hell,* based on
Dante's *Inferno* and Baudelaire's *Flowers
of Evil.* Originally inspired by Lorenzo
Ghiberti's *Gates of Paradise* (FIG. 21-10),
which he had seen in Florence, Rodin
quickly abandoned the idea of a series
of framed narrative panels and decided
instead to cover each of the doors with a
continuous writhing mass of tormented
men and women, sinners condemned
to Dante's second circle of Hell for their
lust. Because of the varying height of the
relief, the complex poses, and the effect of
light on the highly textured surfaces, the
figures seem to be in flux, moving in and
out of an undefined space in a reflection
of their psychic turmoil. The dreamlike
(or rather, the nightmarish) vision connects Rodin with the Symbolists, and

28-33A RODIN, *Burghers
of Calais,* 1884–1889.

the pessimistic mood and sensuality embody the fin-de-siècle spirit.
The swirling composition and emotionalism recall Delacroix's *Death
of Sardanapalus* (FIG. 27-15) and Michelangelo's *Last Judgment*
(FIG. 22-19). Rodin's work defies easy stylistic classification.

The nearly 200 figures of *The Gates of Hell* spill over onto the
jambs and the lintel. Rodin also included freestanding figures,
which, cast separately in multiple versions, are among his most
famous works. Above the doors, *The Three Shades* is a trio of twisted
nude male figures, essentially the same figure with elongated arms

10 ft.

28-34 AUGUSTE RODIN, *The Gates of
Hell,* 1880–1900 (cast in 1917). Bronze,
20' 10" × 13' 1". Musée Rodin, Paris.

Rodin's most ambitious work, inspired by
Dante's *Inferno* and Ghiberti's *Gates of Paradise*
(FIG. 21-10), presents nearly 200 tormented
sinners in relief below *The Three Shades* and
The Thinker.

1 in.

28-35 CAMILLE CLAUDEL, *The Waltz*, 1895. Bronze, 1' 4⁷⁄₈" high. Private collection, Paris.

The Waltz was a bold work for a woman artist because it portrays male nudity. The textures and movement are hallmarks of Rodin, but the conception of spiritual and physical union is Claudel's own.

CAMILLE CLAUDEL Because of the physical strength required for carving stone, throughout history women who pursued careers as artists almost universally became painters rather than sculptors. An important exception is CAMILLE CLAUDEL (1864–1943), who met Rodin in 1883 when she was an apprentice in another sculptor's studio. She became his assistant, model, and lover in 1885. Although Claudel produced life-size sculptures for public commissions, she specialized in small-scale bronzes for display in private homes.

The Waltz (FIG. **28-35**), produced over several years in a number of variations, is a characteristic, extremely bold work for a woman artist of this era because it portrays male nudity. It deserves comparison with Klimt's *Kiss* (FIG. 28-30) in its unbridled fin-de-siècle passion and eroticism. But unlike the Austrian painter's kneeling lovers, Claudel's embracing couple is swept up in the motion of their dance, their spiraling movement underscored and enhanced by the flowing drapery of the seminude woman. The influence of Rodin is evident in the variegated texture of the bronze statuette and in Claudel's interest in the movement of the human body, but *The Waltz* is her own conception of spiritual as well as physical union between a man and a woman.

in three different positions. The group evokes Carpeaux's *Ugolino and His Children* (FIG. 28-32), as does *The Thinker*, Rodin's famous seated nude man with a powerful body who rests his chin on his clenched right hand, pondering the fate of the tormented souls on the doors below. *The Thinker* is the alter-ego of both Dante and Rodin.

The *Gates of Hell*, more than 20 feet tall, was Rodin's most ambitious project. It greatly influenced the painters and sculptors of the Expressionist movements of the early 20th century (see page 885). Rodin's ability to capture the quality of the transitory through his highly textured surfaces while revealing larger themes and deeper, lasting sensibilities is another reason he had a strong influence on 20th-century artists. Because many of his works, such as *Walking Man,* were deliberate fragments, he was also instrumental in creating a taste for the incomplete, an aesthetic many later sculptors embraced enthusiastically.

AUGUSTUS SAINT-GAUDENS Outside France, the most renowned sculptor of the late 19th century was an American, AUGUSTUS SAINT-GAUDENS (1848–1907), whose subjects and style differed markedly from those of his French counterparts. Saint-Gaudens produced monumental statues expressing the majestic calm of ancient Greek and Roman sculpture, such as his *Adams Memorial* (FIG. **28-35A**) in Washington, D.C.

📷 **28-35A** SAINT-GAUDENS, *Adams Memorial,* 1886–1891.

ART AND SOCIETY
The Arts and Crafts Movement

One of the clearest cases in history of social, economic, and technological changes giving birth to new art forms is the Arts and Crafts movement in 19th-century England. This movement was shaped by the ideas of John Ruskin, the critic who skewered Whistler's "arrangements" (see "Whistler," page 851), and the artist William Morris. Both men shared a distrust of machines and industrial capitalism, which they believed alienated workers from their own nature. Accordingly, they advocated an art "made by the people for the people as a joy for the maker and the user."* This condemnation of capitalism and support for manual laborers were also consistent with the tenets of socialism, and many artists in the Arts and Crafts movement, especially in England, considered themselves socialists and participated in the labor movement.

This democratic, or at least populist, attitude carried over to the art they produced as well. Members of the Arts and Crafts movement dedicated themselves to making functional objects with high aesthetic value for a wide public. They advocated a style based on natural, rather than artificial, forms, which often consisted of repeated designs of floral or geometric patterns. For Ruskin, Morris, and others in the Arts and Crafts movement, who despised the inferior machine-made products that were flooding the market in England, high-quality artisanship and honest labor were crucial ingredients of superior works of decorative art.

To promote these ideals, Morris formed a decorating firm dedicated to Arts and Crafts principles: Morris, Marshall, Faulkner, and Company, Fine Arts Workmen in Painting, Carving, Furniture, and Metals. His company did a flourishing business producing wallpaper, textiles, tiles, furniture, books, rugs, stained glass, and pottery. In 1867,

28-36 WILLIAM MORRIS, Green Dining Room, South Kensington Museum (now Victoria & Albert Museum), London, England, 1867.

William Morris was a founder of the Arts and Crafts movement. His Green Dining Room exemplifies the group's dedication to creating intricately patterned yet unified and functional environments.

Morris received the commission to decorate the Green Dining Room (FIG. 28-36) at London's South Kensington Museum (now the Victoria & Albert Museum), the center of public art education and home of decorative art collections. The range of room features that Morris created for this unified, beautiful, and functional environment was all-encompassing: wallpaper, ceiling panels, doors, *wainscoting* (paneling on the lower part of interior walls), and lighting. Nothing escaped his eye. Morris's design for this room also reveals the penchant of Arts and Crafts designers for intricate patterning of vegetal and floral motifs.

*Quoted in Eileen Boris, *Art and Labor: Ruskin, Morris, and the Craftsman Ideal in America* (Philadelphia: Temple University Press, 1986), 7.

ARCHITECTURE AND DECORATIVE ARTS

The decisive effects of industrialization were impossible to ignore, and although many artists embraced this manifestation of "modern life" or at least explored its effects, other artists decried the impact of rampant industrialism. Most notable were those associated with the Arts and Crafts movement in England, spearheaded by John Ruskin and WILLIAM MORRIS (1834–1896; see "The Arts and Crafts Movement," above, and FIG. 28-36).

CHARLES RENNIE MACKINTOSH Numerous Arts and Crafts societies in America, England, and Germany carried on the ideal of artisanship championed by Ruskin and Morris. In Scotland,

CHARLES RENNIE MACKINTOSH (1868–1929) designed a number of tea rooms, including the Ladies' Luncheon Room (FIG. 28-37) located in the Ingram Street Tea Room in Glasgow. The room decor is consistent with Morris's vision of functional, exquisitely designed art. The chairs, stained-glass windows, and large panels of colored *gesso* with twine, glass beads, thread, mother-of-pearl, and tin leaf—made by MARGARET MACDONALD MACKINTOSH (1864–1933), an artist-designer and Mackintosh's wife, who collaborated with him on many projects—are all pristinely geometric and rhythmical in design.

ART NOUVEAU An important international architectural and design movement that developed out of the ideas that the Arts and

28-37 CHARLES RENNIE MACKINTOSH and MARGARET MACDONALD MACKINTOSH, **Ladies' Luncheon Room, Ingram Street Tea Room, Glasgow, Scotland, 1900–1912. Reconstructed (1992–1995) in the Glasgow Art Galleries and Museum, Glasgow.**

The Mackintoshes' Ladies' Luncheon Room in Glasgow features functional and exquisitely designed Arts and Crafts decor, including stained-glass windows and pristinely geometric furnishings.

Crafts movement promoted was *Art Nouveau* (New Art), which took its name from a shop in Paris called L'Art Nouveau. Known by that name in France, Belgium, Holland, England, and the United States, the style had other names in other places: *Jugendstil* in Austria and Germany (after the magazine *Der Jugend,* "youth"), *Modernismo* in Spain, and *Stile Floreale* in Italy. Proponents of this movement tried to synthesize all the arts in a determined attempt to create art based on natural forms that could be mass-produced for a large audience. The Art Nouveau style adapted the twining-plant form to the needs of architecture, painting, sculpture, and all the decorative arts.

VICTOR HORTA The mature Art Nouveau style of the 1890s is on display in the houses designed by the Belgian architect VICTOR HORTA (1861–1947). A characteristic example is the staircase (FIG. **28-38**) in the Van Eetvelde House, which Horta built in Brussels in 1895, three years after designing the Tassel House

28-38 VICTOR HORTA, **staircase in the Van Eetvelde House, Brussels, Belgium, 1895.**

The Art Nouveau movement was an attempt to create art and architecture based on natural forms. Here, every detail conforms to the theme of the twining plant and functions as part of a living whole.

(FIG. 28-38A), his first major commission. Every detail of the Van Eetvelde interior functions as part of a living whole. Furniture, drapery folds, veining in the lavish stone paneling, and the patterning of the door moldings join with real plants to provide graceful counterpoints for the twining-plant theme. Metallic tendrils curl around the railings and posts, delicate metal tracery fills the glass dome, and floral and leaf motifs spread across the fabric panels of the screen. Flower and plant motifs also figure prominently in the immensely popular stained-glass lamps (FIG. 28-38B) of LOUIS COMFORT TIFFANY (1848–1933).

The Art Nouveau style reflects several influences. In addition to the rich, foliated two-dimensional ornamentation of Arts and Crafts design and that movement's respect for materials, the sinuous whiplash curve of Japanese print designs (FIG. 34-13) inspired Art Nouveau artists. Art Nouveau also borrowed from the expressively patterned styles

🔼 **28-38A** HORTA, Tassel House, Brussels, 1892–1893.

🔼 **28-38B** TIFFANY, water lily lamp, 1904–1915.

of van Gogh (FIGS. 28-18 and 28-19), Gauguin (FIGS. 28-20 and 28-21), and their Post-Impressionist and Symbolist contemporaries (compare, for example, Toulouse-Lautrec's posters [FIG. 28-15]). In addition, the style is a distant descendant of the Rococo aesthetic (see page 764), which was also derived from natural forms.

ANTONIO GAUDI Art Nouveau achieved its most personal expression in the work of the Spanish architect ANTONIO GAUDI (1852–1926). Before becoming an architect, Gaudi had trained as an ironworker. Like many young artists of his time, he longed to create a style both modern and appropriate to his country. Taking inspiration from Moorish architecture and from the simple architecture of his native Catalonia, Gaudi developed a distinctive personal aesthetic. He conceived a building as a whole and molded it almost as a sculptor might shape a figure from clay, approaching architectural design as if buildings were organic, living forms. Although work on his designs proceeded slowly under the guidance of his intuition and imagination, Gaudi was a master who invented many new structural techniques that facilitated construction of his visions.

Gaudi's Barcelona apartment house, Casa Milá (FIG. 28-39), is a wondrously free-form mass wrapped around a street corner. Lacy iron railings enliven the swelling curves of the cut-stone facade, which are echoed in the undulating walls of the interior courtyard. Dormer windows peep from the undulating tiled roof, from which fantastically writhing chimneys poke energetically into the air

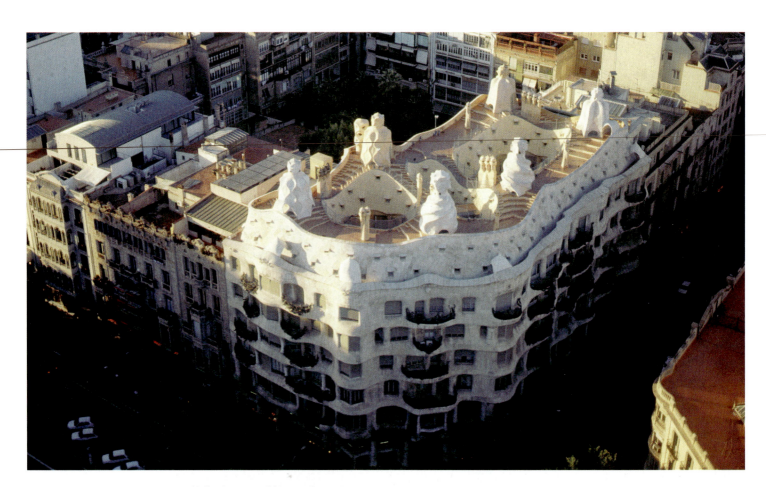

28-39 ANTONIO GAUDI, Casa Milá (looking north), Barcelona, Spain, 1907.

Spanish Art Nouveau architect Gaudi conceived this Barcelona apartment house as if it were a gigantic sculpture to be molded from clay. Twisting chimneys cap the undulating roof and walls.

above. The rough surfaces of the stone walls suggest naturally worn rock. The entrance portals look like eroded sea caves. Their design also may reflect the excitement that swept Spain following the 1879 discovery of Paleolithic cave paintings at Altamira (FIG. 1-8).

ALEXANDRE-GUSTAVE EIFFEL In the later 19th century, new technologies and the changing needs of urbanized, industrialized society affected architecture throughout the Western world. Since the 18th century, bridges had been built of cast iron (FIG. 26-13), which enabled engineering advancements in the construction of larger, stronger, and more fire-resistant structures. Steel, available after 1860, made it possible for architects to enclose ever larger spaces, such as those found in railroad stations (FIG. 28-4) and exposition halls. The Realist impulse

also encouraged architectural designs that honestly expressed a building's purpose, rather than elaborately disguising its function.

The elegant metal-skeleton structures of the French engineer-architect ALEXANDRE-GUSTAVE EIFFEL (1832–1923) were responses to this idea, and they constituted an important contribution to the development of the 20th-century skyscraper. A native of Burgundy, Eiffel trained in Paris before beginning a distinguished career designing exhibition halls, bridges, and the interior armature for France's anniversary gift to the United States—the *Statue of Liberty* by Frédéric Auguste Bartholdi (1834–1904).

Eiffel designed his best-known work, the Eiffel Tower (FIG. 28-40), for an exhibition in Paris in 1889. Although the tower pays tribute to traditional architectural forms, such as the Roman

28-40 ALEXANDRE-GUSTAVE EIFFEL, Eiffel Tower (looking southeast), Paris, France, 1889.

New materials and technologies and the modernist aesthetic fueled radically new architectural designs in the late 19th century. Eiffel jolted the world with the exposed iron skeleton of his tower.

28-43 Louis Henry Sullivan, Carson, Pirie, Scott Building (looking southeast), Chicago, 1899–1904.

Sullivan's architectural motto was "form follows function." He tailored the design of this steel, glass, and stone Chicago department store to meet the needs of its employees and customers.

Sullivan also designed the Carson, Pirie, Scott Building (FIG. 28-43) in Chicago. Built between 1899 and 1904, this department store required broad, open, well-illuminated display spaces. Sullivan again used a minimal structural steel skeleton to achieve this goal. The architect gave over the lowest two levels of the building to an ornament in cast iron (of his invention) made of wildly fantastic motifs. He regarded the display windows as pictures, which merited elaborate frames. As in the Guaranty Building, Sullivan revealed his profound understanding of the maturing consumer economy and tailored the Carson, Pirie, Scott Building to meet the functional and symbolic needs of its users.

Thus, in architecture as well as in the pictorial arts, the late 19th century was a period during which artists challenged traditional modes of expression, often emphatically rejecting the past. Architects, painters, and sculptors as different as Sullivan, Monet, van Gogh, Cézanne, and Rodin, each in his own way, contributed significantly to the entrenchment of modernism as the new cultural orthodoxy of the early 20th century.

28-42 Louis Henry Sullivan, Guaranty (Prudential) Building (looking southwest), Buffalo, New York, 1894–1896.

Sullivan drew on the latest technologies to create this light-filled, well-ventilated Buffalo office building. He added ornate surface embellishments to impart a sense of refinement and taste.

28-42A Sullivan, Wainwright Building, St. Louis, 1890–1891.

the use of iron for many building programs, especially commercial ones. Designers in both England and the United States enthusiastically developed cast-iron architecture until a series of disastrous fires in the early 1870s in New York, Boston, and Chicago demonstrated that cast iron by itself was far from impervious to fire. This discovery led to encasing the metal in masonry, combining the first material's strength with the second's fire resistance (see "The First Skyscrapers," page 876, and FIG. 28-41).

LOUIS HENRY SULLIVAN As skyscrapers proliferated, architects refined the visual vocabulary of the new inhabitable towers. Louis Henry Sullivan (1856–1924), whom many architectural

historians call the first truly modern architect, arrived at a synthesis of industrial structure and ornamentation that perfectly expressed the spirit of late-19th-century commerce. To achieve this, he used the latest technological developments to create light-filled, well-ventilated office buildings and adorned both exteriors and interiors with ornate embellishments. Such decoration served to connect commerce and culture, and imbued these white-collar workspaces with a sense of refinement and taste.

These characteristics are evident in Sullivan's Guaranty (Prudential) Building (FIG. 28-42) in Buffalo, built between 1894 and 1896, and in his earlier Wainwright Building (FIG. 28-42A) in St. Louis. The Buffalo skyscraper is steel, sheathed with terracotta. The imposing scale of the building and the regularity of the window placements served as an expression of the large-scale, refined, and orderly office work taking place within. Sullivan tempered the severity of the structure with lively ornamentation, both on the piers and cornice on the exterior of the building and on the stairway balustrades, elevator cages, and ceiling in the interior. The Guaranty Building illustrates Sullivan's famous dictum "form follows function," which became the slogan of many early-20th-century architects. Still, Sullivan did not advocate a rigid and doctrinaire correspondence between exterior and interior design. Rather, he espoused a free and flexible relationship—one that his pupil Frank Lloyd Wright (see page 917) later described as similar to that between the hand's bones and tissue.

28-43 Louis Henry Sullivan, Carson, Pirie, Scott Building (looking southeast), Chicago, 1899–1904.

Sullivan's architectural motto was "form follows function." He tailored the design of this steel, glass, and stone Chicago department store to meet the needs of its employees and customers.

Sullivan also designed the Carson, Pirie, Scott Building (FIG. 28-43) in Chicago. Built between 1899 and 1904, this department store required broad, open, well-illuminated display spaces. Sullivan again used a minimal structural steel skeleton to achieve this goal. The architect gave over the lowest two levels of the building to an ornament in cast iron (of his invention) made of wildly fantastic motifs. He regarded the display windows as pictures, which merited elaborate frames. As in the Guaranty Building, Sullivan revealed his profound understanding of the maturing consumer economy and tailored the Carson, Pirie, Scott Building to meet the functional and symbolic needs of its users.

Thus, in architecture as well as in the pictorial arts, the late 19th century was a period during which artists challenged traditional modes of expression, often emphatically rejecting the past. Architects, painters, and sculptors as different as Sullivan, Monet, van Gogh, Cézanne, and Rodin, each in his own way, contributed significantly to the entrenchment of modernism as the new cultural orthodoxy of the early 20th century.

above. The rough surfaces of the stone walls suggest naturally worn rock. The entrance portals look like eroded sea caves. Their design also may reflect the excitement that swept Spain following the 1879 discovery of Paleolithic cave paintings at Altamira (FIG. 1-8).

ALEXANDRE-GUSTAVE EIFFEL In the later 19th century, new technologies and the changing needs of urbanized, industrialized society affected architecture throughout the Western world. Since the 18th century, bridges had been built of cast iron (FIG. 26-13), which enabled engineering advancements in the construction of larger, stronger, and more fire-resistant structures. Steel, available after 1860, made it possible for architects to enclose ever larger spaces, such as those found in railroad stations (FIG. 28-4) and exposition halls. The Realist impulse

also encouraged architectural designs that honestly expressed a building's purpose, rather than elaborately disguising its function.

The elegant metal-skeleton structures of the French engineer-architect ALEXANDRE-GUSTAVE EIFFEL (1832–1923) were responses to this idea, and they constituted an important contribution to the development of the 20th-century skyscraper. A native of Burgundy, Eiffel trained in Paris before beginning a distinguished career designing exhibition halls, bridges, and the interior armature for France's anniversary gift to the United States—the *Statue of Liberty* by Frédéric Auguste Bartholdi (1834–1904).

Eiffel designed his best-known work, the Eiffel Tower (FIG. 28-40), for an exhibition in Paris in 1889. Although the tower pays tribute to traditional architectural forms, such as the Roman

28-40 ALEXANDRE-GUSTAVE EIFFEL, **Eiffel Tower (looking southeast), Paris, France, 1889.**

New materials and technologies and the modernist aesthetic fueled radically new architectural designs in the late 19th century. Eiffel jolted the world with the exposed iron skeleton of his tower.

PROBLEMS AND SOLUTIONS
The First Skyscrapers

In cities, convenience required closely grouped buildings, and increased property values forced architects literally to raise the roof. Even an attic could command high rent if the builders installed one of the new elevators, used for the first time in the Equitable Building in New York, constructed between 1868 and 1871. Iron and steel, which could support these towering structures, gave birth to the American skyscraper.

One of the pioneers in designing these modern commercial towers was HENRY HOBSON RICHARDSON (1838–1886), but he also had a profound respect for earlier architectural styles. Because Richardson had a special fondness for the Romanesque architecture of the Auvergne area in France, he frequently used heavy round arches and massive masonry walls. Architectural historians sometimes consider his work to constitute a Romanesque revival related to the Neo-Gothic style (FIGS. 27-43 and 27-43A). This designation, however, does not do justice to the originality and quality of most of the buildings that Richardson designed during his brief 18-year practice. Trinity Church in Boston and his smaller public libraries, residences, railroad stations, and courthouses in New England and elsewhere best demonstrate his vivid imagination and the solidity (the sense of enclosure and permanence) so characteristic of his style.

Nevertheless, Richardson's most important and influential building was the Marshall Field wholesale store (FIG. 28-41) in Chicago, begun in 1885 and demolished in 1930. In this vast building, which occupied an entire city block, Richardson solved the problem of designing a structure to satisfy the needs of commerce while paying homage to historical styles without imitating them—an approach that would be revived a century later in *postmodern* architecture (see "After Modernism: Postmodernist Architecture," page 949). The tripartite elevation of a Renaissance palace (FIG. 21-35) or of the Roman aqueduct (FIG. 7-33) near Nîmes, France, may have influenced Richardson's design. But he used no classical ornamentation, made much of the massive courses of masonry, and, in the strong horizontality of the windowsills and the interrupted courses defining the levels,

28-41 HENRY HOBSON RICHARDSON, Marshall Field wholesale store, Chicago, 1885–1887 (demolished 1930).

Richardson was a pioneer in designing commercial structures using a cast-iron skeleton encased in fire-resistant masonry. This construction technique enabled the insertion of large windows in the walls.

stressed the long sweep of the building's lines, as well as the edifice's ponderous weight. Although the structural frame still lay behind and in conjunction with the masonry screen, the great glazed arcades opened up the walls of the monumental store. They pointed the way to 20th-century skyscrapers characterized by the total penetration of walls and the transformation of them into mere screens or curtains that serve both to echo the underlying structural grid and to protect the interior spaces from the weather (compare FIG. 30-45).

---

arch and the Gothic spire, it immediately—and justly—became the iconic symbol of modern Paris. Eiffel's elegant iron tower thrusts its needle shaft 984 feet above the city, making it at the time of its construction until the erection of the Empire State Building in New York City in 1931 the world's tallest structure. The tower rests on four giant supports connected by gracefully arching open-frame skirts that provide a pleasing mask for the heavy horizontal girders needed to strengthen the legs as well as anchor the structure against powerful wind gusts. Visitors can take two successive elevators to the top, or they can use the internal staircase. Either way, the view of Paris and the Seine from the tower is incomparable, as is the design of the tower itself. The transparency of Eiffel's struc-

ture blurs the distinction between interior and exterior to an extent never before achieved or even attempted. This interpenetration of inner and outer space became a hallmark of 20th-century art and architecture. Eiffel's tower and the earlier iron skeletal frames designed by Labrouste (FIG. 27-46) and Paxton (FIG. 27-47) jolted the architectural profession into a realization that modern materials and processes could germinate a completely new style and a radically innovative approach to architectural design (see "Prefabricated Architecture," page 833).

AMERICAN SKYSCRAPERS The desire for greater speed and economy in building, as well as for a reduction in fire hazards, prompted

IMPRESSIONISM, POST-IMPRESSIONISM, SYMBOLISM: EUROPE AND AMERICA, 1870 TO 1900

Impressionism

- A hostile critic applied the term *Impressionism* to the paintings of Claude Monet because of their sketchy quality. The Impressionists—Monet, Pierre-Auguste Renoir, Edgar Degas, and others—were a diverse group. Some strove to capture fleeting moments and transient effects of light and climate on canvas. Others focused on recording the contemporary urban scene in Paris, frequently painting bars, dance halls, the ballet, wide boulevards, and railroad stations. What united them was not a uniform style or technique but an interest in depicting the transitory nature of modern life.

- Impressionist canvases vary in composition as well as technique, but many feature figures seen at sharply oblique angles and arbitrarily cut off by the frame. These compositions reflect the influence of Japanese prints and of photography.

Degas, *The Rehearsal*, 1874

Post-Impressionism and Symbolism

- Post-Impressionism is not a unified style. The term refers to the group of late-19th-century artists, including Georges Seurat, Vincent van Gogh, Paul Gauguin, and Paul Cézanne, who followed the Impressionists and took painting in new directions. Seurat refined the Impressionist approach to color and light into pointillism—the disciplined application of pure color in tiny daubs. Van Gogh explored the capabilities of colors and distorted forms to express emotions. Gauguin moved away from Impressionism in favor of large areas of flat color bounded by firm lines, as in the Japanese prints that he and his contemporaries admired. Cézanne replaced the transitory visual effects of the Impressionists with a rigorous analysis of the lines, planes, and colors that make up landscapes and still lifes.

- Gustave Moreau, Odilon Redon, and Henri Rousseau were the leading French Symbolists. They disdained Realism as trivial and sought to depict a reality beyond that of the everyday world, rejecting materialism and celebrating fantasy and imagination. The subjects of their paintings were often mysterious, exotic, and sensuous.

Gauguin, *Vision after the Sermon*, 1888

Rousseau, *Sleeping Gypsy*, 1897

Sculpture

- At the end of the 19th century, French artists also led the world in sculpture. Jean-Baptiste Carpeaux, an admirer of Michelangelo and Greco-Roman statuary, added a Realist dimension to his models in groups such as *Ugolino. The Waltz,* by Camille Claudel, exemplifies fin-de-siècle passion and eroticism.

- The leading sculptor of the era was Auguste Rodin, who explored Realist themes and the representation of movement. His vision of tormented, writhing figures in Hell connects his work with the Symbolists. Rodin also made statues that were deliberate fragments, creating a taste for the incomplete that appealed to many later sculptors.

Claudel, *The Waltz*, 1895

Architecture and Decorative Arts

- Not all artists embraced the industrialization transforming daily life during the 19th century. The Arts and Crafts movement in England and the international Art Nouveau style formed in opposition to modern mass production. Both schools advocated natural forms and high-quality craftsmanship.

- New technologies and the changing needs of urbanized, industrialized society transformed architecture in the late 19th century. The exposed iron skeleton of the Eiffel Tower jolted architects into realizing that modern materials and processes could revolutionize architectural design. Henry Hobson Richardson and Louis Sullivan were pioneers in designing the first metal, stone, and glass skyscrapers.

Eiffel, Eiffel Tower, Paris, 1889

29-1 PABLO PICASSO, *Les Demoiselles d'Avignon*, 1907. Oil on canvas, 8' × 7' 8".
Museum of Modern Art, New York (acquired through the Lillie P. Bliss Bequest).

1 ft.

▲ **29-1a** "Primitive" art helped inspire Picasso's radical break with traditional Western norms of pictorial representation. Ancient Iberian sculptures were the sources of the features of the three young women at the left.

▲ **29-1b** The striated features of the distorted heads of the two young Avignon Street prostitutes at the right grew directly from Picasso's increasing fascination with African artworks, which he studied and collected.

▲ **29-1c** By breaking the figures of the demoiselles into ambiguous planes, as if the viewer were seeing them from more than one place in space at once, Picasso disrupted the standards of Western art since the Renaissance.

Modernism in Europe and America, 1900 to 1945

PICASSO DISRUPTS THE WESTERN PICTORIAL TRADITION

An artist whose importance to the history of art is uncontested, PABLO PICASSO (1881–1973) was blessed with boundless talent and an inquisitive intellect that led him to make groundbreaking contributions to Western pictorial art. In 1907, with *Les Demoiselles d'Avignon* (*The Young Ladies of Avignon*; FIG. **29-1**), he opened the door to a radically new method of representing forms in space. Picasso began the work as a symbolic picture to be titled *Philosophical Bordello,* portraying two male clients (who, based on surviving drawings, had features resembling Picasso's) intermingling with women in the reception room of a brothel on Avignon Street in Barcelona. One was a sailor. The other carried a skull, an obvious reference to death. By the time the artist finished, he had eliminated both men and simplified the room's details to a suggestion of drapery and a schematic foreground still life. Picasso had become wholly absorbed in the problem of finding a new way to represent the five women in their interior space. Instead of depicting the figures as continuous volumes, he fractured their shapes and interwove them with the equally jagged planes representing drapery and empty space. Indeed, the space, so entwined with the bodies, is virtually illegible. The tension between Picasso's representation of three-dimensional space and his modernist conviction that a painting is a two-dimensional design on the surface of a stretched canvas is a tension between representation and abstraction.

The artist extended the radical nature of *Les Demoiselles d'Avignon* even further by depicting the figures inconsistently. Ancient Iberian sculptures inspired the calm, ideal features of the three prostitutes at the left. The energetic, violently striated features of the heads of the two women at the right emerged late in Picasso's production of the work and grew directly from his increasing fascination with African sculpture. Perhaps responding to the energy of these two new heads, Picasso also revised the women's bodies. He broke them into more ambiguous planes suggesting a combination of views, as if the observer sees the figures from more than one place in space at once. The woman seated at the lower right shows these multiple angles most clearly, seeming to present the observer simultaneously with a three-quarter back view from the left, another from the right, and a front view of the head that suggests seeing the figure frontally as well. Gone is the traditional Renaissance concept of an orderly, constructed, and unified pictorial space mirroring the world. In its place are the rudimentary beginnings of a new approach to representing the world—as a dynamic interplay of time and space. Picasso's *Les Demoiselles d'Avignon* was nothing less than a dramatic departure from and disruption of the Western pictorial tradition. It set the stage for many other artistic revolutions in the 20th century.

GLOBAL UPHEAVAL AND ARTISTIC REVOLUTION

The first half of the 20th century was a period of significant upheaval worldwide. Between 1900 and 1945, the major industrial powers fought two global wars (MAP 29-1); witnessed the rise of Communism, Fascism, and Nazism; and suffered the Great Depression.

These decades were also a time of radical change in the arts when painters and sculptors challenged some of the most basic assumptions about the purpose of art and what form an artwork should take. Throughout history, artistic revolution has often accompanied political, social, and economic upheaval, but never before had the new directions that artists explored been as pronounced or as long-lasting as those born during the first half of the last century (see "Picasso Disrupts the Western Pictorial Tradition," page 881).

MAP 29-1 Europe at the end of World War I.

AVANT-GARDE As did other members of society, artists felt deeply the effects of the political and economic disruptions of the early 20th century. As the old social orders collapsed and new ones, from Communism to corporate capitalism, took their places, artists searched for new definitions of and uses for art in a changed world. This fundamental questioning of the nature and goals of artistic production had many precedents in the 19th century, when each successive modernist movement had challenged artistic conventions with ever-greater intensity. This relentless questioning of the status quo gave rise to the notion of an artistic *avant-garde*. The term, which means "front guard," derives from 19th-century French military usage. The avant-garde were the troops sent ahead of the army's main body to scout the enemy's position and strength. Politicians who deemed themselves visionary and forward-thinking subsequently adopted the term. It then migrated to the art world in the 1880s, when artists and critics used it to refer to the Realists, Impressionists, and Post-Impressionists—artists who were ahead of their time and who transgressed the limits of established art forms.

These trailblazing rebels rejected the classical and the academic, and questioned the premises and formal qualities of traditional Western painting, sculpture, and other media. Although the general public found avant-garde art incomprehensible, the principles underlying 19th-century modernism appealed to increasing numbers of artists as the 20th century dawned.

EUROPE, 1900 TO 1920

Avant-garde artists in all their diversity became a major force during the opening decades of the 20th century, beginning with the artistic movement known as *Fauvism*.

Fauvism

In 1905, at the third Salon d'Automne (Autumn Salon) in Paris, a group of young painters exhibited canvases so simplified in design and so shockingly bright in color that a startled critic, Louis Vauxcelles (1870–1943), described the artists as *fauves* (wild beasts). The Fauves were totally independent of the French Academy and the "official" Salon (see "Academic Salons and Independent Art Exhibitions," page 844). Driving the Fauve movement was a desire to develop an art having the directness of Impressionism but employing intense color juxtapositions for expressive ends.

Building on the legacy of artists such as Vincent van Gogh and Paul Gauguin (FIGS. 28-18 to 28-21), the Fauves went even further in liberating color from its descriptive function and exploring the effects that different colors have on emotions. The Fauves produced portraits, landscapes, still lifes, and nudes of spontaneity and verve, with rich surface textures, lively linear patterns, and, above all, bold colors. In an effort to release internal feelings, they employed startling contrasts of vermilion and emerald green and of cerulean blue and vivid orange held together by sweeping brushstrokes and bold patterns.

The Fauve painters never officially organized, and the looseness of both personal connections and stylistic affinities caused the Fauve movement to begin to disintegrate almost as soon as it emerged. Within five years, most of the artists had departed from a strict adherence to Fauve principles and developed their own more personal styles. During its brief existence, however, Fauvism made a remarkable contribution to the direction of art by demonstrating color's structural, expressive, and aesthetic capabilities.

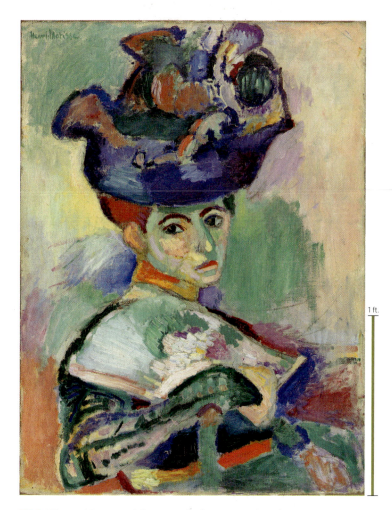

29-2 HENRI MATISSE, *Woman with the Hat*, 1905. Oil on canvas, 2' 7¾" × 1' 11½". San Francisco Museum of Modern Art, San Francisco (bequest of Elise S. Haas).

Matisse's portrayal of his wife, Amélie, features patches and splotches of seemingly arbitrary colors. He and the other Fauve painters used color not to imitate nature but to produce a reaction in the viewer.

HENRI MATISSE The dominant figure of the Fauve group was HENRI MATISSE (1869–1954), who believed that color could play a primary role in conveying meaning, and consequently focused his efforts on developing this notion. In an early painting, *Woman with the Hat* (FIG. 29-2), Matisse depicted his wife, Amélie, in a rather conventional manner compositionally, but the seemingly arbitrary colors immediately startle the viewer, as does the sketchiness of the forms. The entire image—the woman's face, clothes, hat, and background—consists of patches and splotches of color juxtaposed in ways that sometimes produce jarring contrasts. Matisse explained his approach: "What characterized Fauvism was that we rejected imitative colors, and that with pure colors we obtained stronger reactions."[1] For Matisse and the Fauves, therefore, color became the formal element most responsible for pictorial coherence and the primary conveyor of meaning (see "Henri Matisse on Color," page 884, and FIG. 29-2A).

29-2A MATISSE, *Le Bonheur de Vivre*, 1905–1906.

ARTISTS ON ART
Henri Matisse on Color

In an essay titled "Notes of a Painter," published in the Parisian journal *La Grande Revue* on Christmas Day 1908, Henri Matisse responded to his critics and set forth his principles and goals as a painter. The following excerpts help explain what Matisse was trying to achieve in paintings such as *Harmony in Red* (FIG. 29-3).

What I am after, above all, is expression.... Expression, for me, does not reside in passions glowing in a human face or manifested by violent movement. The entire arrangement of my picture is expressive: the place occupied by the figures, the empty spaces around them, the proportions, everything has its share. Composition is the art of arranging in a decorative manner the diverse elements at the painter's command to express his feelings....

Both harmonies and dissonances of color can produce agreeable effects.... Suppose I have to paint an interior: I have before me a cupboard; it gives me a sensation of vivid red, and I put down a red which satisfies me. A relation is established between this red and the white of the canvas. Let me put a green near the red, and make the floor yellow; and again there will be relationships between

the green or yellow and the white of the canvas which will satisfy me.... A new combination of colors will succeed the first and render the totality of my representation. I am forced to transpose until finally my picture may seem completely changed when, after successive modifications, the red has succeeded the green as the dominant color. I cannot copy nature in a servile way; I am forced to interpret nature and submit it to the spirit of the picture. From the relationship I have found in all the tones there must result a living harmony of colors, a harmony analogous to that of a musical composition....

The chief function of color should be to serve expression as well as possible.... My choice of colors does not rest on any scientific theory; it is based on observation, on sensitivity, on felt experiences.... I simply try to put down colors which render my sensation. There is an impelling proportion of tones that may lead me to change the shape of a figure or to transform my composition. Until I have achieved this proportion in all parts of the composition I strive towards it and keep on working. Then a moment comes when all the parts have found their definite relationships, and from then on it would be impossible for me to add a stroke to my picture without having to repaint it entirely.[*]

[*]Translated by Jack D. Flam, *Matisse on Art* (London: Phaidon, 1973), 32–40.

1 ft.

29-3 HENRI MATISSE, *Red Room* (*Harmony in Red*), 1908–1909. Oil on canvas, 5' 11" × 8' 1". State Hermitage Museum, Saint Petersburg.

Matisse believed that painters should choose compositions and colors that express their feelings. Here, the table and wall seem to merge because they are the same color and have identical patterning.

29-4 ANDRÉ DERAIN, *Mountains at Collioure,* 1905. Oil on canvas, 2' 8" × 3' 3½". National Gallery of Art, Washington, D.C. (John Hay Whitney Collection).

Mountains at Collioure owes much to the landscapes of the Impressionists, van Gogh, and Gauguin, but Derain went further in liberating color from its traditional role of imitating nature.

tance of color for striking the right chord in the viewer. Initially, this work was predominantly green. Then Matisse repainted it blue, but blue also did not seem appropriate to him. Not until he repainted the canvas red did Matisse feel that he had found the right color for the "harmony" he wished to compose.

ANDRÉ DERAIN The landscape setting of Matisse's *Le Bonheur de Vivre* (FIG. 29-2A) is Collioure, on the southeastern coast of France near the border with Spain. In 1905, Matisse painted there beside his friend and fellow Fauve, André Derain (1880–1954). Although Derain also produced many figure studies (for example, FIG. 29-5), at Collioure he frequently painted pure landscapes in the open air, as did the Impressionists before him. *Mountains at Collioure* (FIG. 29-4) is probably the best of that series. Much smaller than *Le Bonheur de Vivre,* Derain's representation of Collioure succeeds in capturing the vast panorama of the Mediterranean mountains, olive groves, and sky seen from a high vantage point. The painting owes much not only to Impressionism but also to Derain's close study of the Post-Impressionists. The short, energetic brushstrokes of pure color, for example, reveal Derain's familiarity with the landscapes of Vincent van Gogh (FIG. 28-19), whose influence is especially clear in the way Derain alternated staccato strokes of green with exposed white canvas in the foreground. The broad, flat areas of unmodulated color in the mountains and sky derive from Paul Gauguin (FIGS. 28-20 and 28-21).

Mountains at Collioure is no mere synthesis of earlier styles, however. Derain went further than either van Gogh or Gauguin in liberating color from its traditional role of imitating the appearance of nature. Like Matisse, Derain used color to create a mood—to express the energy he perceived in the landscape. In Derain's *The Dance* (FIG. 29-5), a lush landscape is merely the background for a study of several large figures, some nude, others clothed, which dominate the canvas.

HARMONY IN RED These color discoveries reached maturity in Matisse's *Red Room* (*Harmony in Red*; FIG. 29-3). The subject is the interior of a comfortable, prosperous household with a maid placing fruit and wine on the table, but Matisse's canvas is radically different from traditional paintings of domestic interiors (for example, FIGS. 25-18C and 25-19). The Fauve painter depicted objects in simplified and schematized fashion and flattened out the forms. For example, Matisse eliminated the front edge of the table, rendering the table, with its identical patterning, as flat as the wall behind it. The window at the upper left could also be a painting on the wall, further flattening the space. Everywhere, the colors contrast richly and intensely. Matisse's process of overpainting reveals the impor-

29-5 ANDRÉ DERAIN, *The Dance,* 1906. Oil on canvas, 6' ⅞" × 6' 10¼". Fridart Foundation, London.

Derain worked closely with Matisse, but the tropical setting and the bold colors of *The Dance* also reflect Derain's study of Gauguin's paintings (FIGS. 28-20 and 28-21), as does the flattened perspective.

29-6 ERNST-LUDWIG KIRCHNER, *Street, Dresden,* 1908 (dated 1907). Oil on canvas, 4' 11$\frac{1}{4}$" × 6' 6$\frac{7}{8}$". Museum of Modern Art, New York.

Kirchner's perspective distortions, disquieting figures, and color choices reflect the influence of the Fauves and of Edvard Munch (FIG. 28-29), who made similar expressive use of formal elements.

The tropical setting and the bold colors again reflect Derain's study of Gauguin, as does the flattened perspective, but the the Fauve painter's colors are often jarring juxtapositions of complementary colors, which Derain referred to as "deliberate disharmonies." They are precisely what generated the hostility directed at the Fauves when they first presented their work to the public at the Salon d'Automne of 1905.

German Expressionism

The immediacy and boldness of the Fauve images appealed to many artists, including two groups of painters in Germany who called themselves *Die Brücke* ("the Bridge") and *Der Blaue Reiter* ("the Blue Rider"). Together, they produced dramatic and often emotional canvases that art historians classify under the general heading German *Expressionism.* However, although color plays a prominent role in German painting of the early 20th century, the "expressiveness" of many of the German images is due as much to the Expressionists' wrenching distortions of form, ragged outlines, and agitated brushstrokes.

ERNST LUDWIG KIRCHNER Die Brücke, the first group of German Expressionists, gathered in Dresden in 1905 under the leadership of ERNST LUDWIG KIRCHNER (1880–1938). The group members thought of themselves as paving the way for a more perfect age by bridging the old age and the new, hence their name. Kirchner's early studies in architecture, painting, and the graphic arts had instilled

in him a deep admiration for German medieval art. Like the British artists associated with the Arts and Crafts movement, such as William Morris (FIG. 28-36), Die Brücke artists modeled themselves on medieval craft guilds whose members lived together and practiced all the arts equally. Kirchner described their lofty goals in a ringing 1913 statement published in the form of a *woodcut* titled *Chronik der Brücke:*

> With faith in progress and in a new generation of creators and specta-
> tors we call together all youth. As youth, we carry the future and want
> to create for ourselves freedom of life and of movement against the
> long-established older forces. Everyone who reproduces that which
> drives him to creation with directness and authenticity belongs to us.[2]

Die Brücke artists protested the hypocrisy and materialistic decadence of those in power. Kirchner, in particular, focused much of his attention on the detrimental effects of industrialization, such as the alienation of individuals in cities, which he felt fostered a mechanized and impersonal society. The tensions leading to World War I further intensified the discomfort and anxiety of the German Expressionists.

Kirchner's *Street, Dresden* (FIG. **29-6**) provides a glimpse into the frenzied urban activity of a bustling German city before World War I. Rather than offering the distant, panoramic urban view of the Impressionists (FIG. 28-5), Kirchner's street scene is jarring and dissonant in both composition and color, conveying the disquieting and alienating character of Dresden in the early 20th century. The women in the foreground loom large, approaching somewhat menacingly. The steep perspective of the street, which threatens to push the women directly into the viewer's space, increases their confrontational nature. Harshly rendered, the women's features make them appear ghoulish, and the garish, clashing colors—juxtapositions of bright orange, emerald green, chartreuse, and pink—add to the expressive impact of the image. Kirchner's perspective distortions, disquieting figures, and color choices reflect the influence of the work of Edvard Munch, who made similar expressive use of formal elements in *The Scream* (FIG. 28-29).

VASSILY KANDINSKY Der Blaue Reiter, the second major German Expressionist group, formed in Munich in 1911. The two founding members, Vassily Kandinsky and Franz Marc, whimsically selected this name because of their mutual interest in horses and the color

blue. Like Die Brücke, this group produced paintings that captured their feelings in visual form while also eliciting intense emotional responses from viewers.

Born in Russia, VASSILY KANDINSKY (1866–1944) moved to Munich in 1896 and soon developed a spontaneous expressive style. Indeed, Kandinsky was one of the first artists to reject representation and explore abstraction as the "subject" of his paintings, as in *Improvisation 28* (FIG. 29-7). Kandinsky's elimination of recognizable forms from his canvases grew in part from his interest in theosophy (a religious and philosophical belief system incorporating a wide range of tenets from, among other sources, Buddhism and mysticism) and the occult, but it also reflected his interest in the latest advances in science. A true intellectual, widely read in philosophy, religion, history, and the other arts, especially music, Kandinsky was also one of the few early modernist artists to read with some comprehension the new scientific theories of the era

ART AND SOCIETY
Science and Art in the Early 20th Century

In the early 20th century, radical new ways of thinking emerged in both science and art, forcing people to revise how they understood the world. In particular, the values and ideals that were the legacy of the Enlightenment (see page 771) began to yield to new perspectives. Intellectuals countered 18th- and 19th-century assumptions about progress and reason with ideas challenging traditional notions about the physical universe, the structure of society, and human nature. Modernist artists fully participated in this reassessment and formulated innovative theoretical bases for their work. Accordingly, much early-20th-century Western art is a rejection of traditional limitations and definitions both of art and of the universe.

Fundamental to the Enlightenment was faith in science (see "Joseph Wright of Derby and the Industrial Revolution," page 772). Because of its basis in empirical, or observable, fact, science provided a mechanistic conception of the universe, which reassured a populace that was finding traditional religions less certain. As promoted in the classic physics of Isaac Newton (1642–1727), the universe was a huge machine consisting of time, space, and matter. In the early 20th century, many scientists challenged this model of the universe in what amounted to a second scientific and technological revolution. Particularly noteworthy was the work of physicists Max Planck (1858–1947), Albert Einstein (1879–1955), Ernest Rutherford (1871–1937), and Niels Bohr (1885–1962). With their discoveries, each of these scientists shattered the

existing faith in the objective reality of matter and, in so doing, paved the way for a new model of the universe.

Planck's quantum theory (1900) raised questions about the emission of atomic energy. In his 1905 paper "The Electrodynamics of Moving Bodies," Einstein carried Planck's work further by introducing his theory of relativity. He argued that space and time are not absolute, as postulated in Newtonian physics. Rather, Einstein explained, time and space are relative to the observer and linked in what he called a four-dimensional space-time continuum. He also concluded that matter was not a solid, tangible reality, but another form of energy. Einstein's famous equation, $E = mc^2$, where E stands for energy, m for mass, and c for the speed of light, provided a formula for understanding atomic energy. Rutherford's and Bohr's exploration of atomic structure between 1906 and 1913 contributed to this new perception of matter and energy.

Together, all these scientific discoveries constituted a changed view of physical nature and contributed to the growing interest in abstraction, as opposed to naturalism—the representation of the world as it appears to the eye—among early-20th-century artists, especially Vassily Kandinsky (FIG. 29-7).

29-7 VASSILY KANDINSKY, *Improvisation 28* (second version), 1912. Oil on canvas, 3' 7$\frac{7}{8}$" × 5' 3$\frac{7}{8}$". Solomon R. Guggenheim Museum, New York (gift of Solomon R. Guggenheim, 1937).

The theories of Einstein and Rutherford convinced Kandinsky that material objects had no real substance. He was one of the first painters to reject representation in favor of abstraction in his canvases.

1 ft.

29-8 FRANZ MARC, *Fate of the Animals*, 1913. Oil on canvas, 6' 4¾" × 8' 9½". Kunstmuseum Basel, Basel.

Marc developed a system of correspondences between specific colors and feelings or ideas. In this apocalyptic scene of animals trapped in a forest, the colors of severity and brutality dominate.

(see "Science and Art in the Early 20th Century," page 887). Scientists' exploration of atomic structure, for example, convinced Kandinsky that material objects had no real substance, thereby shattering his faith in a world of tangible things. He articulated his ideas in an influential treatise, *Concerning the Spiritual in Art,* published in 1912, the same year that he painted *Improvisation 28.* Artists, Kandinsky believed, must express their innermost feelings by orchestrating color, form, line, and space, much like composers create music out of notes, which do not mimic the sounds of nature. In his *Improvisation* series, Kandinsky sought to convey feelings solely by color juxtapositions, intersecting linear elements, and implied spatial relationships. Ultimately, Kandinsky saw these abstractions as evolving blueprints for a more enlightened and liberated society emphasizing spirituality.

FRANZ MARC Like many of the other German Expressionists, FRANZ MARC (1880–1916), the cofounder of Der Blaue Reiter, grew increasingly pessimistic about the state of humanity, especially as World War I loomed on the horizon. His perception of human beings as deeply flawed prompted him to turn to the animal world for his subjects. Animals, he believed, were more pure than humans and thus more appropriate vehicles for expressing an inner truth. In his quest to imbue his paintings with greater emotional intensity, Marc focused on color and developed a system of correspondences between specific colors and feelings or ideas. In a letter to a fellow "blue rider," Marc explained: "Blue is the *male* principle, severe and spiritual. Yellow is the *female* principle, gentle, happy and sensual. Red is *matter,* brutal and heavy."[3]

Fate of the Animals (FIG. 29-8) represents the culmination of Marc's efforts to create, in a sense, an iconography of color. Painted in 1913, when the horrific tension of impending warfare had pervaded society, the animals appear trapped in a forest amid falling trees, some apocalyptic event destroying both the forest and the animals

inhabiting it. The painter distorted the entire scene and shattered it into fragments. Significantly, the lighter and brighter colors—the passive, gentle, and cheerful ones—are absent, and the colors of severity and brutality dominate the work. On the back of the canvas, Marc wrote: "All being is flaming suffering." The artist discovered just how well his painting portended war's anguish and tragedy when he ended up at the front the following year. His experiences in battle prompted him to tell his wife in a letter: "[*Fate of the Animals*] is like a premonition of this war—horrible and shattering. I can hardly conceive that I painted it."[4] Marc's contempt for people's inhumanity and his attempt to express that through his art ended, with tragic irony, in his death in action in 1916.

29-9 KÄTHE KOLLWITZ, *Woman with Dead Child,* 1903. Etching and soft-ground etching, overprinted lithographically with a gold-tone plate, 1' 4⅝" × 1' 7⅛". British Museum, London.

The theme of the mother mourning over her dead child comes from images of the *Pietà* in Christian art, but Kollwitz transformed it into a powerful universal statement of maternal loss and grief.

KÄTHE KOLLWITZ The emotional range of German Expressionism extends from passionate protest and satirical bitterness to the poignantly expressed pity for the poor in the prints of KÄTHE KOLLWITZ (1867–1945)—for example, *Woman with Dead Child* (FIG. 29-9). Kollwitz and her younger contemporary PAULA MODERSOHN-BECKER (1876–1907; FIG. 29-9A) studied at the Union of Berlin Women Artists and had no formal association with any Expressionist group. Working in a variety of printmaking techniques, including woodcut, lithography, and etching, Kollwitz explored a range of issues from the overtly political to the deeply personal.

⬈ **29-9A** MODERSOHN-BECKER, *Self-Portrait*, 1906.

One image that Kollwitz explored in depth, producing a number of print variations, was a mother with her dead child. Although she initially derived the theme from the Christian *Pietà,* Kollwitz transformed it into a universal statement of maternal loss and grief. In the etching and lithograph illustrated here (FIG. 29-9), she replaced the reverence and grace pervading most depictions of Mary holding the dead Christ (FIG. 22-12) with an animalistic passion. The grieving mother ferociously grips the body of her dead child. The primal nature of the undeniably powerful image is in keeping with the aims of the Expressionists. Not since the Gothic age in Germany (FIG. 13-50) had any artist produced a mother-and-son group with a comparable emotional impact. Because Kollwitz used her younger son, Peter, as the model for the dead child, the image was no doubt all the more personal to her. The print stands as a poignant premonition. Peter died fighting in World War I at age 21.

EGON SCHIELE Another painter of highly expressive works featuring distorted forms but not associated with any German Expressionist group was the Austrian artist EGON SCHIELE (1890–1918), who during his tragically brief but prolific career produced more than 3,000 paintings and drawings. The bulk of them are nude figure studies of men and women in *gouache* and watercolor on paper, including approximately a hundred self-portraits exemplifying early-20th-century Expressionist painters' intense interest in emotional states. As a teenager, Schiele watched the slow, painful deterioration of his father, who contracted syphilis and died when Egon was 15. The experience had a profound impact on the artist, who ever after associated sex with physical and emotional pain and death.

Schiele began formal art training the year after his father died. He enrolled in Vienna's Academy of Fine Art in 1906, where he became a protégé of Gustav Klimt (FIG. 28-30), who invited Schiele to exhibit some of his works with his own and

⬈ **29-9B** LEHMBRUCK, *Seated Youth*, 1917.

those of, among others, Vincent van Gogh and Edvard Munch. The emotional content of their work made a deep impression on Schiele, who nonetheless far surpassed van Gogh, Munch, and all of his contemporaries, including the sculptor WILHELM LEHMBRUCK (1881–1919; FIG. 29-9B), in the portrayal of emaciated bodies and tormented

psyches. Indeed, Schiele once spent 24 days in prison for producing what a judge ruled was pornographic art.

Schiele's 1910 nude portrait of himself grimacing (FIG. 29-10) is a characteristic example of his mature work. He stands frontally, staring at himself in the large mirror he kept in his studio. There is no background. The edges of the paper sever his lower legs and right elbow. In some portraits, Schiele portrayed himself with amputated limbs, and his body is always that of a malnourished man whose muscles show through transparent flesh. The pose is awkward, twisted, and pained. The elongated fingers of the hands seem useless, incapable of holding anything. It is hard to imagine a nude body breaking more sharply with the classical tradition of heroic male nudity. Schiele's self-portrait is that of a martyr who has suffered both physically and psychologically. (He portrayed himself in several paintings as Saint Sebastian pierced by arrows.) Schiele's unhappy life ended when he contracted the Spanish flu in 1918. He was only 28 years old.

29-10 EGON SCHIELE, *Nude Self-Portrait, Grimacing*, 1910. Gouache, watercolor, and pencil on paper, 1' 10" × 1' 2$\frac{3}{8}$". Albertina, Vienna.

Breaking sharply with the academic tradition of heroic male nudity, Schiele, a Viennese Expressionist, often portrayed himself with an emaciated body, twisted limbs, and a grimacing expression.

Primitivism and Cubism

The Expressionist departure from any strict adherence to illusionism in art was a path that other early-20th-century artists followed. Among those who most radically challenged prevailing artistic conventions and moved most deliberately into the realm of abstraction was Pablo Picasso (see "Picasso Disrupts the Western Pictorial Tradition," page 881).

PABLO PICASSO Born in Spain four years after Gustave Courbet's death, Picasso had mastered all aspects of late-19th-century Realist technique by the time he entered the Barcelona Academy of Fine Art in the late 1890s. His restless mind and limitless energy led him to experiment with a wide range of visual expression, first in Spain and then in Paris, where he settled in 1904. Perhaps the most prolific artist in history, Picasso explored virtually every artistic medium during his lengthy career, but remained a traditional artist in making careful preparatory studies for each major work. Nonetheless, Picasso exemplified modernism in his enduring quest for innovation, which resulted in sudden shifts from one style to another. By the time he settled permanently in Paris, Picasso's work had evolved from Spanish painting's sober Realism through an Impressionistic phase to the so-called Blue Period (1901–1904), when, in a melancholy state of mind, he used primarily blue colors to depict worn, pathetic, and alienated figures. In 1904, Picasso's palette changed to lighter and brighter colors during his Rose (or Pink) Period (1904–1906), but some of the canvases he painted during those years, such as *Family of Saltimbanques* (FIG. **29-10A**), retain the pessimistic overtones of the Blue Period.

↗ **29-10A** PICASSO, *Family of Saltimbanques*, 1905.

Gertrude and Leo Stein and the Avant-Garde

One of the many unexpected developments in the history of art is that two Americans—Gertrude (1874–1946) and Leo (1872–1947) Stein—played pivotal roles in the history of the European avant-garde. The Steins provided a hospitable environment in their Paris home for artists, writers, musicians, collectors, and critics to socialize and discuss progressive art and ideas. Born in Pennsylvania, the Stein siblings moved to 27 rue de Fleurus in Paris in 1903. Gertrude's experimental writing stimulated her interest in the latest developments in the arts. Conversely, the avant-garde ideas discussed in her home influenced Gertrude's unique poetry, plays, and other works. She is perhaps best known for *The Autobiography of Alice B. Toklas* (1933), a unique memoir written in the persona of her lover and longtime companion.

The Steins' interest in the exciting and invigorating debates taking place in avant-garde circles led them to welcome visitors to their Saturday salons, which included lectures, thoughtful discussions, and spirited arguments. Often, these gatherings lasted until dawn and included not only their French friends but also visiting Americans, Britons, Swedes, Germans, Hungarians, Spaniards, Poles, and Russians. Among the hundreds who visited the Steins were artists Henri Matisse, Pablo Picasso, Georges Braque, Mary Cassatt, Marcel Duchamp, Alfred Stieglitz, and Arthur B. Davies; writers Ernest Hemingway, F. Scott Fitzgerald, John dos Passos, Jean Cocteau, and Guillaume Apollinaire; art dealers Daniel Kahnweiler and Ambroise Vollard; critics Roger Fry and Clive Bell; and collectors Sergei Shchukin and Ivan Morosov.

The Steins were themselves avid art collectors, and the works they hung in their home attracted many visitors. One of the first paintings Leo purchased was Matisse's notorious *Woman with the Hat* (FIG. 29-2), and he subsequently bought many more by Matisse—including *Le Bonheur de Vivre* (FIG. 29-2A)—along with works by Gauguin, Cézanne, Renoir, Picasso, and Braque. Sarah Stein and her husband, Michael, who was Leo and Gertrude's older brother, were also major, if more focused, collectors. They acquired many works by Matisse and lent some of them to the 1913 Armory Show in New York, which introduced avant-garde European art to America (see "The Armory Show," page 909).

29-11 PABLO PICASSO, *Gertrude Stein*, 1906–1907. Oil on canvas, 3' 3 3/8" × 2' 8". Metropolitan Museum of Art, New York (bequest of Gertrude Stein, 1947).

Picasso had left this portrait of his friend and patron unfinished until he decided to incorporate the planar simplicity of ancient Iberian stone sculptures into his depiction of her face.

Gertrude developed an especially close relationship with Picasso, who painted her portrait (FIG. 29-11) in 1907. Gertrude loved the painting so much that she kept it by her all her life and bequeathed it to the Metropolitan Museum of Art only upon her death in 1946.

GERTRUDE STEIN By 1906, Picasso was searching restlessly for new ways to depict form. He found clues in the ancient Iberian sculpture of his homeland and other "primitive" cultures. Inspired by these sources, Picasso returned to an unfinished portrait he had been preparing for Gertrude Stein (FIG. 29-11), his friend and patron (see "Gertrude and Leo Stein and the Avant-Garde," page 890). Stein had posed for more than 80 sittings earlier in the year, but Picasso was still not satisfied with the results. On resuming work, Picasso painted Stein's head as a simplified planar form, incorporating aspects derived from Iberian stone heads. Although the disparity between the style of the face and the rest of the figure is striking, together they provide an insightful portrait of a forceful, confident woman. More important, Picasso had discovered a new approach to the representation of the human form.

ART AND SOCIETY
Primitivism and Colonialism

The art of Africa, Oceania, and the native peoples of the Americas was a major source of inspiration for many early-20th-century modernist artists. Art historians refer to the incorporation of stylistic elements from these non-Western cultures as *primitivism*. Both "primitive" and "non-Western" are adjectives that imply the superiority of Western civilization and Western art, but many modernist artists admired the artworks of these cultures precisely because they embodied different stylistic preferences and standards. Some artists—for example Henri Matisse and Pablo Picasso (FIG. 29-12)—became enthusiastic collectors of "primitive art," but all of them could view non-Western objects in the many European and American anthropological and ethnographic museums that had begun to proliferate during the second half of the 19th century.

In 1882, the Musée d'Ethnographie du Trocadéro (now the Musée du quai Branly) in Paris opened its doors to the public. The Musée Permanent des Colonies (now the Musée National des Arts d'Afrique et d'Océanie) in Paris also provided the public with a wide array of objects—weapons, tools, basketwork, headdresses—from colonial territories, as did the Musée Africain in Marseilles. In Berlin, the Museum für Völkerkunde housed almost 10,000 African objects by 1886, when it opened for public viewing. Even the Expositions Universelles—regularly scheduled exhibitions in France designed to celebrate industrial progress—included products from Oceania and Africa after 1851. By the beginning of the 20th century, significant non-Western collections were on view in museums in Liverpool, Glasgow, Edinburgh, London, Hamburg, Stuttgart, Vienna, Berlin, Munich, Leiden, Copenhagen, and Chicago.

The formation of these collections was a by-product of the frenzied imperialist expansion central to the geopolitical dynamics of the 19th century and much of the 20th century. Most of the Western powers maintained colonies as sources of raw materials, as manufacturing markets, and as territorial acquisitions. For example, the United States, France, and Holland all kept a colonial presence in the Pacific. Britain, France, Germany, Belgium, Holland, Spain, and Portugal divided up the African continent. Social Darwinists, most notably Herbert Spencer (1820–1903), justified this colonization in terms of the survival of the most economically fit industrialized countries. Europeans and Americans often perceived the cultures they colonized as "primitive" and referred to many of the non-Western artifacts displayed in museums as "artificial curiosities" or "fetish objects." Indeed, the exhibition of these objects collected during expeditions to the colonies served to reinforce the "need" for a colonial presence in these countries. Colonialism often had a missionary dimension. These objects, which often depicted strange gods or creatures, reinforced the perception that these peoples were "barbarians" who needed to be "civilized" or "saved," and this perception justified colonialism and its missionary aspects worldwide.

Whether avant-garde artists were aware of the imperialistic implications of their appropriation of non-Western culture is unclear.

29-12 FRANK GELETT BURGESS, photograph of Pablo Picasso in his studio in the rue Ravignan, Paris, France, 1908. Musée Picasso, Paris.

Picasso was familiar with ancient Iberian art from his homeland and studied African and other "primitive" art in Paris's Trocadéro museum. He kept his own collection of primitive art in his studio.

Certainly, however, many artists reveled in the energy and freshness of non-Western images and forms. These different cultural products provided Western artists with new ways of looking at their own art. Matisse always maintained that he saw African sculptures as simply "good sculptures . . . like any other."* Picasso, in contrast, believed that "the masks weren't just like any other pieces of sculpture. Not at all. They were magic things. . . . mediators" between humans and the forces of evil, and he sought to capture their power as well as their forms in his paintings. "[In the Trocadéro] I understood why I was a painter. . . . All alone in that awful museum, with masks, dolls . . . *Les Demoiselles d'Avignon* [FIG. 29-1] must have come to me that day."† "Primitive art" seemed to embody a directness, closeness to nature, and honesty that appealed to modernist artists determined to reject conventional models. Non-Western art served as an important revitalizing and energizing force in Western art.

*Jean-Louis Paudrat, "From Africa," in William Rubin, ed., *"Primitivism" in 20th Century Art: Affinity of the Tribal and the Modern* (New York: Museum of Modern Art, 1984), 1:141.
†Ibid.

DEMOISELLES D'AVIGNON Later in 1907, Picasso carried his new approach to the representation of human form much further in his *Les Demoiselles d'Avignon* (FIG. 29-1). Although Picasso's painting incorporates references to the Western pictorial tradition—for example, a variation on an Archaic Greek *kouros* statue (FIG. 5-9) for the standing woman at the left and a doubtless intentional tribute to Manet's *Déjeuner sur l'Herbe* (FIG. 27-32) for the seated woman at the right—*Demoiselles* stands apart from that tradition not only in formal terms but in the representation of nude women as threatening rather than as passive figures on display for the pleasure of male viewers. However, Picasso's break with the formal vocabulary of Western art was far more radical than Manet's (see "Picasso Disrupts the Western Pictorial Tradition," page 881). Picasso's rethinking of the premises of Western art was largely inspired by his fascination with "primitive" art, which he had studied in Paris's Trocadéro ethnography museum and collected and kept in his Paris studio (see "Primitivism and Colonialism," page 891, and FIG. 29-12).

GEORGES BRAQUE AND CUBISM For many years, Picasso showed *Les Demoiselles* only to other painters. One of the first to see it was GEORGES BRAQUE (1882–1963), a Fauve painter who found it so challenging that he began to rethink his own painting style. Using the painting's revolutionary elements as a point of departure, together Braque and Picasso formulated *Cubism* around 1908 in the belief that the art of painting had to move far beyond the description of visual reality. Cubism represented a radical turning point in the history of art, nothing less than a dismissal of the pictorial illusionism that had dominated Western art since the Renaissance. The Cubists rejected naturalistic depictions, preferring compositions of shapes and forms abstracted from the conventionally perceived world. As Picasso once explained: "I paint forms as I think them, not as I see them."[5] Together, Picasso and Braque pursued the analysis of form central to Cézanne's artistic explorations (see page 860 and FIGS. 28-22 to 28-23A) by dissecting everything around them into its many constituent features, which they then recomposed, by a new logic of design, into a coherent, independent aesthetic picture. The Cubists' rejection of accepted artistic practice illustrates both the period's avant-garde critique of pictorial convention and the artists' dwindling faith in a safe, concrete Newtonian world in the face of the physics of Einstein and others (see "Science and Art," page 887).

The new style received its name after Matisse described some of Braque's work to the critic Louis Vauxcelles as having been painted "with little cubes." In his review, Vauxcelles described the new paintings as "cubic oddities."[6] The French writer and theorist Guillaume Apollinaire (1880–1918) summarized well the central concepts of Cubism in 1913:

> Authentic cubism [is] the art of depicting new wholes with formal elements borrowed not from the reality of vision, but from that of conception. This tendency leads to a poetic kind of painting which stands outside the world of observation; for, even in a simple cubism, the geometrical surfaces of an object must be opened out in order to give a complete representation of it. . . . Everyone must agree that a chair, from whichever side it is viewed, never ceases to have four legs, a seat and a back, and that, if it is robbed of one of these elements, it is robbed of an important part.[7]

ANALYTIC CUBISM Most art historians refer to the first phase of Cubism, developed jointly by Picasso and Braque, as *Analytic Cubism,* because in essence it is a painterly analysis of the structure of form. Because Cubists could not achieve the kind of total view Apollinaire described by the traditional method of drawing or painting models from one position, they began to dissect the forms of their subjects and to present their analysis of form across the canvas surface.

Georges Braque's painting *The Portuguese* (FIG. 29-13) exemplifies Analytic Cubism. The subject is a Portuguese musician whom the artist recalled seeing years earlier in a bar in Marseilles. Braque dissected the man and his instrument and placed the resulting forms in dynamic interaction with the space around them. Unlike the Fauves and German Expressionists, who used vibrant colors, the Cubists chose subdued hues—here solely brown tones—in order to focus attention on form. In *The Portuguese,* Braque carried his analysis so far that viewers must work diligently to discover clues to the subject. The construction of large intersecting planes suggests the forms of a man and a guitar. Smaller shapes interpenetrate and hover in the large planes. The way Braque treated light and shadow reveals his departure from conventional artistic practice. Light and dark passages suggest both chiaroscuro modeling and transparent planes that enable viewers to see through one level to another. Solid forms emerge only to be canceled almost immediately by a different reading of the subject.

1 ft.

29-13 GEORGES BRAQUE, *The Portuguese,* 1911. Oil on canvas, 3' 10$\frac{1}{8}$" × 2' 8". Kunstmuseum Basel, Basel (gift of Raoul La Roche, 1952).

The Cubists rejected the pictorial illusionism that had dominated Western art for centuries. Here, Braque concentrated on dissecting form and placing it in dynamic interaction with space.

Pablo Picasso on Cubism

In 1923, almost a decade after Picasso and Braque launched an artistic revolution with their Analytic (FIG. 29-13) and Synthetic (FIG. 29-14) Cubist paintings, Picasso granted an interview to the painter and critic Marius de Zayas (1880–1961). Born in Mexico, de Zayas had settled in New York City in 1907, and in 1911 had been instrumental in mounting the first exhibition in the United States of Picasso's works. In their conversation, the approved English translation of which appeared in the journal *The Arts* under the title "Picasso Speaks," the artist set forth his views about Cubism and the nature of art in general.

> We all know that Art is not truth. Art is a lie that makes us realize truth, at least the truth that is given us to understand. The artist must know the manner whereby to convince others of the truthfulness of his lies. . . . They speak of naturalism in opposition to modern painting. I would like to know if anyone has ever seen a natural work of art. Nature and art, being two different things, cannot be the same thing. Through art we express our conception of what nature is not. . . .
>
> Cubism is no different from any other school of painting. The same principles and the same elements are common to all. . . . Many think that Cubism is an art of transition, an experiment which is to bring ulterior results. Those who think that way have not understood it. Cubism is not either a seed or a foetus, but an art dealing primarily with forms, and when a form is realized it is there to live its own life. . . . Mathematics, trigonometry, chemistry, psychoanalysis, music, and whatnot, have been related to Cubism to give it an easier interpretation. All this has been pure literature, not to say nonsense, . . . Cubism has kept itself within the limits and limitations of painting, never pretending to go beyond it. Drawing, design, and color are understood and practiced

29-14 PABLO PICASSO, *Still Life with Chair-Caning*, 1912. Oil, oilcloth, and rope on canvas, $10\frac{5}{8}$" × 1' $1\frac{3}{4}$". Musée Picasso, Paris.

This painting includes a piece of oilcloth imprinted with the photolithographed pattern of a cane chair seat. Framed with a piece of rope, the still life challenges the viewer's understanding of reality.

> in Cubism in the spirit and manner that they are understood and practiced in all other schools. Our subjects might be different, as we have introduced into painting objects and forms that were formerly ignored. . . . [I]n our subjects, we keep the joy of discovery, the pleasure of the unexpected; our subject itself must be a source of interest.*

*Marius de Zayas, "Picasso Speaks," *The Arts* (May 1923), 315–326. Reprinted in Herschel B. Chipp, *Theories of Modern Art: A Source Book by Artists and Critics* (Berkeley and Los Angeles: University of California Press, 1968), 263–266.

The stenciled letters and numbers that Braque included add to the painting's complexity. Letters and numbers are flat shapes, but as elements of a Cubist painting such as *The Portuguese*, they enable the painter to play with the viewer's perception of two- and three-dimensional space. The letters and numbers lie flat on the painted canvas surface, yet the shading and shapes of other forms seem to flow behind and underneath them, pushing the letters and numbers forward into the viewing space. Occasionally, they seem attached to the surface of some object within the painting. Ultimately, the constantly shifting imagery makes it impossible to arrive at any definitive or final reading of the composition. Examining this kind of painting is a disconcerting excursion into ambiguity and doubt, especially because the letters and numbers seem to anchor the painting in the world of representation, thereby heightening the tension between representation and abstraction. Analytical Cubist paintings radically disrupt expectations about the representation of space and time.

SYNTHETIC CUBISM In 1912, Cubism entered a new phase that art historians have dubbed *Synthetic Cubism*. In this later Cubist style, instead of dissecting forms, artists constructed paintings and draw-

ings from objects and shapes cut from paper or other materials. The work marking the point of departure for this new style was Picasso's *Still Life with Chair-Caning* (FIG. 29-14), a mixed-media painting in which Picasso imprinted a photolithographed pattern of a cane chair seat on the canvas and then pasted a piece of oilcloth on it. Framed with rope, this work challenges the viewer's understanding of reality. The photographically replicated chair caning seems so "real" that the viewer expects the holes to break any brushstrokes laid on it. But the chair caning, although optically suggestive of the real, is only an illusion or representation of an object. In contrast, the painted abstract areas do not refer to tangible objects in the real world. Yet the fact that they do not imitate anything makes them more "real" than the chair caning. No pretense exists. Picasso extended the visual play by making the letter *U* escape from the space of the accompanying *J* and *O* and partially covering it with a cylindrical shape that pushes across its left side. The letters *JOU*, which appear in many Cubist paintings, formed part of the masthead of the daily French newspapers (*journaux*) often found among the objects represented. Picasso and Braque especially delighted in the punning references to *jouer* and *jouir*—the French verbs meaning "to play" and "to enjoy."

Although most discussions of Cubism focus on the formal innovations of Picasso and Braque, it is important to note that contemporary critics also viewed the revolutionary nature of Cubism in sociopolitical terms. Many considered Cubism's challenge to artistic convention and tradition a subversive attack on 20th-century society. In fact, many modernist artists and writers of the period did ally themselves with various anarchist groups whose social critiques and utopian visions appealed to progressive thinkers. It was, therefore, not difficult to see radical art, such as Cubism, as having political ramifications. The French press consistently equated Cubism's disdain for tradition with anarchism and revolution. Picasso himself, however, never viewed Cubism as a protest movement or even different in kind from traditional painting (see "Pablo Picasso on Cubism," page 893).

COLLAGE After *Still Life with Chair-Caning,* both Picasso and Braque continued to explore the medium of *collage* introduced into the realm of "high art" (as opposed to unself-conscious "folk art") in that work. From the French word *coller,* meaning "to stick," a collage is a composition of bits of objects, such as newspaper or cloth, glued to a surface. Braque's *Bottle, Newspaper, Pipe, and Glass* (FIG. **29-15**) is a type of collage called *papier collé* ("stuck paper") in which the artist glues assorted paper shapes to a drawing or painting. In Braque's papier collé, charcoal lines and shadows provide clues to the Cubist multiple views of various surfaces and objects. Roughly rectangular strips of printed and colored paper dominate the composition. The paper imprinted with wood grain and moldings provides an illusion whose concreteness contrasts with the lightly rendered objects on the right. Five pieces of paper overlap each other in the center of the composition to create a layering of flat planes that both echo the space that the lines suggest and establish the flatness of the work's surface. All shapes in the image seem to oscillate, pushing forward and dropping back in space. Shading seems to carve space into flat planes in some places and to turn planes into transparent surfaces in others. The pipe in the foreground illustrates this complex visual interplay especially well. Although it appears to lie on the newspaper, it is in fact a form cut through the printed paper to reveal the canvas surface, which Braque lightly modeled with charcoal. The artist thus kept his audience aware that *Bottle, Newspaper, Pipe, and Glass* is an artwork, a visual game to be deciphered, and not an attempt to reproduce nature.

Picasso explained the goals of Cubist collage in this way:

> Not only did we try to displace reality; reality was no longer in the object. . . . [In] the *papier collé* . . . [w]e didn't any longer want to fool the eye; we wanted to fool the mind. . . . If a piece of newspaper can be a bottle, that gives us something to think about in connection with both newspapers and bottles, too.[8]

Like all collage, the papier collé technique was modern in its medium—mass-produced materials never before found in high art—and modern in the way that the artist embedded the art's "message" in the imagery and in the nature of these everyday materials.

GUERNICA Picasso continued to experiment with different artistic styles and media right up until his death in 1973. Celebrated primarily for his brilliant formal innovations, in the late 1930s Picasso became openly involved in political issues as he watched his homeland descend into civil war. The result was *Guernica* (FIG. **29-16**), one of the greatest works of 20th-century art in any genre. At the time, Picasso declared: "[P]ainting is not made to decorate apartments. It is an instrument for offensive and defensive war against the enemy."[9] The artist got the opportunity to use his craft as a weapon in January 1937 when the Spanish Republican government-in-exile in Paris asked Picasso to produce a major work for the Spanish Pavilion at the Paris International Exposition that summer. He did not formally accept the invitation, however, until he received word that Guernica, the capital of the Basque region (an area in southern France and northern Spain populated by Basque speakers), had been almost totally destroyed in an air raid on April 26, 1937. Nazi pilots acting on behalf of the rebel general Francisco Franco (1892–1975) bombed the city at the busiest hour of a market day, killing or wounding many of Guernica's 7,000 citizens as well as leveling buildings. The event jolted Picasso into action. By the end of June, he had completed *Guernica,* a mural-sized canvas of immense power.

Despite the painting's title, Picasso made no specific reference to the event in *Guernica.* The imagery includes no bombs and no

29-15 GEORGES BRAQUE, *Bottle, Newspaper, Pipe, and Glass,* 1913. Charcoal and various papers pasted on paper, 1' 6$\frac{7}{8}$" × 2' 1$\frac{1}{4}$". Private collection, New York.

This Cubist collage of glued paper is a visual game to be deciphered. The pipe in the foreground, for example, seems to lie on the newspaper, but it is a cutout revealing the canvas surface.

1 in.

29-16 PABLO PICASSO, *Guernica*, 1937. Oil on canvas, 11′ 5½″ × 25′ 5¾″. Museo Nacional Centro de Arte Reina Sofía, Madrid.

Picasso used Cubist techniques, especially the fragmentation of objects and dislocation of anatomical features, to expressive effect in this condemnation of the Nazi bombing of the Basque capital.

29-17 PABLO PICASSO, maquette for *Guitar,* 1912. Cardboard, string, and wire (restored), 2′ 1¼″ × 1′ 1″ × 7½″. Museum of Modern Art, New York.

In this model for a sculpture of sheet metal, Picasso presented what is essentially a cutaway view of a guitar, enabling the viewer to examine both surface and interior space, both mass and void.

German planes. It is a universal outcry of human grief. In the center, along the lower edge of the painting, lies a slain warrior clutching a broken and useless sword. A gored horse tramples him and rears back in fright as it dies. On the left, a shrieking, anguished woman cradles her dead child. On the far right, a woman on fire runs screaming from a burning building, while another woman flees mindlessly. In the upper right corner, a woman, represented by only a head, emerges from the burning building, thrusting forth a light to illuminate the horror. Overlooking the destruction is a bull, which, according to the artist, represents "brutality and darkness."[10]

In *Guernica,* Picasso brilliantly used aspects of his earlier Cubist discoveries to expressive effect, particularly the fragmentation of objects and the dislocation of anatomical features. This Cubist fragmentation gave visual form to the horror of the aerial bombardment of the Basque people. What happened to these figures in the artist's act of painting—the dissections and contortions of the human form—paralleled what happened to them in real life. To emphasize the scene's severity and starkness, Picasso reduced his palette to black, white, and shades of gray, suppressing color once again, as he had in his Analytic Cubist works.

GUITAR Cubism not only opened new avenues for representing form on two-dimensional surfaces but also inspired new approaches to sculpture. Picasso created *Guitar* (FIG. **29-17**) in 1912. Like his Cubist paintings, this sculpture operates at the intersection of two- and three-dimensionality. Picasso took the form of a guitar—an image that surfaces in many of his paintings as well, including *Three Musicians* (FIG. **29-17A**)—and explored its volume using only flat pieces of cardboard. (The work reproduced in FIG. 29-17 is Picasso's *maquette,* or

29-17A PICASSO, *Three Musicians,* 1921.

model. The finished sculpture was to be made of sheet metal.) By presenting what is essentially a *cutaway* view of a guitar, Picasso enabled the viewer to examine both surface and interior space, both mass and void. This, of course, was completely in keeping with the Cubist program. Some scholars have suggested that Picasso derived the cylindrical form that serves as the sound hole on the guitar from the eyes on masks from the Ivory Coast of Africa. African masks were a continuing and persistent source of inspiration for the artist (see "Primitivism," page 891). Here, however, Picasso seems to have transformed the anatomical features of African masks into a part of a musical instrument—dramatic evidence of his unique, innovative artistic vision. Ironically—and intentionally—the sound hole, the central void in a real guitar, is, in Picasso's *Guitar,* the only solid form.

ALEKSANDR ARCHIPENKO The Russian sculptor ALEKSANDR ARCHIPENKO (1887–1964) similarly explored the Cubist notion of spatial ambiguity and the relationship between solid forms and space. In *Woman Combing Her Hair* (FIG. **29-18**), Archipenko introduced, in place of the head, a void with a shape of its own that figures importantly in the whole design. Enclosed spaces have always existed in figurative sculpture—for example, the space between the arm and the body when the hand rests on the hip (FIG. 21-12). But in Archipenko's statuette, the space penetrates the figure's continuous mass and is a defined form equal in importance to the mass of the bronze. It is not simply the negative counterpart to the volume as it is in traditional statues. Archipenko's *Woman* shows the same fluid intersecting planes seen in Cubist painting, and the relation of the planes to each other is similarly complex. Thus, both in painting and sculpture, the Cubists broke through traditional limits and transformed these media.

29-18 ALEKSANDR ARCHIPENKO, *Woman Combing Her Hair,* 1915. Bronze, 1' 1¾" high. Museum of Modern Art, New York (acquired through the Lillie P. Bliss Bequest).

In this statuette, Archipenko introduced, in place of the head, a void with a shape of its own that figures importantly in the whole design. The void is not simply the negative counterpart of the volume.

JULIO GONZÁLEZ Among the other notable sculptors of the early 20th century were JACQUES LIPCHITZ (1891–1973) and JULIO GONZÁLEZ (1876–1942). Lipchitz's works, such as *Bather* (FIG. **29-18A**), are three-dimensional equivalents of the Analytical Cubist canvases of Picasso and Braque (FIG. 29-13). González was a friend of Picasso who shared his interest in the artistic possibilities of new materials and new methods borrowed from both industrial technology and traditional metalworking. Born into a family of metalworkers in Barcelona, González helped Picasso construct a number of welded sculptures. This contact with Picasso in turn enabled González to refine his own sculptural vocabulary.

29-18A LIPCHITZ, *Bather,* 1917.

Using prefabricated bars, sheets, or rods of welded or wrought iron and bronze, González created dynamic sculptures with both linear elements and volumetric forms. A comparison between his *Woman Combing Her Hair* (FIG. **29-19**) and Archipenko's version of the same subject (FIG. 29-18) is instructive. Archipenko's figure still incorporates the basic shapes of a woman's body. González reduced his figure to an interplay of curves, lines, and planes—virtually a complete abstraction without any vestiges of traditional representational art. Although González's sculpture received only limited exposure during his lifetime, his work greatly influenced later abstract artists working in welded metal (FIG. 30-17).

29-19 JULIO GONZÁLEZ, *Woman Combing Her Hair,* 1936. Iron, 4' 4" high. Museum of Modern Art, New York (Mrs. Simon Guggenheim Fund).

Using prefabricated metal pieces, González reduced his figure to an interplay of curves, lines, and planes—virtually a complete abstraction without any vestiges of traditional representational art.

Delaunay, Orphism, and the Representation of Modern Life

Robert Delaunay developed his ideas about color use in dialogue with his Russian-born wife, Sonia (1885–1974), also an important modernist artist. She created paintings, quilts and other textile arts, and book covers that exploited the expressive capabilities of color. As a result of their artistic explorations, both Delaunays became convinced that the best solution to the problem of representing the rhythms of modern life was to build on the Cubist breakthroughs of Picasso and Braque and enrich their approach to representation through the use of color harmonies and dissonances.

Delaunay called his method *Simultané-isme,* although it is better known under the name Guillaume Apollinaire proposed: *Orphism.* Simultaneity/Orphism for Delaunay meant the application of 19th-century theories about the perception and psychology of color (see "19th-Century Color Theory," page 855) to create spatial effects and kaleidoscopic movement solely through color contrasts. He insisted that color in painting was both form and subject, and as early as 1912 he began to paint purely abstract compositions with titles such as *Simultaneous Disks, Simultaneous Windows,* and *Simultaneous Contrasts.*

A salient feature of modern life for Delaunay was technological innovation, a belief he shared with the Futurists in Italy (see page 898). Consequently, the engineering marvels of the late 19th and early 20th centuries figure prominently in Delaunay's paintings. For example, in 1914, he immortalized the engineer, inventor, and aviator Louis Blériot (1872–1936) in one of his boldest Orphic canvases. *Homage to Blériot* (FIG. **29-20**) is a mostly abstract composition that retains representational elements in celebration of Blériot's unprecedented achievement of flying across the English Channel. The 22-mile flight—in a monoplane of his own design—from Les Barraques, near Calais, France, to Dover, England, on July 25, 1909, lasted 37 minutes and made Blériot an instant international celebrity. It also brought him a prize of 1,000 British pounds, which a London newspaper had offered as a challenge to all aviators. At the time Delaunay commemorated the event, Blériot was manufacturing warplanes for use by French pilots and their allies during World War I. One of Blériot's planes appears at the upper right of Delaunay's painting, above another triumph of French engineering, the Eiffel Tower (FIG. 28-40), one of Delaunay's

29-20 Robert Delaunay, *Homage to Blériot,* 1914. Oil on canvas, 8' 2$\frac{1}{2}$" × 8' 3". Kunstmuseum Basel, Basel (Emanuel Hoffman Foundation).

In this canvas celebrating modern technological innovation, Delaunay paid tribute to the first pilot to fly across the English Channel. The swirling shapes and bold colors convey explosive energy.

favorite subjects (FIG. **29-20A**). Filling the rest of the canvas are a propeller (at the lower left) and mostly circular abstract shapes suggestive of whirling propellers and blazing suns. The swirling abstract and semiabstract shapes and the bold colors together convey explosive energy, and produce an exhilarating effect in the eye and mind of the viewer.

Delaunay's experiments with color dynamics strongly influenced the German Expressionists (he exhibited with Der Blaue Reiter as well as with Cubists)

29-20A Delaunay, *Champs de Mars,* 1911.

and the Futurists. These artists found in his art means for intensifying expression by suggesting violent motion through shape and color.

ROBERT DELAUNAY AND ORPHISM Art historians generally regard the suppression of color as crucial to the success of Cubist painting, but Robert Delaunay (1885–1941), Picasso's and Braque's contemporary, worked toward a kind of color Cubism. Apollinaire gave the name *Orphism* to Delaunay's version of Cubism, after Orpheus, the mythical Greek musician. Apollinaire believed that art, like music, was distinct from the representation of the visible world. But Delaunay's own name for his art was *Simultanéisme* (see "Delaunay, Orphism, and the Representation of Modern Life," above, and FIGS. 29-20 and 29-20A).

PROBLEMS AND SOLUTIONS

Léger, the Machine Aesthetic, and the Representation of Modern Life

Robert Delaunay (FIGS. 29-20 and 29-20A) was by no means the only early-20th-century artist who sought to capture the dynamism of modern life on canvas. Another was the Purist Fernand Léger, a champion of the "machine aesthetic." But Léger's solution to the problem differed markedly from Delaunay's.

Léger devised an effective compromise of tastes, bringing together meticulous Cubist analysis of form with Purism's broad simplification and machinelike finish of the design components. He retained from his Cubist practice a preference for cylindrical and tube-shaped motifs, suggestive of machined parts such as pistons and cylinders. Léger's works have the sharp precision of the machine, whose beauty and quality he was one of the first artists to appreciate. For example, in his film *Ballet Mécanique* (*Mechanical Ballet*; 1924), Léger contrasted inanimate objects such as functioning machines with humans in dance-like variations.

Preeminently a painter of modern urban life, Léger incorporated into works such as *The City* (FIG. **29-21**) the massive effects of modern posters and billboard advertisements, the harsh flashing of electric lights, and the noise of traffic. The monumental scale of *The City*, an early work incorporating the aesthetic of Synthetic Cubism, suggests that Léger, had he been given the opportunity, would have been one of the great mural painters of his age. In a defini-

29-21 FERNAND LÉGER, *The City*, 1919. Oil on canvas, 7' 7" × 9' 9½". Philadelphia Museum of Art, Philadelphia (A. E. Gallatin Collection).

Léger championed the "machine aesthetic." In *The City*, he captured the mechanical commotion of urban life, incorporating the effects of billboard ads, flashing lights, and noisy traffic.

tive way, he depicted the mechanical commotion of urban life, including the robotic movements of mechanized people (FIG. **29-21A**).

⬈ **29-21A** LÉGER, *Three Women*, 1921.

FERNAND LÉGER AND PURISM Best known today as one of the most important modernist architects, Le Corbusier (FIG. 29-69) was also a painter. In 1918, he founded a movement called *Purism,* which opposed Synthetic Cubism on the grounds that it was becoming merely an esoteric, decorative art out of touch with the machine age. Purists maintained that machinery's clean functional lines and the pure forms of its parts should direct artists' experiments in design, whether in painting, architecture, or industrially produced objects. This "machine aesthetic" inspired FERNAND LÉGER (1881–1955), a French artist who had painted with the Cubists (see "Léger, the Machine Aesthetic, and the Representation of Modern Life," above, and FIGS. 29-21 and 29-21A).

Futurism

Artists associated with another early-20th-century movement, *Futurism,* pursued many of the ideas that the Cubists explored. Equally important to the Futurists, however, was their well-defined sociopolitical agenda. Inaugurated and given its name by the charismatic Italian poet and playwright Filippo Tommaso Marinetti (1876–1944) in 1909, Futurism began as a literary movement but soon encompassed the visual arts, cinema, theater, music, and architecture. Indignant over the political and cultural decline of Italy, the Futurists published numerous manifestos in which they aggressively advocated revolution, both in society and in art (see "Futurist Manifestos," page 899). Like Die Brücke artists, the Futurists aimed at ushering in a new, more enlightened era.

In their quest to launch Italian society toward a glorious future, the Futurists championed war as a means of washing away the stagnant past. Indeed, they saw war as a cleansing agent. Marinetti declared: "We will glorify war—the only true hygiene of the world."[11] The Futurists agitated for the destruction of museums, libraries, and similar repositories of accumulated culture, which they described as mausoleums. They also called for radical innovation in the arts. Of particular interest to the Futurists were the speed and dynamism of modern technology, an interest shared by Delaunay (FIGS. 29-20 and 29-20A) and Léger (FIGS. 29-21 and 29-21A). Marinetti insisted that a racing "automobile adorned with great pipes like serpents with explosive breath . . . is more beautiful than the *Victory of Samothrace*"[12]—a reference to the Greek statue (FIG. 5-83) in the Louvre that for early-20th-century artists represented classicism and the glories of past civilizations. Appropriately, Futurist art often focused on motion in time and space, incorporating the Cubist discoveries derived from the analysis of form.

Futurist Manifestos

On April 11, 1910, a group of young Italian artists published *Futurist Painting: Technical Manifesto* in Milan in an attempt to apply the writer Filippo Tommaso Marinetti's views on literature to the visual arts. Signed jointly by Giacomo Balla (FIG. 29-22), Umberto Boccioni (FIG. 29-23), Carlo Carrà, Luigi Russolo, and Gino Severini, the manifesto also appeared in an English translation supervised by Marinetti himself. It states in part:

> On account of the persistency of an image on the retina, moving objects constantly multiply themselves [and] their form changes . . . Thus a running horse has not four legs, but twenty. . . .

> What was true for the painters of yesterday is but a falsehood today. . . . To paint a human figure you must not paint it; you must render the whole of its surrounding atmosphere. . . . [T]he vivifying current of science [must] soon deliver painting from academic tradition. . . . The shadows which we shall paint shall be more luminous than the highlights of our predecessors, and our pictures, next to those of the museums, will shine like blinding daylight compared with deepest night. . . .

> We declare . . . that all forms of imitation must be despised, all forms of originality glorified . . . that all subjects previously used must be swept aside in order to express our whirling life of steel, of pride, of fever and of speed . . . that movement and light destroy the materiality of bodies.*

Two years later, Boccioni published a *Technical Manifesto of Futurist Sculpture*, in which he argued that traditional sculpture was "a monstrous anachronism" and modern sculpture should be

> a translation, in plaster, bronze, glass, wood or any other material, of those atmospheric planes which bind and intersect things. . . . Let's . . . proclaim the absolute and complete abolition of finite lines and the contained statue. Let's split open our figures and place the environment inside them. We declare that the environment must form part of the plastic whole.†

The sculptures of Boccioni (FIG. 29-23) and the paintings of Balla (FIG. 29-22) and Severini (FIG. 29-24) perfectly express these Futurist principles and goals.

Futurist Painting: Technical Manifesto (*Poesia*, April 11, 1910). Translated by Filippo Tommaso Marinetti, in Umbro Apollonio, ed. *Futurist Manifestos* (Boston: Museum of Fine Arts, 1970), 27–31.

†Translated by Robert Brain, in Apollonio, *Futurist Manifestos*, 51–65.

1 ft.

29-22 GIACOMO BALLA, *Dynamism of a Dog on a Leash*, 1912. Oil on canvas, 2' 11$\frac{3}{8}$" × 3' 7$\frac{1}{4}$". Albright-Knox Art Gallery, Buffalo (bequest of A. Conger Goodyear, gift of George F. Goodyear, 1964).

The Futurists' interest in motion and in the Cubist dissection of form is evident in Balla's painting of a passing dog and its owner. Simultaneity of views was central to the Futurist program.

1 ft.

29-23 UMBERTO BOCCIONI, *Unique Forms of Continuity in Space*, 1913 (cast 1931). Bronze, 3' 7$\frac{7}{8}$" high. Museum of Modern Art, New York (acquired through the Lillie P. Bliss Bequest).

Boccioni's Futurist manifesto for sculpture advocated abolishing the enclosed statue. This running figure's body is so expanded that it almost disappears behind the blur of its movement.

GIACOMO BALLA The Futurists' interest in motion and in the Cubist dissection of form is evident in *Dynamism of a Dog on a Leash* (FIG. 29-22), in which GIACOMO BALLA (1871–1958) represented a passing dog and its owner, whose skirts are just within visual range. Balla achieved the effect of motion by repeating shapes—for example, the dog's legs and tail and the swinging line of the leash. Simultaneity of views, as in Cubism, was central to the Futurist program.

UMBERTO BOCCIONI One of the cosigners of the Futurist manifesto (see "Futurist Manifestos," page 899) was UMBERTO BOCCIONI (1882–1916), who produced what is the definitive work of Futurist sculpture, *Unique Forms of Continuity in Space* (FIG. 29-23). This piece highlights the formal and spatial effects of motion rather than their source, the striding human figure. The figure is so expanded, interrupted, and broken in plane and contour that it almost disappears behind the blur of its movement—just as people, buildings, and stationary objects become blurred when seen from an automobile traveling at great speed on a highway or a train racing through the countryside along its steel rails. Boccioni's search for sculptural means of expressing dynamic movement reached definitive expression in *Unique Forms*. In its power and sense of vital activity, this sculpture surpasses similar efforts in Futurist painting to create images symbolic of the dynamic quality of modern life. Although Boccioni's figure bears a curious resemblance to the *Nike of Samothrace* (FIG. 5-83), the ancient sculptor suggested motion only through posture and agitated drapery, not through distortion and fragmentation of the human body—an approach to representation that is the antithesis of the core principles of classical art.

This Futurist representation of motion in sculpture has its limitations, however. The eventual development of the motion picture, based on the rapid sequential projection of fixed images (see page 838 and FIG. 27-53), produced more convincing illusions of movement. And several decades later, Alexander Calder (FIG. 29-79) pioneered the development of kinetic sculpture—sculptures with parts that really move. But in the early 20th century, Boccioni was unsurpassed for his ability to capture the sensation of motion in statuary.

GINO SEVERINI The painting *Armored Train* (FIG. **29-24**) by GINO SEVERINI (1883–1966) also encapsulates the Futurist program—politically as well as artistically. Severini depicted a high-tech armored train with its rivets glistening and a huge booming cannon protruding from the top. Submerged in the bowels of the train, soldiers in a row point guns at an unseen target. In Cubist fashion, Severini depicted all of the elements of the painting, from the soldiers to the smoke emanating from the cannon, broken into facets and planes, suggesting action and movement. *Armored Train* reflects both the Futurists' passion for speed and the "whirling life of steel" and their faith in the cleansing action of war. Not only are the colors predominantly light and bright, but death and destruction—the tragic consequences of war—are absent from Severini's painting. This sanitized depiction of armed conflict contrasts sharply with Francisco Goya's *Third of May, 1808* (FIG. 27-12), which also depicts a uniform row of anonymous soldiers in the act of shooting. Goya, however, graphically presented the dead and those about to be shot, and the dark tones he used cast a dramatic and sobering pall.

Once World War I broke out, the Futurist group began to disintegrate, largely because so many of them felt compelled (given the Futurist support for the war) to join the Italian army. Some of them, including Umberto Boccioni, died in the war.

Dada

Although the Futurists celebrated World War I—the "Great War"—and the changes that they hoped it would effect, the mass destruction and chaos that the conflict unleashed horrified other artists. Humanity had never before witnessed such wholesale slaughter on so grand a scale over such an extended period. More than nine million soldiers died in four years. Millions more sustained grievous wounds in great battles. Britain alone lost 60,000 men on the opening day of the

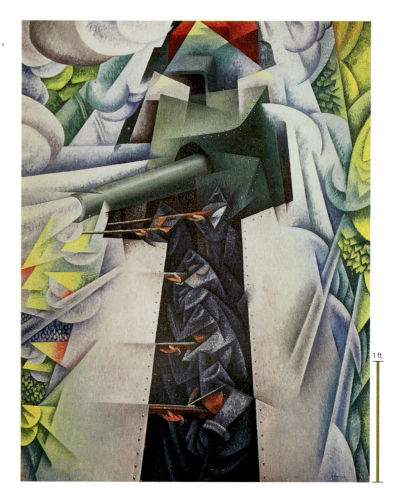

1 ft.

29-24 GINO SEVERINI, *Armored Train*, 1915. Oil on canvas, 3' 10" × 2' 10⅛". Collection of Richard S. Zeisler, New York.

Severini's glistening armored train with protruding cannon reflects the Futurist faith in the cleansing action of war. The painting captures the dynamism and motion central to the Futurist manifesto.

battle of the Somme in 1916. In the same year, the battle of Verdun, which lasted 10 months, produced half a million casualties. The new technology of armaments, bred of the age of steel, made the Great War a "war of the guns." In the face of massed artillery hurling millions of tons of high explosives and gas shells and in the sheets of fire from thousands of machine guns in armored vehicles of the kind celebrated in Severini's *Armored Train* (FIG. 29-24), attack was suicidal. Military campaigns no longer consisted of troop movements designed to capture territory. Warfare became a frustrating stalemate of soldiers holed up in trenches stretching from the English Channel almost to Switzerland. The mud, filth, and blood of the trenches, the pounding and shattering of incessant shell fire, and the terrible deaths and mutilations were a devastating psychological, as well as physical, experience for a generation brought up with the doctrine of progress and a belief in the fundamental values of civilization. The introduction of poison gas in 1915 added to the horror of humankind's inhumanity. The negotiated formal end of hostilities finally arrived in 1919, but peace could not erase the scars of a global conflict that had destroyed the lives of millions and altered the worldview of many millions more.

One major consequence of the Great War was the emergence of an artistic movement known as *Dada*. The Dadaists believed that Enlightenment reasoning had been responsible for the insane spectacle of collective homicide and global devastation that was World War I, and they concluded that the only route to salvation was through political anarchy, the irrational, and the intuitive. Although

Dada began independently in New York and Zurich, it also took root in Paris, Berlin, and Cologne, among other cities. Dada was more a mind-set or attitude than a single identifiable style. As André Breton (1896–1966), founder of the slightly later Surrealist movement (see page 922), explained: "Cubism was a school of painting, futurism a political movement: DADA is a state of mind."[13] Thus an element of absurdity is a cornerstone of Dada—reflected in the movement's very name. Many explanations exist for the choice of "Dada," but according to an oft-repeated anecdote, the Dadaists chose the word at random by sticking a knife into a French-German dictionary. Dada is French for a child's hobby horse. The word satisfied the Dadaists' desire for something nonsensical.

The Dadaists' pessimism and disgust surfaced in their disdain for convention and tradition. These artists made a concerted and sustained attempt to undermine cherished notions and assumptions about art. Because of this iconoclastic dimension, art historians often describe Dada as a destructive enterprise. Dada's negativity and derisive iconoclasm can be read at random from the Dadaists' numerous manifestos and declarations of intent. For example:

> Dada knows everything. Dada spits on everything. Dada says "knowthing," Dada has no fixed ideas. Dada does not catch flies. Dada is bitterness laughing at everything that has been accomplished, sanctified. . . . Dada is never right. . . . No more painters, no more writers, no more religions, no more royalists, no more anarchists, no more socialists, no more police, no more airplanes, no more urinary passages. . . . Like everything in life, Dada is useless, everything happens in a completely idiotic way. . . . We are incapable of treating seriously any subject whatsoever, let alone this subject: ourselves.[14]

Although cynicism and pessimism inspired the Dadaists, what they developed was phenomenally influential and powerful. By attacking convention and logic, the Dada artists unlocked new avenues for creative invention, thereby fostering a more serious examination of the basic premises of art than prior movements had. But the Dadaists could also be lighthearted in their subversiveness. Although horror and disgust about the war initially prompted Dada, an undercurrent of often irreverent humor and whimsy runs through much of the art. For example, Marcel Duchamp painted a moustache and goatee on a reproduction of Leonardo's *Mona Lisa* (FIG. 29-26A). The French painter Francis Picabia (1879–1953), Duchamp's collaborator in establishing Dada in New York, nailed a toy monkey to a board and labeled it *Portrait of Cézanne*.

In its emphasis on the spontaneous and intuitive, Dada paralleled the views of Sigmund Freud (1856–1939) and Carl Jung (1875–1961). Freud was a Viennese doctor who developed the fundamental principles for what became known as psychoanalysis. In his book *The Interpretation of Dreams* (1900), Freud argued that unconscious and inner drives (of which people are largely unaware) control human behavior. Jung, a Swiss psychiatrist who developed Freud's theories further, believed that the unconscious is composed of two facets, a personal unconscious and a collective unconscious. The collective unconscious comprises memories and associations that all humans share, such as archetypes and mental constructions. According to Jung, the collective unconscious accounts for the development of myths, religions, and philosophies.

Particularly interested in the exploration of the unconscious that Freud advocated, the Dada artists believed that art was a powerfully practical means of self-revelation and healing, and that the images arising out of the subconscious mind had a truth of their own, independent of conventional vision. A Dada filmmaker, Hans Richter (1888–1976), summarized the attitude of the Dadaists:

Possessed, as we were, of the ability to entrust ourselves to "chance," to our conscious as well as our unconscious minds, we became a sort of public secret society. . . . We laughed at everything. . . . But laughter was only the expression of our new discoveries, not their essence and not their purpose. Pandemonium, destruction, anarchy, anti-everything of the World War? How could Dada have been anything but destructive, aggressive, insolent, on principle and with gusto?[15]

JEAN ARP One prominent Dada artist whose works illustrate Richter's element of chance was Zurich-based JEAN (HANS) ARP (1887–1966). Arp pioneered the use of chance in composing his images. Tiring of the look of the Cubist-related collages he was making, he took several sheets of paper, tore them into roughly shaped squares, haphazardly dropped them onto a sheet of paper on the floor, and glued them into the resulting arrangement. The rectilinearity of the shapes guaranteed a somewhat regular design (which Arp no doubt enhanced by adjusting the random arrangement into a quasi-grid), but chance had introduced an imbalance that seemed to Arp to restore to his work a special mysterious vitality that he wanted to preserve. *Collage Arranged According to the Laws of Chance* (FIG. 29-25) is one of the works that Arp created by this method. The operations of chance were for Dadaists a crucial part of this kind of

1 in.

29-25 JEAN (HANS) ARP, *Collage Arranged According to the Laws of Chance,* 1916–1917. Torn and pasted paper, 1' 7$\frac{1}{8}$" × 1' 1$\frac{5}{8}$". Museum of Modern Art, New York.

In this collage, Arp dropped torn paper squares onto a sheet of paper and then glued them where they fell. His reliance on chance in composing images reinforced the anarchy inherent in Dada.

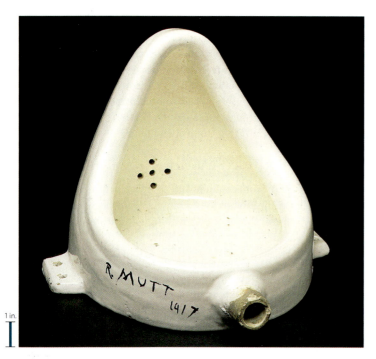

29-26 MARCEL DUCHAMP, *Fountain* (second version), 1950 (original version produced 1917). Glazed sanitary china with black paint, 1' high. Philadelphia Museum of Art, Philadelphia.

Duchamp's "readymade" sculptures were mass-produced objects that the Dada artist modified. In *Fountain,* he conferred the status of art on a urinal and forced people to see the object in a new light.

improvisation. As Richter stated: "For us chance was the 'unconscious mind' that Freud had discovered in 1900. . . . Adoption of chance had another purpose, a secret one. This was to restore to the work of art its primeval magic power and to find a way back to the immediacy it had lost through contact with . . . classicism."[16] Arp's renunciation of artistic control and reliance on chance when creating his compositions reinforced the anarchy and subversiveness inherent in Dada.

MARCEL DUCHAMP Perhaps the most influential Dadaist was MARCEL DUCHAMP (1887–1968), a Frenchman who became the central artist of New York Dada but was also active in Paris. In 1913, he exhibited his first "readymade" sculptures, which were mass-produced common objects—"found objects" that the artist selected and sometimes "rectified" by modifying their substance or combining them with another object. The creation of readymades, Duchamp insisted, was free from any consideration of either good or bad taste, qualities shaped by a society that he and other Dada artists found aesthetically bankrupt. Perhaps his most outrageous readymade was *Fountain* (FIG. 29-26), a porcelain urinal presented on its back, signed "R. Mutt," and dated (1917). The "artist's signature" was, in fact, a witty pseudonym derived from the Mott plumbing company's name and that of the taller man of the then-popular Mutt and Jeff comic-strip duo. As with Duchamp's other readymades and "assisted readymades" such as *L.H.O.O.Q.* (FIG. 29-26A), he did not select the urinal for exhibition because of its aesthetic qualities. The "art" of this "artwork" lay in the artist's choice of object, which had the effect of conferring the status of art on it and forcing viewers to

⬀ 29-26A DUCHAMP, *L.H.O.O.Q.,* 1919.

see the object in a new light. As Duchamp wrote in a "defense" published in 1917, after an exhibition committee rejected *Fountain* for display: "Whether Mr. Mutt with his own hands made the fountain or not has no importance. He CHOSE it. He took an ordinary article of life, placed it so that its useful significance disappeared under the new title and point of view—created a new thought for that object."[17] It is hard to imagine a more direct challenge to artistic conventions than Dada works such as *Fountain.*

THE LARGE GLASS Among the most visually and conceptually challenging of Duchamp's works is *The Bride Stripped Bare by Her Bachelors, Even* (FIG. 29-27), often called *The Large Glass.* Begun in 1915 and abandoned by Duchamp as unfinished in 1923, *The Large Glass* is a simultaneously playful and serious examination of humans as machines. Consisting of oil paint, wire, and lead foil sandwiched in between two large glass panels, the artwork presents an array of images, some apparently mechanical, others diagrammatic, and yet others seemingly abstract in nature. Duchamp provided some clues to the intriguing imagery in a series of notes accompanying the

29-27 MARCEL DUCHAMP, *The Bride Stripped Bare by Her Bachelors, Even (The Large Glass),* 1915–1923. Oil, lead, wire, foil, dust, and varnish on glass, 9' 1½" × 5' 9⅛". Philadelphia Museum of Art, Philadelphia (Katherine S. Dreier Bequest).

The Large Glass is a simultaneously playful and serious examination of humans as machines. The bride is a motor fueled by "love gasoline," and the male figures in the lower half also move mechanically.

work. The top half of *The Large Glass* represents "the bride," whom Duchamp has depicted as "basically a motor" fueled by "love gasoline." In contrast, the bachelors appear as uniformed male figures in the lower half of the composition. They too move mechanically. The chocolate grinder in the center of the lower glass pane represents masturbation ("the bachelor grinds his own chocolate"). In *The Large Glass,* Duchamp provided his own whimsical but insightful reflections on desire and sexuality. In true Dadaist fashion, chance completed the work. During the transportation of *The Large Glass* from an exhibition in 1927, the glass panes shattered. Rather than replace the broken glass, Duchamp painstakingly pieced together the glass fragments. After encasing the reconstructed work, broken panes and all, between two heavier panes of glass, Duchamp declared the work completed "by chance."

Duchamp (and the generations of artists after him profoundly influenced by his art and especially his attitude) considered life and art matters of chance and choice freed from the conventions of society and tradition. In Duchamp's approach to art and life, each act was individual and unique. Every person's choice of found objects would be different, for example, and each person's throw of the dice would be at a different instant and would probably yield a different number. This philosophy of utter freedom for artists was fundamental to the history of art in the 20th century—in America as well as Europe. Duchamp spent much of World War I in New York, where he painted *Nude Descending a Staircase* (FIG. 29-35) and inspired a group of American artists and collectors with his radical rethinking of the role of artists and of the nature of art.

HANNAH HÖCH Dada spread throughout much of western Europe, arriving as early as 1917 in Berlin, where it soon took on an activist political edge, partially in response to the economic, social, and political chaos in that city in the years at the end of and immediately after World War I. The Berlin Dadaists developed to a new intensity a technique that had been used in private and popular arts long before the 20th century to create a composition by pasting together pieces of paper. A few years earlier, the Cubists had named the process "collage." The Berliners christened their version of the technique *photomontage.* Unlike Cubist collage, the parts of a Dada collage consisted almost entirely of "found" details, such as pieces of magazine photographs, usually combined into deliberately antilogical compositions. Collage lent itself well to the Dada desire to use chance when creating art—and anti-art—but not all Dada collage was as savagely aggressive as that of the Berlin photomontagists.

One of the Berlin Dadaists who perfected the photomontage technique was HANNAH HÖCH (1889–1978). Höch's photomontages advanced the absurd illogic of Dada by presenting the viewer with chaotic, contradictory, and satiric compositions. They also provided scathing and insightful commentary on two of the most dramatic developments during the Weimar Republic (1918–1933) in Germany— the redefinition of women's social roles and the explosive growth of mass print media. Höch, a passionate early feminist, revealed these combined themes in *Cut with the Kitchen Knife Dada through the Last Weimar Beer Belly Cultural Epoch of Germany* (FIG. 29-28). In this work, whose title

1 ft.

29-28 HANNAH HÖCH, *Cut with the Kitchen Knife Dada through the Last Weimar Beer Belly Cultural Epoch of Germany,* 1919–1920. Photomontage, 3′ 9″ × 2′ 11½″. Neue Nationalgalerie, Staatliche Museen zu Berlin, Berlin.

Photographs of some of Höch's fellow Dadaists appear among images of Marx and Lenin, and the artist juxtaposed herself with a map of Europe showing the progress of women's right to vote.

refers to the story that the name "Dada" resulted from thrusting a knife into a dictionary (see page 901), Höch arranged an eclectic mixture of cutout photos in seemingly haphazard fashion. Closer inspection, however, reveals the artist's careful selection and placement of the photographs. For example, the key figures in the Weimar Republic are together at the upper right (identified as the "anti-Dada movement"). Some of Höch's fellow Dadaists appear among images of Karl Marx and Vladimir Lenin, aligning Dada with other revolutionary forces in what she prominently labeled with cutout lettering *Die grosse Welt dada* ("the great Dada world"). Certainly, juxtaposing the heads of German military leaders with exotic dancers' bodies provided the wickedly humorous critique central to much of Dada. Höch also positioned herself in the topsy-turvy Dada world that she created. A photograph of her head appears in the lower right corner, juxtaposed with a map of Europe showing which countries had granted women the right to vote—a commentary on the power that both women and Dada had to destabilize society.

KURT SCHWITTERS In Hanover, KURT SCHWITTERS (1887–1948) followed a gentler muse. Inspired by Cubist collage but working nonobjectively, Schwitters found visual poetry in the cast-off junk of modern society and scavenged in trash bins for materials, which he pasted and nailed together into designs such as *Merz 19* (FIG. **29-29**). The term *Merz,* which Schwitters used as a generic title for a series of collages, derived nonsensically from the German word *Kommerzbank* ("commerce bank") and appeared as a word fragment in one of his compositions. Although nonobjective, his collages still resonate with the meaning of the fragmented found objects they contain. The recycled elements of Schwitters's collages, like Duchamp's readymades, acquire changed meanings through their new uses and locations. Elevating objects that are essentially trash to the status of high art certainly fits within the parameters of the Dada program and parallels the absurdist dimension of much of Dada art. Contradiction, paradox, irony, and even blasphemy were Dada's bequest to later artists.

Suprematism and Constructivism

Dada was a movement born of pessimism and cynicism. However, not all early-20th-century artists reacted to the profound turmoil of the times by retreating from society. Some artists promoted utopian ideals, believing staunchly in art's ability to contribute to improving society and all humankind. These efforts often surfaced in the face of significant political upheaval, as was the case with Suprematism and Constructivism in Russia.

KAZIMIR MALEVICH Despite Russia's distance from Paris, the center of the international art world in the early 20th century, Russians had a long history of cultural contact and interaction with western Europe. Wealthy Russians, such as Ivan Morozov (1871–1921) and Sergei Shchukin (1854–1936), amassed extensive collections of Impressionist, Post-Impressionist, and avant-garde paintings. Both Morozov and Shchukin had participated in the salons at the Steins' home in Paris (see "Gertrude and Leo Stein," page 890),

1 in.

29-29 KURT SCHWITTERS, *Merz 19*, 1920. Paper collage, $7\frac{1}{4}" \times 5\frac{7}{8}"$. Yale University Art Gallery, New Haven (gift of Collection Société Anonyme).

Inspired by Cubist collage but working nonobjectively, Schwitters found visual poetry in the cast-off junk of modern society, which he pasted and nailed together into striking Dada compositions.

and Shchukin became particularly enamored of the work of both Picasso and Matisse. By the mid-1910s, he had acquired 37 paintings by Matisse and 51 by Picasso. Because of their access to collections such as these, Russian artists were familiar with the latest artistic developments, especially Fauvism, Cubism, and Futurism.

One Russian artist who contributed significantly to the avant-garde nature of early-20th-century art was KAZIMIR MALEVICH (1878–1935). Malevich developed an abstract style to convey his belief that the supreme reality in the world is "pure feeling," which attaches to no object. Thus this belief called for new, nonobjective forms in art—shapes not related to objects in the visible world. Malevich had studied painting, sculpture, and architecture and had worked his way through most of the avant-garde styles of his youth before deciding that none could express pure feeling. He christened his new artistic approach *Suprematism,* explaining: "Under Suprematism I understand the supremacy of pure feeling in creative art. To the Suprematist, the visual phenomena of the objective world are, in themselves, meaningless; the significant thing is feeling, as such, quite apart from the environment in which it is called forth."[18]

1 in.

29-30 Kᴀᴢɪᴍɪʀ Mᴀʟᴇᴠɪᴄʜ, *Suprematist Composition: Airplane Flying,* 1915 (dated 1914). Oil on canvas, 1' 10 $\frac{7}{8}$" × 1' 7". Museum of Modern Art, New York.

Malevich developed an abstract style that he called Suprematism to convey that the supreme reality in the world is pure feeling. Here, the brightly colored rectilinear shapes float against white space.

The basic form of Malevich's new Suprematist nonobjective art was the square. Combined with its relatives, the straight line and the rectangle, the square soon filled his paintings, such as *Suprematist Composition: Airplane Flying* (ꜰɪɢ. **29-30**). In this work, the brightly colored shapes float against and within a white space, and the artist placed them in dynamic relationship to one another. Malevich believed that all peoples would easily understand his new art because of the universality of its symbols. It used the pure language of shape and color, to which everyone could respond intuitively.

RUSSIAN REVOLUTION In 1917, as a result of widespread dissatisfaction with the regime of Tsar Nicholas II (r. 1894–1917), Russian workers staged a general strike in protest, and the tsar abdicated in March. In late 1917, the Bolsheviks, a faction of Russian Social Democrats that promoted violent revolution, wrested control of the country from the ruling provisional government. Once in power, their leader, Vladimir Lenin (1870–1924), nationalized the land and turned it over to the local rural soviets (councils of workers' and soldiers' deputies). After extensive civil war, the Communists, as they now called themselves, succeeded in retaining control of Russia and taking over an assortment of satellite countries in eastern Europe. This new state adopted the official name Union of Soviet Socialist Republics (USSR, or Soviet Union) in 1923.

Malevich, who held influential teaching posts in Vitebsk and Petrograd from 1919 to 1927, viewed the revolution as an opportunity to wipe out past traditions and begin a new culture. He believed that his art could play a major role in that effort because of its universal accessibility. But, after a short period during which the new regime tolerated avant-garde art, the political leaders of the Soviet Union decided that their new communist society needed a more "practical" art. Soviet authorities promoted a "realistic," illusionistic art that they thought a wide public could understand and that they hoped would teach citizens about their new government. This horrified Malevich. To him, true art could never have a practical connection with life:

> Every social idea, however great and important it may be, stems from the sensation of hunger; every art work, regardless of how small and insignificant it may seem, originates in pictorial or plastic feeling. It is high time for us to realize that the problems of art lie far apart from those of the stomach or the intellect.[19]

Disappointed and unappreciated by the public, Malevich continued to produce art but began to gravitate toward other disciplines, such as mathematical theory and geometry, logical fields given his interest in pure abstraction. His work and his theories, if ignored by the masses, nonetheless made a profound impression on other artists, especially in Russia. These included Lʏᴜʙᴏᴠ Pᴏᴩᴏᴠᴀ (1889–1924), who joined Malevich's Suprematist movement in 1916. Popova's most notable works are the series of canvases she named *Architectonic Paintings* (ꜰɪɢ. **29-30A**).

⬈**29-30A** Pᴏᴩᴏᴠᴀ, *Architectonic Painting,* 1916–1917.

NAUM GABO The Russian-born sculptor Nᴀᴜᴍ Gᴀʙᴏ (1890–1977) also wanted to create an innovative art to express a new reality, and like Malevich, he believed that art should spring from sources separate from the everyday world. For Gabo, the new reality was the space-time world described by early-20th-century scientists (see "Science and Art," page 887). As he wrote in *The Realistic Manifesto,* published with his brother Anton Pevsner (1886–1962) in 1920:

> Space and time are the only forms on which life is built and hence art must be constructed. . . . The realization of our perceptions of the world in the forms of space and time is the only aim of our pictorial and plastic art. . . . We renounce the thousand-year-old delusion in art that held the static rhythms as the only elements of the plastic and pictorial arts. We affirm in these arts a new element, the kinetic rhythms, as the basic forms of our perception of real time.[20]

Gabo was one of the Russian sculptors known as Constructivists. The name *Constructivism* may have come originally from the title *Construction,* which the Russian artist Vladimir Tatlin (FIG. 29-32) used for some relief sculptures he made in 1913 and 1914. Gabo explained that he called himself a Constructivist partly because he built up his sculptures piece by piece in space, instead of carving or modeling them in the traditional way. Although Gabo experimented briefly with real motion in his work, most of his sculptures relied on the relationship of mass and space to suggest the nature of space-time. To indicate the volumes of mass and space more clearly in his sculpture, Gabo used some of the new synthetic plastic materials, including celluloid, nylon, and Lucite, to create constructions whose space seems to flow through as well as around the transparent materials. In works such as *Column* (FIG. **29-31**), Gabo opened up the column's circular mass so that the viewer can experience the volume of space it occupies. Two transparent planes extend through its diameter, crossing at right angles at the center of the implied cylindrical column shape. The opaque colored planes at the base and the inclined open ring set up counter-rhythms to the crossed upright planes. They establish the sense of dynamic kinetic movement that Gabo always sought to express as an essential part of reality.

Architecture

One of the goals of the Russian Constructivists was to design a better environment for human beings, a goal best achieved by architects.

VLADIMIR TATLIN The Russian Revolution was the signal to Vladimir Tatlin (1885–1953), as it had been to Malevich, that the hated old order was about to end. In utopian fashion, he aspired to play a significant role in creating a new world, one that would fully use the power of industrialization to benefit all people. Initially, like Malevich and Gabo, Tatlin believed that nonobjective art was ideal for the new society, free as such art was from any past symbolism. But after the 1917 revolution, Tatlin enthusiastically abandoned abstract art for "functional art" and designed products such as an efficient stove and workers' clothing.

Tatlin's most famous work is *Monument to the Third International* (FIG. **29-32**), an architectural design that, in its reductive geometry, connects his work to the artistic programs of the Suprematists and Constructivists, although Tatlin was not a member of either group. Tatlin received the commission from the Department of Artistic Work of the People's Commissariat for Enlightenment

29-31 Naum Gabo, *Column,* ca. 1923 (reconstructed 1937). Perspex, wood, metal, and glass, 3′ 5″ × 2′ 5″ × 2′ 5″. Solomon R. Guggenheim Museum, New York.

Gabo's Constructivist sculptures rely on the relationship of mass and space to suggest the nature of space-time. Space seems to flow through as well as around the transparent materials he used.

29-32 Vladimir Tatlin, *Monument to the Third International,* 1919–1920. Reconstruction of the lost model, 1992–1993. Kunsthalle, Düsseldorf.

"Tatlin's Tower" was an ambitious avant-garde design for a Soviet governmental building with three geometrically shaped chambers rotating at different speeds within a dynamically tilted spiral cage.

in early 1919 to honor the Russian Revolution. He envisioned a huge glass-and-iron building that—at 1,300 feet—would have been one-third taller than the Eiffel Tower (FIG. 28-40). Widely influential, "Tatlin's Tower," as it became known, served as a model for those seeking to encourage socially committed and functional art. On its proposed site straddling the Moscow River at the center of the city, it would have functioned as a propaganda and news center for the Soviet people. Within a dynamically tilted spiral cage, three geometrically shaped chambers were to rotate around a central axis, each chamber housing facilities for a different type of governmental activity and rotating at a different speed. The one at the bottom, a huge cylindrical glass structure for lectures and meetings, was to revolve once a year. Higher up was a cone-shaped chamber that would rotate monthly and serve administrative functions. At the top, above a cubic information center designed to revolve daily, Tatlin placed an open-air news screen (illuminated at night) and a special instrument designed to project news bulletins and proclamations on the clouds on any overcast day. The proposed decreasing size of the chambers as visitors ascended the monument paralleled the decision-making hierarchy in the political system, with the most authoritative, smallest groups near the building's apex. Unfortunately, due to Russia's desperate economic situation in the 1920s, Tatlin's Tower was never built. But Tatlin worked out his ambitious design in now-lost metal and wood models exhibited on various official occasions. The only records of these models are a few drawings and photographs, but they have permitted faithful reconstructions of the design, such as the one reproduced in FIG. 29-32.

29-33 ADOLF LOOS, Villa Müller (looking north), Prague, Czech Republic, 1928–1930.

For Loos, decoration was a "criminal" waste of labor and materials. His Villa Müller is a white stucco cubical mass devoid of any ornamentation and without even moldings separating the floors.

ADOLF LOOS In Germany, the most influential architectural theorist during the opening decades of the 20th century was ADOLF LOOS (1870–1933). Loos trained as an architect at the Dresden College of Technology and then traveled to the United States to attend the 1893 Columbia Exposition in Chicago. Although he apparently found no work as an architect in Chicago, he remained there three years. During that time, he became familiar with the buildings (FIGS. 28-42, 28-42A, and 28-43) and theories of Louis Sullivan, whose essay "Ornament in Architecture," published in *The Engineering Magazine* in August 1892, affected Loos profoundly. In that treatise, Sullivan suggested that architects consider banishing all ornamentation from their buildings for a period of years "in order that our thought might concentrate acutely upon the production of buildings well formed and comely in the nude."

Loos carried Sullivan's ideas even further in a series of essays in which he railed against the excesses of the Art Nouveau style (FIGS. 28-38 and 28-38A), which was the rage in Europe at the turn of the century. He published his major statement on the subject in 1908 under the title *Ornament and Crime*. Loos equated architectural ornamentation with the "amoral" tattoos of Papua New Guinea (see "Tattoo in Polynesia," page 1115, and FIGS. I-19 and 36-16) and asserted that modern men who tattooed themselves were either criminals or degenerates. Ornamentation in architecture was also a crime, both on aesthetic grounds and because it wasted labor and materials.

Loos put his ideas to work early on in his 1910 design for the Viennese home of the painter Lilly Steiner (1884–1962) and in many other buildings, of which the Villa Müller (FIG. **29-33**) in Prague is perhaps the purest example of his architectural philosophy. The villa, restored to its former glory in 2000, was the grandiose private residence of the Czech engineer František Müller (1890–1951), the co-owner of a construction company that specialized in providing reinforced concrete for industrial projects and public buildings. Müller's new home was to be, in part, a showcase for the construction materials that brought him his personal fortune. Cubical in form, the Villa Müller has a reinforced-concrete skeleton and a severe white stucco shell without ornamentation of any kind, even moldings separating the floors. The only design elements breaking up the planar severity of the exterior walls are the windows and doors. Walter Gropius would later build on Loos's ideas about pure, functional architectural design at the Bauhaus (see "Walter Gropius and the Bauhaus," page 933, and FIG. 29-67), where he promoted "avoiding all romantic embellishment and whimsy."

UNITED STATES, 1900 TO 1930

Avant-garde experiments in the arts were not limited to Europe. Increasingly common transatlantic travel during the later 19th and early 20th centuries resulted in a lively exchange of artistic ideas among European and American artists. For example, John Singer Sargent (FIG. 27-37), James Abbott McNeil Whistler (FIG. 28-11), and Mary Cassatt (FIG. 28-12) spent much of their productive careers in Europe, whereas many European artists ended their careers in the United States, especially in anticipation of and, later, in the wake of World War I.

Painting and Sculpture

In the opening decade of the 20th century, when most American artists knew little about the revolutionary work of their European counterparts, the goal of many of the leading painters was to present a realistic, unvarnished look at American life. In this regard, their work parallels that of the French Realists in the mid-19th century (see page 815).

JOHN SLOAN AND THE EIGHT The most important group of American Realist artists was The Eight—eight painters who gravitated into the circle of the influential and evangelical artist and teacher Robert Henri (1865–1929). Henri urged his followers to make "pictures from life,"[21] and accordingly, these artists pursued with zeal the production of images depicting the rapidly changing urban landscape of New York City. Because these vignettes often captured the bleak and seedy aspects of city life, The Eight eventually became known as the Ash Can School. Some critics referred to them as "the apostles of ugliness."

A prominent member of The Eight was JOHN SLOAN (1871–1951). A self-described "incorrigible window watcher,"[22] Sloan constantly wandered the streets of New York, observing human drama. He focused much of his attention on the working class, which he perceived as embodying the realities of life. So sympathetic was Sloan to the plight of workers that he joined the Socialist Party in 1909 and eventually ran for public office on the Socialist ticket. In paintings such as *Sixth Avenue and 30th Street, New York City* (FIG. 29-34), Sloan revealed his ability to capture both the visual and social realities of American urban life. When he painted this image in 1907, Sloan lived on West 23rd Street, on the outskirts of the Tenderloin District, an area cluttered with brothels, dance halls, saloons, gambling dens, and cheap hotels. *Sixth Avenue* depicts a bustling intersection. Bracketing the throngs of people filling the intersection are elevated train tracks on the left and a row of storefronts and apartment buildings on the right. These two defining elements of city life converge in the far center background of the painting.

Sloan's portrayals of New York also feature a cross-section of the population of the city at the opening of the 20th century. In the foreground of *Sixth Avenue,* Sloan prominently placed three women. One, in a shabby white dress, is a drunkard, stumbling along with her pail of beer. All around her are the residents of the Tenderloin, who barely take notice of her, save for two elegantly dressed women who are passing through the area on their way somewhere else. They stare at the disoriented woman with disdain. At a time when traditional art centered on genteel and proper society, the comfortable world of the two fashionable women, Sloan forthrightly depicted the street life of New York's underclass, for whom the painter clearly had deep sympathy.

ARMORY SHOW The relative isolation of American artists from developments across the Atlantic came to an abrupt end in early 1913 when the Armory Show opened in New York City (see "The Armory Show," page 909). Although later recognized as the foundational event in the development of American modernist art, the

29-34 JOHN SLOAN, *Sixth Avenue and Thirtieth Street, New York City,* 1907. Oil on canvas, 2' $\frac{1}{4}$" × 2' 8". Philadelphia Museum of Art, Philadelphia (gift of Meyer P. Potamkin and Vivian O. Potamkin, 2000).

A prominent member of the American Realist group called The Eight, Sloan captured in his paintings the bleak and seedy aspects of the rapidly changing urban landscape of New York City.

1 ft.

ART AND SOCIETY

The Armory Show

From February 17 to March 15, 1913, the American public flocked in large numbers to view the International Exhibition of Modern Art at the 69th Regiment Armory in New York City. The "Armory Show," as it universally came to be called, was an ambitious endeavor organized primarily by two artists, Walt Kuhn (1877–1949) and Arthur B. Davies (1862–1928). The show included more than 1,600 artworks by American and European artists. Among the European artists represented were Matisse, Derain, Picasso, Braque, Duchamp (FIG. 29-35), Kandinsky, Kirchner, Lehmbruck, and Brancusi. In addition to exposing American artists and the public to the latest European artistic developments, the Armory Show also provided American artists with a prime showcase for their work. The foreword to the exhibition catalog spelled out the goals of the organizers:

> The American artists exhibiting here consider the exhibition of equal importance for themselves as for the public. The less they find their work showing signs of the developments indicated in the Europeans, the more reason they will have to consider whether or not painters or sculptors here have fallen behind . . . the forces that have manifested themselves on the other side of the Atlantic.*

On its opening, this provocative exhibition served as a lightning rod for commentary, immediately attracting heated controversy. The *New York Times* described the show as "pathological" and called the modernist artists "cousins to the anarchists," while the magazine *Art and Progress* compared them to "bomb throwers, lunatics, depravers."† Other critics demanded that the exhibition be closed as a menace to public morality. The *New York Herald,* for example, asserted: "The United States is invaded by aliens, thousands of whom constitute so many perils to the health of the body politic. Modernism is of precisely the same heterogeneous alien origin and is imperiling the republic of art in the same way."‡

Nonetheless, the exhibition was an important milestone in the history of art in the United States. The Armory Show traveled to Chicago and Boston after it closed in New York and was a significant catalyst for the reevaluation of the nature and purpose of American art.

*Quoted in Herschel B. Chipp, *Theories of Modern Art: A Source Book by Artists and Critics* (Berkeley and Los Angeles: University of California Press, 1968), 503.
†Quoted in Sam Hunter, John Jacobus, and Daniel Wheeler, *Modern Art,* rev. 3d. ed. (Upper Saddle River, N.J.: Prentice Hall, 2005), 250.
‡Quoted in Francis K. Pohl, *Framing America: A Social History of American Art,* 2d ed. (New York: Thames & Hudson, 2002), 341.

1 ft.

29-35 MARCEL DUCHAMP, *Nude Descending a Staircase, No. 2,* 1912. Oil on canvas, 4' 10" × 2' 11". Philadelphia Museum of Art, Philadelphia (Louise and Walter Arensberg Collection).

The Armory Show introduced European modernism to America. Duchamp's figure moving in a time continuum owes a debt to Cubism and Futurism. The press gave his painting a hostile reception.

exhibition received a hostile response from the press. The work that the journalists and critics most maligned was Marcel Duchamp's *Nude Descending a Staircase, No. 2* (FIG. 29-35). The painting represents a single figure moving in a time continuum and suggests the effect of a sequence of overlaid film stills. Unlike the Dada works by Duchamp (FIGS. 29-26, 29-26A, and 29-27), *Nude Descending a Staircase* shares many characteristics with the work of the Cubists and the Futurists. The monochromatic palette is reminiscent of Analytic Cubism, as is Duchamp's faceted presentation of the human form. The artist's interest in depicting the figure in motion reveals an affinity for the Futurists' ideas. One critic described this work as "an explosion in a shingle factory,"[23] and newspaper cartoonists delighted in lampooning the painting.

ARTHUR DOVE Among the American modernists who exhibited their work in the Armory Show was ARTHUR DOVE (1880–1946). After graduating from Cornell University, Dove worked briefly as a commercial artist in New York City and then in 1907 left for Paris, where he encountered the paintings of Henri Matisse (FIGS. 29-2, 29-2A, and 29-3) and André Derain (FIGS. 29-4 and 29-5). Dove returned to New York in 1910. He occupies a special place in the evolution of modernist art in the United States because he began painting completely nonobjective paintings at about the same time as Vassily Kandinsky but apparently without any knowledge of Kandinsky's *Improvisation* series (for example, FIG. 29-7).

Dove spent most of his life on farms in rural New York and Connecticut and loved the textures and colors of the American

29-36 ARTHUR DOVE, *Nature Symbolized No. 2*, ca. 1911. Pastel on paper, 1' 6" × 1' 9⅝". Art Institute of Chicago, Chicago (Alfred Stieglitz Collection).

Dove was one of the first painters to produce completely nonobjective canvases. Using only abstract shapes and color, he sought to capture the essence of nature and of pulsating organic growth.

landscape. He sought to capture in his paintings the essence of nature, especially its pulsating energy, but without representing nature directly. A characteristic and aptly named example of his abstract renditions of fields, vegetation, and sky is *Nature Symbolized No. 2* (FIG. 29-36), which he probably painted in 1911. Incorporating some of the principles and forms of Cubism but without representing any identifiable objects or landscape elements, Dove used swirling and jagged lines and a palette of mostly green, black, and sandy yellow to capture the essence of vegetation sprouting gloriously from fertile soil beneath patches of blue sky. He once described his goal as the creation of "rhythmic paintings" expressing nature's "spirit" through shape and color.

MAN RAY Another American artist who incorporated the latest European trends in his work was Emmanuel Radnitzky, who assumed the name MAN RAY (1890–1976). He was a close associate of Duchamp's in the 1920s and produced art having a decidedly Dada spirit, often incorporating found objects in his paintings, sculptures, movies, and photographs. Trained as an architectural draftsman, he earned his living as a graphic designer and portrait photographer, and developed an innovative photographic technique. In contrast to traditional photographs, Man Ray produced his images without using a camera by placing objects directly on photographic paper and then exposing the paper to light. He dubbed the resulting photographs, which in effect created themselves, *Rayographs*.

With many other artists of this period, Man Ray shared a keen interest in mass-produced objects and technology, as well as a dedication to exploring the psychological realm of human perception of the exterior world. Like Schwitters, he used the dislocation of ordinary things from their everyday settings to surprise the viewer into new awareness. His displacement of found objects was particularly effective in works such as *Cadeau* (*Gift*; FIG. 29-37). For this sculpture, with characteristic Dada humor, he equipped a laundry iron with a row of wicked-looking tacks, subverting its proper function. Ray's "gift" would rip to shreds any garment that the recipient tried to press with it.

MARSDEN HARTLEY One American artist who developed a personal style influenced by European avant-garde art movements was MARSDEN HARTLEY (1877–1943). In 1912, Hartley traveled to Europe, visiting Paris, where he became acquainted with the work of the Cubists, and Munich, where he gravitated to the Blaue Reiter circle. Kandinsky's work particularly impressed Hartley, and he developed a style that he called "Cosmic Cubism." In 1913, he moved to Berlin. With the heightened militarism in Germany and the eventual outbreak of World War I, Hartley immersed himself in military imagery.

Portrait of a German Officer (FIG. 29-38) is one of Hartley's best paintings of this period. It depicts an array of military-related images:

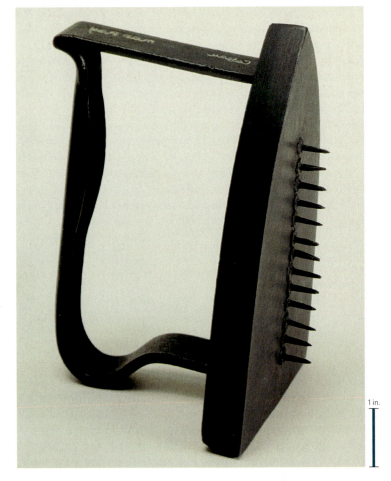

29-37 MAN RAY, *Cadeau* (*Gift*), ca. 1958 (replica of 1921 original). Painted flatiron with row of 13 tacks with heads glued to the bottom, 6⅛" × 3⅝" × 4½". Museum of Modern Art, New York (James Thrall Soby Fund).

With characteristic Dada humor, the American artist Man Ray equipped a laundry iron with a row of wicked-looking spikes, subverting its proper function of smoothing and pressing.

German imperial flags, regimental insignia, badges, and emblems such as the Iron Cross. Although this image resonates in the general context of wartime militarism, important elements in the painting had personal significance for Hartley. In particular, the painting includes references to his lover, Lieutenant Karl von Freyberg, who lost his life in battle a few months before Hartley painted this "portrait." Von Freyberg's initials appear in the lower left corner. His age when he died (24) appears in the lower right corner, and his regiment number (4) appears in the center of the painting. Also incorporated is the letter *E* for von Freyberg's regiment, the Bavarian Eisenbahn. The influence of Synthetic Cubism is evident in the flattened, planar presentation of the elements, which almost appear as abstract patterns. The somber black background against which the artist placed the colorful stripes, patches, and shapes casts an elegiac pall over the painting.

STUART DAVIS Philadelphia-born STUART DAVIS (1894–1964) created what he believed was a modern American art style by combining the flat shapes of Synthetic Cubism with his sense of jazz

tempos and his perception of the energy of fast-paced American culture. *Lucky Strike* (FIG. **29-39**) is one of several tobacco still lifes Davis began in 1921. Davis was a heavy smoker, and tobacco products and their packaging fascinated him. He insisted that the introduction of packaging in the late 19th century was evidence of high civilization and the progressiveness of American culture. Davis depicted the Lucky Strike package in fragmented form, reminiscent of Synthetic Cubist collages. However, the flat printed elements that the work incorporates are illusionistically painted, rather than glued onto the canvas. The discontinuities and the interlocking planes

29-38 MARSDEN HARTLEY, *Portrait of a German Officer*, 1914. Oil on canvas, 5' 8$\frac{1}{4}$" × 3' 5$\frac{3}{8}$". Metropolitan Museum of Art, New York (Alfred Stieglitz Collection).

In this elegy to a lover killed in battle, Hartley arranged military-related images against a somber black background. The flattened, planar presentation reveals the influence of Synthetic Cubism.

29-39 STUART DAVIS, *Lucky Strike*, 1921. Oil on canvas, 2' 9$\frac{1}{4}$" × 1' 6". Museum of Modern Art, New York (gift of the American Tobacco Company, Inc.). Art © Estate of Stuart Davis/Licensed by VAGA, New York.

Tobacco products fascinated Davis, a heavy smoker. In *Lucky Strike,* he depicted a cigarette package in fragmented form, recalling Cubism, and imbued his painting with an American jazz rhythm.

ART AND SOCIETY

Aaron Douglas and the Harlem Renaissance

Spearheaded by writers and editors Alain Locke (1886–1953) and Charles Spurgeon Johnson (1883–1956), the Harlem Renaissance was a manifestation of the desire of African Americans to promote their cultural accomplishments. Locke and Johnson also aimed to cultivate pride among fellow African Americans and to foster racial tolerance across the United States. Expansive and diverse, the fruits of the Harlem Renaissance included the writings of authors such as Langston Hughes, Countee Cullen, and Zora Neale Hurston; the jazz and blues of Duke Ellington, Bessie Smith, Eubie Blake, Fats Waller, and Louis Armstrong; the photographs of James Van Der Zee and Prentice H. Polk; and the paintings and sculptures of Meta Warrick Fuller and Augusta Savage. The best-known artist associated with the Harlem Renaissance is, however, Aaron Douglas (FIGS. 29-40 and 29-40A).

Douglas arrived in New York City in 1924 and quickly became one of the most sought-after graphic artists in the African American community. Encouraged to create art that would express the cultural history of his race, Douglas incorporated motifs from African sculpture, broadly defined to include ancient Egyptian works, into compositions painted in a version of Synthetic Cubism stressing transparent angular planes. In 1927, Douglas observed:

> While it is absurd to take African sculpture and literally transplant it and inject it into Negro American life, we can go to African life and get . . . understanding, form and color and use this [in] an expression which interprets our life.*

Noah's Ark (FIG. **29-40**) is one of seven paintings Douglas produced based on a book of poems by James Weldon Johnson (1871–1938) called *God's Trombones: Seven Negro Sermons in Verse*. Egyptian influence is evident in Douglas's figures with rounded crania and frontal eyes in profile heads (compare FIG. 3-29). In *Noah's Ark*, he used flat planes to evoke a sense of mystical space and miraculous happenings. Lightning strikes and rays of light crisscross the pairs of animals entering the ark, while men load supplies in preparation for departure. Douglas suggested deep space by differentiating the size of the large human head and shoulders of the worker at the bottom and the small person at work on the far deck of the ship. Yet the composition's unmodulated color shapes create a pattern on the Masonite surface that cancels any illusion of three-dimensional depth. Here, Douglas used Cubism's formal language to express a powerful religious vision.

Seven years later, employed by the U.S. government to create murals for the Harlem branch of the New York Public Library, he addressed a contemporary rather than a biblical subject: the history of Africans in America (FIG. **29-40A**).

29-40 AARON DOUGLAS, *Noah's Ark*, ca. 1927. Oil on Masonite, 4' × 3'. Fisk University Galleries, University of Tennessee, Nashville.

In *Noah's Ark* and other paintings of the cultural history of African Americans, Douglas incorporated motifs from African sculpture and the transparent angular planes characteristic of Synthetic Cubism.

⬈ **29-40A** DOUGLAS, *Slavery through Reconstruction*, 1934.

*Quoted by Caroline Goeser, *Picturing the New Negro* (Lawrence: University of Kansas Press, 2007), 32.

---

imbue *Lucky Strike* with a dynamism and rhythm not unlike American jazz or the pace of life in a lively American metropolis. *Lucky Strike* is decidedly both American and modern.

AARON DOUGLAS Also deriving his personal style from Synthetic Cubism was African American artist AARON DOUGLAS (1898–1979), who used the style to represent symbolically the historical and cultural memories of African Americans. Born in Kansas, Douglas studied in Nebraska and Paris before settling in

New York City, where he became part of the flowering of art and literature in the 1920s known as the Harlem Renaissance (see "Aaron Douglas and the Harlem Renaissance," above).

PRECISIONISM One of the distinctly American art movements that developed in the post–Armory Show period was *Precisionism*. Although not an organized group, the Precisionists shared a fascination with the machine's "precision" and its importance in modern life. Although new technologies captured the imaginations of many

ART AND SOCIETY

Art "Matronage" in the United States

Until the 20th century, a leading reason for the dearth of women artists was that professional institutions restricted women's access to artistic training. For example, the proscription against women participating in life-drawing classes, a staple of academic artistic training, in effect denied women the opportunity to become professional artists. Another explanation for the absence of women from the traditional art historical canon is that art historians have not considered as "high art" many of the art objects that women have traditionally produced (for example, quilts or basketry).

By the early 20th century, however, many of the impediments to a woman's becoming a recognized artist had been removed. Today, women are a major presence in the art world, as the roster of artists discussed in Chapter 31 highlights. One of the developments in the early 20th century that laid the groundwork for this change was the prominent role that American women played as art patrons. These "art matrons" provided financial, moral, and political support to cultivate the advancement of the arts in America. Chief among them were Gertrude Vanderbilt Whitney, Lillie P. Bliss, Mary Quinn Sullivan, Abby Aldrich Rockefeller, Isabella Stewart Gardner, Peggy Guggenheim, and Jane Stanford.*

Gertrude Vanderbilt Whitney (1875–1942) was a practicing sculptor and enthusiastic collector. To assist young American artists such as Robert Henri and John Sloan (FIG. 29-34) in exhibiting their work, she opened the Whitney Studio in 1914. By 1929, dissatisfied with the recognition accorded young, progressive American artists, she offered her entire collection of 500 works to the Metropolitan Museum of Art in New York City. Her offer rejected, she founded her own museum in New York, the Whitney Museum of American Art, and provided funds to purchase additional works by American artists, such as Charles Demuth's *My Egypt* (FIG. **29-41**). She chose Juliana Force (1876–1948) as the first director, a visionary and energetic woman who inaugurated a pioneering series of monographs on living American artists, and organized lecture series by influential art historians and critics. Through the efforts of these two women, the Whitney Museum became a major factor in the enhanced prestige of American art.

A trip to Paris in 1920 whetted the interest of Peggy Guggenheim (1898–1979) in avant-garde art. Like Whitney, Guggenheim collected art and eventually opened a gallery in England to exhibit the work of innovative artists. She continued her support for modernist art after her return to the United States. Guggenheim's New York gallery, called Art of This Century, was instrumental in advancing the careers of many artists, including her husband, Max Ernst (FIG. 29-53). She eventually moved her art collection to a lavish Venetian palace, where the public can still view the important artworks that she acquired.

Other women who contributed significantly to the arts were Lillie P. Bliss (1864–1931), Mary Quinn Sullivan (1877–1939), and Abby Aldrich Rockefeller (1874–1948). Philanthropists, art collectors, and educators, these influential and farsighted women saw the need for a museum to collect and exhibit modernist art. Together they established the Museum of Modern Art in New York City in 1929, which became (and continues to be) the most influential museum of modern art in the world (see "The Museum of Modern Art," page 945).

29-41 CHARLES DEMUTH, *My Egypt*, 1927. Oil on composition board, 2′ 11¾″ × 2′ 6″. Whitney Museum of American Art, New York (purchased with funds from Gertrude Vanderbilt Whitney).

Demuth was one of the leading Precisionists—American artists who extolled the machine age. This painting depicts grain elevators reduced to geometric forms amid Cubist transparent diagonal planes.

Isabella Stewart Gardner (1840–1924) and Jane Stanford (1828–1905) also undertook the ambitious project of founding museums. The Isabella Stewart Gardner Museum in Boston, established in 1903, houses a well-chosen and comprehensive collection of art of many periods. The Stanford University Museum of Art (now the Iris B. and Gerald Cantor Center for Visual Arts), the first American museum west of the Mississippi, got its start in 1891 at the university that Leland Stanford Sr. and Jane Stanford founded after the tragic death of their son. The Cantor Center houses a wide range of objects, including archaeological and ethnographic artifacts. Both women committed much of their time, energy, and financial resources to ensure the success of their museums, and were intimately involved in their institutions' day-to-day operations.

The museums that these women established flourish today, attesting to the extraordinary vision of these "art matrons" and the remarkable contributions they made to the advancement of art in the United States.

*Art historian Wanda Corn coined the term "art matronage" in the catalog *Cultural Leadership in America: Art Matronage and Patronage* (Boston: Isabella Stewart Gardner Museum, 1997).

European artists, especially Delaunay, Léger, and the Futurists, Americans generally seemed more enamored of the prospects of a mechanized society than did Europeans. Even the Frenchman Francis Picabia, Duchamp's collaborator, noted: "Since machinery is the soul of the modern world, and since the genius of machinery attains its highest expression in America, why is it not reasonable to believe that in America the art of the future will flower most brilliantly?"[24] Precisionism, however, expanded beyond the exploration of machine imagery. Many artists associated with this group gravitated toward Synthetic Cubism's flat, sharply delineated planes as an appropriate visual idiom for their imagery, adding to the clarity and precision of their work. Eventually, Precisionism came to be characterized by a merging of a familiar native style in American architecture and artifacts with a modernist vocabulary derived largely from Synthetic Cubism.

CHARLES DEMUTH Two of the leading Precisionists hailed from Pennsylvania—Charles Sheeler (1883–1965) and CHARLES DEMUTH (1883–1935). Sheeler traveled to Italy and France in 1909, and Demuth spent the years 1912–1914 in Paris, but both artists rejected pure abstraction and favored American subjects, especially industrial landscapes. Demuth's *My Egypt* (FIG. 29-41) is one of many artworks acquired by Gertrude Vanderbilt Whitney, the leading patron of American modernist artists in the period between the two world wars (see "Art 'Matronage' in the United States," page 913). The painting incorporates the spatial discontinuities characteristic of Cubism into a typically Precisionist depiction of an industrial site near Lancaster, the painter's birthplace. Demuth reduced the John W. Eshelman and Sons grain elevators to simple geometric forms. The grain elevators remain recognizable and solid, but the "beams" of transparent planes and the diagonal force lines threaten to destabilize the image and recall Cubist fragmentation of space. The degree to which Demuth intended to extol the American industrial scene is unclear. The title, *My Egypt,* is sufficiently ambiguous in tone to accommodate differing readings. On the one hand, Demuth could have been suggesting a favorable comparison between the Egyptian pyramids and American grain elevators as cultural icons. On the other hand, the title could be read cynically, as a negative comment on the limitations of American culture. Or Demuth might have been making a biblical reference to Joseph's granaries, which fed Egypt during seven years of famine.

GEORGIA O'KEEFFE The work of Wisconsin-born GEORGIA O'KEEFFE (1887–1986) changed stylistically throughout her career. During the 1920s, O'Keeffe was a Precisionist. She had moved from the tiny town of Canyon, Texas, to New York City in 1918, and although she had visited the city before, what she found there excited her. "You have to live in today," she told a friend. "Today the city is something bigger, more complex than ever before in history. And nothing can be gained from running away. I couldn't even if I could."[25] While in New York, O'Keeffe met Alfred Stieglitz (FIGS. 29-43 and 29-43A), who played a major role in promoting the avant-garde in the United States. Stieglitz had established an art gallery at 291 Fifth Avenue in New York. In "291," as the gallery came to be called, he exhibited the latest in both European and American art. Thus 291, like the Armory Show, played an important role in the history of early-20th-century art in America. Stieglitz had seen and exhibited some of O'Keeffe's earlier work, and he drew her into his avant-garde circle of painters and photographers. He became one of O'Keeffe's staunchest supporters and, eventually, her husband. The interest of Stieglitz and his circle in capturing the sensibility of the machine age intersected with O'Keeffe's fascination with the fast pace of city life. During this period, she produced paintings such as *New York, Night* (FIG. **29-42**), featuring the soaring skyscrapers dominating the city, which, for many, were symbols of the modern world and of America's preeminence in architecture and engineering. Like other Precisionists, O'Keeffe reduced her images to simple planes, here punctuated by small rectangular windows that add rhythm and energy to the image, countering the monolithic darkness of the looming buildings.

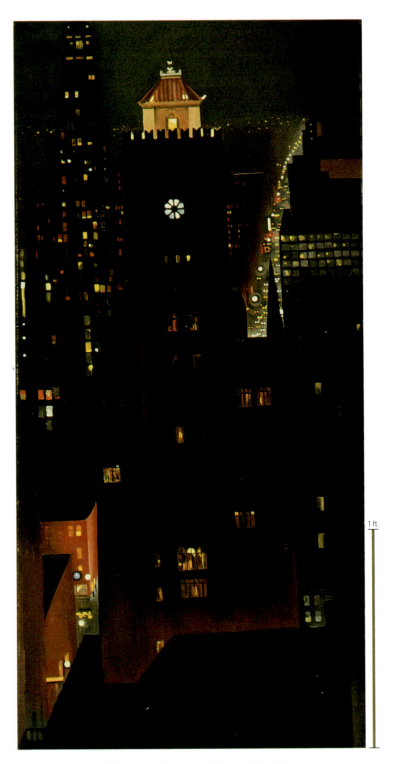

29-42 GEORGIA O'KEEFFE, *New York, Night,* 1929. Oil on canvas, 3' 4⅛" × 1' 7⅛". Sheldon Memorial Art Gallery, Lincoln (Nebraska Art Association, Thomas C. Woods Memorial Collection).

O'Keeffe's Precisionist representation of New York's soaring skyscrapers reduces the buildings to large, simple, dark planes punctuated by small windows that add rhythm and energy to the image.

Despite O'Keeffe's affiliation with the Precisionist movement and New York, she is best known for her paintings of cow skulls and of flowers. For example, in *Jack-in-the-Pulpit No. 4* (FIG. I-5), she reveals her interest in stripping subjects to their purest forms and colors to heighten their expressive power. In this work, O'Keeffe reduced the curved planes and contours of the flower to a symphony of basic

Alfred Stieglitz on "Straight Photography"

Taking his camera everywhere he went, Alfred Stieglitz photographed whatever he saw around him, from the bustling streets of New York City to cloudscapes in upstate New York and the faces of friends and relatives. He believed in making only "straight, unmanipulated" photographs. Thus he exposed and printed them using basic photographic processes, without resorting to techniques such as double-exposure or double-printing that would add information absent in the subject when he released the shutter. Stieglitz said that he wanted the photographs he made with this direct technique "to hold a moment, to record something so completely that those who see it would relive an equivalent of what has been expressed."*

Stieglitz's photographic work is noteworthy for his insistence on seeing his subjects in terms of arrangements of forms and of the "colors" of his black-and-white materials. His aesthetic approach crystallized during the making of *The Steerage* (FIG. **29-43**), a photograph he took during a sea voyage to Europe with his first wife and daughter in 1907. Traveling first class, Stieglitz rapidly grew bored with the company of the prosperous passengers in his section of the ship. He walked as far forward on the first-class level as he could, when the rail around the opening onto the lower deck brought him up short. This level was for the steerage passengers whom the government sent back to Europe after refusing them entrance into the United States. Later, Stieglitz described what happened next:

> The scene fascinated me: A round hat; the funnel leaning left, the stairway leaning right; the white drawbridge, its railing made of chain; white suspenders crossed on the back of a man below; circular iron machinery; a mast that cut into the sky, completing a triangle. I stood spellbound. I saw shapes related to one another— a picture of shapes, and underlying it, a new vision that held me: simple people; the feeling of ship, ocean, sky; a sense of release that I was away from the mob called rich. Rembrandt came into my mind and I wondered would he have felt as I did. . . . I had only one plate holder with one unexposed plate. Could I catch what I saw and felt? I released the shutter. If I had captured what I wanted, the photograph would go far beyond any of my previous prints. It would be a picture based on related shapes and deepest human feeling—a step in my own evolution, a spontaneous discovery.†

This description reveals Stieglitz's abiding interest in the formal elements of the photograph—an insistently modernist focus that

29-43 ALFRED STIEGLITZ, *The Steerage*, 1907 (print 1915). Photogravure (on tissue), $1' \frac{3}{8}'' \times 10\frac{1}{8}''$. Amon Carter Museum, Fort Worth.

Stieglitz waged a lifelong campaign for photography as a fine art. This 1907 "straight photographic" image taken on an ocean liner is a haunting mixture of human activity and found patterns of forms.

emerges in even more extreme form in his *Equivalent* series (FIG. **29-43A**) of the 1920s. The finished print fulfilled Stieglitz's vision so well that it shaped his future photographic work, and its haunting mixture of found patterns and human activity has continued to stir viewers' emotions to this day.

29-43A STIEGLITZ, *Equivalent*, 1923.

*Dorothy Norman, *Alfred Stieglitz: An American Seer* (Millerton, N.Y.: Aperture, 1973), 9–10.
†Ibid., 161.

---

colors, shapes, textures, and vital rhythms, simplifying the forms almost to the point of complete abstraction. The fluid planes unfold like undulant petals from a subtly placed axis—the white jetlike streak—in a vision of the slow, controlled motion of growing life. O'Keeffe's painting, in its graceful, quiet poetry, reveals the organic reality of the object by strengthening its characteristic features.

Photography

Among the most significant artistic developments during the decades between the two world wars was the emergence of photography as a respected branch of the fine arts in the United States. The person most responsible for elevating the stature of photography was Alfred Stieglitz.

ALFRED STIEGLITZ While a student of photochemistry in Germany, ALFRED STIEGLITZ (1864–1946) began a lifelong campaign to win a place for photography among the fine arts. In New York, he founded the Photo-Secession group, which mounted traveling exhibitions in the United States and sent loan collections abroad, and he published an influential journal titled *Camera Work*. Stieglitz's many recorded comments on the art of photography clearly set forth his philosophy of picture making using film instead of paint (see "Alfred Stieglitz on 'Straight Photography,'" above).

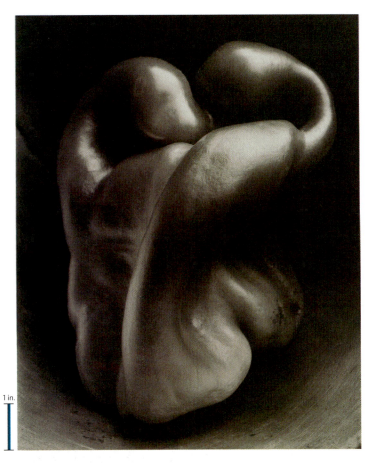

29-44 EDWARD WESTON, *Pepper No. 30*, 1930. Gelatin silver print, $9\frac{1}{2}$" × $7\frac{1}{2}$". Center for Creative Photography, University of Arizona, Tucson.

Weston "previsualized" his still lifes, choosing the exact angle, lighting, and framing he desired. His vegetables often resemble human bodies, in this case a seated nude seen from behind.

EDWARD WESTON Like Alfred Stieglitz, EDWARD WESTON (1886–1958) played a major role in establishing photography as an important artistic medium. But unlike Stieglitz, who worked outdoors and sought to capture transitory moments in his photographs, Weston meticulously composed his subjects in a controlled setting, whether he was doing still lifes of peppers, shells, and other natural forms of irregular shape, or figure studies. The 1930 photograph of a pepper illustrated here (FIG. 29-44) is the 30th in a large series and an outstanding example of this genre. In contrast to Weston's photographs of sections of nude human bodies (FIG. 29-44A), his still-life photographs show the entire object, albeit tightly framed. (Compare Georgia O'Keeffe's *Jack-in-the-Pulpit No. 4* [FIG. I-5] painted the same year.) The lighting accentuates the undulating surfaces and

29-44A WESTON, *Nude*, 1925.

crevices of the vegetable. Weston left nothing to chance, choosing the exact angle and play of light over the object, "previsualizing" the final photographic print before snapping the camera's shutter.

In a kind of reversal of his approach to photographing nudes, which he often transformed into landscapes, Weston frequently chose peppers whose shapes reminded him of human bodies.

Pepper No. 30 looks like a seated nude figure seen from behind with raised arms emerging from broad shoulders. Viewers can read the vertical crease down the center of the vegetable as the spinal column leading to the buttocks. Although highly successful as a purely abstract composition of shapes and of light and dark, Weston's still life also conveys mystery and sensuality through its dramatic lighting and rich texture.

Architecture

Like other artists, many early-20th-century architects in the United States looked to Europe for inspiration, but distinctive American styles also emerged that in turn had a major influence on architectural design worldwide.

FRANK LLOYD WRIGHT One of the most striking personalities in the development of modern architecture on either side of the Atlantic was FRANK LLOYD WRIGHT (1867–1959). Born in Wisconsin, Wright moved to Chicago, where he eventually joined the firm headed by Louis Sullivan (FIGS. 28-42, 28-42A, and 28-43). Wright set out to create an American "architecture of democracy" (see "Frank Lloyd Wright on Organic Architecture," page 917).

Wright's vigorous originality emerged early, and by 1900 he had arrived at a style entirely his own. In his work during the first decade of the 20th century, his cross-axial plan and his fabric of continuous roof planes and screens defined a new American domestic architecture. He fully expressed these elements and concepts in the Robie House (FIG. 29-45), built between 1907 and 1909. Like other buildings in the Chicago area that Wright designed at about the same time, he called this home a "prairie house." Wright conceived the long, sweeping, ground-hugging lines, unconfined by abrupt wall limits, as reaching out toward and capturing the expansiveness of the Midwest's great flatlands. Abandoning all symmetry, he eliminated a facade, extended the roofs far beyond the walls, and all but concealed the entrance. Wright filled the house's "wandering" plan (FIG. 29-46) with intricately joined spaces (some large and open, others closed), grouped freely around a great central fireplace. (He believed strongly in the hearth's age-old domestic significance as well as in its ability to keep a house's inhabitants warm in Chicago's frigid winters.) Wright designed enclosed patios, overhanging roofs (essential to provide shade in the summer heat), and strip windows to provide unexpected light sources and glimpses of the outdoors as the inhabitants moved through the interior space. These elements, together with the open ground plan, created a sense of space in motion, inside and out. Wright matched his new and fundamental interior spatial arrangement in his exterior treatment. For example, the flow of interior space determined the sharp angular placement of exterior walls.

ART DECO Although Adolf Loos (FIG. 29-33) had strongly condemned ornamentation in the design of buildings, popular taste still favored decoration as an important element in architecture. *Art Deco* was a movement in the 1920s and 1930s whose adherents sought to upgrade industrial design in competition with "fine art." Proponents wanted to work new materials into decorative patterns that could be either machined or handcrafted and could, to a degree, reflect the simplifying trend in architecture. A remote descendant of Art Nouveau (see page 872), Art Deco acquired its name at the Exposition des Arts Décoratifs et Industriels Modernes (Exposition of Modern Decorative and Industrial Arts), held in Paris in 1925. Art Deco had universal application—to buildings, interiors,

ARTISTS ON ART

Frank Lloyd Wright on Organic Architecture

Always a believer in "natural" and "organic" buildings, Wright envisioned an "architecture of democracy"*—that is, buildings designed to serve free individuals who have the right to move within a "free" space. Wright equated free space with a nonsymmetrical design interacting spatially with its natural surroundings, as in his 1907–1909 Robie House (FIGS. 29-45 and 29-46) in Chicago. In his architectural designs, Wright sought to develop an organic unity of planning, structure, materials, and site, and identified the principle of "continuity" as fundamental to understanding his view of organic unity.

> Classic architecture was all fixation. . . . Now why not let walls, ceilings, floors become seen as component parts of each other? . . . You may see the appearance in the surface of your hand contrasted with the articulation of the bony structure itself. This ideal, profound in its architectural implications . . . I called . . . continuity.†

> In Organic Architecture . . . it is quite impossible to consider the building as one thing, its furnishings another and its setting and environment still another. The Spirit in which these buildings are conceived sees all these together at work as one thing. All are to be studiously foreseen and provided for in the nature of the structure. All these should become mere details of the character and completeness of the structure. . . . To thus make of a human dwelling-place a complete work of art, in itself expressive and beautiful, intimately related to modern life and fit to live in, lending itself more freely and suitably to the individual needs of the dwellers . . . this is the tall modern American opportunity in Architecture. True basis of a true Culture. . . . I believe this Ideal will become a new Tradition: a vast step in advance of the prescribed fashion in a day when a dwelling was a composite of cells arranged as separate rooms. . . . An organic-entity, this modern building as contrasted with that former insensate aggregation of parts. . . . One great thing instead of a quarrelling collection of so many little things.‡

*Quoted in Vincent Scully Jr., *Frank Lloyd Wright* (New York: Braziller, 1960), 18.

†Quoted in Edgar Kauffmann, ed., *Frank Lloyd Wright, An American Architecture* (New York: Horizon, 1955), 205, 208.

‡Quoted in Ulrich Conrads, ed., *Programs and Manifestoes on 20th-Century Architecture* (Cambridge, Mass.: MIT Press, 1970), 25.

29-45 FRANK LLOYD WRIGHT, Robie House (looking northeast), Chicago, Illinois, 1907–1909.

The Robie House is an example of Wright's "architecture of democracy," in which free individuals move within a "free" space—a nonsymmetrical design interacting spatially with its natural surroundings.

29-46 FRANK LLOYD WRIGHT, plan of the second (main) level of the Robie House, Chicago, Illinois, 1907–1909.

Typical of Wright's "prairie houses," the Robie House has a bold "wandering" asymmetrical plan with intricately joined open and closed spaces grouped freely around a great central fireplace.

furniture, utensils, jewelry, fashions, illustration, and commercial products of every sort. Art Deco products have a "streamlined," elongated symmetrical aspect. Simple, flat shapes alternate with shallow volumes in hard patterns. Derived from nature, these simple forms are inherently aerodynamic, making them technologically efficient (because of their reduced resistance as they move through air or water) as well as aesthetically pleasing. Designers adopted streamlined designs for trains and cars, and the popular appeal of these designs led to their use in an array of objects, from machines to consumer products.

Art Deco architecture's exemplary masterpiece is the stainless-steel spire of the Chrysler Building (FIG. **29-47**) in New York City, designed by WILLIAM VAN ALEN (1882–1954). The building and spire are monuments to the fabulous 1920s, when American millionaires and corporations competed with one another to raise the tallest skyscrapers in the biggest cities (compare FIG. 29-42). Built up of diminishing fan shapes, the spire glitters triumphantly in the sky, a resplendent crown honoring the business achievements of the great auto manufacturer. As a temple of commerce, the Chrysler Building celebrated the principles and success of American business before the onset of the Great Depression.

EUROPE, 1920 TO 1945

Because World War I was fought entirely on European soil, European artists experienced its devastating effects to a much greater degree than did American artists. The war had a profound effect on Europe's geopolitical terrain (MAP 29-1), on individual and national psyches, and on European art of the 1920s and 1930s.

Neue Sachlichkeit

In Germany, World War I gave rise to an artistic movement called *Neue Sachlichkeit* (New Objectivity). All of the artists associated with Neue Sachlichkeit served, at some point, in the German army. Their military experiences deeply influenced their worldviews and informed their art. "New Objectivity" captures the group's aim—to present a clear-eyed, direct, and honest image of the world, especially the "Great War" and its effects.

GEORGE GROSZ One of the leading Neue Sachlichkeit artists was GEORGE GROSZ (1893–1958), who was, for a time, associated with the Dada group in Berlin. Grosz observed the onset of World War I with horrified fascination that soon turned to anger and frustration:

> Of course, there was a kind of mass enthusiasm at the start. But this intoxication soon evaporated, leaving a huge vacuum. . . . And then after a few years when everything bogged down, when we were defeated, when everything went to pieces, all that remained, at least for me and most of my friends, were disgust and horror.[26]

Many of Grosz's paintings and drawings—for example, *Fit for Active Service* (FIG. **29-47A**)—depict the war itself. However, the largest canvas he ever painted—*The Eclipse of the Sun* (FIG. **29-48**)—does not, although it is a stinging indictment of the militarism and capitalism that Grosz believed were the root causes of the global conflict. *Eclipse of the Sun* takes its name from the large red German coin at the upper left blocking the sun and signifying

⊿ 29-47A GROSZ, *Fit for Active Service*, 1916–1917.

that capitalism has brought darkness to the world. Also at the top are burning buildings. At the lower right are a skull and bones. Filling the rest of the canvas are the agents of this destruction seated at a table seen at a sharp angle from above. The main figure is the president of Germany, Paul von Hindenburg (r. 1925–1934), who wears his army uniform and war medals. His bloody sword is on the table before him, and on his head is the laurel wreath of victory. He presides over a meeting with four headless ministers—men who act on his orders without question. Grosz, however, also portrayed the president as a puppet leader. A wealthy industrialist wearing a top hat whispers

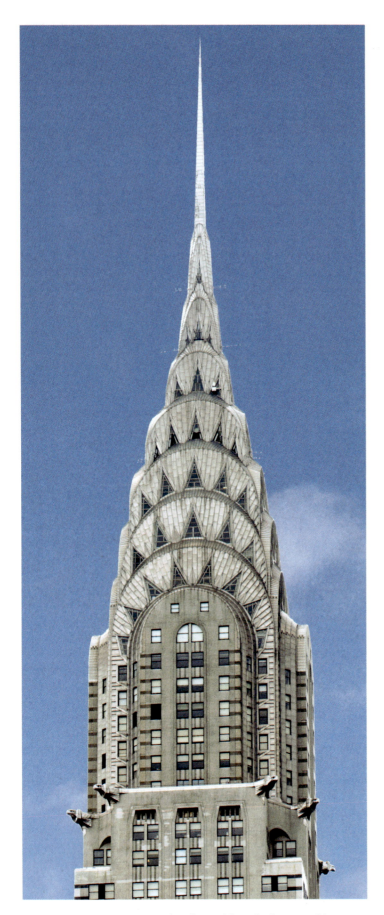

29-47 WILLIAM VAN ALEN, Chrysler Building (looking south), New York, New York, 1928–1930.

The Chrysler Building's stainless steel spire epitomizes Art Deco architecture. The skyscraper's glittering crown of diminishing fan shapes has a streamlined form popular in America during the 1920s.

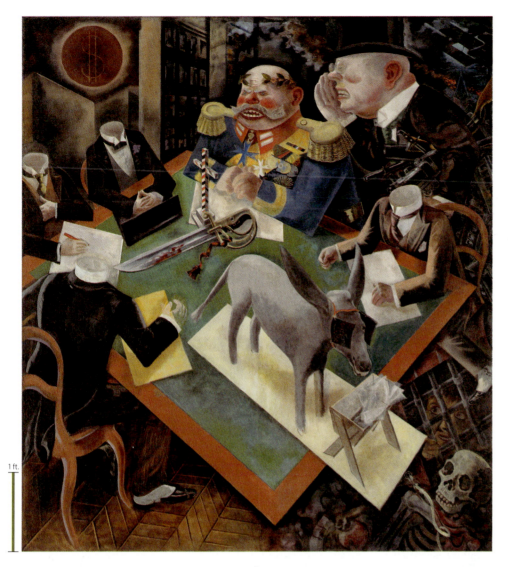

29-48 GEORGE GROSZ, *The Eclipse of the Sun*, 1926. Oil on canvas, 6' 9⅝" × 5' 11⅞". Heckscher Museum of Art, Huntington.

In Grosz's indictment of militarism and capitalism, an industrialist whispers instructions in the ear of the uniformed president of Germany, who meets with four of his headless ministers.

instructions in von Hindenburg's ear. The painting is also a commentary on the gullibility of the public, personified here as a donkey who eats newspapers—that is, as a mindless creature who swallows the propagandistic lies promoted by the government- and business-friendly press.

MAX BECKMANN Another major German artist who enlisted in the German army and initially rationalized the Great War was MAX BECKMANN (1884–1950). He believed that a better society would emerge from the chaos that the armed conflict unleashed, but over time the massive loss of life and widespread destruction increasingly disillusioned him. Soon Beckmann's work began to emphasize the horrors of war and of a society that he regarded as descending into madness. His disturbing view of wartime Germany is evident in *Night* (FIG. **29-49**), which depicts a cramped room that three intruders have forcefully invaded. A bound woman, apparently raped, is splayed across the foreground of the painting. Her husband appears on the left. One of the intruders hangs him, while another one twists his left arm out of its socket. An unidentified woman cowers in the background. On the far right, the third intruder prepares to flee with the child.

Although this image does not depict a war scene, the wrenching brutality and violence pervading the home are searing and horrifying comments on society's condition. Beckmann also injected a personal reference by using himself, his wife, and his son as the models for the three family members. The stilted angularity of the figures and the roughness of the paint surface contribute to the image's savageness. In addition, the artist's treatment of forms and space reflects the world's violence. Objects seem dislocated

29-49 MAX BECKMANN, *Night,* 1918–1919. Oil on canvas, 4' 4⅜" × 5' 1¼". Kunstsammlung Nordrhein-Westfalen, Düsseldorf.

Beckmann's treatment of forms and space in *Night* matched his view of the brutality of early-20th-century society. Objects seem dislocated and contorted, and the space appears buckled and illogical.

and contorted, and the space appears buckled and illogical. For example, the woman's hands are bound to the window opening from the room's back wall, but her body appears to hang vertically, rather than lying across the plane of the intervening table.

OTTO DIX The third artist most closely associated with Neue Sachlichkeit was OTTO DIX (1891–1969). Having served as both a machine gunner and an aerial observer, Dix was well acquainted with the Great War's effects. Like Grosz and Beckmann, Dix initially tried to find redeeming value in the apocalyptic event: "The war was a horrible thing, but there was something tremendous about it, too. . . . You have to have seen human beings in this unleashed state to know what human nature is. . . . I need to experience all the depths of life for myself, that's why I go out, and that's why I volunteered."[27] This idea of experiencing the "depths of life" stemmed from Dix's interest in the philosophy of Friedrich Nietzsche (1844–1900). In particular, Dix avidly read Nietzsche's *The Joyous Science,* deriving from it a belief in life's cyclical nature—procreation and death, building up and tearing down, and growth and decay.

As the war progressed, however, Dix's faith in the potential improvement of society faded, and he began to produce unflinchingly direct and provocative artworks. His triptych titled *Der Krieg* (*The War*; FIG. **29-50**) vividly captures the panoramic devastation that war inflicts, both on the terrain and on humans. In the left panel,

armed and uniformed soldiers march off into the distance. Dix graphically displayed the horrific results in the center and right panels, where mangled bodies, many riddled with bullet holes, are scattered throughout the eerily lit apocalyptic landscape. As if to emphasize the intensely personal nature of this scene, the artist painted himself into the right panel as the ghostly but determined soldier who drags a comrade to safety. In the bottom panel, in a coffinlike bunker, lie sleeping—or perhaps dead—soldiers. Significantly, Dix chose to present this sequence of images in the format of an altarpiece, and the work recalls triptychs such as Matthias Grünewald's *Isenheim Altarpiece* (FIG. 23-2). However, Dix's "altarpiece" presents a bleaker outlook than Grünewald's. The hope of salvation extended to viewers of the *Isenheim Altarpiece* through Christ's eventual resurrection is absent from *Der Krieg*. As did his fellow Neue Sachlichkeit artists, Dix felt compelled to lay bare the realities of his time, which the war's violence dominated. Even years later, Dix still maintained:

> You have to see things the way they are. You have to be able to say yes to the human manifestations that exist and will always exist. That doesn't mean saying yes to war, but to a fate that approaches you under certain conditions and in which you have to prove yourself. Abnormal situations bring out all the depravity, the bestiality of human beings. . . . I portrayed states, states that the war brought about, and the results of war, as states.[28]

29-50 OTTO DIX, *Der Krieg* (*The War*), 1929–1932. Oil and tempera on wood, 8' 8" (including predella) × 13' 4¾". Staatliche Kunstsammlungen, Gemäldegalerie Neue Meister, Dresden.

In this triptych recalling earlier altarpieces, Dix captured the panoramic devastation that war inflicts on the terrain and on humans. He depicted himself as a soldier dragging a comrade to safety.

ERNST BARLACH A work more spiritual in its expression is the *War Monument* (FIG. 29-51) fashioned by the German sculptor ERNST BARLACH (1870–1938) for the cathedral in his hometown of Güstrow in 1927. Working often in wood, Barlach sculpted single figures usually dressed in flowing robes and portrayed in strong, simple poses embodying deep human emotions and experiences such as grief, vigilance, or self-comfort. Barlach's works combine sharp, smoothly planed forms with intense expression. The cast-bronze hovering figure of his *War Monument* is one of the most poignant memorials of World War I. Unlike traditional war memorials depicting heroic military figures, often engaged in battle, the hauntingly symbolic figure that Barlach created speaks to the experience of all caught in the conflict of war. The floating human form, suspended above a tomb inscribed with the dates 1914–1918 (and later also 1939–1945), suggests a dying soul at the moment when it is about to awaken to everlasting life—the theme of death and transfiguration. The rigid economy of surfaces concentrates attention on the simple but expressive head. So powerful was this sculpture that

the Nazis had it removed from the cathedral in 1937 and melted it down for ammunition. Luckily, a friend hid another version that Barlach had made. A Protestant parish in Cologne purchased it, and bronze workers made a new cast of the figure for the Güstrow cathedral.

Surrealism

The exuberantly aggressive momentum of the Dada movement that emerged during World War I lasted for only a short time. By 1924, with André Breton's publication in France of the *First Surrealist Manifesto*, most of the artists associated with Dada had joined the *Surrealism* movement, which had begun as a literary movement (see "André Breton's *First Surrealist Manifesto*," page 922). The Surrealists were determined to explore ways to express in art the world of dreams and the unconscious. Not surprisingly, the Surrealists incorporated many of the Dadaists' improvisational techniques. They believed that these methods were important for engaging the elements of fantasy and activating the unconscious forces deep within every human being. Inspired in part by the ideas of the psychoanalysts Sigmund Freud and Carl Jung, the Surrealists focused on the inner world of the psyche and had a special interest in the nature of dreams, an interest already central to the Italian Metaphysical Painting movement of Giorgio de Chirico (FIG. 29-52). They viewed dreams as occurring at the level connecting all human consciousness and as constituting the arena in which people could move beyond their environment's constricting forces to reengage with the deeper selves that society had long suppressed.

Thus the Surrealists' dominant motivation was to bring the aspects of outer and inner "reality" together into a single position, in much the same way that life's seemingly unrelated fragments combine in the vivid world of dreams. The projection in visible form of this new conception required new techniques of pictorial construction. The Surrealists adapted some Dada devices and invented new methods such as automatic writing (spontaneous writing using free association), not so much to reveal a world without meaning as to provoke reactions closely related to subconscious experience.

Surrealism developed along two lines. In *Naturalistic Surrealism*, artists presented recognizable scenes that seem to have metamorphosed into a dream or nightmare image. The artists Salvador Dalí (FIG. 29-55) and René Magritte (FIGS. 29-56 and 29-56A) were the most famous practitioners of this variant of Surrealism. In contrast, some artists gravitated toward an interest in *Biomorphic Surrealism*. In Biomorphic ("life forms") Surrealism, *automatism*—the creation of art without conscious control—predominated. Biomorphic Surrealists such as Joan Miró (FIG. 29-58) produced largely abstract compositions, although the imagery sometimes suggests organisms or natural forms.

29-51 ERNST BARLACH, *War Monument*, Güstrow Cathedral, Güstrow, Germany, 1927. Bronze.

In this World War I memorial, which the Nazis melted down for ammunition, a human form floating above a tomb suggests a dying soul at the moment that it is about to awaken to everlasting life.

André Breton's *First Surrealist Manifesto*

A poet, novelist, and critic rather than a visual artist, André Breton nonetheless played a leading role in the formation of two of the 20th century's most important art movements: Dada (see page 900) and Surrealism. Although it was Guillaume Apollinaire who first proposed the term "Surrealism," the movement did not begin to take firm shape until 1924, when Breton published the *First Surrealist Manifesto* in the inaugural issue of *La revolution surréaliste*.

Some excerpts:

The mere word "freedom" is the only one that still excites me. . . . We are still living under the reign of logic . . . The absolute rationalism that is still in vogue allows us to consider only facts relating directly to our experience. . . . Under the pretense of civilization and progress, we have managed to banish from the mind everything that may rightly or wrongly be termed superstition, or fancy; forbidden is any kind of search for truth which is not in conformance with accepted practices. . . . [T]hanks to the discoveries of Sigmund Freud . . . [t]he imagination is perhaps on the point of reasserting itself, of reclaiming its rights. . . . Freud very rightly brought his critical faculties to bear upon the dream. . . . I have always been amazed at the way an ordinary observer lends so much more credence and attaches so much more importance to waking events than to those occurring in dreams. . . . I believe in the future resolution of these two states, dream and reality, which are seemingly so contradictory, into a kind of absolute reality, a "surreality," if one may so speak. It is in quest of this surreality that I am going . . .

Surrealism . . . is [p]sychic automatism in its pure state, by which one proposes to express—verbally . . . or in any other manner—the actual function of thought. . . . Surrealism is based on the belief in the superior reality of certain forms of previously neglected associations, in the omnipotence of dream, in the disinterested play of thought. It tends to ruin once and for all all other psychic mechanisms and to substitute itself for them in solving all the principal problems of life.*

*Translated by Richard Seaver and Helen R. Lane, *André Breton: Manifestoes of Surrealism* (Ann Arbor: University of Michigan Press, 1969), 3–47.

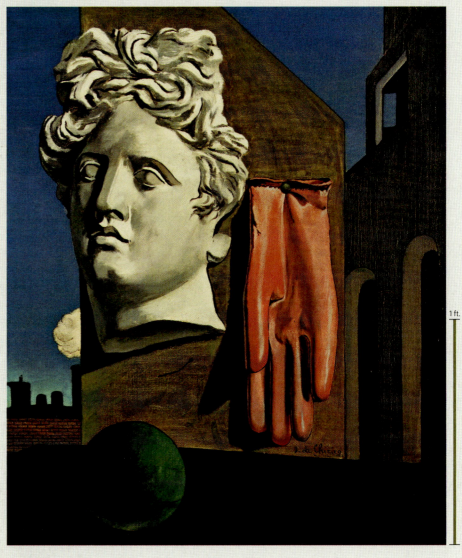

29-52 GIORGIO DE CHIRICO, *The Song of Love*, 1914. Oil on canvas, 2' 4¾" × 1' 11⅜". Museum of Modern Art, New York (Nelson A. Rockefeller bequest).

De Chirico's Metaphysical Painting movement was a precursor of Surrealism. In this dreamlike scene set in a deserted square, a classical head of Apollo floats mysteriously next to a gigantic red glove.

GIORGIO DE CHIRICO The widely recognized precursor of Surrealism was the Italian painter GIORGIO DE CHIRICO (1888–1978). De Chirico's intentionally ambiguous paintings of cityscapes are the most famous examples of a movement called *Pittura Metafisica*, or Metaphysical Painting. Returning to Italy after studying in Munich, de Chirico found hidden reality revealed through strange juxtapositions, such as those seen on late autumn afternoons in the city of Turin, when the long shadows of the setting sun transformed vast open squares and silent public monuments into what the painter called "metaphysical towns."

De Chirico translated this vision into paint in works such as *The Song of Love* (FIG. 29-52), a dreamlike scene set in the deserted piazza of an Italian town. A huge marble head—a fragment of the famous *Apollo Belvedere* in the Vatican—is suspended in midair above a large green ball. To the right is a gigantic red glove nailed to a wall. The buildings and the three over-life-size objects cast shadows that direct the viewer's eye to the left and to a locomotive puffing smoke—a favorite Futurist motif, here shown in slow motion and incongruously placed near the central square. The choice of the term *metaphysical* to describe de Chirico's paintings

29-53 MAX ERNST, *Two Children Are Threatened by a Nightingale*, 1924. Oil on wood with wood construction, 2' 3½" × 1' 10½" × 4½". Museum of Modern Art, New York.

In this early Surrealist painting with an intentionally ambiguous title, Ernst used traditional perspective to represent the setting, but the three sketchily rendered figures belong to a dream world.

with marvels. In autobiographical notes, written mostly in the third person, he said of his birth:

> Max Ernst had his first contact with the world of sense on the 2nd April 1891 at 9:45 a.m., when he emerged from the egg which his mother had laid in an eagle's nest and which the bird had incubated for seven years.[30]

Ernst's service in the German army during World War I swept away his early success as an Expressionist. In his own words:

> Max Ernst died on 1st August 1914. He returned to life on 11th November 1918, a young man who wanted to become a magician and find the central myth of his age. From time to time he consulted the eagle which had guarded the egg of his prenatal existence. The bird's advice can be detected in his work.[31]

Before joining the Surrealists, Ernst explored every means of achieving the sense of the psychic in his art. Like other Dadaists, Ernst set out to incorporate found objects and chance into his works, often combining fragments of images that he had cut from old books, magazines, and prints to form one hallucinatory collage. He also began making paintings that shared the mysterious dreamlike effect of his collages.

In 1920, Ernst met Breton, who instantly recognized the German artist's affinity with the Surrealist group. In 1922, Ernst moved to Paris, where two years later he painted *Two Children Are Threatened by a Nightingale* (FIG. **29-53**). In it, Ernst displayed a private dream challenging the Renaissance idea that a painting should resemble a window looking into a "real" scene rendered illusionistically three-dimensional through mathematical perspective. He painted the landscape, the distant city, and the tiny flying bird in conventional fashion, following all the established rules of linear and atmospheric perspective. The three sketchily rendered figures, however, clearly belong to a dream world, and the literally three-dimensional miniature gate, the odd button knob, and the strange closed building "violate" the bulky frame's space. Additional dislocation occurs in the traditional museum identification label, which Ernst displaced into a cutaway part of the frame. Handwritten, it announces the work's title (taken from a poem that Ernst wrote before he painted this), adding another note of irrational mystery.

As is true of many Surrealist works, the title, *Two Children Are Threatened by a Nightingale,* is ambiguous and relates uneasily to what the spectator sees. The viewer must struggle to decipher connections between the image and the words. When Surrealists (and Dadaists and Metaphysical artists before them) used puzzling titles (for example, de Chirico's *Song of Love*), they intended the seeming contradiction between title and picture to knock the audience off balance with all their expectations challenged. Much of the impact of Surrealist works begins with the viewer's sudden awareness of the

suggests that these images transcend their physical appearances. *The Song of Love,* for all its clarity and simplicity, takes on a rather sinister air. The sense of strangeness that de Chirico could conjure with familiar objects and scenes recalls Nietzsche's "foreboding that underneath this reality in which we live and have our being, another and altogether different reality lies concealed."[29]

Reproductions of de Chirico's paintings appeared in periodicals almost as soon as he completed them, and his works quickly influenced artists outside Italy, including both the Dadaists and, later, the Surrealists. The incongruities in his work intrigued the Dadaists, whereas the eerie mood and visionary quality of paintings such as *The Song of Love* excited and inspired Surrealist artists who sought to portray the world of dreams.

MAX ERNST Originally a Dada activist in Germany, MAX ERNST (1891–1976) became one of the early adherents of the Surrealist circle anchored by André Breton. As a child living in a small community near Cologne, Ernst had found his existence fantastic and filled

ART AND SOCIETY

Degenerate Art

Although avant-garde artists often had to endure public ridicule both in Europe and America (see "The Armory Show," page 909), they suffered outright political persecution in Germany in the 1930s and 1940s. The most dramatic example of this persecution was the infamous *Entartete Kunst* (Degenerate Art) exhibition that Adolf Hitler (1889–1945) and the Nazis mounted in 1937.

Hitler aspired to become an artist himself and produced numerous drawings and paintings reflecting his firm belief that 19th-century realistic genre painting represented the zenith of Aryan art development. Accordingly, Hitler denigrated anything that did not conform to that standard—in particular, avant-garde art. Turning his criticism into action, Hitler ordered the confiscation of more than 16,000 artworks that he considered "degenerate." To publicize his condemnation of this art, he ordered his minister for public enlightenment and propaganda, Joseph Goebbels (1897–1945), to organize a massive exhibition of this "degenerate art." Hitler designated as degenerate those artworks that "insult German feeling, or destroy or confuse natural form, or simply reveal an absence of adequate manual and artistic skill."*

The term "degenerate" also had other specific connotations at the time. The Nazis used it to identify supposedly inferior racial, sexual, and moral types. Hitler's order to Goebbels to target 20th-century avant-garde art for inclusion in the *Entartete Kunst* exhibition aimed to impress on the public the general inferiority of the artists producing this work. To make that point all the more dramatic, Hitler ordered the organization of another exhibition, the *Grosse Deutsche Kunstausstellung* (Great German Art Exhibition), which ran concurrently and presented an extensive array of Nazi-approved conservative art.

Entartete Kunst opened in Munich on July 19, 1937, and included more than 650 paintings, sculptures, prints, and books. The exhibition was immensely popular. Roughly 20,000 people visited the show daily. By the end of its four-month run, it had attracted more than two million visitors, and nearly a million more viewed it as it traveled through Germany and Austria. Among the 112 artists whose works the Nazis presented for ridicule were Ernst Barlach, Max Beckmann, Otto Dix, Max Ernst, George Grosz, Vassily Kandinsky, Ernst Kirchner, Paul Klee, Wilhelm Lehmbruck, Franz Marc, and Kurt Schwitters. In a memorable photograph (FIG. 29-54) taken during Hitler's preview visit to the exhibition on July 16, 1937, the Nazi leader pauses in front of the Dada wall. Behind him are works by Schwitters, Klee, and Kandinsky, which the

29-54 Adolf Hitler, accompanied by Nazi commission members, including photographer Heinrich Hoffmann, Wolfgang Willrich, Walter Hansen, and painter Adolf Ziegler, viewing the "Entartete Kunst" show on July 16, 1937.

For Hitler's visit, the curators deliberately hung askew the works of Kandinsky, Klee, and Schwitters. In Nazi Germany, no avant-garde artist was safe from persecution, and many fled the country.

organizers deliberately hung askew on the wall. (They subsequently straightened them for the duration of the exhibition.)

In Germany in the 1930s and 1940s, in the face of Nazi persecution, artists committed to pursuing avant-garde ideas required courage and a resoluteness that extended beyond issues of aesthetics and beyond the confines of the art world. No modernist artist was safe from Hitler's attack. (Only six of the artists in the exhibition were Jewish.) For example, despite his status as a charter member of the Nazi Party, the German Expressionist painter Emil Nolde (1867–1956) received particularly harsh treatment. The Nazis confiscated more than 1,000 of Nolde's works from German museums and included 27 of them in the exhibition, more than for almost any other artist. Max Beckmann and his wife fled to Amsterdam on the opening day of the *Entartete Kunst* exhibit, never to return to their homeland. Ernst Kirchner responded to the stress of Nazi pressure by destroying all his woodblocks and burning many of his works. A year later, in 1938, he committed suicide.

*Stephanie Barron, ed., "Degenerate Art": The Fate of the Avant-Garde in Nazi Germany (Los Angeles: Los Angeles County Museum of Art, 1991), 19.

---

incongruity and absurdity of what the artist pictured. These were precisely the qualities that subjected the Dadaists and Surrealists to public condemnation and, in Germany under Adolf Hitler (1889–1945), to governmental persecution (see "Degenerate Art," above, and FIG. 29-54).

SALVADOR DALÍ The Surrealists' exploration of the human psyche and dreams reached new heights in the works of Spanish-born SALVADOR DALÍ (1904–1989). In his paintings, sculptures, jewelry, and designs for furniture and movies, Dalí probed a deeply erotic dimension, studying the writings of Richard von Krafft-Ebing (1840–1902) and Sigmund Freud, and inventing what he called the "paranoiac-critical method" to assist his creative process. As he described it, in his painting he aimed "to materialize the images of

concrete irrationality with the most imperialistic fury of precision . . . in order that the world of imagination and of concrete irrationality may be as objectively evident . . . as that of the exterior world of phenomenal reality."[32]

In *The Persistence of Memory* (FIG. 29-55), Dalí created a haunting allegory of empty space where time has ended. An eerie, never-setting sun illuminates the barren landscape. An amorphous creature draped with a limp pocket watch sleeps in the foreground. Another watch hangs from the branch of a dead tree springing unexpectedly from a blocky architectural form. A third watch hangs half over the edge of the rectangular form, beside a small timepiece resting dial-down on the block's surface. Ants swarm mysteriously over the small watch, while a fly walks along the face of its large neighbor, almost as if this assembly of watches were decaying

29-55 SALVADOR DALÍ, *The Persistence of Memory,* 1931. Oil on canvas, $9\frac{1}{2}"$ × 1' 1". Museum of Modern Art, New York.

Dalí painted "images of concrete irrationality." In this realistically rendered landscape featuring three "decaying" watches, he created a haunting allegory of empty space where time has ended.

organisms—soft and sticky. Dalí rendered every detail of this dreamscape with precise control, striving to make the world of his paintings convincingly real—in his words, to make the irrational concrete.

RENÉ MAGRITTE The Belgian painter RENÉ MAGRITTE (1898–1967) encountered the work of Giorgio de Chirico (FIG. 29-52) in 1922. The Italian artist's disquieting combinations of motifs rendered in a realistic manner deeply impressed the younger artist, who produced his first Surrealist painting, *The Lost Jockey,* in 1926. The next year, Magritte moved to Paris, where he joined the intellectual circle of André Breton and remained in France until 1930. In 1929, Magritte

published an important essay in the Surrealist journal *La revolution surréaliste* in which he discussed the disjunction between objects, pictures of objects, and names of objects and pictures. The essay explains the intellectual basis for *The Treachery (or Perfidy) of Images* (FIG. 29-56), in which Magritte presented a meticulously rendered *trompe l'oeil* depiction of a briar pipe. The caption beneath the image, however, contradicts what seems obvious: "Ceci n'est pas une pipe" ("This is not a pipe"). The discrepancy between image and caption clearly challenges the assumptions underlying the reading of visual art. As is true of the other Surrealists' work, Magritte's paintings—for example, *The False Mirror* (FIG. 29-56A)—wreak havoc on the viewer's reliance on the conscious and the rational.

Ceci n'est pas une pipe.

29-56 RENÉ MAGRITTE, *The Treachery (or Perfidy) of Images,* 1928–1929. Oil on canvas, 1' $11\frac{5}{8}"$ × 3' 1". Los Angeles County Museum of Art, Los Angeles (purchased with funds provided by the Mr. and Mrs. William Preston Harrison Collection).

The discrepancy between Magritte's meticulously painted briar pipe and his caption, "This is not a pipe," challenges the viewer's reliance on the conscious and rational in the reading of visual art.

⊿ 29-56A MAGRITTE, *The False Mirror,* 1928.

29-57 MERET OPPENHEIM, *Object* (*Le Déjeuner en fourrure*), 1936. Fur-covered cup, $4\frac{3}{8}$" diameter; saucer, $9\frac{3}{8}$" diameter; spoon, 8" long. Museum of Modern Art, New York.

The Surrealists loved the concrete tangibility of sculpture, which made their art even more disquieting. Oppenheim's fur-covered object captures the Surrealist flair for magical transformation.

MERET OPPENHEIM Sculpture especially appealed to the Surrealists because its concrete tangibility made their art all the more disquieting. *Object* (FIG. 29-57), also called *Le Déjeuner en fourrure* (*Luncheon in Fur*), by Swiss artist MERET OPPENHEIM (1913–1985) captures the incongruity, humor, visual appeal, and, often, eroticism characterizing Surrealism. The artist presented a fur-lined teacup inspired by a conversation with Picasso. After admiring a bracelet that Oppenheim had made from a piece of brass covered with fur, Picasso noted that anything might be covered with fur. When her tea grew cold, Oppenheim responded to Picasso's comment by ordering "un peu plus de fourrure" (a little more fur), and the sculpture had its genesis. *Object* takes on an anthropomorphic quality, animated by the quirky combination of fur, exclusive to living organisms, with a stationary manufactured object. Further, the sculpture captures the Surrealist flair for alchemical, seemingly magical or mystical, transformation. It incorporates a sensuality and eroticism (seen here in the seductively soft, tactile fur lining the concave form) that are also components of much of Surrealist art.

JOAN MIRÓ Like the Dadaists, the Surrealists used many methods to free the creative process from reliance on the kind of conscious control that they believed society had shaped too much. Dalí used his paranoiac-critical approach to encourage the free play of association as he worked. Other Surrealists used automatism and various types of planned "accidents" to provoke reactions closely related to subconscious experience. Dalí's older countryman JOAN MIRÓ (1893–1983) was a master of this approach. Although Miró resisted formal association with any movement or group, including the Surrealists, André Breton identified him as "the most Surrealist of us all."[33]

29-58 JOAN MIRÓ, *Painting*, 1933. Oil on canvas, 5' $8\frac{1}{2}$" × 6' $5\frac{1}{4}$". Museum of Modern Art, New York (Loula D. Lasker bequest by exchange).

Miró promoted automatism, the creation of art without conscious control. He began this painting with random doodles and completed the composition with forms suggesting floating amoebic organisms.

From the beginning, Miró's work contained an element of fantasy and hallucination. After Surrealist poets in Paris introduced him to the use of chance in the creation of art, the young Spaniard devised a new painting method that enabled him to create works such as *Painting* (FIG. 29-58). Miró began this painting by making random doodles. The abstract curvilinear forms became motifs that the artist freely reshaped on the canvas to create black silhouettes—solid or in outline, with dramatic accents of white and vermilion. They suggest, in the painting, a host of amoebic organisms or extraterrestrial constellations floating in an immaterial background space filled with soft reds, blues, and greens.

Miró described his creative process as a switching back and forth between unconscious and conscious image-making: "Rather than setting out to paint something, I begin painting and as I paint the picture begins to assert itself, or suggest itself under my brush. The form becomes a sign for a woman or a bird as I work. . . . The first stage is free, unconscious. . . . The second stage is carefully calculated."[34] Even the artist could not always explain the meanings of pictures such as *Painting*. They are, in the truest sense, spontaneous and intuitive expressions of the little-understood, submerged unconscious part of life.

PAUL KLEE Perhaps the most inventive artist using fantasy images to represent the nonvisible world was the Swiss-German painter PAUL KLEE (1879–1940). Like Miró, he shunned formal association with groups such as the Dadaists and Surrealists, but pursued their interest in the subconscious. Klee sought clues to humanity's deeper nature in primitive shapes and symbols. Like Jung, Klee seems to have accepted the existence of a collective unconscious that reveals itself in archaic signs and patterns and is everywhere evident in the art of "primitive" cultures (see "Primitivism," page 891). The son of a professional musician and himself an accomplished violinist, Klee thought of painting as similar to music in its ability to express feelings through color, form, and line. In 1920, Klee set down his "creative credo," which reads in part:

> Art does not reproduce the visible; rather it makes visible. . . . The formal elements of graphic art are dot, line, plane, and space—the last

1 ft.

29-59 PAUL KLEE, *Twittering Machine*, 1922. Watercolor and pen and ink, on oil transfer drawing on paper, mounted on cardboard, 2' 1" × 1' 7". Museum of Modern Art, New York.

Although based on forms in the tangible world easily read as birds, Klee's *Twittering Machine* is a fanciful vision of a mysterious place presented in a simplified, almost childlike manner.

three charged with energy of various kinds. . . . Formerly we used to represent things visible on earth, things we either liked to look at or would have liked to see. Today we reveal the reality that is behind visible things.[35]

To penetrate "the reality behind visible things," Klee studied nature avidly, taking special interest in analyzing processes of growth and change. He coded these studies in diagrammatic form in notebooks. Thus the root of his work was nature, but nature filtered through his mind. Upon starting an image, Klee would allow the pencil or brush to lead him until an image emerged, to which he would then respond to complete the idea.

Twittering Machine (FIG. **29-59**) reveals Klee's fanciful vision. The painting, although based on forms in the tangible world easily read as birds, is far from illusionistic. Klee presented the scene in a simplified, almost childlike manner, imbuing the work with a poetic lyricism. The inclusion of a crank-driven mechanism added a touch of whimsy. The small size of Klee's works enhances their impact. A viewer must draw near to decipher the delicately rendered forms and enter his mysterious dream world. Perhaps no other artist of the 20th century matched Klee's subtlety as he deftly created a world of ambiguity and understatement that draws each viewer into finding a unique interpretation of the work.

WIFREDO LAM Also loosely associated with the Surrealists was WIFREDO LAM (1902–1982), an artist whose work is as distinctive as his background. Cuban by birth, Lam was the son of a Chinese immigrant father and a mother of Cuban-African descent. He studied painting in Havana and later in Madrid, where he fought alongside the Republicans in the Spanish Civil War. That endeared Lam to Picasso, whom he met in Paris in 1938. Picasso introduced Lam to Braque and Breton and many other avant-garde artists and critics, and Lam's mature work, although the distinctive by-product of his Caribbean-African heritage, shows the influence of both Cubism and Surrealism.

After an 18-year sojourn in Europe, Lam returned to Havana in 1941, where two years later he produced *The Jungle* (FIG. **29-60**), which

1 ft.

29-60 WIFREDO LAM, *The Jungle*, 1943. Gouache on paper mounted on canvas, 7' 10$\frac{1}{4}$" × 7' 6$\frac{1}{2}$". Museum of Modern Art, New York (Inter-American Fund).

In Lam's tropical jungle stand four composite creatures with long legs, prominent buttocks, and faces resembling African masks. The painting draws on Cubism, Surrealism, and Cuban religious ritual.

Piet Mondrian on Neoplasticism

Initially attracted to the exciting efforts of the Cubists to rethink the Western pictorial tradition (see page 892), the Dutch De Stijl artist Piet Mondrian soon moved beyond Cubism because he felt that "Cubism did not accept the logical consequences of its own discoveries; it was not developing towards its own goal, the expression of pure plastics."* In 1914, he eloquently articulated his own view of what art should be.

> What first captivated us does not captivate us afterward (like toys). If one has loved the surface of things for a long time, later on one will look for something more. . . . The interior of things shows through the surface; thus as we look at the surface the inner image is formed in our soul. It is this inner image that should be represented. For the natural surface of things is beautiful, but the imitation of it is without life. . . . Art is higher than reality and has no direct relation to reality. . . . To approach the spiritual in art, one will make as little use as possible of reality, because reality is opposed to the spiritual. . . . [W]e find ourselves in the presence of an abstract art. Art should be above reality, otherwise it would have no value for man.†

Caught by the outbreak of hostilities while on a visit to Holland, Mondrian remained there during World War I, developing his theories for what he called *Neoplasticism*—the new "pure plastic art." He believed that all great art had polar but coexistent goals, the attempt to create "universal beauty" and the desire for "aesthetic expression of oneself."‡ The first goal is objective in nature, whereas the second is subjective, existing within the individual's mind and heart. To create a universal expression, an artist must communicate "a real equation of the universal and the individual."§

To express this vision, Mondrian eventually limited his formal vocabulary to the three primary colors (red, yellow, and blue), the three primary values (black, white, and gray), and the two primary directions (horizontal and vertical). Basing his ideas on a combination of teachings, he concluded that primary colors and values are the purest colors and therefore are the perfect tools to help an artist construct a harmonious composition. Using this system, he created numerous paintings locking color planes into a grid of intersecting vertical and horizontal lines, as in *Composition with Red, Blue, and Yellow* (FIG. 29-61). In each of these paintings, Mondrian altered the grid patterns and the size and

1 in.

29-61 PIET MONDRIAN, *Composition with Red, Blue, and Yellow*, 1930. Oil on canvas, 1' 6$\frac{1}{8}$" × 1' 6$\frac{1}{8}$". Kunsthaus, Zürich. © 2014 Mondrian/ Holtzman Trust c/o HCR International USA.

Mondrian's "pure plastic" paintings consist of primary colors locked into a grid of intersecting vertical and horizontal lines. By altering the grid patterns, he created a "dynamic equilibrium."

placement of the color planes to create an internal cohesion and harmony. This did not mean inertia. Rather, Mondrian worked to maintain what he called a "dynamic equilibrium" in his paintings by precisely determining the size and position of lines, shapes, and colors.

*Piet Mondrian, *Plastic Art and Pure Plastic Art* (1937), quoted in George Heard Hamilton, *Painting and Sculpture in Europe, 1880–1940*, 6th ed. (New Haven, Conn.: Yale University Press, 1993), 319.
†Quoted in Michel Seuphor, *Piet Mondrian: Life and Work* (New York: Abrams, 1956), 117.
‡Mondrian, *Plastic Art*, quoted in Herschel B. Chipp, *Theories of Modern Art: A Source Book by Artists and Critics* (Berkeley and Los Angeles: University of California Press, 1968), 349.
§Ibid., 350.

many art historians consider his greatest work. The complex, crowded composition indeed suggests a dense jungle, populated by Surrealistic creatures whose fragmented forms recall Cubism. Inspired also by Santería, the Cuban religion that is a blend of African ritual and European Catholicism, *The Jungle* depicts four hybrid figures with long legs, prominent buttocks, and heads that resemble African masks. (Many scholars believe the painting is Lam's response, 35 years later, to Picasso's *Demoiselles d'Avignon* [FIG. 29-1].) Lam's composite creatures inhabit a tropical jungle of sugarcane and tobacco plants. Two of them have a horse's tail. The figure at the right holds a scissors—as if she, not the artist, is the one responsible for dismembering herself and her companions. In

many ways, *The Jungle* is a bridge between Cubism, Surrealism, and the nonrepresentational canvases of the New York School Abstract Expressionists of the 1940s and 1950s (see page 953).

De Stijl

The utopian spirit and ideals of the Suprematists and Constructivists (FIGS. 29-31 and 29-32) in Russia were shared in western Europe by a group of young Dutch artists. They formed a new movement in 1917 and began publishing a magazine, calling both the movement and magazine *De Stijl* (The Style). The group's cofounders were the painters Piet Mondrian (FIG. 29-61) and Theo van Doesburg

(1883–1931). In addition to promoting utopian ideals, De Stijl artists believed in the birth of a new age in the wake of World War I. They felt that it was a time of balance between individual and universal values, when the machine would assure ease of living. In their first manifesto of De Stijl, the artists declared: "There is an old and a new consciousness of time. The old is connected with the individual. The new is connected with the universal."[36] The goal, according to van Doesburg and architect Cor van Eesteren (1897–1988), was a total integration of art and life:

> We must realize that life and art are no longer separate domains. That is why the "idea" of "art" as an illusion separate from real life must disappear. The word "Art" no longer means anything to us. In its place we demand the construction of our environment in accordance with creative laws based upon a fixed principle. These laws, following those of economics, mathematics, technique, sanitation, etc., are leading to a new, plastic unity.[37]

PIET MONDRIAN Toward this goal of integration, PIET MONDRIAN (1872–1944) created a new style based on a single ideal principle. The choice of the term "De Stijl" reflected Mondrian's confidence that this style—*the* style—revealed the underlying eternal structure of existence. Accordingly, De Stijl artists reduced their artistic vocabulary to simple geometric elements. Time spent in Paris just before World War I introduced Mondrian to Cubism and other modes of abstraction. However, as his attraction to theological writings grew, Mondrian sought to purge his art of every overt reference to individual objects in the external world. He initially favored the teachings of theosophy, a tradition basing knowledge of nature and the human condition on knowledge of the divine nature or spiritual powers. (His fellow theosophist Vassily Kandinsky pursued a similar path.) Mondrian, however, quickly abandoned the strictures of theosophy and turned toward a conception of nonobjective design—"pure plastic art"—that he believed expressed universal reality (see "Piet Mondrian on Neoplasticism," page 928, and FIG. **29-61**).

Sculpture

It was impossible for early-20th-century artists to ignore the increasing expansion of mechanization and growth of technology in everyone's life. The Futurists had embraced these developments, but other artists did not. They attempted to overcome the predominance of mechanization in society by immersing themselves in a search for the organic and natural.

CONSTANTIN BRANCUSI One artist who was eager to produce works emphasizing the natural or organic was Romanian sculptor CONSTANTIN BRANCUSI (1876–1957). Brancusi sought to move beyond surface appearances to capture the essence or spirit of objects in rhythmic, elegant sculptures (see "Brancusi, Hepworth, and Moore on Abstract Sculpture," page 930). The softly curving surfaces and ovoid form of his sculptures refer, directly or indirectly, to the cycle of life. Brancusi's *The Newborn* (FIG. **29-61A**) is not a literal depiction of a head, nor does his *Bird in Space* (FIG. **29-62**) mimic a real bird's shape. The abstract form of both

29-61A BRANCUSI, *The Newborn*, 1915.

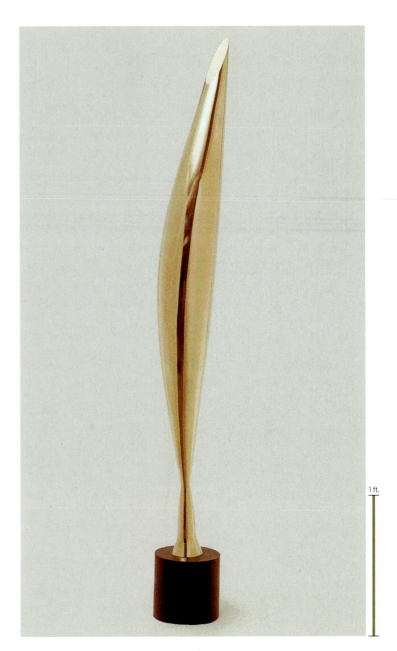

1 ft.

29-62 CONSTANTIN BRANCUSI, *Bird in Space,* 1924. Bronze, 4' 2 5/16" high. Philadelphia Museum of Art, Philadelphia (Louise and Walter Arensberg Collection, 1950).

Although not a literal depiction of a bird, Brancusi's softly curving light-reflecting abstract sculpture in polished bronze suggests a bird about to soar in free flight through the heavens.

works is the final result of a long process. For *Bird in Space,* Brancusi started with the image of a bird at rest with its wings folded at its sides, and ended with a gently curving columnar form sharply tapered at each end. Despite the abstraction, the sculpture retains the suggestion of a bird about to soar in free flight through the heavens. The highly reflective surface of the polished bronze does not allow the viewer's eye to linger on the sculpture itself (as do, for example, Rodin's agitated and textured surfaces; FIGS. 28-33, 28-33A, and 28-34). Instead, the eye follows the gleaming reflection along the delicate curves right off the tip of the work, thereby inducing a feeling of flight. Brancusi stated, "All my life I have sought the essence of flight. Don't look for mysteries. I give you pure joy. Look at the sculptures until you see them. Those nearest to God have seen them."[38]

Brancusi, Hepworth, and Moore on Abstract Sculpture

Many early-20th-century sculptors rejected the notion that reproducing the physical world of nature was the purpose of sculpture. Instead, they championed abstraction as the sculptor's proper goal. Among those who not only produced enduring masterpieces of abstract sculpture but also wrote eloquently about the theoretical basis of their work were Constantin Brancusi (FIGS. 29-61A and 29-62), Barbara Hepworth (FIG. 29-63), and Henry Moore (FIG. 29-64). Some excerpts from their writings on sculpture illustrate their commitment to abstraction as their guiding principle.

- **Constantin Brancusi** Simplicity is not an objective in art, but one achieves simplicity despite oneself by entering into the real sense of things.* . . . What is real is not the external form but the essence of things. Starting from this truth it is impossible for anyone to express anything essentially real by imitating its exterior surface.[†]

- **Barbara Hepworth** The forms which have had special meaning for me since childhood have been the standing form (which is the translation of my feeling towards the human being standing in landscape); the two forms (which is the tender relationship of one living thing beside another); and the closed form, such as the oval, spherical, or pierced form (sometimes incorporating color) which translates for me the association and meaning of gesture in the landscape. . . . In all these shapes the translation of what one feels about man and nature must be conveyed by the sculptor in terms of mass, inner tension, and rhythm, scale in relation to our human size, and the quality of surface which speaks through our hands and eyes.[‡]

- **Henry Moore** Since the Gothic, European sculpture had become overgrown with moss, weeds—all sorts of surface excrescences which completely concealed shape. It has been Brancusi's special mission to get rid of this overgrowth, and to make us once more shape-conscious. To do this he has had to concentrate on very simple direct shapes . . . Abstract qualities of design are essen-

29-63 BARBARA HEPWORTH, *Oval Sculpture (No. 2)*, 1943. Plaster cast, $11\frac{1}{4}$" × 1' $4\frac{1}{4}$" × 10". Tate, London.

Hepworth's major contribution to the history of sculpture was the introduction of the hole, or negative space, as an abstract element that is as integral and important to the sculpture as its mass.

tial to the value of a work . . . Because a work does not aim at reproducing natural appearances, it is not, therefore, an escape from life—but may be a penetration into reality. . . . My sculpture is becoming less representational, less an outward visual copy . . . but only because I believe that in this way I can present the human psychological content of my work with greatest directness and intensity.[§]

*Quoted in Herschel B. Chipp, *Theories of Modern Art: A Source Book by Artists and Critics* (Berkeley and Los Angeles: University of California Press, 1968), 364–365.

[†]Quoted in George Heard Hamilton, *Painting and Sculpture in Europe, 1880–1940,* 6th ed. (New Haven, Conn.: Yale University Press, 1993), 426.

[‡]Barbara Hepworth, *A Pictorial Autobiography* (London: Tate, 1978), 9, 53.

[§]Quoted in Robert L. Herbert, *Modern Artists on Art,* 2d ed. (Mineola, N.Y.: Dover, 2000), 173–179.

BARBARA HEPWORTH In England, BARBARA HEPWORTH (1903–1975) developed her own kind of essential sculptural form, combining pristine shape with a sense of organic vitality. She sought a sculptural idiom that would express her sense both of nature and the landscape and of the person who is in and observes nature (see "Brancusi, Hepworth, and Moore," above). By 1929, Hepworth arrived at a breakthrough that evolved into an enduring and commanding element in her work from that point on. It represents her major contribution to the history of sculpture: the use of the hole, or void. Earlier sculptors, such as Archipenko (FIG. 29-18) had experimented with sculptural voids, but Hepworth introduced holes in her sculptures as abstract elements. The holes do not represent anything specific. They are simply negative space, but are as integral and important to the sculptures as their mass. *Oval Sculpture (No. 2)* is a plaster cast (FIG. **29-63**) of an earlier wood sculpture that Hepworth carved in 1943. Pierced in four places, the work is as much defined by the smooth, curving edges of the holes as by the volume

of white plaster. Like the forms in all of Hepworth's mature works, those in *Oval Sculpture* are basic and universal, expressing a sense of timelessness.

HENRY MOORE Fellow Briton HENRY MOORE (1898–1986) shared Hepworth's interest in the hole, or void, as an important element in sculptural design, but his sculptures, such as *Reclining Figure* (FIG. **29-64**), although abstracted, always remain recognizable. This statue is one of a long series of reclining female nudes inspired originally by a photograph that Moore acquired of a *chacmool* (FIG. 18-16) from pre-Columbian Mexico. Moore believed that the simple and massive shapes of his statues expressed a universal truth beyond the physical world (see "Brancusi, Hepworth, and Moore," above).

Reclining Figure is also characteristic of Moore's work in exploiting the natural beauty of different materials—here, elm. Moore maintained that every "material has its own individual qualities" and that these qualities could play a role in the creative process: "It is

29-64 Henry Moore, *Reclining Figure*, 1939. Elm wood, 3' 1" × 6' 7" × 2' 6". Detroit Institute of Arts, Detroit (Founders Society purchase with funds from the Dexter M. Ferry Jr. Trustee Corporation).

The reclining female figure was a major theme in Moore's sculptures. Inspired by a Mexican chacmool (FIG. 18-16), he simplified and abstracted the body form in a way that recalls Biomorphic Surrealism.

1 ft.

only when the sculptor works direct, when there is an active relationship with his material, that the material can take its part in the shaping of an idea."[39] Accordingly, the contours of *Reclining Figure* follow the grain of the wood. The abstracted shapes suggest Surrealist biomorphic forms (FIG. 29-58), but Moore's recumbent woman is also a powerful earth mother whose swelling forms and hollows suggest nurturing human energy. Similarly, the body shapes evoke the contours of the Yorkshire hills of Moore's childhood and the windpolished surfaces of weathered wood and stone. Moore heightened the allusions to landscape (compare FIG. 29-44A) and to Surrealist organic forms in his work by interplaying mass and void, based on the intriguing qualities of cavities in nature. For Moore, the hole was not an abstract shape. It represented "the mysterious fascination of caves in hillsides and cliffs."[40] *Reclining Figure* uses the organic vocabulary central to Moore's philosophy—bone shapes, eroded rocks, and geologic formations—to describe the human form.

VERA MUKHINA Not all European sculptors of this period pursued abstraction. *Worker and Collective Farm Woman* (FIG. 29-65) by Russian artist Vera Mukhina (1889–1963) presents a vivid contrast to the work of Brancusi, Hepworth, and Moore. Produced in 1937 for the International Exposition in Paris—the same venue in which Picasso displayed *Guernica* (FIG. 29-16)—Mukhina's overlife-size stainless-steel sculpture glorifies the communal labor of the Soviet people. Whereas Picasso employed Cubist abstraction to convey the horror of wartime bombing, Mukhina's representation of two exemplars of the Soviet citizenry was based on traditional figural sculpture. Specifically, Mukhina's primary source was an early-fifth-century BCE Greek group representing two Athenian citizens, Harmodios and Aristogeiton, who were celebrated for slaying a hated tyrant and restoring rule by the people—an appropriate model in the egalitarian Soviet state. Her statuary group, which stood on the top of the Soviet Pavilion at the exposition, depicts a male factory worker, holding aloft the tool of his trade, the hammer, and a farm woman, raising her sickle to the sky. The juxtaposed hammer and sickle at the apex of the sculpture replicate their appearance on the Soviet flag. Mukhina augmented the heroic tenor of the work by emphasizing the solidity of the figures, who stride forward with their clothes blowing dramatically behind them. Mukhina had studied in Paris and was familiar with abstraction,

10 ft.

29-65 Vera Mukhina, *Worker and Collective Farm Woman,* Soviet Pavilion, Paris Exposition, 1937. Stainless steel, 78' high. Art © Estate of Vera Mukhina/RAO, Moscow/VAGA, New York.

In contrast to contemporaneous abstract sculpture, Mukhina's realistic representation of a male factory worker and a female farm worker glorified the communal labor of the Soviet people.

29-66 Gerrit Thomas Rietveld, Schröder House (looking northwest), Utrecht, the Netherlands, 1924.

The De Stijl Schröder House has an open plan and an exterior that is a kind of three-dimensional projection of the carefully proportioned flat color rectangles in Mondrian's paintings (FIG. 29-61).

especially Cubism, but felt that a commitment to realism tempered with idealism—note the muscled arms and chest of the man and the blemishless features of both faces—produced the most powerful sculpture. This approach to figural sculpture was, in fact, since 1934 the officially approved style of the Communist government. Mukhina's eager embrace of the official style, called Soviet Realism, earned high praise for her art and for this sculpture in particular. Indeed, Russian citizens cherished *Worker and Collective Farm Woman* as a national symbol for decades.

Architecture

As in the opening decades of the century, developments in European architecture after World War I closely paralleled the stylistic and theoretical concerns of painters and sculptors.

GERRIT RIETVELD The ideas that Piet Mondrian, Theo van Doesburg, and De Stijl artists advanced found their architectural equivalent in the designs of GERRIT THOMAS RIETVELD (1888–1964). His Schröder House (FIG. **29-66**) in Utrecht, built in 1924, perfectly expresses van Doesburg's definition of De Stijl architecture:

> The new architecture is anti-cubic, i.e., it does not strive to contain the different functional space cells in a single closed cube, but it throws the functional space (as well as canopy planes, balcony volumes, etc.) out from the center of the cube, so that height, width, and depth plus time become a completely new plastic expression in open spaces. . . . The plastic architect . . . has to construct in the new field, time-space.[41]

The main public rooms of the Schröder House are on the second floor, with the private living quarters on the ground floor. Rietveld's house has an open plan and a relationship to nature more like the houses of American architect Frank Lloyd Wright (FIGS. 29-45 and 29-46). Rietveld designed the entire second floor with sliding partitions that can be closed to define separate rooms or pushed back to create one open space broken into units only by the furni-

ture arrangement. This shifting quality appears also on the outside, where railings, free-floating walls, and long rectangular windows give the effect of cubic units breaking up before the viewer's eyes. Rectangular planes seem to slide across each other on the Schröder House facade like movable panels, making this structure a kind of three-dimensional projection of the rigid but carefully proportioned flat color rectangles in Mondrian's paintings (FIG. 29-61).

WALTER GROPIUS De Stijl architects not only developed an appealing simplified geometric style but also promoted the notion that art should be thoroughly incorporated into living environments. As Mondrian had insisted, "[A]rt and life are *one*; art and life are both expressions of truth."[42] In Germany, WALTER GROPIUS (1883–1969) developed a particular vision of "total architecture." He made this concept the foundation of not only his own work but also the work of generations of pupils under his influence at a school called the *Bauhaus* (see "Walter Gropius and the Bauhaus," page 933, and FIG. **29-67**).

The building that Gropius designed for the Bauhaus in 1925 after the school relocated to Dessau was the Bauhaus's architectural manifesto. The Dessau Bauhaus consisted of workshop and class areas, a dining room, a theater, a gymnasium, a wing with studio apartments, and an enclosed two-story bridge housing administrative offices. Of the major wings, the most dramatic was the Shop Block (FIG. 29-67). Three stories tall, the Shop Block housed a printing shop and dye works facility, in addition to other work areas. The builders constructed the skeleton of reinforced concrete but set these supports well back, sheathing the entire structure in glass, creating a streamlined and light effect. This design's simplicity followed Gropius's dictum that architecture should avoid "all romantic embellishment and whimsy." Further, he realized the "economy in the use of space" articulated in his list of Bauhaus principles in his interior layout of the Shop Block, which consisted of large areas of free-flowing undivided space. Gropius believed that this kind of spatial organization encouraged interaction and the sharing of ideas.

Walter Gropius and the Bauhaus

In 1919, Walter Gropius became the director of the Weimar School of Arts and Crafts in Germany, founded in 1906. Under Gropius, the school assumed a new name—Das Staatliche Bauhaus (State School of Building). Gropius's goal was to train artists, architects, and designers to accept and anticipate 20th-century needs. He developed an extensive curriculum based on certain principles set forth in the *Bauhaus Manifesto,* published in April 1919.

29-67 WALTER GROPIUS, Shop Block (looking northeast), the Bauhaus, Dessau, Germany, 1925–1926.

Gropius constructed this Bauhaus building by sheathing a reinforced concrete skeleton in glass. The design followed his dictum that architecture should avoid "all romantic embellishment and whimsy."

BAUHAUS MANIFESTO

The first principle that Gropius staunchly advocated in the 1919 manifesto was the importance of strong basic design (including principles of composition, two- and three-dimensionality, and color theory) and craftsmanship as fundamental to good art and architecture. He asserted that there was no essential difference between the artist and the craftsperson.

> The Bauhaus strives to coordinate all creative effort, to achieve, in a new architecture, the unification of all training in art and design. The ultimate, if distant, goal of the Bauhaus is the collective work of art—the Building—in which no barriers exist between the structural and the decorative arts.*

To encourage the elimination of those boundaries that traditionally separated art from architecture and art from craft, the Bauhaus offered courses in a wide range of artistic disciplines. These included carpentry, furniture design (by MARCEL BREUER [1902–1981]; FIG. **29-67A**), weaving (by GUNTA STÖLZL [1897–1983]; FIG. **29-67B**), pottery, bookbinding, metalwork, stained glass, mural painting, stage design, and advertising and typography, in addition to painting, sculpture, and architecture. Both a technical instructor and a "teacher of form"—an artist—taught in each department. Among the teachers whom Gropius hired were Vassily Kandinsky (FIG. 29-7) and Paul Klee (FIG. 29-59).

29-67A BREUER, Wassily chair, 1925.

29-67B STÖLZL, Gobelin tapestry, 1927–1928.

In addition, because Gropius wanted the Bauhaus to produce graduates who could design progressive environments that satisfied 20th-century needs, he emphasized thorough knowledge of machine-age technologies and materials. He felt that to produce truly successful designs, the artist-architect-craftsperson had to understand industry and mass production. Ultimately, Gropius hoped for a marriage between art and industry—a synthesis of design and production. As did the De Stijl movement, the Bauhaus philosophy had its roots in utopian principles. Gropius's declaration reveals the idealism of the entire Bauhaus enterprise:

> Let us collectively desire, conceive, and create the new building of the future, which will be everything in one structure: architecture and sculpture and painting, which, from the million hands of craftsmen, will one day rise towards heaven as the crystalline symbol of a new and coming faith.†

In its reference to a unity of workers, this statement also reveals the undercurrent of socialism present in Germany at the time.

BAUHAUS IN DESSAU

After encountering increasing hostility from a new government elected in 1924, the Bauhaus moved north from Weimar to Dessau (FIG. 29-67) in early 1925. By this time, the Bauhaus program had matured. In a new statement, Gropius listed the school's goals more clearly:

- A decidedly positive attitude to the living environment of vehicles and machines
- The organic shaping of things in accordance with their own current laws, avoiding all romantic embellishment and whimsy
- Restriction of basic forms and colors to what is typical and universally intelligible
- Simplicity in complexity, economy in the use of space, materials, time, and money‡

*Quoted in Charles Harrison and Paul Wood, eds., *Art in Theory, 1900–2000: An Anthology of Changing Ideas,* 2d ed. (Oxford: Blackwell, 2003), 311.

†Translated by Charles W. Haxthausen, in Barry Bergdoll, ed., *Bauhaus 1919–1933* (New York: Museum of Modern Art, 2009), 64.

‡Quoted in John Willett, *Art and Politics in the Weimar Period: The New Sobriety, 1917–1933* (New York: Da Capo Press, 1978), 119.

LUDWIG MIES VAN DER ROHE In 1928, Gropius left the Bauhaus, and LUDWIG MIES VAN DER ROHE (1886–1969) eventually took over the directorship, moving the school to Berlin in 1932. Taking as his motto "less is more" and calling his architecture "skin and bones," the new Bauhaus director had already fully formed his aesthetic when he conceived the model (FIG. 29-68) for a glass skyscraper building in 1921. In the glass model, which was on display at the first Bauhaus exhibition in 1923, three irregularly shaped towers flow outward from a central court designed to hold a lobby, a porter's room, and a community center. Two cylindrical entrance shafts rise at the ends of the court, each containing elevators, stairways, and toilets. Wholly transparent, the perimeter walls reveal the regular horizontal patterning of the cantilevered floor planes and their thin vertical supporting elements. The bold use of glass sheathing and inset supports was, at the time, technically and aesthetically adventurous. The weblike delicacy of the lines of the model, as well as the illusion of movement created by reflection and by light

changes seen through the glass, appealed to many other architects. A few years later, Gropius pursued it in his design for the Bauhaus building (FIG. 29-67) in Dessau. The legacy of Mies van der Rohe's design can be seen in the glass-and-steel skyscrapers found in major cities throughout the world today.

END OF THE BAUHAUS One of Hitler's first acts after coming to power was to close the Bauhaus in 1933. The student body had become radicalized, and the Nazis suspected that the school housed a press that printed Communist-inspired anti-Nazi brochures. During its 14-year existence, the beleaguered school graduated fewer than 500 students, yet it achieved legendary status. Its phenomenal influence extended beyond painting, sculpture, and architecture to interior design, graphic design, and advertising. Moreover, art schools everywhere began to structure their curricula in line with the program that the Bauhaus pioneered. The numerous Bauhaus instructors who fled Nazi Germany disseminated the school's philosophy and aesthetic. Many Bauhaus members came to the United States. Gropius and Breuer (FIG. 29-67A) ended up at Harvard University. Mies van der Rohe moved to Chicago and taught there.

LE CORBUSIER The simple geometric aesthetic developed by Gropius and Mies van der Rohe became known as the *International Style* because of its widespread popularity. The first and purest exponent of this style was the Swiss architect Charles-Edouard Jeanneret, who adopted his maternal grandfather's name—LE CORBUSIER (1887–1965). Trained in Paris and Berlin, he was also a painter, but Le Corbusier had the greatest influence as an architect and theorist on modern architecture. As such, he applied himself to designing a functional living space, which he described as a "machine for living."

Le Corbusier maintained that the basic physical and psychological needs of every human being were sun, space, and vegetation combined with controlled temperature, good ventilation, and insulation against harmful and undesired noise. He also advocated basing dwelling designs on human scale, because the house is humankind's assertion within nature. All these qualities characterize Le Corbusier's Villa Savoye (FIG. 29-69), built at Poissy-sur-Seine near Paris on commission from Pierre Savoye, the director of a major insurance company. The country house, a place of retreat from the city for the wealthy businessman, sits at the center of a large plot of land cleared of trees and shrubs, but windows on all sides and the villa's roof-terrace provided Savoye and his wife, Emilie, with broad views of the surrounding landscape. Several colors appear on the exterior—originally, a dark-green base, cream walls, and a rose-and-blue windscreen on top. They were deliberately analogous to the colors in the machine-inspired Purist style of painting (FIG. 29-21) that Le Corbusier practiced.

A cube of lightly enclosed and deeply penetrated space, the Villa Savoye has only a partially confined ground floor (containing, originally, a three-car garage, bedrooms, a bathroom, and utility rooms, and today a ticket counter and small gift shop for visitors). Much of the house's interior is open space, with thin columns supporting the main living floor and the roof garden area. The major living rooms in the Villa Savoye are on the second floor, wrapping around an open central court. Strip windows running along the membranelike exterior walls provide illumination to the rooms as well as views out to nature. From the second-floor court, a ramp leads up to the roof-terrace and an interior garden protected by a curving windbreak along the north side.

The Villa Savoye has no traditional facade. The ostensible approach to the house does not define an entrance. Visitors must

29-68 LUDWIG MIES VAN DER ROHE, model for a glass skyscraper, Berlin, Germany, 1922 (no longer extant).

In this technically and aesthetically adventurous design, the architect whose motto was "less is more" proposed a transparent building that revealed its cantilevered floor planes and thin supports.

29-69 LE CORBUSIER, Villa Savoye (looking southeast), Poissy-sur-Seine, France, 1929.

Steel and ferroconcrete made it possible for Le Corbusier to invert the traditional practice of placing light architectural elements above heavy ones and to eliminate weight-bearing walls on the ground story.

walk around and through the house to comprehend its layout, which incorporates several changes of direction and spiral staircases. Spaces and masses interpenetrate so fluidly that inside and outside space intermingle. The machine-planed smoothness of the unadorned surfaces, the slender ribbons of continuous windows, and the buoyant lightness of the whole fabric—all combine to reverse the effect of traditional country houses (FIG. 22-28). By placing heavy elements above and light ones below, and by refusing to enclose the ground story of the Villa Savoye with masonry walls, Le Corbusier inverted traditional design practice. This openness, made possible by the use of steel and *ferroconcrete* (concrete strengthened by a skeleton of iron bars) as construction materials, makes the "load" of the Villa Savoye's upper stories appear to hover lightly on the slender columnar supports.

MARSEILLES AND CHANDIGARH As noted, Le Corbusier designed the Villa Savoye as a private home, but like De Stijl architects, he dreamed of extending his ideas of the house as a "machine for living" to designs for efficient and humane cities. He saw great cities as spiritual workshops, and he proposed to correct the deficiencies in existing cities caused by poor traffic circulation, inadequate living units, and the lack of space for recreation and exercise. He proposed replacing traditional cities with three types of new communities. Vertical cities would house workers and the business and service industries. Linear-industrial cities would run as belts along the routes between the vertical cities and would serve as centers for the people and processes involved in manufacturing. Finally, separate centers would be constructed for people involved in intensive agricultural activity. Le Corbusier's cities would provide for human cultural needs in addition to serving every person's need for physical, mental, and emotional comfort.

Later in his career, Le Corbusier designed a few vertical cities, most notably the Unité d'Habitation in Marseilles (1945–1952). He also created the master plan for the entire city of Chandigarh, the capital city of the Punjab, India (1950–1957). The ever-innovative architect ended his career with the Chapel of Notre Dame du Haut (FIGS. 30-41 and 30-42) at Ronchamp, France, one of the most adventurous building designs of the first half of the 20th century.

UNITED STATES AND MEXICO, 1930 TO 1945

In the 1930s, much of the Western world plunged into the Great Depression, which had a particularly acute effect in the United States. The decade following the catastrophic stock market crash of October 1929 dramatically changed the nation, and artists were among the millions of economic victims. The limited art market virtually disappeared, and museums curtailed both their purchases and exhibition schedules. Many artists sought financial support from the federal government, which established numerous programs to provide relief, assist recovery, and promote reform. Among the programs supporting artists were the Treasury Relief Art Project, founded in 1934 to commission art for federal buildings, and the Works Progress Administration (WPA), founded in 1935 to relieve widespread unemployment. Under the WPA, varied activities of the Federal Art Project paid artists, writers, and theater people a regular wage in exchange for work in their professions.

Despite the economic hardships facing artists during the Great Depression, the United States became a haven for European painters, sculptors, and architects seeking to escape from Hitler and the Nazis. Among those who abandoned their homelands for America during the years leading up to World War II were Léger, Lipchitz, Beckmann, Grosz, Ernst, and Dalí. This influx of European artists searching for freedom from political and religious persecution and a more hospitable environment for their art was as significant a factor in exposing American artists to modernist European art as the Armory Show of 1913 (see "The Armory Show," page 909).

A complementary factor was the desire on the part of American museums to demonstrate their familiarity and connection with the most progressive European art by mounting exhibitions centered on the latest European artistic developments. In 1938, for example, the City Art Museum of Saint Louis presented an exhibition of Beckmann's work, and the Art Institute of Chicago organized *George Grosz: A Survey of His Art from 1918–1938*. This interest in exhibiting the work of persecuted artists driven from their homelands also had political overtones. In the highly charged atmosphere of the late 1930s leading to the onset of World War II, Americans often perceived support for these artists and their work as support for freedom and democracy. For example, in 1942, Alfred H. Barr Jr. (1902–1981), the director of the Museum of Modern Art, stated:

> Among the freedoms which the Nazis have destroyed, none has been more cynically perverted, more brutally stamped upon, than the Freedom of Art. For not only must the artist of Nazi Germany bow to political tyranny, he must also conform to the personal taste of that great art connoisseur, Adolf Hitler. . . . But German artists of spirit and integrity have refused to conform. They have gone into exile or slipped into anxious obscurity. . . . Their paintings and sculptures, too, have been hidden or exiled. . . . But in free countries they can still be seen, can still bear witness to the survival of a free German culture.[43]

Despite this moral support for exiled artists, once the United States formally entered the war, Germany officially became the enemy. It became much more difficult for the American art world to promote German artists, however persecuted. Many émigré artists, including Léger, Grosz, Ernst, and Dalí, returned to Europe after the war ended. Their collective presence in the United States until then, however, was critical for the development of American art.

Painting

Although the political, social, and economic developments of the 1930s and 1940s brought many modernist European artists to the United States, the leading American painters of this period were primarily figural artists who had only a limited interest in abstract composition.

BEN SHAHN Born in Lithuania, BEN SHAHN (1898–1969) came to the United States in 1906 and trained as a lithographer before broadening the media in which he worked to include easel and mural painting and photography. He focused on the lives of ordinary people and the injustices often done to them by the structure of an impersonal, bureaucratic society. In the early 1930s, he completed a cycle of 23 paintings and prints inspired by the trial and execution of two Italian anarchists, Nicola Sacco and Bartolomeo Vanzetti. Accused of killing two men in a holdup in 1920 in South Braintree, Massachusetts, the Italians were convicted in a trial that

many people thought resulted in a grave miscarriage of justice. Shahn felt that he had found in this story a subject the equal of any in Western art history: "Suddenly I realized . . . I was living through another crucifixion."[44] Basing many of the works in this cycle on newspaper photographs of the events, Shahn devised a style that adapted his knowledge of Synthetic Cubism and his training in commercial art to an emotionally expressive use of flat, intense color in figural compositions filled with sharp, dry, angular forms. He called the major work in the series *The Passion of Sacco and Vanzetti* (FIG. I-6), drawing a parallel to Christ's passion. This tall, narrow painting condenses the narrative in terms of both time and space. The two executed men lie in coffins at the bottom of the composition. Presiding over them are the three members of the commission chaired by Harvard University president A. Laurence Lowell, who declared the original trial fair and cleared the way for the executions to take place. A framed portrait of Judge Webster Thayer, who handed down the initial sentence, hangs on the wall of a simplified government building. The gray pallor of the dead men, the stylized mask-faces of the mock-pious mourning commissioners, and the haughty judge all contribute to the mood of anguished commentary that Shahn sought. *The Passion of Sacco and Vanzetti* is one of the most powerful American artworks of the era.

EDWARD HOPPER Trained as a commercial artist, EDWARD HOPPER (1882–1967) studied painting and printmaking in New York and then in Paris. When he returned to the United States, he concentrated on scenes of contemporary American city and country life. His paintings depict buildings, streets, and landscapes that are curiously muted, still, and filled with empty spaces, evoking the national mindset during the Depression era. Hopper did not paint historically specific scenes. He took as his subject the more generalized theme of the overwhelming loneliness and echoing isolation of modern life in the United States. In his paintings, motion is stopped and time suspended.

From the darkened streets outside a restaurant in Hopper's *Nighthawks* (FIG. **29-70**), the viewer glimpses the lighted interior through huge plate-glass windows, which lend the inner space the paradoxical sense of being both a safe refuge and a vulnerable place

29-70 EDWARD HOPPER, *Nighthawks*, 1942. Oil on canvas, 2' 6" × 4' 8 $\frac{11}{16}$". Art Institute of Chicago, Chicago (Friends of American Art Collection).

The seeming indifference of Hopper's characters to one another, and the echoing spaces surrounding them, evoke the overwhelming loneliness and isolation of Depression-era life in the United States.

1 ft.

ART AND SOCIETY

Jacob Lawrence's *Migration of the Negro*

Disillusioned with their lives in the South, hundreds of thousands of African Americans migrated north in the years following World War I, seeking improved economic opportunities and a more hospitable political and social environment. But the conditions that African Americans encountered both during their migration and in the North were often as difficult and discriminatory as those they had left behind in the South, as the artist Jacob Lawrence knew from his own experience. Lawrence was an African American whose family had migrated from the rural south to Atlantic City, New Jersey, where he was born. He moved to Harlem when he was 13 years old.

> I was part of the migration, as was my family, my mother, my sister, and my brother. . . . I grew up hearing tales about people "coming up," another family arriving. . . . I didn't realize what was happening until about the middle of the 1930s, and that's when the *Migration* series began to take form in my mind.*

Lawrence sought funding for his project from the Julius Rosenwald Fund. In his successful fellowship application, Lawrence argued that his proposal was of high educational value. He stated:

> It is important as a part of the evolution of America, since this Migration has affected the whole of America mentally, economically and socially. Since it has had this effect, I feel that my project would lay before the Negroes themselves a little of what part they have played in the History of the United States. In addition the whole of America might learn some of the history of this particular minority group, of which they know very little.†

His plan was to depict the history of the great African American migration northward in eight sections: Causes of the Migration; Stimulation of the Migration; The Spread of the Migration; The Efforts to Check the Migration; Public Opinion Regarding the Migration; The Effects of the Migration on the South; The Effects of the Migration on Various Parts of the North; and The Effects of the Migration on the Negro. The resulting series consists of 60 panels, all with explanatory captions—for example, "They did not always leave because they were promised work in the North. Many of them left because of Southern conditions, one of them being great floods that ruined the crops, and therefore they were unable to make a living where they were" (*No. 8*) and "They also found discrimination in the North although it was much different from that which they had known in the South" (*No. 49*; FIG. **29-71**).

29-71 JACOB LAWRENCE, *No. 49* from *The Migration of the Negro*, 1940–1941. Tempera on Masonite, 1' 6" × 1'. Phillips Collection, Washington, D.C.

The 49th in a series of 60 paintings documenting African American life in the North, Lawrence's depiction of a segregated dining room underscored that the migrants had not left discrimination behind.

*Quoted in Henry Louis Gates Jr., "New Negroes, Migration, and Cultural Exchange," in Elizabeth Hutton Turner, ed., *Jacob Lawrence: The Migration Series* (Washington, D.C.: Phillips Collection, 1993), 20.

†Quoted in Patricia Hills, *Painting Harlem Modern: The Art of Jacob Lawrence* (Berkeley and Los Angeles: University of California Press, 2009), 98.

for the three customers and the man behind the counter. The seeming indifference of Hopper's characters to one another as well as the echoing spaces surrounding them evoke the pervasive loneliness of modern humans. In *Nighthawks* and other works, Hopper created a Realist vision recalling that of 19th-century artists such as Thomas Eakins (FIG. 27-36) and Henry Ossawa Tanner (FIG. 27-38), but in keeping with more recent trends in painting, he simplified the shapes, moving toward abstraction.

JACOB LAWRENCE African American artist JACOB LAWRENCE (1917–2000) moved to Harlem, New York, in 1927 while still a

boy. There, he came under the spell of the African art and the African American history he found in lectures and exhibitions and in the special programs sponsored by the 135th Street branch of the New York Public Library, which had outstanding collections of African American art and archival data. Inspired by the politically oriented art of Goya (FIG. 27-12), Daumier (FIG. 27-29), and Orozco (FIG. 29-74), and influenced by the many artists and writers of the Harlem Renaissance whom he met, including Aaron Douglas (see "Aaron Douglas and the Harlem Renaissance," page 912, and FIGS. 29-40 and 29-40A), Lawrence found his subjects in the everyday life of Harlem and in African American history.

ARTISTS ON ART

Grant Wood's *Revolt against the City*

Grant Wood and the Regionalists, sometimes referred to as the American Scene Painters, turned their attention away not only from Europe but also from America's cities. The Regionalists found their subjects instead in the rural life of America, which they considered its cultural backbone. Wood set forth his philosophy most clearly in *Revolt against the City,* a pamphlet he published in Iowa City in 1935, five years after completing his masterpiece, *American Gothic* (FIG. 29-72).

> [American] painting has declared its independence from Europe, and is retreating from the cities to the more American village and country life. Paris is no longer the Mecca of the American artist. The American public, which used to be interested solely in foreign and imitative work, has readily acquired a strong interest in the distinctly indigenous art of its own land; and our buyers of paintings and patrons of art have naturally and honestly fallen in with the movement away from Paris and the American pseudo-Parisians. . . . This is no mere chauvinism. If it is patriotic, it is so because a feeling for one's own milieu and for the validity of one's own life and its surroundings is patriotic. . . . No longer is it necessary for [the American artist] to migrate even to New York, or to seek any great metropolis. No longer is it necessary for him to suffer the confusing cosmopolitanism, the noise, the too intimate gregariousness of the large city.
>
> Let me try to state the basic idea of the regional movement. Each section has a personality of its own, in physiography, industry, psychology. Thinking painters and writers who have passed their formative years in these regions, will, by care-taking analysis, work out and interpret in their productions these varying personalities. When the different regions develop characteristics of their own, they will come into competition with each other; and out of this competition a rich American culture will grow.*

*Grant Wood, *Revolt against the City* (Iowa City: Frank Luther Mott, 1935). Reprinted in James M. Dennis, *Grant Wood: A Study in American Art and Culture* (New York: Viking, 1975).

29-72 GRANT WOOD, *American Gothic,* 1930. Oil on beaverboard, 2' 5⅞" × 2' ⅞". Art Institute of Chicago, Chicago (Friends of American Art Collection).

In reaction to modernist abstract painting, the Midwestern Regionalism movement focused on American subjects. Wood's painting of an Iowa farmer and his daughter became an American icon.

In 1941, Lawrence began a 60-painting series titled *The Migration of the Negro* in which he defined his vision of the continuing African American struggle against discrimination (see "Jacob Lawrence's *Migration of the Negro,*" page 937). Unlike his earlier historical paintings depicting important figures in American history, such as the abolitionists Frederick Douglass and Harriet Tubman, this series called attention to a contemporaneous event—the ongoing exodus of black labor from the southern United States.

Lawrence's *Migration* paintings provide numerous vignettes capturing the experiences of the African Americans who had moved to the North. Often, a sense of the bleakness and degradation of their new life dominates the images. In *No. 49* (FIG. 29-71), which tells of the unexpected and different kind of discrimination that African Americans encountered in the North, Lawrence depicted a blatantly segregated dining room with a barrier running down the room's center separating the whites on the left from the African Americans on the right. To ensure a continuity and visual integrity among all 60 paintings, Lawrence interpreted his themes systematically in rhythmic arrangements of bold, flat, and strongly colored shapes. His style drew equally from his interest in the push-pull effects of Cubist space and his memories of the patterns made by the colored scatter rugs brightening the floors of his childhood homes. He unified the narrative with a consistent palette of bluish green, orange, yellow, and grayish brown throughout the entire series.

GRANT WOOD Although many American artists, such as the Precisionists (FIGS. 29-41 and 29-42), preferred to depict the city or rapidly developing technological advances, others avoided subjects tied to modern life. At a 1931 arts conference, GRANT WOOD (1891–1942) announced a new movement developing in the Midwest, known as *Regionalism,* which he described as focused on American subjects and as standing in reaction to the modernist abstraction of Europe and New York. Four years later, Wood published a pamphlet titled *Revolt against the City,* which underscored their new focus (see "Grant Wood's *Revolt against the City,*" above). Wood's paintings, for example, portray the people of rural Iowa, where he was born and raised.

The work that catapulted Wood to national prominence was *American Gothic* (FIG. 29-72), which became an American icon. The artist depicted his dentist and his sister posing as a farmer and his spinster daughter standing in front of a neat house with a small *lancet* window, a motif originating in Gothic architecture and associated with churches and religious piety. The man and woman wear traditional attire. He appears in worn overalls and she in an apron trimmed with rickrack. The dour expression on both faces gives the painting a severe quality, which Wood enhanced with his meticulous brushwork. The public and professional critics agreed that *American Gothic* was "quaint, humorous, and AMERICAN" and embodied "strength, dignity, fortitude, resoluteness, integrity," qualities that represented the true spirit of America.[45]

Wood's Regionalist vision involved more than his subjects. It extended to a rejection of avant-garde styles in favor of a clearly readable, Realist style. Surely, this approach appealed to many people alienated by the increasing presence of abstraction in art. However, despite the accolades this painting received, it also attracted criticism. Not everyone saw the painting as a sympathetic portrayal of Midwestern life. Indeed, some Iowans considered the depiction of life in their state insulting. In addition, despite the seemingly reportorial nature of *American Gothic,* some viewed it as a political statement—one of staunch nationalism. In light of the problematic nationalism in Germany at the time, many observers found Wood's nationalistic attitude disturbing. Nonetheless, during the Great Depression, Regionalist paintings had a popular appeal because they often projected a reassuring image of America's heartland. The public saw Regionalism as a means of coping with the national crisis through a search for cultural roots. Thus people deemed acceptable any nostalgia implicit in Regionalist paintings or the mythologies these works perpetuated, because they served a larger purpose.

THOMAS HART BENTON Another major Regionalist artist was THOMAS HART BENTON (1889–1975). Whereas Wood focused his attention on Iowa, Benton turned to scenes from his native Missouri. He produced one of his major works, a series of murals titled *A Social History of the State of Missouri,* in 1936 for the Missouri State Capitol. The murals depict a collection of images from the state's historical and legendary past, such as primitive agriculture, horse trading, a vigilante lynching, an old-fashioned political meeting, and Mark Twain's Huckleberry Finn and Jim on their raft. Other scenes portray the mining industry, grain elevators, Native Americans, and family life. One segment, *Pioneer Days and Early Settlers* (FIG. 29-73), shows a white man using whisky as a bartering tool with a Native American (*left*), along with scenes documenting the building of Missouri (*right*). Part documentary and part invention, Benton's images include both positive and negative aspects of Missouri's history, as these examples illustrate. Although the public perceived the Regionalists as dedicated to glorifying Midwestern life, that was not their aim. Indeed, Grant Wood observed, "Your true regionalist is not a mere eulogist; he may

29-73 THOMAS HART BENTON, *Pioneer Days and Early Settlers,* fresco in the State Capitol, Jefferson City, Missouri, 1936.
Art © T. H. Benton and R. P. Benton Testamentary Trusts/UMB Bank Trustee/Licensed by VAGA, New York.

Benton's mural for Missouri's State Capitol is one of the major Regionalist artworks. Part documentary and part invention, the images include both positive and negative aspects of state history.

29-74 José Clemente Orozco, *Epic of American Civilization: Hispano-America* (panel 16), fresco in Baker Memorial Library, Dartmouth College, Hanover, New Hampshire, ca. 1932–1934. Art © Orozco Valladares Family/SOMAAP, Mexico/Licensed by VAGA, New York.

One of 24 panels depicting the history of Mexico from ancient times, this scene focuses on a heroic peasant soldier of the Mexican Revolution surrounded by symbolic figures of his oppressors.

even be a severe critic."[46] Benton, like Wood, championed a visually accessible style, but he developed a highly personal aesthetic that included complex compositions, a fluidity of imagery, and simplified figures depicted with a rubbery distortion.

JOSÉ CLEMENTE OROZCO During the period between the two world wars, several Mexican painters achieved international renown for their work both in Mexico and the United States. The eldest was José Clemente Orozco (1883–1949), one of a group of Mexican artists determined to base their art on the indigenous history and culture existing in Mexico before the arrival of Europeans. The movement that these artists formed was part of the idealistic rethinking of society that occurred in conjunction with the Mexican Revolution (1910–1920) and the lingering political turmoil of the 1920s. Among the projects that these politically motivated artists undertook were vast mural cycles placed in public buildings to dramatize and validate the history of Mexico's native peoples. Orozco worked on one of the first major cycles, painted in 1922 on the walls of the National Training School in Mexico City. He carried the ideas of this mural revolution to the United States, completing many commissions for wall paintings between 1927 and 1934, notably a major mural cycle in the Baker Library at Dartmouth College in New Hampshire. The college let Orozco choose the subject, and he designed 14 large panels and 10 smaller ones that together formed a panoramic and symbolic history of ancient and modern Mexico.

The murals recount Mexican history from the early mythic days of the feathered-serpent god Quetzalcoatl (see pages 514 and 1088) to a contemporary and bitterly satiric vision of modern education.

The imagery in panel 16, *Epic of American Civilization: Hispano-America* (FIG. **29-74**), revolves around the monumental figure of a heroic Mexican peasant who has become a soldier in the Mexican Revolution. Looming on either side of him are mounds crammed with symbolic figures of his oppressors—bankers, government soldiers, officials, gangsters, and the rich. Money-grubbers empty huge bags of gold coins at the feet of the incorruptible armed peasant, cannons threaten him, and a general bedecked with medals raises a dagger to stab him in the back. Orozco's training as an architect gave him a sense of the framed wall surface, which he easily commanded, projecting his clearly defined figures onto the solid mural plane in monumental scale. In addition, Orozco's early experience as a maker of political prints and as a newspaper artist had taught him the rhetorical strength of graphic brevity, which he used here to assure that his allegory could be read easily. His skillful merging of the graphic and mural media effects gives his work an originality and force rarely seen in mural painting after the Renaissance and Baroque periods.

DIEGO RIVERA A second Mexican who received great acclaim for his murals, both in Mexico and in the United States, was Diego Rivera (1886–1957), who lived in Paris from 1911 to 1919 and

Diego Rivera on Art for the People

Diego Rivera was an avid proponent of a social and political role for art in the lives of common people and wrote passionately about the proper goals for an artist—goals he fully met in his own murals depicting Mexican history (FIG. 29-75). Rivera's views stand in sharp contrast to the growing interest in abstraction on the part of many early-20th-century painters and sculptors.

> Art has always been employed by the different social classes who hold the balance of power as one instrument of domination—hence, as a political instrument. One can analyze epoch after epoch—from the stone age to our own day—and see that there is no form of art which does not also play an essential political role. . . . What is it then that we really need? . . . An art with revolution as its subject: because the principal interest in the worker's life has to be touched first. It is necessary that he find aesthetic satisfaction and the highest pleasure appareled in the essential interest of his life. . . . The subject is to the painter what the rails are to a locomotive. He cannot do without it. In fact, when he refuses to seek or accept a subject, his own plastic methods and his own aesthetic theories become his subject instead. . . . [H]e himself becomes the subject of his work. He becomes nothing but an illustrator of his own state of mind . . . That is the deception practiced under the name of "Pure Art."*

*Quoted in Robert Goldwater and Marco Treves, eds., *Artists on Art from the XIV to the XX Century* (New York: Pantheon, 1945), 475–477.

29-75 DIEGO RIVERA, *Ancient Mexico,* detail of *History of Mexico,* fresco in the Palacio Nacional, Mexico City, 1929–1935.

A staunch Marxist, Rivera painted vast mural cycles in public buildings to dramatize the history of his native land. This fresco depicts the conflicts between indigenous Mexicans and Spanish colonizers.

traveled to Italy to study Renaissance frescoes. A staunch Marxist, Rivera strove to develop an art that served his people's needs (see "Diego Rivera on Art for the People," above, and FIG. 29-75.). Toward that end, inspired in part by ancient murals in his homeland, he sought to create a national Mexican style focusing on Mexico's history and also incorporating a popular, generally accessible aesthetic in keeping with the socialist spirit of the Mexican Revolution. Rivera produced numerous large murals in public buildings, among them a series lining the staircase of the National Palace in Mexico City. In these images, painted between 1929 and 1935, he depicted scenes from Mexico's history, of which *Ancient Mexico* (FIG. 29-75) is one. This section of the mural represents the conflicts between the indigenous people and the Spanish colonizers. Rivera included portraits of important figures in Mexican history, especially those involved in the struggle for Mexican independence. Although the composition is complex, the simple monumental shapes and areas of bold color make the story easily legible.

FRIDA KAHLO Born to a Mexican mother and German father, the painter FRIDA KAHLO (1907–1954), who married Diego Rivera, used the details of her life as powerful symbols for the psychological pain of human existence. Art historians often consider Kahlo a Surrealist due to the psychic, autobiographical issues she dealt with

in her art. Indeed, André Breton himself deemed her a Natural Surrealist. (The work of her older contemporary, RUFINO TAMAYO [1899–1991; FIG. 29-75A] has also been compared with Natural Surrealism.) Kahlo herself, however, rejected any association with the Surrealists. She began painting seriously as a young student, during

29-75A TAMAYO, *Friend of the Birds,* 1944.

convalescence from an accident that tragically left her in constant pain. Her life became a heroic and tumultuous battle for survival against illness and stormy personal relationships.

Typical of her long series of unflinching self-portraits is *The Two Fridas* (FIG. 29-76), one of the few large-scale canvases Kahlo ever produced. The twin figures sit side by side on a low bench in a

29-76 FRIDA KAHLO, *The Two Fridas,* 1939. Oil on canvas, 5' 7" × 5' 7". Museo de Arte Moderno, Mexico City.

Kahlo's deeply personal paintings touch sensual and psychological memories in her audience. Here, twin self-portraits linked by clasped hands and a common artery suggest two sides of her personality.

barren landscape under a stormy sky. The figures suggest different sides of the artist's personality, inextricably linked by the clasped hands and by the thin artery stretching between them, joining their exposed hearts. The artery ends on one side in surgical forceps and on the other in a miniature portrait of her husband as a child. Her deeply personal paintings touch sensual and psychological memories in her audience.

To read Kahlo's paintings solely as autobiographical overlooks the powerful political dimension of her art. Kahlo was deeply nationalistic and committed to her Mexican heritage. Politically active, she joined the Communist Party in 1927 and participated in public political protests. *The Two Fridas* incorporates Kahlo's commentary on the struggle facing Mexicans in the early 20th century in defining their national cultural identity. The Frida on the right (representing indigenous culture) appears in a Tehuana dress, the traditional costume of Zapotec women from the Isthmus of Tehuantepec, whereas the Frida on the left (representing imperialist forces) wears a European-style white lace dress. The heart, depicted here in such dramatic fashion, was an important symbol in the art of the Aztecs, whom Mexican nationalists idealized as the last inde-

pendent rulers of their land. Thus *The Two Fridas* represents both Kahlo's personal struggles and the struggles of her homeland.

Photography

Today, Frida Kahlo is the most famous female artist of her generation, but other women achieved prominence in the arts in the period between the two world wars. Especially noteworthy are the photographers Dorothea Lange and Margaret Bourke-White.

DOROTHEA LANGE One of the most important programs the U.S. government initiated during the 1930s was the Resettlement Administration (RA), better known by its later name, the Farm Security Administration. The RA oversaw emergency aid programs for farm families struggling to survive the Great Depression. The RA hired DOROTHEA LANGE (1895–1965) in 1935, and dispatched her to document the deplorable living conditions of the rural poor. At the end of an assignment photographing migratory pea pickers in California, Lange stopped at a camp in Nipomo and found the migrant workers there starving because the crops had frozen in the

fields. Among the pictures Lange made on this occasion was *Migrant Mother, Nipomo Valley* (FIG. **29-77**), in which she captured the mixture of strength and worry in the raised hand and careworn face of a young mother, who holds a baby on her lap. Two older children cling to their mother trustfully while turning their faces away from the camera. Lange described how she got the picture:

> [I] saw and approached the hungry and desperate mother, as if drawn by a magnet. I do not remember how I explained my presence or my camera to her, but I remember she asked me no questions. I made five exposures, working closer and closer from the same direction. . . . There she sat in that lean-to tent with her children huddled around her, and she seemed to know that my pictures might help her, and so she helped me.[47]

Within days after Lange's photograph appeared in a San Francisco newspaper, people rushed food to Nipomo to feed the hungry workers.

29-77 DOROTHEA LANGE, *Migrant Mother, Nipomo Valley,* 1935. Gelatin silver print, 1' 1" × 9". Oakland Museum of California, Oakland (gift of Paul S. Taylor).

While documenting the lives of migratory farm workers during the Depression, Lange made this unforgettable photograph of a mother in which she captured the woman's strength and worry.

1 in.

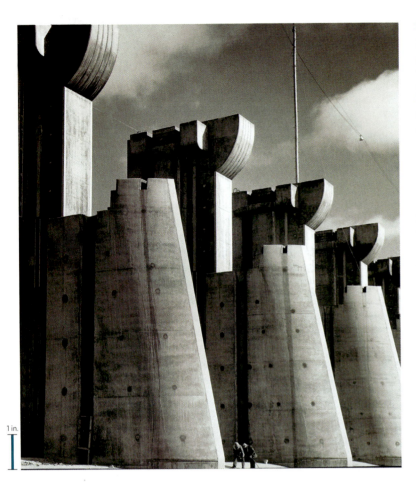

1 in.

29-78 MARGARET BOURKE-WHITE, *Fort Peck Dam, Montana,* 1936. Gelatin silver print, 1' 1" × 10½". Metropolitan Museum of Art, New York (gift of Ford Motor Company and John C. Waddell, 1987).

Bourke-White's dramatic photograph of Fort Peck Dam graced the cover of the first issue of *Life* magazine and celebrated the achievements of American engineering during the depths of the Great Depression.

fortress.) She chose a sharp angle from below to communicate the dam's soaring height, underscoring the immense scale by including two dwarfed figures of men in the foreground. The tight framing, which shuts out all of the landscape and much of the sky, transforms the dam into an almost abstract composition, a kind of still life, like Edward Weston's peppers (FIG. 29-44). Bourke-White's photographs celebrate modern American engineering as heir to the architectural achievements of the ancient world's great civilizations, and bear comparison with the paintings of Charles Demuth (FIG. 29-41).

Sculpture

In striking contrast to the leading American painters and photographers of the 1930s, the most renowned sculptor of this period rose to international prominence because of his contributions to the development of abstract art.

MARGARET BOURKE-WHITE Almost 10 years younger than Dorothea Lange, MARGARET BOURKE-WHITE (1904–1971) also made her reputation as a photojournalist in Depression-era America. She was the first staff photographer that Henry Luce (1898–1967) hired to furnish illustrations for the magazines in his publishing empire. Beginning in 1929, Bourke-White worked for *Fortune,* then for *Life* when Luce launched the famous newsweekly in 1936. During her long career, she photographed Midwestern farmers in their drought-stricken fields, impoverished Southern sharecroppers, black gold miners in South Africa, the Nazi concentration camp at Buchenwald, and the Korean War.

Bourke-White's most famous photographs, however, were not of people or events but of the triumphs of 20th-century engineering, many of which appeared in Luce's magazines and served to instill pride in an American public severely lacking in confidence during the Depression. She photographed the Chrysler Building (FIG. 29-47) while it was under construction in New York, attracting media attention for her daring balancing act on steel girders high above the pavement. She also achieved renown as the first woman to fly a combat mission when she was an official U.S. Air Force photographer during World War II.

For the first issue of *Life* (November 23, 1936), Bourke-White not only provided the cover photograph—*Fort Peck Dam, Montana* (FIG. 29-78)—but also wrote and illustrated with 16 additional photographs the lead story on the town of New Deal, home to the workers who constructed the dam during the depths of the Depression. Fort Peck Dam was at the time the largest earth-filled dam in the world. Bourke-White photographed the still unfinished dam before the installation of the elevated highway at its summit. (The supports for that highway fortuitously conjure the image of a crenellated medieval

ALEXANDER CALDER The son and grandson of sculptors, ALEXANDER CALDER (1898–1976) initially studied mechanical engineering. Fascinated all his life by motion, he explored movement in relationship to three-dimensional form in much of his work. As a young artist in Paris in the late 1920s, Calder invented a circus full of wire-based miniature performers that mimicked the motion of their real-life counterparts. After a visit to Piet Mondrian's studio in the early 1930s, Calder set out to put the Dutch painter's brightly colored rectangular shapes (FIG. 29-61) into motion. (Marcel Duchamp, intrigued by Calder's early motorized and hand-cranked examples of moving abstract pieces, named them *mobiles.*) Calder soon used his engineering skills to fashion a series of balanced structures hanging from rods, wires, and colorful, organically shaped plates. This new kind of sculpture, which combined nonobjective organic forms and motion, succeeded in expressing the innate dynamism of the natural world.

An early Calder mobile is *Lobster Trap and Fish Tail* (FIG. 29-79), which the artist created in 1939 under a commission from the Museum of Modern Art in New York City for the stairwell of the museum's new building on West 53rd Street (see "The Museum of Modern Art as Collector and Patron," page 945). Calder carefully planned each nonmechanized mobile so that any air current would set the parts moving to create a constantly shifting dance in space. Mondrian's work may have provided the initial inspiration for the mobiles, but their organic shapes resemble those in Joan Miró's Surrealist paintings (FIG. 29-58). Indeed, viewers can read Calder's forms as either geometric or organic. Geometrically, the lines suggest circuitry and rigging, and the shapes derive from circles and ovoid forms. Organically, the lines suggest nerve axons, and the shapes resemble cells, leaves, fins, wings, and other bioforms.

THE PATRON'S VOICE

The Museum of Modern Art as Collector and Patron

People understandably think of museums as repositories of artworks, often donated by wealthy private individuals. Indeed, the interests and tastes of donors can be the primary determinants of the character of a museum's collection. Although some world-famous museums—for example, the Metropolitan Museum of Art in New York and the Musée du Louvre in Paris—boast comprehensive art collections of all periods and places, most museums have much narrower acquisition policies. All museums, but especially the richest and largest, have the power to elevate the stature of individual artists or particular kinds of art by featuring them in exhibitions. And sometimes museums become influential patrons themselves by directly commissioning works of art.

The Museum of Modern Art (MoMA) in New York City is an excellent case study of the role of museums as art patrons. Established in 1929, MoMA owes its existence to a trio of women—Lillie P. Bliss, Mary Quinn Sullivan, and Abby Aldrich Rockefeller (see "Art 'Matron-age' in the United States," page 913)—who saw the need for a museum to collect and exhibit modernist art. Within a short period of time, the institution that they founded became the most important museum of modern art in the world. Their success was extraordinary considering the skepticism and hostility greeting modernist art in the years before MoMA's inception. Indeed, few American museums then exhibited late-19th- and 20th-century art at all.

In its quest to expose the public to the energy and challenge of modernist, particularly avant-garde, art, MoMA developed ground-breaking, progressive exhibitions. Among those that the museum mounted during the early years of its existence were *Cubism and Abstract Art* and *Fantastic Art, Dada, Surrealism* (1936). Two other note-worthy shows were *American Sources of Modern Art* (Aztec, Maya, Inca) in 1933 and *African Negro Art* in 1935, both among the first exhibitions to deal with "primitive" artifacts in artistic rather than anthropological terms (see "Primitivism and Colonialism," page 891).

The organization of MoMA's administrative structure and the scope of the museum's early activities were also remarkable. The museum's first director, Alfred H. Barr Jr., insisted on establishing departments not only for painting and sculpture but also for photography, prints and draw-ing, architecture, and the decorative arts. He developed a library of books on modern art and a film library, both of which have become world-class collections, as well as an extensive publishing program.

It is the museum's art collection, however, that has drawn the most attention. By cultivating an influential group of benefactors, MoMA has developed an extensive and enviable collection of late-19th- and 20th-century art. The museum owns a long list of important works, such as van Gogh's *Starry Night* (FIG. 28-19), Picasso's *Les Demoiselles d'Avignon* (FIG. 29-1), and Dalí's *The Persistence of Memory* (FIG. 29-55), as well as many others illustrated in this book, including 23 in this chapter alone. MoMA has also played a role in the history of 20th-century art through its patronage of modernist artists. For example, in 1939, just a decade after the institution's founding, it commissioned Alexander Calder to produce the mobile *Lobster Trap and Fish Tail* (FIG. 29-79) for display in a prominent location in its midtown Manhattan building.

1 ft.

29-79 ALEXANDER CALDER, *Lobster Trap and Fish Tail,* 1939. Painted sheet aluminum and steel wire, 8' 6" × 9' 6". Museum of Modern Art, New York.

Commissioned by the Museum of Modern Art, Calder used his thorough knowledge of engineering to create a new kind of sculpture—the mobile—that expressed nature's innate dynamism.

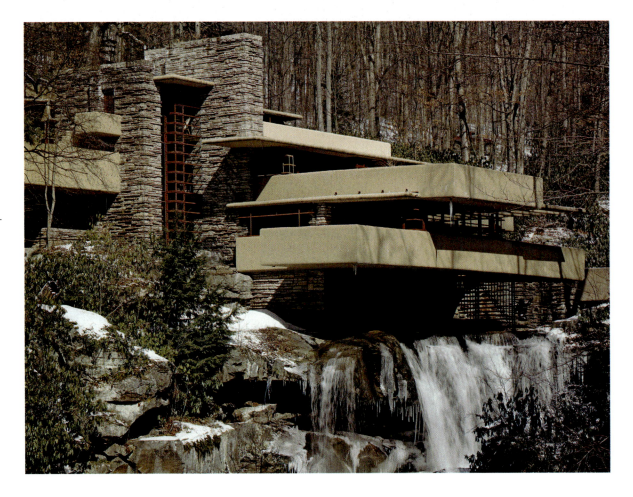

29-80 FRANK LLOYD WRIGHT, Kaufmann House (Fallingwater; looking northeast), Bear Run, Pennsylvania, 1936–1939.

Perched on a rocky hillside over a waterfall, Wright's Fallingwater has long, sweeping lines, unconfined by abrupt wall limits, reaching out and capturing the expansiveness of the natural environment.

Architecture

The most influential American architect of the 1930s, as during the opening decades of the century, was the ever-inventive Frank Lloyd Wright.

FALLINGWATER Wright's universally acclaimed masterpiece of this period is the Kaufmann House (FIG. **29-80**), which he designed as a weekend retreat at Bear Run, Pennsylvania, for Pittsburgh department store magnate Edgar Kaufmann Sr. Perched on a rocky hillside over a small waterfall, the house, nicknamed Fallingwater, has become an icon of modernist architectural design. In keeping with his commitment to "organic architecture" (see page 917), Wright sought to find a way to incorporate the structure fully into its site in order to ensure a fluid, dynamic exchange between the interior of the house and the natural environment outside. Rather than build the house overlooking or next to the waterfall, Wright decided to build it over the waterfall, because he believed that the Kaufmanns would become desensitized to the waterfall's presence and power if they merely overlooked it. In Fallingwater, Wright took the blocky masses characterizing his earlier Robie House (FIGS. 29-45 and 29-46) and extended them in all four directions. To take advantage of the location, he designed a series of terraces that extend on three levels from a central core structure. The contrast in textures among concrete, painted metal, and natural stones in the house's terraces and walls enlivens its shapes, as does Wright's use of full-length strip windows to create a stunning interweaving of interior and exterior space.

The implied message of Wright's new architecture was space, not mass—a space designed to fit the patron's life and enclosed and divided as required. Wright took special pains to meet his clients' requirements, often designing all the accessories of a house (including, in at least one case, gowns for his client's wife). In the late 1930s, he acted on a cherished dream to provide good architectural design for less prosperous people by adapting the ideas of his prairie houses (see page 916) to plans for smaller, less expensive dwellings with neither attics nor basements. These residences, known as *Usonian* houses (for "United States of North America"), became templates for suburban housing developments in the post–World War II housing boom.

The publication of Wright's plans brought him a measure of fame in Europe, especially in Holland and Germany. The issuance in Berlin in 1910 of a portfolio of his work and an exhibition of his designs the following year stimulated younger architects to adopt some of his ideas about open plans that afforded clients freedom. Some 40 years before his career ended, his work was already of revolutionary significance. Mies van der Rohe wrote in 1940: "[The] dynamic impulse from [Wright's] work invigorated a whole generation. His influence was strongly felt even when it was not actually visible."[48]

Frank Lloyd Wright's influence in Europe was exceptional for any American artist before World War II. However, in the decades following that global conflict, American painters, sculptors, and architects often took the lead in establishing new styles that artists elsewhere quickly emulated. This new preeminence of the United States in the arts is the subject of Chapter 30.

MODERNISM IN EUROPE AND AMERICA, 1900 TO 1945

Europe 1900 to 1920

- In the early 1900s, avant-garde artists searched for new definitions of art in a changed world. Matisse and the Fauves used bold colors as the primary means of conveying feeling. German Expressionist paintings by Die Brücke featured clashing colors, disquieting figures, and perspective distortions.

- Pablo Picasso and Georges Braque radically challenged prevailing artistic conventions with Cubism. The Cubists dissected forms and placed them in interaction with the space around them.

- The Futurists focused on motion in time and space in their effort to create paintings and sculptures that captured the dynamic quality of modern life. The Dadaists celebrated the spontaneous and intuitive, exploring the role of chance in art and often incorporating found objects in their works.

Boccioni, *Unique Forms of Continuity in Space*, 1913

United States 1900 to 1930

- The Armory Show of 1913 introduced avant-garde European art to American artists. Man Ray, for example, embraced Dada's fondness for the displacement of ordinary items, and Stuart Davis adopted the Cubist interest in fragmented form.

- The Harlem Renaissance brought African American artists to the forefront, including Aaron Douglas, whose paintings drew on Cubist principles. Charles Demuth, Georgia O'Keeffe, and the Precisionists used European modernist techniques to celebrate contemporary American subjects.

- Photography emerged as an important American art form in the work of Alfred Stieglitz and Edward Weston, who emphasized the careful arrangement of forms and patterns of light and dark.

Douglas, *Noah's Ark*, ca. 1927

Europe 1920 to 1945

- World War I gave rise to the Neue Sachlichkeit movement in Germany. "New Objectivity" artists depicted the horrors of war and explored the themes of death and transfiguration.

- The Surrealists investigated ways to express in art the world of dreams and the unconscious. Natural Surrealists aimed for "concrete irrationality" in their naturalistic paintings of dreamlike scenes. Biomorphic Surrealists experimented with automatism and employed abstract imagery.

- Many European modernists pursued utopian ideals. The Suprematists developed an abstract style to express pure feeling. The Constructivists used nonobjective forms to suggest the nature of space-time. De Stijl artists reduced their formal vocabulary to simple geometric forms in their search for "pure plastic art."

- Brancusi, Hepworth, Moore, and other sculptors increasingly turned to abstraction, often emphasizing voids as well as masses in their work.

- The Bauhaus in Germany promoted the vision of "total architecture," which called for the integration of all the arts in constructing modern living environments. Bauhaus buildings were unembellished glass and steel designs. In France, Le Corbusier used modern construction materials to build "machines for living"—houses with open plans and unadorned surfaces.

Dalí, *The Persistence of Memory*, 1931

Hepworth, *Oval Sculpture (No. 2)*, 1943

United States and Mexico 1930 to 1945

- Between the wars, Alexander Calder created mobiles (abstract sculptures with moving parts), but other American artists favored figural art. Lange and Shahn chronicled social injustice. Hopper explored the loneliness of life in the Depression era. Lawrence recorded the struggle of African Americans. Wood depicted life in rural Iowa.

- Mexican artists Orozco and Rivera painted epic mural cycles of the history of Mexico. Kahlo's powerful paintings explored the human psyche and were frequently autobiographical.

- The leading American architect of the first half of the 20th century was Frank Lloyd Wright, who promoted "organic architecture," in which free individuals move in a "free" space.

Wright, Fallingwater, 1936–1939

30-1a Moore's circular postmodern Italian plaza incorporates elements drawn from classical architecture, including a portico inspired by ancient Roman fora and an exedra loosely based on a triumphal arch.

30-1b Postmodernist architects frequently incorporate references to historical styles in their designs. In addition to motifs based on Roman buildings, Moore included modern versions of medieval flying buttresses.

30-1 CHARLES MOORE, Piazza d'Italia (looking northeast), New Orleans, 1976–1980.

▲ **30-1c** Many of Moore's historical motifs are rendered in high-tech materials unavailable to earlier architects—for example, stainless-steel columns and capitals and neon lighting for multicolored nighttime illumination.

Modernism and Postmodernism in Europe and America, 1945 to 1980

AFTER MODERNISM: POSTMODERNIST ARCHITECTURE

One of the most significant developments in later-20th-century architecture (as well as in contemporaneous painting and sculpture) was *postmodernism*. Postmodernist architects rejected the severity and simplicity of the modernist idiom pioneered by Gropius (FIG. 29-67), Mies van der Rohe (FIG. 29-68), Le Corbusier (FIG. 29-69), and their postwar successors. Instead, they celebrated complexity and incorporated historical references in their designs, often rendered in high-tech materials unavailable to earlier architects.

An outstanding example of a postmodernist design that creates a dialogue between the past and the present is Piazza d'Italia (Plaza of Italy; FIG. **30-1**) in New Orleans by American architect CHARLES MOORE (1925–1993), dean of the Yale School of Architecture from 1965 to 1970. Designed in the late 1970s and restored after sustaining serious damage in the wake of Hurricane Katrina in 2005, Piazza d'Italia is dedicated to the city's Italian American community. Appropriately, Moore selected elements relating specifically to Italian history, all the way back to ancient Roman culture.

Piazza d'Italia is an open circular area partially formed by short segments of colonnades arranged in staggered concentric arcs, which direct the eye to the focal point of the composition—an *exedra*. This recessed area on a raised platform serves as a *rostrum* (speaker's platform) during the annual festivities of Saint Joseph's Day. Moore inlaid the piazza's pavement with a map of Italy centered on Sicily, from which the majority of the city's Italian families originated. From there, the map's Italian "boot" stretches to the steps, which correspond to the Alps, and ascends the rostrum.

The piazza's most immediate historical references are to the porticos of an ancient Roman forum (FIGS. 7-12 and 7-44) and to triumphal arches (FIGS. 7-40 and 7-44A), but the irregular placement of the concentrically arranged colonnade fragments inserts a note of instability into the design reminiscent of Mannerism (FIG. 22-56). Illusionistic devices, such as the continuation of the piazza's pavement design (apparently through a building and out into the street), are Baroque in character (FIG. 24-4). Moore incorporated all the classical orders—most with whimsical modifications, such as the stainless-steel columns and capitals, neon collars around the column necks, and neon lights framing various parts of the exedra and porticos for dramatic multicolored nighttime illumination. He even made references to medieval architecture by including modern versions of *flying buttresses,* and alternating white and gray-green stones in emulation of medieval buildings in Florence, Siena, and Orvieto (FIGS. 12-30, 12-30A, 14-13, and 14-13A). This kind of architectural eclecticism, especially rich in Piazza d'Italia, epitomizes postmodernism.

THE AFTERMATH OF WORLD WAR II

World War II, with the global devastation it unleashed on all dimensions of life—political, economic, and psychological—set the stage for the second half of the 20th century. The dropping of atomic bombs by the United States on the Japanese cities of Hiroshima and Nagasaki in 1945 signaled a turning point not only in the war itself but in the geopolitical balance and the nature of international conflict as well. For the postwar generation, nuclear attack became a very real threat. Indeed, the two nuclear superpowers, the United States and the Soviet Union, divided the world into spheres of influence, and each regularly intervened politically, economically, and militarily wherever and whenever it considered its interests to be at stake.

The cessation of global warfare did not bring global peace. On the contrary, regional conflicts erupted throughout the world during the decades after World War II. In 1947, the British left India, which precipitated a murderous Hindu-Muslim war that divided South Asia into two new hostile nations—India and Pakistan. After a bloody civil war, Communists came to power in China in 1949. North Korea invaded South Korea in 1950 and fought a grim war with the United States and its allies. The Soviets brutally suppressed uprisings in their subject nations—East Germany, Poland, Hungary, and Czechoslovakia. The United States intervened in disputes in Central and South America. Almost as soon as many of the colonial nations of Africa—Kenya, Uganda, Nigeria, Angola, Mozambique, the Sudan, Rwanda, and the Congo—won their independence, civil wars devastated them. In Indonesia, civil war left more than 100,000 dead. Algeria expelled France in 1962 after the French waged a prolonged war with Algeria's Muslim natives. After 15 years of bitter war in Southeast Asia, the United States suffered defeat in Vietnam.

The period from 1945 to 1980 also brought upheaval in the cultural sphere. In the United States, for example, the struggles for civil rights for African Americans, for free speech on university campuses, and for disengagement from the Vietnam War led to a rebellion of the young, who took to the streets in often raucous demonstrations, some with violent repercussions. The prolonged ferment produced a new system of values, a "youth culture," expressed in the radical rejection not only of national policies but often also of the society generating them. Young Americans mocked their elders' lifestyles and adopted unconventional dress, manners, habits, and morals deliberately subversive of mainstream social standards, a phenomenon that continues today in different forms—for example, "punk" fashion. The postwar youth era witnessed the sexual revolution, the widespread use and abuse of drugs, and the development of rock music, then an exclusively youthful art form. Young people "dropped out" of regulated society, embraced alternative belief systems, and rejected Western university curricula as irrelevant.

This counterculture had considerable societal impact. The civil rights movement of the 1960s and later the women's liberation movement of the 1970s reflected the spirit of rebellion, coupled with the rejection of racism and sexism. In keeping with the growing resistance to established authority, women systematically began to challenge the male-dominated culture, which they perceived as having limited their political power and economic opportunities for centuries. Feminists charged that the political, social, and economic institutions of Western society, as well as the traditional family unit headed by a patriarch, perpetuated male power and the subordination of women.

Increasingly, individuals and groups actively challenged the status quo and sought to change the balance of power. For example, by adapting strategies developed first in the civil rights movement and later in feminism, various ethnic groups and gays and lesbians mounted challenges to discriminatory policies and attitudes. These groups fought for recognition, respect, and legal protection and battled discrimination with political action, an effort that recently has begun to yield significant results—for example, in the increasing acceptance of same-sex marriage. In addition, the growing scrutiny in numerous academic fields—cultural studies, literary theory, and colonial and postcolonial studies—of the dynamics and exercise of power also contributed to the dialogue on these issues. As a result, identity (both individual and group) emerged as a potent arena for discussion and action—and as a persistent and compelling subject for artists.

PAINTING, SCULPTURE, AND PHOTOGRAPHY

The end of World War II in 1945 left devastated cities, ruptured economies, and governments in chaos throughout Europe. These factors, coupled with the massive loss of life and the indelible horrors of the bombing of Hiroshima and Nagasaki and of the Holocaust, in which six million Jews died at the hands of the Nazis, resulted in a pervasive sense of despair, disillusionment, and skepticism. Although many people (for example, the Futurists in Italy; see page 898) had tried to find redemptive value in World War I, it was nearly impossible to do the same with World War II, coming as it did so soon after the "war to end all wars." Further, the "Great War" was largely a European conflict that left roughly 10 million people dead, whereas World War II was a truly global catastrophe, claiming 35 million lives.

MODERNISM AND POSTMODERNISM, 1945 TO 1980

1945–1960

- European Expressionists capture in paintings and sculptures the revulsion and cynicism that emerged in the wake of World War II
- New York School painters develop Abstract Expressionism, emphasizing form and raw energy over subject matter
- Sleek, geometrically rigid modernist skyscrapers become familiar sights in cities throughout the world

1960–1970

- Post-Painterly Abstractionists reject the passion and texture of action painting and celebrate the flatness of pigment on canvas
- Op artists produce the illusion of motion and depth using only geometric forms
- Minimalists reduce sculpture to basic shapes and emphasize their works' "objecthood"
- Pop artists find inspiration in popular culture and represent commonplace commercial products
- Superrealists create paintings and sculptures characterized by scrupulous reproduction of the appearance of people and objects
- Performance artists replace traditional stationary artworks with temporal action-artworks

1970–1980

- Artists play a leading role in the feminist movement by promoting women's themes and employing materials traditionally associated with women, such as china and fabric
- Postmodern architects erect complex and eclectic buildings that often incorporate references to historical styles
- Environmental artists redefine what constitutes "art" by manipulating natural materials in monumental earthworks
- Artists increasingly embrace new media—video recorders, computers—as tools for creating artworks

Postwar Expressionism in Europe

The cynicism pervading Europe in the 1940s found a voice in *existentialism*, a philosophy asserting the absurdity of human existence and the impossibility of achieving certitude. Many who embraced existentialism also promoted atheism and questioned the possibility of situating God within a systematic philosophy. Scholars trace the roots of existentialism to the Danish theologian Søren Kierkegaard (1813–1855), but in the postwar period, the writings of French author Jean-Paul Sartre (1905–1980) most clearly captured the existentialist spirit. According to Sartre, if God does not exist, then individuals must constantly struggle in isolation with the anguish of making decisions in a world without absolutes or traditional values. This spirit of pessimism and despair emerged frequently in European art of the immediate postwar period. A brutality or roughness appropriately expressing both the artist's state of mind and the larger cultural sensibility characterized the work of many European sculptors and painters.

ALBERTO GIACOMETTI The sculptures of Swiss artist ALBERTO GIACOMETTI (1901–1966) perhaps best express the existentialist spirit. Although Giacometti never claimed that he pursued existentialist ideas in his art, his works brilliantly capture the spirit of that philosophy. Indeed, Sartre, Giacometti's friend, saw the artist's figurative sculptures as the personification of existentialist humanity—alienated, solitary, and lost in the world's immensity. Giacometti's sculptures of the 1940s, such as *Man Pointing No. 5* (FIG. 30-2), are thin, nearly featureless figures with rough, agitated surfaces. Rather than conveying the solidity and mass of conventional bronze sculpture, these thin and elongated figures seem

1 ft.

30-3 FRANCIS BACON, *Painting*, 1946. Oil and pastel on linen, 6' 5$\frac{7}{8}$" × 4' 4". Museum of Modern Art, New York.

Painted in the aftermath of World War II, this intentionally revolting image of a powerful figure presiding over a slaughter is a reflection of war's butchery. It is Bacon's indictment of humanity.

30-2 ALBERTO GIACOMETTI, *Man Pointing No. 5*, 1947. Bronze, 5' 10" high. Des Moines Art Center, Des Moines (Nathan Emory Coffin Collection).

The writer Jean-Paul Sartre saw Giacometti's thin and virtually featureless sculpted figures as the personification of existentialist humanity—alienated, solitary, and lost in the world's immensity.

1 ft.

swallowed up by the space surrounding them, imparting a sense of isolation and fragility. Giacometti's evocative sculptures spoke to the pervasive despair that emerged in the aftermath of world war.

FRANCIS BACON Although born in Dublin, Ireland, FRANCIS BACON (1910–1992) was the son of a well-to-do Englishman. He spent most of his life in London, where he experienced firsthand the destruction of lives and property that the Nazi bombing wrought on the city during World War II. *Painting* (FIG. 30-3) is characteristic of Bacon's work—a reflection of war's butchery and an indictment of humanity. The artist presented a compelling and revolting image of a powerful, stocky man with a gaping mouth and a vivid red stain on his upper lip, as if he were a carnivore devouring the raw meat sitting on the railing surrounding him (compare FIG. 30-3A). Bacon may have based his depiction of this central figure on news photos of similarly dressed European

⤴ 30-3A BACON, *Figure with Meat*, 1954.

Jean Dubuffet on Crude Art

In the introductory essay to the catalog of the Autumn 1949 group exhibition of the Compagnie de l'Art Brut at the Galerie René Drouin in Paris, Jean Dubuffet (FIG. 30-4) explained the rationale for Crude Art in what became the movement's manifesto:

> [T]he approved art of the museums, galleries and salons—let us call it "cultural art" . . . [is not] representative of art in general, rather merely the activity of a particular clique: a cohort of careerist intellectuals. . . . There are still people, particularly the intellectuals, who do not clearly see that the intelligent are hopeless cases, and one needs to rely on the so-called imbeciles for moments of lucidity . . . [I]n July 1945 we [the Compagnie de l'Art Brut] undertook . . . methodical research into the relevant ways of producing that which we now call Crude Art. We understand by this works created by those untouched by artistic culture, in which copying has little part, unlike the art of intellectuals. Similarly, the artists take everything . . . from their own inner being, not from the canons of classical or fashionable art. We engage in an artistic enterprise that is completely pure, basic; totally guided in all its phases solely by the creator's own impulses.*

Not surprisingly, among the founding members of the Crude Art group was André Breton, the key intellectual champion of Dada and Surrealism (see "André Breton's First Surrealist Manifesto," page 922).

*Jean Dubuffet, *L'art brut préferé aux arts culturels* (Paris: Galerie René Drouin, 1949), n.p. Translated by Charles Harrison and Paul Wood, eds., *Art and Theory 1900–2000: An Anthology of Changing Ideas* (Malden, Mass.: Blackwell, 2002), 606–607.

30-4 Jean Dubuffet, *Vie Inquiète* (*Uneasy Life*), 1953. Oil on canvas, 4' 3" × 6' 4". Tate Modern, London (gift of the artist, 1966).

Dubuffet expressed a tortured vision of the world through thickly encrusted painted surfaces and crude images of the kind that children and the insane produce. He called it Art Brut—untaught Crude Art.

1 ft.

and American officials. The umbrella in particular recalls images of Neville Chamberlain (1869–1940), the wartime British prime minister who frequently appeared in photographs with an umbrella. Bacon added to the gut-wrenching impact of the painting by depicting the flayed carcass hanging behind the central figure like a crucified human form. Although the specific sources for the imagery in *Painting* are uncertain, the work is unmistakably "an attempt to remake the violence of reality itself," as Bacon often described his art, based on what he referred to as "the brutality of fact."[1]

JEAN DUBUFFET Although less specific, the works of French artist JEAN DUBUFFET (1901–1985) also express a tortured vision of the world through manipulated materials. In works such as *Vie Inquiète* (*Uneasy Life*; FIG. 30-4), Dubuffet first built up an *impasto* (a layer of thickly applied pigment) of plaster, glue, sand, asphalt, and other common materials, on which he painted or incised crude images of the kind that children, the insane, and scrawlers of graffiti produce. Scribblings interspersed with the images heighten the impression of smeared and gashed surfaces of crumbling walls and worn pavements marked by random individuals. Dubuffet believed that the art of children, the mentally unbalanced, prisoners, and outcasts was more direct and genuine because those who created it did so unrestrained by conventional standards of art. He promoted *Art Brut*—untaught *Crude Art* (see "Jean Dubuffet on Crude Art," above).

GERHARD RICHTER Artistic repercussions of the devastation of World War II were not confined to England and France. Powerful, frightening memories of the destruction wrought in Europe during the war lingered forever after in the minds of all who lived through it. Decades later in Germany, GERHARD RICHTER (b. 1932) would paint a series of grey "damaged landscapes"—for example, *Townscape Paris* (FIG. **30-4A**)—that conjured the aerial bombardments of the 1940s.

Abstract Expressionism

The devastation that World War II had inflicted across Europe resulted in an influx of émigré artists escaping to the United States. In the 1950s, the center of the Western art world shifted from Paris to New York. It was there that the first major American avant-garde art movement—*Abstract Expressionism*—emerged. The most important forerunner of the Abstract Expressionists, however, was an Armenian immigrant who arrived in New York in 1924.

ARSHILE GORKY Born a Christian in Islamic Turkish Armenia, Vosdanik Manoog Adoian was four years old when his father escaped being drafted into the Turkish army by fleeing the country. His mother died of starvation in her 15-year-old son's arms in a refugee camp for victims of the Turkish campaign of genocide against the Christian minority. The penniless Vosdanik managed in 1920 to make his way to America, where a relative took him into his home near Boston. Four years later, then a young man, Vosdanik changed his name to ARSHILE GORKY (1904–1948)—"Bitter Achilles" in Russian—and moved to New York City, where he continued the art education that he had begun in Boston. In 1948, Gorky hanged himself after suffering a series of misfortunes: a fire destroyed much of his recent work, he discovered his wife's infidelity, and an automobile accident robbed him of the use of his right arm. The injury

might have been only temporary, but the depressed Gorky thought he would never be able to paint again. In a career lasting only two decades, the Armenian immigrant contributed significantly to the artistic revolution born in New York. His work is the bridge between the Biomorphic Surrealism of Joan Miró (FIG. 29-58) and the totally abstract canvases of Jackson Pollock (FIG. 30-6).

Garden in Sochi (FIG. **30-5**), painted in 1943, is the third in a series of canvases with identical titles named after a Black Sea resort but inspired by Gorky's childhood memories of the Garden of Wish Fulfillment in his birthplace. The women of the Armenian village of Khorkom believed that their wishes would be granted if they rubbed their bare breasts against a rock in that garden beneath a tree to which they tied torn strips of their clothing. The brightly colored and thinly outlined forms in *Garden in Sochi,* which initially appear to be purely abstract biomorphic shapes, are loose sketches representing, at the left, a bare-breasted woman, and, at the center, a tree trunk with fluttering fabric. At the bottom are two oversized shoes—the Armenian slippers that Gorky's father gave his son shortly before abandoning the family.

CLEMENT GREENBERG The few traces of representational art in Gorky's work disappeared in Abstract Expressionism. As the name suggests, the artists associated with the New York School of Abstract Expressionism produced paintings that are, for the most part, abstract but express the artist's state of mind, with the goal also of striking emotional chords in the viewer. The most important champion of this strict *formalism*—an emphasis on an artwork's visual elements rather than its subject—was the American art critic Clement Greenberg (1909–1994), who wielded considerable influence from the 1940s through the 1970s. Greenberg helped redefine the parameters of modernism by advocating the rejection of illusionism and the exploration of the properties of each artistic medium.

1 ft.

30-5 ARSHILE GORKY, *Garden in Sochi*, ca. 1943. Oil on canvas, 2' 7" × 3' 3". Museum of Modern Art, New York (acquired through the Lillie P. Bliss Bequest).

Gorky's paintings of the 1940s, which still incorporate recognizable forms, are the bridge between the Biomorphic Surrealist canvases of Miró and the Abstract Expressionist paintings of Pollock.

WRITTEN SOURCES
Greenbergian Formalism

Clement Greenberg, the most important critic of modern art in the postwar period, modified his complex ideas about art over the years, but consistently expounded certain basic concepts. He argued, for example, that Abstract Expressionism was no different than more traditional modes of painting in the sense that "abstract art like every other cultural phenomenon reflects the social and other circumstances of the age in which its creators live."* Greenberg championed abstract art because he believed that it represented purity in art: "Purity in art consists in the acceptance, willing acceptance, of the limitations of the medium of the specific art. . . . The purely plastic or abstract qualities of the work of art are the only ones that count."† In other words, Greenberg thought that artists should strive for a more explicit focus on the properties exclusive to each medium—for example, two-dimensionality or flatness in painting, and three-dimensionality in sculpture:

> [T]he unique and proper area of competence of each art coincide[s] with all that [is] unique to the nature of its medium.‡

> It follows that a modernist work of art must try, in principle, to avoid communication with any order of experience not inherent in the most literally and essentially construed nature of its medium. Among other things, this means renouncing illusion and explicit subject matter. The arts are to achieve concreteness, "purity," by

dealing solely with their respective selves—that is, by becoming "abstract" or nonfigurative.§

The Abstract Expressionists turned inward to create, and the resulting works convey a rough spontaneity and palpable energy. The New York School painters—Jackson Pollock (FIGS. 30-6 and 30-7), Mark Rothko (FIG. 30-11), and others—wanted the viewer to grasp the content of their art intuitively, in a mental state free from structured thinking. Rothko himself explained:

> We assert man's absolute emotions. We don't need props or legends. We create images whose realities are self evident. Free ourselves from memory, association, nostalgia, legend, myth. Instead of making cathedrals out of Christ, man or life, we make it out of ourselves, out of our own feelings. The image we produce is understood by anyone who looks at it without nostalgic glasses of history.**

*Clement Greenberg, "Toward a Newer Laocoon," *Partisan Review* 7, no. 4 (July–August 1940): 296.

†Ibid., 305.

‡Clement Greenberg, "Sculpture in Our Time," *Arts Magazine* 32, no. 9 (June 1956): 22.

§Clement Greenberg, "Modernist Painting," *Art & Literature* 4 (Spring 1965): 195.

**Marcus Rothko and Adolph Gottlieb, quoted in Edward Alden Jewell, "The Realm of Art: A New Platform and Other Matters: 'Globalism' Pops into View," *New York Times*, June 13, 1943, 9.

30-6 JACKSON POLLOCK, *Number 1, 1950* (*Lavender Mist*), 1950. Oil, enamel, and aluminum paint on canvas, 7' 3" × 9' 10". National Gallery of Art, Washington, D.C. (Ailsa Mellon Bruce Fund).

Pollock's paintings are pure abstractions that emphasize the creative process. His mural-size canvases consist of rhythmic drips, splatters, and dribbles of paint that draw viewers into a lacy spider web.

So dominant was Greenberg that scholars often refer to the general modernist tenets during this period as Greenbergian formalism (see "Greenbergian Formalism," above).

The Abstract Expressionist movement developed along two lines—*gestural abstraction* and *chromatic abstraction*. The gestural abstractionists relied on the expressiveness of energetically applied pigment. In contrast, the chromatic abstractionists focused on color's emotional resonance.

JACKSON POLLOCK The artist whose work best exemplifies gestural abstraction is JACKSON POLLOCK (1912–1956), who developed his signature style in the mid-1940s. By 1950, Pollock had refined his technique and was producing large-scale abstract paintings such as *Number 1, 1950* (*Lavender Mist*; FIG. **30-6**), which consist of rhythmic drips, splatters, and dribbles of paint. The mural-sized fields of energetic skeins of pigment envelop viewers, drawing them into a lacy spider web. Using sticks or brushes, Pollock flung, poured, and

ARTISTS ON ART
Jackson Pollock on Easel and Mural Painting

Jackson Pollock's canvases (FIG. 30-6) constitute a revolution in the art of painting, not only because of their purely abstract form but also in the artist's rejection of the centuries-old tradition of applying pigment to stretched canvases supported vertically on an easel. In two statements Pollock made in 1947, one as part of his application for a Guggenheim Fellowship and one in a published essay, the artist explained the motivations for his new kind of "action painting" and described the tools he used and the way he produced his monumental canvases (FIG. 30-7).

> I intend to paint large movable pictures which will function between the easel and mural. . . . I believe the easel picture to be a dying form, and the tendency of modern feeling is towards the wall picture or mural.*
>
> My painting does not come from the easel. I hardly ever stretch my canvas before painting. I prefer to tack the unstretched canvas to the hard wall or the floor. I need the resistance of a hard surface. On the floor I am more at ease. I feel nearer, more a part of the painting, since this way I can walk around it, work from the four sides and literally be *in* the painting. This is akin to the method of the Indian sand painters of the West [see page 1093]. I continue to get further away from the usual painter's tools such as easel, palette, brushes, etc. I prefer sticks, trowels, knives and dripping fluid paint or a heavy impasto with sand, broken glass and other foreign matter added. When I am *in* my painting, I'm not aware of what I'm doing. . . . [T]he painting has a life of its own. I try to let it come through. . . . The source of my painting is the unconscious.†

Indeed, art historians have linked Pollock's ideas about improvisation in the creative process to his interest in what psychiatrist Carl Jung called the collective unconscious. The improvisational nature of Pollock's work and his reliance on the subconscious also have parallels in the "psychic automatism" of Surrealism and the work of Vassily Kandinsky (FIG. 29-7), whom critics described as an Abstract Expressionist as early as 1919. In addition to Pollock's unique working methods and the expansive scale of his canvases, the lack of a well-defined compositional focus in his paintings significantly departed from conventional easel painting.

30-7 HANS NAMUTH, *Jackson Pollock painting in his studio in Springs, Long Island, New York,* 1950. Gelatin silver print, 8" × 10". Center for Creative Photography, University of Arizona, Tucson.

"Gestural abstraction" nicely describes Pollock's working technique. Using sticks or brushes, he flung, poured, and dripped paint onto a section of canvas that he simply unrolled across his studio floor.

*Quoted in Francis V. O'Connor, *Jackson Pollock* (New York: Museum of Modern Art, 1967), 39.
†Ibid., 39-40.

dripped paint (not only traditional oil paints but aluminum paints and household enamels as well) onto a section of canvas that he simply unrolled across his studio floor (see "Jackson Pollock on Easel and Mural Painting," above, and FIG. 30-7). This working method earned Pollock the derisive nickname "Jack the Dripper." Responding to the image as it developed, he created art that was spontaneous yet choreographed. Pollock's painting technique highlights the most significant aspect of gestural abstraction—its emphasis on the creative process. Indeed, Pollock literally immersed himself in the painting during its creation.

LEE KRASNER A towering figure in 20th-century art, Pollock tragically died in a car accident at age 44, cutting short the development of his innovative artistic vision. Surviving him was his wife, LEE KRASNER (1908–1984), whom art historians recognize as a major Abstract Expressionist painter (FIG. 30-7A), although overshadowed by Pollock during her lifetime.

30-7A KRASNER, *The Seasons,* 1957.

WILLEM DE KOONING Despite the public's skepticism about Pollock's art, other artists enthusiastically pursued similar avenues of expression. Dutch-born WILLEM DE KOONING (1904–1997) also developed a gestural abstractionist style. Even images such as *Woman I* (FIG. **30-8**), although rooted in figuration, display the sweeping gestural brushstrokes and energetic application of pigment typical of gestural abstraction. Out of the jumbled array of slashing lines and agitated patches of color appears a ferocious-looking woman with staring eyes and ponderous breasts. Her toothy smile, inspired by an ad for Camel cigarettes, seems to devolve into a grimace. Female models on advertising billboards partly inspired *Woman I* and de Kooning's other paintings of women. However, he did not consider the figures to be pictures of individual women but images of fertility goddesses or a satiric inversion of the traditional image of Venus, the goddess of love.

Process was important to de Kooning, as it was to Pollock. Continually working on *Woman I* for almost two years, de Kooning painted an image and then scraped it away the next day and began anew. His wife, Elaine, also an accomplished painter, estimated that he painted approximately 200 scraped-away images of women on this canvas before settling on the final one.

In addition to his *Woman* series, de Kooning created nonrepresentational works dominated by huge swaths and splashes of pigment. The images suggest rawness and intensity. His dealer, Sidney Janis (1896–1989), confirmed this impression, recalling that de Kooning occasionally brought him paintings with ragged holes in them, the result of overly vigorous painting. Like Pollock, de Kooning was very much "in" his paintings. Vigorous physical interaction between the painter and the canvas led the critic Harold Rosenberg (1906–1978) to describe the work of the New York School as *action painting*. In his influential 1952 article, "The American Action Painters," Rosenberg described the attempts of Pollock, de Kooning, and others to get "inside the canvas," although he did not name any individual painters in his essay.

> At a certain moment the canvas began to appear to one American painter after another as an arena in which to act—rather than as a space in which to reproduce, redesign, analyze or "express" an object, actual or imagined. What was to go on the canvas was not a picture but an event. The painter no longer approached his easel with an image in his mind; he went up to it with material in his hand to do something to that other piece of material in front of him. The image would be the result of this encounter.... With traditional aesthetic references discarded as irrelevant, what gives the canvas its meaning is ... the way the artist organizes his emotional and intellectual energy as if he were in a living situation. The interest lies in the kind of act taking place in the four-sided arena, a dramatic interest. Criticism must begin by recognizing in the painting the assumptions inherent in its mode of creation. Since the painter has become an actor, the spectator has to think in a vocabulary of action.[2]

JOAN MITCHELL Critics and the public at large regarded action painting as a violent, heroic, and distinctly masculine art form, but some of the most prominent Abstract Expressionists were women,

1 ft.

30-8 WILLEM DE KOONING, *Woman I*, 1950–1952. Oil on canvas, 6' 3⅞" × 4' 10". Museum of Modern Art, New York.

Although rooted in figuration, including pictures of female models on advertising billboards, de Kooning's *Woman I* displays the energetic application of pigment typical of gestural abstraction.

1 in.

30-9 JOAN MITCHELL, *Untitled*, ca. 1955. Oil on canvas, 1' 5" × 1' 4". Butler Institute of American Art, Youngstown (gift of Marilynn Meeker, 1986).

Influenced by de Kooning and Kline, Mitchell's abstract paintings of the 1950s feature asymmetrical compositions of broad intersecting bands of bright color mixed with narrower curving strokes.

notably Lee Krasner (FIG. 30-7A), Helen Frankenthaler (FIG. 30-14), and JOAN MITCHELL (1925–1992). Mitchell enjoyed a privileged childhood in a wealthy and socially prominent Chicago family. She attended Smith College and the Art Institute of Chicago before moving to New York City in 1947 and the next year to France, returning to New York in 1949, where she took up in earnest her career as a painter. She returned to France often between 1955 and 1959 and painted there exclusively from 1959 on. Gorky (FIG. 30-5) and de Kooning (FIG. 30-8) were major influences on her early work—for example, the painting illustrated here (FIG. 30-9), one of Mitchell's characteristically untitled canvases. It features the energetic application of pigment seen in the work of other gestural abstractionists, including broad intersecting bands of red, black, and white, mixed with shorter, narrower, curving brushstrokes that fill almost the entire surface of the canvas. In contrast to the central placement of the main motif in most works in the Western tradition, both figural and abstract, this composition's focus of attention is off-center at the upper left.

Once, when asked to define her style and technique, Mitchell responded:

> Abstract is not a style. I simply want to make a surface work. This is just a use of space and form: it's an ambivalence of forms and space. Style in painting has to do with labels. Lots of painters are obsessed with inventing something. When I was young, it never occurred to me to invent. All I wanted to do was paint.[3]

30-9A KLINE, *Mahoning*, 1956.

Among the other prominent New York School Abstract Expressionists were Pennsylvania-born FRANZ KLINE (1910–1962), whose predominantly black-and-white paintings (FIG. 30-9A) resemble Chinese and Japanese calligraphy, and ROBERT MOTHERWELL

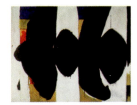

30-9B MOTHERWELL, *Elegy to Spanish Republic*, 1953–1954.

(1915–1991), best known for his series of paintings inspired by the Spanish civil war (FIG. 30-9B). In the 1970s and later, a new generation of artists, including SUSAN ROTHENBERG (b. 1945; FIG. 30-9C), reinvigorated Abstract Expressionism in a movement that art historians have dubbed *Neo-Expressionism* (see page 1012).

30-9C ROTHENBERG, *Tattoo*, 1979.

BARNETT NEWMAN In contrast to the aggressively energetic images of the gestural abstractionists, the paintings produced by the chromatic abstractionists exude a quieter aesthetic, exemplified by the work of Barnett Newman and Mark Rothko. The emotional resonance of their canvases derives from their eloquent use of color. In his early paintings, New York native BARNETT NEWMAN (1905–1970) presented organic abstractions inspired by his study of biology and his fascination with Native American art. He soon simplified his compositions so that each canvas—for example, the enormous Latin-titled *Vir Heroicus Sublimis* (*Sublime Heroic Man*; FIG. 30-10)—consists of a single slightly modulated color field split by narrow bands that the artist called "zips," which run from one edge of the painting to the other. As Newman explained it, "The streak was always going through an atmosphere; I kept trying to create a world around it."[4] He did not intend the viewer to perceive the zips as specific entities, separate from the ground, but as accents or interruptions energizing the large color fields and giving them scale. By simplifying his compositions, Newman increased color's capacity to communicate and to express his feelings about the tragic condition of modern life and the human struggle to survive. He claimed that "the artist's problem . . . [is] the

30-10 BARNETT NEWMAN, *Vir Heroicus Sublimis* (*Sublime Heroic Man*), 1950–1951. Oil on canvas, 7' 11$\frac{3}{8}$" × 17' 9$\frac{1}{4}$". Museum of Modern Art, New York (gift of Mr. and Mrs. Ben Heller).

Newman's canvases consist of a single slightly modulated color field split by "zips" (narrow bands) running from one edge of the painting to the other, energizing the color field and giving it scale.

idea-complex that makes contact with mystery—of life, of men, of nature, of the hard black chaos that is death, or the grayer, softer chaos that is tragedy."[5] Confronted by one of Newman's grandiose colored canvases, viewers truly feel as if they are in the presence of the epic.

MARK ROTHKO The work of MARK ROTHKO (1903–1970) also deals with universal themes. Born in Russia, Rothko moved with his family to the United States when he was 10. His early paintings were figural, but he soon came to believe that references to anything specific in the physical world conflicted with the sublime idea of the universal, supernatural "spirit of myth," which he saw as the core of meaning in art. In a statement cowritten with Newman and artist Adolph Gottlieb (1903–1974), Rothko expressed his beliefs about art:

> We favor the simple expression of the complex thought. We are for the large shape because it has the impact of the unequivocal. . . . We assert that . . . only that subject matter is valid which is tragic and timeless. That is why we profess spiritual kinship with primitive and archaic art.[6]

Rothko's paintings became compositionally simple, and he increasingly focused on color as the primary conveyor of meaning. In works such as *No. 14* (FIG. **30-11**), Rothko created compelling visual experiences by confining his compositions to two or three large rectangles of pure color with hazy edges. The forms seem to float on the canvas surface, hovering in front of a colored background. Rothko often displayed his paintings in rows so that the several canvases together presented shimmering veils of intensely luminous colors. Although the color juxtapositions are visually captivating, Rothko intended them as more than decorative. He saw color as a doorway to another reality, and insisted that color could express "basic human emotions—tragedy, ecstasy, doom. . . . The people who weep before my pictures are having the same religious experience I had when I painted them. And if you, as you say, are moved only by their color relationships, then you miss the point."[7] Like the other Abstract Expressionists, Rothko produced highly evocative paintings reliant on formal elements rather than on specific representational content to elicit emotional responses in the viewer.

Post-Painterly Abstraction

Post-Painterly Abstraction, another postwar American art movement, developed out of Abstract Expressionism. Indeed, many of the artists associated with Post-Painterly Abstraction produced Abstract Expressionist work early in their careers. Yet Post-Painterly Abstraction, a term coined by Clement Greenberg, manifests a sensibility radically different from Abstract Expressionism. Whereas Abstract Expressionism conveys a feeling of intense passion, Post-Painterly Abstraction is characterized by a cool, detached rationality emphasizing tighter pictorial control. Greenberg saw this art as contrasting with "painterly" art, characterized by loose, visible pigment application. Evidence of the artist's hand, so prominent in gestural abstraction, is conspicuously absent in Post-Painterly Abstraction. Greenberg championed this art form because it embodied his idea of purity in art.

ELLSWORTH KELLY Attempting to arrive at pure painting, the Post-Painterly Abstractionists distilled painting down to its essential elements, producing spare, elemental images. A key figure in the Post-Painterly Abstraction movement is ELLSWORTH KELLY (b.

30-11 MARK ROTHKO, *No. 14,* 1960. Oil on canvas, 9' 6" × 8' 9". San Francisco Museum of Modern Art, San Francisco (Helen Crocker Russell Fund Purchase).

Rothko's chromatic abstractionist paintings—consisting of hazy rectangles of pure color hovering in front of a colored background—are compositionally simple but compelling visual experiences.

1923). Born in Newburgh on the Hudson River north of New York City, Kelly studied at the Pratt Institute in Brooklyn, at the School of the Museum of Fine Arts in Boston, and at the École des Beaux-Arts in Paris. Kelly's independence from any formal school was influenced by his experiences in France between 1948 and 1954. With its razor-sharp edges and clearly delineated simple abstract shapes, Red Blue Green (FIG. **30-12**) is a characteristic example of his work from the 1960s. Since the beginning of his career, Kelly's emphasis on pure form and color and his impulse to suppress gesture in favor of creating spatial unity have played a pivotal role in the development of abstract art in America.

FRANK STELLA Another artist associated with the movement of the 1960s is Massachusetts-born FRANK STELLA (b. 1936), the leading Post-Painterly Abstraction exponent of hard-edge painting. Stella studied history at Princeton University and moved to New York City in 1958, but did not favor the rough, expressive brushwork of the Abstract Expressionists. In works such as *Mas o Menos* (*More or Less;* FIG. **30-13**), Stella eliminated many of the variables associated with painting. His simplified images of thin, evenly spaced pinstripes on colored grounds have no central focus, no painterly or expressive elements, only limited surface modulation, and no tactile quality. His systematic painting illustrates Greenberg's insistence on purity in art. The artist's own famous comment on his work, "What you see is what you see," reinforces the notions that painters interested in producing advanced art must reduce their work to its essential elements and that the viewer must acknowledge that a painting is simply pigment on a flat surface.

30-12 **ELLSWORTH KELLY**, *Red Blue Green*, 1963. Oil on canvas, 6' 11⅝" × 11' 3⅞". Museum of Contemporary Art, San Diego (gift of Dr. and Mrs. Jack M. Farris).

Suppressing gesture in favor of spatial unity, Kelly distills painting to its essential elements emphasizing pure line, form, and color.

30-13 **FRANK STELLA**, *Mas o Menos* (*More or Less*), 1964. Metallic powder in acrylic emulsion on canvas, 9' 10" × 13' 8½". Musée National d'Art Moderne, Centre Georges Pompidou, Paris (purchase 1983 with participation of Scaler Foundation).

In his hard-edge paintings, Stella tried to achieve purity in painting using evenly spaced pinstripes on colored grounds. His canvases have no central focus, no painterly or expressive elements, and no tactile quality.

Helen Frankenthaler on Color-Field Painting

Helen Frankenthaler, the daughter of a New York State Supreme Court justice, began her study of art at the Dalton School in New York City under Rufino Tamayo (FIG. 29-75A). She painted in New York for virtually her entire career, and in 1958 married fellow abstract painter Robert Motherwell (FIG. 30-9B). In 1965, the art critic Henry Geldzahler (1935–1994) interviewed Frankenthaler about her work as a color-field painter. In the following excerpt, Frankenthaler described the approach that she took to placing color on canvas in *The Bay* (FIG. 30-14) and similar abstract paintings she produced in the early 1960s, and compared her method with the way earlier modernist artists used color in their paintings.

> I will sometimes start a picture feeling "What will happen if I work with three blues and another color, and maybe more or less of the other color than the combined blues?" And very often midway through the picture I have to change the basis of the experience. Or I add and add to the canvas. And if it's over-worked and beyond help I throw it away. I used to try to work from a given, made shape. But I'm less involved now with the shape as such. . . . When you first saw a Cubist or Impressionist picture there was a whole way of instructing the eye or the subconscious. Dabs of color had to stand for real things; it was an abstraction of a guitar or a hillside. The opposite is going on now. If you have bands of blue, green, and pink, the mind doesn't think sky, grass, and flesh. These are colors and the question is what are they doing with themselves and with each other. Sentiment and nuance are being squeezed out so that if something is not altogether flatly painted then there might be a hint of edge, chiaroscuro, shadow and if one wants just that pure thing these associations get in the way.*

Frankenthaler's "unsentimental" abstract canvases are very different from Matisse's emotive Fauve representations of recognizable

30-14 HELEN FRANKENTHALER, *The Bay*, 1963. Acrylic on canvas, $6' 8\frac{7}{8}'' \times 6' 9\frac{7}{8}''$. Detroit Institute of Arts, Detroit.

Frankenthaler and other color-field painters poured paint onto plain canvas, allowing the pigments to soak into the fabric. Their works underscore that a painting is simply pigment on a flat surface.

figures, objects, and places, but her comments on a painter's struggle to find the right combination of colors without regard to colors in nature echo those of Matisse almost 60 years before (see "Henri Matisse on Color," page 884).

*Henry Geldzahler, "Interview with Helen Frankenthaler," *Artforum* 4, no. 2 (October 1965): 36–38.

HELEN FRANKENTHALER *Color-field painting,* another variant of Post-Painterly Abstraction, also emphasized painting's basic properties. However, rather than produce sharp, unmodulated shapes as the hard-edge artists had done, the color-field painters poured diluted paint onto plain canvas and allowed the pigments to soak in. It is hard to conceive of another painting method resulting in such literal flatness. The images created, such as *The Bay* (FIG. 30-14) by HELEN FRANKENTHALER (1928–2011), appear spontaneous and almost accidental (see "Helen Frankenthaler on Color-Field Painting," above). These works differ from those by Rothko and Newman in that Frankenthaler subordinated the emotional component, so integral to Abstract Expressionism, in favor of resolving formal problems.

MORRIS LOUIS Baltimore native MORRIS LOUIS (1912–1962), who spent most of his career in Washington, D.C., also became a champion of color-field painting. Clement Greenberg, an admirer of Frankenthaler's paintings, took Louis to her studio, where she introduced him to the possibilities presented by the staining technique.

Louis used this method of pouring diluted paint onto the surface of unprimed canvas in several series of paintings. *Saraband* (FIG. 30-15) is one of the works in Louis's *Veils* series. By holding up the canvas edges and pouring diluted acrylic resin, Louis created billowy, fluid, transparent shapes running down the length of the canvas. Like Frankenthaler, Louis reduced painting to the concrete fact of the paint-impregnated material.

CLYFFORD STILL Although not a member of the New York School, another American painter whose work art historians usually classify as Post-Painterly Abstraction was CLYFFORD STILL (1904–1980), whom Clement Greenberg held in very high esteem. Born in North Dakota, Still spent most of his career on the West Coast or in Maryland. He is best known for the large series of canvases that he titled simply with their dates, underscoring his rejection of the very notion that the purpose of art is to represent places, people, or objects. Nonetheless, Still's paintings remind many viewers of vast landscapes seen from the air, even though the artist's canvases make no reference to any forms in nature. His paintings, for example,

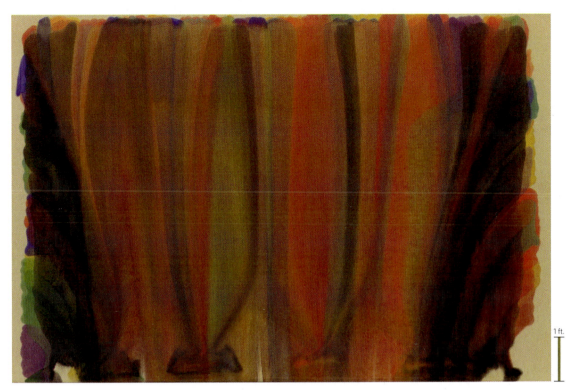

30-15 MORRIS LOUIS, *Saraband*, 1959. Acrylic resin on canvas, 8' 5 1/8" × 12' 5". Solomon R. Guggenheim Foundation, New York.

Louis created his color-field paintings by holding up the canvas edges and pouring diluted acrylic resin to produce billowy, fluid, transparent shapes running down the length of the fabric.

1 ft.

1948-C (FIG. I-2), are pure exercises in the expressive use of color, shape, and texture. Said Greenberg of Still's work: "Clifford Still . . . is one of the great innovators of modernist art . . . The picture no longer divided itself into shapes or even patches, but into zones and areas and fields of color."[8]

Op Art

A major artistic movement of the 1960s was *Op Art* (short for Optical Art), in which painters sought to produce optical illusions of motion and depth using only geometric forms on two-dimensional surfaces. Among the primary sources of the movement was the work of Josef Albers, whose series of paintings called *Homage to the Square* (FIG. I-11) explored the optical effects of placing different colors next to each other. Ultimately, Op Art can be traced to 19th-century theories of color perception and the pointillism of Georges Seurat (see "Pointillism and 19th-Century Color Theory," page 855, and FIGS. 28-16 and 28-17).

BRIDGET RILEY The artist whose name is synonymous with Op Art is the British artist BRIDGET RILEY (b. 1931), who painted in a neo-pointillist manner in the 1950s before developing her signature black-and-white Op Art style. Her paintings—for example, *Fission* (FIG. **30-16**) of 1963—came to the public's attention after being featured in the December 1964 issue of *Life* magazine. The publicity unleashed a craze for Op Art designs in clothing. In 1965, the exhibition *The Responsive Eye* at the Museum of Modern Art, which also featured paintings by Ellsworth Kelly and Morris Louis, among others, bestowed an official stamp of approval on the movement.

In *Fission,* Riley filled the canvas with black dots of varied sizes and shapes, creating the illusion of a pulsating surface that caves in at the center (hence the painting's title). The effect on the viewer of Op Art paintings such as *Fission* is disorienting and sometimes disturbing, and some works can even induce motion sickness. Thoroughly modernist is the Op artist's insistence that a painting

is a two-dimensional surface covered with pigment and not a representation of any person, object, or place. Nonetheless, the Op Art movement embraced the Renaissance notion that the painter can create the illusion of depth through perspective.

1 ft.

30-16 BRIDGET RILEY, *Fission*, 1963. Tempera on composition board, 2' 11" × 2' 10". Museum of Modern Art, New York (gift of Philip Johnson).

Op Art paintings create the illusion of motion and depth using only geometric forms. The effect can be disorienting. The pattern of black dots in Riley's *Fission* appears to cave in at the center.

ARTISTS ON ART
David Smith on Outdoor Sculpture

From ancient times, sculptors have frequently created statues for display in the open air, whether a portrait of a Roman emperor in a forum or Michelangelo's *David* (FIG. 22-13) in Florence's Piazza della Signoria. But rarely have sculptors taken into consideration the effects of sunlight in the conception of their works. American sculptor David Smith was an exception.

Smith learned to weld in an automobile plant in 1925 and later applied to his art the technical expertise in handling metals that he gained there. In addition, working on industrial-scale projects helped him visualize the possibilities for large-scale metal sculpture. Nonetheless, his works—for example, *Cubi XII* (FIG. 30-17)—differ from machine-made parts in important ways. Smith usually added gestural elements reminiscent of Abstract Expressionism by burnishing the metal with steel wool, producing swirling, random-looking patterns that draw attention to the two-dimensionality of the sculptural surface. This treatment, which captures the light hitting the artwork, activates the surface and imparts a texture to his pieces, a key element of all of his sculptures, which he designed for display outdoors. Indeed, the *Cubi* lose much of their character in the sterile lighting of a museum.

> I like outdoor sculpture and the most practical thing for outdoor sculpture is stainless steel, and I make them and I polish them in such a way that on a dull day, they take on the dull blue, or the color of the sky in the late afternoon sun, the glow, golden like the rays, the colors of nature. And in a particular sense, I have used atmosphere in a reflective way on the surfaces. They are colored by the sky and the surroundings, the green or blue of water. Some are down by the water and some are by the mountains. They reflect the colors. They are designed for the outdoors.*

*Quoted in Cleve Gray, ed., *David Smith by David Smith* (New York: Holt, Rinehart, and Winston, 1968), 133.

30-17 DAVID SMITH, *Cubi XII*, 1963. Stainless steel, 9' 1⅝" high. Hirshhorn Museum and Sculpture Garden, Smithsonian Institution, Washington, D.C. (gift of the Joseph H. Hirshhorn Foundation, 1972). Art © Estate of David Smith/Licensed by VAGA, New York, NY.

David Smith designed his abstract metal sculptures of simple geometric forms to reflect the natural light and color of their outdoor settings, not the sterile illumination of a museum gallery.

1 ft.

Abstraction in Sculpture

Painters were not the only artists interested in Clement Greenberg's formalist ideas (see "Greenbergian Formalism," page 954). American sculptors also strove to arrive at purity in their medium. While painters worked to emphasize flatness, sculptors, understandably, chose to focus on three-dimensionality as the essential characteristic and inherent limitation of the sculptural medium.

DAVID SMITH After experimenting with a variety of sculptural styles and materials, Indiana-born and Ohio-raised DAVID SMITH (1906–1965) produced metal sculptures that have affinities with the Abstract Expressionist movement in painting. In the 1960s, he produced a series of large-scale works called *Cubi* that he created to be seen in the open air (see "David Smith on Outdoor Sculpture," above). *Cubi XII* (FIG. 30-17), a characteristic example, consists of simple geometric forms—cubes and rectangular bars. Made of stainless-steel sections piled on top of one another, often at unstable angles, and then welded together, the *Cubi* sculptures make a striking visual statement.

TONY SMITH A predominantly sculptural movement that emerged in the 1960s among artists seeking Greenbergian purity of form was *Minimalism.* One of the leading Minimalist sculptors was New Jersey native TONY SMITH (1912–1980), who created simple volumetric sculptures such as *Die* (FIG. 30-18). Minimalist artworks generally lack identifiable subjects, colors, surface textures, and narrative elements, and are perhaps best described simply as three-dimensional objects. By rejecting illusionism and reducing sculpture to basic geometric forms, Smith and other Minimalists emphatically emphasized their art's "objecthood" and concrete tangibility. In so doing, they reduced experience to its most fundamental level, preventing viewers from drawing on assumptions or preconceptions when dealing with the art before them.

DONALD JUDD Another important Minimalist sculptor was DONALD JUDD (1928–1994), who embraced a spare, universal aesthetic corresponding to the core tenets of the movement. Born in Missouri, Judd studied philosophy and art history at Columbia University in New York City, where he produced most of his major works. Judd's determination to arrive at a visual vocabulary devoid of deception or ambiguity propelled him away from representation and toward precise and simple sculpture. For Judd, a work's power derived from its character as a whole and from the specificity of its materials (see "Donald Judd on Sculpture and Industrial Materials," page 963). *Untitled* (FIG. 30-19) presents basic geometric boxes constructed of brass and red Plexiglas, undisguised by paint or

30-18 Tony Smith, *Die*, 1962. Steel, 6' × 6' × 6'. Museum of Modern Art, New York (gift of Jane Smith in honor of Agnes Gund).

By rejecting illusionism and symbolism and reducing sculpture to basic geometric forms, Minimalist Tony Smith emphasized the "objecthood" and concrete tangibility of his sculptures.

other materials. The artist did not intend the work to be metaphorical or symbolic. It is a straightforward declaration of sculpture's objecthood. Judd used Plexiglas because its translucency enables the viewer access to the interior, thereby rendering the sculpture both open and enclosed. This aspect of the design reflects Judd's desire to banish ambiguity or falseness from his works.

Perhaps surprisingly, despite the ostensible connections between Minimalism and Greenbergian formalism, the critic did not embrace this direction in art:

> Minimal Art remains too much a feat of ideation [the mental formation of ideas], and not enough anything else. Its idea remains an idea, something deduced instead of felt and discovered. The geometrical and modular simplicity may announce and signify the artistically furthest-out, but the fact that the signals are understood for what they want to mean betrays them artistically. There is hardly any aesthetic surprise in Minimal Art. . . . Aesthetic surprise hangs on forever—it is there in Raphael as it is in Pollock—and ideas alone cannot achieve it.[9]

LOUISE NEVELSON Although Minimalism was a dominant sculptural trend in the 1960s, many sculptors, including the German artist Eva Hesse

---

ARTISTS ON ART
Donald Judd on Sculpture and Industrial Materials

In a 1965 essay titled "Specific Objects," the Minimalist sculptor Donald Judd described the advantages of sculpture over painting and the attractions of using industrial materials for his works, such as his 1969 Plexiglas sculpture characteristically called *Untitled* (FIG. 30-19).

> Three dimensions are real space. That gets rid of the problem of illusionism . . . one of the salient and most objectionable relics of European art. The several limits of painting are no longer present. A work can be as powerful as it can be thought to be. Actual space is intrinsically more powerful and specific than paint on a flat surface. . . . The use of three dimensions makes it possible to see all sorts of materials and colors. Most of [my] work involves new materials, either recent inventions or things not used before in art. Little was done until lately with the wide range of industrial products. . . . Materials vary greatly and are simply materials—formica, aluminum, cold-rolled steel, plexiglas, red and common brass, and so forth. They are specific. If they are used directly, they are more specific. Also, they are usually aggressive. There is an objectivity to the obdurate identity of a material. . . . The form of a work of art and its materials are closely related. In earlier work the structure and the imagery were executed in some neutral and homogeneous material.*

*Donald Judd, *Complete Writings 1959–1975* (New York: New York University Press, 1975), 181–189.

30-19 Donald Judd, *Untitled*, 1969. Brass and colored fluorescent Plexiglas on steel brackets, 10 units, $6\frac{1}{8}"$ × 2' × 2' 3" each, with 6" intervals. Hirshhorn Museum and Sculpture Garden, Smithsonian Institution, Washington, D.C. (gift of Joseph H. Hirshhorn, 1972). © Donald Judd Estate/Licensed by VAGA, New York, NY.

Judd's Minimalist sculpture incorporates boxes fashioned from undisguised industrial materials. The artist used Plexiglas because its translucency gives the viewer access to the work's interior.

(1936–1970; FIG. **30-19A**) and Russian-born LOUISE NEVELSON (1899–1988), pursued other styles. Nevelson created sculptures combining a sense of the architectural fragment with the power of Dada and Surrealist found objects to express her personal sense of life's underlying significance. Multiplicity of meaning was important to Nevelson. She sought "the in-between place. . . . The dawns and the dusks"[10]—the transitional realm between one state of being and another.

30-19A HESSE, *Hang-Up*, 1965.

Beginning in the late 1950s, Nevelson assembled sculptures of found wood objects and forms. She enclosed small sculptural compositions in boxes of varied sizes, and joined the boxes to one another to form "walls." She then painted the forms in a single hue—usually black, white, or gold. This monochromatic color scheme unifies the diverse parts of pieces such as *Tropical Garden II* (FIG. **30-20**) and creates a mysterious field of shapes and shadows. The structures suggest magical environments resembling the treasured secret hideaways dimly remembered from childhood. Yet the boxy frames and the precision of the manufactured found objects create a rough geometric structure that the eye roams over freely, lingering on some details, including occasional pieces of unmodified driftwood. The parts of a Nevelson sculpture and their interrelation recall the *Merz* constructions of Kurt Schwitters (FIG. 29-29). The effect is also rather like viewing the side of an apartment building from a moving elevated train or looking down on a city from the air.

LOUISE BOURGEOIS In contrast to the architectural nature of Nevelson's work, a sensuous organic quality recalling the evocative Biomorphic Surrealist forms of Joan Miró (FIG. 29-58) pervades the work of French-American artist LOUISE BOURGEOIS (1911–2010). *Cumul I* (FIG. **30-21**) is a collection of round-headed units huddled, with their heads protruding, within a collective cloak dotted with holes. The units differ in size, and their position within the group lends a distinctive personality to each. Although the shapes remain abstract, they refer strongly to human figures. Bourgeois used a wide variety of materials in her works, including wood, plaster, latex, and plastics, in addition to alabaster, marble, and bronze. She exploited each material's qualities to suit the expressiveness of the piece.

In *Cumul I,* the alternating high gloss and matte finish of the marble increases the sensuous distinction between the group of swelling forms and the soft folds swaddling them. Like Barbara Hepworth (FIG. 29-63), Bourgeois connected her sculpture with the body's multiple relationships to landscape: "[My pieces] are anthropomorphic and they are landscape also, since our body could be considered from a topographical point of view, as a land with mounds and valleys and caves and holes."[11] However, Bourgeois's sculptures are more personal and more openly sexual than Hepworth's. *Cumul I* perfectly represents the allusions Bourgeois sought: "There has always been sexual suggestiveness in my work. Sometimes I am totally concerned with female shapes—characters of breasts like clouds—but often I merge the activity—phallic breasts, male and female, active and passive."[12]

30-20 LOUISE NEVELSON, *Tropical Garden II,* 1957–1959. Wood painted black, 5' 11½" × 10' 11¾" × 1'. Musée National d'Art Moderne, Centre Georges Pompidou, Paris.

The monochromatic color scheme unifies the diverse sculpted forms and found objects in Nevelson's "walls" and creates a mysterious field of shapes and shadows suggesting magical environments.

1 ft.

30-21 Louise Bourgeois, *Cumul I*, 1969. Marble, 1' 10 $\frac{3}{8}$" × 4' 2" × 4'. Musée National d'Art Moderne, Centre Georges Pompidou, Paris. © Louise Bourgeois/Licensed by VAGA, New York, NY.

Bourgeois's sculptures are made up of sensuous organic forms that recall the Biomorphic Surrealist forms of Miró (FIG. 29-58). Although the shapes remain abstract, they refer strongly to human figures.

30-22 Isamu Noguchi, *Shodo Shima Stone Study,* 1978. Granite, 5' 6" × 5' 9". Walker Art Center, Minneapolis (gift of the artist, 1978).

Japanese American sculptor Noguchi here created a miniature Japanese rock garden. Two irregularly shaped pieces of granite frame a trio of egglike stones suggesting birth from a primordial nest.

ISAMU NOGUCHI Another sculptor often considered a Minimalist because of pure geometric works such as *Red Cube,* which he created for the sidewalk in front of a New York City skyscraper, is ISAMU NOGUCHI (1904–1988). His work defies easy classification, however. Although born in Los Angeles, Noguchi, the son of a Japanese poet and an American writer, spent most of his childhood in Japan. In 1926 he won a Guggenheim Fellowship to study sculpture in Paris, where he worked as an apprentice to Constantin Brancusi (FIGS. 29-61A and 29-62). During his long career, Noguchi completed a wide range of commissions in the United States, Europe, and Asia in a variety of styles ranging from the abstract *Kouros* of 1944, strongly influenced by Miró's Biomorphic Surrealism (FIG. 29-58), to the Minimalist *Red Cube* of 1968. Some of his most interesting works, however, wed the traditions of the West with those of the East, especially his designs for gardens and garden sculptures, which reflect his Japanese heritage.

A little-known work of great beauty in the last category is *Shodo Shima Stone Study* (FIG. 30-22), a miniature version of a Japanese garden in which two roughly shaped pieces of granite form a rectangular frame for a trio of egglike granite stones. Shodo Shima (Magical Island) is an island off the coast of Japan and the source of the stone that Noguchi used for this work. In form it recalls the design of Zen Buddhist gardens (FIG. 34-2) and a bird's nest. Noguchi observed: "In Japan the rocks in a garden are so planted as to suggest a protuberance from the primordial mass below. Every rock gains enormous weight, and that is why the whole garden may be said to be a sculpture, whose roots are joined way below."[13] The "eggs" in Noguchi's miniature rock garden in the Walker Art Center suggest a birth out of a primordial nest.

Pop Art

Despite their differences, the Abstract Expressionists, Post-Painterly Abstractionists, Op Art painters, and Minimalist sculptors all adopted an artistic vocabulary of pure abstraction. Other artists, however, observing that the insular and introspective attitude of the avant-garde had alienated the public, sought to harness the communicative power of art to reach a wide audience. Thus was born the art movement that came to be known as Pop. Art historians trace the roots of *Pop Art* to the young British artists, architects, and writers who formed the Independent Group at the Institute of Contemporary Art in London in 1952. They sought to initiate fresh thinking in art, in part by sharing their fascination with the aesthetics and content of such facets of popular culture as advertising, comic books, and movies (see "Pop Art and Consumer Culture," page 966). In 1956, an Independent Group member, RICHARD HAMILTON (1922–2011), made

ART AND SOCIETY
Pop Art and Consumer Culture

Although the acceptance of pure abstraction as an artistic mode had gained significant momentum in the decades after the end of World War II, many artists, as well as the general public, reacted against pure formalism in painting and sculpture. In the 1950s and 1960s, the artists of the *Pop Art* movement reintroduced all the devices that the postwar abstractionists had purged from their artworks. Pop artists revived the tools traditionally used to convey meaning in art, such as signs, symbols, metaphors, allusions, illusions, and figural imagery. They not only embraced representation but also firmly grounded their art in the consumer culture and mass media of the postwar period, thereby making it much more accessible and understandable to the average person. Indeed, the name "Pop Art"—credited to the British art critic Lawrence Alloway (1926–1990)—is short for "popular art" and referred to the popular mass culture and familiar imagery of the contemporary urban environment, such as the collection of everyday objects, advertisements, and celebrity photographs featured in Richard Hamilton's collage *Just What Is It That Makes Today's Homes So Different, So Appealing?* (FIG. 30-23).

The fantasy interior in Hamilton's collage reflects the values of mid-20th-century consumer culture through figures and objects cut from glossy magazines. *Just What Is It?* includes references to mass media (the television, the theater marquee outside the window, the newspaper), to advertising (Hoover vacuum cleaners, Ford cars, Armour hams, Tootsie Pops), and to popular culture (the "girlie magazine," the body builder Charles Atlas, romance comic books). Artworks

of this sort stimulated viewers' wide-ranging speculation about society's values. This kind of intellectual toying with mass-media meaning and imagery typified Pop Art both in Europe and America.

Alloway eloquently described the intellectual basis of Pop Art in a 1958 essay:

> The definition of culture is changing as the result of the pressure of the great audience . . . [I]t is no longer sufficient to define culture solely as something that a minority guards for the few and the future . . . Our definition of culture is being stretched beyond the fine art limits imposed on it by Renaissance theory, and refers now, increasingly, to the whole complex of human activities. Within this definition, rejection of the mass produced arts is not, as critics think, a defense of culture but an attack on it.*

*Lawrence Alloway, "The Arts and the Mass Media," *Architectural Design* (February 1958): 34–35.

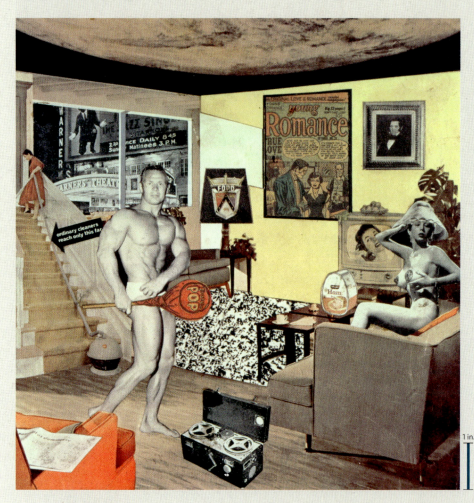

30-23 Richard Hamilton, *Just What Is It That Makes Today's Homes So Different, So Appealing?* 1956. Collage, $10\frac{1}{4}'' \times 9\frac{3}{4}''$. Kunsthalle Tübingen, Tübingen.

The fantasy interior in Hamilton's collage of figures and objects cut from glossy magazines reflects the values of modern consumer culture. Toying with mass-media imagery typifies British Pop Art.

---

a small collage, *Just What Is It That Makes Today's Homes So Different, So Appealing?* (FIG. **30-23**), which exemplifies British Pop Art. Trained as an engineering draftsman, exhibition designer, and painter, Hamilton studied the way that advertising shapes public attitudes. Long intrigued by Marcel Duchamp's ideas (see page 902), Hamilton consistently combined elements of popular art and fine art, seeing both as belonging to the whole world of visual communication. He created *Just What Is It?* for the poster and catalog of one section of an exhibition titled *This Is Tomorrow*, which included images from Hollywood cinema, science fiction, and the mass media.

JASPER JOHNS Although Pop Art originated in England, the movement found its greatest articulation and success in the United States, in large part because the more fully matured American consumer culture provided a fertile environment in which the movement flourished through the 1960s. Indeed, Independent Group members claimed that their inspiration came from Hollywood, Detroit, and New York's Madison Avenue, paying homage to America's predominance in the realms of mass media, mass production, and advertising.

One of the artists pivotal to the early development of American Pop Art was JASPER JOHNS (b. 1930), who grew up in South Carolina

30-24 JASPER JOHNS, *Three Flags,* 1958. Encaustic on canvas, 2' 6⅞" × 3' 9½". Whitney Museum of American Art, New York (50th Anniversary Gift of the Gilman Foundation, the Lauder Foundation, and A. Alfred Taubman). Art © Jasper Johns/Licensed by VAGA, New York, NY.

American Pop artist Jasper Johns wanted to draw attention to common objects that people view frequently but rarely scrutinize. He made many paintings of targets, flags, numbers, and alphabets.

dimensional objects attached to the surface. In the 1950s, Rauschenberg's assemblages usually contained an array of art reproductions, magazine and newspaper clippings, and passages painted in an Abstract Expressionist style. In the early 1960s, he adopted the commercial medium of *silk-screen printing,* first in black and white and then in color, and began filling entire canvases with appropriated news images and anonymous photographs of city scenes.

Canyon (FIG. **30-25**) is typical of Rauschenberg's combines. Pieces of printed paper and photographs cover parts of the canvas.

and moved to New York City in 1952. Johns sought to draw attention to common objects in the world—what he called things "seen but not looked at."[14] To this end, he did several series of paintings of numbers, alphabets, flags, and maps of the United States—all of which are items that people view frequently but rarely scrutinize. He created his first flag painting in 1954 at the height of the Cold War. Initially labeled a Neo-Dadaist because of the kinship of his works to Marcel Duchamp's readymades (FIG. 29-26), Johns also had strong ties to the Surrealists, especially René Magritte, whose painting of a pipe labeled "This is not a pipe" (FIG. 29-56) is conceptually a forerunner of Johns's flags—for example, *Three Flags* (FIG. **30-24**), which could easily carry the label "These are not flags." In fact, when asked why he chose the American flag as a subject, Johns replied that he had a dream in which he saw himself painting a flag. The world of dreams was central to Surrealism (see "André Breton's First Surrealist Manifesto," page 922).

In *Three Flags,* Johns painted a trio of overlapping American national banners of decreasing size, with the smallest closest to the viewer, reversing traditional perspective, which calls for diminution of size with distance. Johns drained meaning from the patriotic emblem by reducing it to a repetitive pattern—not the flag itself but three pictures of a flag in one. Nevertheless, the heritage of Abstract Expressionism is still apparent. Although Johns rejected the heroic, highly personalized application of pigment championed by the 1950s action painters, he painted his flags in *encaustic* (liquid wax and dissolved pigment; see "Encaustic Painting," page 217) mixed with newsprint on three overlapping canvases. His flags thus retain a pronounced surface texture, emphasizing that the viewer is looking at a handmade painting, not a machine-made fabric. The painting, like the flags, is an object, not an illusion of other objects.

ROBERT RAUSCHENBERG A close friend of Johns's, ROBERT RAUSCHENBERG (1925–2008) began using mass-media images in his work in the 1950s. Rauschenberg set out to create works that would be open and indeterminate, and he began by making multimedia works that he called *combines,* which intersperse painted passages with sculptural elements. Rauschenberg's combines are, in a sense, his personal variation on *assemblages,* artworks constructed from already existing objects. At times, these combines seem to be sculptures with painting incorporated into certain sections. Others seem to be paintings with three-

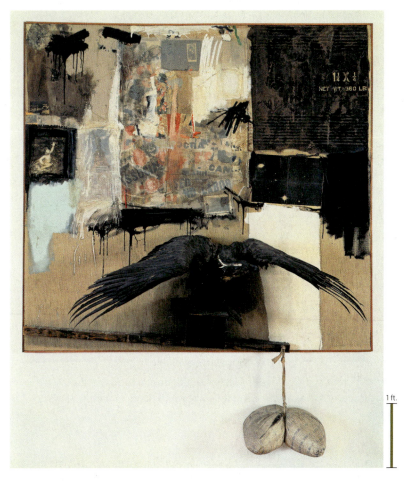

30-25 ROBERT RAUSCHENBERG, *Canyon,* 1959. Oil, pencil, paper, fabric, metal, cardboard box, printed paper, printed reproductions, photograph, wood, paint tube, and mirror on canvas, with oil on bald eagle, string, and pillow, 6' 9¾" × 5' 10" × 2'. Sonnabend Collection, New York. Art © Estate of Robert Rauschenberg/Licensed by VAGA, New York, NY.

Rauschenberg's "combines" intersperse painted passages with sculptural elements. *Canyon* incorporates pigment on canvas with pieces of printed paper, photographs, a pillow, and a stuffed eagle.

ARTISTS ON ART
Roy Lichtenstein on Pop Art and Comic Books

In November 1963, Roy Lichtenstein was one of eight painters interviewed for a profile on Pop Art in *Art News.* Gene R. Swenson posed the questions. Some of Lichtenstein's answers follow.

[Pop Art is] the use of commercial art as a subject matter in painting . . . [Pop artists portray] what I think to be the most brazen and threatening characteristics of our culture, things we hate, but which are also so powerful in their impingement on us. . . . I paint directly . . . [without] perspective or shading. It doesn't look like a painting *of* something, it looks like the thing itself. Instead of looking like a painting *of* a billboard . . . Pop art seems to be the actual thing. It is an intensification, a stylistic intensification of the excitement which the subject matter has for me; but the style is . . . cool. One of the things a cartoon does is to express violent emotion and passion in a completely mechanized and removed style. To express this thing in a painterly style would dilute it.

Everybody has called Pop Art "American" painting, but it's actually industrial painting. America was hit by industrialism and capitalism harder and sooner . . . I think the meaning of my work is that it's industrial, it's what all the world will soon become. Europe will be the same way, soon, so it won't be American; it will be universal.*

The influence of comic books is evident in Lichtenstein's mature works—for example, his 1963 painting titled *Hopeless* (FIG. 30-26). Here, Lichtenstein excerpted an image from a comic book, a form of entertainment meant to be read and discarded, and immortalized the image on a large canvas. Aside from that modification, Lichtenstein remained remarkably faithful to the original comic-strip image. His subjects were typically the melodramatic scenes that were mainstays of romance comic books popular at the time, and included "balloons" with the words that the characters speak. Lichtenstein also used the

30-26 ROY LICHTENSTEIN, *Hopeless,* 1963. Oil and synthetic polymer paint on canvas, 3' 8" × 3' 8". Kunstmuseum Basel, Basel. © Estate of Roy Lichtenstein.

Comic books appealed to Lichtenstein because they were a mainstay of popular culture, meant to be read and discarded. The Pop artist immortalized their images on large canvases.

visual vocabulary of the comic strip, with its dark black outlines and unmodulated color areas, and retained the familiar square dimensions. Moreover, by emulating the printing technique called *benday dots,* he called attention to the mass-produced derivation of the image. Named after its inventor, the newspaper printer Benjamin Day (1810–1889), the benday-dot system involves the modulation of colors through the placement and size of colored dots. Lichtenstein thus transferred the visual shorthand language of the comic book to the realm of monumental painting.

*G. R. Swenson, "What Is Pop Art? Interviews with Eight Painters," *Art News* 62, no. 7 (November 1963): 25, 64.

Much of the unevenly painted surface consists of pigment roughly applied in a manner reminiscent of de Kooning's work (FIG. 30-8). A stuffed bald eagle attached to the lower part of the combine spreads its wings as if lifting off in flight toward the viewer. Completing the combine, a pillow dangles from a string attached to a wood stick below the eagle. The artist presented the work's components in a jumbled fashion. He tilted or turned some of the images

sideways, and each overlays part of another image. The compositional confusion may resemble that of a Dada collage, but the parts of Rauschenberg's combines maintain their individuality more than those, for example, in a Schwitters piece (FIG. 29-29). The eye scans a Rauschenberg canvas much as it might survey the environment on a walk through a city. The various recognizable images and objects seem unrelated and defy a consistent reading, although Rauschenberg chose all the elements of his combines with specific meanings in mind. For example, Rauschenberg based *Canyon* on a Rembrandt painting of Jupiter in the form of an eagle carrying the boy Ganymede heavenward. The photo in the combine is a reference to the Greek boy, and the hanging bag is a visual pun on his buttocks.

ROY LICHTENSTEIN As the Pop Art movement matured, the images became more concrete and tightly controlled. ROY LICHTENSTEIN (1923–1997), who was born in Manhattan not far from Madison Avenue, the center of the American advertising industry, developed an interest in art in elementary school and as a teenager took weekend painting classes at the Parsons School of Design before enrolling at Ohio State University. He served in the army during World War II and was stationed in France, where he was able to visit the Musée du Louvre and Chartres Cathedral. In the late 1950s, however, he turned his attention to commercial art and especially to the comic book as a mainstay of American popular culture (see "Roy Lichtenstein on Pop Art and Comic Books," page 968, and FIG. **30-26**).

ANDY WARHOL The quintessential American Pop artist was ANDY WARHOL (1928–1987). An early successful career as a commercial artist and illustrator grounded Warhol in the sensibility and visual rhetoric of advertising and the mass media. This knowledge proved useful for his Pop artworks, which often depicted icons of mass-produced consumer culture, such as *Green Coca-Cola Bottles* (FIG. **30-27**), and Hollywood celebrities, such as Marilyn Monroe (1926–1962; FIG. **30-27A**). Warhol favored reassuringly familiar objects and people. He explained his attraction to the ubiquitous curved Coke bottle:

🔼 **30-27A** WARHOL, *Marilyn Diptych*, 1962.

> What's great about this country is that America started the tradition where the richest consumers buy essentially the same things as the poorest. You can be watching TV and see Coca-Cola, and you can know that the President drinks Coke, Liz Taylor drinks Coke, and just think, you can drink Coke, too. A Coke is a Coke and no amount of money can get you a better Coke.[15]

As did other Pop artists, Warhol used a visual vocabulary and a printing method that reinforced the image's connections to consumer culture. The silk-screen technique enabled Warhol to print the image endlessly (although he varied each bottle slightly). The repetition and redundancy of the Coke bottle reflect the saturation of this product in American society—in homes, at work, literally everywhere, including gas stations, as immortalized by GEORGE SEGAL (1924–2000) in 1963 (FIG. **30-27B**). So immersed was Warhol in a culture of mass production that he not only produced numerous canvases of the same image but also named his studio "the Factory."

1 ft.

30-27 ANDY WARHOL, *Green Coca-Cola Bottles,* 1962. Oil on canvas, 6' 10½" × 4' 9". Whitney Museum of American Art, New York.

Warhol was the quintessential American Pop artist. Here, he selected an icon of mass-produced consumer culture and then multiplied it, reflecting Coke's omnipresence in American society.

Art © Estate of George Segal/Licensed by VAGA, New York, NY

🔼 **30-27B** SEGAL, *Gas Station,* 1963.

JAMES ROSENQUIST Because of the close connection between Pop Art and consumer culture, many Pop artworks also incorporated social commentary. That is especially true of the work of JAMES ROSENQUIST (b. 1933). Born in Grand Forks, North Dakota, Rosenquist studied painting at the Minneapolis Art Institute and the University of Minnesota and initially supported himself by painting commercial billboards. In 1955, he moved to New York City and met several of the most innovative artists of the day, including Ellsworth Kelly, Jasper Johns, Robert Rauschenberg, and Claes Oldenburg. In addition to painting billboards in Times Square and elsewhere, Rosenquist created window displays for upscale jewelry and fashion stores Tiffany and Bonwit Teller until he established his reputation as an artist with his first (sold-out) solo exhibition in 1962.

ARTISTS ON ART

James Rosenquist on *F-111*

F-111 (FIG. 30-28) is James Rosenquist's most ambitious work. It exemplifies his singular contribution to the Pop Art movement in its grandiose scale (comparable to the billboards he painted to earn a living), its imagery drawn from America's consumer culture, and its implied social and political commentary. The F-111 was the latest technological marvel, an enormously costly fighter jet that, for Rosenquist, was emblematic of the U.S. "military-industrial complex" that produced the Vietnam War, the subject of widespread protest demonstrations at the time (1965). The gigantic aircraft fills the full length of *F-111*, but interspersed are meticulously painted motifs from daily life, including spaghetti, a lightbulb, an automobile tire, a smiling girl under a hairdryer that resembles a missile head, and an atomic explosion under a beach umbrella. Rosenquist's idea was to show the F-111, a war machine, flying through consumer society, and to suggest complicity between the two. He explained:

> [The F-111] is the newest, latest fighter-bomber . . . This first of its type cost many million dollars. People are planning their lives through work on this bomber . . . A man has a contract from the company making the bomber, and he plans his third automobile and his fifth child because he is a technician and has work for the next couple of years. Then the original idea is expanded, another thing is invented; and the plane already seems obsolete. The prime force of this thing has been to keep people working, an economic tool; but behind it, this is a war machine.

In the same interview, Rosenquist also talked about his approach to painting and about the scale of *F-111*.

> The style I use was gained by doing outdoor commercial work as hard and as fast as I could. My techniques for me are still anti-style. I have an idea what I want to do, what it will look like when I want it finished—in between is just a hell of a lot of work. When they say the Rosenquist style is very precise, maybe they just know that painting style as they know it is going out of style. . . . The *F-111* was enclosed—four walls of a room in a gallery. My idea was to make an extension of ways of showing art in a gallery, instead of showing single pictures with wall space that usually gives your eye a relief. In this picture, because it did seal up all the walls, I could set the dial and put in the stops and rests for the person's eye in the whole room instead of allowing the eye to wander and think in an empty space.*

*G. R. Swenson, "The F-111: An Interview with James Rosenquist," *Partisan Review* 32, no. 4 (Autumn 1965): 589–601.

30-28 JAMES ROSENQUIST, *F-111*, 1965. Oil on canvas and aluminum, 10' × 86'. Museum of Modern Art, New York. (Gift, by exchange, of Mr. and Mrs. Alex L. Hillman and Lillie P. Bliss Bequest.) Art © James Rosenquist/Licensed by VAGA, New York, NY.

In this billboard-like Pop Art masterpiece, Rosenquist interspersed everyday images with a fighter jet to comment on the connection between the "military-industrial complex" and the American consumer.

Rosenquist's largest and most important work is *F-111* (FIG. 30-28), a 23-panel, 10-foot-high and 86-foot-long mural-like painting designed to wrap around the four walls of the main room of the Leo Castelli Gallery in Manhattan (see "James Rosenquist on *F-111*," above).

CLAES OLDENBURG In the 1960s, CLAES OLDENBURG (b. 1929) also produced Pop artworks that incisively commented on American consumer culture, but his medium was sculpture. The son of a Swedish diplomat who moved to the United States in 1936, Oldenburg attended school in Chicago and graduated from Yale

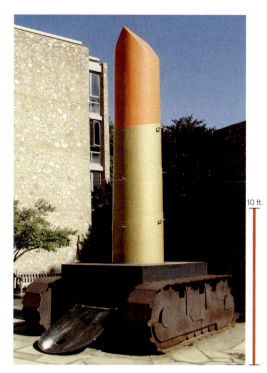

30-29 CLAES OLDENBURG, *Lipstick (Ascending) on Caterpillar Tracks*, 1969; reworked, 1974. Painted steel, aluminum, and fiberglass, 21' high. Morse College, Yale University, New Haven (gift of Colossal Keepsake Corporation).

Designed as a speaker's platform for antiwar protesters, *Lipstick* humorously combines phallic and militaristic imagery. Originally, the lipstick tip was soft red vinyl and had to be inflated.

10 ft.

NIKI DE SAINT-PHALLE Also usually classified as a Pop Art sculptor was French-born NIKI DE SAINT-PHALLE (1930–2002), because her sculptures remind many viewers of dolls and folk art. Her most famous works are the series of polyester statues of women she called "Nanas" (FIG. 30-29A), oversized, brightly colored sculptures that are feminist commentaries on popular stereotypes of female beauty.

Superrealism

Like the Pop artists, the artists associated with *Superrealism* sought a form of artistic communication more accessible to the public than the remote, unfamiliar visual language of the

30-29A SAINT-PHALLE, *Black Venus*, 1965–1967.

Abstract Expressionists, Post-Painterly Abstractionists, and Minimalists. The Superrealists expanded Pop's iconography in both painting and sculpture by making images in the late 1960s and 1970s involving scrupulous fidelity to optical fact. Because many Superrealists used photographs as sources for their imagery, art historians also refer to this postwar art movement as *Photorealism*.

AUDREY FLACK One of Superrealism's pioneers was lifelong New Yorker AUDREY FLACK (b. 1931), who studied the history of art at New York University's Institute of Fine Arts after graduating from Yale. Her paintings, such as *Marilyn* (FIG. 30-30), are not simply technical exercises in recording objects in minute detail. They are also conceptual inquiries into the nature of photography and the extent to which photography constructs an understanding of reality. Flack observed: "[Photography is] my whole life, I studied art

University in 1950. His early works consisted of plaster reliefs of food and clothing items. Oldenburg constructed these sculptures of plaster layered on chicken wire and muslin, painting them with cheap commercial house enamel. In later works, focused on the same subjects, he shifted to large-scale stuffed sculptures of sewn vinyl or canvas, many of which he exhibited in a show he titled *The Store*—an appropriate comment on the function of art as a commodity in a consumer society.

Oldenburg is best known, however, for his mammoth outdoor sculptures. In 1966, a group of graduate students at the Yale School of Architecture, calling themselves the Colossal Keepsake Corporation, raised funds for materials for a giant sculpture that Oldenburg agreed to create (in secret and without a fee) as a gift to his alma mater. The work, *Lipstick (Ascending) on Caterpillar Tracks* (FIG. 30-29), was Oldenburg's first large-scale public sculpture. He installed *Lipstick* on Ascension Day, May 15, 1969, on Beineke Plaza across from the office of the university's president, the site of many raucous protests against the Vietnam War. Oldenburg's characteristic humor emerges unmistakably in the combination of phallic and militaristic imagery, especially in the double irony of the "phallus" being a woman's cosmetic item, and the Caterpillar-type endless-loop metal tracks suggesting not a tractor-earthmover for construction work but a military tank designed for destruction in warfare. *Lipstick* was to be a speaker's platform for protesters, and originally the lipstick tip was a drooping red vinyl balloon that the speaker had to inflate, underscoring the sexual innuendo. (Oldenburg once remarked that art collectors preferred nudes, so he produced nude cars, nude telephones, and nude electric plugs to please them.)

Vandalism and exposure to the elements (the original tractor was plywood) caused so much damage to *Lipstick* that it had to be removed, and Oldenburg reconstructed it in metal and fiberglass. Yale formally accepted the controversial and unsolicited repaired gift in 1974, when the architectural historian Vincent Scully (b. 1920), then master of Yale's Morse College, offered a permanent home for *Lipstick* in the college courtyard. Oldenburg expressed mixed feelings about the recognition of what he viewed as a political statement as a "work of art."

1 ft.

30-30 AUDREY FLACK, *Marilyn*, 1977. Oil over acrylic on canvas, 8' × 8'. University of Arizona Museum, Tucson (museum purchase with funds provided by the Edward J. Gallagher Jr. Memorial Fund).

Flack's pioneering Photorealist still lifes record objects with great optical fidelity. *Marilyn* alludes to Dutch vanitas paintings (FIG. 25-21) and incorporates multiple references to the transience of life.

Chuck Close on Photorealist Portrait Painting

Chuck Close (FIG. 30-31) based his paintings of the late 1960s and early 1970s on photographs, and his main goal was to translate photographic information into painted information. Because he aimed simply to record visual information about his subject's appearance, Close deliberately avoided creative compositions, flattering lighting effects, and revealing facial expressions. Not interested in providing great insight into the personalities of those portrayed, Close painted anonymous and generic people, mostly friends. By reducing the variables in his paintings (even their canvas size is a constant 9 by 7 feet), he could focus on employing his methodical presentations of faces, thereby encouraging the viewer to deal with the formal aspects of his works. Indeed, because of the large scale of Close's paintings, careful scrutiny causes the images to dissolve into abstract patterns.

In a widely read 1970 interview in the journal *Artforum,* art critic Cindy Nemser (b. 1937) asked Close about the scale of his huge portraits and the relationship of his Photorealist canvases to the photographs that lie behind them. He answered in part:

> The large scale allows me to deal with information that is overlooked in an eight-by-ten inch photograph . . . My large scale forces the viewer to focus on one area at a time. In that way he is made aware of the blurred areas that are seen with peripheral vision. Normally we never take those peripheral areas into account. When we focus on an area it is sharp. As we turn our attention to adjacent areas they sharpen up too. In my work, the blurred areas don't come into focus, but they are too large to be ignored. . . . In order to . . . make [my painted] information stack up with photographic information, I tried to purge my work of as much of the baggage of traditional portrait painting as I could. To avoid a painterly brush stroke and surface, I use some pretty devious means, such as razor blades, electric drills and airbrushes. I also work as thinly as possible and I don't use white paint as it tends to build up and become chalky and opaque. In fact, in a nine-by-seven foot picture, I only use a couple of tablespoons of black paint to cover the entire canvas.*

30-31 CHUCK CLOSE, *Big Self-Portrait,* 1967–1968. Acrylic on canvas, 8' 11" × 6' 11". Walker Art Center, Minneapolis (Art Center Acquisition Fund, 1969).

Close's goal was to translate photographic information into painted information. In his portraits, he deliberately avoided creative compositions, flattering lighting effects, and revealing facial expressions.

*Cindy Nemser, "Chuck Close: Interview with Cindy Nemser," *Artforum* 8, no. 5 (January 1970): 51–55.

history, it was always photographs, I never saw the paintings, they were in Europe. . . . Look at TV and at magazines and reproductions, they're all influenced by photo-vision."[16] The photograph's formal qualities also intrigued her, and she used photographic techniques by first projecting an image in slide form onto the canvas. By next using an *airbrush* (a device originally designed as a photo-retouching tool that sprays paint with compressed air), Flack could duplicate the smooth gradations of tone and color found in photographs.

Most of Flack's paintings are still lifes that present the viewer with a collection of familiar objects painted with great optical fidelity. *Marilyn* is a still life incorporating photographs of the face of famed Hollywood actress Marilyn Monroe. It is a poignant commentary on Monroe's tragic life and differs markedly from Warhol's *Marilyn Diptych* (FIG. 30-27A), which celebrates celebrity and makes no allusion to the death of the glamorous star. Flack's still life includes multiple references to death and alludes to Dutch *vanitas* paintings (FIG. 25-21). In addition to the black-and-white photo-

graphs of a youthful, smiling Monroe, Flack painted fresh fruit, an hourglass, a burning candle, a watch, and a calendar, all of which refer to the passage of time and the transience of life on earth.

CHUCK CLOSE Perhaps the most famous Superrealist is CHUCK CLOSE (b. 1940), who grew up near Seattle and attended the University of Washington and Yale University. He is best known for his large-scale portraits, such as *Big Self-Portrait* (FIG. **30-31**). However, Close felt that his connection to the Photorealists was tenuous, because for him, realism was not an end in itself but rather the result of an intellectually rigorous, systematic approach to painting (see "Chuck Close on Photorealist Portrait Painting," above).

LUCIAN FREUD Born in Berlin in 1922, LUCIAN FREUD (1922–2011) moved to London with his family in 1933 when Adolph Hitler became German chancellor. The grandson of Sigmund Freud, the painter is best known for his unflattering close-up views of faces in

1 ft.

30-32 Lucian Freud, *Naked Portrait*, 1972–1973. Oil on canvas 2' × 2'. Tate Modern, London.

Freud's brutally realistic portrait of an unnamed woman lying on a bed in an awkward position gives the impression that the viewer is an intruder in a private space, but the setting is the artist's studio.

whose poses he determined, his paintings convey the impression that the artist and the viewer are intruders in a private realm.

In *Naked Portrait* (FIG. **30-32**), the viewer observes an unnamed woman lying in an uncomfortable, almost fetal, position at the foot of a bed. Freud depicted her from a sharp angle above and to the left. In the foreground is a small table with the painter's tools on it, revealing that this is not the woman's bedroom but the painter's studio and that the woman is the subject of intense scrutiny by the artist. Freud's models do not have perfect bodies. Some are overweight, and many are well beyond their prime. These are truly "naked portraits" of real people. They break sharply with the Western tradition from Greek antiquity to the Renaissance and into the modern era of depicting idealized Venuses, Eves, and courtesans in graceful and often erotic poses. Freud explained his interest in nudity: "I'm really interested in people as animals. Part of my liking to work from them naked is for that reason. Because I can see more."[17] Regarding the setting of his paintings, Freud observed: "I work from people that interest me, and that I care about and think about, in rooms that I live in and know."[18]

which the sitter seems almost unaware of the painter's presence, and for his portrayals of female and male nudes in foreshortened and often contorted poses. Although Freud always used living models

DUANE HANSON Not surprisingly, many sculptors also were Superrealists, including Minnesota-born Duane Hanson (1925–1996), who spent much of his career in southern Florida. Hanson perfected a casting technique that enabled him to create life-size figurative sculptures that many viewers mistake at first for real people. Hanson began by making plaster molds from live models and then filled the molds with polyester resin. After the resin hardened, he removed the outer molds and cleaned, painted with an airbrush, and decorated the sculptures with wigs, clothes, and other accessories. These works, such as *Supermarket Shopper* (FIG. **30-33**), depict stereotypical average Americans, striking chords with the

1 ft.

30-33 Duane Hanson, *Supermarket Shopper*, 1970. Polyester resin and fiberglass polychromed in oil, with clothing, steel cart, and groceries, life-size. Nachfolgeinstitut, Neue Galerie, Sammlung Ludwig, Aachen. Art © Estate of Duane Hanson/Licensed by VAGA, New York, NY.

Hanson used molds from live models to create his Superrealist life-size painted plaster sculptures. His aim was to capture the emptiness and loneliness of average Americans in familiar settings.

public specifically because of their familiarity. Hanson explained his choice of imagery:

> The subject matter that I like best deals with the familiar lower- and middle-class American types of today. To me, the resignation, emptiness and loneliness of their existence captures the true reality of life for these people. . . . I want to achieve a certain tough realism which speaks of the fascinating idiosyncrasies of our time.[19]

Photography

Although Superrealist artists admired the ability of photography to reproduce faithfully the appearance of people, objects, and places, photographers themselves used their medium to pursue varied ends. The photographs of Edward Weston (FIGS. 29-44 and 29-44A) and Dorothea Lange (FIG. 29-77) represent the two poles of American photography between the world wars—the art photograph (Weston), which transforms the real into the abstract, and the documentary photograph (Lange), which records people and events directly, without artifice. In the postwar period, leading photographers adopted both approaches.

One documentary photographer who achieved a prominent position in the circle of innovative photographers was Diane Arbus (1923–1971). Often described as a "photographer of freaks," Arbus

1 in.

specialized in taking black-and-white photographs (not illustrated) of ordinary people with all their blemishes, both physical and psychological. Among her subjects were people with physical deformities, and people at the margins of society—transvestites, a Mexican dwarf, a man tattooed from head to foot, a young man smoking with his hair in curlers, another of enormous height ("a Jewish giant") at home with his diminutive parents, a boy in New York's Central Park menacingly holding a toy hand grenade—in short, people who were rarely the chosen subjects of professional photographers.

MINOR WHITE The other pole of mid-20th-century photography in America is perhaps best represented by the work of Minneapolis native MINOR WHITE (1908–1976), who moved to Portland, Oregon in 1938 and became a photographer for the Works Progress Administration. He served in the United States Army in World War II and then settled in New York City in 1945, where he met Alfred Stieglitz, whose *Equivalent* photographs (FIG. 29-43A) he greatly admired. Deeply influenced by Zen Buddhism (see "Zen Buddhism," page 1067), White sought to incorporate a mystical element in his own work.

His 1962 photograph (FIG. **30-34**) of a rock formation in Utah is a characteristic example. A "straight photograph" in the tradition of Stieglitz and Weston, it is also an abstract composition of jagged shapes and contrasts of light and dark reminiscent of Abstract Expressionist paintings (FIG. 30-9). Viewers of *Moencopi Strata, Capitol Reef, Utah* may recognize White's nominal subject as a detail of a landscape, but in his hands, nature becomes the springboard for meditation. As one of the founders and the longtime editor (1952–1975) of *Aperture,* the leading art photography magazine of the time, White had a profound influence on the development of the medium in the postwar period.

Feminist Art

With the renewed interest in representation that the Pop artists and Superrealists introduced in the 1960s and 1970s, artists once again began to embrace the persuasive powers of art to communicate with a wide audience. In the 1970s, many artists began to investigate the social dynamics of power and privilege, especially in relation to gender, although racial, ethnic, and sexual orientation issues have also figured prominently in the art of recent decades (see Chapter 31). Women artists played a significant role in the feminist movement, which sought equal rights for women in contemporary society and focused attention on the subservient place of women in societies throughout history. Spearheading the feminist art movement of the 1970s were Judy Chicago (FIG. **30-35**) and Miriam Schapiro

30-34 MINOR WHITE, *Moencopi Strata, Capitol Reef, Utah,* 1962. Gelatin silver print, $1' \frac{1}{8}"\times 9\frac{1}{4}"$. Museum of Modern Art, New York. © The Minor White Archive, Princeton University.

White's "straight photograph" of a natural rock formation is also an abstract composition of jagged shapes and contrasts of light and dark reminiscent of Abstract Expressionist paintings.

ARTISTS ON ART

Judy Chicago on *The Dinner Party*

One of the acknowledged masterpieces of feminist art is Judy Chicago's *The Dinner Party* (FIG. 30-35), which required a team of nearly 400 to create and assemble. In 1979, Chicago published a book explaining the genesis and symbolism of the work.

[By 1974] I had discarded [my original] idea of painting a hundred abstract portraits on plates, each paying tribute to a different historic female figure. . . . In my research I realized over and over again that women's achievements had been left out of history . . . My new idea was to try to symbolize this. . . . [I thought] about putting the plates on a table with silver, glasses, napkins, and tablecloths, and over the next year and a half the concept of *The Dinner Party* slowly evolved. I began to think about the piece as a reinterpretation of the Last Supper from the point of view of women, who, throughout history, had prepared the meals and set the table. In my "Last Supper," however, the women would be the honored guests. Their representation in the form of plates set on the table would express the way women had been confined, and the piece would thus reflect both women's achievements and their oppression. . . . My goal with *The Dinner Party* was . . . to forge a new kind of art expressing women's experience . . . [It] seemed appropriate to relate our history through art, particularly through techniques traditionally associated with women—china-painting and needlework.*

The Dinner Party rests on a triangular white tile floor inscribed with the names of 999 additional women of achievement to signify that the accomplishments of the 39 honored guests rest on a founda-

tion that other women had laid. Among those with place settings at the table are the Egyptian pharaoh Hatshepsut (FIG. 3-21), the Minoan snake goddess (FIG. 4-13), the Byzantine empress Theodora (FIG. 9-14), the medieval nun Hildegard of Bingen (FIG. 12-25), and the painters Artemisia Gentileschi (FIG. 24-19 and 24-20) and Georgia O'Keeffe (FIGS. I-5 and 29-42). Other women artists among the 999 names include Lavinia Fontana (FIG. 22-40A), Élisabeth-Louise Vigée-Lebrun (FIGS. 26-15A and 26-16), Adélaïde Labille-Guiard (FIG. 26-17), Angelica Kauffman (FIG. 26-1), Mary Cassatt (FIG. 28-12), Berthe Morisot (FIGS. 28-13 and 28-13A), Gertrude Käsebier (FIG. 28-31), Käthe Kollwitz (FIG. 29-9), Paula Modersohn-Becker (FIG. 29-9A), Barbara Hepworth (FIG. 29-63), Dorothea Lange (FIG. 29-77), and Louise Nevelson (FIG. 30-20).

Each woman's place has identical eating utensils and a goblet, but features a unique oversized porcelain plate and a long place mat or table runner covered with imagery reflecting significant facts about that woman's life and culture. The plates range from simple concave shapes with china-painted imagery to dishes whose sculptured three-dimensional designs almost seem to struggle to free themselves. The designs on each plate incorporate both butterfly and vulval motifs—the butterfly as the ancient symbol of liberation and the vulva as the symbol of female sexuality. Each table runner combines traditional needlework techniques, including needlepoint, embroidery, crochet, beading, patchwork, and appliqué.

The Dinner Party is more than the sum of its parts, however. Of monumental size, as so many great works of public art have been throughout the ages, Chicago's 1979 masterwork provides viewers with a powerful launching point for considering broad feminist concerns.

*Judy Chicago, "The Dinner Party": A Symbol of Our Heritage (Garden City, N.Y.: Anchor Press, 1979), 11–12.

10 ft.

30-35 JUDY CHICAGO, *The Dinner Party,* 1979. Multimedia, including ceramics and stitchery, 48' × 48' × 48'. The Brooklyn Museum, Brooklyn.

Chicago's *Dinner Party* honors 39 women from antiquity to 20th-century America. The triangular form and the materials—painted china and fabric—are traditionally associated with women.

(FIG. 30-36). Chicago and a group of students at California State University in Fresno founded the Feminist Art Program, and Chicago and Schapiro coordinated it at the California Institute of the Arts in Valencia. In 1972, as part of this program, teachers and students joined to create projects such as Womanhouse, an abandoned house in Los Angeles that they completely converted into a suite of "environments," each based on a different aspect of women's lives and fantasies.

JUDY CHICAGO A major goal of Chicago native Judy Cohen, who took the name JUDY CHICAGO (b. 1939), was to educate the public about women's role in history and the fine arts and to establish a respect for women and their art. Chicago sought to forge a new kind of art expressing women's experiences and to find a way to make that art accessible to a large audience. Inspired early in her career by the work of Barbara Hepworth (FIG. 29-63), Georgia O'Keeffe (FIGS. I-5 and 29-42), and Louise Nevelson (FIG. 30-20), Chicago developed a personal painting style that consciously included abstract organic vaginal images.

In the early 1970s, Chicago began planning an ambitious piece, *The Dinner Party* (FIG. 30-35), using craft techniques (such as china painting and needlework) traditionally practiced by women, to celebrate the achievements and contributions that women had made throughout history (see "Judy Chicago on *The Dinner Party*," page 975). She originally conceived the work as a feminist *Last Supper* for 13 "honored guests," as in the biblical account of Christ's passion, but at Chicago's table, the guests are women instead of men. The number of women in a witches' coven is also 13, and the artist intended her feminist *Dinner Party* additionally to refer to witchcraft and the worship of the Mother Goddess. But because Chicago had uncovered so many worthy women in the course of her research, she tripled the number of guests and placed table settings for 39 women around a triangular table 48 feet long on each side. The triangular form refers to the ancient symbol for both woman and the Goddess. The notion of a dinner party also alludes to women's traditional role as homemakers.

MIRIAM SCHAPIRO After enjoying a thriving career as a hard-edge painter in California in the late 1960s, Toronto-born MIRIAM SCHAPIRO (b. 1923) became fascinated with the hidden metaphors for womanhood that she then saw in her abstract paintings. Intrigued by the materials she had used to create a doll's house for her part in Womanhouse, in the 1970s Schapiro began to make huge sewn collages, assembled from fabrics, quilts, buttons, sequins, lace trim, and rickrack collected at antique shows and fairs. She called these works *femmages*—from the French *femme* ("woman") and an inversion of the French *homage* ("homage") from *homme* ("man"). She wanted to make the point that women had been doing collages using these materials long before Pablo Picasso (FIG. 29-14) introduced them to the art world. *Anatomy of a Kimono* (FIG. **30-36**) is one of a series of gigantic femmages based on the patterns of Japanese kimonos, fans, and robes. This vast 10-panel composition is more than 52 feet long and almost 7 feet high and repeats the kimono shape in a rich array of fabric fragments.

CINDY SHERMAN After studying painting in Buffalo, CINDY SHERMAN (b. 1954) switched to photography as her primary means of expression. She addresses in her work the way that much of Western art presents female beauty for the enjoyment of the "male gaze," a primary focus of contemporary feminist theory, which explores gender as a socially constructed concept. Since 1977, Sherman has produced a series of more than 80 black-and-white photographs called *Untitled Film Stills*. She got the idea for the series after examining soft-core pornography magazines and noting the stereotypical ways that they depicted women. She decided to produce her own series of photographs, designing, acting in, directing, and photographing the works. In so doing, she took control of her own image and constructed her own identity, a primary feminist concern.

In works from the series, such as *Untitled Film Still #35* (FIG. **30-37**), Sherman appears, often in costume and wig, in a photograph that seems to be a film still. Most of the images in this series recall popular film genres but are sufficiently generic that the viewer cannot relate them to specific movies. Sherman often reveals the constructed nature of these images by holding in her hand the shutter release cable used to take the pictures. (The cord runs across the floor in *#35*.) Although the artist is still the object of the viewer's gaze in these images, the identity is one that she alone chose to assume by posing for the photographs.

1 ft.

30-36 MIRIAM SCHAPIRO, *Anatomy of a Kimono* (detail of 2 panels of a 10-panel composition), 1976. Fabric and acrylic on canvas, entire work 6′ 8″ × 52′ 2½″. Collection of Bruno Bischofberger, Zurich.

Schapiro calls her huge sewn collages "femmages" to make the point that women had been doing collages of fabric long before Picasso (FIG. 29-14). This femmage incorporates patterns from Japanese kimonos.

30-37 CINDY SHERMAN, *Untitled Film Still #35,* 1979. Gelatin silverprint, 10" × 8". Private collection.

Sherman here assumed a role for one of 80 photographs resembling film stills in which she addressed the way that women have traditionally been presented in Western art for the enjoyment of the "male gaze."

ANA MENDIETA Two other feminist artists who used their bodies as key components of their artworks were New Yorker HANNAH WILKE (1940–1993; FIG. **30-37A**) and Cuban-born ANA MENDIETA (1948–1985; FIG. **30-38**), who left her native land as a child when Fidel Castro came to

⬈**30-37A** WILKE, *S.O.S.,* 1974–1982.

power. Although gender issues concerned Mendieta, her art also deals with issues of spirituality and cultural heritage. The artist's best-known series, *Silueta* (*Silhouettes*), consists of approximately 200 earth/body works completed between 1973 and 1980. These works represented Mendieta's attempt to carry on, as she described, "a dialogue between the landscape and the female body (based on my own silhouette)."[20]

Flowers on Body (FIG. 30-38) is a documentary photograph of the first of the earth/body sculptures in the *Silueta* series. In this work, Mendieta appears covered with flowers in an earthen, womblike cavity. Executed at El Yagul, a Mexican archaeological site, the

work speaks to the issues of birth and death, the female experience of childbirth, and the human connection to the earth. Objects and locations from nature play an important role in Mendieta's art. She explained the centrality of this connection to nature:

> I believe this has been a direct result of my having been torn from my homeland during my adolescence. I am overwhelmed by the feeling of having been cast from the womb (nature). My art is the way I reestablish the bonds that unite me to the universe. It is a return to the maternal source. Through my earth/body sculptures I become one with the earth.[21]

Beyond their sensual, moving presence, Mendieta's works also generate a palpable spiritual force. In longing for her homeland, she sought the cultural understanding and acceptance of the spiritual powers inherent in nature that modern Western societies often seem to reject in favor of scientific and technological developments. Mendieta's art is lyrical and passionate and operates at the intersection of cultural, spiritual, physical, and feminist concerns.

30-38 ANA MENDIETA, *Flowers on Body,* 1973. Color photograph of earth/body work with flowers, executed at El Yagul, Mexico. Courtesy of the Estate of Ana Mendieta and Galerie Lelong, New York.

In this earth/body sculpture, Mendieta appears covered with flowers in a womblike cavity to address issues of birth and death, as well as the human connection to the earth.

1 in.

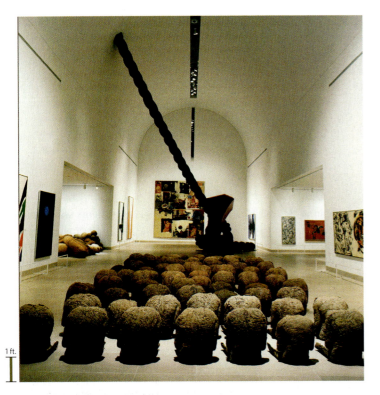

30-39 Magdalena Abakanowicz, *80 Backs,* 1976–1980. Burlap and resin, each 2′ 3″ high. Museum of Modern Art, Dallas.

Polish fiber artist Abakanowicz explored the stoic, everyday toughness of the human spirit in this group of nearly identical sculptures that serve as symbols of distinctive individuals lost in the crowd.

MAGDALENA ABAKANOWICZ Not strictly feminist in subject, but created using materials traditionally associated with women, are the sculptures of Polish fiber artist MAGDALENA ABAKANOWICZ (b. 1930). A leader in the exploration of the expressive power of weaving techniques in large-scale artworks, Abakanowicz gained fame with experimental freestanding figural works expressing the stoic, everyday toughness of the human spirit. For Abakanowicz, fiber materials are deeply symbolic:

> I see fiber as the basic element constructing the organic world on our planet, as the greatest mystery of our environment. It is from fiber that all living organisms are built—the tissues of plants and ourselves. . . . Fabric is our covering and our attire. Made with our hands, it is a record of our souls.[22]

Abakanowicz's sculptures are to a great degree reflections of her early life experiences as a member of an aristocratic family disturbed by the dislocations of World War II and its aftermath. Initially attracted to weaving as a medium easily adaptable to the small studio space she had available,

Abakanowicz gradually developed huge abstract hangings that she called Abakans, which suggest organic spaces as well as giant pieces of clothing. She returned to a smaller scale with works based on human forms—*Heads, Seated Figures,* and *Backs*—multiplying each type for exhibition in groups as symbols for the individual in society lost in the crowd yet retaining some distinctiveness.

This impression is especially powerful in *80 Backs* (FIG. 30-39). Abakanowicz made each piece by pressing layers of natural organic fibers into a plaster mold. Every sculpture depicts the slumping shoulders, back, and arms of a figure of indeterminate gender, and rests legless directly on the floor. The repeated pose of the figures in *80 Backs* suggests meditation, submission, and anticipation. Although made from a single mold, the figures achieve a touching sense of individuality because each assumed a slightly different posture as the material dried and because the artist imprinted a different pattern of fiber texture on each.

ARCHITECTURE AND SITE-SPECIFIC ART

Some of the most innovative architects of the first half of the 20th century, most notably Frank Lloyd Wright (FIGS. 29-45, 29-46, and 29-80), Ludwig Mies van der Rohe (FIG. 29-68), and Le Corbusier (FIG. 29-69), concluded their long and productive careers in the postwar period. At the same time, younger architects rose to international prominence, some working in the modernist idiom but others taking architectural design in new "postmodern" directions (see "After Modernism: Postmodernist Architecture," page 949, and "Robert Venturi and Postmodernist Complexity and Contradiction," page 982).

Modernism

In parallel with the progressive movement toward formal abstraction in painting and sculpture in the decades following World War II, modernist architects became increasingly concerned with a formalism stressing simplicity. They articulated this in buildings that retained intriguing organic sculptural qualities, as well as in buildings adhering to a more rigid geometry.

FRANK LLOYD WRIGHT The last great building that Frank Lloyd Wright designed was the Solomon R. Guggenheim Museum

30-40 FRANK LLOYD WRIGHT, Solomon R. Guggenheim Museum (looking southeast), New York, 1943–1959.

Using reinforced concrete almost as a sculptor might use resilient clay, Wright designed a snail shell–shaped museum with a winding, gently inclined interior ramp for the display of artworks.

30-41 Le Corbusier, Notre-Dame-du-Haut (looking northwest), Ronchamp, France, 1950–1955.

The organic forms of Le Corbusier's mountaintop chapel present a fusion of architecture and sculpture. The architect based the shapes on praying hands, a dove's wings, and a ship's prow.

30-42 Le Corbusier, interior of Notre-Dame-du-Haut (looking southwest), Ronchamp, France, 1950–1955.

Constructed of concrete sprayed on a frame of steel and metal mesh, the heavy walls of the Ronchamp chapel enclose an intimate and mysteriously lit interior that has the aura of a sacred cave.

(FIG. 30-40) in New York City. Using reinforced concrete almost as a sculptor might use resilient clay, Wright, who often described his architecture as "organic" (see "Frank Lloyd Wright on Organic Architecture," page 917), designed a structure inspired by the spiral of a snail's shell. Wright had introduced curves and circles into some of his plans in the 1930s, and as the architectural historian Peter Blake noted, "The spiral was the next logical step; it is the circle brought into the third and fourth dimensions."[23] Inside the building (FIG. 31-34), the shape of the shell expands toward the top, and a winding interior ramp spirals to connect the gallery bays. A skylight strip embedded in the museum's outer wall provides illumination to the ramp, which visitors can stroll down at a leisurely pace after taking an elevator to the top of the building, viewing the artworks displayed along the gently sloping pathway. Thick walls and the solid organic shape give the building, outside and inside, the sense of turning in on itself, and the long interior viewing area opening onto a 90-foot central well of space creates a sheltered environment, secure from the bustling city outside.

LE CORBUSIER Compared with his pristine geometric design for Villa Savoye (FIG. 29-69), the organic forms of Le Corbusier's Notre-Dame-du-Haut (FIG. 30-41) come as a startling surprise. Completed in 1955 at Ronchamp, France, the chapel attests to the boundless creativity of this great architect. A fusion of architecture and sculpture, the small chapel, which replaced a building destroyed in World War II, occupies a pilgrimage site in the Vosges Mountains. The monumental impression of Notre-Dame-du-Haut seen from afar is somewhat deceptive. Although one massive exterior wall (FIG. 30-41, *right*) contains a pulpit resembling a balcony that faces a spacious outdoor area for large-scale open-air services on holy days, the interior (FIG. 30-42) holds at most 200 people. The intimate scale, stark and heavy walls, and mysterious illumination (jewel tones cast from the deeply recessed stained-glass windows) give this space an aura reminiscent of a sacred cave or a medieval monastery.

Notre-Dame-du-Haut's structure may look free-form to the untrained eye, but Le Corbusier, like the designers of Romanesque and Gothic cathedrals, based it on an underlying mathematical system. The pilgrimage church has a frame of steel and metal mesh, which the builders sprayed with concrete (an engineering innovation pioneered in Italy by Pier Luigi Nervi (1891–1979; FIG. 30-42A) and painted

30-42A Nervi, Palazzetto dello Sport, 1958–1959.

white, except for two interior private chapel niches with colored walls and the roof, which Le Corbusier wished to have darken naturally with the passage of time. The roof appears to float freely above the worshipers in their pews (FIG. 30-42), intensifying the quality of mystery in the interior space. In reality, a series of nearly invisible blocks holds up the roof. The mystery of the roof's means of support recalls the reaction to Hagia Sophia's miraculously floating dome (FIG. 9-8) a millennium and a half before in Byzantium. Le Corbusier's preliminary sketches for the building indicate that he linked the design with the shape of praying hands, with the wings of a dove (representing both peace and the Holy Spirit), and with the prow of a ship (a reminder that the term for the central aisle in a traditional basilican church is *nave*—Latin for "ship"). Le Corbusier hoped that in the mystical interior he created and in the rolling hills around the church, men and women would reflect on the sacred and the natural. No one who has visited Notre-Dame-du-Haut, whether on a bright sunlit day or in a thundering storm, has come away unmoved.

EERO SAARINEN Dramatic, sweeping, curvilinear reinforced concrete rooflines are also characteristic features of the buildings de-

30-43 EERO SAARINEN, Terminal 5 (JetBlue Airways terminal, formerly the Trans World Airlines terminal), John F. Kennedy International Airport, New York, 1956–1962. *Top:* exterior looking southeast; *bottom:* interior.

Saarinen based his design on the theme of motion. The concrete-and-glass air terminal's dramatic, sweeping rooflines suggest expansive wings and flight. The interior features the same curvilinear vocabulary.

signed by Finnish-born architect EERO SAARINEN (1910–1961). One of his signature buildings of the late 1950s is the former Trans World Airlines terminal (now the JetBlue Airways terminal, FIG. **30-43,** *top*) at New York's John F. Kennedy International Airport. The terminal, which Saarinen based on the theme of motion, consists of two immense concrete shells split down the middle and slightly rotated, giving the building a fluid curved outline that fits its corner site. The shells immediately suggest expansive wings and flight. Saarinen also designed every detail of the spacious, light-filled interior (FIG. 30-43, *bottom*), including the furniture, ventilation ducts, and signboards, with this same curvilinear vocabulary in mind. The design brilliantly combines symbolism, drama, and function.

JOERN UTZON Saarinen was responsible for selecting a kindred spirit, the Danish architect JOERN UTZON (1918–2008) to build the Sydney Opera House (FIG. **30-44**) in Australia. Utzon's design is a bold composition of organic forms on a colossal scale. Utzon worked briefly with Frank Lloyd Wright at Taliesin (Wright's Wisconsin residence), and the style of the Sydney Opera House resonates distantly with the graceful curvature of New York's Guggenheim Museum. Clusters of immense concrete shells—the largest is 200 feet tall—rise from massive platforms and soar to delicate peaks. Recalling at first the *ogival* (pointed) shapes of Gothic vaults, the shells also suggest both the buoyancy of seabird wings and the billowing sails of the tall ships of the European settlers who emigrated to Australia in the 18th and 19th centuries. These architectural metaphors are appropriate to the harbor surrounding Bennelong Point, whose bedrock foundations support the building. Utzon's matching of the structure with its site and atmosphere adds to the organic nature of the design.

Although construction of the building began in 1959, completion of the opera house had to wait until 1972, primarily because Utzon's daring design required construction technology not yet developed. Today the opera house is Sydney's defining symbol, a monument of civic pride that functions as the city's cultural center. In addition to the opera auditorium, the complex houses auxiliary halls and rooms for concerts, the performing arts, motion pictures, lectures, art exhibitions, and conventions.

MIES VAN DER ROHE Sculpturesque building design was not the only manifestation of postwar modernist architecture. From the mid-1950s through the 1970s, other architects created massive, sleek, and geometrically rigid buildings. They designed most of these structures following Bauhaus architect Mies van der Rohe's contention that "less is more." Many of these more Minimalist designs are powerful, heroic presences in the urban landscape, effectively symbolizing the giant corporations that often were the skyscrapers' primary tenants.

The purest example of these corporate skyscrapers is the mid-1950s rectilinear glass-and-bronze Seagram Building (FIG. **30-45**) in Manhattan, designed by Mies van der Rohe and American architect Philip Johnson (FIG. 30-48). By this time, the concrete-steel-and-glass towers pioneered by Louis Sullivan (FIGS. 28-42, 28-42A, and 28-43) and carried further by Mies van der Rohe himself (FIG. 29-68) had become a familiar sight in cities all over the world. Appealing in its structural logic and clarity, the style, easily imitated, quickly became the norm

The soaring clusters of concrete shells of Utzon's opera house on an immense platform in Sydney's harbor suggest both the buoyancy of seabird wings and the billowing sails of tall ships.

for postwar commercial high-rise buildings. The architects of the Seagram Building deliberately designed it as a thin shaft, leaving the front quarter of its midtown site as an open pedestrian plaza. The tower appears to rise from the pavement on stilts. Glass walls even surround the recessed lobby. The building's recessed structural elements make it appear to have a glass skin, interrupted only by the thin strips of bronze anchoring the windows. The bronze metal and the amber glass windows give the tower a richness found in few of its neighbors. Mies van der Rohe and Johnson carefully planned every detail of the Seagram Building, inside and out, to create an elegant whole. They even designed the interior and exterior lighting to make the edifice an impressive sight both day and night.

30-45 LUDWIG MIES VAN DER ROHE and PHILIP JOHNSON, Seagram Building (looking northeast), New York, 1956–1958.

Massive, sleek, and geometrically rigid, this modernist skyscraper has a bronze-and-glass skin masking its concrete-and-steel frame. The giant corporate tower appears to rise from the pavement on stilts.

SKIDMORE, OWINGS & MERRILL The architectural firm SKIDMORE, OWINGS & MERRILL (SOM), perhaps the purest proponent of Miesian-inspired structures, designed a number of these simple rectilinear glass-sheathed buildings, and SOM's success indicates the popularity of this building type. By 1970, the company comprised more than a thousand architects and had offices in New York, Chicago, San Francisco, Portland, and Washington, D.C. In 1974, the firm completed the Sears Tower (now Willis Tower; FIG. **30-46**), a mammoth corporate

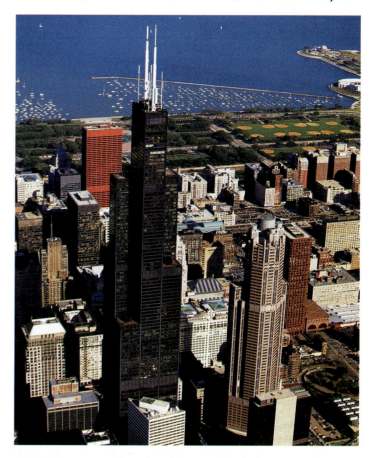

30-46 SKIDMORE, OWINGS & MERRILL, Willis Tower (formerly Sears Tower; looking east), Chicago, 1974.

Consisting of nine black aluminum and smoked glass shafts soaring to 110 stories, the Willis (Sears) Tower dominates Chicago's skyline. It was the world's tallest building at the time of its construction.

Robert Venturi and Postmodernist Complexity and Contradiction

The restrictiveness of modernist architecture and the impersonality and sterility of many modernist structures eventually led to a rejection of modernism's authority in architecture. But the question faced by architects dissatisfied with the modernist mode was what to put in its place. The answer was the diversity of solutions that architectural historians use the generic term *postmodernism* to describe. Postmodernist architecture is not a unified style. It is a widespread cultural phenomenon far more encompassing and accepting than the more rigid confines of modernist practice, which, critics believed, failed to respond to the unique character of the cities and neighborhoods in which modernist architects erected their buildings. In contrast to modernist architecture, which features simple shapes and little ornamentation, postmodern architecture is complex and eclectic. Whereas the modernist program was reductive, the postmodern vocabulary is expansive and inclusive.

Among the first to explore this new direction in architecture were Jane Jacobs (1916–2006) and ROBERT VENTURI (b. 1925). In their influential books *The Death and Life of Great American Cities* (Jacobs, 1961) and *Complexity and Contradiction in Architecture* (Venturi, 1966), Jacobs and Venturi argued that the uniformity and anonymity of modernist architecture (in particular, corporate skyscrapers, such as the Seagram Building [FIG. 30-45] and the Sears Tower [FIG. 30-46] that then domi-

nated many urban skylines) were unsuited to human social interaction. Jacobs and Venturi further maintained that diversity is the great advantage of urban life. Postmodern architects accepted, indeed embraced, the messy and chaotic nature of big-city life.

When designing these varied buildings, many postmodern architects consciously selected past architectural elements or references and juxtaposed them with contemporary elements or fashioned them of high-tech materials, thereby creating a dialogue between past and present, as Charles Moore did in Piazza d'Italia (FIG. 30-1). Postmodern architecture incorporates references not only to traditional architecture but also to mass culture and popular imagery. This was precisely the "complexity and contradiction" Venturi referred to in the title of his book and that he explored further in *Learning from Las Vegas* (1972), coauthored with Denise Scott Brown (b. 1931) and Steven Izenour (1940–2001).

An early example of Venturi's work is the house (FIG. 30-47) he designed in 1962 for his mother. A fundamental axiom of modernism is that a building's form must arise directly and logically from its function and structure. Against this rule, Venturi asserted that form should be separate from function and structure. Thus the Vanna Venturi house has an oversized gable roof that recalls classical temple design more than domestic architecture. However, the gable has a missing central section, which reveals the house's "chimney" (a penthouse suite). Moreover, Venturi inserted an arch motif over the doorway's lintel, and the placement of the windows violates the symmetry of both classical and modernist design.

30-47 ROBERT VENTURI, Vanna Venturi house, Chestnut Hill, Pennsylvania, 1962.

Venturi advocated complexity and contradiction in architectural design, in contrast to modernist simplicity and uniformity. An early example of the postmodern approach that he championed is his mother's house.

building in Chicago. Consisting of nine clustered shafts soaring vertically, this 110-floor building provides offices for more than 12,000 workers. Original plans called for 104 stories, but the architects acquiesced to Sears's insistence on making the building the tallest (measured to the structural top) in the world at the time. The tower's size, coupled with the black aluminum sheathing it and the smoked glass, establishes a dominant presence in a city of many corporate skyscrapers—exactly the image Sears executives wanted to project.

Postmodernism

Within a few years of the completion of the Seagram Building (FIG. 30-45) in the heart of New York City, some architects were already questioning the validity of the modernist approach to architectural design. Thus was born the diverse and complex style called *postmodernism* (see page 949 and "Robert Venturi and Postmodernist Complexity and Contradiction," above, and FIG. 30-47).

ARTISTS ON ART
Philip Johnson on Postmodern Architecture

Philip Johnson, who died in 2005 at age 98, had a distinguished career spanning almost the entire 20th century, during which he transformed himself from a modernist closely associated with Mies van der Rohe (FIG. 30-45) into one of the leading postmodernists, whose AT&T (now Sony) Building (FIG. 30-48) in New York City remains an icon of 1970s postmodernism. In the following passages, Johnson commented on his early "Miesian" style and about the incorporation of various historical styles in postmodernist buildings.

> My eyes are set by the Miesian tradition . . . The continuity with my Miesian approach also shows through in my classicism. . . . [But in] 1952, about the same time that my whole generation did, I became very restless. . . . In the last decade there has been such a violent switch that it is almost embarrassing. But it isn't a switch, so much as a centrifugal splintering of architecture, to a degree that I don't think has been seen in the past few hundred years. Perfectly responsible architects build, even in one year, buildings that you cannot believe are done by the same person.*
>
> Structural honesty seems to me one of the bugaboos that we should free ourselves from very quickly. The Greeks with their marble columns imitating wood, and covering up the roofs inside! The Gothic designers with their wooden roofs above to protect their delicate vaulting. And Michelangelo, the greatest architect in history, with his Mannerist column! There is only one absolute today and this is change. There are no rules, surely no certainties in any of the arts. There is only the feeling of a wonderful freedom, of endless possibilities to investigate, of endless past years of historically great buildings to enjoy.†

*Quoted in Paul Heyer, *Architects on Architecture: New Directions in America* (New York: Van Nostrand Reinhold, 1993), 285–286.

†Ibid., 279.

30-48 Philip Johnson and John Burgee (with Simmons Architects), Sony Building (formerly AT&T Building; looking northeast), New York, 1978–1984.

In a startling shift of style, modernist Johnson (FIG. 30-45) designed this postmodern skyscraper with more granite than glass and with a variation on a classical pediment as the crowning motif.

PHILIP JOHNSON Even architects instrumental in the proliferation of the modernist idiom embraced postmodernism. Early in his career, PHILIP JOHNSON (1906–2005), for example, had been a leading proponent of modernism and worked with Mies van der Rohe on the design of the Seagram Building (FIG. 30-45). Johnson even served as director of the Department of Architecture at New York's Museum of Modern Art, the bastion of modernism, in 1930–1934 and 1946–1954. Yet he made one of the most startling shifts of style in 20th-century architecture, eventually moving away from the severe geometric formalism exemplified by the Seagram Building to a classical transformation of it in his AT&T (American Telephone and Telegraph) Building—now the Sony Building (FIG. **30-48**)—in New York City. Architect JOHN BURGEE (b. 1933) codesigned the Manhattan skyscraper with assistance from the firm SIMMONS ARCHITECTS. This structure was influential in turning architectural taste and practice away from modernism and toward postmodernism—from organic "concrete sculpture" and the rigid "glass box" to elaborate shapes, motifs, and silhouettes freely adapted from his-

torical styles (see "Philip Johnson on Postmodernist Architecture," above).

The 660-foot-high slab of the former AT&T Building is mostly granite. Johnson reduced the window space to some 30 percent of the structure, in contrast to modernist glass-sheathed skyscrapers. His design of its exterior elevation is classically tripartite, having an arcaded base and arched portal; a tall, shaftlike body segmented by slender *mullions* (vertical elements dividing a window); and a crowning pediment broken by an *orbiculum* (a disclike opening). The arrangement refers to the base, column, and entablature system of classical architecture (FIG. 5-13). More specifically, the pediment, indented by the circular space, resembles the crown of a typical 18th-century Chippendale high chest of drawers. It rises among the monotonously flat-topped glass towers of the New York skyline as an ironic rebuke to the rigid uniformity of modernist architecture.

MICHAEL GRAVES Philip Johnson at first endorsed, then disapproved of, a building that rode considerably farther on the wave

30-49 MICHAEL GRAVES, Portland Building (looking northeast), Portland, 1980.

In this early example of postmodern architecture, Graves reasserted the horizontality and solidity of the wall. He drew attention to the wall surfaces through polychromy and ornamental motifs.

of postmodernism than did his AT&T tower. The Portland Building (FIG. **30-49**) by Indianapolis-born architect MICHAEL GRAVES (b. 1934) reasserts the wall's horizontality against the verticality of the tall, window-filled shaft. Graves favored the square's solidity and stability, making it the main body of his composition (echoed in the windows), which rests on a wider base and carries a set-back penthouse crown. Narrow vertical windows tying together seven stories open two paired facades. These support capital-like large hoods on one pair of opposite facades and a frieze of stylized Baroque roundels tied by bands on the other pair. A huge painted keystone motif joins five upper levels on one facade pair, and painted surfaces further define the building's base, body, and penthouse levels.

The modernist purist surely would not welcome the ornamental wall, color painting, or symbolic references. These features, taken together, raised an even greater storm of criticism than greeted the Sydney Opera House or the AT&T Building. Various critics denounced Graves's Portland Building as "an enlarged jukebox," an "oversized Christmas package," a "marzipan monstrosity," a "histrionic masquerade," and a kind of "pop surrealism." Yet others approvingly noted its classical references as constituting a "symbolic temple" and praised the building as a courageous architectural adventure. Whatever history's verdict will be, the Portland Building, like the AT&T tower, is an early marker of postmodernist innovation that borrowed from the lively, if more-or-less garish, language of pop culture. The night-lit dazzle of entertainment sites such as Las Vegas, and the carnival colors, costumes, and fantasy of theme-park props all lie behind the Portland Building design, which many critics regard as a vindication of architectural populism against the pretension of modernist elitism.

ROGERS AND PIANO During their short-lived partnership, British architect RICHARD ROGERS (b. 1933) and Italian architect RENZO PIANO (b. 1937) used motifs and techniques from ordinary industrial buildings in their design for the Georges Pompidou National Center of Art and Culture in Paris (FIG. **30-50**). The architects fully exposed the anatomy of this six-level building, which is a kind of updated version of the Crystal Palace (FIG. 27-47), and made its "metabolism" visible. They color-coded pipes, ducts, tubes, and corridors according to function (red for the movement of people, green for water, blue for air-conditioning, and yellow for electricity), much as in a sophisticated factory.

Critics who deplore the building's industrial qualities disparagingly refer to the complex as a "cultural supermarket" and point out that its exposed entrails require excessive maintenance to protect them from the elements. Nevertheless, the Pompidou Center has

30-50 RICHARD ROGERS and RENZO PIANO, Centre Georges Pompidou (the "Beaubourg," looking northeast), Paris, France, 1977.

The architects fully exposed the anatomy of this six-level building, as in the century-earlier Crystal Palace (FIG. 27-47), and color-coded the internal parts according to function, as in a factory.

been immensely popular with visitors since it opened. The flexible interior spaces and the colorful structural body provide a festive environment for the crowds flowing through the building and enjoying its art galleries, industrial design center, library, science and music centers, conference rooms, research and archival facilities, movie theaters, rest areas, and restaurant (which looks down and through the building to the terraces outside), as well as dramatic panoramas of Paris from its terrace. The sloping plaza in front of the main entrance has become part of the local scene. Peddlers, street performers, Parisians, and tourists fill this square at almost all hours of the day and night. The kind of secular activity that once occurred in the open spaces in front of cathedral entrances now takes place next to a center for culture and popular entertainment.

Environmental and Site-Specific Art

One of the most exciting developments in postwar art and architecture has been *Environmental Art,* sometimes called *earthworks.* Environmental Art stands at the intersection of architecture and sculpture. It emerged as a major form of artistic expression in the 1960s and includes a wide range of artworks, most of which are *site-specific* (created for a unique location) and in the open air. Many artists associated with the Environmental Art movement also used natural or organic materials, including the land itself. It is no coincidence that this art form developed during a period of increased concern for the environment. The ecology movement of the 1960s and 1970s aimed to publicize and combat escalating pollution, depletion of natural resources, and the dangers of toxic waste. The problems of public aesthetics (for example, litter, urban sprawl, and compromised scenic areas) were also at issue. Widespread concern in the United States about the environment led to the passage of the National Environmental Policy Act in 1969 and the creation of the federal Environmental Protection Agency. Environmental artists used their art to call attention to the landscape and, in so doing, were part of this national dialogue.

As an innovative artistic genre challenging traditional assumptions about art making, Environmental Art clearly has an avant-garde, progressive dimension. But as Pop artists did in their time, Environmental artists insist on moving art out of the rarefied atmosphere of museums and galleries and into the public sphere. Most encourage spectator interaction with their works. Ironically, the remote locations of many earthworks have limited public access to them.

ROBERT SMITHSON One of the pioneering Environmental artists was New Jersey–born Robert Smithson (1938–1973), who used industrial construction equipment to manipulate vast quantities of earth and rock on isolated sites. Smithson's best-known project is *Spiral Jetty* (FIG. **30-51**), a mammoth 1,500-foot-long coil of black basalt, limestone rocks, and earth extending out into Utah's Great Salt Lake. As he was driving by the lake one day, Smithson came across some abandoned mining equipment, left there by a company that had tried and failed to extract oil from the site. Smithson saw this as a testament to the enduring power of nature and the inability of humans to conquer it. He decided to create an artwork in the lake that ultimately became a monumental spiral curving out from the shoreline and running 1,500 feet into the water. Smithson insisted on designing his work in response to the location itself. He wanted to avoid the arrogance of an artist merely imposing an unrelated concept on the site. The spiral idea grew from Smithson's first impression of the location. Then, while researching Great Salt Lake, Smithson discovered that the molecular structure of the salt crystals coating the rocks at the water's edge is spiral in form.

> As I looked at the site, it reverberated out to the horizons only to suggest an immobile cyclone while flickering light made the entire landscape appear to quake. A dormant earthquake spread into the fluttering stillness, into a spinning sensation without movement. The site was a rotary that enclosed itself in an immense roundness. From that gyrating space emerged the possibility of the Spiral Jetty. [24]

Smithson not only recorded *Spiral Jetty* in photographs, but also filmed its construction in a movie describing the forms and life of the whole site. The photographs and film have become increasingly important, because fluctuations in Great Salt Lake's water level often place *Spiral Jetty* underwater. Smithson tragically died at age 35 in a plane crash while surveying a site for a new earthwork at Amarillo, Texas.

30-51 Robert Smithson, *Spiral Jetty* (looking northeast), Great Salt Lake, Utah, 1970. Art © Estate of Robert Smithson/ Licensed by VAGA, New York, NY.

Smithson used industrial equipment to create Environmental artworks by manipulating earth and rock. *Spiral Jetty* is a mammoth coil of black basalt, limestone, and earth extending into Great Salt Lake.

PERFORMANCE AND CONCEPTUAL ART AND NEW MEDIA

Environmental Art, although a singular artistic phenomenon, typifies postwar developments in the art world in redefining the nature of an "artwork" and expanding the range of works that artists and the general public consider "art." Some of the new types of artworks are the result of the invention of new media, such as computers and video cameras. But the new art forms also reflect avant-garde artists' continued questioning of the status quo.

Performance Art

An important new artistic genre that emerged in the decades following World War II was *Performance Art.* Performance artists replace traditional stationary artworks with movements, gestures, and sounds performed before an audience, whose members may or may not participate in the performance. The informal and spontaneous events that early Performance artists staged anticipated the rebellion and youthful exuberance of the 1960s and at first pushed art outside the confines of the mainstream art institutions—museums and galleries. Performance Art also served as an antidote to the pretentiousness of most traditional art objects and challenged art's function as a commodity. In the later 1960s, however, museums began to commission performances with increasing frequency, thereby neutralizing much of the subversiveness characteristic of this new art form. Unfortunately, because the earliest Performance artists created their works before the widespread availability of inexpensive handheld video cameras, the only records of their performances are the documentary photographs taken during the events. Photographs are unsatisfying, if invaluable, records because they lack the elements of sound and motion integral to Performance Art.

ARTISTS ON ART
Carolee Schneemann on Painting, Performance Art, and Art History

Born in Pennsylvania, Carolee Schneemann (FIG. **30-52**) studied painting at Bard College and the University of Illinois before settling in New York City in 1962, where she became one of the pioneering Performance artists of the 1960s. In notes she wrote in 1962–1963, Schneemann reflected on the nature of art production and contrasted her kinetic works with more traditional art forms.

> Environments, happenings—concretions—are an extension of my painting-constructions which often have moving (motorized) sections. . . . [But the] steady exploration and repeated viewing which the eye is required to make with my painting-constructions is reversed in the performance situation where the spectator is overwhelmed with changing recognitions, carried emotionally by a flux of evocative actions and led or held by the specified time sequence which marks the duration of a performance. In this way the audience is actually *visually* more *passive* than when confronting a . . . "still" work . . . With paintings, constructions and sculptures the viewers are able to carry out repeated examinations of the work, to select and vary viewing positions (to walk with the eye), to touch surfaces and to freely indulge responses to areas of color and texture at their chosen speed.*

Readers of this book will also take special interest in Schneemann's 1975 essay titled "Woman in the Year 2000," in which she envisioned what introductory art history courses would be like at the beginning of the 21st century:

> By the year 2000 [every] young woman will study Art Istory [sic] courses enriched by the inclusion, discovery, and re-evaluation of works by women artists: works (and lives) until recently buried away, willfully destroyed, [or] ignored.†

A comparison between this 15th edition of *Art through the Ages* and editions published in the 1960s and 1970s will immediately reveal the accuracy of Schneemann's prediction.

*Quoted in Bruce McPherson, ed., *More Than Meat Joy: Complete Performance Works and Selected Writings* (New Paltz, N.Y.: Documentext, 1979), 10–11.
†Ibid., 198.

30-52 **CAROLEE SCHNEEMANN,** *Meat Joy* (performance at Judson Church, New York City), 1964.

In her performances, Schneemann transformed the nature of Performance Art by introducing a feminist dimension through the use of her body (often nude) to challenge traditional gender roles.

JOHN CAGE Many of the artists instrumental in the development of Performance Art were students or associates of the charismatic American teacher and composer John Cage (1912–1992). Cage encouraged his students at both the New School for Social Research in New York and Black Mountain College in North Carolina to link their art directly with life. He brought to music composition some of the ideas of Duchamp and of Eastern philosophy. Cage used methods such as chance to avoid the closed structures marking traditional music and, in his view, separating it from the unpredictable and multilayered qualities of daily existence. For example, the score for one of Cage's piano compositions instructs the performer to appear, sit down at the piano, raise the keyboard cover to mark the beginning of the piece, remain motionless at the instrument for 4 minutes and 33 seconds, and then close the keyboard cover, rise, and bow to signal the end of the work. The "music" would be the unplanned sounds and noises (such as coughs and whispers) emanating from the audience during the "performance."

ALLAN KAPROW One of Cage's students in the 1950s was ALLAN KAPROW (1927–2006). Schooled in art history as well as music composition, Kaprow sought to explore the intersection of art and life. He believed, for example, that Jackson Pollock's actions when producing a painting (FIG. 30-7) were more important than the finished painting. This led Kaprow to develop a type of event known as a *Happening*. He described a Happening as

> an assemblage of events performed or perceived in more than one time and place. Its material environments may be constructed, taken over directly from what is available, or altered slightly: just as its activities may be invented or commonplace. A Happening, unlike a stage play, may occur at a supermarket, driving along a highway, under a pile of rags, and in a friend's kitchen, either at once or sequentially. If sequentially, time may extend to more than a year. The Happening is performed according to plan but without rehearsal, audience, or repetition. It is art but seems closer to life.[25]

Happenings were often participatory. One Happening consisted of a constructed setting with partitions on which viewers wrote phrases, while another involved spectators walking on a pile of tires. One of Kaprow's first Happenings, titled *18 Happenings in Six Parts,* took place in 1959 in the Reuben Gallery in New York City. For the event, he divided the gallery space into three sections with translucent plastic sheets. Over the course of the 90-minute piece, performers, including Kaprow's artist friends, bounced balls, read from placards, extended their arms like wings, and played records as slides and lights switched on and off in programmed sequences.

FLUXUS Other Cage students interested in the composer's search to find aesthetic potential in the nontraditional and commonplace formed the *Fluxus* group. Eventually expanding to include European and Japanese artists, this group's performances were more theatrical than Happenings. To distinguish their performances from Happenings, the artists associated with Fluxus coined the term *Events* to describe their work. Events focused on single actions, such as turning a light on and off or watching falling snow—what Fluxus artist La Monte Young (b. 1935) called "the theater of the single event."[26] Events usually took place on a stage separating the performers from the audience but without costumes or added decor. Events were not spontaneous. They followed a compositional "score," which, given the restricted nature of these performances, was short.

CAROLEE SCHNEEMANN Some artists, notably CAROLEE SCHNEEMANN (b. 1939) in the United States and members of the Concrete Art Association (FIG. 34-19) in Japan, produced artworks integrating painting and performance (see "Carolee Schneemann on Painting, Performance Art, and Art History," page 986). Schneemann's self-described "kinetic theater" radically transformed the nature of Performance Art by introducing a feminist dimension through the use of her body (often nude) to challenge "the psychic territorial power lines by which women were admitted to the Art Stud Club."[27] In her 1964 performance, *Meat Joy* (FIG. 30-52), which was designed to be both erotic and revolting, Schneemann cavorted with male performers and reveled in the taste, smell, and feel of raw sausages, chickens, and fish.

JOSEPH BEUYS The leftist politics of the Fluxus group in the early 1960s strongly influenced German artist JOSEPH BEUYS (1921–1986; FIG. **30-53**). Drawing on Happenings and Fluxus, Beuys created actions aimed at illuminating the condition of modern humanity.

30-53 JOSEPH BEUYS, *How to Explain Pictures to a Dead Hare* (**performance at Schmela Gallery, Düsseldorf**), 1965.

In this one-person event, Beuys coated his head with honey and gold leaf and spoke to a dead hare. Assuming the role of a shaman, he used stylized actions to evoke a sense of mystery and sacred ritual.

He wanted to make a new kind of sculptural object that would include "Thinking Forms: how we mold our thoughts or Spoken Forms: how we shape our thoughts into words or Social Sculpture: how we mold and shape the world in which we live."[28]

Beuys's commitment to artworks stimulating thought about art and life derived in part from his experiences as a pilot during World War II. After the enemy shot down his plane over Crimea, nomadic Tatars nursed him back to health by swaddling his body in fat and felt to warm him. Fat and felt thus symbolized healing and regeneration to Beuys, and he incorporated these materials into many of his sculptures and actions, such as *How to Explain Pictures to a Dead Hare* (FIG. 30-53), in which the seated Beuys rests his left foot on soft felt and, to make a contrast with the often cold and unyielding contemporary world, rests his right foot on steel. In this one-person event, Beuys performed stylized actions evoking a sense of mystery and sacred ritual. He appeared in a room hung with his drawings, cradling a dead hare to which he spoke softly. Beuys coated his head with honey covered with gold leaf, creating a shimmering mask. In this manner, he took on the role of the shaman, an individual with special spiritual powers. As a shaman, Beuys believed he was acting to help revolutionize human thought so that each human being could become a truly free and creative person. But the impossibility of communicating with a dead hare symbolized the difficulty of achieving successful exchanges among alienated people in modern society.

JEAN TINGUELY The paradoxical notion of destruction as an act of creation surfaces in a number of kinetic artworks, most notably in the sculpture of JEAN TINGUELY (1925–1991). Trained as a painter in his native Switzerland, Tinguely gravitated to motion sculpture. In the 1950s, he made a series of motor-driven devices that he called *metamatics,* which produced instant abstract paintings. He programmed these metamatics electronically to act with an antimechanical unpredictability when someone inserted a felt-tipped marking pen into a pincer and pressed a button to initiate the pen's motion across a small sheet of paper clipped to an "easel." Participants in his metamatic demonstrations could use different-colored markers in succession and could stop and start the device to achieve some degree of control over the final image. These operations created a series of small works resembling Abstract Expressionist paintings.

In 1960, Tinguely expanded the scale of his work with a kinetic piece designed to "perform" and then destroy itself in the sculpture garden of the Museum of Modern Art in New York City. He created *Homage to New York* (FIG. **30-54**) with the aid of engineer Billy Klüver (1927–2004), who helped him scrounge wheels and other moving objects from a dump near Manhattan. The completed structure, painted white for visibility against the dark night sky, included a player piano modified into a metamatic painting machine, a weather balloon that inflated during the performance, vials of colored smoke, and a host of gears, pulleys, wheels, and other found machine parts.

Homage to New York premiered (and instantly self-destructed) on March 17, 1960, with the state's governor, Nelson Rockefeller (1908–1979), an array of other distinguished guests, and three television crews in attendance. Once Tinguely turned on the machine, smoke poured from its interior and the piano caught fire. Various

30-54 JEAN TINGUELY, *Homage to New York,* 1960, just prior to its self-destruction in the garden of the Museum of Modern Art, New York.

Tinguely produced motor-driven devices programmed to make instant abstract paintings. To explore the notion of destruction as an act of creation, he designed this one to perform and then destroy itself.

PROBLEMS AND SOLUTIONS
Rethinking "Art": Conceptual Art

In many ways, the most radical of avant-garde art movements of the postwar era was Conceptual Art, which reconsidered the very definition of what "art" is. Conceptual artists maintained that the "art-fulness" of art lay in the artist's idea, rather than in its final expression. These artists regarded the idea, or concept, as the defining component of the artwork. Indeed, in their effort to solve the problem of creating artworks that are ideas instead of tangible objects, some Conceptual artists do not create new objects at all.

One of the leading Conceptual artists and theorists was Joseph Kosuth. Born in Toledo, Ohio, and educated at the School of Visual Arts in New York City, Kosuth summarized the intellectual transformation that he and other Conceptual artists had to undergo in their effort to rethink everything they had been taught about art.

> Like everyone else I inherited the idea of art as a set of *formal* problems. So when I began to re-think my ideas of art, I had to re-think that thinking process . . . [T]he radical shift, was in changing the idea of art itself. . . . It meant you could have an art work which was that *idea* of an art work, and its formal components weren't

important. I felt I had found a way to make art without formal components being confused for an expressionist composition. The expression was in the idea, not the form—the forms were only a device in the service of the idea.*

Kosuth's work operates at the intersection of language and vision, dealing with the relationship between the abstract and the concrete. For example, in *One and Three Chairs* (FIG. 30-55), Kosuth juxtaposed a real chair, a full-scale photograph of the same chair, and an enlarged reproduction of a dictionary definition of the word "chair." By so doing, the Conceptual artist asked viewers to ponder the notion of what constitutes "chairness."

Other Conceptual artists pursued the notion that the idea itself is a work of art by creating works involving invisible materials, such as inert gases, radioactive isotopes, or radio waves. In each case, viewers must base their understanding of the artwork on what they know about the properties of these materials, rather than on any visible empirical data, and must depend on the artist's linguistic description of the work. Ultimately, the Conceptual artists challenged the very premises of artistic production, pushing art's boundaries to a point where no concrete definition of art is possible.

*"Joseph Kosuth: Art as Idea as Idea," in Jeanne Siegel, ed., *Artwords: Discourse on the 60s and 70s* (Ann Arbor, Mich.: UMI Research Press, 1985), 221, 225.

30-55 JOSEPH KOSUTH, *One and Three Chairs*, 1965. Wood folding chair, photographic copy of a chair, and photographic enlargement of a dictionary definition of a chair; chair, 2' 8$\frac{3}{8}$" × 1' 2$\frac{7}{8}$" × 1' 8$\frac{7}{8}$"; photo panel, 3' × 2' $\frac{1}{8}$"; text panel, 2' × 2' $\frac{1}{8}$". Museum of Modern Art, New York (Larry Aldrich Foundation Fund).

Conceptual artists regard the concept as an artwork's defining component. To portray "chairness," Kosuth juxtaposed a chair, a photograph of the chair, and a dictionary definition of "chair."

1 ft.

parts of the machine broke off and rambled away, while one of the metamatics tried but failed to produce an abstract painting. Finally, Tinguely summoned a firefighter to extinguish the blaze and ensure the demise of his artwork-machine with an ax. Like Tinguely's other kinetic sculptures, *Homage to New York* recalls the satiric Dadaist spirit and the droll import of Klee's *Twittering Machine* (FIG. 29-59). But Tinguely deliberately made the wacky behavior of *Homage to New York* more playful and more endearing. Having been given a freedom of eccentric behavior unprecedented in the mechanical

world, Tinguely's creations often seemed to behave with the whimsical individuality of human actors.

Conceptual Art

The relentless challenges to artistic convention fundamental to the historical avant-garde reached a logical conclusion with *Conceptual Art* in the mid-1960s and the work of JOSEPH KOSUTH (b. 1945; FIG. 30-55) and others (see "Rethinking 'Art': Conceptual Art," above).

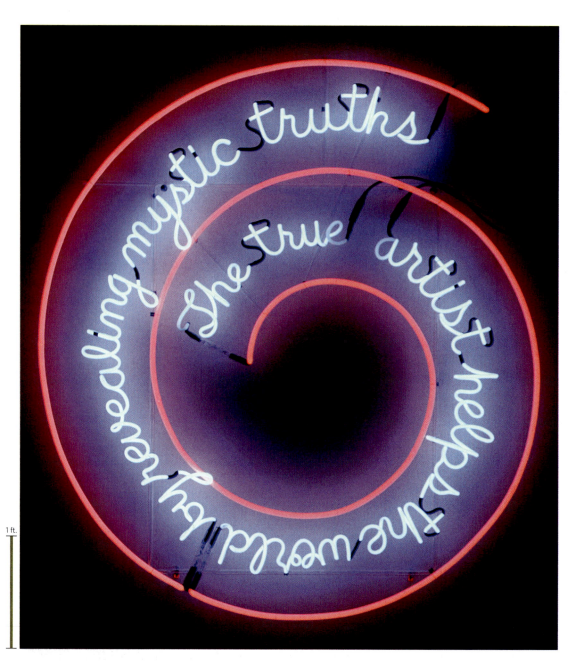

30-56 Bruce Nauman, *The True Artist Helps the World by Revealing Mystic Truths,* 1967. Neon with glass tubing suspension frame, 4' 11" high. Private collection.

In his art, Nauman explores his interest in language and wordplay. He described this Conceptual neon sculpture's emphatic assertion as "a totally silly idea," but an idea he believed.

the foundation of much of his art, and in his interest in language and wordplay.

The True Artist Helps the World by Revealing Mystic Truths (FIG. 30-56) was the first of Nauman's many neon sculptures. Nauman selected neon, which Charles Moore also employed to great effect in his postmodern Piazza d'Italia (FIG. 30-1), because he wanted to find a medium that would be identified with a nonartistic function. Determined to discover a way to connect objects with words, he drew on the method outlined in *Philosophical Investigations,* in which the Austrian philosopher Ludwig Wittgenstein (1889–1951) encouraged contradictory and nonsensical arguments. Nauman's neon sculpture spins out an emphatic assertion, which is also the work's title, but as Nauman explained, "[The statement] was kind of a test—like when you say something out loud to see if you believe it. . . . [I]t was on the one hand a totally silly idea and yet, on the other hand, I believed it."[29]

New Media

During the 1960s and 1970s, many avant-garde artists eagerly embraced technologies previously unavailable in their attempt to find new avenues of artistic expression. Among the most popular new media were video recording and computer graphics.

VIDEO Initially, only commercial television studios possessed video equipment, but in the 1960s, with the development of relatively inexpensive portable video recorders and of electronic devices allowing manipulation of recorded video material, artists began to explore in earnest the expressive possibilities of this new technology. In its basic form, video recording involves a special motion-picture

BRUCE NAUMAN About the time that Kosuth made *One and Three Chairs* (FIG. 30-55), his slightly older contemporary, Indiana native BRUCE NAUMAN (b. 1941), made his artistic presence known in California when he abandoned painting and turned to object-making. Since then, his work, produced since 1979 in New Mexico, has been extremely varied. In addition to sculptural pieces constructed from different materials, including neon lights (FIG. 30-56), rubber, fiberglass, and cardboard, he has also produced photographs (FIG. 30-56A), films, videos, books, and large room installations, as well as Performance Art.

30-56A Nauman, *Self-Portrait as Fountain,* 1966–1967.

Nauman's work of the 1960s intersected with that of the Conceptual artists, especially in terms of the philosophical exploration that was

30-57 NAM JUNE PAIK, video still from *Global Groove*, 1973. $\frac{3}{4}''$ videotape, color, sound, 30 minutes. Collection of the artist.

Korean-born video artist Paik's best-known work is a cascade of fragmented sequences of performances and commercials intended as a sample of the rich worldwide television menu of the future.

camera that captures visible images and translates them into electronic data for display on a video monitor or television screen. Video pictures resemble photographs in the amount of detail they contain, but, like computer graphics, a video image consists of a series of points of light on a grid, giving the impression of soft focus. Viewers looking at television or video art are not aware of the monitor's surface. Instead, fulfilling the ideal of Renaissance artists, they concentrate on the image and look through the glass surface, as through a window, into the "space" beyond. Video images combine the optical realism of photography with the sense that the subjects move in real time in a deep space "inside" the monitor.

NAM JUNE PAIK When video introduced the possibility of manipulating subjects in real time, artists such as Korean-born NAM JUNE PAIK (1932–2006) were eager to work with the medium. After studying music performance, art history, and Eastern philosophy in Korea and Japan, Paik worked with electronic music in Germany in the late 1950s. In 1965, after relocating to New York City, Paik acquired the first inexpensive video recorder sold in Manhattan (the Sony Porta-Pak) and immediately recorded everything he saw out the window of his taxi on the return trip to his studio downtown. Experience acquired as artist-in-residence at television stations WGBH in Boston and WNET in New York enabled him to experiment with the most advanced broadcast video technology.

A grant permitted Paik to collaborate with the gifted Japanese engineer-inventor Shuya Abe (b. 1932) in developing a video synthesizer. This instrument enables artists to manipulate and change the electronic video information in various ways, causing images or parts of images to stretch, shrink, change color, or break up. With the synthesizer, artists can also layer images, inset one image into another, or merge images from various cameras with those from video recorders to make a single visual kaleidoscopic "time-collage." This kind of compositional freedom enabled Paik to combine his interests in painting, music, Eastern philosophy, global politics for survival, humanized technology, and cybernetics. Inspired by the ideas of John Cage, Paik called his video works "physical music" and said his musical background enabled him to understand time better than could video artists trained in painting or sculpture.

Paik's best-known video work, *Global Groove* (FIG. **30-57**), was commissioned for broadcast over the United Nations satellite. The video combines in quick succession fragmented sequences of female tap dancers, poet Allen Ginsberg (1926–1997) reading his work, a performance by Fluxus artist and cellist Charlotte Moorman (1933–1991) using a man's back as her instrument, Pepsi commercials from Japanese television, Korean drummers, and a shot of the Living Theatre group performing a controversial piece called *Paradise Now*. The cascade of imagery in *Global Groove* gives viewers a glimpse of the rich worldwide television menu that Paik predicted would be available in the future—a prediction that has been fulfilled with the advent of affordable cable and satellite television service.

COMPUTER GRAPHICS Perhaps the most promising new medium for creating and manipulating illusionistic three-dimensional forms is computer graphics. This new medium uses light to make images and, like photography, can incorporate specially recorded camera images. Unlike video recording, computer graphic art enables artists to work with wholly invented forms, as painters can. Developed during the 1960s and 1970s, this technology opened up new possibilities for both abstract and figural art. It involves electronic programs dividing the surface of the computer monitor's

30-58 David Em, *Nora*, 1979. Computer-generated color photograph, 1' 5" × 1' 11". Private collection.

Unlike video recording, computer graphic art enables the creation of wholly invented forms, as in painting. Em builds fantastic digital images of imaginary landscapes out of tiny boxes called pixels.

1 in.

cathode-ray tube into a grid of tiny boxes called "picture elements," or *pixels*. Artists can electronically address pixels individually to create a design, much as knitting or weaving patterns have a grid matrix as a guide for making a design in fabric. Once created, parts of a computer graphic design can be changed quickly through an electronic program, enabling artists to revise or duplicate shapes in the design and to manipulate at will the color, texture, size, number, and position of any desired detail. Computer graphic pictures appear in luminous color on the cathode-ray tube. The effect suggests a view into a vast world existing inside the tube.

DAVID EM One of the pioneering artists working in this electronic painting mode, David Em (b. 1952) uses what he terms "computer imaging" to fashion fantastic imaginary landscapes. These have an eerily believable existence within the "window" of the computer monitor. When he was artist-in-residence at the California Institute of Technology's Jet Propulsion Laboratory, Em created brilliantly colored scenes of alien worlds using the laboratory's advanced computer graphics equipment. He also had access to software programs developed to create computer graphic simulations of NASA's missions in outer space. Creating images with the computer afforded Em great flexibility in manipulating simple geometric shapes—shrinking or enlarging them, stretching or reversing them, repeating them, adding texture to their surfaces, and creating the illusion of light and shadow. In images such as *Nora* (FIG. **30-58**), Em created futuristic geometric versions of Surrealistic dreamscapes whose forms seem familiar and strange at the same time. The illusion of space in these works is immensely vivid and seductive. It almost seems possible to wander through the tubelike foreground "frame" and up the inclined foreground plane or to hop aboard the hovering globe at the lower left for a journey through the strange patterns and textures of this mysterious labyrinthine setting.

AFTER 1980 The decades following the conclusion of World War II were unparalleled in art history for innovation in form and content and for the development of new media. Those exciting trends have continued unabated since 1980—and with an increasingly international dimension that will be explored in Chapter 31.

MODERNISM AND POSTMODERNISM IN EUROPE AND AMERICA, 1945 TO 1980

Painting, Sculpture, and Photography

- The art of the decades following World War II reflects cultural upheaval—the rejection of traditional values, the civil rights and feminist movements, and the new consumer society.

- The first major postwar avant-garde art movement was Abstract Expressionism, which championed an artwork's formal elements rather than its subject. Gestural abstractionists, such as Pollock, de Kooning, Krasner, and Mitchell, sought expressiveness through energetically applied pigment. Chromatic abstractionists, such as Rothko, struck emotional chords through large areas of pure color.

- Post-Painterly Abstraction promoted a cool rationality in contrast to Abstract Expressionism's passion. Both hard-edge painters, such as Kelly and Stella, and color-field painters, such as Frankenthaler and Louis, pursued purity in art by emphasizing the flatness of pigment on canvas.

- Pop artists, such as Johns, Lichtenstein, and Warhol, rejected abstraction to represent subjects grounded in popular culture—flags, comic strips, Coca-Cola bottles—sometimes employing commercial printing techniques. Rosenquist incorporated social and political commentary into his billboard-size paintings.

- Riley and other Op artists sought to produce optical illusions of motion and depth using only geometric forms on two-dimensional surfaces.

- Superrealists, such as Flack, Close, and Hanson—kindred spirits to Pop artists in many ways—created paintings and sculptures featuring scrupulous fidelity to optical fact.

- The leading sculptural movement of this period was Minimalism. Tony Smith and Judd created artworks consisting of simple and unadorned geometric shapes to underscore the "objecthood" of their sculptures.

- Arbus and White represent the two poles of photography in the postwar period—documentary photography and art photography.

- Many artists pursued social agendas in their work. Postwar feminist artists include Chicago, whose *Dinner Party* honors important women throughout history and features crafts traditionally associated with women; Sherman, who explored the "male gaze" in her photographs resembling film stills; and Mendieta and Wilke, whose bodies were their subjects.

Mitchell, *Untitled*, ca. 1953–1954

Lichtenstein, *Hopeless*, 1963

Sherman, *Untitled Film Still #35*, 1979

Architecture and Site-Specific Art

- Some of the leading early-20th-century modernist architects remained active after 1945. Wright built the snail-shell Guggenheim Museum, Le Corbusier the sculpturesque Notre-Dame-du-Haut, and Mies van der Rohe the Minimalist Seagram skyscraper. Younger architects Saarinen and Utzon designed structures with dramatic curvilinear rooflines.

- In contrast to modernist architecture, postmodernist architecture is complex and eclectic and often incorporates references to historical styles. Among the best-known postmodern projects are Moore's Piazza d'Italia and Graves's Portland Building, both of which incorporate classical motifs.

- Site-specific art stands at the intersection of architecture and sculpture. Smithson's *Spiral Jetty* is a mammoth coil of natural materials in Utah's Great Salt Lake.

Moore, Piazza d'Italia, New Orleans, 1976–1980

Performance and Conceptual Art and New Media

- Among the most significant developments in the art world after World War II has been the expansion of the range of works considered "art."

- Performance artists, notably Schneemann and Beuys, replace traditional stationary artworks with movements and sounds performed before an audience. Performance Art often addresses the same social and political issues that contemporaneous painters and sculptors explore.

- Kosuth and other Conceptual artists believe that the "artfulness" of art is in the artist's idea, not the work resulting from the idea.

- Paik and others have embraced video recording technology to produce artworks combining images and sounds.

- Em was a pioneer in exploring computer graphics as an art form. Unlike video recording, computer art enables artists to work with wholly invented forms, as painters can.

Beuys, *How to Explain Pictures to a Dead Hare*, 1965

▲ **31-1a** Smith's *Trade* celebrates her Native American identity. The cheap trinkets she offers in return for confiscated land include sports team memorabilia with offensive names, such as Braves and Redskins.

▲ **31-1b** Newspaper clippings chronicle the conquest of Native America by Europeans and include references to the problems facing those living on reservations today—poverty, alcoholism, and disease.

1 ft.

31-1   JAUNE QUICK-TO-SEE SMITH, *Trade (Gifts for Trading Land with White People)*, 1992. Oil and mixed media on canvas, 5' × 14' 2". Chrysler Museum of Art, Norfolk.

▶ **31-1c** Overlapping the collage and the central motif of the canoe in Smith's anti–Columbus Quincentenary Celebration is dripping red paint, symbolic of the shedding of Native American blood.

Contemporary Art Worldwide

ART AS SOCIOPOLITICAL MESSAGE

Although televisions, smartphones, and the Internet have brought people all over the world closer together than ever before in history, national, ethnic, religious, and racial conflicts are also an unfortunate and pervasive characteristic of contemporary life. Some of the most eloquent voices raised in protest about the major political and social issues of the day have been those of painters and sculptors, who can harness the power of art to amplify the power of the written and spoken word.

JAUNE QUICK-TO-SEE SMITH (b. 1940) is a Native American artist descended from the Shoshone, Salish, and Cree peoples. Raised on the Flatrock Reservation in Montana, she is steeped in the traditional culture of her ancestors, but she trained as an artist in the European American tradition at Framingham State University in Massachusetts and at the University of New Mexico. Smith's ethnic heritage has always informed her art, however, and her concern about the invisibility of Native American artists has led her to organize exhibitions of their art. Her self-identity has also been the central theme of her mature work as an artist.

In 1992, Smith created what many critics consider her masterpiece: *Trade* (FIG. **31-1**), subtitled *Gifts for Trading Land with White People*. A complex multimedia work of imposing size, *Trade* is Smith's response to what she called "the Quincentenary Non-Celebration"—that is, white America's celebration of the 500th anniversary of Christopher Columbus's arrival in what Europeans called the New World. *Trade* incorporates collage elements and attached objects, reminiscent of a Rauschenberg *combine* (FIG. 30-25), with energetic brushwork recalling Willem de Kooning's Abstract Expressionist canvases (FIG. 30-8). Among the items in *Trade*'s collage are clippings from Native American newspapers featuring images chronicling the conquest of Native America by Europeans and references to the problems facing those living on reservations today—poverty, alcoholism, and disease. The dripping red paint overlaying the collage with the central motif of the canoe is symbolic of the shedding of Native American blood.

Above the painting, as if hung from a clothesline, is an array of objects. These include Native American artifacts, such as beaded belts and feather headdresses, plastic tomahawks, "Indian princess" dolls, and contemporary sports memorabilia from teams with American Indian–derived names: the Cleveland Indians, Atlanta Braves, and Washington Redskins. The inclusion of these objects reminds viewers of the vocal opposition to the use of these and similar names for high school and college as well as professional sports teams. All the cheap artifacts together also have a deeper significance. As the title indicates and Smith explained: "Why won't you consider trading the land we handed over to you for these silly trinkets that so honor us? Sound like a bad deal? Well, that's the deal you gave us."[1]

ART TODAY

This is an "incomplete" or "unfinished" chapter, because the story of the art of the present generation—that is, the history of the art and architecture of the past 35 to 40 years—is still unfolding, and the body of material to be surveyed is increasing literally daily. It is both impractical and unwise to try to impose a strict chronological development scheme on the extraordinarily diverse range of paintings, sculptures, photographs and videos, buildings and monuments, and multimedia works produced worldwide since 1980. Instead, this survey of contemporary art is organized thematically and stylistically and, to a lesser degree, by medium, under the following headings: Personal and Group Identity; Political and Social Commentary; Representation and Abstraction; New Media; Environmental and Site-Specific Art; and Architecture. It is important to note, however, that most contemporary artworks fall into more than one of these categories. For example, a painting that explores personal and group identity, such as Jaune Quick-to-See Smith's *Trade* (FIG. 31-1), can also be a work of social commentary and combine representation and abstraction and several different media. Nevertheless, these six categories constitute a useful way to approach the complex phenomenon of contemporary art and architecture.

PERSONAL AND GROUP IDENTITY

Trade is the unique product of Smith's heritage as a Native American who has sought to bridge native and European artistic traditions, but her work parallels that of many other innovative artists of the decades since 1980 in addressing contemporary life. This focus on the content and meaning of art represents, as did the earlier work of the Pop artists and Superrealists (see pages 965–973), a rejection of modernist formalist doctrine and a desire on the part of artists once again to embrace the persuasive power of art to communicate with a wide audience—an audience that, thanks to smartphones, the Internet, and other technological breakthroughs, is now instantly international in character. It also represents in many respects a return to the core principle of the 19th-century Realists, as defined by Gustave Courbet (see page 816): "[A]rt in painting should consist only of the representation of things that are visible and tangible to the artist. Every age should be represented only by its own artists, that is to say, by the artists who have lived in it."[2]

The multicultural diversity of the world today has made almost everybody keenly aware of her or his distinct national, ethnic, racial, and religious identity. Not surprisingly, many contemporary artists have made their personal and group identity the focus of their work.

African American Art

Prominent among those for whom race has been a key element of the art that they have produced during the past few decades are African Americans. This is a very significant development in the history of art because outside Africa, Africans and people of African descent have rarely been the subject of artworks produced by European and American artists except in marginal and often demeaning

31-2 KEHINDE WILEY, *Napoleon Leading the Army over the Alps,* 2005. Oil on canvas, 9' × 9'. Brooklyn Museum, Brooklyn (Collection of Suzi and Andrew B. Cohen).

Wiley's trademark paintings are reworkings of famous portraits (FIG. 27-2A) in which he substitutes young African American men in contemporary dress in order to situate them in "the field of power."

roles. Black artists have also been omitted from most histories of Western art until recently.

KEHINDE WILEY One leading living African American artist who has lamented the near-total absence of blacks in Western painting and sculpture—and who has set out to correct that discriminatory imbalance—is Los Angeles native KEHINDE WILEY (b. 1977). Wiley earned his BFA at the San Francisco Art Institute and his MFA at Yale University and is currently based in New York City, where he was artist-in-residence at the Studio Museum in Harlem in 2001–2002. Wiley has achieved renown for his large-scale portraits of young urban African American men. His trademark paintings, however, are reworkings of historically important portraits in which he substitutes figures of young black men in contemporary dress in order to situate them in what he calls "the field of power."

A characteristic example is *Napoleon Leading the Army over the Alps* (FIG. **31-2**) based on Jacques-Louis David's painting (FIG. 27-2A) of the same subject. To evoke the era of the original, Wiley presented his portrait of an African American Napoleon on horseback in a gilt wood frame. Although in many details an accurate reproduction of David's canvas, Wiley's version is by no means a mechanical copy. His heroic narrative unfolds against a vibrantly colored ornate wallpaper-like background instead of a dramatic sky—a distinctly modernist reminder to the viewer that this is a painting and not a window onto an Alpine landscape.

JEAN-MICHEL BASQUIAT Among other contemporary artists whose work has focused on the experiences of American men of African descent are MELVIN EDWARDS (b. 1937; FIG. **31-2A**) and JEAN-MICHEL BASQUIAT (1960–1988), whose father was an accountant from Haiti and whose mother was a black Puerto Rican. Basquiat grew up in a comfortable middle-class home in Brooklyn, but he rebelled against his parents'

⊿ **31-2A** EDWARDS, *Tambo*, 1993.

values, dropped out of school at 17, and took to the streets. He first burst onto the New York art scene as the anonymous author of witty graffiti in Lower Manhattan signed SAMO (a dual reference to the derogatory name *Sambo* for African Americans and to "same old shit"). Basquiat first drew attention as an artist in 1980 when he participated in a group show—the "Times Square Show"—in an abandoned 42nd Street building. Eight years later, after a meteoric rise to fame, he died of a heroin overdose at age 27.

Basquiat was self-taught, both as an artist and about the history of art, but he was not a "primitive." His sophisticated style owes a debt to diverse sources, including the late paintings of Pablo Picasso, Abstract Expressionism, and the "art brut" of Jean Dubuffet (FIG. 30-4). Many of Basquiat's paintings celebrate black heroes—for example, the legendary jazz musicians Charlie "Bird" Parker and Dizzy Gillespie, whom he memorialized in *Horn Players* (FIG. **31-3**). The fractured figures, the bold colors against a black background, and the deliberately scrawled, crossed-out, and misspelled graffiti

31-3 JEAN-MICHEL BASQUIAT, *Horn Players,* 1983. Acrylic and oil paintstick on three canvas panels, 8' × 6' 3". Broad Art Foundation, Santa Monica.

In this tribute to two legendary African American musicians, Basquiat combined bold colors, fractured figures, and graffiti to capture the dynamic rhythms of jazz and the excitement of New York.

("ornithology"—the study of birds—is a pun on Parker's nickname and also the title of one of Parker's musical compositions) create a dynamic composition suggesting the rhythms of jazz music and the excitement of the streets of New York, "the city that never sleeps."

FAITH RINGGOLD Just as Wiley, Basquiat, and Edwards have examined the lives of African American men in their art, several leading contemporary black women artists have made the challenges faced by African American women the subject of their artworks. One of them is Harlem native FAITH RINGGOLD (b. 1930), who studied painting at the City College of New York and taught art in the New York public schools for 18 years. In the 1960s, Ringgold produced numerous works that provided incisive commentary on the realities of racial prejudice. She increasingly incorporated references to gender as well and, in the 1970s, turned to fabric as the predominant material in her art. Using fabric enabled Ringgold to make more pointed reference to the domestic sphere, traditionally associated with women, and to collaborate with her mother, Willi Posey, a fashion designer.

After her mother's death in 1981, Ringgold created *Who's Afraid of Aunt Jemima?* (FIG. 31-4), a quilt composed of dyed, painted, and pieced fabric. A moving tribute to her mother, this "story quilt"—Ringgold's signature art form—merges the personal and the political. Combining words with pictures, as did Basquiat (FIG. 31-3) and many other contemporary artists (FIGS. 31-6 and 31-8), Ringgold incorporates a narrative in her quilt. *Aunt Jemima* tells the witty story of the family of the stereotypical black "mammy" in the mind of the public, but here Jemima is a successful African American businesswoman. Ringgold narrates the story using black dialect interspersed with embroidered portraits and traditional patterned squares. *Aunt Jemima,* while incorporating autobiographical references, also speaks to the larger issues of the history of African American culture and the struggles of women to overcome oppression.

CARRIE MAE WEEMS Among the other contemporary feminist artists who have addressed the racial and social issues of concern to African American women are LORNA SIMPSON (b. 1960; FIG. 31-4A) and CARRIE MAE WEEMS (b. 1953), both of whom have chosen photography as their favored medium of expression. Oregon-born Weems trained at the California Institute of the Arts in Valencia and the University of California, San Diego, and now lives in Syracuse, New York. Her critically acclaimed work as a photographer and video artist includes the *Kitchen Table* series of 20 photographs interwoven with 13 text panels and audio recordings examining the domestic life of an African American family. The *Kitchen Table* pictorial, verbal, and audio narratives resonate with a much broader audience, however.

The setting of each photo is a kitchen table, with the viewer positioned at one end and Weems seated at the other. A ceiling fixture resembling a lamp in an interrogation cell illuminates the small room. In *Man Smoking/Malcolm X* (FIG. 31-5), Weems and a man smoking a cigarette play cards while consuming alcohol. Weems stares at her companion, attempting not only to determine the cards he holds but to size up the man's character. Behind her on the wall is a large photograph of Malcolm X (1925–1965) preaching, flanked

▶ **31-4A** SIMPSON, *Stereo Styles*, 1988.

by smaller personal photographs revealing Weems's own character. Like the other 19 images in the *Kitchen Table* series, this photograph tells a universal story about personal relationships in addition to capturing a characteristic moment in one African American household (compare FIG. 27-38). As Weems explained,

> I'm not simply describing African-American culture. I'm really involved with other levels of description that move across several different kinds of categories. On the one hand, I might be interested in what's happening in gender with men and women, black and white and Asian, and maybe I'm interested in questions of globalism and class.[3]

Gender and Sexuality

The interest in feminist issues among African American women artists is but one aspect of a more general concern among contemporary artists of all races and nationalities with gender and sexuality

[Quilt image with caption:]

31-4 FAITH RINGGOLD, *Who's Afraid of Aunt Jemima?* 1983. Acrylic on canvas with fabric borders, quilted, 7' 6" × 6' 8". Private collection.

In this quilt, a medium associated with women, Ringgold presented a tribute to her mother that also addresses African American culture and the struggles of women to overcome oppression.

1 ft.

31-5 CARRIE MAE WEEMS, *Man Smoking/Malcolm X,* from the *Kitchen Table* series, 1990. Gelatin silver print, 2' 4¼" × 2' 4¼". Brooklyn Museum, Brooklyn (Caroline A.L. Pratt Fund).

Weems appears in each of the photographs in her *Kitchen Table* series, which records the domestic life of an African American family, but the issues addressed resonate with a much wider audience.

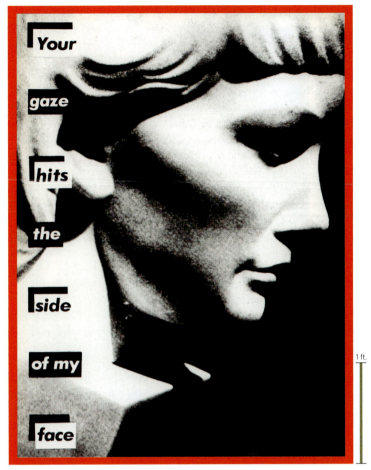

31-6 BARBARA KRUGER, *Your Gaze Hits the Side of My Face,* 1981. Photograph, red painted frame, 4' 7" × 3' 5". © Barbara Kruger/ Courtesy Mary Boone Gallery, New York.

Kruger has explored the "male gaze" in her art. Using the layout techniques of mass media, she constructed this word-and-photograph collage to challenge culturally constructed notions of gender.

as core elements of their personal identity. Feminism and homosexuality are the central themes explored by a diverse group of artists, including Barbara Kruger, Robert Mapplethorpe, and David Wojnarowicz in America and the Pakistani artist Shahzia Sikander.

BARBARA KRUGER In the 1970s, some feminist artists, chief among them Cindy Sherman (FIG. 30-37), used their art to explore the "male gaze" and the culturally constructed notion of gender. BARBARA KRUGER (b. 1945), who studied at Syracuse University and then at the Parsons School of Design in New York under Diane Arbus, examines similar issues in her photographs. The strategies and techniques of contemporary mass media have fascinated Kruger, who was a commercial graphic designer early in her career and the art director of *Mademoiselle* magazine in the late 1960s. In *Your Gaze Hits the Side of My Face* (FIG. **31-6**), Kruger incorporated the layout techniques that magazine and billboard designers use to sell consumer goods. Although she chose the reassuringly familiar format and look of advertising for *Your Gaze* and similar works, Kruger's goal was to subvert the typical use of advertising imagery. She aimed to expose the deceptiveness of the media messages that viewers complacently absorb. Kruger wants to undermine the myths—particularly those about women—that the media constantly reinforce. Her large (often 4-by-6-foot) word-and-photograph collages challenge the cultural attitudes embedded in commercial advertising. She often uses T-shirts, postcards, matchbooks, and billboards to present her work to a wide public audience.

In *Your Gaze,* Kruger overlaid a photograph of a classically beautiful sculpted head of a woman (compare FIG. 5-62A) with a vertical row of text composed of eight words. The words cannot be taken in with a single glance. Reading them is a staccato exercise, with an overlaid cumulative quality that delays understanding and intensifies the meaning (rather like a series of words painted on the pavement to be read by a driver in a moving car). Kruger's use of text in her work is significant. Many cultural theorists have asserted that language is one of the most powerful vehicles for internalizing stereotypes and conditioned roles. The combined pictorial and verbal message in this case is that the woman being viewed not only feels the viewer's gaze but can repel it, reversing the power relationship between the male observer and the observed woman. In fact, some feminist artists, most notably the GUERRILLA GIRLS (FIG. **31-6A**), have created powerful artworks consisting only of words—presented in a style and format reminiscent of the same kinds of magazine ads that Kruger incorporates in her photo-collages.

31-6A GUERRILLA GIRLS, *Advantages of Being a Woman Artist,* 1988.

ROBERT MAPPLETHORPE For many artists, their homosexuality is as important an element of their personal identity as their gender, ethnicity, or race—often more important. One brilliant

ART AND SOCIETY

Public Funding of Controversial Art

Although art can be beautiful and uplifting, throughout history art has also often challenged and offended. Since the early 1980s, a number of heated controversies about art have surfaced in the United States. There have been many calls to remove "offensive" works from public view (see "Richard Serra's *Tilted Arc*," page 1022) and, in reaction, accusations of censorship. The central questions in all cases have been whether there are limits to what art can appropriately be exhibited and whether governmental authorities have the right to monitor and pass judgment on creative endeavors. A related question is whether the acceptability of a work should be a criterion in determining the public funding of art.

Two exhibits in 1989 placed the National Endowment for the Arts (NEA), a U.S. government agency charged with distributing federal funds to support the arts, squarely in the middle of this debate. One of the exhibitions, devoted to recipients of the Awards for the Visual Arts (AVA), took place at the Southeastern Center for Contemporary Art in North Carolina. Among the award winners was Andres Serrano, whose *Piss Christ*, a photograph of a crucifix submerged in urine, sparked an uproar. Responding to this artwork, Reverend Donald Wildmon, an evangelical minister from Mississippi and head of the American Family Association, expressed outrage that this kind of work was in an exhibition funded by the NEA and the Equitable Life Assurance Society (a sponsor of the AVA). He demanded that the work be removed, and launched a letter-writing campaign that caused Equitable Life to cancel its sponsorship of the awards. To Wildmon and other staunch conservatives, this exhibition, along with *Robert Mapplethorpe: The Perfect Moment*, which included erotic homosexual images of the artist (FIG. 31-7) and others, served as evidence of cultural depravity and immorality. These critics insisted that art of an offensive character should not be funded by government agencies such as the NEA.

As a result of media furor over *The Perfect Moment*, the director of the Corcoran Museum of Art in Washington, D.C., decided to cancel the scheduled exhibition of this traveling show. But Dennis Barrie, director of the Contemporary Arts Center in Cincinnati, chose to mount the exhibition. The government indicted Barrie on charges of obscenity, but a jury acquitted him six months later.

These controversies intensified public criticism of the NEA and its funding practices. The next year, the head of the NEA, John Frohnmayer, vetoed grants for four lesbian, gay, or feminist performance artists—Karen Finley, John Fleck, Holly Hughes, and Tim Miller—who became known as the "NEA Four." Infuriated by what they perceived as governmental censorship, the artists filed suit, eventually settling the case and winning reinstatement of their grants. Congress responded by dramatically reducing the NEA's budget, and the agency no longer awards grants or fellowships to individual artists.

31-7 Robert Mapplethorpe, *Self-Portrait*, 1980. Gelatin silver print, $7\frac{3}{4}'' \times 7\frac{3}{4}''$. Robert Mapplethorpe Foundation, New York.

Mapplethorpe's *Perfect Moment* show led to a landmark court case on freedom of expression for artists. In this self-portrait, an androgynous Mapplethorpe confronts the viewer with a steady gaze.

Controversies have also erupted on the municipal level. In 1999, Rudolph Giuliani, then mayor of New York, joined a number of individuals and groups protesting the inclusion of several artworks in the exhibition *Sensation: Young British Artists from the Saatchi Collection* at the Brooklyn Museum. Chris Ofili's *The Holy Virgin Mary* (FIG. 31-10), a collage of Mary incorporating cutouts from pornographic magazines and shellacked clumps of elephant dung, became the flashpoint for public furor. Denouncing the show as "sick stuff," the mayor threatened to cut off all city subsidies to the museum.

Art that seeks to unsettle and challenge is critical to the cultural, political, and psychological life of a society. The regularity with which this kind of art raises controversy suggests that it operates at the intersection of two competing principles: free speech and artistic expression on the one hand, and a reluctance to impose images on an audience that finds them repugnant or offensive on the other. What these controversies do demonstrate, beyond doubt, is the enduring power of art—and artists.

gay artist who became the central figure in a heated debate in the halls of the U.S. Congress as well as among the public at large was ROBERT MAPPLETHORPE (1946–1989). Born in Queens, New York, Mapplethorpe studied drawing, painting, and sculpture at the Pratt Institute in Brooklyn, but after he purchased a Polaroid camera in 1970, he became increasingly interested in photography. Mapplethorpe's *The Perfect Moment* traveling exhibition, funded in part by the National Endowment for the Arts, featured an extensive series of his photographs, including many of people, often nude, some depicting children, some openly homoerotic and sadomasochistic in nature. The show led to a landmark court case in Cincinnati on freedom of expression for artists and prompted new legislation establishing restrictions on government funding of the arts (see "Public Funding of Controversial Art," above).

Never at issue was Mapplethorpe's technical mastery of the photographic medium. His gelatin silver prints have glowing tex-

When I put my hands on your body on your flesh I feel the history of that body. Not just the beginning of its forming in that distant lake but all the way beyond its ending. I feel the warmth and texture and simultaneously I see the flesh unwrap from the layers of fat and disappear. I see the fat disappear from the muscle. I see the muscle disappearing from around the organs and detaching itself from the bones. I see the organs gradually fade into transparency leaving a gleaming skeleton gleaming like ivory that slowly revolves until it becomes dust. I am consumed in the sense of your weight the way your flesh occupies momentary space the fullness of it beneath my palms. I am amazed at how perfectly your body fits to the curves of my hands. If I could attach our blood vessels so we could become each other I would. If I could attach our blood vessels in order to anchor you to the earth to this present time to me I would. If I could open your body and slip up inside your skin and look out your eyes and forever have my lips fused with yours I would. It makes me weep to feel the history of you of your flesh beneath my hands in a time of so much loss. It makes me weep to feel the movement of your flesh beneath my palms as you twist and turn over to one side to create a series of gestures to reach up around my neck to draw me nearer. All these moments will be lost in time like tears in the rain.

1 ft.

31-8 DAVID WOJNAROWICZ, *When I Put My Hands on Your Body,* 1990. Gelatin silver print and silk-screened text on museum board, 2' 2" × 3' 2". Private collection.

In this disturbing yet eloquent print, Wojnarowicz overlaid typed commentary on a photograph of skeletal remains. He movingly communicated his feelings about watching a loved one die of AIDS.

tures with rich tonal gradations of black, gray, and white. In many ways, Mapplethorpe was the heir of Edward Weston, whose innovative compositions of still lifes (FIG. 29-44) and nudes (FIG. 29-44A) helped establish photography as an art form on a par with painting and sculpture. What shocked the public was not nudity per se—a traditional subject with roots in antiquity, indeed at the very birth of art during the Old Stone Age (FIGS. 1-4, 1-5, and 1-5A)—but the openly gay character of many of Mapplethorpe's images. *The Perfect Moment* photographs included, in addition to some very graphic images of homosexual men, a series of self-portraits documenting Mapplethorpe's changing appearance almost up until he died from having contracted AIDS only months after the show opened in Philadelphia in December 1988. The self-portrait reproduced here (FIG. 31-7) presents Mapplethorpe as an androgynous young man with long hair and makeup, confronting the viewer with a steady gaze. Mapplethorpe's photographs, like the work of David Wojnarowicz (FIG. 31-8) and other gay and lesbian artists of the time, are inextricably bound up with the social upheavals in American society and the struggle for equal rights for women, homosexuals, minorities, and the disabled that emerged in the decades following World War II.

DAVID WOJNAROWICZ The disease that killed Mapplethorpe in 1989 and cut short the careers of many other gay artists in the 1980s and 1990s was a most unwelcome reinforcement of these artists' self-identification. Some sculptors and painters responded to the devastating impact of AIDS in the gay community by producing deeply moving works of art. DAVID WOJNAROWICZ (1955–1992) was a gay-rights activist who dropped out of high school in his hometown of Red Bank, New Jersey, and moved to New York City, where he lived on the streets before achieving success as an artist. As did so many others in the gay community, Wojnarowicz watched

his lover and many of his friends die of AIDS. He reacted by creating disturbing yet eloquent works about the tragedy of this disease, which eventually claimed his own life.

In *When I Put My Hands on Your Body* (FIG. **31-8**), Wojnarowicz overlaid a photograph of a pile of skeletal remains with evenly spaced typed commentary communicating his feelings about watching a loved one dying of AIDS. Wojnarowicz movingly describes the effects of AIDS on the human body and soul:

> When I put my hands on your body on your flesh I feel the history of that body. . . . I see the flesh unwrap from the layers of fat and disappear. . . . I see the organs gradually fade into transparency. . . . It makes me weep to feel the history of you of your flesh beneath my hands.

Wojnarowicz's juxtaposition of text and imagery, as in the works by Barbara Kruger (FIG. 31-6) and the Guerrilla Girls (FIG. 31-6A), paralleled the use of both words and images in advertising. The public's familiarity with this format ensured greater receptivity to these artists' messages.

SHAHZIA SIKANDER The struggle for recognition and equal rights has never been confined to the United States, least of all in the present era of instant global communication. In the Muslim world, women and homosexuals face especially difficult challenges, which SHAHZIA SIKANDER (b. 1969) brilliantly addresses in her work. Born in Lahore, Pakistan, and trained at the National College of Arts in the demanding South Asian/Persian art of miniature painting (see "Indian Miniature Painting," page 1037), Sikander earned an MFA from the Rhode Island School of Design and now lives in New York City. So thoroughly immersed in the methods of miniature painting that she makes her own paper, pigments, and squirrel-hair brushes, Sikander nonetheless imbues this traditional art form with

1 in.

31-9 Shahzia Sikander, *Perilous Order*, 1994–1997. Vegetable color, dry pigment, watercolor, and tea on Wasli paper, $10\frac{1}{2}'' \times 8''$. Whitney Museum of American Art, New York (purchased with funds from the Drawing Committee).

Imbuing miniature painting with a contemporary message about hypocrisy and intolerance, Sikander portrayed a gay friend as a homosexual Mughal emperor who enforced Muslim orthodoxy.

ial homeland figures prominently in his art. One of the major themes Ofili has addressed is religion, as interpreted through the eyes of an artist with his racial and national background. His *The Holy Virgin Mary* (FIG. **31-10**) depicts Mary in a manner that departs radically from conventional Renaissance representations. Ofili's work presents the Virgin in simplified form, and she appears to float in an indeterminate space. The artist employed brightly colored pigments applied to the canvas in multiple layers of beadlike dots (inspired by images from ancient caves in Zimbabwe). Surrounding the Virgin, whose face is that of an African woman, are tiny images of genitalia and buttocks cut out from pornographic magazines, which, to the artist, parallel the putti often surrounding Mary in Renaissance paintings. Another reference to Ofili's African heritage surfaces in the clumps of elephant dung—one forming the Virgin's breast, and two more serving as supports for the canvas. The dung enabled Ofili to incorporate Africa into his work in a literal way. Still, he wants the viewer to move beyond the cultural associations of the materials and see them in new ways.

Not surprisingly, *The Holy Virgin Mary* elicited strong reactions, as Ofili clearly intended it to do when he decided to merge the sacred and the vile. The paint-

contemporary meaning. In *Perilous Order* (FIG. **31-9**), she addresses homosexuality, intolerance, and hypocrisy by portraying a gay friend in the guise of the Mughal emperor Aurangzeb (r. 1658–1707), who was a strict enforcer of Islamic orthodoxy although reputed to be a homosexual. Sikander depicted him framed against a magnificent marbleized background ringed by voluptuous nude Hindu nymphs and behind the shadow of a veiled Hindu goddess. *Perilous Order* thus also incorporates a reference to the tensions between the Muslim and Hindu populations of Pakistan and India today.

National Identity

As in the case of Shahzia Sikander, a person's birthplace is often a central component of personal identity, even if the artist has migrated to another country. National identity looms large in the work of many contemporary artists.

CHRIS OFILI A British-born Catholic of Nigerian descent, Chris Ofili (b. 1968) is one of the leading European artists whose famil-

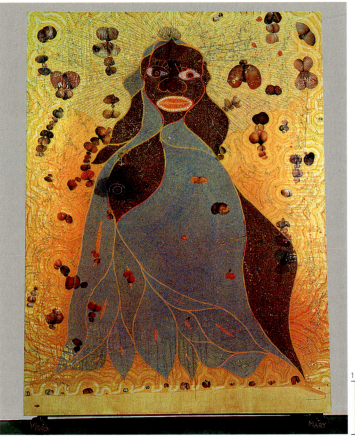

31-10 Chris Ofili, *The Holy Virgin Mary*, 1996. Paper collage, oil paint, glitter, polyester resin, map pins, elephant dung on linen, 7′ 11″ × 5′ 11$\frac{5}{16}$″. Museum of Old and New Art, Hobart.

Ofili, a British-born Catholic of Nigerian descent, represented the Virgin Mary with African elephant dung as a breast and with genitalia and buttocks surrounding her. The painting produced a public outcry.

ARTISTS ON ART

Shirin Neshat on Iran after the Revolution

In an interview with Arthur C. Danto in 2000, expatriate Iranian artist Shirin Neshat discussed how the Islamic Revolution of 1979 affected her work as an artist.

[I]n 1993 . . . I began to seriously make artworks again. . . . I thought photography was the most appropriate medium for my subject as it had the realism that I needed. In the 1990s I finally began going back to Iran. I had been away for over ten years—since the Islamic Revolution. As I traveled back and forth a lot of things started to go through my mind, which eventually led me to develop the work that I have. My focus from the beginning was the subject of women in relation to the Iranian society and the revolution, so I produced a series of photographic images that explored that topic. . . . The first group of photographic work I produced in 1993 certainly reflected the point of view of an Iranian living abroad, looking back in time and trying to analyze and comprehend the changes that had taken place in Iran since the revolution. It was the approach of an artist who had been away for a long time, and it was an important turning point for me artistically and personally, as it became more than art making but a type of journey back to my native country. I was deeply invested in understanding the ideological and philosophical ideas behind contemporary Islam, most of all the origin of the revolution and how it had transformed my country. I knew the subject was very complex and broad so I minimized my focus to something tangible and specific. I chose to concentrate on the meanings behind "martyrdom," a concept which became the heart of the Islamic government's mission at the time, particularly during the Iran/Iraq War. It promoted faith, self-sacrifice, rejection of the material world, and ultimately, life after death. Mostly, I was interested in how their ideas of spirituality, politics and violence were and still are so interconnected and inseparable from one another.*

Neshat often poses for her photographs wearing a veil—which is for her a symbol both of ethnic pride and of the repression of Muslim women—and with her face and exposed parts of her body covered with Farsi (Persian) messages. Unlike the words in the photographs and posters of Simpson (FIG. 31-4A), Kruger (FIG. 31-6), the Guerrilla Girls (FIG. 31-6A), and Wojnarowicz (FIG. 31-8), which evoke commercial typography, Neshat's handwritten additions to her photographs remind the viewer of the long tradition of calligraphy in Persian art (see page 297). A rifle also often figures prominently in Neshat's photographs as an emblem of militant feminism, a notion foreign to the Muslim faith.

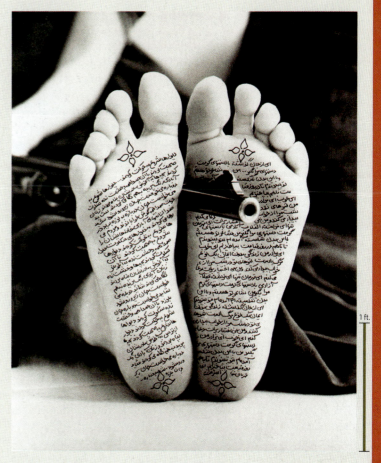

31-11 SHIRIN NESHAT, *Allegiance and Wakefulness*, 1994. Offset print with ink calligraphy, 3' 5¼" × 2' 9". Israel Museum, Jerusalem (anonymous gift, New York, to American Friends of the Israel Museum).

Neshat's photographs address the repression of women in postrevolutionary Iran. She poses in traditional veiled garb but wields a rifle and displays militant Farsi poetry on her exposed body parts.

In *Allegiance and Wakefulness* (FIG. **31-11**) from her *Women of Allah* series, Neshat omitted her face and most of her body, and focused on her feet covered with verses of militant Farsi poetry and on the barrel of a rifle she points menacingly toward the viewer.

*Kristine Stiles and Peter Selz, *Theories and Documents of Contemporary Art: A Sourcebook of Artists' Writings*, 2d ed. (Berkeley: University of California Press, 2012), 547–548.

---

ing's inclusion in the *Sensation* exhibition at the Brooklyn Museum in 1999 with other "sensational" works by young British artists prompted indignant (but unsuccessful) demands for cancellation of the show and countercharges of censorship (see "Public Funding of Controversial Art," page 1000).

SHIRIN NESHAT Born in Iran, SHIRIN NESHAT (b. 1957) grew up in a Westernized home and attended a Catholic boarding school in Tehran before leaving her homeland to study art in California, where she earned undergraduate and graduate degrees from the University of California, Berkeley. Today she lives in New York City and produces films, videos, and photographs critical of the funda-

mentalist Islamic regime in Iran, especially its treatment of women (see "Shirin Neshat on Iran after the Revolution," above).

Not every artist who has achieved an international reputation has migrated to the West to pursue a career. CLIFF WHITING (TE WHANAU-A-APANUI, b. 1936) of New Zealand, for example, continues the Maori tradition of woodcarving, but in a distinctly modern style in works such as *Tawhiri-Matea* (FIG. **31-11A**).

31-11A WHITING, *Tawhiri-Matea*, 1984.

POLITICAL AND SOCIAL COMMENTARY

Although almost all of the works discussed thus far are commentaries on contemporary society (seen through the lens of the artists' personal experiences), they do not incorporate references to specific events, nor do they address conditions affecting all people regardless of their race, national origin, gender, or sexual orientation—for example, homelessness, industrial pollution, and street violence. Other artists, however, have confronted precisely those aspects of late 20th- and early 21st-century life in their work.

KRZYSZTOF WODICZKO Polish-born KRZYSZTOF WODICZKO (b. 1943) is one of many living artists who focus on some of these more universal concerns in his art. When working in Canada in 1980, he developed artworks involving the outdoor display of enormous slide images. He projected photographs on specific buildings to expose how civic buildings embody, legitimize, and perpetuate power. When Wodiczko moved to New York City in 1983, he became troubled by the pervasive homelessness in a city that is the financial capital of the world and home to many of America's wealthiest families. He resolved to use his art to publicize this problem, and got the opportunity in 1987, albeit in Boston instead of New York. On Boston Common, as part of the city's New Year's celebration, Wodiczko produced *The Homeless Projection* (FIG. **31-12**), a temporary artwork consisting of images of homeless people projected on all four sides of the Civil War Soldiers and Sailors Monument. In these photos, the homeless appear flanked by plastic bags filled with their few possessions. At the top of the monument, Wodiczko projected a local condominium construction site, which helped viewers make a connection between urban development and homelessness.

EDWARD BURTYNSKY The destructive effects of industrial plants and mines on the environment have been the motivation for the photographs of "manufactured landscapes" by Canadian EDWARD BURTYNSKY (b. 1955). The son of a Ukrainian immigrant who worked in the General Motors plant in St. Catharines, Ontario, Burtynsky studied photography and graphic design at Ryerson University and Niagara College. He uses a large-format field camera to produce high-resolution negatives of industrial landscapes littered with tires, scrap metal, and industrial refuse. His choice of subjects is itself an unambiguous negative commentary on modern manufacturing processes, but Burtynsky transforms ugliness into beauty in his color prints. For example, his photograph (FIG. **31-13**) of a Toronto recycling plant from his *Urban Mines* series converts bundles of compressed scrap metal into a striking abstract composition of multicolored rectangles. Burtynsky's work thus merges documentary and fine-art photography and bears comparison with the photographs of Margaret Bourke-White (FIG. 29-78) and Minor White (FIG. 30-34).

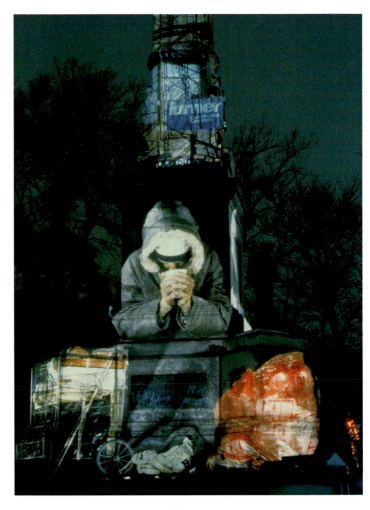

31-12 KRZYSZTOF WODICZKO, *The Homeless Projection*, 1986. Outdoor slide projection at the Civil War Soldiers and Sailors Monument, Boston Common, Boston.

To publicize the plight of the homeless, Wodiczko projected on the walls of a monument on Boston Common images of them with their plastic bags containing their few possessions.

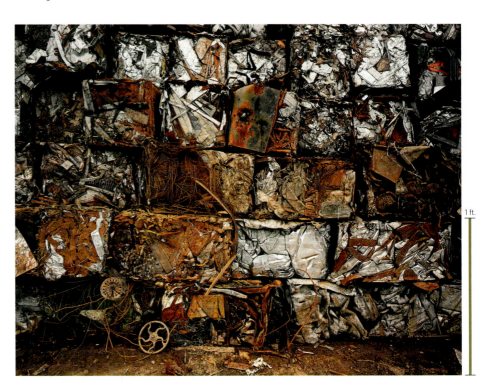

1 ft.

31-13 EDWARD BURTYNSKY, *Densified Scrap Metal #3A, Toronto, Ontario,* 1997. Dye coupler print, 2' 2¾" × 2' 10⅜". National Gallery of Canada, Ottawa (gift of the artist, 1998).

Burtynsky's "manufactured landscapes" are commentaries on the destructive effects on the environment of industrial plants and mines, but his photographs transform ugliness into beauty.

ARTISTS ON ART
Leon Golub on *Mercenaries*

Mercenaries IV (FIG. 31-14), which rivals the huge history paintings of the 19th century in size, presents a mysterious tableau of five tough freelance military professionals willing, for a price, to fight for anyone willing to pay. The three clustering at the right side of the canvas react with tense physical gestures to something one of the two other mercenaries standing at the far left is saying. The dark uniforms and skin tones of the four black fighters flatten their figures and make them stand out against the searing dark red background. The slightly modulated background seems to push their forms forward up against the picture plane and becomes an echoing void in the space between the two groups. Golub painted the mercenaries so that the viewer's eye is level with the menacing figures' knees. He placed the men so close to the front plane of the work that the lower edge of the painting cuts off their feet, thereby trapping the viewer in the painting's compressed space. The feeling of peril confronts viewers mercilessly. They become one with all the victims caught in today's political battles.

Golub emphasized both the scarred light tones of the white mercenary's skin and the weapons. Modeled with shadow and gleaming highlights, the guns contrast with the harshly scraped, flattened surfaces of the figures. The rawness of the canvas reinforces the rawness of the imagery. Indeed, Golub's working method is, appropriately, itself violent, as he explained in a 1981 interview with Matthew Baigell:

> [My *Mercenaries* paintings] arise out of the contemporary world as given to us by the media: the uses of mercenaries or irregulars . . . to enforce political ends. The mercenary is not a common subject of art, but is a near-universal means of establishing or maintaining control under volatile or up-for-grabs political circumstances.
>
> I do not have the total conceptual framework for a painting in mind until the later stages. I orient the figures, their gestures, their glances, their intentions. I reinterpret these on the basis of changing body stances. For example, I intend a figure to act out a certain gesture. As I work, the psychic dimensions of that individual and what he portends might shift. The figure gets more or less menacing, more or less active. My original intentions shift considerably in the balancing of energies which move across the canvas. I may use drawings or parts of photographs enlarged through an opaque projector onto the vertical hanging canvas. A figure might develop from two or three or half a dozen photographs or drawings. Other figures are then located in stressed tension to the first. I then evolve the drawing to precise military dress, weapons, and, most important, intention. . . . The particular individual has to both typify and illustrate mercenaries and to appear to possess an idiosyncratic, singular experience. The figures are outlined and partially shaded in black paint. Then a coat of white paint is put on for highlights and lighter areas. I then apply layers of local colors to define skin, metal, wood, cloth, etc. The painting is then laid on the floor. Areas are partially dissolved with solvents and scraped with sculpture tools, more recently, a meat cleaver, to erode the paint skin. . . . I continue to reconstruct and erode until I get to the point where . . . the different figures, their gestures, grins and leers, etc., are in some sort of achieved tension.*

*Kristine Stiles and Peter Selz, *Theories and Documents of Contemporary Art: A Sourcebook of Artists' Writings*, 2d ed. (Berkeley: University of California Press, 2012), 266–268.

31-14 LEON GOLUB, *Mercenaries IV*, 1980. Acrylic on linen, 10' × 19' 2". Courtesy Ronald Feldman Fine Arts, New York. Art © Estate of Leon Golub/ Licensed by VAGA, New York, NY.

The violence of contemporary life is the subject of Golub's huge paintings. Here, five mercenaries loom over the viewer, instilling a feeling of peril. The rough textures reinforce the raw imagery.

1 ft.

LEON GOLUB The brutality of urban life and warfare was the focus of painter LEON GOLUB (1922–2004) during his long career. Born in Chicago and trained at the University of Chicago and the Art Institute of Chicago, Golub is best known for his two series of paintings titled *Assassins* and *Mercenaries* (FIG. 31-14). In these large-scale works, anonymous characters inspired by newspaper and magazine photographs of urban gangs and Latin American death squads participate in atrocious street violence and military operations (see "Leon Golub on *Mercenaries*," above). The paintings have a universal impact because they suggest not specific stories but a condition of being. This impression is fostered in large part by Golub's removal of the figures from time and space by placing them against a featureless red background, which, although inspired by and modeled freely on ancient Roman mural paintings (compare FIG. 7-18), also is the color of the blood shed by the victims of Golub's assassins.

MARTHA ROSLER Street violence and armed combat are themes that have also been explored in depth by SANDOW BIRK (b. 1962) in paintings such as *Death of Manuel* (FIG. **31-14A**) and by MARTHA ROSLER (b. 1943), especially in a series of photomontages called *Bringing the War Home: House Beautiful*. Born in Brooklyn, Rosler graduated from Brooklyn College and earned an MFA at the University of California, San Diego. A professor at Rutgers University for three decades and a prolific writer, Rosler has

↗ **31-14A** BIRK, *Death of Manuel*, 1992.

produced a diverse body of artistic work, including videos and performance art as well as photography. Throughout her career, Rosler has focused on social and political commentary, primarily issues concerning women, housing and homelessness, and war and its depiction in the media.

Gladiators (FIG. **31-15**) is one of the recent additions to the *House Beautiful* series, originally created between 1967 and 1972 as a critical commentary on the Vietnam War but expanded in 2004 in reaction to the war in Iraq. Like the other photomontages in the series, *Gladiators* brings disturbing images of combat into the domestic sphere by inserting armed soldiers (modern "gladiators") into the tranquil living rooms of upscale houses, literally "bringing the war home" to those whose sons and daughters, unlike those of working-class families, rarely enlist in the armed forces and fight for their country.

FERNANDO BOTERO Perhaps the most emotionally wrenching recent artworks to express outrage against war in general and specifically the inhumane treatment of prisoners is the large series of paintings and drawings by Colombian artist FERNANDO BOTERO (b. 1932). Still active in his 80s, Botero, who has lived and worked in Paris for decades, reacted with horror to the news reports and photographs of the humiliation and torture of Iraqi prisoners at the hands of American military personnel at Abu Ghraib prison. The paintings—for example, *Abu Ghraib 46* (FIG. **31-16**)—are peopled by Botero's trademark larger-than-life inflated bodies, but they differ markedly from his usually tranquil domestic subjects. As in the published photographs from Abu Ghraib, the men

in Botero's paintings are stripped of their clothes, blindfolded, bound, beaten, and bloodied, and are often threatened by ferocious dogs or forced to wear women's underwear. Critics have compared these graphic depictions of physical and mental torture to the passion of Christ and the martyrdom of saints. Botero has insisted that the paintings are not intended as anti-American but as a broad condemnation of cruelty in violation of the Geneva Convention. He has refused to profit from sales of the Abu Ghraib paintings and has donated them to museums—many, including the illustrated example, are gifts to the University of California's Berkeley Art Museum—on the condition that they forever remain on display.

WILLIE BESTER The use of their craft by artists such as Botero, Golub, and Rosler to express outrage at violence, warfare, and social and political injustices of all kinds is indeed a global phenomenon in the late 20th and early 21st centuries, but it is not new in the history of art. Beckmann's *Night* (FIG. 29-49), Picasso's *Guernica* (FIG. 29-16), Goya's *Third of May, 1808* (FIG. 27-12), Géricault's *Raft of the Medusa* (FIG. 27-1), and Turner's *Slave Ship* (FIG. 27-22) are but a few notable examples. In South Africa, many artists became vocal critics of apartheid (government-sponsored racial separation) and used painting as a potent means of protesting the oppression of blacks by the minority white government.

WILLIE BESTER (b. 1956) is probably the most prominent South African artist to take up that cause. His 1992 *Homage to Steve Biko* (FIG. **31-17**) is a tribute to the gentle and heroic leader of the South African Black Consciousness Movement whom the authorities killed while he was in detention. The exoneration of the two white doctors in charge of him sparked protests around the world. Bester packed his picture with references to death and injustice. Biko's portrait, at the center, is near another of the police minister, James Kruger, who had him transported 1,100 kilometers (almost 700 miles) to Pretoria in the yellow Land Rover ambulance seen left of center and again beneath Biko's portrait. Bester portrayed Biko with his chained fists raised in the classic worldwide protest gesture. This portrait memorializes both Biko and the many other antiapartheid activists, as indicated by the white graveyard crosses above a blue sea of skulls

31-15 MARTHA ROSLER, *Gladiators*, 2004, from *Bringing the War Home: House Beautiful*. Photomontage, 1′ 8″ × 2′. Mitchell-Innes & Nash Gallery, New York.

Rosler's *House Beautiful* photomontages disturbingly insert images of armed soldiers (modern "gladiators") into the tranquil living rooms of upscale houses, literally "bringing the war home."

1 ft.

31-16 FERNANDO BOTERO, *Abu Ghraib 46*, 2005. Oil on canvas, 4' 9$\frac{1}{2}$" × 5' 9$\frac{5}{8}$". Berkeley Art Museum, Berkeley (gift of the artist).

Botero's *Abu Ghraib* series is a condemnation of the humiliation and torture of Iraqi prisoners by American military personnel. Critics have compared the paintings to scenes of martyrdom.

The red crosses on this vehicle's door and on Kruger's reflective dark glasses repeat, with sad irony, the graveyard crosses.

Blood-red and ambulance-yellow are in fact unifying colors dripped or painted on many parts of the canvas. Writing and numbers, found fragments, and stenciled and painted signs—favorite Cubist motifs (FIGS. 29-13 and 29-14; compare FIG. 31-3)—also appear throughout the composition. Numbers refer to the dehumanized life of blacks under apartheid. Found objects—wire, sticks, cardboard, sheet metal, cans, and other discards—from which the poor construct fragile, impermanent township dwellings, remind viewers of the degraded lives of most South

beside Biko's head. The crosses stand out against a red background, recalling the inferno of burned townships. The stop sign (lower left) seems to mean "stop Kruger," or perhaps "stop apartheid." The tagged foot, as if in a morgue, above the ambulance also refers to Biko's death.

African people of color. The oilcan guitar (bottom center), another recurrent Bester symbol, refers both to the social harmony and joy provided by music and to the control imposed by apartheid policies. The whole composition is rich in texture and dense in its collage combinations of objects, photographs, signs, symbols, and pigment. *Homage to Steve Biko* is a powerful critique of an oppressive sociopolitical system, and it exemplifies the extent to which art can be invoked in the political process.

Protests against apartheid have taken many forms, however—for example, opposition to corporate investment in South Africa, the approach taken by German artist HANS HAACKE (b. 1936) in *MetroMobiltan* (FIG. **31-17A**).

⏎ 31-17A HAACKE, *MetroMobiltan*, 1985.

31-17 WILLIE BESTER, *Homage to Steve Biko*, 1992. Mixed media, 3' 7$\frac{5}{6}$" × 3' 7$\frac{5}{6}$". Collection of the artist.

Homage to Steve Biko is a tribute to a leader of the Black Consciousness Movement, which protested apartheid in South Africa. References to the injustice of Biko's death fill this complex painting.

31-18 Trigo Piula, *Ta Tele,* 1988. Oil on canvas, 3' 3$\frac{3}{8}$" × 3' 4$\frac{3}{8}$". National Museum of African Art, Washington, D.C.

Ta Tele is a commentary on contemporary life showing Congolese citizens transfixed by television pictures of the world outside Africa. Even the traditional power figure at the center has a TV screen for a chest.

TRIGO PIULA The Democratic Republic of Congo's Trigo Piula (b. ca. 1950) is a painter trained in Western artistic techniques and styles who creates works that fuse Western and Congolese images and objects in a pictorial blend providing social commentary on present-day Congolese culture. *Ta Tele* (FIG. **31-18**) depicts a group of Congolese citizens staring transfixed at colorful pictures of life beyond Africa displayed on 14 television screens. The TV images include references to travel to exotic places (such as Paris, symbolized by the Eiffel Tower, FIG. 28-40), sports events, love, the earth seen from a satellite, and Western worldly goods. A traditional Kongo power figure (compare FIG. 37-5) associated with warfare and divination stands at the composition's center as a visual mediator between the anonymous foreground viewers and the multiple TV images. In traditional Kongo contexts, this figure's feather headdress links it to supernatural and magical powers from the sky, such as lightning and storms. In Piula's rendition, the headdress perhaps refers to the power of airborne televised pictures. In the stomach area, where Kongo power figures often have glass in front of a medicine packet, Piula painted a television screen showing a second power figure, as if to double the figure's power. The artist shows most of the television viewers with a small white image of a foreign object—for example, a car, shoe, or bottle—on the backs of their heads.

One meaning of this picture appears to be that television messages have deadened the minds of Congolese people to anything but modern Western thoughts or commodities. Two speaker cabinets set against the back wall beneath the TV screens have wires leading to the power figure, implying that even this ancient symbol of native power has been subjected to the greater power of modern television. Clearly, Piula suggests, the contemporary world's new television-induced consumerism is poisoning the minds and souls of Congolese people as if by magic or sorcery.

ZHANG XIAOGANG Political and social commentary is also the principal interest of Chinese painter Zhang Xiaogang (b. 1958). Zhang is best known for his *Bloodline* portraits—for example, *Big Family*

31-19 Zhang Xiaogang, *Bloodline: Big Family No. 2,* 1995. Oil on canvas, 5' 11" × 7' 6$\frac{5}{8}$". Private collection.

Ironically titled *Big Family* in reaction to the government's one-child policy, Zhang's generic, personality-less portraits intentionally recall black-and-white family photographs of the Mao era in China.

No. 2 (FIG. **31-19**). Based on the black-and-white photographs of Chinese families popular during the Cultural Revolution, the *Bloodline* paintings are not really portraits. Instead, they depict generic, personality-less fathers, mothers, and children wearing the approved plain clothes of the Mao era in China. Ironically titled *Big Family,* these somber three-figure groups are also commentaries on the longstanding, though recently eased, government policy of restricting most married couples to having only a single child, a policy that has led many families to seek abortions, often in order to raise a boy instead of a girl. The *Bloodline* series takes its name from of the meaninglessness of contemporary political language and as a commentary on the illegibility of the past. Xu himself has characterized the work as intentionally ambiguous:

People have so many perspectives on *Book from the Sky* because the work is empty. The work does not present any clear message. . . . I used every possible method to force people to believe in the legitimacy of this work, while at the same time extracting all content completely. . . . The artwork itself is a contradiction because it makes a parody of culture while also placing culture in a temple to be taken very seriously. *Book from the Sky* invites your desire to understand it and pushes you away at the same time. It treats everyone as equal—educated or uneducated, Chinese or non-Chinese—because no one can "read" it.[4]

Like many postmodern artists, who, like postmodern architects, reject pure formalism and emphasize content and historical references (see "After Modernism: Postmodern Architecture," page 949), Xu created *A Book from the Sky* to be read on many levels.

31-20 Xu Bing, *A Book from the Sky,* 1987. Installation of woodblock printed books at the Elvehjem (now Chazen) Museum of Art, University of Wisconsin, Madison, 1991.

Xu trained as a printmaker in Beijing. *A Book from the Sky,* with its invented Chinese woodblock characters, may be a stinging critique of the meaninglessness of contemporary political language.

the faint red lines connecting the figures—a device used earlier by Frida Kahlo (FIG. 29-76). The red bloodlines are the only touches of color in Zhang's otherwise intentionally subdued palette, save for, in the illustrated example, the yellow that draws attention to the highly desirable male child.

XU BING A different kind of commentary on Chinese culture has been the hallmark of the work of Xu Bing (b. 1955), a Chongqing, China, native who was forced to work in the countryside with peasants during the Cultural Revolution of 1966 to 1976 under Mao Tse-tung (1893–1976). Xu later studied printmaking in Beijing at the Central Academy of Fine Arts, where he is now professor and vice president. In 1990, however, Xu moved to the United States at the invitation of the University of Wisconsin, where two years earlier he had exhibited his most famous work, a large *installation* (an assemblage that creates an artistic environment in a room or gallery) called *A Book from the Sky* (FIG. 31-20). First exhibited in China before being installed at Wisconsin's Elvehjem (now Chazen) Museum of Art, the work presents an enormous number of *woodblock*-printed texts in *characters* evocative of Chinese writing but invented by the artist. Producing them required both an intimate knowledge of genuine Chinese characters and extensive training in woodblock carving. Xu's work, however, is no hymn to tradition. Critics have interpreted it both as a stinging critique

REPRESENTATION AND ABSTRACTION

Despite the high visibility of contemporary artists whose work deals with the pressing social and political issues of the world, some critically acclaimed living or recently deceased artists have produced innovative modernist art during the postmodern era. Abstraction remains a valid and compelling approach to painting and sculpture in the 21st century, as does more traditional representational art, both figural and landscape.

Figural Art and Landscape

Recent decades have brought a revival of interest in figural art, both in painting and sculpture, a trend best exemplified in the earlier postwar period by Lucian Freud (FIG. 30-32), who remained an active and influential painter until his death in July 2011.

JENNY SAVILLE Fellow Briton Jenny Saville (b. 1970) is the leading figure painter in the Freud mold of the younger generation of European and American artists. Born in Cambridge, England, and trained at the Glasgow School of Art in Scotland, Saville lives and paints in an old palace in Palermo, Italy. Her best-known works are over-life-size self-portraits in which she exaggerates the girth of her body and delights in depicting heavy folds of flesh with visible veins in minute detail and from a sharply foreshortened angle, which further distorts the body's proportions. Her nude self-portraits deserve comparison not only with those of Freud but also of Egon Schiele (FIG. 29-10), despite the vivid contrast between Schiele's emaciated body and Saville's (false) obesity.

1 ft.

31-21 JENNY SAVILLE, *Branded*, 1992. Oil on canvas, 7' × 6'. Saatchi Gallery, London.

Saville's unflattering foreshortened self-portrait "branded" with words such as "delicate" and "petite" underscores the dichotomy between the perfect bodies of fashion models and those of most people.

Saville's paintings are a commentary on the contemporary obsession with the lithe bodies of fashion models. In *Branded* (FIG. **31-21**), she underscores the dichotomy between the popular notion of a beautiful body and the imperfect bodies of most people by "branding" her body with words inscribed in her flesh—"delicate," "decorative," "petite." Art critic Michelle Meagher has described Saville's paintings as embodying a "feminist aesthetics of disgust."[5]

KIKI SMITH A distinctly unflattering approach to the representation of the human body is also the hallmark of New York–based KIKI SMITH (b. 1954), the daughter of Minimalist sculptor Tony Smith (FIG. 30-18). In her work, Smith has explored the question of who controls the human body, an interest that grew out of her training as an emergency medical service technician. Her studies of bodies afflicted by illnesses deserve comparison with other artists' works addressing the physical devastation brought on by AIDS (see page 1001), but Smith's goals are different. She wants to reveal the socially constructed nature of the body, and she encourages the viewer to consider how external forces shape people's perceptions of their bodies. In works such as *Untitled* (FIG. **31-22**), the artist dramatically departed from conventional representations of the body, both in art and in the media. She suspended two life-size wax figures, one male and one female, both nude, from metal stands. Smith marked each of the sculptures with long white drips—body fluids running from the woman's breasts and down the man's leg. She commented:

> Most of the functions of the body are hidden . . . from society. . . . [W]e separate our bodies from our lives. But, when people are dying, they are

1 ft.

31-22 KIKI SMITH, *Untitled*, 1990. Beeswax and microcrystalline wax figures on metal stands, female figure installed height 6' $1\frac{1}{2}$" and male figure installed height 6' $4\frac{15}{16}$". Whitney Museum of American Art, New York (purchased with funds from the Painting and Sculpture Committee).

Asking "Who controls the body?" Kiki Smith sculpted two life-size wax figures of a nude man and woman with body fluids running from the woman's breasts and down the man's leg.

losing control of their bodies. That loss of function can seem humiliating and frightening. But, on the other hand, you can look at it as a kind of liberation of the body. It seems like a nice metaphor—a way to think about the social—that people lose control despite the many agendas of different ideologies in society, which are trying to control the body(ies) . . . medicine, religion, law, etc. Just thinking about control—who has control of the body? . . . Does the mind have control of the body? Does the social?[6]

Underscoring the diversity of contemporary art, not all recent figure painters have worked in a realistic mode. It is hard to imagine a more vivid contrast with the figures portrayed by Saville and Smith than the exuberantly animated, joyful cartoon-like figures in the paintings of KEITH HARING (1958–1990; FIG. **31-22A**), who, like Jean-Michel Basquiat (FIG. 31-3), began his career as a street artist in New York City.

31-22A HARING, *Tuttomondo*, 1989.

JEFF KOONS Haring's painted figures are firmly rooted in popular culture, as are the sculptures of JEFF KOONS (b. 1955). Trained at the Maryland Institute College of Art in Baltimore, Koons worked early in his career as a commodities broker. He first became prominent in the art world for a series of works in the early 1980s involving the exhibition of everyday commercial products such as vacuum cleaners. Clearly following in the footsteps of Marcel Duchamp (FIG. 29-26), Koons made no attempt to manipulate or alter the machine-made objects. More recently, he, like Californian ROBERT ARNESON (1930–1992; FIG. 31-22B), turned to ceramic sculpture. In *Pink Panther* (FIG. 31-23), Koons, who divides his time between his hometown of York, Pennsylvania, and New York City, playfully intertwined a pin-up nude with a famous cartoon character. He reinforced the trite and kitschy nature of this imagery by titling the exhibition of which this work was a part *The Banality Show*. Koons intends his work to draw attention to everything that he believes is wrong with contemporary American society. His prominence in the art world is based on his acute understanding of the dynamics of consumer culture. Haring too enjoyed great commercial success owing to his sensitivity to popular taste and his shrewd marketing of his trademark motifs to the general public.

🔗 **31-22B** ARNESON, *California Artist,* 1982.

MARISOL Known simply by her first name, MARISOL ESCOBAR (b. 1930) grew up in a wealthy, widely traveled Venezuelan family. Born in Paris and educated there, in Los Angeles, and in New York City, Marisol first studied painting and drawing, but after discovering Pre-Columbian art in 1951, she pursued a career as a sculptor. Marisol also spent time in Italy, where she developed a deep admiration for Renaissance art.

In the 1960s, Marisol was one of the inner circle of New York Pop artists, and she appeared in two of Andy Warhol's films. Some of her works at that time portrayed prominent public figures, including the Hollywood actor John Wayne and the family of U.S.

31-23 JEFF KOONS, *Pink Panther,* 1988. Porcelain, 3' 5" high. Museum of Contemporary Art, Chicago (Gerald S. Elliot Collection).

Koons creates sculptures highlighting everything that he considers wrong with contemporary American consumer culture. In this work, he intertwined a centerfold nude and a cartoon character.

president John F. Kennedy. Her subjects were always people, however, not the commercial products of consumer culture that fascinated most leading Pop artists and still are prominent in the art of Jeff Koons and others.

Marisol retained her interest in figural sculpture long after Pop Art gave way to other movements. One of her most ambitious works (FIG. 31-24) is a multimedia three-dimensional version of Leonardo da Vinci's *Last Supper* (FIG. 22-4), including the walls and windows of the dining room in order to replicate the Renaissance master's application of linear perspective. By reproducing the fresco in three dimensions, Marisol transformed it into an object. The figures in her version of Leonardo's composition are painted wood, with the exception of Christ, whose stone body is the physical and emotional anchor of the composition. In many of her sculptures, the female figures have Marisol's features, and in this tableau she added a

31-24 MARISOL, *Self-Portrait Looking at the Last Supper,* 1982–1984. Painted wood, stone, plaster, and aluminum, 10' 1½" × 29' 10" × 5' 1". Metropolitan Museum of Art, New York (gift of Mr. and Mrs. Roberto C. Polo, 1986). Art © Marisol Escobar/Licensed by VAGA, New York, NY.

In a tribute to the Renaissance master, Marisol created a sculptural replica of Leonardo da Vinci's *Last Supper* (FIG. 22-4), transforming the fresco into an object. She is the seated viewer as well as the artist.

31-25 ANSELM KIEFER, *Nigredo*, 1984. Oil paint on photosensitized fabric, acrylic emulsion, straw, shellac, relief paint on paper pulled from painted wood, 11' × 18'. Philadelphia Museum of Art, Philadelphia (gift of Friends of the Philadelphia Museum of Art).

Kiefer's paintings have thickly encrusted surfaces incorporating materials such as straw. Here, the German artist used perspective to pull the viewer into an incinerated landscape alluding to the Holocaust.

seated armless portrait of herself looking at the *Last Supper*. Catholic and deeply religious—as a teenager she emulated martyr saints by inflicting physical harm on herself—Marisol may have wanted to show herself as a witness to Christ's last meal. But more likely her presence here is a tribute to the 16th-century painter. (She also made a sculptural replica of Leonardo's *Madonna and Child with Saint Anne* [FIG. 22-3].)

Marisol's *Self-Portrait Looking at the Last Supper* is a commentary on the artist not only as a creator but also as a viewer of the works of earlier artists, a link in an artistic chain extending back to antiquity. One pervasive element in the work of contemporary artists is a self-consciousness of the postmodern painter's or sculptor's position in the continuum of art history, as noted earlier in the discussions of Kehinde Wiley's *Napoleon* (FIG. 31-2) and Sandow Birk's *Manuel* (FIG. 31-14A). However, no one better exemplifies that aspect of contemporary art than MARK TANSEY (b. 1949; FIG. 31-24A).

⊿ 31-24A TANSEY, *A Short History of Modernist Painting*, 1982.

ANSELM KIEFER Traditional realistic landscape painting remains a popular mode of artistic expression in the early 21st century, but some of the most innovative landscapes of the past few decades have verged on abstraction. German artist ANSELM KIEFER (b. 1945) studied art in Düsseldorf with Joseph Beuys (FIG. 30-53) in the early 1970s, and has lived and worked in Barjac, France, since 1992. His canvases, such as *Nigredo* (FIG. 31-25), are large in scale and feature highly textured surfaces of pigment mixed with nontraditional materials such as straw and lead. It is not merely the impressive physicality of Kiefer's paintings that accounts for the impact of his work, however. His images function on a mythological or metaphorical level as well as on a historically specific one. Many of Kiefer's works involve a reexamination of German history, particularly the painful Nazi era of 1933–1945, and evoke a feeling of despair. Kiefer believes that Germany's participation in World War II and the Holocaust left permanent scars on the souls of the German people and on the souls of all humanity.

Nigredo ("blackening") pulls the viewer into an expansive landscape depicted using Renaissance perspective principles. This landscape, however, is far from pastoral or carefully cultivated. Rather, it appears bleak and charred. Although it does not make specific reference to the Holocaust, this incinerated landscape indirectly alludes to the horrors of that tragic event. More generally, the blackness of the landscape may refer to the notion of alchemical change or transformation, a concept of great interest to Kiefer. Black is one of the four symbolic colors of the alchemist—a color referencing both death and the molten, chaotic state of substances broken down by fire. Because the alchemist focuses on the transformation of substances, the emphasis on blackness is not absolute, but can also be perceived as part of a process of renewal and redemption. Kiefer thus imbued his work with a deep symbolic meaning that, when combined with the intriguing visual quality of his parched, congealed surfaces, results in paintings of enduring power.

Abstract Painting and Sculpture

In the 1970s, Susan Rothenberg (FIG. 30-9C) had produced large-scale "Neo-Expressionist" paintings inspired by German Expressionism and American Abstract Expressionism. Today, many artists continue to explore this dynamic style, including some who, like Anselm Kiefer, have produced works with landscape as the central theme—for example, *Summer Trees* (FIG. 31-25A) by Korean painter SONG SU-NAM (b. 1938) and *Wild Vines with Flowers Like Pearls* (FIG. 31-25B) by the recently deceased Chinese painter WU GUANZHONG (1919–2010).

⊿ 31-25A SONG, *Summer Trees*, 1983.

⊿ 31-25B WU, *Wild Vines*, 1997.

JULIAN SCHNABEL In the United States, New Yorker JULIAN SCHNABEL (b. 1951), who wrote and directed a 1996 film about fellow artist Jean-Michel Basquiat (FIG. 31-3), has, like Anselm Kiefer (FIG. 31-25), experimented widely with media and materials

31-26 Julian Schnabel, *The Walk Home*, 1984–1985. Oil, plates, copper, bronze, fiberglass, and Bondo on six wood panels, 9' 4" × 19' 4". Broad Art Foundation, Santa Monica.

Schnabel's paintings recall the work of the midcentury American gestural abstractionists, but he employs an amalgamation of media, bringing together painting, mosaic, and low-relief sculpture.

in his forceful restatements of the premises of Abstract Expressionism. Schnabel's Neo-Expressionist works range from paint on velvet and tarpaulin to a mixture of pigment and fragmented china plates bonded to wood. He has a special interest in the physicality of objects, and by combining broken crockery and paint, as in *The Walk Home* (FIG. 31-26), he has found an extension of what paint can do. Superficially, Schnabel's paintings recall the work of the gestural abstractionists, especially the spontaneous drips of Jackson Pollock (FIG. 30-6) and the energetic brushstrokes of Willem de Kooning (FIG. 30-8), but their Abstract Expressionist works lack the thick, mosaic-like texture of Schnabel's canvases. The amalgamation

of media brings together painting, mosaic, and low-relief sculpture, and considerably amplifies the expressive impact of his paintings.

ELIZABETH MURRAY AND HELEN OJI One of the few things that paintings as diverse as those examined so far have in common is that they share the standard rectilinear format that has characterized paintings on wood, canvas, or silk from antiquity to the present day. Two contemporary artists who have experimented with alternate shapes are ELIZABETH MURRAY (1940–2007)—see "Rethinking the Shape of Painting," below, and FIG. 31-27)—and HELEN OJI (b. 1950).

PROBLEMS AND SOLUTIONS
Rethinking the Shape of Painting

Rectangular frames for paintings have been since antiquity the norm worldwide for decorated vases, wood panels, frescoed walls, oil-on-canvas, manuscript illustrations, and silk scrolls alike. Even during the past century, when artists have rethought almost every traditional tenet of the art of painting, the vertically or horizontally oriented rectilinear painting surface has with few exceptions (for example, FIG. 30-13) reigned supreme, even among artists who have abandoned easel painting in favor of applying pigment to unstretched canvas spread out on the floor (FIG. 30-7). Recently, however, some artists have experimented not merely with other geometric shapes but with highly irregular formats.

Chief among them is Elizabeth Murray. Born in Chicago, Murray graduated from that city's famed Art Institute and then earned an MFA at Mills College. She moved to New York City in 1967 and painted there until her death in 2007, the year after a major retrospective exhibition of her work was mounted at the Museum of Modern Art—a rare honor accorded to few women before her.

Can You Hear Me? (FIG. 31-27) is typical of Murray's innovative approach to abstract painting. It is an irregularly shaped composite of several small canvas-on-wood panels that bear comparison not only to Abstract Expressionist works but to the Biomorphic Surrealist paintings of Joan Miró (FIG. 29-58) and also to cartoon art. The central—although almost unnoticed at first—motif of *Can You Hear Me?* is a face with a wide-open mouth out of which emerges a shape resembling an elongated comic-strip balloon but without words—the reason the

31-27 Elizabeth Murray, *Can You Hear Me?* 1984. Oil on canvas on wood, 8' 10" × 13' 3" × 1'. Dallas Museum of Art, Dallas (Foundation for the Arts Collection).

Elizabeth Murray is the most prominent contemporary artist who rejected the traditional rectilinear format for painting in favor of a multilayered composite of canvas-on-wood panels.

viewer cannot hear what the face is saying. Murray has acknowledged that Edvard Munch's *Scream* (FIG. 28-29) was the source of inspiration for her painting, but in *Can You Hear Me?* emotional frenzy is expressed by purely abstract means, most notably through the centrifugal force of the propeller-like shape of the painting itself.

Representation and Abstraction **1013**

Shaped like a kimono in acknowledgment of the artist's Japanese heritage, Oji's *Mount St. Helens* is a highly textured abstract landscape celebrating the eruptive power of Washington State's active volcano.

1 ft.

Born in Sacramento, California, and trained at California State University's Sacramento campus, where she earned both BA and MA degrees in art, Oji has lived and worked in New York City since 1976. *Mount St. Helens* (FIG. 31-28) is one of a series of acrylic and glitter paintings in the shape of a kimono (compare FIG. 30-36) in acknowledgment of Oji's Japanese heritage. But the decoration of the "garment" bears little resemblance to traditional textile design. Oji's kimono is a highly textured abstract landscape that has much in common with the canvases of Kiefer (FIG. 31-25) and Schnabel (FIG. 31-26). It captures and celebrates the raw power of Washington State's Mount St. Helens, one of the world's few still-active volcanoes, which erupted in 1980, inspiring this painting.

YAYOI KUSAMA One of the most successful—and certainly one of the most market-savvy—abstract artists active today is YAYOI KUSAMA (b. 1929) of Japan. Now in her 80s, during her long career Kusama has worked in many artistic genres, including painting, sculpture, film, and performance art, and has written poems and novels. She is best known for her brightly colored compositions ("psychedelic" is a common adjective used to describe her paintings) that recall in some ways the Biomorphic Surrealist canvases of Joan Miró (FIG. 29-58) reinterpreted in a mode that draws on both Pop Art and Abstract Expressionism. Kusama's signature motif is the polka dot, and in the illustrated photograph (FIG. 31-29), taken in 2012 at a retrospective exhibition of her abstract paintings at the Whitney Museum of American Art in New York, she wears a dress of her own design, one item in a complete line of clothing, shoes, watches, jewelry, and leather goods distributed worldwide by Louis Vuitton. Kusama personifies the conjunction of art, popular culture, advertising, and marketing that increasingly characterizes the art world of the 21st century but has its roots in the launching of a line of clothing based on Bridget Riley's Op Art paintings of the 1960s (see page 961 and FIG. 30-16).

31-29 YAYOI KUSAMA seated in a wheelchair in front of a selection of her acrylic-on-canvas paintings at the Whitney Museum of American Art in New York City, July 9, 2012.

Multifaceted octogenarian Japanese artist Yayoi Kusama is best known for her psychedelically colored paintings that draw on Biomorphic Surrealism, Pop Art, and Abstraction Expressionism.

31-30 Tara Donovan, *Untitled,* 2003. Styrofoam cups and hot glue, variable dimensions. Installation at the Ace Gallery, Los Angeles, 2005.

Donovan's sculptures consist of everyday components, such as straws, plastic cups, toothpicks, and wire. The abstract shapes suggest rolling landscapes, clouds, fungus, and other natural forms.

TARA DONOVAN For sculptors as well as painters, abstraction remains a compelling mode of artistic expression today. Brooklynite Tara Donovan (b. 1969) is one of the leading contemporary sculptors producing abstract work. The first recipient (in 2005) of the Alexander Calder Foundation's Calder Prize for sculpture, Donovan studied at the School of Visual Arts in New York City, the Corcoran College of Art and Design in Washington, D.C., and Virginia Commonwealth University in Richmond. She has earned an international reputation for her installations, such as *Untitled* (FIG. **31-30**), composed of thousands of small everyday objects— for example, toothpicks, straws, pins, paper plates, plastic cups, and electrical wire. Her large-scale abstract sculptures often suggest rolling landscapes, clouds, fungus, and other natural forms, although she seeks in her work not to mimic those forms but to capture nature's dynamic growth. Some of Donovan's installations are unstable and can change shape during the course of an exhibition.

KIMIO TSUCHIYA Unlike the paintings of Yayoi Kusama (FIG. 31-29), which are firmly in the Western tradition in style, content, and technique, the works produced by some contemporary Japanese artists are rooted in traditions integral to and distinctive of native Japanese culture. For example, the Shinto beliefs in the generative forces in nature and in humankind's position as part of the totality of nature (see "Shinto," page 495) hold great appeal for Kimio Tsuchiya (b. 1955), who studied sculpture in London and Tokyo. Tsuchiya is best known for his large-scale sculptures (FIG. **31-31**) constructed of branches or driftwood. Despite their abstract nature, his works assert the life forces found in natural materials, thereby engaging viewers in a consideration of their own relationship to nature. Tsuchiya does not specifically invoke Shinto when speaking about his art, but it is clear that he has internalized Shinto principles. He identifies as his goal "to bring out and present the life of nature emanating from this energy of trees. . . . It is as though the wood is part of myself, as though the wood has the same kind of life force."[7]

31-31 Kimio Tsuchiya, *Symptom,* 1987. Branches, 13' $1\frac{1}{2}$" × 14' $9\frac{1}{8}$" × 3' $11\frac{1}{4}$". Installation at the exhibition *Jeune Sculpture '87,* Paris 1987.

Tsuchiya's sculptures consist of branches or driftwood, and despite their abstract nature, they assert the life forces found in natural materials. His approach to sculpture reflects ancient Shinto beliefs.

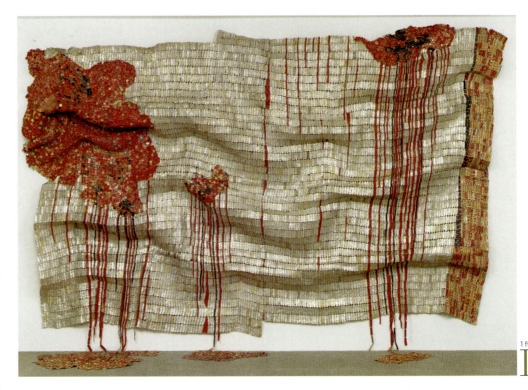

EL ANATSUI Probably the most unusual abstract artworks being created today are those of Ghana-born and -educated EL ANATSUI (b. 1944), who, unique among African artists, established his international reputation without moving his studio to Europe or America. Anatsui has spent his entire adult life in Nigeria and, even more remarkably, did not begin producing the art that has made him famous until his 60s. *Bleeding Takari II* (FIG. 31-32) is a characteristic example of the artistic genre that Anatsui invented, a kind of artwork that is so different from all others that art historians have yet to agree on a label for it. A cross between sculpture and textile design, Anatsui's "metal hangings" (as they are often called) are labor-intensive constructions of crushed bottle caps and lids of aluminum cans pierced and stitched together using copper wire. The colors (primarily red, gold, and black) that Anatsui uses have close parallels in Asante *kente* cloth (FIG. 37-24), and his works can be rolled and folded like fabric. When displayed on museum walls or hanging from a ceiling—or even draped on a building's facade—the metal sheets undulate with any breeze. Anatsui's artworks-in-motion deserve comparison with Alexander Calder's pioneering *mobiles* (FIG. 29-79). They are, however, thoroughly in tune with 21st-century concerns in being assembled (by a large team of assistants) almost entirely from recycled materials.

NEW MEDIA

In addition to taking the ancient arts of painting and sculpture in new directions, contemporary artists have continued to explore the expressive possibilities of the various new media developed in the postwar period, especially digital photography, computer graphics, and video.

31-34 JENNY HOLZER, *Untitled* (selections from *Truisms, Inflammatory Essays, The Living Series, The Survival Series, Under a Rock, Laments,* and *Child Text*), 1989. Extended helical tricolor LED electronic display signboard, 16' × 162' × 6'. Installation at the Solomon R. Guggenheim Museum, New York, December 1989–February 1990 (partial gift of the artist, 1989).

Holzer's 1989 installation consisted of electronic signs created using LED technology. The continuous display of texts wound around the Guggenheim Museum's spiral interior ramp.

ANDREAS GURSKY German photographer ANDREAS GURSKY (b. 1955) grew up in Düsseldorf, where his father was a commercial photographer. Andreas studied photography at Düsseldorf's Kunstakademie (Academy of Art) and since the mid-1990s has used computer and digital technology to produce gigantic color prints in which he combines and manipulates photographs taken with a wide-angle lens, usually from a high vantage point. The size of his photographs, sometimes almost a dozen feet wide, intentionally rivals 19th-century history paintings. But as was true of Gustave Courbet (FIGS. 27-26 and 27-27) in his day, Gursky chooses his subjects from everyday life. He records the mundane world of the modern global economy—vast industrial plants, major department stores, hotel lobbies, and stock and commodity exchanges—and transforms the commonplace into striking, almost abstract, compositions. (Compare the photographs of Edward Burtynsky, FIG. 31-13.)

Gursky's nearly 12-foot-wide 1999 print (FIG. 31-33) documenting the frenzied activity on the main floor of the Chicago Board of Trade is a characteristic example of his work. He took a series of photographs from a gallery, creating a panoramic view of the traders in their brightly colored jackets. He then combined several digital images using commercial photo-editing software to produce a blurred tableau of bodies, desks, computer terminals, and strewn paper in which both mass and color are so evenly distributed as to negate the traditional Renaissance notion of perspective. In using the computer to modify the "objective truth" and spatial recession of "straight photography," Gursky blurs the distinction between painting and photography.

JENNY HOLZER Gallipolis, Ohio, native JENNY HOLZER (b. 1950) studied art at Ohio University and the Rhode Island School of Design. In 1990, she became the first woman to represent the United States at the prestigious Venice Biennale art exhibition. Holzer has won renown for several series of artworks using electronic signs, most involving light-emitting diode (LED) technology, and has created light-projection shows worldwide. In 1989, she assembled a major installation at the Solomon R. Guggenheim Museum in New York that included elements from her previous series and consisted of a large continuous LED display spiraling around the interior ramp (FIG. 31-34) of Frank Lloyd Wright's landmark building (FIG. 30-40). Holzer believes in the communicative power of language, and her installation focused specifically on text. She invented sayings with an authoritative tone for her LED displays—for example, "Protect me from what I want," "Abuse of power comes as no surprise," and "Romantic love was invented to manipulate women." The statements, which people could read from a distance, were intentionally vague and, in some cases, contradictory.

BILL VIOLA The successors of pioneering video artist Nam June Paik (FIG. 30-57) include ADRIAN PIPER (b. 1948; FIG. 31-34A) and BILL VIOLA (b. 1951), who have explored the capabilities of digitized imagery, producing many and varied video installations. Viola often focuses on sensory perception. His pieces not only heighten viewer awareness of

31-34A PIPER, *Cornered*, 1988.

the senses but also suggest an exploration into the spiritual realm. After majoring in art and music at Syracuse University, Viola spent years seriously studying Buddhist, Christian, Sufi, and Zen mysticism. Because he fervently believes in art's transformative power and in a spiritual view of human nature, Viola designs works encouraging spectator introspection. His video projects make use of contrasts in scale, shifts in focus, mirrored reflections, extreme slow motion, staccato editing, and multiple or layered screens to achieve dramatic effects.

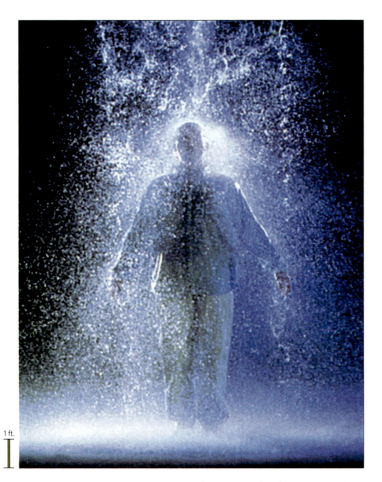

1 ft.

31-35 BILL VIOLA, *The Crossing*, 1996. Video/sound installation with two channels of color video projection onto screens 16' high.

Viola's video projects use contrasts in scale, shifts in focus, mirrored reflections, extreme slow motion, and staccato editing to create dramatic sensory experiences rooted in tangible reality.

The power of Viola's work is evident in *The Crossing* (FIG. **31-35**), an installation piece involving two color video channels projected on 16-foot-high screens. The artist either shows the two projections on the front and back of the same screen or on two separate screens in the same installation. In these two companion videos, shown simultaneously on the two screens, a man surrounded in darkness appears, moving closer until he fills the screen. On one screen, drops of water fall from above onto the man's head, while on the other screen, a small fire breaks out at the man's feet. Over the next few minutes, the water and fire increase in intensity until the man disappears in a torrent of water on one screen (FIG. 31-35) and flames consume the man on the other screen. The deafening roar of a raging fire and a torrential downpour accompany these visual images. Eventually, everything subsides and fades into darkness. This installation's elemental nature and its presentation in a dark space immerse viewers in a pure sensory experience very much rooted in tangible reality.

TONY OURSLER Whereas Viola, Piper, and other artists present video and digital imagery to their audiences on familiar flat screens, thus reproducing the format in which we most often come into contact with electronic images, New Yorker TONY OURSLER (b. 1957), who studied art at the California Institute of the Arts, manipulates his images, projecting them onto sculptural objects. This has the effect of taking the images out of the digital world and insinuating them into the "real" world. Accompanied by sound tapes, Oursler's

1 ft.

31-36 TONY OURSLER, *Mansheshe*, 1997. Ceramic, glass, video player, videocassette, CPJ-200 video projector, sound, 11" × 7" × 8" each. Courtesy of the artist and Metro Pictures, New York.

Video artist Oursler projects his digital images onto sculptural objects, insinuating them into the "real" world. Here, he projected talking heads onto egg-shaped forms suspended from poles.

installations, such as *Mansheshe* (FIG. **31-36**), not only engage but often challenge the viewer. In this example, Oursler projected talking heads onto egg-shaped forms suspended from poles. Because the projected images of people look directly at the viewer, the statements they make about religious beliefs, sexual identity, and interpersonal relationships cannot be easily dismissed.

MATTHEW BARNEY A major trend in the art world today is the relaxation of the traditional boundaries between artistic media—and not just those between painting, photography, sculpture, and textile art. Many contemporary artists are combining new and traditional media to create vast and complex multimedia installations. One of these artists is MATTHEW BARNEY (b. 1967), who studied art at Yale University. The 2003 installation (FIG. **31-37**) of his epic *Cremaster* cycle (1994–2002) at the Solomon R. Guggenheim Museum in New York typifies the expansive scale of many contemporary works. A multimedia extravaganza involving drawings, photographs, sculptures, videos, films, and performances (presented in videos), the *Cremaster* cycle is a lengthy narrative set in a self-enclosed universe that Barney created. The title of the work refers to the cremaster muscle, which controls testicular contractions in response to external stimuli. Barney uses the development of this muscle in the embryonic process of sexual differentiation as the conceptual springboard for the entire *Cremaster* project, in which he explores the notion of creation in expansive and complicated ways.

The cycle's narrative, revealed in the five 35-millimeter feature-length films and the artworks, makes reference to, among other things, a musical revue in Boise, Idaho (where San Francisco–born Barney grew up), the life cycle of bees, the execution of convicted murderer Gary Gilmore, the construction of the Chrysler Building (FIG. 29-47), Celtic mythology, Masonic rituals, a motorcycle race, and a lyric opera set in late-19th-century Budapest. In the installation, Barney tied the artworks together conceptually with a five-channel video piece projected on screens hanging in the Guggenheim's rotunda. Immersion in Barney's constructed world is disorienting and overwhelming and has a force that competes with the immense scale and often frenzied pace of contemporary life.

ENVIRONMENTAL AND SITE-SPECIFIC ART

When Robert Smithson created *Spiral Jetty* (FIG. 30-51) in Utah's Great Salt Lake in 1970, he was a trailblazer in the new genre of Environmental Art, or earthworks. In recent decades, earthworks and other site-specific artworks that bridge the gap between architecture and sculpture have become an established mode of artistic expression. As is true of all other media in the postmodern era, these artworks take a dazzling variety of forms—and some of them have engendered heated controversies.

CHRISTO AND JEANNE-CLAUDE The most prominent heir today to Smithson's earthworks movement is Canadian ANDY GOLDSWORTHY (b. 1956; FIG. **31-37A**), but the most famous Environmental artists of the past few decades are CHRISTO (b. 1935) and JEANNE-CLAUDE (1935–2009). In their works, the couple sought to intensify the viewer's awareness of the space and features of rural and urban sites. However, rather than physically alter the land itself, as Smithson often did, Christo and Jeanne-Claude prompted this awareness by temporarily modifying the landscape with cloth.

⬈ **31-37A** GOLDSWORTHY, *Cracked Rock Spiral*, 1985.

Christo studied art in his native Bulgaria and in Austria. After moving from Vienna to Paris, he began to encase objects in clumsy wrappings, thereby appropriating bits of the real world into the mysterious world of the unopened package whose contents can be dimly seen in silhouette under the wrap. Starting in 1961, a year before their marriage, Christo and Jeanne-Claude began to collaborate on large-scale projects normally dealing with the environment itself. For example, in 1969 they wrapped more than a million square feet of Australian coastline and in 1972 hung a vast curtain across a valley at Rifle Gap, Colorado. Their projects require years of preparation and research, and scores of meetings with local authorities and interested groups of local citizens. These temporary artworks are usually on view for only a few weeks.

Surrounded Islands 1980–83 (FIG. **31-38**), created in Biscayne Bay in Miami, Florida, for

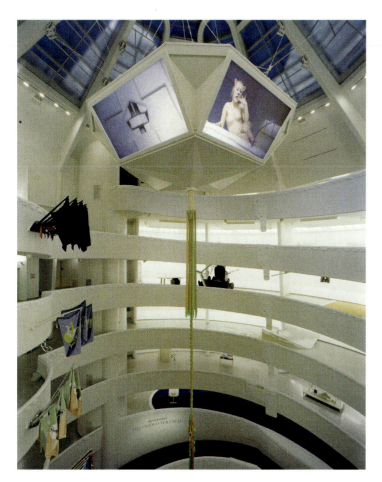

31-37 MATTHEW BARNEY, *Cremaster* cycle, installation at the Solomon R. Guggenheim Museum, New York, 2003.

Barney's vast multimedia installations of drawings, photographs, sculptures, and videos typify the relaxation at the opening of the 21st century of the traditional boundaries among artistic media.

31-38 CHRISTO AND JEANNE-CLAUDE, *Surrounded Islands, Biscayne Bay, Greater Miami, Florida, 1980–83*, 1980–1983.

Christo and Jeanne-Claude created this Environmental artwork by surrounding 11 small islands with 6.5 million square feet of pink fabric. Characteristically, the work existed for only two weeks.

ART AND SOCIETY

Maya Lin's Vietnam Veterans Memorial

Maya Lin's design for the Vietnam Veterans Memorial (FIG. 31-39) is, like Minimalist sculptures (FIGS. 30-18 and 30-19), an unadorned geometric form. Yet the monument, despite its serene simplicity, actively engages viewers in a psychological dialogue, rather than standing mute. This dialogue gives visitors the opportunity to explore their feelings about the Vietnam War and perhaps arrive at some sense of closure.

The history of the Vietnam Veterans Memorial provides dramatic testimony to this monument's power. In 1981, a jury of architects, sculptors, and landscape architects selected Lin's design from among 1,400 entries in a blind competition for a memorial to be placed in Constitution Gardens in Washington, D.C. Conceivably, the jury not only found her design compelling but also thought that its simplicity would be the least likely to provoke controversy. But when the jury made its selection public, heated debate ensued. Even the wall's color came under attack. One veteran charged that black is "the universal color of shame, sorrow and degradation in all races, all societies worldwide."* But the sharpest protests concerned the form and siting of the monument. Because of the stark contrast between the massive white memorials (the Washington Monument and the Lincoln Memorial) bracketing Lin's sunken wall, some people interpreted her Minimalist design as minimizing the Vietnam War and, by extension, the efforts of those who fought in the conflict. Lin herself, however, described the wall as follows:

> The Vietnam Veterans Memorial is not an object inserted into the earth but a work formed from the act of cutting open the earth and polishing the earth's surface—dematerializing the stone to pure

surface, creating an interface between the world of the light and the quieter world beyond the names.[†]

Because of the vocal opposition, a compromise was necessary to ensure the memorial's completion. The Commission of Fine Arts, the federal group overseeing the project, commissioned an additional memorial from artist Frederick Hart (1943–1999) in 1983. This larger-than-life-size realistic bronze sculpture of three soldiers, armed and uniformed, now stands approximately 120 feet from Lin's wall. Several years later, a group of nurses, organized as the Vietnam Women's Memorial Project, received approval for a sculpture honoring women's service in the Vietnam War. The 7-foot-tall bronze statue by Glenna Goodacre (b. 1939) depicts three female figures, one cradling a wounded soldier in her arms. Unveiled in 1993, the work occupies a site about 300 feet south of the Lin memorial.

Whether celebrated or condemned, Lin's Vietnam Veterans Memorial generates dramatic responses. Commonly, visitors react very emotionally, even those who knew none of the soldiers named on the monument. The polished granite surface prompts individual soul-searching—viewers see themselves reflected among the names. Many visitors leave mementos at the foot of the wall in memory of loved ones whom they lost in the Vietnam War or make rubbings from the incised names. It can be argued that much of this memorial's power derives from its Minimalist simplicity. Like Minimalist sculpture, it does not dictate response and therefore successfully encourages personal exploration.

*Elizabeth Hess, "A Tale of Two Memorials," *Art in America* 71, no. 4 (April 1983): 122.
[†]Excerpt from an unpublished 1995 lecture, quoted in Kristine Stiles and Peter Selz, *Theories and Documents of Contemporary Art: A Sourcebook of Artists' Writings* (Berkeley and Los Angeles: University of California Press, 1996), 525.

31-39 MAYA LIN, Vietnam Veterans Memorial (looking north), Washington, D.C., 1981–1983.

Like Minimalist sculpture, Lin's memorial to veterans of the Vietnam War is a simple geometric form. Its inscribed polished walls actively engage viewers in a psychological dialogue about the war.

two weeks in May 1983, typifies Christo and Jeanne-Claude's work. For this project, they surrounded 11 small artificial islands in the bay (created from a dredging project) with 6.5 million square feet of specially fabricated pink polypropylene floating fabric. This Environmental artwork required three years of preparation to obtain the required permits, assemble the labor force, and obtain the $3.2 million needed to complete the project. The artists raised the money by selling preparatory drawings, collages, and models of works they created in the 1950s and 1960s. Huge crowds watched as crews removed accumulated trash from the 11 islands (to assure maximum contrast between their dark colors, the pink of the cloth, and the blue of the bay) and then unfurled the fabric "cocoons" to form magical floating "skirts" around each tiny bit of land. Despite the brevity of its existence, *Surrounded Islands 1980–83* lives on in the host of photographs, films, and books documenting the project.

MAYA LIN Often classified as either a work of Minimalist sculpture or as an architectural monument, the Vietnam Veterans Memorial (FIG. **31-39**) in Washington, D.C., is perhaps best considered under the heading of site-specific art. The now-acclaimed war memorial was designed in 1981 by MAYA YING LIN (b. 1960) when she was a 21-year-old student at the Yale School of Architecture. Austere and simple, the Vietnam memorial takes the form of a V-shaped wall constructed of polished black granite panels. The two 246-foot-long wings of the wall begin at ground level at each end and gradually ascend to a height of 10 feet at the center of the V. Lin set the memorial into the landscape, enhancing visitors' awareness of descent as they walk along the wall toward the center. The names of the Vietnam War's 57,939 American casualties (and those missing in action) inscribed on the two wings (in the order of their deaths) contribute to the memorial's dramatic effect.

When Lin designed this pristinely simple monument, she gave a great deal of thought to the purpose of war memorials. She was determined to create a memorial that would

> be honest about the reality of war and be for the people who gave their lives. . . . [I] didn't want a static object that people would just look at, but something they could relate to as on a journey, or passage, that would bring each to his own conclusions. . . . I wanted to work with the land and not dominate it. I had an impulse to cut open the earth . . .

an initial violence that in time would heal. The grass would grow back, but the cut would remain.[8]

In light of the tragedy of the war, this unpretentious memorial's allusion to a wound and long-lasting scar contributes to its visual and psychological impact (see "Maya Lin's Vietnam Veterans Memorial," page 1020).

RACHEL WHITEREAD Another controversial memorial commissioned for a specific historical setting is the Viennese Holocaust Memorial (FIG. **31-40**) by British sculptor RACHEL WHITEREAD (b. 1963). In 1996, the city of Vienna chose Whiteread as the winner of the competition to design a commemorative monument to the 65,000 Austrian Jews who perished at the hands of the Nazis during World War II. The decision to focus attention on a past that most Austrians wished to forget unleashed a controversy that delayed construction of the monument until 2000. Also controversial was the Minimalist severity of Whiteread's massive block of concrete planted in a Baroque square at the heart of the Austrian capital—as was, at least initially, the understated form of Lin's Vietnam monument (FIG. 31-39) juxtaposed with the Washington and Lincoln Monuments in Washington, D.C.

Whiteread modulated the surface of the Holocaust memorial only slightly by depicting in low relief the shapes of two doors and hundreds of identical books on shelves, with the edges of the covers and the pages rather than the spines facing outward. The book motif was a reference both to Jews as "People of the Book" and to the book burnings that accompanied Jewish persecutions throughout the centuries and under the Nazis. Around the base, Whiteread inscribed the names of Nazi concentration camps in German, Hebrew, and English. The setting for the memorial is Judenplatz (Jewish Square), the site of a synagogue destroyed in 1421. The brutality of the tomblike monument—it cannot be entered, and its shape suggests a prison block—is a visual as well as psychological shock in that beautiful Viennese square. Whiteread's purpose, however, was not to please but to create a memorial that met the jury's charge to "combine dignity with reserve and spark an aesthetic dialogue with the past in a place that is replete with history."

Whiteread had gained fame in 1992 for her monument commemorating the demolition of a working-class neighborhood in East London. *House* took the form of a concrete cast of the space inside the last standing Victorian house on the site. She had also made sculptures of "negative spaces"—for example, the space beneath a chair or mattress or sink. In Vienna, she represented the space behind the shelves of a library. In drawing viewers' attention to the voids between and inside objects and buildings, Whiteread pursued in a different way the same goal as Pop Art innovator Jasper Johns (FIG. 30-24), who painted things "seen but not looked at."

31-40 RACHEL WHITEREAD, Holocaust Memorial (looking northwest), Judenplatz, Vienna, Austria, 2000.

Whiteread's monument to the 65,000 Austrian Jews who perished in the Holocaust is a tomblike concrete block with doors that cannot be opened and library books seen from behind.

ART AND SOCIETY

Richard Serra's *Tilted Arc*

When Richard Serra installed *Tilted Arc* (FIG. 31-41) in the plaza in front of the Javits Federal Building in New York City in 1981, much of the public immediately responded with hostile criticism. Prompting the chorus of complaints was the uncompromising presence of a Minimalist sculpture bisecting the plaza. Many argued that *Tilted Arc* was ugly, attracted graffiti, interfered with the view across the plaza, and prevented use of the plaza for performances or concerts. Because of the sustained barrage of protests and petitions demanding the removal of *Tilted Arc*, the General Services Administration, which had commissioned the sculpture, held a series of public hearings. Afterward, the agency decided to remove Serra's sculpture despite its prior approval of the artist's model. Understandably, this infuriated Serra, who had a legally binding contract acknowledging the site-specific nature of *Tilted Arc*. "To remove the work is to destroy the work," the artist stated.[*]

This episode raised intriguing issues about the nature of public art, including the public reception of experimental art, the artist's responsibilities and rights when executing public commissions, censorship in the arts, and the purpose of public art. If an artwork is on display in a public space outside the relatively private confines of a museum or gallery, do different guidelines apply? As one participant in the *Tilted Arc* saga asked, "Should an artist have the right to impose his values and taste on a public that now rejects his taste and values?"[†] Historically, one of the express functions of the artistic avant-garde was to challenge convention by rejecting tradition and disrupting the complacency of the viewer. Will placing experimental art in a public place always cause controversy? From Serra's statements, it is clear that he intended the sculpture to challenge the public.

Another issue that *Tilted Arc* presented involved the rights of the artist, who in this case accused the GSA of censorship. Serra filed a lawsuit against the federal government for infringement of his First Amendment rights and insisted that "the artist's work must be uncensored, respected, and tolerated, although deemed abhorrent, or perceived as challenging, or experienced as threatening."[‡] Did removal of the work constitute censorship? A U.S. district court held that it did not.

Ultimately, who should decide what artworks are appropriate for the public arena? One artist argued, "We cannot have public art by plebiscite [popular vote]."[§] But to avoid recurrences of the *Tilted Arc* controversy, the GSA changed its procedures and now solicits input from a wide range of civic and neighborhood groups before commissioning public artworks. Despite the removal of *Tilted Arc* (now languishing in storage), the sculpture maintains a powerful presence in all discussions of the aesthetics, politics, and dynamics of public art.

[*]Grace Glueck, "What Part Should the Public Play in Choosing Public Art?" *New York Times,* February 3, 1985, 27.
[†]Calvin Tomkins, "The Art World: Tilted Arc," *New Yorker,* May 20, 1985, 98.
[‡]Ibid., 98–99.
[§]Ibid., 98.

31-41 RICHARD SERRA, *Tilted Arc,* as installed before its removal from Jacob K. Javits Federal Plaza (looking southwest), New York City, 1981.

Serra intended his Minimalist *Tilted Arc* to alter the character of an existing public space. He succeeded, but unleashed a storm of protest that caused the government to remove the work.

RICHARD SERRA Also unleashing an emotional public debate, but for different reasons and with a decidedly different outcome, was *Tilted Arc* (FIG. **31-41**) by San Franciscan RICHARD SERRA (b. 1939), who worked in steel mills in California before studying art at Yale University. He now lives in New York, where he received a commission in 1979 from the General Services Administration (GSA), the federal agency responsible for overseeing the selection and installa-

tion of artworks for government buildings, to install a 120-foot-long, 12-foot-high curved wall of Cor-Ten steel in the plaza in front of the Jacob K. Javits Federal Building in lower Manhattan. He completed the project in 1981. Serra wished *Tilted Arc* to "dislocate or alter the decorative function of the plaza and actively bring people into the sculpture's context."[9] In pursuit of that goal, Serra situated the sculpture so that it bisected and consequently significantly altered the space

Kapoor's enormous polished stainless steel sculpture has delighted visitors to Chicago's Millennium Park, who enjoy seeing distorted views of themselves and the city's skyline in *Cloud Gate*'s curving mirrored surface.

10 ft.

31-43 DO-HO SUH, *Bridging Home,* 2010. Korean house installation in Duke Street, Liverpool, England.

Bridging Home is an empty Korean house wedged between two buildings in Liverpool. It effectively communicates Suh's sense of displacement as a nomad dividing his life between Seoul and New York.

of the open plaza and interrupted the traffic flow across the square. By creating such an intrusive presence in this large public space, Serra forced viewers to reconsider the plaza's physical space as a sculptural form—but only temporarily, because the public succeeded in having the sculpture removed (see "Richard Serra's *Tilted Arc,*" page 1022).

ANISH KAPOOR The public reacted very differently to the installation in 2004 in Chicago's Millennium Park of *Cloud Gate* (FIG. **31-42**), a 33-foot-tall and 66-foot-long polished stainless steel abstract sculpture by the recently knighted Mumbai-born British sculptor ANISH KAPOOR (b. 1954). Affectionately known to Chicagoans as the Bean, Kapoor's gigantic, gently curving sculpture is large enough that people can walk under its swelling arched form, hence its title *Cloud Gate.* Rather than disrupting activity in the park, as Serra's *Tilted Arc* (FIG. 31-41) did in Manhattan, Kapoor's *Cloud Gate* encourages viewers to interact with it. Indeed, most people delight in seeing their reflection (with the backdrop of the panorama of Chicago's skyline) in the mirrorlike surface. On many days, *Cloud Gate* also reflects clouds of similar bean shape. The reflections of people, buildings, and clouds, however, are distorted by the Bean's curved surface, as Kapoor intended them to be, adding another dimension to the pleasure of looking at the work.

DO-HO SUH Some of the most interesting site-specific artworks being created today are the work of Korean DO-HO SUH (b. 1962), who studied at Seoul National University, the Rhode Island School of Design, and Yale University. Suh maintains a studio in Seoul, but his installations are designed for display on several continents. His pieces are to a large extent autobiographical in that they often are based on the modest houses and apartments in which he has lived. An outstanding example is *Bridging Home* (FIG. **31-43**), which Suh wedged between two buildings on Duke Street in Liverpool, England, for the 2010 International Festival of Contemporary Arts. The title—*Bridging Home*—is a reference to Suh's dividing his personal and professional life between Seoul and New York City. The insertion of an empty Korean home into a Liverpool street effectively communicated Suh's sense of rootlessness and displacement as a nomadic citizen of the world.

31-44 Davıd Hammons, *Public Enemy,* installation at Museum of Modern Art, New York, 1991. Photographs, balloons, sandbags, guns, and other mixed media.

Hammons intended this multimedia installation, with Theodore Roosevelt flanked by an African American and a Native American as servants, to reveal the racism embedded in America's cultural heritage.

DAVID HAMMONS Suh's works have been exhibited in many museums as well as outdoors. In fact, museums throughout the world have in recent decades increasingly allocated more of their limited exhibition space to installation art. One example of this kind of indoor site-specific art that encourages viewer interaction at the same time that it makes a powerful statement about racism in America is *Public Enemy* (FIG. 31-44) by David Hammons (b. 1943), which he created for an exhibition at the Museum of Modern Art in New York in 1991. Born in Springfield, Illinois, Hammons, an African American, moved to Los Angeles in 1962, where he studied art at the Chouinard and Otis Art Institutes before settling in Harlem in 1974. In his installations, Hammons combines sharp social commentary with beguiling sensory elements.

In *Public Enemy,* he enticed viewers to interact with the installation by scattering fragrant autumn leaves on the floor and positioning helium-filled balloons throughout the gallery. The leaves crunched underfoot, and the dangling strings of the balloons gently brushed spectators walking around the installation. Once drawn into the environment, viewers encountered the centerpiece of *Public Enemy*—large black-and-white photographs of a public monument in front of the American Museum of Natural History in New York City depicting President Theodore Roosevelt (1858–1919) triumphantly seated on a horse, flanked by an African American man and a Native American man, both men appearing in the role of servant. Around the edge of the installation, circling the photographs of the monument, were piles of sandbags with both real and toy guns propped on top, aimed at the statue. By selecting evocative found objects and presenting them in a dynamic manner, encouraging viewer interaction, Hammons attracted an audience and then revealed the racism embedded in received cultural heritage and prompted reexamination of American values and cultural emblems.

ARCHITECTURE

The work of architects today is as varied as that of contemporary painters, sculptors, and new-media artists, but the common denominator in the diversity of contemporary architectural design is the breaking down of national boundaries, with leading practitioners working in several countries and even on several continents, often simultaneously. In the late 20th and early 21st centuries, one of the by-products of the globalization of the world's economy has been that in the rapidly developing emerging markets of Asia, the Middle East, Africa, Latin America, and elsewhere, virtually every architect with an international reputation can list on his or her résumé a recent building in a bustling new urban center. In this brief survey of contemporary architecture, the projects of eight internationally acclaimed architects are considered under three major headings: Postmodernism, Deconstructivism, and High-Tech and Green architecture.

Postmodernism

The decades following the conclusion of World War II witnessed the rejection of the unadorned modernist aesthetic in architecture, exemplified by the Seagram Building (FIG. 30-45) in New York City, even by that building's codesigner, in favor of a more complex architectural vocabulary incorporating references to historical styles (see "After Modernism: Postmodern Architecture" and "Philip Johnson on Postmodern Architecture," pages 949 and 983). Architectural postmodernism remains a major stylistic trend today. Two internationally renowned architects who have produced significant postmodern buildings are I. M. Pei and James Stirling.

I. M. PEI The latest chapter in the long architectural history of the Louvre—the former French royal residence (FIGS. 20-16, 23-23, and 25-25), now one of the world's greatest art museums—is a monumental glass-and-steel pyramid erected in the palace's main courtyard in 1988. Designed by the Chinese American architect I. M. (Ieoh Ming) Pei (b. 1917), the Grand Louvre Pyramid (FIG. 31-45) is the dramatic glass-and-steel entryway to the museum's priceless

31-45 I. M. PEI, Grand Louvre Pyramide (looking southwest), Musée du Louvre, Paris, France, 1988.

Egyptian stone architecture inspired Pei's postmodern entryway to the Louvre, but his glass-and-steel pyramid is a transparent tent serving as a skylight for the underground extension of the old museum.

collections. Although initially controversial because conservative critics considered it a jarring, dissonant intrusion in a hallowed public space left untouched for centuries, Pei's pyramid, like Rogers and Piano's Pompidou Center (FIG. 30-50) a decade before, quickly captured the French public's imagination and admiration.

In fact, Pei erected four glass pyramids in the Louvre courtyard: the grand central pyramid plus the three small echoes of it bordering the large fountain-filled pool surrounding the dominating glass entryway. Consistent with postmodern aesthetics, Pei turned to the past for inspiration, choosing the quintessential emblem of ancient Egypt (FIG. 3-8), an appropriate choice given the Louvre's rich collection of Egyptian art. But Pei transformed his ancient solid stone models (see "Building the Great Pyramids," page 62) into a transparent "tent," simultaneously permitting an almost uninterrupted view of the wings of the royal palace courtyard and serving as a skylight for the new underground network of ticket booths, offices, shops, restaurants, and conference rooms that he also designed.

JAMES STIRLING In England, the leading postmodern architect was JAMES STIRLING (1926–1994). Like other architects who achieved critical acclaim, Stirling received commissions for buildings throughout Europe and North America. His masterpiece may be the Neue Staatsgalerie (FIG. **31-46**) in Stuttgart, a brilliant solution to a challenging commission calling for an addition to a Renaissance Revival museum on a difficult hillside site wedged between existing terraced buildings and an eight-lane traffic-clogged thoroughfare. Stirling's sprawling design—which is impossible to encompass in a single photograph other than an aerial view and cannot be fully appreciated except from the ground—intentionally recalls Karl Friedrich Schinkel's Altes Museum (FIG. 27-42) in Berlin in having a central rotunda. But at Stuttgart, the rotunda (FIG. 31-46, *bottom*) is an open

31-46 JAMES STIRLING, Neue Staatsgalerie, Stuttgart, Germany, 1977–1983. *Top:* facade (looking north); *bottom:* courtyard (looking northwest).

Stirling's postmodern design for Stuttgart's new museum complex incorporates Egyptian and Greco-Roman architectural references as well as contemporary High-Tech design elements.

31-47 GÜNTER BEHNISCH, Hysolar Institute (looking south), University of Stuttgart, Stuttgart, Germany, 1987.

The roof, walls, and windows of the Deconstructivist Hysolar Institute seem to explode, avoiding any suggestion of stable masses and frustrating viewers' expectations of how a building should look.

courtyard that forms the centerpiece of an asymmetrical plan that breaks sharply from the rules of classical architectural design.

Like most art museums today—which are income-producing cultural supermarkets with restaurants, shops, theaters, and reception areas for gala events, in addition to exhibition halls with related curatorial offices and workshops—the Staatsgalerie is a multifaceted, multifunctional building. It also incorporates multiple historical references, which are unexpectedly revealed to visitors as they move from one part of the architectural complex to another. The sandstone ramps and pylonlike walls of the facade facing the roadway (FIG. 31-46, *top*) owe their inspiration to ancient Egyptian temples (FIGS. 3-20, 3-24, 3-24A, and 3-39), but Stirling also included an undulating glass wall based on the shape of a grand piano, a red-and-blue steel glass-roofed taxi stand, and, in the courtyard (FIG. 31-46, *bottom*), Greco-Roman columns and architraves scattered like abandoned ruins. The historical eclecticism of Stirling's Staatsgalerie is quintessentially postmodern.

Deconstructivism

Perhaps the most radical development in architectural design during the closing decades of the 20th century was *Deconstructivism.* Deconstructivist architects attempt to disrupt the conventional categories of architecture and to rupture the viewer's expectations based on them. Destabilization plays a major role in Deconstructivist architecture. Disorder, dissonance, imbalance, asymmetry, irregularity, and confusion replace their opposites—order, harmony, balance, symmetry, regularity, and clarity. The seemingly haphazardly presented volumes, masses, planes, borders, lighting, locations, directions, and spatial relations, as well as the disguised structural facts of Deconstructivist design, challenge the viewer's assumptions about architectural form as it relates to function. According to Deconstructivist principles, the very absence of the stability of traditional categories of architecture in a structure announces a "deconstructed" building.

GÜNTER BEHNISCH An early example of this audacious architectural mode is the Hysolar Institute (FIG. 31-47) at the University of Stuttgart, Germany, by GÜNTER BEHNISCH (1922–2010). Behnisch, who gained international attention as the architect of the Olympic Park in Munich for the 1972 Olympic Games, designed the institute as part of a joint German–Saudi Arabian research project on the technology of solar energy. In the Hysolar Institute, Behnisch intended to deny the possibility of spatial enclosure altogether, and his apparently chaotic arrangement of the structural units defies easy analysis. The shapes of the roof, walls, and windows seem to explode, avoiding any suggestion of clear, stable masses. Behnisch aggressively played with the traditional concepts of architectural design, frustrating the viewer's expectations of how a building should look. The disordered architectural elements appear precarious, seemingly prevented from collapsing only by a curved red steel cable running through the building and anchored to the ground on each end.

FRANK GEHRY The architect most closely identified with Deconstructivist architecture is Canadian-born American FRANK GEHRY (b. 1929). Trained in sculpture, and at different times a collaborator with Donald Judd (FIG. 30-19) and Claes Oldenburg (FIG. 30-29), Gehry works up his designs by constructing models and then cutting them up and arranging the parts until he has a satisfying composition. Among Gehry's most notable projects is the Guggenheim Museum (FIGS. 31-48 and 31-49) in Bilbao, Spain, one of several art museum projects of the past few decades—including the Grand Louvre Pyramid (FIG. 31-45), the Neue Staatsgalerie (FIG. 31-46), and the Denver Art Museum (FIG. **31-47A**) by DANIEL LIBESKIND (b. 1946)—that are as notable for their innovative architectural designs as for the important art collections they house.

↗ **31-47A** LIBESKIND, Denver Art Museum, 2006.

Frank Gehry on Architectural Design and Materials

Frank Gehry has been designing buildings since the 1950s, but only in the 1970s did he begin to break away from the rectilinearity of modernist architecture and develop the dramatic sculptural style seen in buildings such as the Guggenheim Museum (FIGS. **31-48** and **31-49**) in Bilbao. In 1999, the Deconstructivist architect reflected on his career and his many projects in a book simply titled *Gehry Talks.*

> My early work was rectilinear because you take baby steps. I guess the work has become a kind of sculpture as architecture. . . . I'm a strict modernist in the sense of believing in purity, that you shouldn't decorate. And yet buildings need decoration, because they need scaling elements. They need to be human scale, in my opinion. They can't just be faceless things. That's how some modernism failed.*

They teach materials and methods in architecture school, as a separate course. I'm a craftsman. . . . It seems to me that when you're doing architecture, you're building something out of something. There are social issues, there's context, and then there's how do you make the enclosure and what do you make it with? . . . I explored metal: how it dealt with the light . . . It does beautiful things with light. . . . Flat was a fetish, and everybody was doing that. I found out that I could use metal if I didn't worry about it being flat; I could do it cheaper. It was intuitive. I just went with it. I liked it. Then when I saw it on the building, I loved it. . . . Bilbao . . . [is] titanium. . . . [I] prefer titanium because it's stronger; it's an element, a pure element, and it doesn't oxidize. It stays the same forever. They give a hundred-year guarantee!†

*Milton Friedman, ed., *Gehry Talks: Architecture + Process,* rev. ed. (New York: Universe, 2002), 47–48.

†Ibid., 44, 47.

31-48 FRANK GEHRY, Guggenheim Bilbao Museo (looking southwest), Bilbao, Spain, 1997.

Gehry's limestone-and-titanium Bilbao museum is an immensely dramatic building. Its disorder and seeming randomness of design epitomize Deconstructivist architectural principles.

31-49 FRANK GEHRY, atrium of the Guggenheim Bilbao Museo (view looking up), Bilbao, Spain, 1997.

The glass-walled atrium of the Guggenheim Bilbao Museum soars skyward 165 feet. The asymmetrical and imbalanced screens and vaults flow into one another, creating a sense of disequilibrium.

Gehry's Bilbao museum appears to be a collapsed or collapsing aggregate of units. Visitors approaching the building see a mass of irregular asymmetrical and imbalanced forms whose profiles change dramatically with every shift of the viewer's position. The limestone- and titanium-clad exterior lends a space-age character to the structure, and highlights further the unique cluster effect of the many forms (see "Frank Gehry on Architectural Design and Materials," page 1027). A group of organic forms that Gehry refers to as a "metallic flower" tops the museum. In the center of the building, an enormous glass-walled atrium (FIG. 31-49) soars 165 feet above the ground, serving as the focal point for the three levels of galleries radiating from it. The seemingly weightless screens, vaults, and volumes of the interior float and flow into one another, guided only by light and dark cues. The Guggenheim Museum in Bilbao is a profoundly compelling structure. Its disorder, its deceptive randomness of design, and the disequilibrium it prompts in viewers exemplify Deconstructivist principles.

31-50 ZAHA HADID, proposal for Signature Towers, Dubai, United Arab Emirates, designed 2006; not yet constructed.

Originally dubbed the Dancing Towers, Hadid's triad of corporate skyscrapers in Dubai features two towers that seem to be in motion. They bend to merge halfway up, enabling passage between them.

ZAHA HADID One of the most innovative living architects is Iraqi Deconstructivist ZAHA HADID (b. 1950), the first woman to win the Pritzker Architecture Prize (in 2004), the architectural equivalent of the Nobel Prize in literature. The first recipient was Philip Johnson in 1979. Other previous winners include Norman Foster (FIGS. 31-51 and 31-53), Frank Gehry, I. M. Pei, Renzo Piano, James Stirling, Joern Utzon, and Robert Venturi. Born in Baghdad, Hadid studied mathematics in Beirut, Lebanon, and architecture in London, and has designed buildings in England, Germany, Austria, France, Italy, Spain, the United States, and elsewhere. Deeply influenced by the Suprematist theories and paintings of Kazimir Malevich (FIG. 29-30), who championed the use of pure colors and abstract geometric shapes to express "the supremacy of pure feeling in creative art," Hadid employs unadorned surfaces (the antithesis of typical postmodernist design) in dynamic arrangements that have an emotional effect on the viewer.

One of her most ambitious projects is a triad of skyscrapers in Dubai, the capital of the oil-rich United Arab Emirates, where many interesting buildings by major architects are being erected today. Originally dubbed the Dancing Towers and now called the Signature Towers (FIG. **31-50**), the three skyscrapers that will house offices, a hotel, a restaurant with a panoramic view, and luxurious private apartments deviate sharply from traditional skyscraper design because Hadid proposes to give the impression that two of the towers "dance." The undulating motion is, of course, illusory. But the towers do bend in order to merge about halfway up to enable people to move from tower to tower without descending to the ground and exiting. The more traditional tower, which also bends, connects to the central tower, but at ground level.

High-Tech and Green Architecture

From its beginnings in the late 19th century (see "The First Skyscrapers," page 876), skyscraper design has always required the collaboration of engineers to provide heating, plumbing, lighting, elevators, and all the other necessities of modern life for the hundreds or thousands of people who work or live in these urban towers. Today, engineering concerns are most readily apparent in the work of technologically savvy architects and especially in the design of buildings that conserve natural resources.

NORMAN FOSTER Pritzker award–winning architect NORMAN FOSTER (b. 1935) began his study of architectural design at the University of Manchester, England. After graduating, he won a fellowship to attend the master's degree program at the Yale School of Architecture, where he met Richard Rogers (FIG. 30-50). The two decided to open a joint architectural firm when they returned to London in 1962, but they established separate practices several years later. Their designs still have much in common, however, because they share a similar outlook. Foster and Rogers are the leading proponents of what critics call *High-Tech architecture,* the roots of which can be traced to Joseph Paxton's mid-19th-century Crystal Palace (FIG. 27-47) in London. High-Tech architects design buildings incorporating the latest innovations in engineering and technology and exposing the structures' component parts. High-Tech architecture, like Deconstructivist architecture, is distinct from other postmodern architectural movements in dispensing with all historical references.

Foster's design for the headquarters (FIG. 31-51) of the Hong Kong and Shanghai Bank Corporation (HSBC), which even a quarter century ago cost $1 billion to build, exemplifies the High-Tech approach to architecture. The banking tower is as different from Philip Johnson's postmodern AT&T Building (FIG. 30-48) as it is from the modernist glass-and-steel Seagram Building (FIG. 30-45)

and Sears Tower (FIG. 30-46). The 47-story Hong Kong skyscraper has an exposed steel skeleton with the elevators and other service elements located in giant piers at the short ends of the building, a design that provides uninterrupted communal working spaces on each cantilevered floor. Foster divided the tower into five horizontal units of six to nine floors each that he calls "villages," suspended from steel girders resembling bridges. Escalators connect the floors in each village—the floors are related by function—but the elevators stop at only one floor in each community of floors. At the base of the building is a plaza opening onto the neighboring streets. Visitors ascend on escalators from the plaza to a spectacular 10-story, 170-foot-tall atrium bordered by balconies with additional workspaces. What Foster calls "sun scoops"—computerized mirrors on the south side of the building—track the movement of the sun across the Hong Kong sky and reflect the sunlight into the atrium and plaza, flooding the dramatic spaces with light at all hours of the day. Not surprisingly, the roof of this High-Tech skyscraper serves as a landing pad for corporate helicopters.

RENZO PIANO The harnessing of solar energy as a power source is one of the key features of what critics commonly refer to as *Green architecture*—ecologically friendly buildings that use "clean energy" and sustain the natural environment. Green architecture is the most important trend in architectural design in the early 21st century. A pioneer in this field is Renzo Piano, the codesigner with Richard Rogers of the Pompidou Center (FIG. 30-50) in Paris. Piano won an international competition to design the Tjibaou Cultural Centre (FIG. 31-52) in Noumea, New Caledonia. Named in honor of the assassinated political leader Jean-Marie Tjibaou (1936–1989), the center consists of 10 beehive-shaped bamboo "huts" nestled in pine trees on a narrow island peninsula in the Pacific Ocean. Rooted in the village architecture of the Kanak people of New Caledonia (see MAP 36-1), each unit of Piano's complex has an adjustable skylight as a roof to provide natural—sustainable—climate control. The curved profile of the Tjibaou pavilions also helps the structures withstand the pressure of the hurricane-force winds common in the South Pacific.

31-51 NORMAN FOSTER, Hong Kong and Shanghai Bank (looking southwest), Hong Kong, China, 1979–1986.

Foster's High-Tech tower has an exposed steel skeleton featuring floors with uninterrupted working spaces. At the base is a 10-story atrium illuminated by computerized mirrors that reflect sunlight.

31-52 RENZO PIANO, Tjibaou Cultural Centre (looking southeast), Noumea, New Caledonia, 1998.

A pioneering example of Green architecture, Piano's complex of 10 bamboo units, based on traditional New Caledonian village huts, has adjustable skylights in the roofs for natural climate control.

PROBLEMS AND SOLUTIONS
Norman Foster, the Gherkin, and Green Architectural Design

One of the major recent additions to the skyline of London is Norman Foster's corporate tower officially called 30 St Mary Axe, formerly named after the global reinsurance company Swiss Re, which commissioned the skyscraper as its U.K. headquarters. However, the building is popularly known as the Gherkin because of its distinctive swelling shape resembling a cucumber. The 590-foot-tall, 40-story tower, the sixth-tallest building in London at the time of its construction, stands in the midst of mostly low-rise buildings in the Canary Wharf district and replaced a 1903 structure damaged in a 1992 bombing by the Irish Republican Army. The Gherkin has consequently figured prominently in debates about the intrusion of gigantic skyscrapers in old historical neighborhoods.

Far more attention, however, has been devoted to its award-winning high-tech design and innovative "green" solution to the problem of constructing massive buildings housing thousands of workers in the heart of a densely populated city, where the conservation of resources such as fossil fuel and electricity are high priorities. For example, the tower's ventilated double skin greatly reduces the need to heat the building in the winter and cool it in the summer. The cavity of the two-layer exterior of the Gherkin traps air and provides natural insulation, and panels installed in the same space capture the sun's rays to produce heat or deflect it to reduce the need for air conditioning. The glass panes that make up most of the building's exterior also provide abundant natural light to the offices within, reducing the need for electrical lighting. Energy consumption is further reduced by light controls throughout the building, which respond to motion and automatically turn off when a space is unoccupied. The building has consequently become the "poster child" for Green architecture in England and, more generally, in the world at large. The Gherkin is pointing the way toward the fully sustainable urban environments of the future.

31-53 Norman Foster, 30 St Mary Axe ("the Gherkin," looking southwest), London, England, erected 2001–2003, opened 2004.

Foster's cucumber-shaped skyscraper, originally built as the headquarters of Swiss Re, is a High-Tech marvel that incorporates the latest innovations in Green design to conserve natural resources.

GHERKIN, LONDON Buildings that conserve energy and provide sustainable living and working environments are especially desirable in densely populated areas, where the demands on the earth's natural resources are greatest. A recent triumph of Green architectural design is the corporate tower in London popularly known as the Gherkin (see "Norman Foster, the Gherkin, and Green Architectural Design," above, and FIG. **31-53**).

WHAT NEXT? No one knows what the next years and decades will bring, but given the expansive scope of postmodern art and architecture, it is certain that no single approach or style will dominate.

New technologies will undoubtedly continue to redefine what constitutes a "work of art" or "a building." The universally expanding presence of computers, digital technology, and the Internet may well erode what few conceptual and geographical boundaries remain, and make art and information about art available to virtually everyone, thereby creating a truly global artistic community. As this chapter has revealed, substantial progress has already been made in that direction.

CONTEMPORARY ART WORLDWIDE

Personal and Group Identity

- The vast number of artworks created since 1980 worldwide are extraordinarily diverse in style, format, content, and technique, but can be classified under a few major themes, including personal and group identity. Many artists of African descent, including Wiley, Basquiat, Edwards, Ringgold, Simpson, and Weems, have produced important works addressing issues of concern to black Americans. Quick-to-See Smith has focused on her Native American heritage. Gender and sexuality are central themes in the work of Kruger, the Guerrilla Girls, Mapplethorpe, Wojnarowicz, and Sikander. National identity looms large in the art created by Neshat (Iran), Ofili (Nigeria), and Whiting (New Zealand).

Weems, *Man Smoking/ Malcolm X*, 1990

Political and Social Commentary

- Other contemporary artists have treated political and economic issues that affect society at large. Polish-born Krystof Wodiczko has used gigantic slide projections to publicize the plight of the homeless. Canadian Edward Burtynsky's photographs of "manufactured landscapes" highlight the destructive effects of industrial pollution.

- The violence of contemporary life has been addressed in America by Golub (urban gangs and Latin American death squads), by Martha Rosler (the effects of war on the home front), and in Paris by Colombian Fernando Botero (torture at Abu Ghraib).

- Willie Bester has protested apartheid in South Africa and Zhang Xiaogang has produced biting commentaries on the Cultural Revolution in China.

Rosler, *Gladiators*, 2004

Zhang, *Big Family No. 2*, 1995

Representation, Abstraction, and New Media

- Contemporary art, both in America and worldwide, encompasses a phenomenal variety of styles ranging from abstraction to brutal realism.

- Among today's best-known figural painters and sculptors are Kiki Smith, Koons, and Venezuelan Marisol in the United States, and expatriate Englishwoman Saville in Italy.

- Leading abstract painters and sculptors include Schnabel, Murray, Oji, and Donovan in the United States, Kusama and Tsuchiya in Japan, Wu Guanzhong in China, and Anatsui in Nigeria.

- Many contemporary artists have harnessed new technologies for their art: Gursky, digital photography; Holzer, LED displays; Piper, Viola, and Oursler, video; and Barney, multimedia installations.

Anatsui, *Bleeding Takari II*, 2007

Site-Specific Art and Architecture

- The site-specific works of Lin, Whiteread, Serra, Kapoor, and Suh bridge the gap between architecture and sculpture, as do the Environmental artworks of Christo and Jean-Claude and of Goldsworthy.

- Postmodern architecture is as diverse as contemporary painting and sculpture. Pei and Stirling incorporate historical references in their buildings. Among the major champions of Deconstructivism are Behnisch, Gehry, Libeskind, and Hadid. Leading Hi-Tech and Green architects include Foster and Piano.

Foster, Gherkin, London, 2001–2003

Notes

INTRODUCTION

1. Quoted in George Heard Hamilton, *Painting and Sculpture in Europe, 1880–1940,* 6th ed. (New Haven, Conn.: Yale University Press, 1993), 345.
2. Quoted in *Josef Albers: Homage to the Square* (New York: Museum of Modern Art, 1964), n.p.

CHAPTER 26

1. Quoted in Thomas A. Bailey, *The American Pageant: A History of the Republic,* 2d ed. (Boston: Heath, 1961), 280.

CHAPTER 27

1. Théophile Gautier, *Histoire de Romantisme* (Paris: Charpentier, 1874), 204.
2. Quoted in Helmut Borsch-Supan, *Caspar David Friedrich* (New York: Braziller, 1974), 7.
3. Ibid., 7–8.
4. Quoted in Frederick Merk, *Manifest Destiny and Mission in American History: A Reinterpretation* (New York: Knopf, 1963), 32.
5. Quoted in Linda Nochlin, *Realism and Tradition in Art 1848–1900* (Upper Saddle River, N.J.: Prentice Hall, 1966), 42.
6. Quoted in George Heard Hamilton, *Manet and His Critics* (New Haven, Conn.: Yale University Press, 1954), 45.
7. Quoted in Charles Harrison, Paul Wood, and Jason Gaiger, eds., *Art in Theory 1815–1900: An Anthology of Changing Ideas* (Oxford: Blackwell, 1998), 515.
8. Ibid., 518.
9. *New York Weekly Tribune,* September 30, 1865.
10. Quoted in Nikolai Cikovsky Jr. and Franklin Kelly, *Winslow Homer* (Washington, D.C.: National Gallery of Art, 1995), 26.
11. Quoted in Lloyd Goodrich, *Thomas Eakins, His Life and Work* (New York: Whitney Museum of American Art, 1933), 51–52.
12. Quoted in Nicholas Pevsner, *An Outline of European Architecture* (Baltimore: Penguin, 1960), 627.
13. Letter from Delaroche to François Arao, quoted in Helmut Gernsheim, *Creative Photography* (New York: Bonanza Books, 1962), 24.
14. Quoted in Naomi Rosenblum, *A World History of Photography,* 4th ed. (New York: Abbeville Press, 2007), 69.
15. Quoted in Kenneth MacGowan, *Behind the Screen* (New York: Delta, 1965), 49.

CHAPTER 28

1. Charles Baudelaire, *Le peintre de la vie moderne* (1863). Translated by Jonathan Mayne, ed., *The Painter of Modern Life and Other Essays by Charles Baudelaire,* 2d ed. (New York: Phaidon, 1995), 12.
2. Clement Greenberg, "Modernist Painting," *Art and Literature,* no. 4 (Spring 1965): 193–194.
3. Translated by Carola Hicks, in Charles Harrison, Paul Wood, and Jason Gaiger, eds., *Art in Theory 1815–1900: An Anthology of Changing Ideas* (Oxford: Blackwell, 1998), 595.
4. Quoted in John McCoubrey, *American Art 1700–1960: Sources and Documents* (Englewood Cliffs, N.J.: Prentice Hall, 1965), 184.
5. Quoted in Robert Goldwater and Marco Treves, eds., *Artists on Art, from the XIV to the XX Century* (New York: Pantheon, 1945), 322.
6. Vincent van Gogh to Theo van Gogh, September 1888, in J. van Gogh-Bonger and V. W. van Gogh, eds., *The Complete Letters of Vincent van Gogh* (Greenwich, Conn.: New York Graphic Society, 1979), 3:534.
7. Vincent van Gogh to Theo van Gogh, July 16, 1888, in W. H. Auden, ed., *Van Gogh: A Self-Portrait. Letters Revealing His Life as a Painter* (New York: Dutton, 1963), 299.
8. Reported by Joachim Gasquet (1873–1921). Quoted in Michael Doran, ed., *Conversations with Cézanne* (Berkeley: University of California Press, 2000), 122.
9. Translated by Akane Kawakami, in Harrison, Wood, and Gaiger, 1066.
10. Quoted in V. Frisch and J. T. Shipley, *Auguste Rodin* (New York: Stokes, 1939), 203.

CHAPTER 29

1. Quoted in John Elderfield, *The "Wild Beasts": Fauvism and Its Affinities* (New York: Museum of Modern Art, 1976), 29.
2. Translated by Charles Harrison and Paul Wood, eds., *Art in Theory 1900–2000: An Anthology of Changing Ideas* (Oxford: Blackwell, 2003), 65.
3. Quoted in Frederick S. Levine, *The Apocalyptic Vision: The Art of Franz Marc as German Expressionism* (New York: Harper & Row, 1979), 57.
4. Quoted in Sam Hunter, John Jacobus, and Daniel Wheeler, *Modern Art,* rev. 3d. ed. (Upper Saddle River, N.J.: Prentice Hall, 2004), 121.
5. Quoted in George Heard Hamilton, *Painting and Sculpture in Europe, 1880–1940,* 6th ed. (New Haven: Yale University Press, 1993), 246.
6. Ibid., 238.
7. Quoted in Edward Fry, ed., *Cubism* (London: Thames & Hudson, 1966), 112–113.
8. Quoted in Françoise Gilot and Carlton Lake, *Life with Picasso* (New York: McGraw-Hill, 1964), 77.
9. Pablo Picasso, "Statement to Simone Téry," in Harrison and Wood, 649.
10. Quoted in Roland Penrose, *Picasso: His Life and Work,* rev. ed. (New York: Harper & Row, 1971), 311.
11. Filippo Tommaso Marinetti, *The Foundation and Manifesto of Futurism* (*Le Figaro,* February 20, 1909). Translated by Joshua C. Taylor, in Herschel B. Chipp, *Theories of Modern Art: A Source Book by Artists and Critics* (Berkeley and Los Angeles: University of California Press, 1968), 284.
12. Ibid., 286.
13. Quoted in Robert Short, *Dada and Surrealism* (London: Octopus Books, 1980), 18.
14. Quoted in Robert Motherwell, ed., *The Dada Painters and Poets: An Anthology,* 2d ed. (Cambridge, Mass.: Belknap Press, 1989).
15. Hans Richter, *Dada: Art and Anti-Art* (London: Thames & Hudson, 1961), 64–65.
16. Ibid., 57.
17. Quoted in Arturo Schwarz, *The Complete Works of Marcel Duchamp* (London: Thames & Hudson, 1965), 466.
18. Translated by Howard Dearstyne, in Robert L. Herbert, *Modern Artists on Art,* 2d ed. (Mineola, N.Y.: Dover, 2000), 117.
19. Ibid., 124.
20. Translated by Herbert Read and Leslie Martin, quoted in Chipp, 325–330.
21. Quoted in Sam Hunter, *American Art of the 20th Century* (New York: Abrams, 1972), 30.
22. Ibid., 37.
23. Charles C. Eldredge, "The Arrival of European Modernism," *Art in America* 61 (July–August 1973): 35.
24. Quoted in Gail Stavitsky, "Reordering Reality: Precisionist Directions in American Art, 1915–1941," in *Precisionism in America 1915–1941: Reordering Reality* (New York: Abrams, 1994), 12.

25. Quoted in Karen Tsujimoto, *Images of America: Precisionist Painting and Modern Photography* (Seattle: University of Washington Press, 1982), 70.

26. Quoted in Matthias Eberle, *World War I and the Weimar Artists: Dix, Grosz, Beckmann, Schlemmer* (New Haven: Yale University Press, 1985), 54.

27. Ibid., 22.

28. Ibid., 42.

29. Quoted in Hamilton, 392.

30. Quoted in Richter, 155.

31. Ibid., 159.

32. Quoted in William S. Rubin, *Dada, Surrealism, and Their Heritage* (New York: Museum of Modern Art, 1968), 111.

33. Quoted in Hunter, Jacobus, and Wheeler, 179.

34. Quoted in William S. Rubin, *Miró in the Collection of the Museum of Modern Art* (New York: Museum of Modern Art, 1973), 32.

35. Translated by Norbert Guterman, quoted in Chipp, 182–186.

36. Translated by Nicholas Bullock, quoted in Harrison and Wood, 281.

37. Quoted in Kenneth Frampton, *Modern Architecture: A Critical History,* 4th ed. (New York: Thames & Hudson, 2007), 147.

38. Quoted in H. H. Arnason and Peter Kalb, *History of Modern Art,* 5th ed. (Upper Saddle River, N.J.: Prentice Hall, 2004), 154.

39. Quoted in Robert L. Herbert, *Modern Artists on Art,* 2d ed. (Mineola, N.Y.: Dover, 2000), 173.

40. Ibid., 177.

41. Quoted in Hans L. C. Jaffé, ed., *De Stijl* (New York: Abrams, 1971), 185–188.

42. Piet Mondrian, *Dialogue on the New Plastic* (1919). Translated by Harry Holzman and Martin S. James, in Harrison and Wood, 285.

43. Quoted in Vivian Endicott Barnett, "Banned German Art: Reception and Institutional Support of Modern German Art in the United States, 1933–45," in Stephanie Barron, *Exiles and Emigrés: The Flight of European Artists from Hitler* (Los Angeles: Los Angeles County Museum of Art, 1997), 283.

44. Quoted in Frances K. Pohl, *Ben Shahn: New Deal Artist in a Cold War Climate, 1947–1954* (Austin: University of Texas Press, 1989), 159.

45. Wanda M. Corn, *Grant Wood: The Regionalist Vision* (New Haven: Yale University Press, 1983), 131.

46. Quoted in Matthew Baigell, *A Concise History of American Painting and Sculpture* (New York: Harper & Row, 1984), 264.

47. Quoted in Milton Meltzer, *Dorothea Lange: A Photographer's Life* (New York: Farrar, Strauss & Giroux, 1978), 133, 220.

48. Quoted in Philip Johnson, *Mies van der Rohe,* rev. ed. (New York: Museum of Modern Art, 1954), 200–201.

CHAPTER 30

1. Dawn Ades and Andrew Forge, *Francis Bacon* (London: Thames & Hudson, 1985), 8; and David Sylvester, *The Brutality of Fact: Interviews with Francis Bacon,* 3d ed. (London: Thames & Hudson, 1987), 182.

2. Harold Rosenberg, "The American Action Painters," *Art News* 51 (December 1952): 22–29; reprinted in Rosenberg, *The Tradition of the New* (New York: Horizon Press, 1959), 23–39.

3. Quoted in an interview by Yves Michaud in *Joan Mitchell: New Paintings* (New York: Xavier Fourcade, 1986), n.p.

4. Quoted in Thomas Hess, *Barnett Newman* (New York: Walker and Company, 1969), 51.

5. Quoted in John P. O'Neill, ed., *Barnett Newman: Selected Writings and Interviews* (New York: Knopf, 1990), 108.

6. Marcus Rothko and Adolph Gottlieb, quoted in Edward Alden Jewell, "The Realm of Art: A New Platform and Other Matters: 'Globalism' Pops into View," *New York Times,* June 13, 1943, 9.

7. Quoted in Selden Rodman, *Conversations with Artists* (New York: Devin-Adair, 1957), 93–94.

8. Clement Greenberg, "After Abstract Expressionism," *Art International* 7, no. 8 (October 1962): 24–32.

9. Clement Greenberg, "Recentness of Sculpture," in Gregory Battcock, ed., *Minimal Art: A Critical Anthology* (New York: Dutton, 1968), 183–184.

10. Louise Nevelson, quoted in John Gordon, *Louise Nevelson* (New York: Praeger, 1967), 12.

11. Quoted in Deborah Wye, *Louise Bourgeois* (New York: Museum of Modern Art, 1982), 22.

12. Ibid., 25.

13. Isamu Noguchi, *A Sculptor's World* (New York: Harper & Row, 1968), 40.

14. Quoted in Richard Francis, *Jasper Johns* (New York: Abbeville Press, 1984), 21.

15. Andy Warhol, *The Philosophy of Andy Warhol* (New York: Harcourt Brace Jovanovich, 1975), 100.

16. Quoted in Christine Lindey, *Superrealist Painting and Sculpture* (London: Orbis, 1980), 50.

17. Quoted in Sebastian Smee, *Lucian Freud: Beholding the Animal* (Cologne: Taschen, 2009), 61.

18. Ibid., 7.

19. Quoted in Lindey, 130.

20. Quoted in Susanna Torruella Leval, "Recapturing History: The (Un)official Story in Contemporary Latin American Art," *Art Journal* 51, no. 4 (Winter 1992): 74.

21. Ibid.

22. Quoted in Mary Jane Jacob, *Magdalena Abakanowicz* (New York: Abbeville, 1982), 94.

23. Peter Blake, *Frank Lloyd Wright* (Harmondsworth: Penguin, 1960), 115.

24. Quoted in Nancy Holt, ed., *The Writings of Robert Smithson* (New York: New York University Press, 1975), 111.

25. Quoted in H. H. Arnason and Peter Kalb, *History of Modern Art,* 5th ed. (Upper Saddle River, N.J.: Prentice Hall, 2004), 489.

26. Quoted in Barbara Haskell, *Blam! The Explosion of Pop, Minimalism, and Performance 1958–1964* (New York: Whitney Museum of American Art), 53.

27. Quoted in Bruce McPherson, ed., *More Than Meat Joy: Complete Performance Works and Selected Writings* (New Paltz, N.Y.: Documentext, 1979), 52.

28. Quoted in Caroline Tisdall, *Joseph Beuys* (New York: Thames & Hudson, 1979), 6.

29. Quoted in Brenda Richardson, *Bruce Nauman: Neons* (Baltimore: Baltimore Museum of Art, 1982), 20.

CHAPTER 31

1. Quoted in Arlene Hirschfelder, *Artists and Craftspeople* (New York: Facts on File, 1994), 115.

2. Translated by Petra ten-Doesschate Chu, *Letters of Gustave Courbet* (Chicago: University of Chicago Press, 1992), 203–204.

3. Interview by Susan Sollins, in Marybeth Sollins, ed., *Art:21 (Art in the Twenty-First Century)* (New York: Abrams, 2009), 5:55.

4. Jerome Silbergeld and Dora C.Y. Ching, eds., *Persistence/Transformation: Text as Image in the Art of Xu Bing* (Princeton, N.J.: Princeton University Press, 2006), 99–101.

5. Michelle Meagher, "Jenny Saville and a Feminist Aesthetics of Disgust," *Hypatia* 18, no. 4 (2003): 23–41.

6. Quoted in Donald Hall, *Corporal Politics* (Cambridge: MIT List Visual Arts Center, 1993), 46.

7. Quoted in Junichi Shiota, *Kimio Tsuchiya, Sculpture 1984–1988* (Tokyo: Morris Gallery, 1988), 3.

8. Quoted in "Vietnam Memorial: America Remembers," *National Geographic* 167, no. 5 (May 1985): 557.

9. Quoted in Calvin Tomkins, "The Art World: Tilted Arc," *New Yorker,* May 20, 1985, 100.

Glossary

NOTE: *Text page references are in parentheses.*
References to bonus image online essays are in blue.

abstract—Nonrepresentational; forms and colors arranged without reference to the depiction of an object. (5)

Abstract Expressionism—The first major American avant-garde movement, Abstract Expressionism emerged in New York City in the 1940s. The artists produced *abstract* paintings that expressed their state of mind and that they hoped would strike emotional chords in viewers. The movement developed along two lines: *gestural abstraction* and *chromatic abstraction.* (953)

action painting—Also called *gestural abstraction.* The kind of *Abstract Expressionism* practiced by Jackson Pollock, in which the emphasis was on the creation process, the artist's gesture in making art. Pollock poured liquid paint in linear webs on his canvases, which he laid out on the floor, thereby physically surrounding himself in the painting during its creation. (956)

additive light—Natural light, or sunlight, the sum of all the wavelengths of the visible *spectrum.* See also *subtractive light.* (7)

additive sculpture—A kind of sculpture *technique* in which materials (for example, clay) are built up or "added" to create form. (11)

airbrush—A tool that uses compressed air to spray paint onto a surface. (972)

aisle—The portion of a basilica flanking the *nave* and separated from it by a row of *columns* or *piers.* (12)

Analytic Cubism—The first phase of *Cubism,* developed jointly by Pablo Picasso and Georges Braque, in which the artists analyzed form from every possible vantage point to combine the various views into one pictorial whole. (892)

ancien régime—French, "old order." The term used to describe the political, social, and religious order in France before the Revolution at the end of the 18th century. (773)

aqueduct—A channel for carrying water, often elevated on *arches.* (774)

armature—The crossed, or diagonal, *arches* that form the skeletal framework of a Gothic rib *vault.* In sculpture, the framework for a clay form. (11)

Art Brut—French, "Crude Art." The mid-20th-century art movement led by Jean Dubuffet that rejected the conventions of traditional art in favor of the untaught art of children and the mentally ill. (952)

Art Deco—Descended from *Art Nouveau,* this movement of the 1920s and 1930s sought to upgrade industrial design as a "fine art" and to work new materials into decorative patterns that could be either machined or handcrafted. Characterized by streamlined, elongated, and symmetrical design. (916)

Art Nouveau—French, "new art." A late-19th- and early-20th-century art movement whose proponents tried to synthesize all the arts in an effort to create art based on natural forms that could be mass produced by technologies of the industrial age. The movement had other names in other countries: Jugendstil in Austria and Germany, Modernismo in Spain, and Stile Floreale in Italy. (873)

assemblage—An artwork constructed from already existing objects. (967)

attribute—(n.) The distinctive identifying aspect of a person—for example, an object held, an associated animal, or a mark on the body. (v.) To make an *attribution.* (5)

attribution—Assignment of a work to a maker or makers. (6)

automatism—In painting, the process of yielding oneself to instinctive motions of the hands after establishing a set of conditions (such as size of paper or *medium*) within which a work is to be created. (921)

avant-garde—French, "advance guard" (in a platoon). Late-19th- and 20th-century artists who emphasized innovation and challenged established convention in their work. Also used as an adjective. (883)

bacchanal—An orgiastic revel in which the followers of the Greco-Roman god Bacchus take part. (28-32A)

bas-relief—See *relief.* (12, 862)

battlement—A low parapet at the top of a circuit wall in a fortification. (26-28A)

Bauhaus—A *school* of architecture in Germany in the 1920s under the aegis of Walter Gropius, who emphasized the unity of art, architecture, and design. (932)

Beaux-Arts—An architectural *style* of the late 19th and early 20th centuries in France. Based on ideas taught at the École des Beaux-Arts in Paris, the Beaux-Arts style incorporated classical principles, such as symmetry in design, and included extensive exterior ornamentation. (831)

benday dots—Named after the newspaper printer Benjamin Day, the benday dot system involves the modulation of *colors* through the placement and size of colored dots. (968)

Biomorphic Surrealism—See *Surrealism.* (921)

burgher—A middle-class citizen. (28-33A)

bust—A freestanding sculpture of the head, shoulders, and chest of a person. (11)

calotype—From the Greek *kalos,* "beautiful." A photographic process in which a positive image is made by shining light through a negative image onto a sheet of sensitized paper. (834, 835)

camera lucida—Latin, "lighted room." A device in which a small lens projects the image of an object downward onto a sheet of paper. (835)

camera obscura—Latin, "dark room." An ancestor of the modern camera in which a tiny pinhole, acting as a lens, projects an image on a screen, the wall of a room, or the ground-glass wall of a box; used by artists in the 17th, 18th, and early 19th centuries as an aid in drawing from nature. (781)

canon—A rule (for example, of proportion). The ancient Greeks considered beauty to be a matter of "correct" proportion and sought a canon of proportion, for the human figure and for buildings. The fifth-century BCE sculptor Polykleitos wrote the *Canon,* a treatise incorporating his formula for the perfectly proportioned *statue.* Also, a church official who preaches, teaches, administers sacraments, and tends to pilgrims and the sick. (10)

carving—A sculptural *technique* in which the artist cuts away material (for example, from a stone block) in order to create a *statue* or a *relief.* (11)

casting—A sculptural *technique* in which the artist pours liquid metal, plaster, clay, or another material into a *mold*. When the material dries, the sculptor removes the cast piece from the mold. (11)

chacmool—A Mesoamerican statuary type depicting a fallen warrior on his back with a receptacle on his chest for sacrificial offerings. (930)

characters—In Chinese writing, signs that record spoken words. (1009)

chasseur—French cavalry officer. (805)

choir—The space reserved for the clergy and singers in the church, usually east of the transept but, in some instances, extending into the *nave*. (12)

chromatic abstraction—A kind of *Abstract Expressionism* that focuses on the emotional resonance of color, as exemplified by the work of Barnett Newman and Mark Rothko. (954)

chronology—In art history, the dating of art objects and buildings. (2)

cloisonné—A decorative metalwork *technique* employing cells made of metal wire or a narrow metal strip soldered edge-up to a metal base to hold enamel, stones, glass, or jewels. (858)

collage—A composition made by combining on a flat surface various materials, such as newspaper, wallpaper, printed text and illustrations, photographs, and cloth. (8, 894)

coller—French, "to stick." (894)

color—The value, or tonality, of a color is the degree of its lightness or darkness. The intensity, or saturation, of a color is its purity, its brightness or dullness. See also *primary colors, secondary colors,* and *complementary colors.* (7)

color-field painting—A variant of *Post-Painterly Abstraction* in which artists sought to reduce painting to its physical essence by pouring diluted paint onto unprimed canvas and letting these pigments soak into the fabric, as exemplified by the work of Helen Frankenthaler and Morris Louis. (960)

column—A vertical, weight-carrying architectural member, circular in cross-*section* and consisting of a base (sometimes omitted), a shaft, and a capital. (10)

combines—The name that American artist Robert Rauschenberg gave to his *assemblages* of painted passages and sculptural elements. (967, 995)

commedia dell'arte—A traditional Italian comic play performed by actors and musicians. (29-17A)

complementary colors—Those pairs of *colors,* such as red and green, that together embrace the entire *spectrum*. The complement of one of the three *primary colors* is a mixture of the other two. (7, 855)

compose—See *composition.* (7)

composition—The way in which an artist organizes *forms* in an artwork, either by placing shapes on a flat surface or arranging forms in space. (7)

Conceptual Art—An American *avant-garde* art movement of the 1960s whose premise was that the "artfulness" of art lay in the artist's idea rather than its final expression. (989)

connoisseur—An expert in *attributing* artworks to one artist rather than another. More generally, an expert on artistic *style.* (6)

Constructivism—An early-20th-century Russian art movement formulated by Naum Gabo, who built up his sculptures piece by piece in space instead of carving or modeling them. In this way, the sculptor worked with "volume of mass" and "volume of space" as different materials. (906)

contour line—In art, a continuous *line* defining the outer shape of an object. (7)

corona civica—Latin, "civic crown." A Roman honorary wreath worn on the head. (7)

crenellation—Alternating solid merlons and open crenels in the notched tops of walls, as in *battlements.* (26-28A)

Crude Art—See *Art Brut.* (951)

Cubism—An early-20th-century art movement that rejected *naturalistic* depictions, preferring *compositions* of shapes and *forms abstracted* from the conventionally perceived world. See also *Analytic Cubism* and *Synthetic Cubism.* (892)

cutaway—An architectural drawing that combines an exterior view with an interior view of part of a building. (12, 896)

Dada—An early-20th-century art movement prompted by a revulsion against the horror of World War I. Dada embraced political anarchy, the irrational, and the intuitive. A disdain for convention, often enlivened by humor or whimsy, is characteristic of the art the Dadaists produced. (900)

daguerreotype—A photograph made by an early method on a plate of chemically treated metal; developed by Louis J. M. Daguerre. (834, 835)

De Stijl—Dutch, "the style." An early-20th-century art movement (and magazine), founded by Piet Mondrian and Theo van Doesburg, whose members promoted utopian ideals and developed a simplified geometric style. (928)

Deconstructivism—A late-20th-century architectural *style*. Deconstructivist architects attempt to disorient the observer by disrupting the conventional categories of architecture. The haphazard presentation of *volumes, masses, planes,* lighting, and so forth challenges the viewer's assumptions about *form* as it relates to function. (1026)

Der Blaue Reiter—German, "the blue rider." An early-20th-century *German Expressionist* art movement founded by Vassily Kandinsky and Franz Marc. The artists selected the whimsical name because of their mutual interest in the color blue and horses. (885)

dictator perpetuo—Dictator for life. (790)

Die Brücke—German, "the bridge." An early-20th-century *German Expressionist* art movement under the leadership of Ernst Ludwig Kirchner. The group thought of itself as the bridge between the old age and the new. (885)

divisionism—See *pointillism.* (854)

documentary evidence—In art history, the examination of written sources in order to determine the date of an artwork, the circumstances of its creation, or the identity of the artist(s) who made it. (2)

earthworks—See *Environmental Art.* (985)

elevation—In architecture, a head-on view of an external or internal wall, showing its features and often other elements that would be visible beyond or before the wall. (12)

empiricism—The search for knowledge based on observation and direct experience. (815)

en plein air—See *plein air.* (843, 845)

enamel—A decorative coating, usually colored, fused onto the surface of metal, glass, or ceramics. (28-25A)

encaustic—A painting *technique* in which pigment is mixed with melted wax and applied to the surface while the mixture is hot. (967)

Enlightenment—The 18th-century Western philosophy based on empirical evidence. The Enlightenment was a new way of thinking critically about the world and about humankind, independently of religion, myth, or tradition. (763)

entablature—The part of a building above the *columns* and below the roof. The entablature has three parts: architrave, frieze, and pediment. (31-17A)

Environmental Art—An American art form that emerged in the 1960s. Often using the land itself as their material, Environmental artists construct monuments of great scale and minimal form. Permanent or impermanent, these works transform some section of the environment, calling attention both to the land itself and to the hand of the artist. Sometimes referred to as earthworks. (985)

Event—See *Fluxus.* (987)

exedra—Recessed area, usually semicircular. (949)

exemplum virtutis—Latin, "example or model of virtue." (763)

existentialism—A philosophy asserting the absurdity of human existence and the improbability of achieving certitude. (951)

Expressionism—Twentieth-century art that is the result of the artist's unique inner or personal vision and that often has an emotional dimension. Expressionism contrasts with art focused on visually describing the empirical world. (885)

fan vault—See *vault.* (26-28A)

fasces—A bundle of rods with an ax attached, an emblem of authority in ancient Rome. (790)

Fauves—French, "wild beasts." See *Fauvism*. (883)

Fauvism—An early-20th-century art movement led by Henri Matisse. For the Fauves, *color* became the formal element most responsible for pictorial coherence and the primary conveyor of meaning. (883)

Favrile—A type of leaded stained glass patented by Louis Comfort Tiffany in the late 19th century. (28-38B)

femmages—The name that American artist Miriam Schapiro gave to her sewn *collages*, assembled from fabrics, quilts, buttons, sequins, lace trim, and rickrack collected at antique shows and fairs. (976)

femme fatale—French, "fatal woman." A destructive temptress of men. (863)

femme savante—French, "learned woman." The term used to describe the cultured hostesses of *Rococo* salons. (765)

ferroconcrete—Concrete strengthened by a skeleton of iron bars; also called reinforced concrete. (935)

fête galante—French, "amorous festival." A type of *Rococo* painting depicting the outdoor amusements of French upper-class society. (768)

fin-de-siècle—French, "end of the century." A period in Western cultural history from the end of the 19th century until just before World War I, when decadence and indulgence masked anxiety about an uncertain future. (866)

Fluxus—A group of American, European, and Japanese artists of the 1960s who created *Performance Art*. Their performances, or Events, often focused on single actions, such as turning a light on and off or watching falling snow, and were more theatrical than *Happenings*. (987)

flying buttress—A buttress is an exterior masonry structure that opposes the lateral thrust of an arch or a vault. A flying buttress consists typically of an inclined member carried on an arch or a series of arches and a solid buttress to which it transmits lateral thrust. (12, 949)

foreshortening (adj. **foreshortened**)—The use of *perspective* to represent in art the apparent visual contraction of an object that extends back in space at an angle to the perpendicular plane of sight. (9)

form—In art, an object's shape and structure, either in two dimensions (for example, a figure painted on a surface) or in three dimensions (such as a *statue*). (7)

formal analysis—The visual analysis of artistic *form*. (7)

formalism—Strict adherence to, or dependence on, stylized shapes and methods of *composition*. An emphasis on an artwork's visual elements rather than its subject. (953)

freestanding sculpture—See *sculpture in the round*. (11)

Futurism—An early-20th-century Italian art movement that championed war as a cleansing agent and that celebrated the speed and dynamism of modern technology. (898)

genre—A *style* or category of art; also, a kind of painting that realistically depicts scenes from everyday life. (5)

German Expressionism—An early-20th-century regional *Expressionist* movement. (885)

gesso—Plaster mixed with a binding material, used as the base coat for paintings on wood panels. (872)

gestural abstraction—Also known as *action painting*. A kind of *abstract* painting in which the gesture, or act of painting, is seen as the subject of art. Its most renowned proponent was Jackson Pollock. See also *Abstract Expressionism*. (954)

gleaning—The collection by peasants of wheat scraps left in the field after a harvest. (818)

Gobelin tapestry—A *tapestry* produced on a vertical loom using a weaving *technique* in which no horizontal threads extend the full width of the fabric. (29-67B)

Gothic Revival—See *Neo-Gothic*. (26-28A)

gouache—A painting *medium* consisting of watercolor mixed with gum. (889)

Grand Manner portraiture—A type of 18th-century portrait painting designed to communicate a person's grace and class through certain standardized conventions, such as the large scale of the figure relative to the canvas, the controlled pose, the *landscape* setting, and the low horizon line. (779)

green architecture—Ecologically friendly architectural design using clean energy to sustain the natural environment. (1029)

Happenings—A term coined by American artist Allan Kaprow in the 1960s to describe loosely structured performances, whose creators were trying to suggest the aesthetic and dynamic qualities of everyday life; as actions, rather than objects, Happenings incorporate the fourth dimension (time). (987)

hard-edge painting—A variant of *Post-Painterly Abstraction* that rigidly excluded all reference to gesture and incorporated smooth knife-edge geometric forms to express the notion that painting should be reduced to its visual components. (958)

hay wain—A hay-filled wagon. (811)

hierarchy of scale—An artistic convention in which greater size indicates greater importance. (11)

high relief—See *relief*. (12)

High-Tech—A contemporary architectural *style* calling for buildings that incorporate the latest innovations in engineering and technology and expose the structures' component parts. (1028)

hookah—A Moroccan water pipe. (808)

hôtel—French, "town house." (764)

hue—The name of a *color*. See also *primary colors, secondary colors,* and *complementary colors*. (7, 855)

iconography—Greek, the "writing of images." The term refers both to the content, or subject, of an artwork and to the study of content in art. It also includes the study of the symbolic, often religious, meaning of objects, persons, or events depicted in works of art. (5)

ikegobo—A Benin royal shrine. (10)

illusionism (adj. **illusionistic**)—The representation of the three-dimensional world on a two-dimensional surface in a manner that creates the illusion that the person, object, or place represented is three-dimensional. See also *perspective*. (8)

impasto—A layer of thickly applied pigment. (952)

Impressionism—A late-19th-century art movement that sought to capture a fleeting moment, thereby conveying the elusiveness and impermanence of images and conditions. (841, 842)

incubus—A demon believed in medieval times to prey, often sexually, on sleeping women. (802)

installation—An artwork that creates an artistic environment in a room or gallery. (1009, 30-27B)

intensity—See *color*. (7)

internal evidence—In art history, the examination of what an artwork represents (people, clothing, hairstyles, and so on) in order to determine its date. Also, the examination of the *style* of an artwork to identify the artist who created it. (3)

International style—A *style* of 20th-century architecture associated with Le Corbusier, whose elegance of design came to influence the look of modern office buildings and skyscrapers. (934)

Japonisme—The French fascination with all things Japanese. Japonisme emerged in the second half of the 19th century. (850)

jouer—French, "to play." (893)

jouir—French, "to enjoy." (893)

journaux—French, "newspapers." (893)

Jugendstil—See *Art Nouveau*. (873)

kente—Brightly colored patterned cloth woven by Asante men on horizontal looms in long, narrow strips sewn together to form toga-like robes. (1016)

Kommerzbank—German, "commerce bank." (904)

kouros (pl. **kouroi**)—Greek, "young man." An Archaic Greek *statue* of a young man. (892)

lancet—In Gothic architecture, a tall narrow window ending in a *pointed arch*. (939, 27-43A)

landscape—A picture showing natural scenery, without narrative content. (5)

lateral section—See *section*. (12)

line—The extension of a point along a path, made concrete in art by drawing on or chiseling into a *plane*. (7)

literati—In China, talented amateur painters and scholars from the landed gentry. (31-25A)

lithograph—See *lithography*. (818)

lithography—A printmaking *technique* in which the artist uses an oil-based crayon to draw directly on a stone plate and then wipes water onto the stone. When ink is rolled onto the plate, it adheres only to the drawing. The *print* produced by this method is a lithograph. (818, 819)

local color—An object's true *color* in white light. (843)

longitudinal section—See *section*. (12)

low relief—See *relief*. (12)

mass—The bulk, density, and weight of matter in *space*. (8)

medium (pl. **media**)—The material (for example, marble, bronze, clay, fresco) in which an artist works; also, in painting, the vehicle (usually liquid) that carries the pigment. (7)

memento mori—Latin, "reminder of death." In painting, a reminder of human mortality, usually represented by a skull. (26-7B, 30-27B)

metamatics—The name that Swiss artist Jean Tinguely gave to the motor-driven devices he constructed to produce instant *abstract* paintings. (988)

miniatures—Small individual Indian paintings intended to be held in the hand and viewed by one or two individuals at one time. (28-25A)

Minimalism—A predominantly sculptural American trend of the 1960s characterized by works featuring a severe reduction of *form*, often to single, homogeneous units. (962)

mobile—A kind of sculpture, invented by Alexander Calder, combining nonobjective organic forms and motion in balanced structures hanging from rods, wires, and colored, organically shaped plates. (944, 1016)

modernism—A movement in Western art that developed in the second half of the 19th century and sought to capture the images and sensibilities of the age. Modernist art goes beyond simply dealing with the present and involves the artist's critical examination of the premises of art itself. (841, 842)

Modernismo—See *Art Nouveau*. (873)

module (adj. **modular**)—A basic unit of which the dimensions of the major parts of a work are multiples. The principle is used in sculpture and other art forms, but it is most often employed in architecture, where the module may be the dimensions of an important part of a building, such as the diameter of a *column*. (10)

mold—A hollow form for *casting*. (11)

mosaic—Patterns or pictures made by embedding small pieces (tesserae) of stone or glass in cement on surfaces such as walls and floors; also, the *technique* of making such works. (28-25A)

mullion—A vertical member that divides a window or that separates one window from another. (983)

Nabis—Hebrew, "prophet." A group of *Symbolist* painters influenced by Paul Gauguin. (863)

Naturalistic Surrealism—See *Surrealism*. (921)

nave—The central area of an ancient Roman basilica or of a church, demarcated from *aisles* by *piers* or *columns*. (980)

Neo-Baroque—The revival of Baroque *style* in later, especially 19th-century, architecture. (830)

Neoclassicism—A *style* of art and architecture that emerged in the late 18th century as part of a general revival of interest in classical cultures. Neoclassical artists adopted themes and *styles* from ancient Greece and Rome. (763)

Neo-Expressionism—An art movement that emerged in the 1970s and that reflects artists' interest in the expressive capability of art, seen earlier in *German Expressionism* and *Abstract Expressionism*. (957, 30-9C)

Neo-Gothic—The revival of the Gothic *style* in architecture, especially in the 19th century. (829, 26-28A)

Neoplasticism—The Dutch artist Piet Mondrian's theory of "pure plastic art," an ideal balance between the universal and the individual using an *abstract* formal vocabulary. (928)

Neue Sachlichkeit—German, "new objectivity." An art movement that grew directly out of the World War I experiences of a group of German artists who sought to show the horrors of the war and its effects. (918)

nirvana—In Buddhism and Hinduism, a blissful state brought about by absorption of the individual soul or consciousness into the supreme spirit. Also called moksha. (28-35A)

odalisque—A woman in a Turkish harem. (801)

ogive (adj. **ogival**)—The diagonal rib of a Gothic *vault*; a pointed, or Gothic, *arch*. (980)

Op Art—An artistic movement of the 1960s in which painters sought to produce optical illusions of motion and depth using only geometric forms on two-dimensional surfaces. (961)

optical mixture—The visual effect of juxtaposed *complementary colors*. (855)

orbiculum—A disklike opening. (983)

Orientalism—The fascination on the part of Westerners with Oriental cultures, especially characteristic of the *Romanticism* movement in 19th-century European painting. (798)

Orphism—A form of *Cubism* developed by the French painter Robert Delaunay in which color plays an important role. (897)

orrery—A mechanical model of the solar system demonstrating how the planets revolve around the sun. (772)

palazzo (pl. **palazzi**)—Italian, "palace." (832)

palette knife—A flat tool used to scrape paint off the palette, a thin board with a thumb hole at one end on which an artist lays and mixes colors; any surface so used. Artists sometimes also use the palette knife in place of a brush to apply paint directly to the canvas. (817)

papier collé—French, "stuck paper." See *collage*. (894)

pastel—A powdery paste of pigment and gum used for making crayons; also, the pastel crayons themselves.

patrician—A Roman freeborn landowner. (790)

Performance Art—An American *avant-garde* art trend of the 1960s that made time an integral element of art. It produced works in which movements, gestures, and sounds of persons communicating with an audience replace physical objects. Documentary photographs are generally the only evidence remaining after these events. See also *Happenings*. (986)

period style—See *style*. (3)

Perpendicular—An English Late Gothic *style* of architecture distinguished by the pronounced verticality of its decorative details. (26-28A)

personal style—See *style*. (4)

personification—An *abstract* idea represented in bodily form. (5)

perspective—A method of presenting an illusion of the three-dimensional world on a two-dimensional surface. In linear perspective, the most common type, all parallel lines or surface edges converge on one, two, or three vanishing points located with reference to the eye level of the viewer (the horizon line of the picture), and associated objects are rendered smaller the farther from the viewer they are intended to seem. Atmospheric, or aerial, perspective creates the illusion of distance by the greater diminution of *color* intensity, the shift in color toward an almost neutral blue, and the blurring of contours as the intended distance between eye and object increases. (8)

philosophe—French, "thinker, philosopher." The term applied to French intellectuals of the *Enlightenment*. (771)

photomontage—A *composition* made by pasting together pictures or parts of pictures, especially photographs. See also *collage*. (903)

Photorealism—See *Superrealism*. (971)

physical evidence—In art history, the examination of the materials used to produce an artwork in order to determine its date. (2)

Picturesque garden—An "unordered" garden designed in accord with the *Enlightenment* taste for the natural. (787)

pier—A vertical, freestanding masonry support. (12)

Pietà—A painted or sculpted representation of the Virgin Mary mourning over the body of the dead Christ. (889)

pinnacle—In Gothic churches, a sharply pointed ornament capping the *piers* or *flying buttresses*; also used on church facades. (27-43A)

Pittura Metafisica—Italian, "metaphysical painting." An early-20th-century Italian art movement led by Giorgio de Chirico, whose work conveys an eerie mood and visionary quality. (922)

pixels—Shortened form of "picture elements." The tiny boxes that make up digital images displayed on a computer monitor. (992)

plan—The horizontal arrangement of the parts of a building or of the buildings and streets of a city or town, or a drawing or diagram showing such an arrangement. In an axial plan, the parts of a building are organized longitudinally, or along a given axis; in a central plan, the parts of the structure are of equal or almost equal dimensions around the center. (12)

plane—A flat surface. (7)

plein air—An approach to painting very popular among the *Impressionists,* in which an artist sketches outdoors to achieve a quick impression of light, air, and *color.* (843, 845)

pointed arch—A narrow *arch* of pointed profile, in contrast to a semicircular arch. (3, 26-28A)

pointillism—A system of painting devised by the 19th-century French painter Georges Seurat. The artist separates *color* into its component parts and then applies the component colors to the canvas in tiny dots (points). The image becomes comprehensible only from a distance, when the viewer's eyes optically blend the pigment dots. Sometimes referred to as divisionism. (854, 855)

Pop Art—A term coined by British art critic Lawrence Alloway to refer to art, first appearing in the 1950s, that incorporated elements from consumer culture, the mass media, and popular culture, such as images from motion pictures and advertising. (965, 966)

positivism—A Western philosophical model that promoted science as the mind's highest achievement. (815)

Post-Impressionism—The term used to describe the stylistically heterogeneous work of the group of late-19th-century painters in France, including van Gogh, Gauguin, Seurat, and Cézanne, who more systematically examined the properties and expressive qualities of *line,* pattern, *form,* and *color* than the *Impressionists* did. (852)

postmodernism—A reaction against *modernist formalism,* which was seen as elitist. Far more encompassing and accepting than the more rigid confines of modernist practice, postmodernism offers something for everyone by accommodating a wide range of *styles,* subjects, and formats, from traditional easel painting to *installation* and from *abstraction* to *illusionistic* scenes. Postmodern art often includes irony or reveals a self-conscious awareness of the position of the artist in the history of art. (876, 949, 982)

Post-Painterly Abstraction—An American art movement that emerged in the 1960s and was characterized by a cool, detached rationality emphasizing tighter pictorial control. See also *color-field painting* and *hard-edge painting.* (958)

Poussiniste—A member of the French Royal Academy of Painting and Sculpture during the early 18th century who followed Nicolas Poussin in insisting that *form* was the most important element of painting. See also *Rubéniste.* (768)

Precisionism—An American art movement of the 1920s and 1930s. The Precisionists concentrated on portraying manmade environments in a clear and concise manner to express the beauty of perfect and precise machine forms. (912)

prefabricated architecture—Construction using structural elements manufactured in advance and transported to the building site ready for assembly. (833)

Pre-Raphaelite art—A 19th-century English art movement whose members wished to create art free from what they considered the artificial manner propagated in the academies by the successors of Raphael. (827)

primary colors—Red, yellow, and blue—the *colors* from which all other colors may be derived. (7, 855)

primitivism—The incorporation in early-20th-century Western art of stylistic elements from the artifacts of Africa, Oceania, and the native peoples of the Americas. (891)

proportion—The relationship in size of the parts of persons, buildings, or objects, often based on a *module.* (10)

provenance—Origin or source; findspot. (3)

Purism—An early-20th-century art movement that embraced the "machine aesthetic" and sought purity of *form* in the clean functional lines of industrial machinery. (898)

putto (pl. **putti**)—A cherubic young boy. (28-32A)

Rayograph—A photograph produced without a camera by placing objects on photographic paper and then exposing the paper to light; named for the American artist Man Ray. (910)

Realism (adj. **Realist**)—A movement that emerged in mid-19th-century France. Realist artists represented the subject matter of everyday life (especially subjects that previously had been considered inappropriate for depiction) in a relatively naturalistic mode. (815, 816)

regional style—See *style.* (3)

Regionalism—A 20th-century American art movement that portrayed American rural life in a clearly readable, *Realist* style. Major Regionalists include Grant Wood and Thomas Hart Benton. (938)

relief—In sculpture, figures projecting from a background of which they are part. The degree of relief is designated high, low (bas), or sunken. In the last, the artist cuts the design into the surface so that the highest projecting parts of the image are no higher than the surface itself. (12)

relief sculpture—See *relief.* (11)

rocaille—See *Rococo.* (764)

Rococo—A style, primarily of interior design, that appeared in France around 1700. Rococo interiors featured lavish decoration, including small sculptures, ornamental mirrors, easel paintings, *tapestries, reliefs,* wall paintings, and elegant furniture. The term Rococo derived from the French word *rocaille* (pebble) and referred to the small stones and shells used to decorate grotto interiors. (764)

Romanticism—A Western cultural phenomenon, beginning around 1750 and ending about 1850, that gave precedence to feeling and imagination over reason and thought. More narrowly, the art movement that flourished from about 1800 to 1840. (790, 793)

rostrum—A speaker's platform. (949)

Rubéniste—A member of the French Royal Academy of Painting and Sculpture during the early 18th century who followed Peter Paul Rubens in insisting that *color* was the most important element of painting. See also *Poussiniste.* (768)

Saint-Simonianism—An early-19th-century utopian movement that emphasized the education and enfranchisement of women. (820)

saltimbanque—An itinerant circus performer. (29-10A)

saturation—See *color.* (7, 855)

satyr—A Greek mythological follower of Dionysos having a man's upper body, a goat's hindquarters and horns, and a horse's ears and tail. (27-33A, 28-32A)

school—A chronological and stylistic classification of works of art with a stipulation of place. (6)

sculpture in the round—Freestanding figures, *carved* or modeled in three dimensions. (11)

secondary colors—Orange, green, and purple, obtained by mixing pairs of *primary colors* (red, yellow, blue). (7, 855)

section—In architecture, a diagram or representation of a part of a structure or building along an imaginary *plane* that passes through it vertically. Drawings showing a theoretical slice across a structure's width are lateral sections. Those cutting through a building's length are longitudinal sections. See also *elevation* and *cutaway.* (12)

silk-screen printing—An industrial printing *technique* that creates a sharp-edged image by pressing ink through a design on silk or a similar tightly woven porous fabric stretched tight on a frame. (967)

Simultanéisme—Robert Delaunay's version of *Cubism* in which he created spatial effects and kaleidoscopic movement solely through *color* contrasts; also known as *Orphism*. (897)

simultaneous contrasts—The phenomenon of juxtaposed *colors* affecting the eye's reception of each, as when a painter places dark green next to light green, making the former appear even darker and the latter even lighter. See also *successive contrasts*. (855)

site-specific art—Art created for a specific location. See also *Environmental Art*. (985)

space—In art history, both the actual area that an object occupies or a building encloses and the *illusionistic* representation of space in painting and sculpture. (8)

spectrum—The range or band of visible *colors* in natural light. (7)

sphinx—A mythical Egyptian beast with the body of a lion and the head of a human. (783)

stained glass—In Gothic architecture, the colored glass used for windows. (12, 858)

statue—A three-dimensional sculpture. (11)

Stile Floreale—See *Art Nouveau*. (873)

still life—A picture depicting an arrangement of inanimate objects. (5)

stoa—In ancient Greek architecture, an open building with a roof supported by a row of *columns* parallel to the back wall. A covered colonnade or portico. (829)

style—A distinctive artistic manner. Period style is the characteristic style of a specific time. Regional style is the style of a particular geographical area. Personal style is an individual artist's unique manner. (3)

stylistic evidence—In art history, the examination of the *style* of an artwork in order to determine its date or the identity of the artist. (3)

subtractive light—The painter's light in art; the light reflected from pigments and objects. See also *additive light*. (7)

subtractive sculpture—A kind of sculpture *technique* in which materials are taken away from the original mass; *carving*. (11)

successive contrasts—The phenomenon of colored afterimages. When a person looks intently at a *color* (green, for example) and then shifts to a white area, the fatigued eye momentarily perceives the *complementary color* (red). See also *simultaneous contrasts*. (855)

Superrealism—A painting and sculpture movement of the 1960s and 1970s that emphasized producing artworks based on scrupulous fidelity to optical fact. The Superrealist painters were also called Photorealists because many used photographs as sources for their imagery. (971)

Suprematism—A type of art formulated by Kazimir Malevich to convey his belief that the supreme reality in the world is pure feeling, which attaches to no object and thus calls for new, nonobjective *forms* in art—shapes not related to objects in the visible world. (904)

Surrealism—A successor to *Dada*, Surrealism incorporated the improvisational nature of its predecessor into its exploration of the ways to express in art the world of dreams and the unconscious. Biomorphic Surrealists, such as Joan Miró, produced largely *abstract compositions*. Naturalistic Surrealists, notably Salvador Dalí, presented recognizable scenes transformed into a dream or nightmare image. (921)

symbol—An image that stands for another image or encapsulates an idea. (5)

Symbolism—A late-19th-century movement based on the idea that the artist was not an imitator of nature but a creator who transformed the facts of nature into a *symbol* of the inner experience of that fact. (863)

Synthetic Cubism—A later phase of *Cubism*, in which paintings and drawings were constructed from objects and shapes cut from paper or other materials to represent parts of a subject, in order to engage the viewer with pictorial issues, such as figuration, realism, and abstraction. (893)

tapestry—A weaving *technique* in which the horizontal (weft) threads are packed densely over the vertical (warp) threads so that the designs are woven directly into the fabric. (764)

technique—The processes artists employ to create *form*, as well as the distinctive, personal ways in which they handle their materials and tools. (7)

terminus ante quem—Latin, "point [date] before which." (2)

terminus post quem—Latin, "point [date] after which." (2)

texture—The quality of a surface (rough, smooth, hard, soft, shiny, dull) as revealed by light. In represented texture, a painter depicts an object as having a certain texture even though the pigment is the real texture. (8)

tonality—See *color*. (7)

tracery—Ornamental stonework for holding *stained glass* in place, characteristic of Gothic cathedrals. In plate tracery, the glass fills only the "punched holes" in the heavy ornamental stonework. In bar tracery, the stained-glass windows fill almost the entire opening, and the stonework is unobtrusive. (26-28A)

tripod—An ancient Greek deep bowl on a tall three-legged stand. (783)

triptych—A three-paneled painting, ivory plaque, or altarpiece. Also, a small, portable shrine with hinged wings used for private devotion. (886)

trompe l'oeil—French, "fools the eye." A form of *illusionistic* painting that aims to deceive viewers into believing that they are seeing real objects rather than a representation of those objects. (26-6A)

ukiyo-e—Japanese, "pictures of the floating world." During the Edo period, *woodcut* prints depicting brothels, popular entertainment, and beautiful women. (28-17B)

Usonian—Frank Lloyd Wright's term for the inexpensive houses he designed for ordinary people. *Usonian* derives from "United States of North America." (946)

value—See *color*. (7, 855)

vanitas—Latin, "vanity." A term describing paintings (particularly 17th-century Dutch *still lifes*) that include references to death. (835, 972, 26-7B)

vault (adj. **vaulted**)—A masonry roof or ceiling constructed on the *arch* principle, or a concrete roof of the same shape. A barrel (or tunnel) vault, semicylindrical in cross-*section*, is in effect a deep arch or an uninterrupted series of arches, one behind the other, over an oblong space. A quadrant vault is a half-barrel vault. A groin (or cross) vault is formed at the point at which two barrel vaults intersect at right angles. In a ribbed vault, there is a framework of ribs or arches under the intersections of the vaulting sections. A sexpartite vault is one whose ribs divide the vault into six compartments. A fan vault is a vault characteristic of English Perpendicular Gothic architecture, in which radiating ribs form a fanlike pattern. (12)

veduta (pl. **vedute**)—Italian, "scenic view." (780, 781)

volume—The *space* that *mass* organizes, divides, or encloses. (8)

wainscoting—Paneling on the lower part of interior walls. (872)

weld—To join metal parts by heating, as in assembling the separate parts of a *statue* made by *casting*. (11)

wet-plate photography—An early photographic process in which the photographic plate is exposed, developed, and fixed while wet. (834)

woodblock—See *woodcut*. (849, 1009)

woodcut—A wood block on the surface of which those parts not intended to print are cut away to a slight depth, leaving the design raised; also, the printed impression made with such a block. (885)

zoopraxiscope—A device invented by Eadweard Muybridge in the 19th century to project sequences of still photographic images; a predecessor of the modern motion-picture projector. (838)

Bibliography

This list of books is very selective, but comprehensive enough to satisfy the reading interests of the beginning art history student and general reader. Significantly expanded from the previous edition, the 15th edition bibliography can also serve as the basis for undergraduate research papers. The resources listed range from works that are valuable primarily for their reproductions to those that are scholarly surveys of schools and periods or monographs on individual artists. The emphasis is on recent in-print books and on books likely to be found in college and municipal libraries. No entries for periodical articles appear, but the bibliography begins with a list of some of the major journals that publish art historical scholarship in English.

Selected Periodicals

African Arts
American Art
American Indian Art
American Journal of Archaeology
Antiquity
Archaeology
Archives of American Art
Archives of Asian Art
Ars Orientalis
Art Bulletin
Art History
Art in America
Art Journal
Artforum International
Artnews
Burlington Magazine
Gesta
History of Photography
Journal of Egyptian Archaeology
Journal of Roman Archaeology
Journal of the Society of Architectural Historians
Journal of the Warburg and Courtauld Institutes
Latin American Antiquity
October
Oxford Art Journal
Women's Art Journal

General Studies

Baxandall, Michael. *Patterns of Intention: On the Historical Explanation of Pictures.* New Haven, Conn.: Yale University Press, 1985.

Bindman, David, ed. *The Thames & Hudson Encyclopedia of British Art.* London: Thames & Hudson, 1988.

Boström, Antonia. *The Encyclopedia of Sculpture.* 3 vols. London: Routledge, 2003.

Broude, Norma, and Mary D. Garrard, eds. *The Expanding Discourse: Feminism and Art History.* New York: Harper Collins, 1992.

Bryson, Norman. *Vision and Painting: The Logic of the Gaze.* New Haven, Conn.: Yale University Press, 1983.

Bryson, Norman, Michael Ann Holly, and Keith Moxey. *Visual Theory: Painting and Interpretation.* New York: Cambridge University Press, 1991.

Burden, Ernest. *Illustrated Dictionary of Architecture.* 2d ed. New York: McGraw-Hill, 2002.

Büttner, Nils. *Landscape Painting: A History.* New York: Abbeville, 2006.

Carrier, David. *A World Art History and Its Objects.* University Park: Pennsylvania State University Press, 2012.

Chadwick, Whitney. *Women, Art, and Society.* 5th ed. New York: Thames & Hudson, 2012.

Cheetham, Mark A., Michael Ann Holly, and Keith Moxey, eds. *The Subjects of Art History: Historical Objects in Contemporary Perspective.* New York: Cambridge University Press, 1998.

Chilvers, Ian, and Harold Osborne, eds. *The Oxford Dictionary of Art.* 3d ed. New York: Oxford University Press, 2004.

Ching, Francis D. K., Mark Jarzombek, and Vikramaditya Prakash. *A Global History of Architecture.* 2d ed. Hoboken, NJ: Wiely, 2010.

Corbin, George A. *Native Arts of North America, Africa, and the South Pacific: An Introduction.* New York: Harper Collins, 1988.

Crouch, Dora P., and June G. Johnson. *Traditions in Architecture: Africa, America, Asia, and Oceania.* New York: Oxford University Press, 2000.

Curl, James Stevens. *Oxford Dictionary of Architecture and Landscape Architecture.* 2d ed. New York: Oxford University Press, 2006.

Davis, Whitney. *A General Theory of Visual Culture.* Princeton, N.J.: Princeton University Press, 2011.

Duby, Georges, ed. *Sculpture: From Antiquity to the Present.* 2 vols. Cologne: Taschen, 1999.

Encyclopedia of World Art. 17 vols. New York: McGraw-Hill, 1959–1987.

Evers, Bernd, and Christof Thoenes. *Architectural Theory from the Renaissance to the Present.* Cologne: Taschen, 2011.

Fielding, Mantle. *Dictionary of American Painters, Sculptors, and Engravers.* 2d ed. Poughkeepsie, N.Y.: Apollo, 1986.

Fine, Sylvia Honig. *Women and Art: A History of Women Painters and Sculptors from the Renaissance to the 20th Century.* Rev. ed. Montclair, N.J.: Alanheld & Schram, 1978.

Fleming, John, Hugh Honour, and Nikolaus Pevsner. *The Penguin Dictionary of Architecture and Landscape Architecture.* 5th ed. New York: Penguin, 2000.

Frazier, Nancy. *The Penguin Concise Dictionary of Art History.* New York: Penguin, 2000.

Freedberg, David. *The Power of Images: Studies in the History and Theory of Response.* Chicago: University of Chicago Press, 1989.

Gaze, Delia, ed. *Dictionary of Women Artists.* 2 vols. London: Routledge, 1997.

Hall, James. *Dictionary of Subjects and Symbols in Art.* 2d ed. Boulder, Colo.: Westview, 2008.

Harris, Anne Sutherland, and Linda Nochlin. *Women Artists: 1550–1950.* Los Angeles: Los Angeles County Museum of Art; New York: Knopf, 1977.

Hauser, Arnold. *The Sociology of Art.* Chicago: University of Chicago Press, 1982.

Hults, Linda C. *The Print in the Western World: An Introductory History.* Madison: University of Wisconsin Press, 1996.

Ingersoll, Richard, and Spiro Kostof. *World Architecture: A Cross-Cultural History.* New York: Oxford University Press, 2012.

Kemp, Martin. *The Science of Art: Optical Themes in Western Art from Brunelleschi to Seurat.* New Haven, Conn.: Yale University Press, 1990.

Kirkham, Pat, and Susan Weber, eds. *History of Design: Decorative Arts and Material Culture, 1400–2000.* New Haven, Conn.: Yale University Press, 2013.

Kostof, Spiro, and Gregory Castillo. *A History of Architecture: Settings and Rituals.* 2d ed. Oxford: Oxford University Press, 1995.

Kultermann, Udo. *The History of Art History.* New York: Abaris, 1993.

Le Fur, Yves, ed. *Musée du Quai Branly: The Collection. Art from Africa, Asia, Oceania, and the Americas.* Paris: Flammarion, 2009.

Lucie-Smith, Edward. *The Thames & Hudson Dictionary of Art Terms.* 2d ed. New York: Thames & Hudson, 2004.

Moffett, Marian, Michael Fazio, and Lawrence Wadehouse. 3d ed. *A World History of Architecture.* London: Laurence King, 2013.

Morgan, Anne Lee. *Oxford Dictionary of American Art and Artists.* New York: Oxford University Press, 2008.

Murray, Peter, and Linda Murray. *The Penguin Dictionary of Art and Artists.* 7th ed. New York: Penguin, 1998.

Nelson, Robert S., and Richard Shiff, eds. *Critical Terms for Art History.* Chicago: University of Chicago Press, 1996.

Pazanelli, Roberta, ed. *The Color of Life: Polychromy in Sculpture from Antiquity to the Present.* Los Angeles: J. Paul Getty Museum, 2008.

Penny, Nicholas. *The Materials of Sculpture.* New Haven, Conn.: Yale University Press, 1993.

Pevsner, Nikolaus. *A History of Building Types.* London: Thames & Hudson, 1987. Reprint of 1979 ed.

———. *An Outline of European Architecture.* 8th ed. Baltimore: Penguin, 1974.

Pierce, James Smith. *From Abacus to Zeus: A Handbook of Art History.* 7th ed. Upper Saddle River, N.J.: Pearson Prentice Hall, 1998.

Placzek, Adolf K., ed. *Macmillan Encyclopedia of Architects.* 4 vols. New York: Macmillan, 1982.

Podro, Michael. *The Critical Historians of Art.* New Haven, Conn.: Yale University Press, 1982.

Pollock, Griselda. *Vision and Difference: Femininity, Feminism, and Histories of Art.* London: Routledge, 1988.

Pregill, Philip, and Nancy Volkman. *Landscapes in History Design and Planning in the Eastern and Western Traditions.* 2d ed. Hoboken, N.J.: Wiley, 1999.

Preziosi, Donald, ed. *The Art of Art History: A Critical Anthology.* New York: Oxford University Press, 1998.

Read, Herbert. *The Thames & Hudson Dictionary of Art and Artists.* Rev. ed. New York: Thames & Hudson, 1994.

Reid, Jane D. *The Oxford Guide to Classical Mythology in the Arts 1300–1990s.* 2 vols. New York: Oxford University Press, 1993.

Rogers, Elizabeth Barlow. *Landscape Design: A Cultural and Architectural History.* New York: Abrams, 2001.

Roth, Leland M. *Understanding Architecture: Its Elements, History, and Meaning.* 2d ed. Boulder, Colo.: Westview, 2006.

Schama, Simon. *The Power of Art.* New York: Ecco, 2006.

Slatkin, Wendy. *Women Artists in History: From Antiquity to the 20th Century.* 4th ed. Upper Saddle River, N.J.: Prentice Hall, 2000.

Squire, Michael. *The Art of the Body: Antiquity and Its Legacy.* New York: Oxford University Press, 2011.

Steer, John, and Antony White. *Atlas of Western Art History: Artists, Sites, and Monuments from Ancient Greece to the Modern Age.* New York: Facts on File, 1994.

Stratton, Arthur. *The Orders of Architecture: Greek, Roman, and Renaissance.* London: Studio, 1986.

Summers, David. *Real Spaces: World Art History and the Rise of Western Modernism.* London: Phaidon, 2003.

Sutcliffe, Antony. *Paris: An Architectural History.* New Haven, Conn.: Yale University Press, 1996.

Sutton, Ian. *Western Architecture: From Ancient Greece to the Present.* New York: Thames & Hudson, 1999.

Trachtenberg, Marvin, and Isabelle Hyman. *Architecture, from Prehistory to Post-Modernism.* 2d ed. Upper Saddle River, N.J.: Prentice Hall, 2003.

Turner, Jane, ed. *The Dictionary of Art.* 34 vols. New ed. New York: Oxford University Press, 2003.

Watkin, David. *A History of Western Architecture.* 5th ed. London: Laurence King, 2011.

Wescoat, Bonna D., and Robert G. Ousterhout, eds. *Architecture of the Sacred: Space, Ritual, and Experience from Classical Greece to Byzantium.* New York: Cambridge University Press, 2012.

West, Shearer. *Portraiture.* New York: Oxford University Press, 2004.

Wittkower, Rudolf. *Sculpture Processes and Principles.* New York: Harper & Row, 1977.

Wren, Linnea H., and Janine M. Carter, eds. *Perspectives on Western Art: Source Documents and Readings from the Ancient Near East through the Middle Ages.* New York: Harper & Row, 1987.

Zijlmans, Kitty, and Wilfried van Damme, eds. *World Art Studies: Exploring Concepts and Approaches.* Amsterdam: Valiz, 2008.

Baroque Art, General

Blunt, Anthony, ed. *Baroque and Rococo: Architecture and Decoration.* Cambridge: Harper & Row, 1982.

Harris, Ann Sutherland. *Seventeenth-Century Art & Architecture.* 2d ed. Upper Saddle River, N.J.: Prentice Hall, 2008.

Harrison, Charles, Paul Wood, and Jason Gaiger, eds. *Art in Theory, 1648–1815: An Anthology of Changing Ideas.* Oxford: Blackwell, 2000.

Held, Julius, and Donald Posner. *17th- and 18th-Century Art: Baroque Painting, Sculpture, Architecture.* New York: Abrams, 1971.

Lagerlöf, Margaretha R. *Ideal Landscape: Annibale Carracci, Nicolas Poussin, and Claude Lorrain.* New Haven, Conn.: Yale University Press, 1990.

Lawrence, Cynthia, ed. *Women and Art in Early Modern Europe: Patrons, Collectors, and Connoisseurs.* University Park: Pennsylvania State University Press, 1997.

Lemerle, Frédérique, and Yves Pauwels. *Baroque Architecture, 1600–1750.* Paris: Flammarion, 2008.

Minor, Vernon Hyde. *Baroque & Rococo: Art & Culture.* New York, Abrams, 1999.

Norberg-Schulz, Christian. *Baroque Architecture.* New York: Rizzoli, 1986.

———. *Late Baroque and Rococo Architecture.* New York: Electa/Rizzoli, 1985.

Tarabra, Daniela, and Claudia Zanlungo. *The Story of Baroque Architecture.* New York: Prestel, 2012.

Toman, Rolf. *Baroque: Architecture, Sculpture, Painting.* Cologne: Könemann, 1998.

CHAPTER 26
Rococo to Neoclassicism: The 18th Century in Europe and America

Beddington, Charles. *Venice: Canaletto and His Rivals.* London: National Gallery, 2010.

Bermingham, Ann. *Landscape and Ideology: The English Rustic Tradition, 1740–1850.* Berkeley: University of California Press, 1986.

Boime, Albert. *Art in the Age of Revolution, 1750–1800.* Chicago: University of Chicago Press, 1987.

Bowron, Edgar Peters, and Joseph J. Rishel, eds. *Art in Rome in the Eighteenth Century.* Philadelphia: Philadelphia Museum of Art, 2000.

Bowron, Edgar Peters, and Peter Björn Kerber. *Pompeo Batoni: Prince of Painters in Eighteenth-Century Rome.* New Haven, Conn.: Yale University Press, 2007.

Braham, Allan. *The Architecture of the French Enlightenment.* Berkeley: University of California Press, 1980.

Conisbee, Philip. *Painting in Eighteenth-Century France.* Ithaca, N.Y.: Phaidon/Cornell University Press, 1981.

Craske, Matthew. *Art in Europe, 1700–1830: A History of the Visual Arts in an Era of Unprecedented Urban Economic Growth.* New York: Oxford University Press, 1997.

Crow, Thomas E. *Painters and Public Life in Eighteenth-Century Paris.* New Haven, Conn.: Yale University Press, 1985.

Goodman, Elise, ed. *Art and Culture in the Eighteenth Century: New Dimensions and Multiple Perspectives.* Newark: University of Delaware Press, 2001.

Harrison, Charles, Paul Wood, and Jason Gaiger, eds. *Art in Theory, 1648–1815: An Anthology of Changing Ideas.* Oxford: Blackwell, 2000.

Hedley, Jo. *François Boucher: Seductive Visions.* London: Wallace Collection, 2004.

Herrmann, Luke. *British Landscape Painting of the Eighteenth Century.* New York: Oxford University Press, 1974.

Honour, Hugh. *Neo-Classicism.* Harmondsworth: Penguin, 1968.

Irwin, David. *Neoclassicism.* London: Phaidon, 1997.

Jarrassé, Dominique. *18th-Century French Painting.* Paris: Terrail, 1999.

Lee, Simon. *David.* London: Phaidon, 1999.

Levey, Michael. *Rococo to Revolution: Major Trends in Eighteenth-Century Painting.* London: Thames & Hudson, 1966.

Plax, Julie-Ann. *Watteau and the Cultural Politics of Eighteenth-Century France.* New York: Cambridge University Press, 2000.

Rosenblum, Robert. *Transformations in Late Eighteenth-Century Art.* Princeton, N.J.: Princeton University Press, 1970.

Roworth, Wendy Wassyng. *Angelica Kauffman: A Continental Artist in Georgian England.* London: Reaktion, 1992.

Rykwert, Joseph. *The First Moderns: Architects of the Eighteenth Century.* Cambridge, Mass.: MIT Press, 1983.

Sheriff, Mary D. *The Exceptional Woman: Elisabeth Vigée-Lebrun and the Cultural Politics of Art.* Chicago: University of Chicago Press, 1996.

Solkin, David. *Painting for Money: The Visual Arts and the Public Sphere in Eighteenth-Century England.* New Haven, Conn.: Paul Mellon Centre for British Art, 1993.

Stillman, Damie. *English Neo-Classical Architecture.* 2 vols. London: Zwemmer, 1988.

Waterhouse, Ellis Kirkham. *Painting in Britain: 1530–1790.* 4th ed. New Haven, Conn.: Yale University Press, 1979.

Wendorf, Richard. *Sir Joshua Reynolds: The Painter in Society.* Cambridge, Mass.: Harvard University Press, 1996.

Wilton, Andrew. *The Swagger Portrait: Grand Manner Portraiture in Britain from Van Dyck to Augustus John, 1630–1930.* London: Tate Gallery, 1992.

19th and 20th Centuries, General

Arnason, H. H., and Peter Kalb. *History of Modern Art: Painting, Sculpture, Architecture, Photography.* 6th ed. Upper Saddle River, N.J.: Prentice Hall, 2009.

Ashton, Dore. *Twentieth-Century Artists on Art.* New York: Pantheon Books, 1985.

Barnitz, Jacueline. *Twentieth-Century Art of Latin America.* Austin: University of Texas Press, 2001.

Brettell, Richard R. *Modern Art, 1851–1929: Capitalism and Representation.* New York: Oxford University Press, 1999.

Brown, Milton, Sam Hunter, and John Jacobus. *American Art: Painting, Sculpture, Architecture, Decorative Arts, Photography.* New York: Abrams, 1979.

Burnham, Jack. *Beyond Modern Sculpture: The Effects of Science and Technology on the Sculpture of This Century.* New York: Braziller, 1968.

Butler, Cornelia, and Alexandra Schwartz, eds. *Modern Women: Women Artists at the Museum of Modern Art.* New York: Museum of Modern Art, 2010.

Chipp, Herschel B. *Theories of Modern Art.* Berkeley: University of California Press, 1968.

Chu, Petra ten-Doesschate. *Nineteenth-Century European Art.* 3d ed. Upper Saddle River, N.J.: Prentice Hall, 2011.

Coke, Van Deren. *The Painter and the Photograph from Delacroix to Warhol.* Rev. ed. Albuquerque: University of New Mexico Press, 1972.

Colquhoun, Alan. *Modern Architecture.* New York: Oxford University Press, 2002.

Craven, Wayne. *American Art: History and Culture.* Rev. ed. New York: McGraw-Hill, 2002.

Dennis, Rafael Cardoso, and Colin Trodd, eds. *Art and the Academy in the Nineteenth Century.* New Brunswick, N.J.: Rutgers University Press, 2000.

Doordan, Dennis P. *Twentieth-Century Architecture.* New York: Abrams, 2002.

Doss, Erika. *Twentieth-Century American Art.* New York: Oxford University Press, 2002.

Driskell, David C. *Two Centuries of Black American Art.* Los Angeles: Los Angeles County Museum of Art; New York: Knopf, 1976.

Eisenmann, Stephen F., ed. *Nineteenth-Century Art: A Critical History.* 4th ed. New York: Thames & Hudson, 2011.

Elsen, Albert. *Origins of Modern Sculpture.* New York: Braziller, 1974.

Facos, Michelle. *An Introduction to Nineteenth-Century Art.* New York: Routledge, 2011.

Foster, Hal, Rosalind Krauss, Yve-Alain Bois, and Benjamin H. D. Buchloh. *Art since 1900: Modernism, Antimodernism, Postmodernism.* 2d ed. New York: Thames & Hudson, 2011.

Frampton, Kenneth. *Modern Architecture: A Critical History.* 4th ed. New York: Thames & Hudson, 2007.

Frascina, Francis, and Charles Harrison, eds. *Modern Art and Modernism: A Critical Anthology.* New York: Harper & Row, 1982.

Giedion, Siegfried. *Space, Time, and Architecture: The Growth of a New Tradition.* 4th ed. Cambridge, Mass.: Harvard University Press, 1965.

Goldwater, Robert, and Marco Treves, eds. *Artists on Art.* 3d ed. New York: Pantheon, 1958.

Greenough, Sarah, Joel Snyder, David Travis, and Colin Westerbeck. *On the Art of Fixing a Shadow: One Hundred and Fifty Years of Photography.* Washington, D.C.: National Gallery of Art; Chicago: Art Institute of Chicago, 1989.

Hamilton, George H. *Painting and Sculpture in Europe, 1880–1940.* 6th ed. New Haven, Conn.: Yale University Press, 1993.

Harrison, Charles, and Paul Wood. *Art in Theory, 1900–2000: An Anthology of Changing Ideas.* Oxford: Blackwell, 2003.

Herbert, Robert L., ed. *Modern Artists on Art.* Upper Saddle River, N.J.: Prentice Hall, 1971.

Hertz, Richard, and Norman M. Klein, eds. *Twentieth-Century Art Theory: Urbanism, Politics, and Mass Culture.* Englewood Cliffs, N.J.: Prentice Hall, 1990.

Heyer, Paul. *Architects on Architecture: New Directions in America.* New York: Van Nostrand Reinhold, 1993.

Hills, Patricia. *Modern Art in the USA: Issues and Controversies of the 20th Century.* Upper Saddle River, N.J.: Prentice Hall, 2000.

Hitchcock, Henry-Russell. *Architecture: Nineteenth and Twentieth Centuries.* 4th ed. New Haven, Conn.: Yale University Press, 1977.

Hunter, Sam, John Jacobus, and Daniel Wheeler. *Modern Art: Painting, Sculpture, Architecture, Photography.* Rev. 3d ed. Upper Saddle River, N.J.: Prentice Hall, 2004.

Janson, Horst W. *19th-Century Sculpture.* New York: Abrams, 1985.

Jencks, Charles. *Modern Movements in Architecture.* Garden City, N.Y.: Anchor; Doubleday, 1973.

Kaufmann, Edgar, Jr., ed. *The Rise of an American Architecture.* New York: Metropolitan Museum of Art; Praeger, 1970.

Krauss, Rosalind E. *The Originality of the Avant-Garde and Other Modernist*

Myths. Cambridge, Mass.: MIT Press, 1985.

———. *Passages in Modern Sculpture.* Cambridge, Mass.: MIT Press, 1981.

Lewis, Samella S. *African American Art and Artists.* Rev. ed. Berkeley: University of California Press, 1994.

Licht, Fred. *Sculpture, Nineteenth and Twentieth Centuries.* Greenwich, Conn.: New York Graphic Society, 1967.

Marien, Mary Warner. *Photography: A Cultural History.* 3d ed. Upper Saddle River, N.J.: Prentice Hall, 2011.

Mason, Jerry, ed. *International Center of Photography Encyclopedia of Photography.* New York: Crown, 1984.

McCoubrey, John W. *American Art, 1700–1960: Sources and Documents.* Englewood Cliffs, N.J.: Prentice Hall, 1965.

Newhall, Beaumont. *The History of Photography.* New York: Museum of Modern Art, 1982.

Osborne, Harold. *The Oxford Companion to Twentieth-Century Art.* New York: Oxford University Press, 1981.

Pohl, Frances K. *Framing America: A Social History of American Art.* 3d ed. New York: Thames & Hudson, 2012.

Rose, Barbara. *American Art since 1900.* Rev. ed. New York: Praeger, 1975.

Rosenblum, Naomi. *A World History of Photography.* 4th ed. New York: Abbeville, 2007.

Rosenblum, Robert. *Modern Painting and the Northern Romantic Tradition: Friedrich to Rothko.* New York: Harper & Row, 1975.

Rosenblum, Robert, and Horst W. Janson. *19th-Century Art.* Rev. ed. Upper Saddle River, N.J.: Prentice Hall, 2005.

Ross, Stephen David, ed. *Art and Its Significance: An Anthology of Aesthetic Theory.* Albany: State University of New York Press, 1987.

Russell, John. *The Meanings of Modern Art.* New York: Museum of Modern Art; Thames & Hudson, 1981.

Scully, Vincent. *Modern Architecture.* Rev. ed. New York: Braziller, 1974.

Spalding, Francis. *British Art since 1900.* London: Thames & Hudson, 1986.

Spencer, Harold. *American Art: Readings from the Colonial Era to the Present.* New York: Scribner, 1980.

Steinberg, Leo. *Other Criteria: Confrontations with 20th-Century Art.* New York: Oxford University Press, 1972.

Szarkowski, John. *Photography until Now.* New York: Museum of Modern Art, 1989.

Upton, Dell. *Architecture in the United States.* Oxford: Oxford University Press, 1998.

Weaver, Mike. *The Art of Photography: 1839–1989.* New Haven, Conn.: Yale University Press, 1989.

Whiffen, Marcus, and Frederick Koeper. *American Architecture, 1607–1976.* Cambridge, Mass.: MIT Press, 1983.

Wilmerding, John. *American Art.* Harmondsworth: Penguin, 1976.

Wilson, Simon. *Holbein to Hockney: A History of British Art.* London: Tate Gallery & Bodley Head, 1979.

CHAPTER 27
Romanticism, Realism, Photography: Europe and America, 1800 to 1870

Amic, Sylvain, et al. *Gustave Courbet.* Ostfildern: Hatje Cantz, 2008.

Athanassaglou-Kallmyer, Nina. *Théodore Géricault.* London: Phaidon, 2008.

Barringer, Tim, Jason Rosenfeld, and Alison Smith, eds. *Pre-Raphaelites: Victorian Art and Design.* New Haven, Conn.: Yale University Press, 2013.

Bartoli, Damien, and Frederick C. Ross. *William Bouguereau.* 2 vols. New York: Antique Collectors' Club, 2010.

Bellenger, Sylvain. *Girodet, 1767–1824.* Paris: Gallimard, 2005.

Bergdoll, Barry. *European Architecture 1750–1890.* New York: Oxford University Press, 2000.

Boime, Albert. *The Academy and French Painting in the 19th Century.* London: Phaidon, 1971.

———. *Art and the French Commune: Imagining Paris after War and Revolution.* Princeton, N.J.: Princeton University Press, 1995.

———. *Art in the Age of Bonapartism, 1800–1815.* Chicago: University of Chicago Press, 1990.

Bordes, Philippe. *Jacques-Louis David: Empire to Exile.* New Haven, Conn.: Yale University Press, 2007.

Brown, David Blayney. *Romanticism.* New York: Phaidon, 2001.

Bryson, Norman. *Tradition and Desire: From David to Delacroix.* New York: Cambridge University Press, 1984.

Burns, Sarah, and John Davis. *American Art to 1900: A Documentary History.* Berkeley and Los Angeles: University of California Press, 2009.

Chu, Petra ten-Doesschate. *The Most Arrogant Man in France: Gustave Courbet and the Nineteenth-Century Media Culture.* Princeton, N.J.: Princeton University Press, 2007.

Clark, T. J. *The Absolute Bourgeois: Artists and Politics in France, 1848–1851.* London: Thames & Hudson, 1973.

———. *Image of the People: Gustave Courbet and the 1848 Revolution.* London: Thames & Hudson, 1973.

———. *The Painting of Modern Life: Paris in the Art of Manet and His Followers.* Princeton, N.J.: Princeton University Press, 1984.

Clay, Jean. *Romanticism.* New York: Phaidon, 1981.

Eitner, Lorenz. *Neoclassicism and Romanticism, 1750–1850: An Anthology of Sources and Documents.* New York: Harper & Row, 1989.

Fried, Michael. *Courbet's Realism.* Chicago: University of Chicago Press, 1982.

———. *Manet's Modernism, or, The Face of Painting in the 1860s.* Chicago: University of Chicago Press, 1996.

Grave, Johannes. *Caspar David Friedrich.* New York: Prestel, 2012.

Harvey, Eleanor Jones. *The Civil War and American Art.* New Haven, Conn.: Yale University Press, 2012.

Hilton, Timothy. *The Pre-Raphaelites.* New York: Oxford University Press, 1970.

Hofmann, Werner. *Caspar David Friedrich.* New York: Thames & Hudson, 2001.

———. *Goya.* New York: Thames & Hudson, 2003.

Holt, Elizabeth Gilmore, ed. *From the Classicists to the Impressionists: A Documentary History of Art and Architecture in the Nineteenth Century.* Garden City, N.J.: Anchor Books; Doubleday, 1966.

Honour, Hugh. *Romanticism.* New York: Harper & Row, 1979.

Koerner, Joseph Leo. *Caspar David Friedrich and the Subject of Landscape.* 2d ed. London: Reaktion, 2009.

Krämer, Felix. *Dark Romanticism: From Goya to Max Ernst.* Ostfildern: Hatje Cantz, 2013.

Krell, Alain. *Manet and the Painters of Contemporary Life.* London: Thames & Hudson, 1996.

Kroeber, Karl. *British Romantic Art.* Berkeley: University of California Press, 1986.

Lampert, Catherine, ed. *Daumier: Visions of Paris.* London: Royal Academy of Arts, 2013.

Le Men, Ségolène. *Courbet.* New York: Abbeville, 2008.

Lewis, Michael J. *The Gothic Revival.* New York: Thames & Hudson, 2002.

Licht, Fred. *Goya.* New York: Abbeville, 2001.

Mainardi, Patricia. *Art and Politics of the Second Empire: The Universal Expositions of 1855 and 1867.* New Haven, Conn.: Yale University Press, 1987.

———. *The End of the Salon: Art and the State in the Early Third Republic.* Cambridge: Cambridge University Press, 1993.

Middleton, Robin. *Architecture of the Nineteenth Century.* London: Phaidon, 2003.

Middleton, Robin, and David Watkin. *Neoclassical and 19th-Century Architecture.* 2 vols. New York: Electa/Rizzoli, 1987.

Needham, Gerald. *19th-Century Realist Art.* New York: Harper & Row, 1988.

Nochlin, Linda. *Realism and Tradition in Art, 1848–1900: Sources and Documents.* Upper Saddle River, N.J.: Prentice Hall, 1966.

Novak, Barbara. *American Painting of the Nineteenth Century: Realism and the American Experience.* New York: Harper & Row, 1979.

Novak, Barbara. *Nature and Culture: American Landscape and Painting, 1825–1875.* 3d ed. New York: Oxford University Press, 2007.

Novotny, Fritz. *Painting and Sculpture in Europe, 1780–1880.* 3d ed. New Haven, Conn.: Yale University Press, 1988.

Porterfield, Todd. *The Allure of Empire: Art in the Service of French Imperialism 1798–1836.* Princeton, N.J.: Princeton University Press, 1998.

Porterfield, Todd, and Susan L. Siegfried. *Staging Empire: Napoleon, Ingres, and David.* University Park: Pennsylvania State University Press, 2006.

Rosen, Charles, and Henri Zerner. *Romanticism and Realism: The Mythology of Nineteenth-Century Art.* New York: Viking, 1984.

Rubin, James Henry. *Courbet.* London: Phaidon, 1997.

———. *Manet: Initial M, Hand and Eye.* Paris: Flammarion, 2010.

Shelton, Andrew Carrington. *Ingres.* London: Phaidon, 2008.

Sloane, Joseph C. *French Painting between the Past and the Present: Artists, Critics, and Traditions from 1848 to 1870.* Princeton, N.J.: Princeton University Press, 1973.

Symmons, Sarah. *Goya.* London: Phaidon, 1998.

Taylor, Joshua, ed. *Nineteenth-Century Theories of Art.* Berkeley: University of California Press, 1987.

Tillier, Betrand, et al. *Gustave Courbet.* New York: Metropolitan Museum of Art, 2008.

Toman, Rolf, ed. *Neoclassicism and Romanticism: Architecture, Sculpture, Painting, Drawings, 1750–1848.* Cologne: Könemann, 2006.

Vaughn, William. *German Romantic Painting.* New Haven, Conn.: Yale University Press, 1980.

Wolf, Bryan Jay. *Romantic Revision: Culture and Consciousness in Nineteenth-Century American Painting and Literature.* Chicago: University of Chicago Press, 1986.

Wood, Christopher. *The Pre-Raphaelites.* New York: Viking, 1981.

CHAPTER 28
Impressionism, Post-Impressionism, Symbolism: Europe and America, 1870 to 1900

Baal-Teshuva, Jacob. *Louis Comfort Tiffany.* Cologne: Taschen, 2008.

Bergdoll, Barry. *European Architecture 1750–1890.* New York: Oxford University Press, 2000.

Breuer, Karin. *Japanesque: The Japanese Print in the Era of Impressionism.* New York: Prestel, 2010.

Bryson, Norman. *Tradition and Desire: From David to Delacroix.* New York: Cambridge University Press, 1984.

Burnham, Helen, ed. *Looking East: Western Artists and the Allure of Japan.* Boston: Museum of Fine Arts, 2014.

Calloway, Stephen. *Aubrey Beardsley.* New York: Harry N. Abrams, 1998.

Clark, T. J. *The Painting of Modern Life: Paris in the Art of Manet and His Followers.* Princeton, N.J.: Princeton University Press, 1984.

Cogeval, Guy, ed. *Claude Monet, 1840–1926.* Paris: Réunion des Musées Nationaux, 2010.

Distel, Anne. *Renoir.* New York: Abbeville, 2010.

Dorra, Henri, ed. *Symbolist Art Theories: A Critical Anthology.* Berkeley and Los Angeles: University of California Press, 1995.

Eitner, Lorenz. *Neoclassicism and Romanticism, 1750–1850: An Anthology of Sources and Documents.* New York: Harper & Row, 1989.

Facos, Michelle. *Symbolism in Context.* Berkeley: University of California Press, 2009.

Hauptmann, Jodi. *Beyond the Visible: The Art of Odilon Redon.* New York: Museum of Modern Art, 2005.

Herbert, Robert L. *Impressionism: Art, Leisure, and Parisian Society.* New Haven, Conn.: Yale University Press, 1988.

Kendall, Richard, and Jill Devonyar. *Degas and the Ballet: Picturing Movement.* London: Royal Academy of Arts, 2011.

Lewis, Mary Tompkins, ed. *Critical Readings in Impressionism and Post-Impressionism: An Anthology.* Berkeley and Los Angeles: University of California Press, 2007.

Loyrette, Henri, Sebastien Allard, and Laurence Des Cars. *Nineteenth Century French Art: From Romanticism to Impressionism, Post-Impressionism, and Art Nouveau.* Paris: Flammarion, 2007.

Masson, Raphaël, and Véronique Mattiussi. *Rodin.* Paris: Flammarion, 2004.

McShine, Kynaston, ed. *Edvard Munch: The Modern Life of the Soul.* New York: Museum of Modern Art, 2006.

Middleton, Robin. *Architecture of the Nineteenth Century.* London: Phaidon, 2003.

Middleton, Robin, and David Watkin. *Neoclassical and 19th-Century Architecture.* 2 vols. New York: Electa/Rizzoli, 1987.

Pfeiffer, Ingrid, et al. *Women Impressionists.* Ostfildern: Hatje Cantz, 2008.

Rey, Jean-Dominique. *Berthe Morisot.* Paris: Flammarion, 2011.

Swinbourne, Anna. *James Ensor.* New York: Museum of Modern Art, 2009.

Thomson, Belinda, ed. *Gauguin: Maker of Myth.* London: Tate, 2010.

Walther, Ingo F., ed. *Impressionist Art 1860–1920.* 2 vols. Cologne: Taschen, 2010.

Zerbst, Rainer. *Gaudí: The Complete Buildings.* Cologne: Taschen, 2005.

CHAPTER 29
Modernism in Europe and America, 1900 to 1945

Antliff, Mark. *Cultural Politics and the Parisian Avant-Garde.* Princeton, N.J.: Princeton University Press, 1993.

Antliff, Mark, and Patricia Leighten. *Cubism and Culture.* New York: Thames & Hudson, 2001.

Arnaldo, Javier, and Max Hollein. *Kirchner.* Ostfildern: Hatje Cantz, 2010.

Baigell, Matthew. *The American Scene: American Painting of the 1930s.* New York: Praeger, 1974.

Barr, Alfred H., Jr. *Cubism and Abstract Art: Painting, Sculpture, Constructions, Photography, Architecture, Industrial Arts, Theatre, Films, Posters, Typography.* Cambridge, Mass.: Belknap, 1986.

Barron, Stephanie. *Exiles and Emigrés: The Flight of European Artists from Hitler.* Los Angeles: Los Angeles County Museum of Art, 1997.

———, ed. *"Degenerate Art": The Fate of the Avant-Garde in Nazi Germany.* Los Angeles: Los Angeles County Museum of Art, 1991.

Bayer, Herbert, Walter Gropius, and Ise Gropius. *Bauhaus, 1919–1928.* New York: Museum of Modern Art, 1975.

Bearden, Romare, and Harry Henderson. *A History of African-American Artists from 1792 to the Present.* New York: Pantheon, 1993.

Bergdoll, Barry. *Bauhaus 1919-1933*. New York: Museum of Modern Art, 2009.

Bouvet, Vincent, and Gérard Durozoi. *Paris between the Wars 1919-1939: Art, Life & Culture*. New York: Vendome, 2010.

Breton, André. *Surrealism and Painting*. New York: Harper & Row, 1972.

Brown, Milton. *Story of the Armory Show: The 1913 Exhibition That Changed American Art*. 2d ed. New York: Abbeville, 1988.

Campbell, Mary Schmidt, David C. Driskell, David Lewis Levering, and Deborah Willis Ryan. *Harlem Renaissance: Art of Black America*. New York: Studio Museum in Harlem; Abrams, 1987.

Clark, T. J. *Picasso and Truth: From Cubism to Guernica*. Princeton, N.J.: Princeton University Press, 2013.

Cowling, Elizabeth, ed. *Picasso: Challenging the Past*. London: National Gallery, 2011.

Cox, Neil. *Cubism*. London: Phaidon, 2000.

Curtis, Penelope. *Sculpture 1900-1945*. New York: Oxford University Press, 1999.

Curtis, William J. R. *Modern Architecture since 1900*. Upper Saddle River, N.J.: Prentice Hall, 1996.

D'Alessandro, Stephanie, ed. *Magritte: The Mystery of the Ordinary, 1926-1938*. New York: Museum of Modern Art, 2013.

Davidson, Abraham A. *Early American Modernist Painting, 1910-1935*. New York: Harper & Row, 1981.

Dickerman, Leah, ed. *Inventing Abstraction, 1910-1925*. New York: Museum of Modern Art, 2013.

Dietrich, Dorothea, ed. *Dada: Zurich, Berlin, Hannover, Cologne, New York, Paris*. Washington, D.C.: National Gallery, 2008.

Du Pont, Diana C. *Tamayo: A Modern Icon Reinterpreted*. Santa Barbara, Calif.: Santa Barbara Museum of Art, 2007.

Eberle, Matthias. *World War I and the Weimar Artists: Dix, Grosz, Beckmann, Schlemmer*. New Haven, Conn.: Yale University Press, 1985.

Edwards, Steve, and Paul Wood, eds. *Art of the Avant-Gardes*. New Haven, Conn.: Yale University Press, 2004.

Elderfield, John. *The "Wild Beasts": Fauvism and Its Affinities*. New York: Museum of Modern Art, 1976.

Favole, Paolo. *The Story of Modern Architecture*. New York: Prestel, 2012.

Fer, Briony, David Batchelor, and Paul Wood. *Realism, Rationalism, Surrealism: Art between the Wars*. New Haven, Conn.: Yale University Press, 1993.

Friedman, Mildred, ed. *De Stijl, 1917-1931: Visions of Utopia*. Minneapolis: Walker Art Center; New York: Abbeville, 1982.

Gale, Matthew. *Dada and Surrealism*. London: Phaidon, 1997.

Gale, Matthew, ed. *Paul Klee: Making Visible*. London: Tate Modern and Thames & Hudson, 2013.

Goldberg, Rose Lee. *Performance: Live Art 1909 to the Present*. New York: Abrams, 1979.

Golding, John. *Cubism: A History and an Analysis, 1907-1914*. Cambridge, Mass.: Belknap, 1988.

Gordon, Donald E. *Expressionism: Art and Idea*. New Haven, Conn.: Yale University Press, 1987.

Harrison, Charles, Francis Frascina, and Gil Perry. *Primitivism, Cubism, Abstraction: The Early Twentieth Century*. New Haven, Conn.: Yale University Press, 1993.

Herbert, James D. *Fauve Painting: The Making of Cultural Politics*. New Haven, Conn.: Yale University Press, 1992.

Herrera, Hayden, ed. *Frida Kahlo*. Minneapolis: Walker Art Center, 2007.

Hills, Patricia. *Painting Harlem Modern: The Art of Jacob Lawrence*. Berkeley and Los Angeles: University of California Press, 2009.

Hitchcock, Henry-Russell, and Philip Johnson. *The International Style*. New York: Norton, 1995.

Hurlburt, Laurance P. *The Mexican Muralists in the United States*. Albuquerque: University of New Mexico Press, 1989.

Jaffé, Hans L. C. *De Stijl, 1917-1931: The Dutch Contribution to Modern Art*. Cambridge, Mass.: Belknap, 1986.

Krauss, Rosalind. *The Originality of the Avant-Garde and Other Modernist Myths*. Cambridge, Mass.: MIT Press, 1986.

Kushner, Marilyn Satin, Kimberly Orcutt, and Casey Nelson Blake, eds. *The Armory Show at 100: Modernism and Revolution*. New York: New York Historical Society, 2013.

Kuspit, Donald. *The Cult of the Avant-Garde Artist*. Cambridge: Cambridge University Press, 1993.

Lloyd, Jill. *German Expressionism: Primitivism and Modernity*. New Haven, Conn.: Yale University Press, 1991.

Lodder, Christina. *Russian Constructivism*. New Haven, Conn.: Yale University Press, 1983.

Lozano, Luis Martin, and Juan Coronel Rivera. *Diego Rivera: The Complete Murals*. Cologne: Taschen, 2008.

Martin, Marianne W. *Futurist Art and Theory*. Oxford: Clarendon, 1968.

McCully, Marilyn. *Picasso in Paris, 1900-1907*. New York: Vendome, 2011.

Messinger, Lisa Mintz, ed. *Stieglitz and His Artists: Matisse to O'Keeffe*. New York: Metropolitan Museum of Art, 2011.

Motherwell, Robert, ed. *The Dada Painters and Poets: An Anthology*. 2d ed. Boston: Hall, 1981.

Mundy, Jennifer. *Duchamp, Man Ray, Picabia*. London: Tate, 2008.

Oles, James. *Art and Architecture in Mexico*. New York: Thames & Hudson, 2013.

Orvell, Miles. *American Photography*. New York: Oxford University Press, 2003.

Peters, Olaf. *Otto Dix*. New York: Prestel, 2010.

Poggi, Christine. *Inventing Futurism: The Art and Politics of Artificial Optimism*. Princeton, N.J.: Princeton University Press, 2009.

Rhodes, Colin. *Primitivism and Modern Art*. New York: Thames & Hudson, 1994.

Richter, Hans. *Dada: Art and Anti-Art*. London: Thames & Hudson, 1961.

Rochfort, Desmond. *Mexican Muralists: Orozco, Rivera, Siqueiros*. San Francisco: Chronicle, 1998.

Rosenblum, Robert. *Cubism and Twentieth-Century Art*. Rev. ed. New York: Abrams, 1984.

Rubin, William S. *Dada and Surrealist Art*. New York: Abrams, 1968.

———, ed. *Pablo Picasso: A Retrospective*. New York: Museum of Modern Art; Boston: New York Graphic Society, 1980.

———. *"Primitivism" in 20th-Century Art: Affinity of the Tribal and the Modern*. 2 vols. New York: Museum of Modern Art, 1984.

Selz, Peter. *German Expressionist Painting*. Berkeley: University of California Press, 1974. Reprint of 1957 edition.

Silver, Kenneth E. *Esprit de Corps: The Art of the Parisian Avant-Garde and the First World War, 1914-1925*. Princeton, N.J.: Princeton University Press, 1989.

Smith, Terry. *Making the Modern: Industry, Art, and Design in America*. Chicago: University of Chicago Press, 1993.

Spieler, Reinhard. *Max Beckmann 1884-1950: The Path to Myth*. Cologne: Taschen, 2011.

Stott, William. *Documentary Expression and Thirties America*. New York: Oxford University Press, 1973.

Taylor, Joshua C. *Futurism*. New York: Museum of Modern Art, 1961.

Taylor, Michael R., ed. *Arshile Gorky: A Retrospective*. New Haven, Conn.: Yale University Press, 2009.

Terraroli, Valerio, ed. *Art of the Twentieth Century, 1900-1919: The Avant-Garde Movements*. Milan: Skira, 2006.

———. *Art of the Twentieth Century, 1920-1945: The Artistic Culture between the Wars*. Milan: Skira, 2006.

Tisdall, Caroline, and Angelo Bozzolla. *Futurism*. New York: Oxford University Press, 1978.

Trachtenberg, Alan. *Reading American Photographs: Images as History—Mathew Brady to Walker Evans*. New York: Hill and Wang, 1989.

Troyen, Carol, ed. *Edward Hopper*. Boston: Museum of Fine Arts, 2007.

Tsujimoto, Karen. *Images of America: Precisionist Painting and Modern Photography*. Seattle: University of Washington Press, 1982.

Tucker, William. *Early Modern Sculpture*. New York: Oxford University Press, 1974.

Vogt, Paul. *Expressionism: German Painting, 1905-1920*. New York: Abrams, 1980.

Weiss, Jeffrey S. *The Popular Culture of Modern Art: Picasso, Duchamp, and Avant-Gardism*. New Haven, Conn.: Yale University Press, 1994.

Whitford, Frank. *Bauhaus*. New York: Thames & Hudson, 1984.

CHAPTER 30
Modernism and Postmodernism in Europe and America, 1945 to 1980

Adamson, Glenn, and Jane Pavitt, eds. *Postmodernism: Style and Subversion, 1970-1990*. London: Victoria & Albert Museum, 2011.

Alloway, Lawrence. *American Pop Art*. New York: Whitney Museum of American Art; Macmillan, 1974.

———. *Topics in American Art since 1945*. New York: Norton, 1975.

Altshuler, Bruce. *Isamu Noguchi*. New York: Abbeville, 1994.

Anfam, David. *Abstract Expressionism*. New York: Thames & Hudson, 1990.

Anreus, Alejandro, Robin Adèle Greeley, and Leonard Folgarait, eds. *Mexican Muralism: A Critical History*. Berkeley and Los Angeles: University of California Press, 2012.

Archer, Michael. *Art since 1960*. New ed. New York: Thames & Hudson, 2002.

Ashton, Dore. *American Art since 1945.* New York: Oxford University Press, 1983.

———. *The New York School: A Cultural Reckoning.* Harmondsworth: Penguin, 1979.

Ballantyne, Andrew, ed. *Architectures: Modernism and After.* Malden, Mass: Blackwell, 2004.

Battcock, Gregory, ed. *Idea Art: A Critical Anthology.* New York: Dutton, 1973.

———. *Minimal Art: A Critical Anthology.* New York: Studio Vista, 1969.

———. *The New Art: A Critical Anthology.* New York: Dutton, 1973.

———. *New Artists Video: A Critical Anthology.* New York: Dutton, 1978.

Battcock, Gregory, and Robert Nickas, eds. *The Art of Performance: A Critical Anthology.* New York: Dutton, 1984.

Beardsley, John, and Jane Livingston. *Hispanic Art in the United States: Thirty Contemporary Painters and Sculptors.* Houston: Museum of Fine Arts; New York: Abbeville, 1987.

Beardsley, Richard. *Earthworks and Beyond: Contemporary Art in the Landscape.* New York: Abbeville, 1984.

Broude, Norma, and Mary D. Garrard. *The Power of Feminist Art: The American Movement of the 1970s, History and Impact.* New York: Abrams, 1994.

Bürger, Peter. *Theory of the Avant-Garde.* Minneapolis: University of Minnesota Press, 1984.

Butler, Cornelia H., ed. *WACK! Art and the Feminist Revolution.* Cambridge, Mass.: MIT Press, 2007.

Causey, Andrew. *Sculpture since 1945.* New York: Oxford University Press, 1998.

Caws, Mary Ann. *Robert Motherwell.* New York: Columbia University Press, 1996.

Celant, Germano, ed. *Louise Nevelson.* Turin: Skira, 2012.

Cockcroft, Eva, John Weber, and James Cockcroft. *Toward a People's Art.* New York: Dutton, 1977.

Cohn, Marjorie, and Eliza Rathbone. *Mark Rothko.* Ostfildern: Hatje Cantz, 2001.

Collins, Bradford R. *Pop Art.* London: Phaidon, 2012.

Crow, Thomas. *The Rise of the Sixties: American and European Art in the Era of Dissent.* New Haven, Conn.: Yale University Press, 2005.

Finch, Christopher. *Chuck Close: Work.* New York: Prestel, 2010.

Fineberg, Jonathan. *Art since 1940: Strategies of Being.* 3d ed. Upper Saddle River, N.J.: Prentice Hall, 2010.

Foster, Hal. *The First Pop Age: Painting and Subjectivity in the Art of Hamilton, Lichtenstein, Warhol, Richter, and Ruscha.* Princeton, N.J.: Princeton University Press, 2011.

Frascina, Francis, ed. *Pollock and After: The Critical Debate.* New York: Harper & Row, 1985.

Gale, Matthew, ed. *Francis Bacon.* New York: Rizzoli, 2009.

Gaugh, Harry F. *Franz Kline.* New York: Abbeville, 1994.

Geldzahler, Henry. *New York Painting and Sculpture, 1940–1970.* New York: Dutton, 1969.

Godfrey, Mark, and Nicholas Serota, eds. *Gerhard Richter: Panorama. A Retrospective.* London: Tate, 2011.

Godfrey, Tony. *Conceptual Art.* London: Phaidon, 1998.

Goldberg, Rose Lee. *Performance Art: From Futurism to the Present.* Rev. ed. New York: Abrams, 1988.

Goldhagen, Sarah Williams, and Réjean Legault. *Anxious Modernisms: Experimentation in Postwar Architectural Culture.* Cambridge, Mass.: MIT Press, 2002.

Goodman, Cynthia. *Digital Visions: Computers and Art.* New York: Abrams, 1987.

Goodyear, Frank H., Jr. *Contemporary American Realism since 1960.* Boston: New York Graphic Society, 1981.

Gouma-Peterson, Thalia. *Miriam Schapiro: Shaping the Fragments of Art and Life.* New York: Abrams, 2000.

Green, Jonathan. *American Photography: A Critical History 1945 to the Present.* New York: Abrams, 1984.

Greenberg, Clement. *Clement Greenberg: The Collected Essays and Criticism.* Edited by J. O'Brien. 4 vols. Chicago: University of Chicago Press, 1986–1993.

Grundberg, Andy. *Photography and Art: Interactions since 1945.* New York: Abbeville, 1987.

Guilbaut, Serge. *How New York Stole the Idea of Modern Art.* Chicago: University of Chicago Press, 1983.

Hays, K. Michael, and Carol Burns, eds. *Thinking the Present: Recent American Architecture.* New York: Princeton Architectural, 1990.

Henri, Adrian. *Total Art: Environments, Happenings, and Performance.* New York: Oxford University Press, 1974.

Hobbs, Robert. *Lee Krasner.* New York: Abbeville, 1993.

Hoffman, Katherine. *Explorations: The Visual Arts since 1945.* New York: Harper Collins, 1991.

Hopkins, David. *After Modern Art, 1945–2000.* New York: Oxford University Press, 2000.

Hughes, Robert. *The Shock of the New.* New York: Knopf, 1981.

Hunter, Sam. *An American Renaissance: Painting and Sculpture since 1940.* New York: Abbeville, 1986.

Jacobs, Jane. *The Death and Life of Great American Cities.* New York: Random House, 1961.

Jacobus, John. *Twentieth-Century Architecture: The Middle Years, 1940–1964.* New York: Praeger, 1966.

Jencks, Charles. *The Language of Post-Modern Architecture.* 6th ed. New York: Rizzoli, 1991.

———. *What Is Post-Modernism?* 3d ed. London: Academy Editions, 1989.

Johnson, Ellen H., ed. *American Artists on Art from 1940 to 1980.* Boulder, Colo.: Westview, 1982.

Joselit, David. *American Art since 1945.* New York: Thames & Hudson, 2003.

Kaprow, Allan. *Assemblage, Environments, and Happenings.* New York: Abrams, 1966.

Kirby, Michael. *Happenings.* New York: Dutton, 1966.

Kotz, Mary Lynn. *Rauschenberg: Art and Life.* New York: Abrams, 2004.

Kramer, Hilton. *The Age of the Avant-Garde: An Art Chronicle of 1956–1972.* New York: Farrar, Straus & Giroux, 1973.

Leja, Michael. *Reframing Abstract Expressionism: Subjectivity and Painting in the 1940s.* New Haven, Conn.: Yale University Press, 1993.

Lippard, Lucy R. *Mixed Blessings: New Art in a Multicultural America.* New York: Pantheon, 1990.

———. *Pop Art.* New York: Praeger, 1966.

———, ed. *From the Center: Feminist Essays on Women's Art.* New York: Dutton, 1976.

———. *Six Years: The Dematerialization of the Art Object from 1966 to 1972.* New York: Praeger, 1973.

Livingston, Jane, ed. *The Paintings of Joan Mitchell.* New York: Whitney Museum of American Art, 2002.

Lobel, Michael. *James Rosenquist: Pop Art, Politics, and History in the 1960s.* Berkeley and Los Angeles: University of California Press, 2009.

Lovejoy, Margot. *Postmodern Currents: Art and Artists in the Age of the Electronic Media.* Ann Arbor, Mich.: UMI Research Press, 1989.

Lucie-Smith, Edward. *Art Now.* Edison, N.J.: Wellfleet, 1989.

———. *Movements in Art since 1945.* New ed. New York: Thames & Hudson, 2001.

Mamiya, Christin J. *Pop Art and Consumer Culture: American Super Market.* Austin: University of Texas Press, 1992.

Marder, Tod A. *The Critical Edge: Controversy in Recent American Architecture.* New Brunswick, N.J.: Rutgers University Press, 1980.

———. *An International Survey of Recent Painting and Sculpture.* New York: Museum of Modern Art, 1984.

Mercurio, Gianni. *Lichtenstein: Meditations on Art.* Milan: Skira, 2010.

Mesch, Claudia. *Art and Politics: A Small History of Art for Social Change since 1945.* New York: I. B. Tauris, 2013.

Meyer, Ursula. *Conceptual Art.* New York: Dutton, 1972.

Mitchell, William J. *The Reconfigured Eye: Visual Truth in the Post-Photographic Era.* Cambridge, Mass.: MIT Press, 1992.

Morris, Francis, ed. *Louise Bourgeois.* New York: Rizzoli, 2008.

Osborne, Peter, ed. *Conceptual Art.* London: Phaidon, 2002.

Polcari, Stephen. *Abstract Expressionism and the Modern Experience.* Cambridge: Cambridge University Press, 1991.

Popper, Frank. *Origins and Development of Kinetic Art.* Translated by Stephen Bann. Greenwich, Conn.: New York Graphic Society, 1968.

Price, Jonathan. *Video Visions: A Medium Discovers Itself.* New York: New American Library, 1977.

Reichardt, Jasia, ed. *Cybernetics, Art, and Ideas.* Greenwich, Conn.: New York Graphics Society, 1971.

Robbins, Corinne. *The Pluralist Era: American Art, 1968–1981.* New York: Harper & Row, 1984.

Rondeau, James, and Sheena Wagstaff, eds. *Roy Lichtenstein: A Retrospective.* Chicago: Art Institute of Chicago, 2012.

Rorimer, Anne. *New Art in the 60s and 70s: Redefining Reality.* New York: Thames & Hudson, 2001.

Rosen, Randy, and Catherine C. Brawer, eds. *Making Their Mark: Women Artists Move into the Mainstream, 1970–1985.* New York: Abbeville, 1989.

Rosenberg, Harold. *The Tradition of the New.* New York: Horizon, 1959.

Rush, Michael. *New Media in Art.* 2d ed. New York: Thames & Hudson, 2005.

Russell, John, and Suzi Gablik. *Pop Art Redefined.* New York: Praeger, 1969.

Sackler, Elizabeth A., ed. *Judy Chicago.* New York: Watson-Guptill, 2002.

Sandford, Mariellen R., ed. *Happenings and Other Acts.* New York: Routledge, 1995.

Sandler, Irving. *Art of the Postmodern Era.* New York: Harper Collins, 1996.

——. *The Triumph of American Painting: A History of Abstract Expressionism.* New York: Praeger, 1970.

Sayre, Henry M. *The Object of Performance: The American Avant-Garde since 1970.* Chicago: University of Chicago Press, 1989.

Schimmel, Paul, ed. *Destroy the Picture: Painting the Void, 1949–1962.* Los Angeles: Museum of Contemporary Art, 2012.

Schneider, Ira, and Beryl Korot. *Video Art: An Anthology.* New York: Harcourt Brace Jovanovich, 1976.

Shapiro, David, and Cecile Shapiro. *Abstract Expressionism: A Critical Record.* New York: Cambridge University Press, 1990.

Shiff, Richard. *Barnett Newman: A Catalogue Raisonné.* New Haven, Conn.: Yale University Press, 2004.

Siegel, Katy. *Since '45: America and the Making of Contemporary Art.* London: Reaktion, 2011.

——, ed. *Abstract Expressionism.* New York: Phaidon, 2011.

Sims, Lowery Stokes. *Wifredo Lam and the International Avant-Garde, 1923–1982.* Austin, Tex.: University of Texas Press, 2002.

Smagula, Howard. *Currents: Contemporary Directions in the Visual Arts.* 2d ed. Upper Saddle River, N.J.: Prentice Hall, 1989.

Smee, Sebastian. *Lucian Freud: Beholding the Animal.* Cologne: Taschen, 2009.

Sonfist, Alan, ed. *Art in the Landscape: A Critical Anthology of Environmental Art.* New York: Dutton, 1983.

Sontag, Susan. *On Photography.* New York: Farrar, Straus & Giroux, 1973.

Stiles, Kristine, and Peter Selz. *Theories and Documents of Contemporary Art: A Sourcebook of Artists' Writings.* Berkeley and Los Angeles: University of California Press, 1996.

Taylor, Brendon. *Contemporary Art: Art since 1970.* Upper Saddle River, N.J.: Prentice Hall, 2005.

Terraroli, Valerio, ed. *Art of the Twentieth Century, 1946–1968: The Birth of Contemporary Art.* Milan: Skira, 2007.

Theriault, Kim S. *Rethinking Arshile Gorky.* University Park: Pennsylvania State University Press, 2009.

Tuchman, Maurice. *American Sculpture of the Sixties.* Los Angeles: Los Angeles County Museum of Art, 1967.

Ursprung, Philip. *Allan Kaprow, Robert Smithson, and the Limits to Art.* Berkeley and Los Angeles: University of California Press, 2013.

Varnedoe, Kirk. *Pictures of Nothing: Abstract Art since Pollock.* Princeton: Princeton University Press, 2006.

Venturi, Robert. *Complexity and Contradiction in Architecture.* New York: Museum of Modern Art, 1966.

Venturi, Robert, Denise Scott-Brown, and Steven Isehour. *Learning from Las Vegas.* Cambridge, Mass.: MIT Press, 1972.

Waldman, Diane. *Collage, Assemblage, and the Found Object.* New York: Abrams, 1992.

Wallis, Brian, ed. *Art after Modernism: Rethinking Representation.* New York: New Museum of Contemporary Art in association with David R. Godine, 1984.

Wheeler, Daniel. *Art since Mid-Century: 1945 to the Present.* Upper Saddle River, N.J.: Prentice Hall, 1991.

Wood, Paul. *Modernism in Dispute: Art since the Forties.* New Haven, Conn.: Yale University Press, 1993.

CHAPTER 31
Contemporary Art Worldwide

Andrews, Julia F., and Kuiyi Shen. *The Art of Modern China.* Berkeley and Los Angeles: University of California Press, 2012.

Anfam, David, ed. *Anish Kapoor.* New York: Phaidon, 2009.

Buchhart, Dieter, et al. *Jean-Michel Basquiat.* Ostfildern: Hatje Cantz, 2010.

Butler, Cornelia H., and Lisa Gabrielle Mark. *WACK!: Art and the Feminist Revolution.* Cambridge, Mass.: MIT Press, 2007.

Celent, Germano. *Anselm Kiefer.* Milan: Skira, 2007.

Chilvers, Ian, and John Glaves-Smith. *Oxford Dictionary of Modern and Contemporary Art.* 2d ed. New York: Oxford University Press, 2009.

Chiu, Melissa, and Benjamin Genocchio. *Asian Art Now.* New York: Monacelli, 2010.

Cook, Peter. *New Spirit in Architecture.* New York: Rizzoli, 1990.

Cummings, P. *Dictionary of Contemporary American Artists.* 6th ed. New York: St. Martin's, 1994.

Dadi, Iftikhar. *Modernism and the Art of Muslim South Asia.* Chapel Hill: University of North Carolina Press, 2010.

Danto, Arthur C., and Marina Abramovic. *Shirin Neshat.* New York: Rizzoli, 2010.

Deepwell, K., ed. *New Feminist Art.* Manchester: Manchester University Press, 1994.

Enwezor, Okwui, and Chika Okeke-Agulu. *Contemporary African Art since 1980.* Bologna: Damiani, 2009.

Favole, Paolo. *The Story of Contemporary Architecture.* New York: Prestel, 2011.

Ferguson, Russell, ed. *Discourses: Conversations in Postmodern Art and Culture.* Cambridge, Mass.: MIT Press, 1990.

Fineberg, Jonathan. *Art since 1940: Strategies of Being.* 3d ed. Upper Saddle River, N.J.: Prentice Hall, 2011.

Galassi, Peter. *Andreas Gursky.* New York: Museum of Modern Art, 2001.

Ghirardo, Diane. *Architecture after Modernism.* New York: Thames & Hudson, 1996.

Goldsworthy, Andy. *Andy Goldsworthy: A Collaboration with Nature.* New York: Abrams, 1990.

Heartney, Eleanor. *Art & Today.* New York: Phaidon, 2008.

Heartney, Eleanor, Helaine Posner, Nancy Princenthal, and Sue Scott. *After the Revolution: Women Who Transformed Contemporary Art.* New York: Prestel, 2007.

Hertz, Richard, ed. *Theories of Contemporary Art.* 2d ed. Upper Saddle River, N.J.: Prentice Hall, 1993.

Hopkins, David. *After Modern Art, 1945–2000.* New York: Oxford University Press, 2000.

Jencks, Charles. *The New Paradigm in Architecture: The Language of Post-Modernism.* New Haven, Conn.: Yale University Press, 2002.

Jodidio, Philip. *100 Contemporary Architects.* Cologne: Taschen, 2008.

Joselit, David. *After Art.* Princeton, N.J.: Princeton University Press, 2013.

Kasfir, Sidney Littlefield. *Contemporary African Art.* New York: Thames & Hudson, 1999.

Kolossa, Alexandra. *Keith Haring 1958–1990: A Life for Art.* Cologne: Taschen, 2009.

Kotz, Mary Lunn. *Rauschenberg: Art and Life.* New York: Abrams, 2004.

Lippard, Lucy R. *Mixed Blessings: New Art in a Multicultural America.* New York: Pantheon, 1990.

Mesch, Claudia. *Art and Politics: A Small History of Art for Social Change since 1945.* New York: I. B. Tauris, 2013.

Moszynska, Anna. *Sculpture Now.* New York: Thames & Hudson, 2013.

Mullins, Charlotte. *Painting People: Figure Painting Today.* New York: Thames & Hudson, 2008.

Neri, Louise, and Takaya Goto, eds. *Yayoi Kusama.* New York: Rizzoli, 2012.

Nesbitt, Judith, ed. *Chris Ofili.* London: Tate, 2010.

Norris, Christopher, and Andrew Benjamin. *What Is Deconstruction?* New York: St. Martin's, 1988.

O'Brien, Elaine, Everlyn Nicodemus, Melissa Chiu, Benjamin Genocchio, Mary K. Coffey, and Roberto Tejada, eds. *Modern Art in Africa, Asia, and Latin America: An Introduction to Global Modernisms.* Malden, Mass.: Wiley-Blackwell, 2013.

Paul, Christiane. *Digital Art.* 2d ed. New York: Thames & Hudson, 2008.

Pauli, Lori, ed. *Manufactured Landscapes: The Photographs of Edward Burtynsky.* New Haven, Conn.: Yale University Press, 2003.

Perry, Gill, and Paul Wood. *Themes in Contemporary Art.* New Haven, Conn.: Yale University Press, 2004.

Raskin, David. *Donald Judd.* New Haven, Conn.: Yale University Press, 2010.

Risatti, Howard, ed. *Postmodern Perspectives: Issues in Contemporary Art.* Upper Saddle River, N.J.: Prentice Hall, 1990.

Sandler, Irving. *Art of the Postmodern Era.* New York: Harper Collins, 1996.

Smith, Terry. *What Is Contemporary Art?* Chicago: University of Chicago Press, 2009.

Sollins, Susan, ed. *Art: 21 (Art in the Twenty-first Century).* 5 vols. New York: Abrams, 2001–2009.

Stiles, Kristine, and Peter Selz. *Theories and Documents of Contemporary Art: A Sourcebook of Artists' Writings.* 2d ed. Berkeley and Los Angeles: University of California Press, 2012.

Storr, Robert. *Elizabeth Murray.* New York: Museum of Modern Art, 2005.

Taylor, Brendon. *Contemporary Art: Art since 1970.* Upper Saddle River, N.J.: Prentice Hall, 2005.

Terraroli, Valerio, ed. *Art of the Twentieth Century, 1969–1999: Neo-avant-gardes, Postmodern and Global Art.* Milan: Skira, 2009.

Vogel, Susan Mullin. *El Anatsui: Art and Life.* New York: Prestel, 2012.

Wands, Bruce. *Art of the Digital Age.* New York: Thames & Hudson, 2007.

Warren, Lynne. *Jeff Koons.* New Haven, Conn.: Yale University Press, 2008.

Wines, James. *Green Architecture.* Cologne: Taschen, 2008.

Credits

The author and publisher are grateful to the proprietors and custodians of various works of art for photographs of these works and permission to reproduce them in this book. Sources not included in the captions are listed here.

NOTE: *All references in the following credits are to figure numbers unless otherwise indicated.*

Introduction—Opener: National Gallery, London/Art Resource, NY; **I-2:** Hirshhorn Museum and Culture Garden, Smithsonian Institution, Washington, DC, Joseph H. Hirshhorn Purchase Fund, 1992 © City and county of Denver, courtesy the Clyfford Still Museum. Photo: akg images; **I-3:** Interior view of the choir, begun after 1284 (photo), French School, (13th century)/Beauvais Cathedral, Beauvais, France/© Paul Maeyaert/The Bridgeman Art Library; **I-4:** akg-images/Rabatti-Domingie; **I-5:** National Gallery of Art, Alfred Stieglitz Collection, Bequest of Georgia O'Keeffe 1987.58.3; **I-6:** Art © Estate of Ben Shahn/Licensed by VAGA, New York, NY. Photo: Whitney Museum of American Art, New York (gift of Edith and Milton Lowenthal in memory of Juliana Force); **I-7:** © Jonathan Poore/Cengage Learning; **I-8:** akg-images; **I-9:** The Metropolitan Museum of Art/Art Resource, NY; **I-10:** Courtesy Saskia Ltd., © Dr. Ron Wiedenhoeft; **I-11:** © 2011 The Josef and Anni Albers Foundation/Artists Rights Society (ARS), New York. Photo: © Whitney Museum of American Art; **I-12:** Photograph © 2011 Museum of Fine Arts, Boston. 11.4584; **I-13:** bpk, Berlin/Staatsgemaeldesammlungen, Munich, Germany/Art Resource, NY; **I-14:** Jürgen Liepe, Berlin; **I-15:** The Trustees of the British Museum/Art Resource, NY; **I-16:** Nimatallah/Art Resource, NY; **I-17:** Scala/Art Resource, NY; **I-18:** Cengage Learning; **I-19 left:** Portrait of Te Pehi Kupe wearing European clothes, c.1826 (w/c), Sylvester, John (fl.1826)/© National Library of Australia, Canberra, Australia/The Bridgeman Art Library; **I-19 right:** Public Domain.

Chapter 26—Opener: Photo: Katherine Wetzel © Virginia Museum of Fine Arts; **26-1A:** Jason Hawkes/Terra/Corbis; **26-2:** Bildarchiv Monheim/akg-images; **26-3:** Erich Lessing/Art Resource, NY; **26-3A:** Hervé Champollion/akg-images; **26-4:** © Jonathan Poore; **26-5:** John Burge; **26-6:** © Jonathan Poore; **26-6A:** Bildarchiv Monheim/akg-images; **26-6B:** Erich Lessing/Art Resource, NY; **26-7:** Scala/Art Resource, NY; **26-7A:** Musée du Louvre Paris/Gianni Dagli Orti/The Art Archive/Picture Desk; **26-7B:** Bildarchiv Preussischer Kulturbesitz/Art Resource, NY; **26-8:** By kind permission of the Trustees of the Wallace Collection, London. **26-9:** © Wallace Collection, London, UK/The Bridgeman Art Library; **26-10:** Image copyright © The Metropolitan Museum of Art/Art Resource, NY; **26-11:** Scala/Ministero per i Beni e le Attività culturali/Art Resource, NY; **26-11A:** © National Gallery, London/Art Resource, NY; **26-12:** Bridgeman-Giraudon/Art Resource, NY; **26-13:** John Meek/The Art Archive/Picture Desk; **26-14:** Réunion des Musées Nationaux/Art Resource, NY; **26-15:** Musée du Louvre Paris/Gianni Dagli Orti/The Art Archive/Picture Desk; **26-15A:** Erich Lessing/Art Resource, NY; **26-16:** Summerfield Press, Ltd.; **26-17:** The Metropolitan Museum of Art/Art Resource, NY; **26-18:** National Gallery, London//Art Resource, NY; **26-19:** The National Gallery of Art; **26-20:** National Gallery, London, UK/The Bridgeman Art Library; **26-21:** National Gallery of Canada; **26-22:** Photograph © 2011 Museum of Fine Arts, Boston, 30.781; **26-23:** Scala/Art Resource, NY; **26-24:** Portrait of Charles John Crowle (1738–1811) of Crowle Park, c. 1761–62 (oil on canvas), Batoni, Pompeo Girolamo (1708–87)/Louvre, Paris, France/Giraudon/The Bridgeman Art Library; **26-25:** Peter Aprahamian/Corbis; **26-25A:** Electa/akg-images; **26-26:** Réunion des Musées Nationaux/Art Resource, Inc.; **26-27:** Scala/Art Resource, NY; **26-28:** © Jonathan Poore/Cengage Learning; **26-28A:** Bildarchiv Monheim/akg-images; **26-29:** Eric Crichton/Encyclopedia/Corbis; **26-29A:** Bildarchiv Monheim/akg-images; **26-30:** ART on FILE/Corbis Art/Corbis; **26-31:** Thomas Jefferson Foundation; **26-32:** Michael Freeman/Value Art/Corbis; **26-33:** Photo © The Library of Virginia; **26-34:** Smithsonian American Art Museum, Washington, DC/Art Resource, NY.

Chapter 27—Opener: Erich Lessing/Art Resource, NY; **27-2:** © Jonathan Poore/Cengage Learning; **27-2A:** Erich Lessing/Art Resource, NY; **27-3:** RMN-Grand Palais/Art Resource, NY; **27-3A:** RMN-Grand Palais/Art Resource, NY; **27-3B:** Erich Lessing/Art Resource, NY; **27-4:** Scala/Ministero per i Beni e le Attività culturali/Art Resource, NY; **27-5:** RMN-Grand Palais/Art Resource, NY; **27-6:** RMN-Grand Palais/Art Resource, NY; **27-6A:** RMN-Grand Palais/Art Resource, NY; **27-7:** RMN-Grand Palais/Art Resource, NY; **27-8:** Réunion

des Musées Nationaux/Art Resource, NY; **27-9:** The Nightmare, 1781 (oil on canvas), Fuseli, Henry (Fussli, Johann Heinrich) (1741–1825)/Detroit Institute of Arts, USA/Founders Society purchase with Mr. and Mrs. Bert L. Smokler/ and Mr. and Mrs. Lawrence A. Fleischman funds/The Bridgeman Art Library; **27-10:** The Pierpont Morgan Library/Art Resource, NY; **27-11:** The Metropolitan Museum of Art/Art Resource, NY; **27-11A:** Erich Lessing/Art Resource, NY; **27-12:** The Art Archive/Museo del Prado Madrid/Gianni Dagli Orti; **27-13:** Erich Lessing/Art Resource, NY; **27-13A:** Bridgeman-Giraudon/Art Resource, NY; **27-14:** RMN-Grand Palais/Art Resource, NY; **27-15:** RMN-Grand Palais/Art Resource, NY; **27-15A:** Erich Lessing/Art Resource, NY; **27-16:** RMN-Grand Palais/Art Resource, NY; **27-16A:** The Art Archive/Musée d'Orsay Paris/Gianni Dagli Orti/Picture Desk; **27-17:** Erich Lessing/Art Resource, NY; **27-18:** © Jonathan Poore/Cengage Learning; **27-18A:** Sharon Adams Poore; **27-19:** Bildarchiv Preussischer Kulturbesitz/Art Resource, NY; **27-20:** Friedrich, Caspar David (1774–1840), Der Wanderer über dem Nebelmeer, ca. 1817. Oil on canvas. Bildarchiv Preussischer Kulturbesitz/Art Resource, NY; **27-21:** National Gallery, London/Art Resource, NY; **27-22:** Photography © 2011 Museum of Fine Arts, Boston, 99.22; **27-23:** The Metropolitan Museum of Art/Art Resource, NY; **27-24:** Smithsonian American Art Museum, Washington, DC/Art Resource, NY; **27-25:** Image © The Cleveland Museum of Art Frederic Edwin Church (American, 1826–1900). Twilight in the Wilderness, 1860. Oil on canvas, 101.6 × 162.6 cm. © The Cleveland Museum of Art. Mr. and Mrs. William H. Marlatt Fund, 1965.233; **27-26:** The Stone Breakers, 1849 (oil on canvas) (destroyed in 1945), Courbet, Gustave (1819–77)/Galerie Neue Meister, Dresden, Germany/ © Staatliche Kunstsammlungen Dresden/The Bridgeman Art Library; **27-27:** Erich Lessing/Art Resource, NY; **27-28:** RMN-Grand Palais/Art Resource, NY; **27-29:** Yale University Art Gallery/Art Resource, NY; **27-30:** The Metropolitan Museum of Art/Art Resource, NY; **27-31:** The Metropolitan Museum of Art/Art Resource, NY; **27-32:** Erich Lessing/Art Resource, NY; **27-33:** Scala/Art Resource, NY; **27-33A:** Nymphs and Satyr, 1873 (oil on canvas), Bouguereau, William-Adolphe (1825–1905)/Sterling & Francine Clark Art Institute, Williamstown, Massachusetts, USA/The Bridgeman Art Library; **27-34:** bpk, Berlin/Hamburger Kunsthalle, Hamburg, Germany/Elke Walford/Art Resource, NY; **27-35:** The Metropolitan Museum of Art/Art Resource, NY; **27-36:** The Philadelphia Museum of Art/Art Resource, NY; **27-37:** Photograph © 2014 Museum of Fine Arts, Boston, 19.124; **27-38:** Art Resource, NY; **27-39:** The Granger Collection, NYC. All rights reserved; **27-40:** Tate, London/Art Resource, NY; **27-41:** Tate, London/Art Resource, NY; **27-41A:** © Jonathan Poore; **27-42:** © Jonathan Poore; **27-43:** Andrew Aitchison/Alamy; **27-43A:** Leo Sorel; **27-44:** Roger Antrobus/Terra/Corbis; **27-45:** © Jonathan Poore/Cengage Learning; **27-46:** LOOK-foto/SuperStock; **27-46A:** Dennis Hallinan/Alamy; **27-47:** Crystal Palace, Sydenham, c. 1862 (colour litho), Martinet, Achille-Louis (1806–77)/Private Collection/The Stapleton Collection/The Bridgeman Art Library; **27-48:** Louis Daguerre/Time & Life Pictures/Getty Images; **27-49:** Massachusetts General Hospital Archives and Special Collections, Boston; **27-49A:** Nadar (1820–1910) elevating Photography to the height of Art, published 1862 (litho), Daumier, Honore (1808–79)/Private Collection/The Stapleton Collection/The Bridgeman Art Library; **27-50:** Nadar/Bettmann/Corbis; **27-51:** Courtesy George Eastman House; **27-52:** New York Public Library/Art Resource, NY; **27-53:** Courtesy George Eastman House; **28-2:** Erich Lessing/Art Resource, NY.

Chapter 28—Opener: A Bar at the Folies-Bergere, 1881–82 (oil on canvas), Manet, Edouard (1832–83)/© Samuel Courtauld Trust, The Courtauld Gallery, London, UK/The Bridgeman Art Library; **28-2A:** Claude Monet, French, 1840–1926, On the Bank of the Seine, Bennecourt, 1868, oil on canvas, 32 1/16 × 39 5/8 in. (81.5 × 100.7 cm), Potter Palmer Collection, 1922.427 Reproduction, The Art Institute of Chicago. **28-2B:** Neue Pinakothek/Bayerische Staatsgemaeldesammlungen/Art Resource, NY; **28-3:** The Metropolitan Museum of Art/Art Resource, NY; **28-4:** Erich Lessing/Art Resource, NY; **28-5:** Photography © The Art Institute of Chicago, 1964.336; **28-6:** Digital Image © 2009 Museum Associates/LACMA/Art Resource, NY; **28-7:** RMN-Grand Palais/Art Resource, NY; **28-8:** © Culture and Sport Glasgow (Museums); **28-9:** RMN-Grand Palais/Art Resource, NY; **28-10:** RMN-Grand Palais/Art Resource, NY; **28-11:** Nocturne in Black and Gold, the Falling Rocket, 1875 (oil on panel), Whistler, James Abbott McNeill (1834–1903)/Detroit Institute of Arts, USA/Gift of Dexter M. Ferry Jr./The Bridgeman Art Library; **28-12:** Photography © The Art Institute of Chicago, 1910.2; **28-13:** Summer's Day, 1879 (oil on canvas), Morisot, Berthe (1841–95)/National Gallery, London, UK/The Bridgeman Art Library; **28-13A:** Photo © The Norton Simon

Hopper © The Whitney Museum of American Art; **29-71:** © 2011 The Jacob and Gwendolyn Lawrence Foundation, Seattle/Artists Rights Society (ARS), NY. Photo: The Phillips Collection, Washington, DC; **29-72:** Art © Figge Art Museum, successors to the Estate of Nan Wood Graham/Licensed by VAGA, New York, NY Photography © The Art Institute of Chicago,1930.934; **29-73:** Art © T. H. Benton and R. P. Benton Testamentary Trusts/UMB Bank Trustee/Licensed by VAGA, New York, NY. Photo © Lloyd Grotjan/Full Spectrum Photo, Jefferson City; **29-74:** © 2011 Orozco Valladares Family/SOMAAP, Mexico. Artists Rights Society (ARS). Photograph: Hood Museum of Art, Dartmouth College; **29-75:** © 2011 Banco de México Trust. Licensed by Artist's Rights Society (ARS), NY. Dirk Bakker, photographer for the Detroit Institute of Arts/The Bridgeman Art Library; **29-75A:** © D. R. Rufino Tamayo/Herederos/Mexico/2011. Fundacion Olga y Rufino Tamayo A.C. Photo: © 2009 Museum Associates/LACMA/Art Resource, NY; **29-76:** © 2011 Banco de México Trust. Licensed by Artists Rights Society (ARS), NY. Photo © Schalkwijk/Art Resource, NY; **29-77:** Courtesy The Dorothea Lange Collection, The Oakland Museum of California; **29-78:** Margaret Bourke-White/Time & Life Pictures/Getty Images; **29-79:** © 2011 Estate of Alexander Calder/Artists Rights Society (ARS), NY. Digital Image © The Museum of Modern Art/Licensed by Scala/Art Resource, NY, 590.1939 a-d; **29-80:** Peter Cook/VIEW View Pictures/Newscom.

Chapter 30—Opener: © Fred S. Kleiner; **30-2:** © 2011 Artists Rights Society (ARS), NY/ADAGP, Paris. Photo: © Des Moines Art Center; **30-3:** © 2011 The Estate of Francis Bacon, ARS, NY/DACS, London. Digital Image © The Museum of Modern Art/Licensed by Scala/Art Resource, NY, 229.1948; **30-3A:** © 2011 The Estate of Francis Bacon. All rights reserved/ARS, New York/DACS, London. Photograph by Bob Hashimoto. Reproduction, The Art Institute of Chicago; **30-4:** © 2011 Artists Rights Society (ARS), NY/ADAGP, Paris. Photo © Tate Gallery, London/Art Resource, NY; **30-4A:** Gerhard Richter Studio; **30-5:** © 2014 The Arshile Gorky Foundation/The Artists Rights Society (ARS), New York. Photograph: © The Museum of Modern Art/Licensed by SCALA/Art Resource, NY; **30-6:** © 2011 The Pollock-Krasner Foundation/Artists Rights Society (ARS), NY. Photo © National Gallery of Art, 1976.37.1; **30-7:** Courtesy Center for Creative Photography, University of Arizona © 1991 Hans Namuth Estate; **30-7A:** © 2011 Pollock-Krasner Foundation/Artists Rights Society (ARS), New York. Photograph: © The Whitney Museum of American Art; **30-8:** © 2011 The Willem de Kooning Foundation/Artists Rights Society (ARS), NY. Digital Image © The Museum of Modern Art/Licensed by Scala/Art Resource, NY, 478.1953; **30-9:** © Estate of Joan Mitchell Photograph: © Butler Institute of American Art, Youngstown, OH, USA/Gift of Marilynn Meeker, 1986 Courtesy of the Joan Mitchell Foundation, NYC/The Bridgeman Art Library International; **30-9A:** © 2011 The Franz Kline Estate/Artists Rights Society (ARS), New York. Photograph: Whitney Museum of American Art, New York; **30-9B:** Albright-Knox Art Gallery/Art Resource, NY. Art © Dedalus Foundation/Licensed by VAGA, New York, NY; **30-9C:** © 2011 Susan Rothenberg/Artists Rights Society (ARS), NY. Photo: Susan Rothenberg, Tattoo, 1979. Acrylic paint on canvas, 5′ 7″ × 8′ 7″. Collection Walker Art Center, Minneapolis. Purchased with the aid of funds from Mr. and Mrs. Edmond R. Ruben, Mr. and Mrs. Julius E. Davis, the Art Center Acquisition Fund, and the National Endowment for the Arts, 1979; **30-10:** Digital Image © The Museum of Modern Art/Licensed by Scala/Art Resource, NY, 240.1969, © 2008 Barnett Newman Foundation/Artists Rights Society (ARS), NY; **30-11:** © 2011 Kate Rothko Prizel & Christopher Rothko. Licensed by Artists Rights Society (ARS), NY. Photo: © San Francisco Museum of Modern Art; **30-12:** © Ellsworth Kelly, photo Philipp Scholz Rittermann; **30-13:** © 2011 Frank Stella/Artists Rights Society (ARS), NY. Photo © CNAC/MNAM/Dist. Réunion des Musées Nationaux/Art Resource, NY; **30-14:** Helen Frankenthaler, The Bay, 1963 (acrylic on canvas), 205.1 × 207.7 cm, Detroit Institute of Arts, USA/© DACS/Founders Society Purchase, Dr. & Mrs. Hilbert H. DeLawter Fund/The Bridgeman Art Library International; **30-15:** © 2011 Helen Frankenthaler/Artists Rights Society (ARS), New York; **30-15:** Solomon R. Guggenheim Museum, NY, 64.1685; **30-16:** The Museum of Modern Art/Licensed by SCALA/Art Resource, NY. © Bridget Riley 2014. All rights reserved, courtesy Karsten Schubert, London; **30-17:** Hirshhorn Museum and Sculpture Garden, Smithsonian Institution. Photo: Lee Stalsworth. Art: Estate of David Smith/Licensed by VAGA, New York, NY; **30-18:** © 2011 Estate of Tony Smith/Artists Rights Society (ARS), NY. Digital Image © The Museum of Modern Art/Licensed by Scala/Art Resource, NY, 333.1998; **30-19:** Art © Judd Foundation/Licensed by VAGA, NY Hirshhorn Museum and Sculpture Garden, Smithsonian Institution, photo Lee Stalsworth, 72.154; **30-19A:** Photography © The Art Institute of Chicago, © 2008 The Estate of Eva Hesse/Galerie Hauser & Wirth, Zürich; **30-20:** © 2012 Estate of Louise Nevelson/Artists Rights Society (ARS), NY. Photo © CNAC/MNAM/Dist. Réunion des Musées Nationaux/Art Resource, NY; **30-21:** Art © Louise Bourgeois Trust/Licensed by VAGA, New York, NY Photo © CNAC/MNAM/Dist. Réunion des Musées Nationaux/Art Resource, NY; **30-22:** © 2011 ISAMU NOGUCHI Licensed by Artist's Rights Society (ARS), New York. Collection Walker Art Center, Minneapolis (gift of the artist, 1978); **30-23:** © 2011 Artists Rights Society (ARS), NY/DACS, London. Photo © The Bridgeman Art Library; **30-24:** Art © Jasper Johns/Licensed by VAGA, New York, NY Photo:Whitney Museum of American Art, New York, USA/© DACS/The Bridgeman Art Library; **30-25:** Art © Estate of Robert Rauschenberg/Licensed by VAGA, New York, NY. Digital Image © The Museum of Modern Art/Licensed by SCALA/Art Resource, NY; **30-26:** © Estate of Roy Lichtenstein; **30-27:** © The Whitney Museum of American Art, New York, Photograph by Geoffrey Clements, © 2012 The Andy Warhol Foundation for the Visual Arts, Inc./Artists Rights Society (ARS), New York; **30-27A:** © 2012 The Andy Warhol Foundation for the Visual Arts, Inc./Artists Rights Society (ARS),

New York Photo: © Tate Gallery, London/Art Resource, NY; **30-27B:** Art © Estate of George Segal/Licensed by VAGA, New York, NY Photo:National Gallery of Canada, Ottawa; **30-28:** Digital Image © The Museum of Modern Art/Licensed by SCALA/Art Resource, NY; **30-29:** Art © Copyright 1969 Claes Oldenburg. Photo: © 2009 Fred S. Kleiner; **30-29A:** © 2011 Niki Charitable Art Foundation. All rights reserved, ARS, NY/ADAGP, Paris. Photograph: © Whitney Museum of American Art, New York; **30-30:** © Audrey Flack, Collection of The University of Arizona Museum of Art & Archive of Visual Arts, Tucson; Museum Purchase with Funds Provided By the Edward J. Gallagher, Jr. Memorial Fund; **30-31:** Close, Chuck Big Self Portrait 1967–68, acrylic on canvas. Collection Walker Art Center Minneapolis. Art Center Acquisition Fund, 1969; **30-32:** Lucian Freud. Licensed by Goodman Derrick, LLP. Photo: © Tate, London/Art Resource, NY; **30-33:** Art © Estate of Duane Hanson/Licensed by VAGA, New York, NY Photo by Anne Gold; **30-34:** Reproduced with permission of the Minor White Archive, Princeton University Art Museum. © Trustees of Princeton University. Digital Image © The Museum of Modern Art/Licensed by SCALA/Art Resource, NY; **30-35:** © 2011 Judy Chicago. Licensed by Artists Rights Society (ARS), NY. Photo: © The Brooklyn Museum; **30-36:** Miriam Schapiro, courtesy Flomenhaft Gallery, NY; **30-37:** Cindy Sherman, courtesy the artist and Metro Pictures; **30-37A:** © Marsie, Emanuelle, Damon and Andrew Scharlatt/Licensed by VAGA, New York, NY. Digital file Courtesy Ron Feldman Fine Arts, New York; **30-38:** © The Estate of Ana Mendieta Collection Courtesy Galerie Lelong, New York; **30-39:** Magdalena Abakanowicz, courtesy Marlborough Gallery, NY; **30-40:** © Jonathan Poore/Cengage Learning; **30-41:** © 2012 Artists Rights Society (ARS), New York/ADAGP, Paris/F.L.C./Photo by Jonathan Poore/Cengage Learning; **30-42:** © 2012 Artists Rights Society (ARS), New York/ADAGP, Paris/F.L.C. Photo: © Francis G. Mayer/CORBIS; **30-42A:** © Jonathan Poore; **30-43 bottom:** © Randy Duchaine/Alamy; **30-43 top:** Photo © Dmitri Kessel/Time & Life Pictures/Getty Images; **30-44:** age fotostock/SuperStock; **30-45:** © Jonathan Poore/Cengage Learning; **30-46:** Alan Schein Photography/Surf/Corbis; **30-47:** Smallbones/Wikimedia Commons; **30-48:** Ambient Images Inc./Alamy; **30-49:** dk/Alamy; **30-50:** © Jonathan Poore/Cengage Learning; **30-51:** Art © Estate of Robert Smithson/Licensed by VAGA, New York, NY//Photo © George Steinmetz/Corbis; **30-52:** © 2011 Carolee Schneemann/Artists Rights Society (ARS), NY. Photo © Al Geise, Courtesy PPOW Gallery; **30-53:** Photo: Ute Klophaus. ARS; **30-54:** © 2011 Artists Rights Society (ARS), NY/ADAGP, Paris Photo Credit: Digital Image © The Museum of Modern Art/Licensed by SCALA/Art Resource, NY; **30-55:** Digital Image © The Museum of Modern Art/Licensed by SCALA/Art Resource, NY; **30-56:** Jean Baptiste Lacroix/WireImage; **30-56A:** Ted Thai/Time & Life Pictures/Getty Images; **30-57:** Courtesy Nam June Paik Studios, Inc.; **30-58:** 1979 David Em.

Chapter 31—Opener: Courtesy artist Jaune Quick-to-See Smith (Salish member of the Confederated Salish and Kootenai Nation, MT, and The Accola Griefen Gallery, New York). Digital Photo: Chrysler Museum of Art; **31-2:** Napoleon Leading the Army Over the Alps © Kehinde Wiley Studio. Used by Permission; **31-2A:** Smithsonian American Art Museum, Washington, DC/Art Resource, NY; **31-3:** The Broad Art Foundation, Santa Monica Photography credit: Douglas M. Parker Studio, Los Angeles, **31-4:** © 1983 Faith Ringgold; **31-4A:** Lorna Simpson; **31-5:** Art: Courtesy of the artist and Jack Shainman Gallery, NY. Photo: Brooklyn Museum of Art, New York, USA/Caroline A.L. Pratt Fund/The Bridgeman Art Library International; **31-6:** COPYRIGHT: BARBARA KRUGER. COURTESY: MARY BOONE GALLERY, NEW YORK; **31-6A:** Copyright © 1988 Guerrilla Girls, courtesy www.guerrillagirls.com; **31-7:** Self-Portrait, 1980 © Copyright The Robert Mapplethorpe Foundation. Courtesy Art + Commerce; **31-8:** Courtesy of the Estate of David Wojnarowicz and P.P.O.W. Gallery, NY; **31-9:** © Shahzia Sikander. Photograph: Sheldan C. Collins, courtesy Whitney Museum of American Art; **31-10:** © Chris Ofili, courtesy Chris Ofili-Afroco and Victoria Miro Gallery, photo by Stephen White; **31-11:** Allegiance with Wakefulness, 1994 (offset print), Neshat, Shirin (b. 1957)/84 × 105 cm/The Israel Museum, Jerusalem, Israel/Anonymous gift, New York/to American Friends of the Israel Museum/The Bridgeman Art Library; **31-11A:** Meteorological Service of New Zealand Ltd. Collection, Wellington; **31-12:** © Krzysztof Wodcizko Courtesy Galerie Lelong, New York; **31-13:** © Edward Burtynsky, courtesy Nicholas Metivier, Toronto/Howard Greenberg & Bryce Wolkowitz, New York; **31-14:** Art © Estate of Leon Golub/Licensed by VAGA, New York, NY Courtesy Ronald Feldman Gallery; **31-14A:** Courtesy of Koplin Del Rio Gallery, Culver City, CA; **31-15:** Photograph by Martha Rosler, Represented by Mitchell-Innes & Nash, NYC; **31-16:** Marlborough Gallery in NY; **31-17:** Willie Bester; **31-17A:** © CNAC/MNAM/Dist. RMN-Grand Palais/Art Resource, NY; **31-18:** Trigo Piula; **31-19:** Bloodline: Big Family, No. 2, 1995 (oil on canvas), Zhang Xiaogang (b. 1958)/Private Collection/Photo © Christie's Images/The Bridgeman Art Library; **31-20:** Copyright © Xu Bing, courtesy Chazen Museum of Art (formerly Elvehjem Museum of Art), University of Wisconsin; **31-21:** Artwork © Jenny Saville; **31-22:** Photo © Whitney Museum of American Art, © Kiki Smith; **31-22A:** Art © The Keith Haring Foundation. Photo © Jonathan Poore/Cengage Learning; **31-22B:** Art © Estate of Robert Arneson/Licensed by VAGA, NY Photo: San Francisco Museum of Modern Art; **31-23:** Museum of Contemporary Art, Chicago © Jeff Koons; **31-24:** Art © Marisol Escobar/Licensed by VAGA, New York, NY; **31-24A:** Mark Tansey, courtesy Gagosian Gallery, NY; **31-25:** © Anselm Kiefer. Courtesy Gagosian Gallery. Photography by Robert McKeever. © Philadelphia Museum of Art, 1985-5-1; **31-25A:** Heritage Images, © The British Museum; **31-25B:** Collection of National Heritage Board, Singapore Art Museum; **31-26:** The Broad Art Foundation, Santa Monica; **31-27:** Dallas Museum of Art, Dallas; **31-28:** Collection of Home Insurance Company, New York. Courtesy of the artist; **31-29:** © Fairchild Photo

Index